McGRAW-HILL PUBLICATIONS IN SOCIOLOGY
EDWARD BYRON REUTER, Consulting Editor

SOCIAL TREATMENT IN
PROBATION AND DELINQUENCY

SOCIAL TREATMENT IN PROBATION AND DELINQUENCY

*Treatise and Casebook for Court Workers,
Probation Officers and Other
Child Welfare Workers*

BY

PAULINE V. YOUNG, Ph.D.

*The University of Southern California;
Co-editor, Social Work Technique*

FOREWORD BY
ROSCOE POUND
Dean of the Law School of Harvard University

INTRODUCTION BY
JUSTIN MILLER
Department of Justice

FIRST EDITION
EIGHTH IMPRESSION

McGRAW-HILL BOOK COMPANY, Inc.
NEW YORK AND LONDON
1937

Dedicated to

ROBERT H. SCOTT, JUDGE

LOS ANGELES COUNTY JUVENILE COURT

*For His Devotion to Children
Science and Social Justice*

PREFACE

It is hoped that this volume may succeed in some measure in developing, partly through empirical methods and partly through tested scientific methods, a planned, rational, many-angled, deliberate, and systematic approach to the problem of delinquency. The discussion of the case data and of the approach to the problem should result in a critical attitude on the part of the reader and in a vigorous concern for the destinies of youth and of the community.

The author first became interested in the problems of the unadjusted child in 1918 while she was living at the Ruth Club in Chicago as assistant to the superintendent, Mrs. Clara Riese, and attending the University of Chicago. Later (1925–1929) she was engaged in several research studies which involved problems of boys, as research assistant in the Boys' Work Survey of Los Angeles conducted under the directorship of Dr. E. S. Bogardus, and as field representative in the study of Boy Scouts conducted under the directorship of Professor Harry P. Fairchild of New York University.

The author also was extended the privilege of carrying on considerable research in the field of probation under the late Warren H. Prescott of the Los Angeles County Probation Department. During these studies and while making the study on *Pilgrims of Russian-Town*, she had the opportunity to study over three thousand cases, fully one half of which were studied in some detail.

A deliberate attempt has been made to pool the varied experiences, points of view, experiments, as well as tested techniques, presented in the work with children in several large communities in this country. A vast literature has grown up in the fields of probation, delinquency, unadjustment, case work, and so on.

There are a number of references not of recent date. Frequently a more recent statement has had to be discarded in preference to an earlier one—on the same subject. It is a major task to gather highly scattered materials on theory and practice in such a form as to give the reader an opportunity to see for himself the validity of the varying points of view and to enable him to further his own thinking on the basis of particular background, experience, and interests.

The book considers the needs of both the practitioner and the student of children's problems. It presents *case-work techniques and processes* suitable for the work of probation departments, juvenile courts, juvenile detention homes, police juvenile bureaus, bureaus of crime prevention, children's protective agencies, and correctional schools. Neither problems of placement nor of administration are considered. It is assumed that the reader has had some general training in social work before going into the specialized field of juvenile delinquency. A knowledge of general case-work techniques, of human nature, and of the social order should be obtained before undertaking to deal with the problems of child unadjustment. Furthermore, this volume does not concern itself with an abstract or general discussion of the causes and problems of juvenile delinquency. There are several comprehensive texts which deal with these matters and the author assumed that the reader is already familiar, or will familiarize himself, with them.

The discussion of problems and causes will be presented here only in so far as they pertain to specific cases under consideration. While the approach to the delinquent is from several different technical standpoints—case work, legal, clinical, and community organization—these techniques are regarded for the present as tools and resources in the hands of case workers. No attempt has been made to discuss each case fully; rather an effort has been made to present only the points under consideration, thus providing the student an opportunity for further analysis, following the samples presented, if desired.

An effort has been made to safeguard carefully the interests of the agencies which were gracious enough to provide material for criticism. Whenever it was impossible to do good work on a case—for whatever reason—the names of the agency and worker are withheld.

In the chapters dealing with the juvenile courts and probation from the standpoint of administrative law—edited by a lawyer— only a few attempts were made to go back to original sources. This is a task for a lawyer. However, every precaution was taken to provide an adequate background by quoting from reliable secondary sources, such as Roscoe Pound, H. H. Lou, Bernard Flexner, Reuben Oppenheimer, F. E. Waite, and others. In writing on the subject of administrative law it is impossible and dangerous to generalize. Only some of the outstanding characteristics were discussed. It will be necessary for the reader to become familiar with the law as well as with the practices of his own community and compare them with the data presented here from a more general standpoint.

The present volume is written from the sociological standpoint. To quote from James Jackson Putman: "It is in each man's social relations that his mental history is mainly written, and it is in his social relations likewise that the causes of the disorders that threaten his happiness and his effectiveness and the means for securing his recovery are to be mainly sought." Unadjustment and delinquency have to do mainly with social situations. Furthermore, whatever competence the author may have lies in the field of sociology and in social work.

PAULINE V. YOUNG.

LOS ANGELES, CALIFORNIA,
   January, 1937.

ACKNOWLEDGMENTS

Many persons and agencies have aided in the preparation of this volume, notable among them being the National Probation Association, the National Committee for Mental Hygiene, Mr. Christopher Ruess of the Los Angeles County Probation Department, the Merrill-Palmer School, who have aided in the compilation of the various bibliographies.

The author has drawn heavily from certain articles published in the Yearbooks of the National Probation Association and wishes to express gratitude to the editors not only for their permission to quote but for the many ways in which they generously extended their help over a period of many months. The White House Conference Reports on Child Health and Protection, the Journal of Criminal Law and Criminology, the Harvard Law Review, the Supplements to the Annual Reports of the Attorney General of the United States, the Annals of the American Academy of Political and Social Science, and others have also contributed many excerpts. The United States Children's Bureau has for many months supplied data, special statistics, and information on various juvenile courts. Miss Alice Nutt deserves special mention for her prompt replies to numerous inquiries. The many authors and publishers who have given permission to quote from their publications are mentioned in the footnotes at the appropriate references.

To her daughter, Harriet, and son, Clarence, the author is greatly indebted for their help in checking the bibliographies, proofreading, form-letter writing, and above all for their simple faith and confidence which only one's own devoted children can inspire. Miss Marion Clark typed the manuscript with the care and loyalty of a devoted friend and scholar.

Mr. William J. Harper, Director, Westchester County Probation Department, New York, for nearly two years has been supplying data and cases and offering suggestions as to the organization and content of the volume, and his assistant, Ethel N. Cherry, was very helpful on the problem of case recording. Miss Irene Kawin, Deputy Chief Probation Officer, Juvenile

Court of Cook County, Illinois, has been of inestimable help. She supplied material and case data, interested other persons in preparing data, read portions of the manuscript, and offered frank and searching criticism.

The following persons have prepared articles especially for this volume or offered criticism on the data prepared by the author: Kenneth Beam, Karl Holton, Kenyon Scudder, E. A. Francis, Patrick L. Palace, Helen Stover, all of the Los Angeles County Probation Department; Rt. Rev. Msgr. Thomas J. O'Dwyer of the Catholic Welfare Bureau of Los Angeles; Lieutenant E. W. Lester, Director, Boy's Division, Los Angeles Police Juvenile Bureau; Irving W. Halperin and Rosalie Supplie of the New York Court of General Sessions; Miss Agnes C. Sullivan, Probation Examiner, State of New York, Department of Correction, Division of Probation; John Plover, State Supervisor of Probation, California; Carl Hyatt and Justin Miller of the Department of Justice; Professors Monachesi, University of Minnesota, E. F. Young, University of Southern California, F. M. Thrasher, New York University; Dr. George J. Mohr, Chicago, psychiatrist; and Mrs. Edith Bogen, Assistance League of Southern California.

The referees of the Los Angeles County Juvenile Court— Mrs. Margaret Pratt and Mrs. Dora Heffner—as well as Commissioner Stanley Sutton, have for many years been most gracious, helpful, and generous when they, under various difficult conditions, made it possible for the author to be present at court hearings and conferences. The secretary, Miss Levitt, also needs to be mentioned.

Karl Holton, Deputy Chief Probation Officer, Los Angeles County Probation Department, has given his time, thought, and energy to personal conferences with the author, to selection of case data, and to reading of the entire manuscript. His sincerity and open-mindedness are particularly appreciated. The late Warren Prescott, Deputy Chief Probation Officer, Los Angeles County, extended to the author many courtesies and for several years made it possible for her to carry on research on case records which to a large extent constitute the groundwork of this volume.

To the Honorable Robert H. Scott, presiding Superior Judge of the Juvenile Court of Los Angeles County, to whom this book is dedicated, the author's debt is unending. He stimulated and encouraged her to study the problem, inspired confidence in herself, made it possible to secure the needed data and to carry on research in the field of probation and delinquency. Without his generous and thoughtful aid since 1926 this volume would never have been written.

To all these people should go the credit for whatever merit this volume may have. The author herself will take the responsibility for the rest.

PAULINE V. YOUNG.

THE UNIVERSITY OF SOUTHERN CALIFORNIA,
LOS ANGELES, CALIFORNIA,
January, 1937.

CONTENTS

PART I
THE SOCIAL CASE STUDY OF UNADJUSTED YOUTH AND PARENTS
THE APPROACH TO INDIVIDUALIZATION OF JUSTICE

CHAPTER I

The Case of Nora Norman and Tom and Dick Dickson—The Wider Social Implications in Nora's Case—Who Is a Juvenile Delinquent?—What Is Juvenile Probation?—Can the Problem of Delinquency Be Dealt with by Case-work Methods Alone? — What Agency Should Deal with Problems of Juveniles?

CHAPTER II

The Social Study of Marilyn Smith—Girl's Own Study—Social Study of Marvin Levkovitz.

CHAPTER III

Steps Prior to Contact with Client—Study of the Offense—Study of the Offender in Relation to His Social World—The Significance of Studying the Underlying and Contributing Factors.

CHAPTER IV

Study of the Family Group—Reactions to the Offense—The Social History of the Child's Development in the Family Circle—

PART III

DYNAMICS OF SOCIAL THERAPY IN THE WORK WITH UNADJUSTED YOUTH AND PARENTS

LIST OF CASE HISTORY MATERIALS AND EXCERPTS

(All Identifying Data Disguised)
Problems and Symptoms Reported

xxi

FOREWORD

As one, not unnaturally, compares Dr. Young's book with two earlier works in somewhat the same field, namely, Miss Richmond's *Social Diagnosis* (1917) and Southard and Jarrett's *The Kingdom of Evils* (1922) he cannot fail to be struck with the great progress in the scope and method and in the fuller understanding of the purposes and possibilities of social work which has been achieved in the past two decades. No less striking is the development of cooperation of agencies of every description with each other and with courts and probation officers and the agencies of prosecution and penal treatment. If that cooperation, in many places and some particulars at least, falls short of what is desirable, one need but recall the American tradition, one might almost say the American habit, of official noncooperation with other officials and governmental agencies, not to speak of habitual noncooperation with extragovernmental agencies, characteristic of the nineteenth century, to perceive a radical and encouraging change.

Miss Richmond's classical book had to do chiefly with the technique of social investigation. Dr. Southard, who came in contact with social work as director of the Boston Psychopathic Hospital, was concerned with diagnosis for social therapy. He sought to determine what agencies to employ for a particular case, as it came to him as a result of some mental or nervous disturbance, finding five major types of evil to be dealt with: diseases and defects of mind and body (calling for cure), educational deficiencies and misinformation (calling for teaching), vices and bad habits (calling for training), legal entanglements (calling for counsel), and poverty and other forms of resourcelessness (calling for aid). Today diagnosis must go forward to much more detail. Ultimately very likely we must ask whether, for example, a particular child presents a case for a court with a probation officer and detention home, or for a social clinic, or for a child guidance clinic with a psychiatrist, or for an institute of social relations, or for some agency looking into the social economic forces behind it.

Much as the progress has been, social case diagnosis is not yet developed. Obviously the process is complex and as things are is largely tentative. There is a complex both of symptoms and of causative factors and there is danger that, as diagnosis must proceed from symptoms, it will become a choice from among symptoms. It is not certain that any one contributing element in delinquency can be termed primary in any individual case. Hence no simple classification of causes is possible. But as one compares Dr. Southard's five major types with Dr. Young's eight elements, each involving a complex of detail, he must be reminded of the contrast between the simple taxonomic schemes of the last century and the more complex and less symmetrical schemes which have taken their place today. It is particularly noticeable that recent thinking recognizes something in individual personality to be taken into account. The law of the past saw nothing more. Later thinking saw only environment. Today, granting that delinquency is relative to time, place, and occasion, on the one hand, it is seen that on the other hand there is something in the individual which these bring out. Law must move with the main body in its cautious advance and not with the advance guard in all its scoutings and reconnoiterings. That it is seldom abreast of the newest thought of the moment is not wholly an evil.

Jurists have had to insist on the limits of effective legal action. The legal order is not equal to the whole task of social control. Much less may the whole be carried on simply by the framing and judicial application of legal precepts. In the same way social workers have to insist that delinquency presents a problem far too complex to be dealt with by any single method and hence not by social case work alone. Accordingly the first part of Dr. Young's book takes up the question how far such work is or may be made effective in the adjustment of delinquents. Here we are brought back to the subject of cooperation and a very wide field is indicated. How is the social worker, who on the one hand works with or for a court and the agencies of the legal order, to cooperate on the other hand with the community organizer, the social engineer, the progressive educator, the social coordinator, the health officer, the clergyman, and the public-spirited promoter of legislation?

Even the lesser task involves all the difficulties encountered in developing administration in every connection in a land and among a people whose tradition knew little or nothing of it and, indeed, has been frankly hostile to it. To link public school and public agencies of preventive justice in a systematic course of dealing not only with the cause and conditions of juvenile delinquency but with individual delinquents, to make judges and probation officers and public school teachers work together efficiently as together exercising the royal function of *parens patriae* is no mean achievement in any English-speaking jurisdiction. It is gratifying to a common-law lawyer to note how all the technique and organized experience of such cooperation have grown from or about unofficial voluntary social work. In this respect the development is characteristically Anglo-American. In view of American habits of thought and action in such matters, it probably could not have been worked out a tithe so well under official auspices. It has been brought about by trial and error on the part of those who did it for its own sake, not as part of an official routine. Thus as we are prepared to use it, we find it worth using.

Cooperation, however, is a means. The end is systematic individualization of treatment, and here we are met with a certain inherent contradiction between system and individualization. This contradiction is a source of difficulty in every field of the administration of justice and especially in punitive justice. To systematize making penal treatment fit the criminal risks losing sight of the individual delinquent in pursuit of system or of system in pursuit of an individual treatment. Reconciling of the general security with the individual life is a fundamental problem of the whole legal order.

What makes the requirement of system, called for to secure the individual life against arbitrary subjection to the will of the magistrate, an irksome one, is that system and method are apt to degenerate into perfunctory routine. In the summary of the Survey of Criminal Justice in Cleveland (1922) I was able to show, on the basis of the several detailed studies, that a tendency to perfunctory routine infected every stage of a criminal prosecution from the police investigation to the ultimate penal treatment. This tendency has brought about disheartening results in the case of almost every improvement in the administration of criminal justice. Yet when I read Dr. Young's pages and think back over

a generation of fairly close experience of social work in connection
with American legal and judicial methods, I am much encouraged.
In truth we have made great strides in a generation.

Happily if we have had little help from any American technique
of administration, something yet to be developed, we have had
ample guidance from the methods and recorded and traditional
experience of our courts of equity. In this respect there is a
significant difference between adult probation and juvenile probation. The latter is not a mode of penal treatment or substitute
for punishment. It is a mode of exercising the authority of the
state as *parens patriae*. As to adult probation the social service
of the courts lags because in our polity the technique of administration generally lags and technique of this particular kind of
administration has had to be developed. But in the juvenile
court, the power to utilize and cooperate with private agencies is
an incident, and a very useful incident, of the discretion of a court
of equity. Probation involves individualization of justice and
socialization of procedure for both of which the organization, traditions, and atmosphere of a common-law criminal tribunal are
ill adapted. On the other hand, great progress has been made in
juvenile court procedure even if not all that could be wished.
The demand for such tribunals grew up so suddenly and there was
so little experience on which to go, that with all allowance for
failures these courts must be pronounced not the least example of
American institutional inventiveness. They present problems
such as are involved in administrative law on every side. Cases
are treated as unique. The tribunal acts on investigation and
report to the judge, not on a controversial trial of the facts. But
courts of equity historically did these very things. The referees
used in some juvenile courts are the equivalent of masters in chancery. The whole method has the flexibility and adjustability of
our classical equity.

Just because the procedure is so flexible and the scope for discretion and individualization of treatment is so great, it is imperative that the judges who sit in these courts be exceptionally
qualified. The practice of rotation, which prevails so generally
in our American judicial organization, has had bad consequences
in this connection. Judges excellently qualified for some forms
of judicial work, exactly because they are so qualified, are not
adapted to the wholly different work of administration. The

action of an ordinary judge, dealing with property or contract, is likely to be reviewed on appeal and his mistakes will be corrected. Moreover what he does is subjected to vigilant scrutiny by the bar. The judge in the juvenile court is not subject to these checks. Nor is it easy to determine how effective but not embarrassing checks are to be devised. Administrative supervision of juvenile courts and juvenile probation involves difficulties because of our constitutional distribution of powers. As the powers of a court of equity belong to the juvenile court there is ample analogy for judicial administrative supervision. A court of equity, as was provided for in the Council Bluffs Bridge case, may if necessary keep a matter on its docket for ninety-nine years in order fully to adjust the relations involved and completely carry out the decree. How to organize effective supervision of the administrative work of a modern court and to coordinate it with supervision of the purely judicial work of the tribunal is not the least of the problems confronting the lawmakers of the immediate future. It is an important part of the whole problem of organization of courts. Lawyers will find much in Dr. Young's book about which they should be thinking in this connection.

If one is inclined to minimize the need of systematic administrative supervision of juvenile probation, let him consider one item. Child placement involves administrative authority over one of the most intimate and cherished of human relations. The powers of the Star Chamber were a trifle in comparison with those of our juvenile courts and courts of domestic relations. The latter may bring about a revolution as easily as did the former. It is well known that too often the placing of a child in a home or even in an institution is done casually or perfunctorily or even arbitrarily. Moreover effective preventive work through these courts requires looking into much more than the bad external conditions of a household, such as poverty or neglect or lack of discipline. Internal conditions, a complex of habits, attitudes, and reactions, may have to be dealt with and this means administrative treatment of the most intimate affairs of life. Even with the most superior personnel, these tribunals call for legal checks.

That individualization may be thought of ultimately as part of a larger question of prevention does not relieve us of the task of making the best of what we have been doing toward individualization. Whatever measures may be devised in the end toward prevention of crime, individual adjustment through case work has been shown to be immediately practicable. Very likely it will always be necessary. One of the chief preventive agencies is the police, and special police technique for handling juvenile cases has been urged. But we must proceed slowly here. It is a grave question whether we can ask for more than enlightened common sense. We cannot reasonably expect the police to do social work or to do the work of child welfare agencies. Any considerable development of the preventive side of the policeman's office adds to the already heavy burden of difficulties involved in making the police adequate to its varied tasks in the American city of today.

At common law the home was relied upon as a chief agency of social control. The parent, or the master in case of apprenticed children, was thought of as having the duties of the crown as *parens patriae* devolved upon him. The internal discipline of the household was privileged. The father or master had the authority of the law behind him. It was over him only in case he exceeded his privilege. Obviously the legal order today is under strain from what may be called the increasing secularization of social control. It is struggling with difficulties of transition from a control recognized and backed up by the law to a control by and through the law immediately. The law has largely to act in gross. Hence when anything is committed to the law there is a tendency to deal with it in the traditional legal manner. Nor can this tendency be overcome entirely. Compromise becomes necessary between general principles and particular rules. For instance, in the household the individual may be treated on the basis of his known precocity or retarded development as the case may be. But the law must fix an exact age at which he ceases to come within the category of "juvenile." Science would, as an ideal, look to the stage of mental and social development of the particular human being. The law must temper regard for the unique individual case with reference to safeguards demanded by the general security. Its reliance for the general security is chiefly upon fixed categories and provisions as to jurisdiction. Its reliance for individualization is chiefly upon probation. But probation must be more than surveillance. It must be social case work backed by law. The family, the church, the neighborhood have largely lost their effectiveness. Newer agencies of social control, the secular school, industrial organization, social institutions, have not yet developed wholly effective substitutes. Thus in treating the individual juvenile delinquent it is needful to some extent to deal with community influences which have made or helped to make him what he is. The family, not the child, may have to be the unit of case work, even if the legal unit in the legal proceeding is the child. The problem child is very likely the child of a problem family. But probation agencies of a juvenile court are not organized or equipped to do family case work. Here is a field for cooperation of legal with extralegal agencies. It shows how important it is to have a modern organization and an enlightened personnel, equal to utilizing to the utmost the possibilities of such cooperation. If we look only at one type of case the probation officer may have to consult a physician, a psychometrist, and a psychologist. In twenty years of experience as dean with nervous breakdowns, insomnia, and nervous scare on the part of ambitious adult students, I have often wished I could combine the special knowledge and technique of all these. The juvenile probation officer has need of access to much more.

Such reflections must lead us to appreciate the need of method. If in devising methods we are threatened on one side by the Scylla of perfunctory routine, we have to avoid on the other the Charybdis of blundering trial and error on the part of each particular magistrate and probation officer. Lack of a clear comprehension of the task, leading to lack of intelligent cooperation between court and probation officer, reliance on magisterial intuition, use of data simply for the court and not as the basis of rehabilitation, are not things to be cured by method. Their causes lie deeper than method can reach. But data gathered for the right purpose and as they should be, and a method constraining a right gathering of them, can do much in directing attention to better purposes and better conceptions.

Method is called for, then, not only in case work and in probation but in the whole field, of which these are parts, so as to make both the whole and the parts effective. The methods have been worked out from different points of view and for different purposes and it is useful to have them coordinated and criticized from their own immediate point of view, from the other points of view, and from the point of view of the whole. If the discussion shows that much remains to be done, it is still gratifying to one who has seen the subject develop that the development has gone so far in relatively so short a time. The matter of records has a special importance because we need a basis for statistical studies which only intelligently planned and carefully kept records can provide.

One special problem of unification of the judicial organization deserves and receives consideration. Is there to be a unified court for family matters, preferably as a branch of a unified court of general jurisdiction? A divorce court with a suit for divorce and alimony before it, a court of law with an action by a grocer for necessaries furnished the wife before it, a criminal court with a prosecution for failure to maintain a wife and child before it, and a juvenile court with an incorrigible child before it, may all be dealing with detached fragments of the single problem of one unhappy household. But our judicial organization is not yet so well developed on modern lines and the possibilities of the juvenile court are not yet so completely worked out as to give us an assured basis on which to build. There is danger of another specialized court, instead of the specialist judges in a unified court—the goal toward which we must be working. Moreover the need first of all is to develop an adequate machinery to sift cases before they reach a particular court or branch of a court and determine whether to refer them to a court, and if so to what court, or to some non-judicial agency. Family courts or courts of domestic relations have a clear advantage in a unified policy and power over situations as a whole. But a well-organized administrative system, intelligently administered, could do much. The juvenile court could be made to coordinate constructively the treatment of all the elements which go to prevent development of a potential or an incipient into a chronic delinquent.

Too much has been expected of probation as a policy which would operate itself. Ex-policemen are still being appointed probation officers on a theory of probation as surveillance. There is little general appreciation of the time needed for each individual case of juvenile probation. There are many types of such officers, and no generally received ideal of one has developed. Because of the mode of appointment and a lack of appreciation of what the position demands, effective officers are somewhat rare. Unhappily too many are merely "holding jobs." This is not wholly an incident of politics. It is one of many survivals of the pioneer American faith in versatility—in the ability of any man to do anything.   Those who may have been discouraged by accounts of some recent studies of the juvenile courts and of probation will take heart from reading Dr. Young's book and seeing how difficult and complicated are the tasks, how much we have done in a relatively short time toward providing for them, how well we now know what we have to do, and how thoroughly the defects in our administration of the new policy have been diagnosed.

Roscoe Pound.

Cambridge, Massachusetts,
   January, 1937

INTRODUCTION

During the last thirty-five years a profound change has taken place in opinions and attitudes regarding the delinquencies of children. The orthodox common law regarded a child under seven years of age as incapable of committing crime and subject only to the disciplines of home, school, and church; it regarded a child over fourteen years of age as fully responsible and subject to punishment as an adult; and a child between seven and fourteen as falling into one or the other of the two groups just described, according to whether or not he possessed the required criminal intent in connection with the commission of the prohibited act. Severe punishments—even death—were sometimes inflicted upon young children for what now seem to us to be very minor infractions of the law.

Approximately thirty-five years ago, the first juvenile courts were established. Since then, they and the philosophy which underlies them have spread throughout the nation. This development has been an uneven one, however. There were some who questioned and there are some who still question its wisdom. Rarely do we find, in any state, uniformly high standards of performance from one county to another.

It is well to remember that a fundamental struggle has been going on between the legalistic thinkers and the social worker group. The lawyers have more or less grudgingly surrendered this area—in fact, in parts of the country they have not yet surrendered it; and even in the federal system there is as yet no provision for a modern disposition of juvenile delinquents, except by outright transfer of cases to state courts—where adequate juvenile courts exist. Although a few lawyers participated understandingly in the early beginnings and later development of juvenile courts and probation systems, many of them have been opposed and are still opposed to these departures from the philosophy and method of the common law. It would be well for those who suggest the exclusive handling of juvenile delinquents by schools or by social agencies to remember that only the concept of a "court" together with the rationalization of "chancery jurisdiction and function" has avoided the necessity for constitutional change and has reconciled lawyer legislators to reluctant relinquishment of this large area of criminal law administration.

It must be admitted, frankly, that public thinking about juvenile delinquency and the work of juvenile courts and probation departments has been largely emotional. Tenderness toward children has been sufficient to offset the primitive desire for vengeance which still dominates public thinking concerning adult delinquency. It is this fact, no doubt, which accounts for the rapid spread of the juvenile court idea; it also explains the too large claims and the false hopes of enthusiastic supporters. Recent investigations, which have seemed to reveal inadequacies in juvenile courts, have come as a shock to many who regarded them as a panacea, adequate to compensate for the failure of home, school, church, and other community agencies. They have come, on the other hand, as an apparent vindication for those who have resented the development of juvenile courts and probation and who, all along, have insisted upon sterner standards of justice for juvenile and adult alike.

Recently there has developed an inclination to appraise, rather than merely to praise or disparage juvenile courts. Gradually some of our sociological engineers have come to realize that a juvenile court alone cannot accomplish miracles. When it is well staffed—both as to judge and probation officers; when it is well equipped—as to detention and clinical facilities; it may perform an extremely important service in revealing the inadequacies and needs of the children who come to it, and, perhaps even more important, the inadequacies and needs of the community itself.

In other words, the problems of child life are problems which require for their solution all the available resources of community life. The only intelligent approach is one which considers the child in its relation to all environmental factors and seeks to improve both the environment and the capacity of the child to react normally thereto. This Dr. Young does in *Social Treatment in Probation and Delinquency*. The name of the book might well have been extended to include delinquent and problem communities, social agencies, schools, and public officials, as well as children and parents.

When we come, honestly, to face the whole problem in these terms, then we ask: "What are the inadequacies of modern community life?" "What are the points of stress in child life?" "What can be done to discover these factors and correct them?" "What of the old institutions, such as home, school, and church?" "What of parents, neighbors, teachers, preachers?" "What are these 'social workers'; what is their method and their place in modern life?" "What new devices have been discovered to compensate for the failures of old social institutions?" "What seems to be needed in addition to or in place of methods and techniques formerly relied upon?" "What do modern thinkers and writers offer?"

With such questions in mind, and seeking to answer the larger question which includes them all, Dr. Young undertakes to show the intricate character of child delinquency by setting out in considerable detail the case histories of typical children who, because of inadequacies within themselves and inadequacies in their environmental surroundings, have failed to fit the conventional pattern of community life. She then analyzes the programs of various agencies, public and private, which have been going through a parallel process of development, equally important, although not so much publicized, perhaps, as that of the juvenile court. Social agencies, schools, crime prevention work in police departments, community recreation programs, clinics of various kinds, probation departments, adult education, that lusty new infant the coordinating council, and others come in for objective interpretation. Generous use is made of professional opinion; the techniques of administrative procedures, practices, and record keeping are explained.

It is a hopeful sign that such books as this are appearing. Whether we agree in every detail is a matter of relatively little consequence. The important fact is that we are beginning to break down the compartmentalized thinking—and acting—of the various professional groups working in this field. We are beginning to get away from the medicine-man method of attempting cures in a vacuum. Having traced adult delinquency back to juvenile delinquency, and juvenile delinquency back to adult delinquency, we are in a fair way toward discovering that neither can be solved on a basis of individual responsibility and mass treatment; but rather that what we need is a recognition of mass—community—responsibility; and treatment applied individually to the individual and collectively to the community at the same time.

There is still left for another book similar treatment, of similar material, but with emphasis rather upon the tremendous and increasing problem faced by every community in the adjustment, guidance, and supervision of inadequate adults—transients, vagrants, habitual drunkards, drug addicts, prostitutes, occasional workers, seasonal workers, unemployed, managers of commercial amusements and recreations, and others. Herein lies a problem of delinquency and social disorder, which most communities are evading, by the use of haphazard, occasional methods of treatment; and which must also be solved, if the problem of juvenile delinquency is to be solved, in any community.

JUSTIN MILLER.

WASHINGTON, D. C.,
January, 1937.

PART I

THE SOCIAL CASE STUDY OF UNADJUSTED YOUTH AND PARENTS

THE APPROACH TO INDIVIDUALIZATION OF JUSTICE

Unless in the future, juvenile courts become case agencies having acceptable standards of work, they are doomed to failure.—FREDERICK A. MORAN

CHAPTER I

A CASE OF UNADJUSTMENT OR DELINQUENCY? WHO SHOULD DEAL WITH THE CASE?

The Case of Nora Norman and Tom and Dick Dickson.—A petition was filed by police officer James Riley on February 25, 1936, in the Juvenile Court of S. County[1] at _____, California, in behalf of Nora Norman, sixteen years of age, who had committed an act of petty theft in a large ready-to-wear shop. She was attempting to buy "a smart outfit and some accessories." As soon as she had the things selected, and the saleslady was making out the check, two small boys, Tom and Dick, who were loitering in front of the store, started a vigorous fight. The saleslady, whose counter faced the street, was distracted, and Nora swiftly disappeared with her "purchases." The boys were held by a store employee, and Nora was followed by the store detective, who apprehended her a block away. He took her back to the store for positive identification and then called the police. She was taken to the Juvenile Detention Home after some questioning by the police officer. (No petition was filed in the case of the boys, but they were detained until their parents called for them.)

Nora's Statement.—Nora—who is large for her age, neat and clean in appearance, smartly dressed, pleasant, friendly, and quick-witted—maintains that she had run away from home (gave address as Platoria, S. County, California) at the age of fourteen years and had found work as an usherette in one of the downtown theaters. She gave her age as seventeen. She still works there three evenings a week. She lives with a girl friend, who is, according to Nora, twenty-four years of age, at _____. She does not attend school; she quit the eighth grade, found it "dull and easy"; does not communicate with her parents, "would rather die than be sent back to a drunken father and a sloppy, irritable stepmother, and half-witted sister." Her father was gassed in the war and "has never fully recovered from gas, wine,

[1] Quoted by permission of S. County Probation Department.

3

and women." Her mother, who was a French war bride, died
in this country from tuberculosis when Nora was seven years old.
"Tuberculosis or a broken heart, I do not know which," Nora
adds under her breath. Her father remarried six months later.
She declares that "nobody could make her stay at home, which is
worse than hell" and is poverty-stricken.

A court record showed that Nora had been arrested about four
months previously in the company of an older woman, Anna
Stagg, at _____, for accosting sailors in a public park. Anna
Stagg was known to the County Welfare Department of S., which
was arranging transportation for her return to her own state,
Wyoming, since she was a nonresident and had been on relief ever
since she arrived in S. County six months before. Nora, who
was only accompanying Anna Stagg, was admonished and warned
to "go straight," to be "a good girl," was released on probation, in
custody of the probation officer, to Mrs. Ida Alden, at _____,
who claimed to be her aunt but was actually a distant relative
with whom Nora lived and who seemed to provide, according to
preliminary investigation, a good home. (The "aunt" verified
Nora's statement regarding her home.) Nora, on the basis of a
clinical examination, had not been involved in any sex relations
with the sailors, but at present admits indulgence in sex intercourse with "a friend at the theater," John X., whom she
"greatly admires and hopes to marry." He is about twenty-two
years old. She was greatly reluctant in giving his full name,
stating that "it was as much my fault as his and I do not wish to
make trouble for him." The medical report from Juvenile
Detention Home shows Nora to be three and one-half months
pregnant, which greatly surprises and worries her (for court
hearing, see pp. 163–165). The petition filed in her behalf alleges
an act of petty theft. The actual situation, however, is much
more serious and involves a number of other offenders.

The Boys' Statement.—Tom and Dick Dickson, eleven and
twelve years of age, live at home with their parents, Mr. and
Mrs. Jacob Dickson, at _____, in Nora's neighborhood. They
have known her only casually. They say that as they were
returning home from school on this day, Nora met them and
promised each a dollar if they rushed into the store screaming
when she gave them a signal. The boys attend Washington
Square School.

Both sets of parents were notified of the whereabouts of their children and of the eventual hearing in the Juvenile Court of S. County. The boys were released to their parents on the following day with instructions to appear in court for the hearing at a stated time and day.

Persons Contributing to Nora's Delinquencies.—Nora, however, is not the only delinquent in this case. Anna Stagg contributed to her delinquency; the woman who claimed to be her aunt and into whose custody the girl was released perjured herself in court by false testimony; the employer for whom Nora works engaged a minor without a work permit and birth certificate; "the friend at the theater" who engaged in sex relations with Nora contributed to a serious delinquency of a minor;[1] the parents, who did not report the girl as missing when she ran away and who for two years did not bother to locate her, contributed to the delinquency of their minor child.

The Wider Social Implications in Nora's Case.—It is apparent that Nora's case is very complex. Her conduct, what she now is and what she has done, to put it in the words of Cyril Burt, "are fruits of a long and complicated process of development." Her present predicament with all its problems and temptations "must be viewed not as the mere sum of its contemporary constituents, but as the product of converging social forces, operating cumulatively throughout her life."[2]

We know little of Nora aside from the legal offenses which she committed. Who is she, viewing her as an individual, as a personality, as an adolescent, as a member of a family and of a community? What does she think, how does she feel about her offenses, about her family, her future, about life itself? What started her on her delinquent career? What are the fundamental contributing factors to her delinquencies? What has life provided for Nora to enable her to avoid disorganizing influences?

She will appear in court, probably accompanied by her parents. In order to make an intelligent disposition of her case the judge will desire a report on her home situation, school, work, health, intelligence, companions, family background and relationships, and a host of other pertinent data in addition to an account of

[1] See REUBEN OPPENHEIMER, *Laws Relating to Sex Offenses against Children*, U. S. Children's Bureau Publication, No. 145 (1925).

[2] *The Young Delinquent*, p. 8.

her delinquencies.   He should also desire an account of the particular forces of our civilization which contrived for or against Nora.

The case is not simple to investigate.   At the age of fourteen Nora was a runaway from home, lied about her age, secured night employment, gave up school before completing the eighth grade. She was unable to get along with her parents; at sixteen years of age she was found in the questionable company of an older woman and accosting sailors; she is a sex delinquent, caught in the act of stealing and involving two minor boys in delinquency. But how did she acquire such a pattern of behavior and why?

What are the circumstances leading up to each new offense and what are the behavior patterns, overt and covert, at each stage of development?   How did she come in contact with those adults who contributed to her delinquencies?   What is their degree of guilt?   What influence do they exert over her?   What are the social relationships which Nora maintains with her parents, friends, lover, employer, roommate, and the urban community at large?

We have cited those who were legally responsible for Nora's misconduct.   What of all those who are indirectly responsible for the delinquency of this minor?   What are the forces leading to her father's reputed drinking and to her stepmother's sloppiness and irritability?   What is contributing to a poverty-stricken home?   Why does a quick-witted girl, capable of making her way in the world alone and under difficult circumstances, able to remain at one job for two years, find school dull and uninteresting?   Why was Nora released to a woman, apparently without sufficient study and investigation, who "claimed to be an aunt"? Why was a girl, in danger of leading a precarious life, released only with an admonition and to a probation officer who did not give careful supervision?   Why were the parents not held responsible for their minor daughter?   Why was not an inquiry undertaken to discover the specific causes of misconduct traceable to the peculiarities of her personality, to the inner content of the mental life of an adolescent, and to her outward, environmental circumstances and conflicting social relations of an urban, competitive, industrial and economic society?

Who Is a Juvenile Delinquent?[1]—Legally Nora is a delinquent by virtue of the fact that the offenses which she committed

---

[1] For the changing conceptions of delinquency see WALTER RECKLESS and MAPHEUS SMITH, *Juvenile Delinquency*, Chap. I.

constitute breaches of the law, which, if committed by adults, would be punishable by imprisonment or fine.   Again, in the eyes of the law, Nora committed offenses which only a juvenile can commit, such as truancy, running away, and incorrigibility at home.   Tom and Dick are not offenders against any explicit legal enactments but their problematic behavior was considered sufficient ground for official court intervention.

In the words of Cyril Burt "a child is to be regarded as technically delinquent when his antisocial tendencies appear so grave that he becomes, or ought to become the object of official action."[1]

The detailed legal specifications of who constitutes a delinquent child have been summarized by H. H. Lou from court statutes of several states:[2]

As delinquency is unknown to the common law, we must look exclusively to the statute for its legal definition.   A delinquent child is commonly defined by statutes as any child under a certain year of age who (1) violates a state law or local ordinance (offenses which, if committed by an adult, are punishable by death, or life imprisonment, are often excepted); (2) is wayward, incorrigible, or habitually disobedient; (3) associates with thieves, criminals, prostitutes, vagrants, or vicious persons; (4) is growing up in idleness or crime; (5) knowingly visits a saloon, pool room, billiard room, or gambling place; (6) knowingly visits a house of ill-fame; (7) wanders about streets at night; (8) wanders about railroad yards, jumps on moving trains, or enters any car or engine without authority; (9) habitually uses or writes vile, indecent, or obscene language; (10) absents himself from home without just cause or without the consent of parent or guardian; (11) is immoral or indecent; or (12) is an habitual truant.

The inclusiveness of the definition of delinquency differs in different states mainly for the reason that some states classify a condition as delinquency which other states consider as dependency or neglect.   The definition of delinquency given above is comprehensive enough to include all children who deport themselves in such a way as to injure or endanger the morals or health of themselves or others.

Students of delinquency have pointed out time and again that "there is no sharp line of cleavage by which the delinquent may be marked off from the non-delinquent.   Between them no deep gulf exists to separate the sinner from the saint, the white sheep

[1] *Op. cit.,* p. 15.

[2] *Juvenile Courts in the United States,* pp. 53–54.   Reprinted by permission of The University of North Carolina Press.

from the black.   It is all a problem of degree, of a brighter or darker grey. . . .   The line of demarcation is thus an arbitrary line, not a natural."[1]

Furthermore, Cyril Burt points out that "delinquency is, at bottom, a social rather than a psychological concept."[2]   Healy disproved long ago, with the publication of his epoch-making volume, *The Individual Delinquent*,[3] that delinquency is purely a biological phenomenon,[4] but delinquency was still largely studied from the standpoint of individual behavior patterns, mentality, temperament, mental conflicts, and complexes.[5]

Nora can no longer be regarded merely from an individual standpoint.   She must also be seen in a network of interrelations with a demoralized social organization which permits the exploitation of minors; she must be viewed in relation to a demoralized family which has lost influence and control over its children, to a society of confused and changing social life and sex mores, to an economic order which facilitates early emancipation of youth and acquirement of a variety of tastes and wishes which can be satisfied legitimately only by a comparatively few.

The extensive and painstaking research carried on by Clifford Shaw in the field of delinquency seems to point conclusively to the fact that delinquents are products of their successive social experiences,[6] or as he states it:

They [delinquencies] are a product of growth and development, a process of summation, which has its origin in the process of interaction between the individual and the situation to which he is responsive. Viewed from this standpoint, a delinquent act is a part of a dynamic life

[1] C. BURT, *op. cit.*, p. 15.

[2] *Ibid.*, p. 15.

[3] Published in 1915.   See also WILLIAM HEALY and AUGUSTA BRONNER, *The Judge Baker Foundation Case Studies*.

[4] See the writings of Cesare Lombroso, who stressed the biological factors in the genesis of crime.

[5] The reader needs, of course, to acquire some mastery over such basic concepts as these and is urged to do a certain indispensable amount of reading in the literature noted in the bibliography at the end of each chapter.

[6] See also E. W. BURGESS, "The Study of the Delinquent as a Person," *American Journal of Sociology*, XXVIII (May, 1923), 657–680; "The Cultural Approach to the Study of Personality," *Mental Hygiene*, XIV (April, 1930), 307–325.

process, which can be understood only in relation to the sequence of experience [and to the social world] of which he is a part.[1]

Who Is a Juvenile?—In the eyes of the California Juvenile Court Law, Nora is a minor and subject to the jurisdiction of the Juvenile Court until she is twenty-one years of age. The age limit for children coming under the jurisdiction of the various juvenile courts in the United States differs from sixteen to twenty-one.

The Social Age of a Juvenile.—Socially, a juvenile is a child who does not conceive himself as playing the role of an adult or who in the eyes of his group is not an adult. Nora undoubtedly conceives herself to be playing the role of an adult because of her emancipation from family, her attempt at economic independence, her sex relations with an adult, and her social contacts and relations with an adult group. The law, however, does not consider social or mental maturity in defining "juvenile," but decides strictly by chronological age.

However, in the process of investigation and treatment, psychological and social conditions, the maturity of the mind of the child, his social age are considered. For administrative purposes it is convenient and expedient to maintain a sharp line of chronological cleavage between juvenile and adult, although such a simple division can hardly be accepted by the scientist. He must regard age, not as a period in chronological history and not a date on the calendar, but as a certain stage of social and mental development.[2]

What Is Juvenile Probation (in theory)?—Nora had a previous court record, defining her, under Section 1, Subdivisions 2 and 11, of the California Juvenile Court Law, as one "who has no parent or guardian actually exercising proper parental control and who is in need of such control"; and who is "in danger of leading an idle, dissolute, lewd, or immoral life." She was placed on probation and was released to her "aunt" in custody of the probation officer.

---

[1] CLIFFORD R. SHAW and HENRY D. McKAY, *Social Factors in Juvenile Delinquency*, p. 347. See also PAULINE V. YOUNG, *Pilgrims of Russian-Town*, Chap. IX, for a study of "Urbanization as a Factor in Juvenile Delinquency."

[2] *Cf.* BURT, *op. cit.*, p. 17.

Theoretically, what does probation mean as applied to juveniles? Varying definitions are offered by different writers depending upon their views, experiences, and philosophies. While these definitions seem to differ on the surface there is more unanimity among the writers and students on the problem than their brief definitions may indicate. We quote here only from Van Waters, Chute, and Johnson.

Probation means a plan of social treatment carried out in the community which enlists the combined forces of home, school, church, settlements, playgrounds and other available social organizations working under skilled personal leadership for a central, well diagnosed goal.[1]

Probation, as it relates to a child, may be defined as a system of treatment for the delinquent child, or, in the case of the neglected or destitute child, for delinquent parents, by means of which the child and parents remain in their ordinary environment and to a great extent at liberty, but, throughout a probation period, subject to the watchful care and personal influence of an agent of the court known as the probation officer.

From the narrower legalistic viewpoint probation is either a definite disposition which the court may make in the child's case in place of commitment or it is an accompaniment or condition of an indefinitely suspended commitment.

More broadly considered, probation, as its Latin origin implies, is the entire system of proving or examining, investigating, and supervising for a period a child brought to the court for treatment. It is a definite follow-up system for court cases with a developing technique. But it is much more. It is a mission to those in need, actuated by the highest ideals of human helpfulness and social service.[2]

Probation may be defined as the suspension of final judgment in a case, giving the offender an opportunity to improve his conduct while living as a member of the community subject to conditions which may be imposed by the Court, and under the supervision and friendly guidance of a probation officer.[3]

We gather that these writers consider probation in its social as well as in its legal aspects; they include in the system of probation not only the juvenile offender but his parents or guardians; they

[1] MIRIAM VAN WATERS, *Youth in Conflict*, pp. 171–172.

[2] CHARLES L. CHUTE, *Probation in Children's Courts*, U. S. Children's Bureau Publications, No. 80 (1921), p. 7.

[3] FRED R. JOHNSON, *Probation for Juveniles and Adults*, p. 3.

see probation as a method of supervision, of guidance, and of
training by agents of the court as well as a method of self-
rehabilitation; they stress the home as well as the school, the
church, the playground, and other available community resources
as potent factors in the reeducation and self-direction of the
offender. They all agree that probation implies guidance and
reeducation "without the walls of the reformatory," that it is a
disciplinary process for the individual and a protection to society
at the same time.

Probation as Case Work and as Individualization of Justice.
The Reverend Michael J. Scanlon[1] is largely correct when he
maintains that "probation [and treatment of delinquency in
general] calls for personal and individual effort. It does not try
to correct mankind; it seeks to correct a man, an individual."

This statement implies that probation departments, strictly
speaking, are doing social case work, that is, they concern themselves primarily with the principles and techniques comprising
what Mary Richmond called those "processes which develop
personality through the adjustments consciously effected individual by individual, between men and their social environment,"[2]
and utilize the principal techniques of social study or investigation, preparation of the social case history, social diagnosis, case
planning, social treatment, and case recording. For this reason,
perhaps Joanna Colcord's definition of probation, from the
point of view of the philosophy which it embodies and the technique which it implies, has become of recent years the most
acceptable to the probation officer: "Probation is simply case work
with the added 'punch' of the law behind it."[3] Jurists, criminol-
ogists, penologists, and social workers alike have come to recognize
the importance of individualization of justice, of punishment (in
the case of the adult), of treatment, as well as of study of the
offender.

The "punch" of the law or the legal aspects of probation consist
of definite court orders, such as suspending commitment, placing
the child under supervision in custody of a probation officer, and
allowing him to remain in his own home or in a foster home rather

---

[1] "Probation in the Social Work Scheme," *Year Book, National Probation
Association* (1930), p. 238.

[2] MARY E. RICHMOND, *What Is Social Case Work?* p. 98.

[3] *Broken Homes*, p. 120.

than committing him to an institution. The legal nature of
probation is governed by statutory provisions and judicial pronouncements, but is supposed to be softened by the human
approach of the juvenile court judge, who is expected to act in the
capacity of a "wise parent."

Since delinquency is the result of manifold causes, all linked into
an intricate pattern affecting various individuals in various ways
and degrees, it can be understood only through intensive, differential study of each individual and curtailed or eliminated
through a carefully worked-out plan of treatment to fit each
situation and personality traits of the offender, that is, through the
application of social case work methods.

Dr. William Healy, pioneer student of the individual delinquent,
points out that the "dynamic center of the whole problem of
delinquency and crime will ever be the individual offender.
. . . Studies of individual cases, and final summary analyses of
these cases form the only way of arriving at the truth . . .
and lead to invaluable understandings of the individuals and to
some idea of that wonderful complex of results which we term
'personality.'"[1]   The National Commission on Law Observance
and Enforcement in its report on *Penal Institutions, Probation and
Parole* raises the vital question of who should be placed on
probation, "Which of the many hundreds, or even thousands of
individuals who come before the court during the year may safely
be released under supervision?"[2]   After a discussion of the various
implications of the classes and the traits of the offenders, of the
risks presented, of the organization of the probation departments,
of the sufficiency of later supervision, this commission arrives
at the conclusion that "the decision in each case must therefore
depend upon a scrutiny of the various elements in the case itself.
It is here perhaps that probation is making its greatest contribution to the court, as well as its most significant contribution
. . . and correctional treatment of the unsocial individual.
Probation is in essence a method of individualization."[3]   Cyril
Burt, from the standpoint of the psychologist, maintains:

The delinquent himself must be approached individually as a unique
human being, with a peculiar constitution, peculiar difficulties, and

[1] *The Individual Delinquent*, pp. 22–25.
[2] P. 155.
[3] *Ibid.*, p. 156.

peculiar problems of his own. The keynote of modern educational thought is individuality . . . by separate adjustments and readjustments for each particular child . . . the aim must be not punishment but treatment; and the target not isolated action, but their causes. Since these causes seldom float conspicuously upon the surface, such authorities must have access to all available information and possess means to make for every case intensive investigations of their own.[1]

Perhaps we can further clarify the nature of juvenile probation by a comparison with the nature of adult probation. Adult probation, in the words of Justin Miller, "is a method of treatment, a procedure which is used before any punishment has been inflicted, following either a plea of guilty or a conviction by a jury."[2] Or adult probation may be defined as an "'arrangement' between the court and the person found guilty of an offense, that he will not be sent to a penal institution if he lives up to the rules for future conduct laid down by the court, acting through and under the supervision of the probation officer."[3]

Sheldon Glueck's definition at one and the same time implies minimal requirements and offers a brief evaluation of adult probation:

What is probation? In any but a most superficial sense, this crime-treatment instrumentality consists of at least three indispensable elements: (1) The suspension, under conditions and for a period imposed by the court, of the imposition or execution of a sentence on a person convicted of crime, and his retention in the community instead of a prison; (2) the taking of such action only after study by the judge of a carefully prepared report that embodies the findings of an investigation into the offender's make-up and career; (3) and the resulting placement of the probationer under the careful supervision of an adequately trained probation officer. These minimal requirements being absent, probation too often consists of just another "lenient disposition" of criminal cases without much discrimination; a practice which only increases the many ill-considered processes of criminal justice that detract from its deterrence and add to its reputation as an elaborate and farcical game of chance.[4]

---

[1] *Op. cit.*, pp. 585–586.

[2] "Law and Probation," *Year Book, National Probation Association* (1931), p. 75.

[3] *Some Facts about Probation in Massachusetts* (pamphlet), p. 1.

[4] SHELDON GLUECK (Editor). *Probation and Criminal Justice*, pp. 3–4.

In the case of juvenile offenders the question is not centered on punishment, on a plea of guilty, on conviction by a jury, since in the eyes of the juvenile court law a juvenile does not commit a crime and is not to be sent to a penal institution.   Adult probation is a substitute for a penalty while juvenile probation is a method of reeducation.[1]

Parole, in the case of adults, is the action taken by a penal institution in remitting the remainder of the prison sentence and permitting the prisoner to return to his community under surveillance of a parole officer on a promise of good behavior.[2] The above definition would apply equally to juveniles, only when the terms "penal institutions," "prison," and "prisoner" are replaced by "correctional schools" and "delinquent."

What Is Probation in Reality?—It may be venturesome to maintain that the above definitions of probation are ideal conceptions of probation and are fully exemplified by only a limited number of probation departments, or by a limited number of cases in a department.   It is not the general rule to find "skilled personal leadership," "well diagnosed cases," "adequate community facilities," intelligent "watchful care" by a trained probation officer.   Most probation officers carry too heavy a load of cases to put into practice the ideals prescribed for them by the idealists. We can agree with Glueck when he maintains that probation, without certain standards, becomes "a farcical game of chance." That is, what probation purposes to be and what it has so far succeeded in becoming are frequently very different matters.

There are still many probation officers and other child welfare workers who believe that every person is the captain of his fate, the master of his soul.   This implies the doctrine that a person does wrong because he wills to do so; and, furthermore, that he can improve his conduct if he only chooses to "go straight" and "do what is right."   In spite of the fact that the juvenile court law is based on the philosophy that a child is not a free moral agent and does not "choose" or "will" to misbehave but does so because he lacks training and discretion, many workers and judges still expect him to conform and to "go straight," to "be a good

[1] For further definitions see E. H. Sutherland, *Principles of Criminology*, p. 349; Clayton J. Ettinger, *The Problem of Crime*, pp. 485–486; Glueck, *op. cit.*, pp. 3–4.

[2] *Cf.* ETTINGER. *op. cit.*, p. 487.

citizen" without providing adequate and tested means for his reeducation and training. Under such circumstances probation is not supervision and reeducation in any proper sense of those terms. The probation officer only too frequently hopes that the court appearance and hearing will "give the offender a big enough jolt and scare him sufficiently to keep him away from trouble." Fear is not conducive to good citizenship. Good citizenship is an art which has to be learned or imbibed through examples. Where such training is lacking, neither fear nor punishment will have the power of providing the concrete knowledge and habits required in the creation of good citizenship. Growth and development do not originate in a social vacuum; they must arise in fruitful experience. It is the function of the case worker to provide the conditions under which a child can succeed. We often realize how difficult it is even for adults to find conditions conducive to success, but we do not hesitate frequently to expect the child to advance and develop under untoward conditions. To demand reform without the propitious conditions generally means to demand the impossible, or, as someone has remarked: "It is the same as asking the fish to soar like the bird or the beast of prey to lie down with the lamb and chew nothing but green blades."

Too much reliance is also frequently placed upon the ability and willingness of the parents to guide and train their wayward child, without aid and motivation from the agency. If they had the knowledge to provide adequate training or were able to adjust their family and marital relations, their children would probably not have fallen victims to delinquency. The parents in many instances need as much training and guidance as, and frequently more than, their young offspring. On the other hand, there are workers who give up in despair because the parents at first blush are unable to handle their children.

In most cases what is needed is not drastic measures but a sustained, consistent, educative training. Old bad habits cannot be broken down abruptly; new habits can be built only slowly by intelligent and enduring training. That is, probation at its best approaches the problems of delinquency from a scientific and not from a moralistic point of view and deals with, or at least takes account of, a vast complex of tangled social and biological forces which it views as determiners of the problematic child's behavior. There are probation departments and probation officers who have had the training and time to do such a piece of work but their number, while steadily increasing, is still at a minimum.

CAN THE PROBLEM OF DELINQUENCY BE DEALT WITH BY CASE WORK METHODS ALONE?

Delinquency is too complex a social problem to be dealt with by any single method.   Case work can only join forces with other social work techniques and with community reorganization programs in the work with delinquent children, their parents, and the neighborhoods in which they live; with the economic forces when they fail to provide their bread; with the educational forces when they fail to develop the youth and assure social progress and adjustment; with the religious forces when they fail to imbue with the spirit of God; and with the legal forces when they fail to sanction social justice.

Perhaps the question: "Can juvenile delinquency be dealt with by case work methods alone?" should be changed to: "What is the nature and extent of social case work in the adjustment of delinquents?"   Let us look at Nora and her like from another angle.

Nora, at the time of her arrest, was sixteen years and five months old.   She was born in August, 1919.   The military record of her father shows that he returned from the World War to this country in January, 1919.   He had brought his French bride of a few months with him.   Nora was born during the postwar hysteria.   Nora's earliest impressions are typical of that period; they were based on stories of mob murder, cynical reactions of gassed fathers, and sentimental attitudes of ardent patriots. Nora, as Maxine Davis would put it, grew up in the midst of "crass materialism," of jazz and the shock of the economic collapse of 1929.   She has seen how fame was achieved by "Al Capone, Huey Long, and Mae West" and their like.   She has heard remotely of "Roosevelt, Einstein, and Jane Addams." She has seen poverty and starvation, and has read of incompetent "heiresses literally tossing away millions."   She had seen "people who wanted to work but could not get it and those who would not work, living on the same level of government bounty."[1]   She has seen persons, families, and groups deny tradition and social norms and live according to their own design and pleasure.

[1] MAXINE DAVIS, *The Lost Generation*, pp. 4–5.

Still, Nora emerges neat and clean, pleasant and friendly, employed, quick-witted. We also find her a determined young lady, resourceful, cynical, and "dangerous." Should Nora be regarded as a delinquent or as a victim of disorganized social and economic forces which failed to supply guidance and support? Or should society be held the defendant and called upon to plead guilty in this case of a girl in trouble?

From the standpoint of a particular technique, we may ask now,[1] is Nora a case for the court to deal with, assisted by a probation officer and detention house, or by an institute of family relations? Or by a social clinic which would undertake to examine, diagnose, and treat those social-economic forces which enter into Nora's situation? Should Nora be examined by a psychiatrist in a child guidance clinic or should the contributors and circumstances leading up to her delinquencies be examined by a sociologist who would concern himself with the maladjustments of group life and social forces? Should the two small boys be called into court as witnesses, or should the war magnates, Wall Street, jazz writers, politicians, skyscraper builders, exploiters of child labor, incompetent schoolteachers, liquor dealers, fathers interested in women and wine, be called to fill the courtroom? Should their cases be heard by a judge—a legal authority—in a juvenile court—a judicial tribunal—and supervised by a probation officer—a representative of the law—or should these cases be heard by antitrust, antiwar, antipoverty, antiliquor, antiignorance leagues? Just how informal can legal people be, with the centuries of legal tradition and precedent behind them, little changed in spite of the current overwhelming social changes? What attitudes does the child form about the procedure, legal in character though unofficially executed, when it barely touches the issues of the lives of adolescents in our civilization? What does the public think about girls and boys arrested and detained in juvenile halls for offenses which are not nearly so gross as many unpunished offenses of crooked politicians, shyster lawyers, "pillars" of society?

These and certain of the following questions are raised to indicate the complexity of the problem of juvenile delinquency and the far-reaching issues involved in its treatment, as well as to

---

[1] Later we shall inquire into what agency should deal with cases of juveniles; see *infra*, pp. 22–30, 239–246.

call attention to the confusion which exists in the current thinking as to the nature and function of the agency which should assume control over the problem.   The formulation of administrative policies is beyond the scope of this book, but the reader must gain insight into the *pro's* and *con's* of the proposals advocated by professional groups in this field and realize the experimental and temporary nature of present work with problematic youth.   It is hoped that such a realization will stimulate the reader to gain a newer and broader vision and greater sympathetic insight and to pursue scientific procedure in work with children.

In large cities and counties the juvenile courts hear thousands of cases annually, coming from every section of the metropolis and of the outlying rural districts in the hinterland.   These cases represent a wide variety of national, cultural, economic, social, educational, and religious elements.   Would it be better for some other social agency (and if so, which one?) well trained in psychology, sociology, pedagogy, but with legal jurisdiction and police powers, to assume responsibility for these cases?[1]   What could child guidance clinics, institutes of family relations, visiting teachers contribute to the adjustment of wayward youth and their parents?   Are these agencies equipped to carry the load? Are their underlying philosophies of human nature in the present social-economic order such that they will be an improvement over a progressive juvenile court?

It follows that the problem of delinquency is in large measure a result of community disorganization and of rapid social and cultural changes.   The swift processes of industrialization and urbanization, the great mobility which characterize modern life, are accompanied by a breakdown of the older social institutions, by an uprooting of established customs and habits, by a reevaluation of existing social controls.   Older institutions and means of social control—the family, the church, the common law, the neighborhood—have lost most of their effectiveness in this era

[1] See THOMAS D. ELIOT, "Case Work for Quasi-delinquent Children by Educational and Other Non-court Methods," *Journal of Delinquency*, IX (January–March, 1925), 50; HELEN T. WOOLEY, "Should the School Take Over the Work of the Children's Courts?" *Proceedings of the National Probation Association* (1919), pp. 105–112; THOMAS D. ELIOT, "Should Courts Do Case Work?" *Survey*, LX (Sept. 15, 1928), 601–603; see also MARJORIE BELL, "Courts and Case Work: A Reply," *Survey*, LXI (Oct. 15, 1928), 91–92.

of transition while the newer institutions—the secular school, industry, social legislation, the social agencies—have not as yet gained sufficient and effective control.

Moreover, the effects of conflicts of culture, of deteriorating areas, of slums, inadequate play space, unsuitable school programs, limited opportunities for proper employment, and so on, are a complex of social problems over which case workers as such have little control.

A group of writers, jurists, and social reformers have started a vigorous campaign of crime prevention.[1] Frederick Thrasher,[2] outstanding student of delinquency and crime, remarks:

A preventive program working with the group and the community promises quicker and more economical realization of the goal of crime prevention than one dealing merely with unadjusted individuals who come to the attention of attendance officers, juvenile courts, guidance clinics and similar agencies. While it is necessary to deal with the individual problem child, from the standpoint of crime prevention, it is probably more important to go out and redeem the so-called "bad companions" who are so often held responsible for the downfall of the individual. The individual product of the gang, the pool-room, or the streets, is but a symptom of the processes of demoralization which are producing delinquents in wholesale lots. Sociologically, therefore, the individual delinquent is far less important than the community influences which create him. If the pool-room or similar hang-out, for instance, is the "cradle of crime," it is far more economical to regulate it rigidly, or to wipe it out entirely by providing more effective substitutes, than it is to maintain an elaborate and expensive social machinery to correct the individual maladjustments which it produces or to protect society from the constant streams of delinquents which emerge from it.

This is the sociological, as contrasted with the individualistic, approach to the problem of crime prevention. It is the community, as contrasted with the institutional, attack on the problem. The failure of the programs of educational, welfare and recreational agencies to prevent crime may be summed up best by the term, "institutional mindedness." This is the collective individualism which puts the supposed success of institutional programs ahead of the community program. Vested interests undoubtedly enter the picture at this point, but whatever the explanation, the fact remains that community

[1] See SHELDON GLUECK and ELEANOR T. GLUECK, (Editors), *Preventing Crime.*

[2] FREDERICK M. THRASHER, "Crime Prevention through Community Planning," *University of Chicago Magazine* (March, 1935), 173–176, 198.

planning for crime prevention and consequent co-ordination and integration of pertinent activities into a well-rounded program is well-nigh impossible under these conditions.

This point of view is not difficult to understand nor does it require any large concessions on the part of social groups and institutions to make verbal acknowledgment of its validity. The real difficulties are encountered when any thorough-going attempt is made to carry it out in a practical program.

Thrasher and his associates and others working in similar fields are fully aware of the wider social and economic implications in crime prevention. They are concentrating on small infested areas, knowing well that their work, like case work, is a stopgap until the larger issues can be cleared up by sound and fundamental methods of social justice and social reorganization.

The philosophy of the case worker is predicated on the belief that it is easier to reconstruct human personality than to change or rebuild the social and economic order. We recall the statement of Maurice Hindus, recognized as a competent authority on Russian life, who maintains that the Russians in their great offensive "for a new world along two vast, all-embracing fronts—that of economics with the aim of creating a new economic order, and of sociology with the aim of creating a new human personality"—have suffered many rebuffs on the economic front, but "within a short space of sixteen years [they have] so 'reboiled' or 'reforged' the human being in Russia that he is a new personage on earth, with a body of new aims, attitudes and responses."[1]

To some extent, the case worker is facing a problem similar to that of the physician during an epidemic. The physician cannot afford to wait in administering treatment, if his patient is to survive, until the epidemic is stopped by public health measures. He must use ameliorative measures in each afflicted case while the slower process of prevention is put into effect, even though he well knows that the patient may again succumb to the prevailing disease.

Prevention of a social ill is perhaps an even more complex process than prevention of a physical ill. The delinquent whose demoralization is an outgrowth of the breakdown of familial, social, economic, religious, political, or communal forces cannot

[1] *The Great Offensive*, p. viii.

wait for adjustment through the reorganization of these forces. His life and that of those associated with him would be wasted while waiting for the change. Both an immediate attack and a long-range program are in urgent demand, when we are dealing "with that most perishable of all commodities: youth," as Maxine Davis[1] states it.

It is evident that there are organizing as well as disorganizing elements in the existing social order. By case work methods the delinquent may be brought into contact with some of the organizing elements. He may be adjusted to some more suitable environment; also by case work methods the existing social situation may be redefined to him and a certain degree of adjustment achieved. Drunkenness of parents, poverty, public aid, unemployment, slums, excessive mobility, and other social ills contributing to delinquency probably cannot be eliminated from a dynamic society within a single lifetime, if ever; and all affected families and their children cannot be removed *en masse* from these conditions. While the social order is slowly reorganizing for the better and preventive measures are being initiated there remains little to do other than to adjust the individual as far as possible to the existing order, abnormal as it is. Needless to say, there will always be persons who will need individual adjustment however well organized the society in which he lives.

Gordon Hamilton's[2] statements regarding the relation of a broad framework of prevention (as the Webbs put it) to preoccupation with individual cases may be applied with equal validity to our problem. Why should one be concerned about individual personalities? Cannot delinquency be dealt with effectively through measures for public health, wholesale recreation, social justice, adequate wage legislation, social education, and other preventive efforts? Much as we need all these measures and efforts, it is not probable that behavior problems will be solved even by the most successful mass treatment. "The more socialized we become the more the individual emerges. . . . What he has to learn is to have satisfaction in group as well as individual purposes. . . . Case work today is in some confusion whether to look outwards to broad avenues of social reform for

[1] *Op. cit.*, p. ix.

[2] GORDON HAMILTON, "Methods of Family Social Work," *Proceedings of the International Conference of Social Work*, II (July, 1932), 178–186.

help or inwards to an increase in man's power of self-knowledge and self-direction. The best case worker does both."

It is often remarked that when children are provided with wholesome activities, congenial school work, adequate play facilities, when they have an opportunity for an outlet for their energies and for self-expression, they do not engage in delinquent behavior. It is obvious then that it should become the concern of every worker to provide such opportunities for every child. The worker should familiarize himself not only with the existing community resources but with the possibilities for creating them wherever they are lacking. For this reason the community approach to delinquency will be presented in this volume in some detail.[1] But it must be remembered, however, that case work is valuable also in group work. Each child finds self-expression in his own, unique, manner.

It is also undoubtedly true that parents, perhaps more so than their children, need individual adjustment. The child welfare worker often spends more time with the parents than with the children. There are many cases where wholesome activities, play, self-expression, etc., will not overcome intense conflicts raging between parents and children, or between home and community, and will not stop conflicts arising because of difference in culture patterns, or because of personal frustration, fears, lack of social and economic status, and numerous other reasons. These problems need the attention of the case worker.

Group activities, well planned and carried out, wholesome recreation, satisfying school work, suitable employment, and so on, are positive assets, as will be seen later, to a case worker in the adjustment of the individual to his unique social setting. The case worker must strive for a correlation of all efforts which will aid the individual in his reorganization.

WHAT AGENCIES SHOULD DEAL WITH PROBLEMS OF JUVENILES?[2]

The Honorable L. B. Day, Judge of the District Court of Omaha, in a paper presented before the National Probation Association in 1926, voiced the opinion of many when he said: "We sentimentally talk in a big hearted way about giving the

[1] See *infra*, pp. 239–246.

[2] This question is here raised only to stimulate independent thinking on controversial issues. The reader is urged to refer to pp. 239–250 and 535–536.

child another chance, when after all, does not every judge feel that it's a case of giving that family another chance to adjust itself? Does not every probation officer know (if they do not, they ought to know) that what they are really doing is family case work?"[1]

Perhaps the judge is assuming too much when he believes that the probation officer is "really doing family case work." Family case work is a tremendous undertaking, and comparatively few of the probation departments or even private child welfare agencies are equipped to carry on family case work. Their personnel is at best rarely trained in more than the specialized field of child welfare and child psychology. They rarely have the administrative facilities of a well-organized family welfare agency. They often have too excessive loads of children's cases to enable them to delve into the problems of family discord, relief, ill-health, unemployment, and so on. But Judge Day is correct when he implies that children's problems need the wholehearted attention of a family case-work agency. It has been repeatedly stated that the family and not the child is the unit of work and treatment in children's problems. Problem families tend to produce problem children.

If we accept this underlying philosophy of work with children we may question the logic, expediency, and legitimacy of child welfare agencies in general, and juvenile courts and probation departments in particular. It is a well-known fact that these workers do not approach the problems pouring into their agencies from the standpoint of the philosophy underlying their work. Many concern themselves for the most part only with the overt manifestations of child misconduct. Under such circumstances they are dealing simply with the symptoms and are attempting to remedy situations which should be attacked at their rotten roots and not at their withered blossoms. This procedure is similar to that of the dentist who would concern himself only with the swelling of the jaw, overlooking the impacted tooth, or as Jonah J. Goldstein[2] observes:

In the treatment of crime we show less judgment than the plumber does with a leaky pipe and a flooded cellar. The plumber bails out the

[1] "A Unified Court Dealing with Family Matters," The Courts and the Prevention of Delinquency, *Proceedings of the National Probation Association* (1926), p. 56.

[2] *The Family in Court*, pp. 102–103.

water, finds and stops the leak.   Legal plumbers bail out the water; no
effort is made to stop the leak.

Courts are conducted on a revolving door basis.   Humans are turned
in, to be turned out, to be turned in, to be turned out—without beginning
and without end.   Why not stop this useless judicial merry-go-round?

However, another assumption should be considered also,
namely, that it is possible to adjust children to their parents
under various conditions of life.   Undoubtedly many children
have been adjusted and have thrived in precarious family and
social environments, but it is doubtful if the bulk of the cases
dealt with by children's agencies can claim any considerable
success, to judge from the findings of the studies made by Drs.
Sheldon and Eleanor Glueck.[1]

There is another consideration which must be mentioned here.
From the work of the family welfare agencies it does not appear
that they too could claim any considerable success in adjusting
broken homes, marital discord, personal and social disorganization
which ravage the modern family.   We need an evaluative study—
let us say, *Five Hundred Disorganized Families*—by which could be
judged the effectiveness of the therapeutic work of a representative, if there be such, family welfare agency.   It must be remembered that procedures of case work agencies should not throw
any reflection on case work itself, since its principles and philosophy are sound within its own sphere—and only await workers
with more training and vision to be put into effect.

The school has also been considered as a possible agency to deal
with children's problems.   Thomas D. Eliot[2] advocated the
unofficial handling of problem cases by the school as early as 1914
and Henrietta Additon and Neva Deardorf[3] in 1919.   The argument for this plan is that the schools can handle the problem
of delinquency more efficiently than the court; that the stigma
attached to court action would be avoided; that the school is in a
more advantageous position to secure the needed information;

---

[1] *One Thousand Juvenile Delinquents; Five Hundred Criminal Careers; Five
Hundred Delinquent Women.*

[2] See *The Juvenile Court and the Community;* also "Welfare Agencies,
Special Education, and the Courts," *American Journal of Sociology*, XXXI
(July, 1925), 58–78.

[3] "That Child," *Survey*, XLII (May 3, 1919), 186–188; see also SUTHER-
LAND, *op. cit.*, pp. 286–292.

that the school can recognize problematic behavior early and deal with it on the spot; and so on. The argument is sound. The statement of William I. Thomas and Dorothy S. Thomas will, however, indicate the actual role of the school in this situation:

The effects of the concentration of "education" in the schools and their lagging response in taking over those functions which cannot be defined as narrowly intellectual have been considered with relation to the child. We have seen the confusion that resulted from the failure of the schools to assume responsibility in these matters, and the multiplicity of agencies that arose to fill the gap. We have further seen new developments in the schools within the last decade or so, whereby they are tending more and more to supplant these other agencies and to assume responsibility for vocational and social adjustments—to become "behavior institutions." But what of that great mass of adults who were turned out upon the world as children half-educated with regard to the adjustments demanded of them, ill-prepared vocationally and bound by traditions which the changing economic and social order made entirely obsolete? Our interest in these adults lies chiefly in their functioning as parents and teachers and in their ability to handle behavior problems of children. We have seen abundant evidence of their limitations in the handling of specific situations.[1]

Grace Abbott argues that "the addition of the psychiatrist and improvement in the probation services have not resulted in the increased percentage of 'cures' that was expected"[2] of the juvenile court when it was first organized in Chicago in 1899. Neither has it appeared that the addition of a psychiatrist, or for that matter a complete psychiatric service, to other agencies, public or private, "resulted in the expected increased percentage of 'cures.'" As far as the juvenile court is concerned, it may be argued that an increased percentage of "cures" is more dependent upon some solution of complexities of modern social and economic life, of the breakdown of the control of social institutions, mores, family life, than upon the services of a psychiatrist, judge, or probation officer. The social sciences and the social arts have not developed to the point where the juvenile courts can profit greatly by their analyses of the problems involved in personal

[1] WILLIAM I. THOMAS and DOROTHY S. THOMAS, *The Child in America*, p. 295.

[2] "The Juvenile Court and a Community Program for Treating and Preventing Delinquency," *The Social Service Review*, X (June, 1936), 234.

and social disorganization. The social service aspects of the court have lagged behind in proportion to the lack of development in the art of social service and in administration in general. Certain judges maintain that as soon as psychiatry, pedagogy, and social work have enough to contribute they will lay down their judicial robes in favor of those who can administer better the principles of socialization (see Judge Hyatt's statement, pp. 534–535).

It may be argued that none of the agencies mentioned above "ever had a fair chance to demonstrate its ability. If they were given enough financial and moral backing by the community or the official bodies the agencies could demonstrate their worth." Perhaps the backing was not forthcoming because these agencies, with few exceptions, have not had the point of view and philosophy which would tend to make their work a success. They have in many instances not shown vision and the grasp of the wider social implications involved in work with children and families. The lack of an adequate social philosophy has made much of their work routine procedure. Under such circumstances it is almost a foregone conclusion that they would fail to win the needed public support.

The pioneers in the juvenile court movement did have vision and established the court on sound and adequate philosophy (see *infra*, pp. 177–181), but under severe pressure of work and with an inadequately trained staff, and perhaps with few educational training facilities, further development and application of the underlying philosophy have been largely overlooked in the daily work with juvenile offenders. A severe blast of criticism has been directed against probation work, with both juveniles and adults. Elsewhere[1] we shall see the limitations of and the handicaps under which probation departments operate. Suffice it to say here that the probation officer gets more serious child unadjustment cases than any social agency, and these come to him only after much harm has been done and frequently after the delinquency pattern has been operating over an extended period of time.

Students of juvenile delinquency have for many years advocated and urged the establishment of a family court[2] with a separate

---

[1] See *infra*, pp. 232–236; also 478–479.

[2] For a discussion of family courts, see pp. 239–243; THOMAS D. ELIOT, *The Juvenile Court and the Community;* also SANFORD BATES, "The Possibility

division for children's cases, based on the belief that if children come in conflict with the law the family should be studied. Such courts are in successful operation in some communities, as will be seen later.[1] Bernard Flexner, Reuben Oppenheimer, and Katherine Lenroot, pioneers and authorities on the juvenile court movement, have long ago pointed out certain problems in the consolidation in one court the jurisdiction over juvenile cases and certain types of adult cases (and their contention still holds true under present conditions):[2]

Those advocating the consolidation in one court of children's cases, cases of adults offending against children, cases of non-support, and desertion, and cases of divorce are impressed with the desirability of enabling the court dealing with children to dispose of related problems that closely affect their welfare and to extend the safeguards of the juvenile court to children who must appear as witnesses in cases against adults. . . .

It may be questioned whether the time, effort, and money devoted to domestic-relations cases should not have been directed first of all toward improving the service rendered in children's cases. In some communities juvenile-court work undoubtedly has been damaged through the effect the family-court movement has had on public opinion. It is a mistake to regard the juvenile court as a task accomplished, as a foundation upon which to rear the structure of a family court before the juvenile court has been given sufficient attention and intelligent criticism to enable it to fulfill its aims.

It is often maintained that because of the delinquent's fear of the court he cannot be adjusted even though it is manned by "trained probation officers, good psychiatric clinics and judges who are intelligent about the value of psychiatric and social treatment."[3] It is believed that the judges should not decide what should be done for a large number of delinquents who require

---

and Methods of Increasing Family Responsibility for Juvenile Delinquency," *Journal of Criminal Law and Criminology*, XII (May, 1921), 61–69.

[1] See pp. 239–243.

[2] *The Child, The Family, and the Court*, U. S. Children's Bureau Publication, No. 193 (1929), pp. 49–50. For a discussion of the limitations of the family court see Roscoe Pound, "The Limits of Effective Legal Action," *Report of the Twenty-second Annual Meeting of the Pennsylvania Bar Association* (1916), pp. 233–238.

[3] GRACE ABBOTT, "Juvenile Courts," *Survey*, LXXII (May 15, 1936), 132.

not legal but social treatment. "This should be the function of the neighborhood center to which parents could turn for help in child training, just as they have learned to turn to child health centers for guidance in the physical care of infants and preschool children."[1] In a small percentage of cases (Judge Hoffman of the Court of Domestic Relations of Cincinnati estimates it to be 10 per cent) where there is an "issue" to settle regarding the legal rights of parents and children, or cases involving disputes as to custody, commitment, and so on, the juvenile court should be used. The juvenile court judge and the probation officer who have vision and training are already referring a large number of cases to private social agencies for care and treatment. The court has been used by some schools and agencies as the "dumping ground" for cases which could and should be handled to greater advantage by nonlegal methods. A more careful assortment of cases should be undertaken by some intake agency, such as was done by the recently organized Bureau of Adjustments of the New York Children's Court.[2] This bureau should decide for all children whether to refer them to the court or to a nonjudicial agency.[3] The trained worker and socialized jurist as well as the worker in any secondary social institution, whether that be a court or a neighborhood center which studies the unadjusted and delinquent child, should take every precaution to eliminate fear. Fear paralyzes the best of intentions and thinking. However, it must be remembered that the neighborhood center is just as much of a stopgap as the court is in the attempt to deal with delinquency.

Cases presenting problems similar to those of Nora are matters for legal consideration since they involve statutory rape and other offenses of adults contributing to the delinquencies of minors, and because they often necessitate institutional commitment and deprivation of parents of the custody of their children—matters upon which only a legal tribunal has power to take action (see pp. 150–159). Under present organization the juvenile court—which is generally a branch of the superior court —can deal with adult contributory cases and avoid the appearance of children in a criminal court and their subjection to cross-examination by defense attorneys in a public court.

[1] *Ibid.*, p. 132.
[2] *Survey*, May 15, 1936, 149.
[3] See statement by Judge Robert Scott, *infra*, pp. 244–246.

Children who live, as stated before, in poverty-stricken homes, discouraged and demoralized families, children who are subject to the exploitation of unscrupulous employers, liquor dealers, mongers of salacious literature and wild movies, whose parents are dependent upon relief, and whose only security is the dole, can rarely be rehabilitated even by the most painstaking efforts of a single social worker or agency. To be effective the neighborhood center should at the same time be a community reorganization agency on a large scale, a promoter of social justice, a stabilizer of urban conditions of life and labor, of changing social mores, of culture conflicts, and other social and economic forces which in a large measure contribute to delinquency and disorganization of the home and the community.

It is of interest to note that Soviet Russia—which has perhaps faced the most difficult problem of child banditry and demoralization—has dealt in the past and still continues to deal with the majority of delinquent and "wild" children under sixteen years of age through a Commission of Cases for Minors. This commission uses casework, vocational, and educational methods in the reconditioning of these children. At present "only the cases of those between sixteen and eighteen are referred to (children's) courts . . . although the measures applied are of a medico-pedagogical nature, very similar to those used for younger children. Only when the circumstances of the crime convince the court that these measures will not be adequate may the minor be sentenced to deprivation of liberty." (According to Mary S. Callcott, *Russian Justice*, pp. 207*ff*.)

In the last analysis the most common argument among progressive jurists, scientists, and social workers in this country centers around a non-legal, educational agency—with some judicial powers—equipped to deal, at least with youth under sixteen years of age whose problematic behavior can be adjusted by means of individualized social treatment. It should be remembered, however, that such an agency must set prevention as its goal and use preventive measures in the eradication of the very sources of delinquency and disorganization.

There are some who believe that there is danger that in the reorganization of the functions of the juvenile court the criminal court will gain jurisdiction over those youths over sixteen, seventeen, or eighteen years of age who had committed some "serious" crime or felony. Great care should be taken that these youth are dealt with either by the juvenile court or other child-caring agency. Minors are not fit subjects for criminal courts and their decisions and need to be kept under juvenile court jurisdiction. While the reorganization of the juvenile court is for the present visionary, the discussion indicates the trend of progressive thinking.

Broadly considered, the philosophy, the social processes, and techniques of social case work with problematic youth should to a large extent be independent of the administrative setup of the particular social work agency dealing with problems of youth. The aim of all agencies dealing with youth is intelligent understanding in order to bring about a lasting adjustment between youth and their social environment. The case work aspects of probation and child welfare work of any agency are not governed by any narrowly defined principles or regulations of some particular administrative setup. Skillful ingenuity, trained insight, and scientific procedure should be the foundations upon which study and treatment of children in any agency are built.

It is clear even from the single case cited that whether delinquencies appear in such complex form as Nora's or with more or fewer concomitants, that before any plan of adjustment is made a great deal must be learned about such Noras, Toms, and Dicks, their past and present behavior patterns, their families, their communities, as well as the entire natural history of their misconduct, which in most instances has a long incubation period.

Much of the blundering in the work with delinquent youth is generally due to a lack of the use of adequate case work processes and techniques. In the following chapters an attempt is made to discuss in some detail and to indicate as far as possible the logic of social case study, social diagnosis, and social adjustment. Later we shall indicate how the modern social case worker can stand in line with the community organizer, the social engineer, the progressive educator, the social coordinator, the health officer, the versatile clergyman, and the new public-spirited legislature. The modern social case worker—the choice of the right personality is assumed—well trained and educated in the wider implications of social pathology, psychology, and sociology, must aid in assuming responsibility in the shaping of social policy, in social engineering, and social justice. The social case worker is perhaps the only one in the unique position of learning at length and from within the needs, pathological processes and their causal factors, interests, and desires of the unadjusted.

Selected Bibliography

1. ADDAMS, JANE: *The Spirit of Youth on the City Streets*, The Macmillan Company, 1909.
2. AICHHORN, AUGUST: *Wayward Youth*, The Viking Press, Inc., 1935.
3. BENEDICT, AGNES E.: *Children at the Crossroads*, Commonwealth Fund, 1930.
4. BOGARDUS, E. S.: *The City Boy and His Problems*, Rotary Club of Los Angeles, 1926.
5. BURT, CYRIL: *The Young Delinquent*, D. Appleton-Century Company, Inc., 1925.
6. COLCORD, JOANNA: *Broken Homes*, Russell Sage Foundation, 1922.
7. COLE, LUELLA: *The Psychology of Adolescence*, Farrar & Rinehart, Inc., 1936.
8. COOLEY, CHARLES H.: *Social Organization*, Charles Scribner's Sons, 1909.
9. ———: *Social Process*, Charles Scribner's Sons, 1918.
10. ———: *Human Nature and the Social Order*, Charles Scribner's Sons, 1922.
11. DAVIS, MAXINE: *The Lost Generation*, The Macmillan Company, 1936.
12. HEALY, WILLIAM: *The Individual Delinquent*, Little, Brown & Company, 1922.
13. JOHNSON, FRED R.: *Probation for Juveniles and Adults*, The Century Company, 1928.
14. KENWORTHY, MARION E., "The Logic of Delinquency," *Publications of the American Sociological Society*, XVI (1921), 197–204.
15. NIMKOFF, MEYER F.: *The Child*, J. B. Lippincott Company, 1934.
16. O'NEIL, JERALD: *That Problem Called the Modern Boy*, Sears Publishing Company, 1931.
17. RECKLESS, WALTER, and MAPHEUS SMITH: *Juvenile Delinquency*, McGraw-Hill Book Company, Inc., 1932.
18. SAYLES, MARY B.: *Three Problem Children*, Commonwealth Fund, 1924.
19. ———: *Child Guidance Cases*, Commonwealth Fund, 1936.
20. SHAW, CLIFFORD, and HENRY D. McKAY: *Social Factors in Juvenile Delinquency*, National Commission on Law Observance and Enforcement, No. 13, Vol. II, 1931.
21. SLAWSON, JOHN: *The Delinquent Boy: A Sociological Study*, Richard G. Badger, 1926.
22. SULLENGER, EARL: *Social Determinants in Juvenile Delinquency*, John Wiley & Sons, Inc., 1936.
23. *The Child, the Clinic and the Court* (A Symposium), New Republic, Inc., 1925.
24. THOM, DOUGLAS A.: *Everyday Problems of Everyday Child.*, D. Appleton-Century Company, Inc., 1927.
25. THOMAS, WILLIAM I.: *The Unadjusted Girl*, Little, Brown & Company, 1924.

26. ———, and DOROTHY S. THOMAS: *The Child in America*, Alfred A. Knopf, Inc., 1928.

27. UNITED STATES CHILDREN'S BUREAU: *Facts about Juvenile Delinquency, Its Prevention and Treatment*, No. 215, 1933.

28. VAN WATERS, MIRIAM: *Youth in Conflict*, New Republic, Inc., 1925.

29. WHITE HOUSE CONFERENCE ON CHILD HEALTH AND PROTECTION: *The Delinquent Child*, IV C-2, The Century Company, 1932.

30. YEOMANS, EDWARD: *Shackled Youth*, Atlantic Monthly Press Publications, 1921.

Suggestions for Further Study

1. To what extent can a case agency deal with problems of delinquency?

2. What is meant by treatment of delinquency? prevention? adjustment?

3. What social forces should be combatted in the work with delinquents?

4. What is the definition in your community of a juvenile? a delinquent? delinquency? crime? How do they differ from those given here?

5. What are the distinctions between physical age, social, anatomical, chronological?

6. Write your own definition of probation and indicate the basis for it.

7. What is meant by individualization of justice? To what extent can it be attained through case work methods? Can these methods be applied to adult offenders?

8. What is the distinction between probation and "another chance"? and parole?

9. What agency should deal with juvenile offenders? what unit of government?

10. What is a better term than juvenile delinquent? Why?

11. On what bases were the above books in the bibliography selected? What additions do you suggest? Indicate the bases for your choice.

12. Compare Burt's and Healy's findings, their methods of study. Compare Burgess and Sayles, Shaw and Addams, as to point of view, significance of suggestions for dealing with delinquency, use of scientific methods, and concepts.

13. What is the significance of the studies by Saul Drucker and Maurice B. Hexter, *Children Astray*, and Agnes E. Benedict, *Children at the Crossroads?*

14. What is the contribution of the recent books published in the field of unadjustment of adolescents?

CHAPTER II

THE COMPREHENSIVE EXPLORATION OF A CASE[1]
ILLUSTRATIVE MATERIAL

"Only through a friendly abbreviated living of the child's life over again with him, following the sequence of time and events, can there be any sound understanding of the genesis of his delinquency. This study of the delinquent can only be carried out by obtaining from those who have known him in school and at play, or from other sources, accounts as truthful as possible of all that he has been through in life. The aim is scientific procedure. If such a study of a human being is not worth the utmost scientific effort, then nothing in the world is."—White House Conference on Child Health and Protection, The Delinquent Child, p. 75.

The following cases of Marilyn Smith[2] and Marvin Levkowitz[3] are illustrative of comprehensive exploration and social study of two problem youths and their problem parents. These youths came from two widely differing social milieus and present interesting contrasts in personal and social traits. While these two cases have never come to the attention of a legal or public agency, their behavior is typical of the cases dealt with daily by these agencies. It was practically impossible to secure from a legal agency an intensive study of a case which would show in detail and from the sociological as well as other angles the various implications of problem cases. The case of Marilyn Smith is presented here as a sample not of recording but of the logic of social study. This case is used for classroom teaching or self-teaching purposes. The rather high economic level of the Smith family is not uncommon in private or public child welfare cases, but the problems presented by the family and the girl are not vastly different from the problems presented in homes on any

[1] The term exploration or social study is much to be preferred to the term investigation. A child needs to be studied and not investigated.

[2] The study was made by Pauline V. Young and is still an active case. Presented in this book with the permission of the parents.

[3] The case was prepared by Gustave K. Kohn, of the Jewish Big Brothers Association of Los Angeles, for the study of the Child Guidance Clinic. Quoted by permission of both agencies.

economic level.   Furthermore, it must be remembered that this book deals with both delinquent and problem youth.   In both cases the studies are presented first, and later the findings and plan of treatment are discussed (see pp. 296–315 and 380–381).

Social Study of Marilyn Smith

10–14–35.   San Bolero High School phoned Mrs. Smith that unless Marilyn's attendance was more regular they would have to file in the juvenile court for truancy and insubordination.   Marilyn has been absent from school on several occasions without legitimate excuse.   She has left home and lived for several days with her aunt or with a friend of hers in Los Angeles.   Her father, who is a well-known physician in his home town (of about 60,000 population and about 45 miles from Los Angeles), asked the assistance of a sociologist in making a study of the girl as well as of the home situation.   He stated that he had consulted a psychiatrist but did not get any practical suggestions and he and his wife are at a loss as to what to do with their daughter.

Andrew C. Smith, M.D.......	48
Alice Smith.................	43
Tom.......................	22
Joe........................	21
Fred.......................	18
Marilyn....................	16 (only survival of triplets)
Charles....................	10
Mrs. Margaret Price........	69 (maternal grandmother)

10–16–35.   Visited family at home.   According to the mother's statement, Marilyn has been defiant, unamenable to discipline, staying out late after midnight, absenting herself from home and school, and "choosing a rather rough crowd of boys and girls to run around with."   Three months ago she found a job working week ends in a drive-in sandwich shop.   She met a Catholic man fifteen years her senior, "became infatuated with him, and the trouble started then."   He has partial paralysis of the left leg.   He is the brother of a girl coworker at the shop.   When the parents objected to her keeping company with "this cripple" Marilyn left home.   Her defiance is of long standing.   "She is stubborn, but she comes by it honestly—from her father's side of the family. . . . She is unfeeling, hard, and hard to deal with.   Mind you, she wants to marry this cripple."

Family Background.—Dr. and Mrs. Smith are American born of American white parentage, nominally of Methodist faith.   They were both reared in a small town in California, and not until after they were married did they live in a large community, although they had access to the city.   Dr. Smith is Mrs. Smith's second husband.   Her first husband, an older brother of the doctor, died in a railroad accident when their first child was four years of age, and the second one three.   "The fact that Dr. Smith is the stepfather of the two oldest boys has never made any difference to any member of the family. The children have never been conscious of any difference and don't even remember their own father."

Mrs. Smith states that her parents moved several times from California to the middle west, where her father owned and operated a grain elevator. He was highly respected by his business associates, but the family had a hard time making a living as her father "was too trusting and suffered serious business reverses." There were times when his ten children had very little food for several days in succession. They were, however, "a strongly united family" and the parents were devoted to each other and to the children. Nothing disturbed her until she was a girl in high school and craved pretty clothes which her mother could not supply. She believes that perhaps she has paid too much attention to Marilyn's wardrobe because of an "unsatisfied desire carried over from her own childhood. But do you believe she appreciates it? She is careless and even ungrateful for the finest clothes she gets."

Dr. Smith was born and raised on a fruit ranch in California. He had two older brothers and a younger sister. His father died of pneumonia when the oldest boy was ten years old. An uncle came to live with them until the boys could manage the ranch. His mother was suffering a great deal with arthritis. They had sufficient financial means to live comfortably, to send the boys through college, to hire needed labor, and to keep improving the ranch. The only outstanding situation in his childhood, which left an impression upon him, was the isolation and loneliness from which the whole family seemed to suffer.

He made his way through a denominational medical college. He was "chiefly interested in surgery but in a small town you just have to practice everything." He decided as a boy to become a doctor because "there was so much illness in the family and the frequent visits from physicians got him interested."

As far as is known by Dr. and Mrs. Smith there have been no outstanding physical ailments, no abnormalities, no insanity, "nor any court troubles" on either side of the family.

Family Relationships.—Marilyn is the only survival of triplets. Her only sister died at birth and her brother died a few days later. She has, however, three older brothers and one younger. Mrs. Smith states that Marilyn, being the only girl in the family, received considerable attention from parents, grandmother, and friends, which did not cease when the last baby was born. "She early acquired a sense of her own importance and expected the family to cater to her whims. As soon as that trait was recognized Marilyn was made to feel and take her place as any child in a large family but she resented this bitterly. She was oversensitive to reprimand, but continued to get under the skin of everybody. This had to stop and we quit paying attention to her. She was then about eight years of age."

"She has been rather seclusive, withdrawing, and even secretive. She reads a great deal, both fiction and nonfiction, and of a high quality." She rarely participated in the entertainment of guests and relatives by her parents. She dislikes her cousins, who are considerably younger than herself. She dislikes helping with any household duties and does not even care for her own room, which is furnished well and with taste.

She does not get along well with her brothers, has never participated in their games and play. On the whole "she is antagonistic to her family, though sweet and charming to strangers whenever she takes a notion."

"As a young child Marilyn was devoted to her mother, but disliked her mother's constant preoccupations with relatives and guests," says Dr. Smith. Mrs. Smith spent considerable time "chauffeuring the child to dancing lessons, music lessons, French lessons," but she was always "on the rush either to entertain at home or to keep an engagement with friends."

There has always been "a close and friendly bond between the two older brothers because of their ages." Ever since the birth of Charles they have regarded him as "the mascot" and paid considerable attention to him. Marilyn was six years old at the time the youngest brother was born. She was very fond of him and frequently played with him. Her interest in this brother waned as he began to acquire boy friends. There has been no conflict, according to the parents, over Charles supplanting Marilyn as "the baby in the family." The sons are friendly and even chummy with their parents. They often participate in the entertainment of friends and relatives.

Husband and Wife Relationship.—Dr. and Mrs. Smith are seemingly unusually devoted to each other. "There have been very few disagreements between us and the older children have never witnessed any conflicts." The parents have always presented a "united front" with respect to child discipline. Dr. Smith maintains that the only time he ever "fusses with his wife is over the lack of responsibility put upon Marilyn."

Others in the Household.—The maternal grandmother has made her home with the Smiths ever since Tom was a baby, and is well liked by all members of the family, particularly Marilyn. The grandmother is reported to be active, in good health, and congenial. She helps with the housework. Mrs. Smith and her mother are very much devoted to each other and spend a good deal of time together. Mrs. Smith is one of a large family, and her five brothers and four sisters visit their mother on frequent occasions. At present the grandmother is visiting a son in the East. She is expected to return in about six weeks.

The Social History of Marilyn's Development in the Smith Family Circle.— As a child Marilyn was pampered a great deal. "The fact that she alone survived while her triplet brother and sister died almost at birth entitled her to some credit. She was very tiny, but normal in every respect. We were delighted to have a daughter. She was always as quick and smart as a whip." She grew up a healthy child; was never food finicky; had good habits. "We did not want to spoil her because she was a girl but we took good care of her. She had a nurse until three years of age."

She started kindergarten at four and a half and at six could read a second-grade book fluently. She skipped three grades. She did not present any serious problems as a child. "When there are so many in the family you can't fuss with one. She was always stubborn and many times had her own way."

She was chiefly interested in reading; had many books given to her. She read the boys' books and sometimes even those the parents drew from the library. She matured quickly and was always very well informed. She was admired by friends and relatives for her brilliance and "early acquired a superior air." There are few family friends of whom she approves and hardly any of the relatives.

Marilyn had taken piano lessons for over five years. She liked to practice on the piano as a girl of seven or eight. Later the lessons became very irksome. At present she rarely touches the piano. She seems satisfied with radio music and jazz. The piano teacher considered her as having exceptional ability and insisted that Marilyn devote all her time to classical music, which was resented. Marilyn and her older brothers used to enjoy playing popular duets together but the teacher made them discontinue.

She dug out the information about sex from books long before the mother thought she was ready for it. However, she did not show any curiosity about sex until about a year ago, when the boys and girls in high school started giving and going to parties. The mother does not believe that Marilyn has ever attended any indecent petting parties. "She is not that kind. But it's hard to know what is going on in that child's head." (The mother frequently referred to Marilyn as "a child" and often repeated that "she comes by her moods and stubbornness honestly, as her paternal uncle and aunt are hard to deal with." She also contradicted herself on several occasions, which is perhaps a sign that she does not know her daughter's situation well. She did not seem to attempt to color or distort the situation.)

The father, more than the mother, realizes that perhaps the social environment, rather than "inborn traits of seclusiveness and selfishness," is responsible for Marilyn's behavior and attitudes. The mother reiterates that "the boys are different and they live in the same environment and receive the same treatment." Both parents realize that Marilyn is more sensitive and more brilliant than her brothers, and, being the only girl, does not have the same companionship as her brothers.

The mother feels that Marilyn does not give anyone a chance to be friendly and chummy with her. "She is a being apart. The nice boys and girls in the neighborhood and in school consider her snobbish and won't have much to do with her. She selects a tough crowd of young people who smoke and are highly sophisticated."

Both parents want her to keep company with nice young men who call at the house and who are satisfied when entertained at the house. They don't mind her keeping company with Catholic boys but object to intermarriage as they "have known too many unfortunate outcomes."

They have "great ambitions" for Marilyn. They want her to pursue her interest in political science, to graduate from the university, and to enter the field of international relations, as she herself had planned before meeting the man who "turned her head."

"It's a case of mere infatuation," the mother repeated frequently. "If she does not listen to reason we shall put her in a convent for two or three years."

The mother frequently referred to the following personality traits in Marilyn: brilliant, daring, industrious and active, "hard" (lacks sympathy), stubborn, seclusive, secretive, uncooperative, selfish, snobbish, and conceited.

Mother's Attitude toward Responsibilities Assumed by Children.— "Children should enjoy themselves as long as they can. They get into the harness soon enough and have to assume responsibilities soon enough. Why burden them when they still live at home?" The boys have always helped their father keep the yard and garage clean. They have helped in keeping the automobile clean and in good repair. During the summer the older boys have had some kind of employment. Marilyn has rarely been asked to help with the housework. When anyone was ill, she was sent to a relative; when the family home was redecorated, she was away from home.

The mother believes that she is the disciplinarian of the children. "The doctor is busy and has never interfered." Marilyn alone resents her attempts at discipline. "Yes, she understands the reason for every attempt at discipline, but she has a very good opinion of herself. I don't believe that I have ever been unreasonable. She has not been whipped since she was five or six years of age. . . . I am not a demonstrative person. She should know my devotion to them all, but I doubt whether I could ever make a show of my affection to anyone."

Housing Conditions.—The Smith home is large and comfortable in a good neighborhood. While there are two or three apartment houses in the same block, the neighborhood is predominantly that of homeowners. The Smiths built their two-story house about fifteen years ago and furnished it well. The house is very well kept both externally and internally. The mother and the grandmother do all the work at present.

The Economic Situation.—Dr. Smith, as a physician in a small town, has a varying net income from $200 to $250 a month. The oldest son is a shoe salesman. He meets his own expenses and those of his brother, Joe, who attends college. The grandmother has a small independent income and frequently contributes to the expenses of the home. She also buys clothes for Marilyn.

The house is unincumbered, but is frequently in need of repair. Its assessed valuation is $5,000. While Dr. Smith has always had a steady income the eight members in the family preclude any opportunity for savings. "Since the depression they have just been able to manage." (Mrs. Smith shows evidences of being a very good manager and housekeeper.)

Marilyn "took it upon herself to look for some work to occupy her time over week ends. She wanted to earn some money for college and saved every dollar she made until she met this man."

The parents were aware of the social conditions facing a young, attractive girl working in a public eating shop but they were confident that "Marilyn was bright enough to foresee all dangers" and, therefore, no interpretation of the situation was attempted. The parents did not inquire, and Marilyn did not volunteer, any information regarding the daily occurrences she met and the acquaintances she made in her work. The parents know little of the girl's thoughts and plans.

Religious Affiliations.—The children attended a Unitarian Sunday school until they were about ten years of age, but later lost interest. Both parents were born Methodists and were married in the Methodist church. They have not attended church since marriage. They "just lost interest in religion." The grandmother attends church irregularly. Her husband was nominally Unitarian, but she was raised a Methodist, and was married in the Methodist church.

Religion has never been a positive force in the lives of the Smiths. They "do the right and proper thing." "One can be upright, moral, and good without church." They "have seen too much bigotry in the church" and do not believe that they could profit from any regular church affiliations.

Recreation.—Entertaining of friends and relatives has been the chief form of recreation. They go on beach parties, hikes, enjoy snow sports in the mountains; they play bridge frequently and serve small amounts of liquor. They disapprove of heavy drinking and drunkenness but "a little drink is very stimulating and socializing. . . . Marilyn has acquired a taste for liquor but she always knows her limit. . . . The doctor is very fond of entertaining friends because, as a child, he was frequently lonesome and isolated."

(At one time the worker arrived at the Smith home when a number of guests were present. It appeared that the parents were very popular and exceptionally well liked by a large circle of friends. Occasionally a guest or a relative would boast of unscrupulous business deals, and the technique of "getting around the law" would be discussed in the presence or within hearing distance of the children. Some of the women appeared somewhat blasé and did not always accept their middle age with grace. On the whole, their friends are of the "higher type" of the modern city and small town dwellers.)

The parents and the children have rarely attended moving pictures together. The children have gone together, in pairs or singly, to shows once or twice a week, but have rarely discussed the pictures with their parents. Marilyn is particularly fond of the cinema.

She and her mother have never taken a hike together. Though both of them have traveled in the West a good deal they have never been on a trip alone. There were always others along.

Frequently when Marilyn entertained her own group of boy and girl friends the parents had left the house after preparing refreshments, either because of their own engagements or because of Marilyn's request to do so. In reality, they do not know most of her friends.

Plan of Family.—"We hardly know what to do. We thought of talking to the man and telling him that such associations can lead to nothing but trouble and to inform him that he might be arrested for contributing to the delinquency of a minor, which is a penitentiary offense. Of course, we have no proof that he hasn't the best of intentions.

"If she does not quit talking about marriage at the age of sixteen, we shall send her for two or three years to a convent even though we are not Catholic. There she will listen to reason.

"She can't return to work at the sandwich shop any more. We shall also take her to the family doctor for a very thorough physical examination."

10–19–35. (Interviewed Marilyn in her own home. She is of pleasing manner and appears a frank, keenly intelligent, well-developed young woman. Her blond, curly hair was well groomed, her blue eyes are large and sparkling. Her eyebrows were carefully plucked and finger-nails painted crimson. She was tastily and well dressed. Her whole appearance gave the impression of great care and individualization. It was not difficult to get acquainted with her.[1] After a few preliminary remarks, she appeared eager to talk and prepared for the interview; she was given every opportunity to tell her story in her own way. Her manners are those of an adult rather than a sixteen-year-old girl.)

Girl's Own Story

"Oh, in a way it feels good to be home again, but I wish I did not live here. I left home because I want to and can be on my own. I had been working week ends and holidays in a drive-in sandwich shop and can support myself. I went to work to save some money for college. I wanted to go away from home.

"I want to live my own life. My parents have lived theirs and they should not be asking me to live according to their design. I am going to live long after they are gone and I should be permitted to order my own life. They object to Arthur. And why?

"Of course, I am in love with him, and shall marry him. They object because he is so much older than myself and a Catholic. But you must realize that I have been going with people much older than myself and they have accepted me as their equal. I despise being looked down and regarded as a 'child.' I am not a child.

"I am unhappy at home. I wish I knew where the difficulty lies. This is not a home to me. It's a big house, with lots of relatives, parties, and company all the time. Mother seems always busy. I do not intend to have her drop everything when I try to talk to her, but she is always doing something while she tries to listen to me.

"I don't care a great deal about school. It's too easy. It does not occupy my mind. I can't forget Arthur. They [the parents] insist on my breaking with him. School won't help me. The only way to forget Art is to bury myself in work at the shop.

"What do you mean I am not old enough to go to work full time? Why do I need a work permit? [Explained.] Well, we all evade the law in some way or another and a little thing like that is not going to hurt anybody. [Explained the possible consequences of evading the law.] None of our friends suffered because of breaking the law. Look how they brag when they can avoid payment of full income tax. They can afford it, but they just like to be smart and get around the law. I even heard an attorney brag

[1] For methods of interviewing see Pauline V. Young, *Interviewing in Social Work.*

about getting around the law and figuring out ways and technicalities which would bring them outside the law. Well, I figure if you can get away with it, it's all right. These friends are regarded as honorable and respectable.

"I don't understand why she [mother] wants to interfere now. She let me do as I pleased before. When I was younger and wanted to consult her, she was always busy. Naturally I had to rely on my own judgment, but now she steps in and wants to upset all my plans. Certainly I do not confide in her. I never did. All I can say is that we are strangers and that I will not allow her to rule over me all at once.

"She buys many things for me. I know I have lots of clothes. She often talks about it and fusses because I do not fuss with clothes. I wish I didn't have so much. What's the use? Well, I don't recall that I ever craved a great deal of affection. I know my mother is proud of me and devoted to me, that she would do anything in her power to please me, except give of herself. Of course, there are many other children in our household, but the boys are different. They always had themselves. I was alone.

"Oh, my brothers have their own interests. They don't interfere with me and I let them alone. My oldest brother thought for a while that he could boss me but he soon found out otherwise. He goes his way now. Fred is a pretty bright fellow and does good work at school, but, I don't know, we seem to fit in well enough in the family but don't have enough in common. I guess I do keep to myself a good deal, but you have to—in a mob like ours.

"Grandma is nice and sweet. Everybody likes her. I wish I could live with her alone. Yes, perhaps because I could do as I please. She and I also enjoy the same things. Occasionally we go with her to the movies.

"No, mother and dad rarely went with us to the show. Ever since I was a little girl mother allowed us to go or sent us to the movies alone or with my older brother. I don't recall the whole family had ever attended the movies together. We go on hikes and to the beach, but there is always a party and some quarrelsome, overbearing youngsters whose mothers allow them to run wild. No, we all have different interests and go on our own way. And why not? We can all be ourselves.

"All at once they threaten to punish me. I recall many times as a child when I thought I would be punished but I never was. Now they tell me they 'will turn me over their knee.' A fat chance they would have. Or that they 'will send me to a convent—and absolutely forbid me to see Art.' Why, they are unreasonable!

"Well, I must admit that as a child I wanted mother home or alone with us but she was very popular and there were always friends calling or inviting her out. And daddy was always busy with his patients and hospital. Oh, I got used to it, I guess. I started to read early and then I made many friends of my own. Perhaps that's why I like Art. He is interested in me and in my ideas and my likes and dislikes. We are very good pals together. And why should I give him up? He is a decent fellow—a good friend to me. I don't feel that he is much older than I. And perhaps that is a good thing.

"Art is a fine fellow. He does not want to marry me at once because of his widowed mother and sister. His mother is not keen about a non-

Catholic girl, but my mother is so strongly prejudiced against a Catholic that she makes up her mind on that score alone. And why should she? We never attend church. We aren't anything. Art and I have no prejudices. Why shouldn't we marry, even though we are of different religions? Religion is nothing in my life.

"I am not sure that he is in good health. I suspect that he is suffering from a heart disease. He had infantile paralysis as a child, but he does not suffer with his leg. That never bothers him. It just looks a little limp, but it isn't. He is not very strong, but he has been feeling better lately.

"He has only graduated from high school, but he is not dumb. He is well read. And the chances are that I will not have further education. He is radio announcer for _____ and, I believe, he makes about $25.00 a week. Of course, he could not support his mother and sister in one home, and a wife and himself in another home. I do not want to live with his mother. But, of course, I would work too if his hours were long and irregular.

"I would not mind living at home if they left me alone and allowed me to see Art. But she [mother] is unreasonable, becomes upset and emotional. She forgets that I can be on my own.

"I had intended to go to college. My greatest interest is in political science. If there is a chance for women in international relations, I would like to qualify myself for that field. But at any rate, I will have to work before entering college. I had wanted to take a business course this summer and work in an office and save money. Dad can't provide everything; business has been pretty bad.

"I get along far better with my father than with her. She and I don't speak the same language. We don't have anything in common. I would like to travel a bit but not with her. I don't enjoy her company well enough. I don't see why she should object to my working in a sandwich shop. The work is easy and as long as I work I may just as well enjoy myself doing it.

"We sure meet some interesting people at work. You never can tell when a fine car will drive up and ask for 'a bite to eat and a drop to wet your whistle.' We all know what that means of course. We can't appear as if we were observing the customers, but you develop a technique of listening and find out what is going on. Oh, I wouldn't accept any date from anybody. I have Art and he would not want me to mix up with these people. And, of course, his sister, Lucy, is there too. She is a fine girl. I am very fond of her. She keeps steady company with an Irishman. Now take her! She has freedom and gets along fine with her mother. They are more like chums. She brings fellows into her own home and her mother welcomes them. Well, my mother does too, except the one I want her to, but she has always had the idea that my friends are tough. I wish you could meet some of them. I'll arrange that.

"Lucy says that she would never marry a man until she had found out whether or not both of them would enjoy each other and would get along sexually. Well, most of our friends think that is a very good plan. Why marry and be divorced on sex grounds when you can try it out first. Personally, I would like to think about it a good deal more. I have not made up my mind on the subject. Some of the girls regard me as a prude because I have not had sex relations. I am telling you Art is a decent fellow. And then I figure that when a man gets everything from a girl without marrying her, he asks why should he marry her?

"Oh yes, I have read enough about sex and know quite a bit on the subject. No, I don't believe that I would consult mother about sex affairs. There is no necessity for it as yet anyway.

"In a way I hate to stay here in this town. We are isolated from real thrills and the life of a big city. Here everybody knows your business. They know I was missing for a few days. I am not going to make any explanations to anyone. They can think what they want. I would like to live in a large city and work in a large city. It takes us nearly an hour and a half to get there so working there is out of the question."

Brief Psychological Examination (given at school).—Marilyn has an I. Q. of 135 (chronological age, sixteen years, two months; mental age, twenty-one years, six months.) She is well informed, widely read, makes exceptionally quick and accurate mental associations. Mentally she is fully a superior adult though only sixteen years of age. She is self-centered, introspective, imaginative, persistent. She does well in all tests.

Physical Examination (given by family physician).—Marilyn is in fairly good health. She is slightly nearsighted and needs glasses. She is subject to frequent colds; has a few carious teeth; and is flat-footed. She eats and sleeps well. Has no bad habits.

Developmental History.—Marilyn had measles, chicken pox, and whooping cough before the age of eight. No aftereffects were noted. Mother states that pregnancy and delivery were normal; child was breast fed. Dentition, walking, talking normal. As a child Marilyn presented no noticeable problems. She was easy to raise and well liked by the family group. Menstruation at thirteen years. No discomforts.

School Accomplishment.—According to the parents and to her report cards Marilyn has been an excellent student at school until the last term. She has been on the honor roll every semester and her deportment is excellent. She is in A-12 grade at the age of sixteen years and two months. She has frequently participated in school events. She is regarded by her teachers as an intellectual.

The girls' vice-principal gives essentially the same account. She believes Marilyn is a very promising student. The teachers report that Marilyn has exceptional ability but is difficult to get acquainted with. She has never presented any problems to them. (For social treatment, see pp. 295–315.)

SOCIAL STUDY OF MARVIN LEVKOWITZ

Referred by Jewish Big Brothers Association to Child Guidance Clinic in November, 1935.

Identifying Data.—Jewish boy, born 4–20–21, Akron, Ohio. (Not verified.) Lives with parents at 0026 West Arden Boulevard; attends Garland Junior High School, A-9 grade.

Problems Presented.—Enuresis; maladjustment, principally at home, and also at school. Ran away from home once; unhappy and depressed.

Developmental History of Patient.—Marvin W. Levkowitz. Normal gestation and birth; no instruments. Mother well during pregnancy. Child was wanted. Weighed 9 pounds at birth. Difficult economic circumstances. Breast fed two or three months; then bottle fed. Exact dates of dentition, walking, and talking unknown. Mother claims, however, that he was normal in this respect, although he began to walk and talk later than her other children. Strong, healthy, normal baby, presenting no problems.

Health.—Measles at four, injury to nose at five, whooping cough at six, chicken pox at eight, attacks of tonsillitis up to age of eight, when tonsils were removed. Following are findings and recommendations from the Lelland Outpatient Department: Tentative diagnosis: "Psychoneurosis. Referred to urology clinic; bladder and prostate normal—3—4—35—Cystoscopic examination negative." No statement of facts upon which diagnosis of psychoneurosis was made found in the records. Boy received psychoanalytic treatment at the Lelland Clinic also. Social workers there state that family was uncooperative and that no satisfactory rapport between doctor and boy and mother was established. Patient and mother have stated that the psychoanalyst advised boy to have complete sex relations. This was the cause of the mother's lack of cooperation, as she resented this advice.

Puberty.—Mother noted that boy's genital organs were underdeveloped at the age of eleven; he was given some glandular treatment. Puberty commenced at twelve, with full sexual development within a year.

Habits.—Falls asleep immediately and sleeps usually about eight hours each night. Does not awaken when enuresis occurs (at least once each night). Is rather careless of personal hygiene but is becoming more particular in this respect. Sucked his thumb as a baby, and bit nails until a few months ago. Used to stutter and stammer until about eight, but improved when sent to a speech correction class at school. Enuresis almost invariably nocturnal. Boy shows an abnormal interest in sex activities. No perversions noted, and masturbation only at rare intervals. Mother states that she informed boy concerning venereal diseases and that she attempted to give him some sex instruction. Boy discusses frankly his sex desires with worker, but assures him with regret that he has never had intercourse.

School.—Normal school placement, A-9 grade, Garland Junior High School. Commenced at six. Has shown some liking for English. Truant only when he ran away from home for three days. Following are statements of teachers and principal:

Miss W., English Teacher: "Marvin is a lad of marked ability in my subject. He has keen insight, clear understanding, ready appreciation of finenesses in expression and effect. His expression (written) is much above the average. His vocabulary is good and his feeling for fit phrases excellent.

"His behavior is quite unsatisfactory—not that he is rude, disorderly, or disobedient—but that one expects responsiveness, effort, from such a boy. He seems very nervous about speaking before the class. He has no interest in his work. It requires pressure to get from him barely satisfactory work He seems apart from his classmates and quite willing to be so. Most of the time he is in the room, his head is hung and he avoids directly looking at me.

"There has been some improvement in his work since I reported to his mother that he was not making a satisfactory record. I feel that Marvin is well worth saving from this present attitude of his and wish I knew how to assist him in realizing his capacity. I try to be understanding."

Miss S., History Teacher: "He is unusually quiet for an A-9. He seems introspective. It is difficult to get him to respond orally. He would rather seem unprepared than respond beyond yes and no. I have not been able to get acquainted, he seems to shut one out.

"Naturally he seems bright and capable. (Often he lacks effort.) He apparently has no close personal friends in the group. He is all boy in appearance (as to cleanliness and neatness). He is courteous but seldom goes out of his way to make the chivalrous gesture."

Mr. F., Printing Teacher: "Behavior good. Attitude toward work, very good. Appearance neat, clean (good). Attitude toward others, fair. Ability, good. Capacity, fair.

"Marvin has made noticeable progress in the last year, particularly in creditable characteristics such as attitude toward work and others. His willingness to apply himself is now a strong point, whereas a year ago, this quality was nil."

Mrs. C., Spanish Teacher: "Marvin has an indifferent attitude about everything he does in school. He is not thorough, not consistent. One day he comes perfectly prepared, the next, he hasn't any conception of what the class is doing. Up until recently I would have said the same thing about his dress, but of late I have seen some change in his personal appearance. On the other hand, he is well able to do fine work. He is also gentlemanly and well behaved in the classroom."

Miss C., Home-room Teacher: "I know this boy only through his ten weeks' membership in home room. He is quiet and courteous to me but wholly indifferent to the usual interests of boys, such as room rivalry, committee competition, and group efforts to excel in home-room records. He has never voluntarily contributed his opinions or criticism to our weekly discussions. He is an inveterate reader and often borrows books and magazines from me.

"Marvin has no particular friend in this group and seems disinterested in efforts of several teachers who have offered him special help to avoid marks that are unsatisfactory. All teachers gave him a satisfactory mark in cooperation, but two considered him unsatisfactory in industry."

Work.—Only odd jobs. Sells newspapers on Saturdays.

Interests, Recreations, Companions.—Boy is primarily interested in his social life away from the school. His companions are boys and girls of junior high-school and high-school ages. He states that many of the others are in the habit of having complete sex relations. They have parties at each others' homes, except his own. After school patient usually assists mother with housework. He cooks, sets the table, cleans the house, and runs errands. He is especially friendly with John, younger brother. In the evenings he leaves home and spends his time either at parties or on the street with newsboys and some of his friends. It is almost impossible to keep boy in the home in the evenings. He is not interested in reading. Attends movies occasionally. Has written a number of poems (see p. 49).

Conduct.—Patient ran away from home early this year and spent two or three nights on a flatcar on a railroad siding. The immediate cause was trivial and involved a scolding and altercation with his parents and older brother, James. Boy has never been involved in delinquent acts. His extreme interest in the opposite sex is worthy of note. His conduct in the home might best be described as cooperative and self-effacing, though he asserts his independence by his refusal to remain home in the evenings.

Summary of Personality Traits.—Patient has better than average intelligence; good memory, extreme curiosity and interest concerning sex matters. Reasons well. Is rather impulsive concerning those things which interest him the most. Is active, lively boy; not overly ambitious with regard to school, but sees a task through and is energetic with regard to other matters. Unless confidence is established he is extremely reticent and gives the appearance of far less intelligence than he really has. He is honest with himself; is self-reliant. Is extremely despondent because he feels his enuresis to be a hopeless problem. Patient has allowed himself to be dominated by the family, and is often self-depreciatory when describing his abilities. He is dependable; appears to lack ambition, probably because of his frequent frustrations. He accepts authority and seems resigned to his position of inferiority in the home, to which he has been assigned by the other members of the family. He is honest, truthful, very sympathetic, generous, sensitive, uncomplaining, kindly. Appears to have a good physique, but is not a bully. When younger he resorted to daydreaming, but appears now to accept an unpleasant reality. He is generally gloomy, placid, unresentful, and even-tempered. Only at rare intervals does he flare up and usually leaves the home rather than resort to loud quarreling. Patient seems to be happiest when his desires for recognition and response are satisfied. He wishes primarily to be accepted as an equal and yearns for friendship, sympathy, and understanding. (See *Habits* for attitude toward sex.)

Family History.—Mike Levkowitz, father, born in Rumania, 1894. Is the fourth of six children. Paternal grandparents are living. Grandfather, seventy-four, is in good health; grandmother, sixty-nine, suffered from a gynecological condition. Father came to the United States at the age of ten. Had high-school education and subsequent business training. He has adjusted to American standards; speaks English fluently. Married mother on 11–12–18. Parents knew each other as children, and attended the same religious school. Man has never provided for the family to the satisfaction of the mother. He has been associated with the retail shoe business both as owner of a store and as a salesman. During the past few years employment has been irregular and until recently family was supported by LACRA. Man is now employed in M. Shoe Department at a salary of $16.00 a week. He does not participate actively in family affairs unless a crisis arises. Mother, however, characterizes him as a gambler, lazy, "a brute," disinterested in the family. Leaves family responsibilities entirely to her. Unintellectual and has only material interests. She described his life as a boy as similar to patient's. States he matured sexually at a very early age, and had a mistress at fifteen. He had frequent sex relations before marriage. His own father ordered the paternal grandmother about, and accepted services from all the children. Mother refers to the paternal relatives as rather ordinary as compared to her own. (Mother.)

Father denies any similarity between his earlier life and that of patient. He worked ever since he was fourteen years old, and claims to have had no particular interest in girls at that age. His own parents were respectable but rather poor. His brother is president of a Zionist organization. Father speaks of his family with modesty, but pride. Economically they were always rather hard pressed. Father intimated that the sex relations between him and wife were compatible, but would not discuss the matter. (Father.)

Worker's Impression of Father.—Man is intelligent, mild mannered, phlegmatic, kindly, and has insight into patient's condition. Either he has suffered a great deal in his associations with his wife, or mother's intimations of his sadism are true. It is worker's feeling that his inarticulateness concerning this matter is a gentlemanly gesture and that the man has considerable insight into his wife's psychological status.

Mother.—Anna Sim Levkowitz; born in Akron, Ohio; 1897. Maternal grandfather born in Russia, died of old age at seventy-seven. Was a semi-invalid throughout life because of a cardiac and stomach condition. Was intelligent, well read. Died in 1929. Lived in America forty-five years. Maternal grandmother died at sixty-two of double pneumonia. Was in good health throughout life. Gave birth to ten children, and managed both business and household affairs for the family. Her general merchandise store at _____ was a source of very good income for a long time. Nine of the children are now married, and all but one have children of their own. Of the collaterals, all are apparently normal, except a maternal aunt, the youngest in the family, who, after the birth of her second child, became insane, and was diagnosed as "schizophrenia," "dementia precox," and "manic depressive." The last diagnosis was given for her commitment to Patton. She was discharged after three months, and is now apparently in normal mental and physical health. Maternal cousins, in one family, are also enuretics. The boys in that family ceased the habit at fifteen; their sister, now fourteen and one-half, is still subject to the habit.

Mother is intelligent; reads good literature. Has become disinterested in household affairs, and is a poor housekeeper. She claims her poor health is responsible for this. The clinic has given a provisional diagnosis of psychoneurosis. She suffers from an ovarian disfunction and "dispareunia," and has been receiving treatment in the gynecological department. Had uterus suspended ten years ago. Woman also suffers from a mild hypothyroidism, and has been given thyroid and ovarian extract hypodermically. Hospital also performed an appendectomy. Mother recently was on the verge of a nervous breakdown and was sent to a rest home for a number of weeks. Mother is a nice-appearing woman, blue eyes, dark hair, fair skin, prominent nose.

Worker's Impression of Mother.—Is apparently neurotic. Protests too much about her affection for patient, but her overt actions show a preference for the other children. Perhaps not too reliable in her evidence, a result of her neurotic condition rather than any dishonesty.

Siblings.—James: born 11–9–19; Akron, Ohio. Delivered by forceps; mother "almost died." Attends View High School; B-12. Member of the honorary scholarship society and track team. Well mannered, but' rather hot-tempered. Is self-centered. Industrious with regard to school, but dislikes home responsibilities. Invariably spends his evenings at home, studying. Dislikes serving father, but responds to discipline. Is attached to mother and apparently prefers her. States there is no family discord.

Patient: 4–20–21.

Agnes: 8–6–22; Los Angeles. Normal birth. Characterized at school as a model pupil. Attends Garland Junior High School; A-8 grade. Loves reading and gets good grades in school. According to mother she gets along well with patient, but resembles older brother in her attitudes and behavior characteristics. Rather nice-appearing girl, presenting no problems at home or at school. Is better liked by father than the older boys.

John: 8–26–26; Los Angeles. Normal birth. Apparently favorite of both parents. B-5 grade, in Opportunity A room. Conversations with boy reveal him as of very superior intelligence, showing an extraordinary interest in such subjects as astronomy. Good-looking child. Plays frequently with patient, and affects a relationship of equality rather than that of younger to older brother.

Home and Home Conditions.—Family resides in a small, frame house located in a lower middle-class district, in the southern part of the city. The father earns $16 a week as a shoe salesman, and family cannot afford even ordinary comforts. Mother formerly supplemented income by employment, but is now too ill. The house is well ventilated and light. The lack of bedrooms is responsible for the three boys sleeping in the same room. There is little religious observance, although the youngest boy attends Hebrew School.

Reciprocal Relationships.—According to mother there is a long history of marital incompatibility, dating almost from the time the couple were married. She states: "His very touch hurts me. He is always brutal." She intimates what may be a sadistic relationship in their sex life. States that husband has always been faithful to her, and that he is excessive in his sex demands of her. Depends upon her entirely for birth-control measures. She has frequently been on the verge of divorcing her husband and claims that when she came to Los Angeles with the two older children, she had actually left him, but that he followed her four months later, and they resumed their married life together. A number of years ago she was attracted to another man with whom she had a sex experience, and from which she derived complete physical satisfaction. For the sake of the children, this relationship was discontinued. She has informed her husband of the affair. How much of this incompatibility the children actually realize is difficult to tell. Mother states that she wishes the father would have an open argument with her. Instead they will merely not speak to each other or they will completely hide their differences. James has spoken to his father in a resentful manner and has told him that he feels that he is being waited on too well by the other members of the family.   Patient often waits on father when James refuses.   In addition he is far more cooperative

POEMS BY MARVIN LEVKOWITZ

I Did the Very Best I Could

When someone needed help
I lent a hand
Dangerous or no
I couldn't be caught
Loafing on my stand.
I sold papers for many bosses
Made many profits and few losses
I shared my bed
I shared my food
I did the very best I could.

Now God is taking me
To a place I long to be.

What I Wish to Be

I want to be a pirate bold
When I grow very big and old,
To ride a ship upon the sea—
Oh! what fun that would be.
I want to be a mailman
And carry mail to every house
To carry a big mail bag
And wear a blue-green blouse.

I want to be a president
And rule all of the folks;
I want to be a funny clown
And crack a lot of jokes.

I want to be an iceman
And put ice in every box;
I want to be a jeweler
And sell all kinds of clocks.

If you were in my place,
Which one would you be?
An iceman, a clown
Or a pirate on the sea?

My Dream

When I grow into my twenties
And get for me a wife
That day that I marry her
Will be the happiest day in my life.

I'll buy her a house to live in
And give her plenty food;
I'll buy her clothes and dishes
And keep her in good mood.
I'll take her to movies, cafes and
      dances
And give her a good time every night.
I'll give her kisses before and after
      work
And we'll never argue or fight.

Who Am I?

I am a homeless hungry boy;
I roam the streets without a cent
For all the money I had before
On clothes and food I spent.

I ran away from home
Because I didn't like to go to bed;
Now I have no place to go
And I wish that I was dead.

Transition

Little snowflakes lightly fall
Form a blanket over all.
They cover up the sleeping flowers
And keep them warm through winter
      hours.
Little raindrops falling fast
Wake the flowers when winter's past.
The little raindrops shine to show
The baby buds 'tis time to grow.

and helpful to mother than the other children.   Father used to call boy a "nut" and was unfair to him when small (mother).   However, this is probably true of the mother also, although they appear now to have insight into boy's feelings of inferiority. Patient has been frequently confronted with the superior achievements of the other children and has continually been compared with them to his own great disadvantage. James's impatience and lack of understanding have been particularly noticeable. His schoolmates are more friendly with patient than he is. However, the fact that the three boys sleep in the same room and have done so for many years must prove a constant source of irritation to the brothers because of patient's enuresis.

Discipline.—Mother is responsible for almost all the family discipline. Father rarely takes an active part. Mother, however, is inconsistent and will favor one or another of the children at various times. Because patient is kinder to his father than any of the other children, and perhaps because of father's insight, he rarely censures the boy. When younger, patient was occasionally thrashed, but this has long since been discontinued.

Plan of Mother.—Mother now feels that boy should be removed from his home environment. She states that the friction existing between him and James, as well as the indifference of the father to the family situation, makes such a plan imperative. On the other hand, the father is inclined to follow a laissez faire attitude. He feels that patient will in time adjust his own problems. Boy will cooperate in any plan.

Summary of Medical and Psychiatric History (by Child Guidance Clinic). The written report of the social history prepared by the Clinic is essentially the same as summarized above by the agency and is, for this reason, not repeated at this point.

Physical Findings.—Patient's long neck and sloping shoulders suggestive of hypergonad build and active reflexes and tremors of hands. Large cyanotic extremities.

Psychological Findings.—He is of high average intelligence according to Binet and educational tests. Superior according to Kohs designs. Is slightly below average on mechanical tests. Seems emotionally mature.

Psychiatric Findings.—Marvin has rather deep feelings of inferiority and insecurity in the presence of a harsh, stern mother and superior brothers and sister who excel him in every possible way. His general demeanor is one of depression and despair. His physique is unattractive; he wets the bed; is the household drudge, etc. He is physiologically advanced from the sex standpoint, hence is easily interested in sex activity as a compensation for what he lacks at home. Fundamentally he has good attitudes and ambitions. All he needs is some praise, understanding, and a chance for self-expression.

The data presented in this case provide a clear picture of the boy, his family, home surroundings, his social environment, school, and associates. However, certain other data should have been included in the records which might be of value in planning a course of treatment for this boy (see pp. 373–374; 380–381).

How does he react to his looks and how do others react to him? Has he ever been a member of a boys' club? Of a character-building agency? What are the reactions of his Big Brother?

From developmental history of patient we learn that he was "strong, healthy, normal baby, presenting no problems." At puberty the boy is already unadjusted. When did the first signs of unadjustment appear? With what were they associated? What were his childhood experiences? How was he accepted in the family circle as a child and particularly after the birth of his younger brother and sister?

There are long statements from the boy's schoolteachers but no account of the boy's personal attitudes and reactions to school are recorded. What attempts has the school made to capitalize his interest in and ability of writing poetry?

About his work very little information is given. How does the boy like his work? Which of the odd jobs does he like best of all? What are his attitudes toward selling papers? How is he accepted by other newsboys? Is he a member of the newsboys' club? What are his experiences while at work on the street? How much does he earn? What are his attitudes toward giving his mother his earnings? What are the family's attitudes toward his working and earning?

This information is essential in providing status for the boy in the family group and in his own eyes if his remunerative work is satisfactory. If disorganizing or not satisfying to the boy, it should be substituted by other work.

The boy ran away from home and spent several nights on a freight car. Only the immediate cause is given. Undoubtedly the boy has thought about the incident. How does he account for his running away? What caused him to return? What are his attitudes toward running away? How else can he solve his problems? What are the boy's reactions to his mother and father? How much does he know of their intimate past? Of their present conflicts? Are there any relatives whom the boy admires? With whom could he live? What is the boy's philosophy of life?

Apparently no notice was taken by the clinic of the content of the poetry which Marvin wrote on many occasions. The boy's interest in writing poetry opens up a line of inquiry which should prove fruitful. The poems selected for reproduction here indicate much of the nature of his social and mental conflicts, his tensions, and the budding of impulses which could be capitalized in further dealing with the boy. The sensitivity to social relations, the urge to independence, the awareness of his own problems, the search for security and response which they reveal make these bits of poetry of high diagnostic value in determining the social needs of the boy and possible treatment methods.

Workers need particularly to become skillful in interpreting these creative efforts of youth which make articulate their inner longings, aspirations, and dream moods. The last poem quoted, if original, indicates particularly good possibilities for his entering into a competitive activity in which he could hope to gain recognition. While few of the boys and girls of a child welfare agency are as articulate as Marvin is, many of them have various means of self-expression which are not taken sufficient cognizance of by the worker.

(To be continued)

CHAPTER III

THE COMPREHENSIVE EXPLORATION OF A CASE[1]
(Continued)

THE STUDY OF THE OFFENDER

While any detailed discussion of social exploration still leaves much to the constructive imagination of the worker, a selective process must be adopted according to the nature of the problem presented by the case and the administrative facilities of the agency.

Where work with juvenile delinquents and problem youth is at its best no means are spared to secure a complete picture of the physical, mental, personal, social, and economic forces (past and present) which exert any appreciable influence upon the life and experiences of the offender in order to provide a basis for intelligent action and adjustment. Care should be taken, however, that exploration of the total situation should never degenerate into mere "history taking," where sight is lost of the relationship between the immediate situation and its problems and the person's past and environmental background.

Pressure of time and lack of perspective often prevent an adequate understanding of the problems and experiences of delinquents. Timely discovery of the causes of unadjustment will often prevent more serious disorganization later. There are few short cuts to efficient work which may not leave in their wake further unadjustment of the offender. Even a very prolonged social investigation, when properly conducted, is more economical of time, energy, and money, to say nothing of the human costs to the offender, than recidivism (repeated or habitual delinquency or criminality). We only seem to shift the problems and costs to other agencies and age levels. Somebody has to face these problems and the longer they are allowed to continue without

[1] See The White House Conference on Child Health and Protection, *The Delinquent Child*, pp. 57-76; also CLIFFORD R. SHAW, *The Jack-Roller; Social Factors in Juvenile Delinquency;* and DOROTHY SWAINE THOMAS and OTHERS, *Some New Techniques for Studying Social Behavior.*

adequate study and attention the harder they will be to deal with and the heavier the ultimate costs.

Of course discretion is needed in securing and weighing the relative importance of facts which would aid in understanding and guiding the delinquent. Some facts may be of little direct significance, yet their relative usefulness may not be seen until a complete view of the total situation is gained. Often apparently unimportant data may lead to the most significant clues.[1] In general, it may be said that the most significant data are those which throw light on what Ada E. Sheffield calls "key conceptions."[2] But considerable sifting is essential.

The worker should seek information regarding the entire life of the individuals in question. He should seek to understand the various aspects of their lives, of their problems, of their environment, and of their character. And as Octavia Hill has pointed out as early as 1869: "By knowledge of character more is meant than whether a man is a drunkard or a woman is dishonest; it means knowledge of the passions, hopes, and history of people; where the temptation will touch them, what is the little scheme they have made of their own lives, or would make, if they had encouragement; what training long past phases of their lives may have afforded; how to move, touch, teach them. Our memories and our hopes are more truly factors of our lives than we often remember."

When we secure the inner life history of a person, Dr. Robert E. Park points out, "we are like a man who opens the door and walks in, and has visible before him what previously he had only guessed at. . . . [Otherwise] we are like a man in the dark looking at the outside of the house and trying to guess what is going on within."[3]

Human behavior can best be explained in relation to the personal, social, and cultural context in which it occurs. To study a person, even his health and biological make-up, apart from his social environment is to study him in a vacuum, and not as an

---

[1] See JANE P. CLARK, "The Interview and the Unimportant," *Journal of Applied Sociology*, X (March–April, 1926), 368–371; see also WILLIAM HEALY, "Study of the Case Preliminary to Treatment," *Journal of Criminal Law and Criminology*, XIII (May, 1922), 78–81.

[2] See *The Social Case History*, pp. 20–41, 146–150.

[3] "Research in Sociology," in Wilson Gee (Editor), *Research in the Social Sciences*, p. 47.

individual who has of necessity established many social relations which are vital to him.

Early experiences and mental associations often influence, shape, and direct the course and behavior trends of a person. Desires, attitudes, fears, plans, and so on, have an antecedent history. To understand their origin will aid in understanding their process of growth and maturation. And as one philosopher has remarked: "Life has a tomorrow and today is understood only if we are able to add the indications of tomorrow to our knowledge of what was yesterday."

It is not sufficient, however, to know the chronological history of events and experiences of the person. It is not the mere enumeration of events, of birth, of movement, of illness, of escapades, of domestic discord, that assumes significance in a person's life, but his *reasons, reactions,* and *attitudes* toward these events and experiences. What counts in addition to getting a job, for instance, is the attitude toward it; what is important in moving about is the cause of, experiences during, and attitude toward mobility.

What is more important than the mere mention of the changes in residence, the amount of rent paid, the landlord's name, and so on, is the significance of the uprooting or maintaining of old habits and associations. Clifford Shaw—in his discussion of what "the own story"[1] reveals—implies that the social explorer is concerned with:

1. The interviewee's point of view—that is, personal attitudes, feelings, interests, the role the person conceives himself to play in relation to others and the interpretation he places on the social situations in which he lives.

2. The social and cultural world in which the person lives. Human behavior can best be explained in relation to the social and cultural context in which it occurred. This milieu reveals not only the traditions, customs, moral standards of the group to which the person is subjected but also "the manner in which these cultural factors become incorporated into the behavior trends of the child" or person. The Gestalt psychologists refer to this social milieu as "the frame of reference" or "configuration" which supplies meaning in the life experience of the person or group. To study a person apart from his social environment is to

[1] *The Jack-Roller,* pp. 3–16.

study him in a vacuum, and not as an individual who has acquired status in the group, who has established many social or group relations which are vital to him.

For the purposes of therapy it is essential to learn the person's "moral struggles, his successes and failures in securing control of his destiny in a world too often at variance with his hopes and ideals"; his social complexes, his sentiment and attitudes, which cooperated with other factors to create his personality. It is essential to know the prestige and incentive to a particular form of behavior.

3. Sequence of events. Early experiences and influences shape and direct the course and behavior trends of a person. The interviewer seeks to visualize the process involved in the fixation of a particular behavior trend, as the successive events of life.[1]

The question may here be raised as to the logic of the social case history, and indeed of social exploration, since "by virtue of differences in personal, social, and group experiences, in culture complexes, in mental and emotional make-ups men are often separated from their fellows by gulfs that are hard to bridge."[2] They may try to "bring their parted natures in closer contact, they may try to convey a sense of themselves to each other, but across the gulf that parts them there is no bridge by which they can wholly enter into one another's life."[3]

Complete exploration of the other's life and personality is probably never effected. We can only "form conceptions of a personal unity out of the fragments of another person in which he alone is accessible to us . . . the unity so formed necessarily depends on that portion of the other which our standpoint of the other permits us to see."[4]   However, living in the same or similar cultures and maintaining, to some degree at least, similar social relations, individuals do grow up to be strikingly similar as well as strikingly differentiated. It is this margin of uniqueness as well as the common grounds which the investigator seeks to explore.

[1] Adapted from PAULINE V. YOUNG, *Interviewing in Social Work*, pp. 97–98.

[2] *Ibid.*, p. 285.

[3] N. S. SHALER, *The Neighbor*, p. 204.

[4] GEORG SIMMEL, "Sociology of Secrecy and Secret Societies," *American Journal of Sociology*, VI (January, 1906), 442.

The question may also be raised from a somewhat different angle: To what extent are data applicable to or true of everybody living in one cultural and national group? As Miss Richmond pointed out a long time ago, we all have some social background, some racial and national characteristics, some family life and traditions; we all live in some form of a social and physical environment; we are all members of some community. "We all have bodies that need intelligent care if we are to keep them in good repair." We have all had some form of education; we have all had some means of subsistence; we all were subject to some social forces exerted by social institutions, traditions, groups; we all have some common personal characteristics. "We are all going someplace and have not yet arrived."[1] It might be added that we all have some common likes and dislikes, some common reactions to situations and persons, some common social attitudes and values, and some shared philosophy of life—as long as we live in the same cultural group.

It is exactly that set of data—in broad ramifications—which is true of everybody in a given cultural area that the investigator can secure best with the aid of a general, flexible, and complete social case history guide. A knowledge of the particular social world in which the persons under consideration live, together with a knowledge of their life experiences, behavior patterns, reactions, and social attitudes, will greatly facilitate the discovery of the unique characteristics of thought and action of these persons.

A trained worker and a skillful interviewer often secures a great deal of pertinent information with a minimum of questioning. The intelligent, stable client who has confidence in the worker will relate his problems without many queries. When it is necessary to ask questions, the worker should know their purpose and note the various implications of the reply. Ideally speaking, the worker should be aware of the logic behind each question. For example, "How much do the parents know of the offense committed by their child?" is not asked merely to learn the parents' part in the offense but also the relations between parents and children; the bonds which unite parent and child; the degree of confidence of the child in his parents; their ability to observe the behavior of their children.

[1] MARY E. RICHMOND, *Social Diagnosis*, p. 377.

The worker will do well to become thoroughly acquainted with the scope of the data he wishes to secure and to weigh carefully each approach to and each question regarding a problem. He should ask himself: "In this particular case what light will the various questions regarding health, school, associates, family relations, and so on, throw on the case—apart from the direct information secured?"

It is assumed, of course, that the worker will safeguard himself against "jumping at conclusions," or evaluating the data prematurely. Certain formulations must be made as the investigation progresses, otherwise the ground will not be covered and the facts in the case will not be seen in their vital relation to each other, but an evaluation of the total situation should be postponed until the case has been studied from various points of view.[1]

STEPS PRIOR TO CONTACT WITH THE CLIENT

Clearance with Social Service Exchange.—Every case coming to the attention of the court or social service agency should be cleared promptly, and as a matter of established routine, with the social service exchange.[2] The social service exchange, or the confidential exchange, as the name implies, is a central clearinghouse of cases for the social service agencies of a community. This service is for the purpose of coordinating the work of social agencies in their dealings with given individuals or families. When a family is accepted for service, the agency generally sends a written inquiry to the exchange which in quick order furnishes the information as to whether this family or any of its members had been in the past or is at present known to any other agency. The files of this exchange contain an alphabetical index of names of families or unattached persons—known to one or more reporting organizations—their addresses, ages of various members, birthplaces, occupations, the names of agencies interested, and other identifying information. No facts about the family history or

---

[1] See WILLIAM HEALY, *The Practical Value of Scientific Study of Juvenile Delinquents*, U. S. Children's Bureau Publication, No. 96 (1922).

[2] For a comprehensive discussion see Margaret F. Buyington, *The Confidential Exchange* (pamphlet); see also Elizabeth A. Hughes and Francelia Stuenkel, *The Social Service Exchange of Chicago;* for an extension of the service beyond the present facilities see Jonah B. Goldstein, *The Family in Court*, pp. 134–142.

treatment of the case are included. This exchange is usually maintained by the council of social agencies or the community chest for the use of all recognized local social agencies.

The terms "clear" and "register" are commonly used by confidential registration bureaus. To clear a case means to inquire of the bureau as to whether or not there are other registrations of the family or the individual about whom the inquiring agency is concerned. To register a case is to record with the bureau the fact that a certain organization, as for example the policewoman's bureau, has worked with an individual or family.[1]

Prompt Contacts with Agencies Listed by the Social Service Exchange.—When the investigator finds that the family under his jurisdiction is also known, let us say, to a relief agency, or a medical agency, or a parent-teacher's organization, or a visiting nurses' organization, or the like, he should promptly make arrangements to read the records or secure reports of these agencies to enable him to learn at least three major points: (1) What is already known about the family? (2) What has already been attempted in working with the family? (3) What degree of success or failure has the given plan had?

Wherever possible it is desirable to consult personally the other visitors on the case and to formulate some uniform plan of procedure which will avoid conflict or duplication of action and advice. At times the investigator may find the case closed or inactive in other agencies. If any of the workers who know the case can still be reached, a conference on the approach to the family, on their attitudes, and on any other points which generally are not recorded in the case history may often prove of value.

The investigator should guard carefully against becoming influenced by any of the biases and prejudices of other workers who, for a variety of reasons, have ceased to view the client or the situation objectively and dispassionately. It is important, however, to learn of the existence of biases and prejudices against a client since such knowledge may aid in explaining his attitude toward the agency and the worker or the proposed plan of action.

Review of Previous Court and Institutional Records.—When a case has been closed at some previous time or the offender was released from probation and the case was later reopened by the

[1] ELEANOR L. HUTZEL and MADELINE L. MACGREGOR, *The Policewoman's Handbook,* p. 142.

same agency because of new delinquent behavior, it is imperative to review the old case history carefully and to consult the supervisor or director in charge.

Previous court records may throw light on the extent and nature of recidivism. The approach to a first offender is different from that to an habitual offender.[1] The worker should aim to learn from the record not only the number and kind of previous offenses committed but also: Why were the offenses committed? How deeply rooted are the habits of misconduct? How much satisfaction does the offender derive from these habits? What are the contributing causes to the persistence of these habits? What has already been attempted in eliminating these habits?

Frequently such information is missing from the case history. In gathering additional data—through personal interviews with either previous workers, teachers, families of the offenders, or the offender himself—these and related points should become a part of the record.

Previous institutional records should also be carefully consulted. Length of stay, methods of rehabilitation, reactions of offender to institution, inmates, discipline, etc., may be of value in understanding present attitudes and behavior problems of offender. It must be remembered, however, that the best and most competent information is supplied by the offender himself and his family. "A well-ordered and properly conducted personal interview with the offender often yields more clues to an understanding of him in his history, habits, and tendencies than all other processes of investigation."[2]

Verification of Data.—Whether dates and records are obtained from the social service exchange or directly from the family, or some other source, it is well to verify births, deaths, marriages, citizenship, immigration records, military service, and others—unless they have already been verified by another agency—to establish as accurate a record as possible. It is of importance to know, for example, the child's age for purposes of issuing work certificates or of transferring the case from the juvenile to the criminal court when he has passed the age of jurisdiction of the former court; it is essential to know whether the children are

[1] See pp. 608–611.
[2] RALPH HALL FERRIS, "The Case History in Probation Service," in Sheldon Glueck (Editor), *Probation and Criminal Justice*, p. 141.

legitimate and entitled to certain property rights; or whether the children are orphaned and entitled to state aid, and so on.

Reporting to Source.—If a case has been referred or a petition filed by another agency or by a private citizen or a relative, it is advisable to report to them that the case in which they are interested is receiving consideration, or is being investigated, or treated according to the particular situation. Thus the referring agency or person will not take steps in referring the case to some other organization nor attempt to do something about the case.

STUDY OF THE OFFENSE

A child is brought to court for delinquent behavior as a result of a complaint made by a police officer, a school, a social agency, a neighbor, or any private citizen, a relative, a parent, and at times the child himself. The offense, from a legal standpoint, is any violation of ordinances, or a misdemeanor, or a felony, as defined by local statutes which may differ widely from state to state. The court worker, though apparently at times paying considerable attention to the offense, actually concerns himself more intensely with the offender. In the eyes of the juvenile court law a minor does not commit a crime. He is not a free moral agent and cannot be expected to distinguish between right and wrong.[1] He commits offenses because of errors in judgment, or because he is an unfortunate victim of social and economic conditions, or because he suffers from physical, mental, or emotional handicaps. His misbehavior is only a symptom of social unadjustment over which a child has little control. The worker should remember that unadjustment or nonconformity does not mean abnormality. For some children asocial and amoral conduct in view of their experiences and social conditions may be natural and normal conduct.

Frequently the petition filed in behalf of the offender will indicate some of the conditions under which the offense was committed. The investigator is concerned with the following:

1. Specific nature of the offense committed: begging, vagrancy, intoxication, incorrigibility, sex immorality, petty larceny, grand larceny, assault, burglary, malicious mischief, robbery, truancy, running away, gambling, forgery, etc.

[1] See *infra*, "Philosophy of the Juvenile Court," pp. 178–185.

2. The circumstances under which the offense was committed: Was it encouraged by adults, by gang associates? Was it committed at night? Was it committed fearlessly? Was it premeditated? and so on.

3. The number of associates in the commitment of the offense: Was he a "lone hand"? Was he a member of a gang which protects him?

4. Weapon used in the commitment of the offense, and degree of bravado and daring exhibited.

5. Disposition of the goods in cases of robbery, burglary, or holdups. Are adults implicated who can be charged with contributing to the delinquency of minors?

A knowledge of these and other points is important in providing clues for further investigation of the offender himself, of his social setting, or his motives, his influences, reactions, and attitudes. As Ralph Hall Ferris points out: "With few exceptions, the specific offense charged is so insignificant for social treatment that for the individual the same treatment would be indicated had he been in court on some other charge."[1]

STUDY OF THE OFFENDER HIMSELF IN RELATION TO HIS SOCIAL WORLD

The study of the offender himself, initiated by Dr. William Healy, has for many years engaged the attention of scientists and practitioners.[2] There is a wealth of material as to what such a study should embrace. It is assumed that the more we know about a given person the better we are able to understand his behavior and to guide him intelligently in self-understanding as well as in reeducation and social rehabilitation.

But to arrive at an adequate understanding of the person himself is not only a very long but also a very difficult process. The person may not be able or willing to give a true account of himself and his circumstances; he may be hiding behind a "mask"; he may be unusually reticent and inarticulate. Often he defies the

---

[1] *Op. cit.*, pp. 136–137.

[2] See WILLIAM HEALY, *The Individual Delinquent;* WALTER C. RECKLESS, "Suggestions for the Sociological Study of Problem Children," *The Journal of Educational Sociology*, II (November, 1928); E. W. BURGESS, "The Study of the Delinquent as a Person," *The American Journal of Sociology*, XXVIII (May, 1923), 657–680; FERRIS, *op. cit.*, pp. 135–164.

best skill of the most competent interviewer. However, it is generally agreed that the proper approach[1] to the person, that establishment of rapport—through respect for his values, appreciation of his difficulties, and broad perspective of the whole situation in which he finds himself—will in most instances break down reticence, and the client will lay aside his mask sufficiently to reveal his true nature.

There are many objective tests and examinations to which the delinquent is subjected and much can be learned from personal observation of his health, intelligence, personality traits, education, recreation, religious training, work habits, social contacts, etc., all of which to a large extent indicate the social world or setting in which he lives. But to understand the delinquent we must also understand his inner world—his ideas, his attitudes and reactions to his outer world and to his group, his beliefs, values, fears, dreams, his relationship to others, his ambitions and outlook on life.[2] He reacts positively or negatively to everything which concerns him, and forms definite attitudes which tend to or actually rouse him to action. Therefore, the worker can never rest satisfied when he has merely learned the state of health of his client, or the type of work in which he engages, or his religious affiliation. He must learn the meaning and the role of these factors in the life of the person.

Within the last decade there has been a noteworthy shift in emphasis from the formal investigation of the outward life, verification of evidence, and so on, to the newer interests in the dynamic, propelling attitudes, motives, interests, ambitions, fears, complexes, to interrelations, and to the individual's own story.[3]

Particularly pertinent is the knowledge of the offender's attitudes toward the complainant, toward the offense, toward those who may have influenced him or instigated the offense; his loyalties to a gang; whether it is necessary to deal with others

[1] For methods of approach and of the technique of interviewing, see Young, *op. cit.*, Chaps. III, IV.

[2] See MIRIAM VAN WATERS, "The Delinquent Attitude: A Study of Juvenile Delinquency from the Standpoint of Human Relationships," *Proceedings of the National Conference of Social Work* (1924), pp. 160–165.

[3] See VIRGINIA ROBINSON, *A Changing Psychology in Social Case Work;* CLIFFORD R. SHAW, *The Jack Roller;* CLIFFORD R. SHAW and OTHERS, *Social Factors in Juvenile Delinquency;* YOUNG, *op. cit.*, Chaps. V, VI.

singly or with whole groups before the offender's habits are reconditioned.

The following case shows the importance of studying attitudes.

The Case of Albert and Richard Richardson (Summary).[1]— Albert, fifteen years, and Richard, sixteen years, were arrested for automobile theft. Albert took and drove a Chevrolet car seventy-five miles without the knowledge and consent of the owner, before he was apprehended by a police officer in a near-by town. Both boys were prowling around cars in a vacant lot but found only the Chevrolet accessible. Richard, as he later confided to a schoolteacher, was much provoked because he "had hard luck" and could only gain a radiator cap of "some tin-can Ford," while he had really hoped "to get a car for himself to take his girl riding." He had little or no concern for a car owner. He swore at his "bad luck" and at his brother. Yet the probation officer, concerning himself chiefly with the nature of the offense, recommended removal of Albert from the home (institutional care or placement in forestry camp) because of grand theft. Richard was released on probation because of petty theft. The teacher, who knows these boys well, maintains that Albert is a responsible boy and if separated from Richard and other offenders would not be involved in any delinquencies. Richard, on the other hand, has a delinquent attitude and while his "hard luck" interfered with his committing grand theft, he is in danger of becoming a serious delinquent.

It will be noted from the following discussion of the various aspects of the life of the offender that at all times both an objective and a subjective study are required, that is, a study of behavior and conditions which can be observed and tested and a study of behavior and conditions which only the offender himself can reveal.

Health (Physical and Mental).[2]—If the offender is detained in a detention home, his health will probably be studied first. If not, the case worker should never attempt to diagnose medical

---

[1] Case reported to writer by a schoolteacher.

[2] For a comprehensive medical social history outline, see RICHARD C. CABOT, *Hospital Social Service* (October, 1929), pp. 269–320; see also LAWRENCE K. FRANK, "Childhood and Youth," in *Recent Social Trends*, pp. 761–769, 784–786; ERNEST R. GROVES and PHYLLIS BLANCHARD, *Readings in Mental Hygiene*, particularly Chap. IV; and JOHN SLAWSON, *The Delinquent Boy*, pp. 270–349.

problems nor to suggest possible medication. This is strictly the function of physicians and psychiatrists. However, he should observe and be sensitive to deviations from what may be termed normal health. Having secured a medical diagnosis from the physician or psychiatrist, at the hospital or the clinic, the worker should learn the relation and effect of ill-health, physical and mental, to misbehavior, complexes, frustrations, and general unadjustment.

In each instance it is important to learn how much the person knows about his problems and what his *attitudes* are regarding them. Some persons are little affected by ill-health or other problems, while others become seriously unadjusted and create tensions and conflicts over even relatively insignificant ailments and handicaps. What attitudes and social conditions stand in the way of carrying out treatment or in removing tensions? (See discussion of developmental history, p. 74 also p. 44.)

Psychological Make-up.—What is the general intelligence of the person? What are his special abilities and disabilities (as established by a competent psychologist or psychiatrist)? What is his emotional make-up? How does he fit into the particular social group of which he is a member? Does he regard himself as superior or inferior? Is he in conflict with other members? What are his personality traits?[1] Dr. Burgess[2] lists under personal behavior patterns:

Objective or direct: (1) Equable, (2) enthusiastic, (3) direct, (4) aggressive, (5) explosive.

Introspective or indirect: (1) Imaginative, (2) secretive, (3) sensitive, (4) inhibited.

Psychopathic or perverse: (1) Eccentric, (2) egocentric, (3) emotionally unstable, (4) psychic inferior.

What are the person's reactions to home? to responsibilities? to himself? How does he accept life in general? What are his interests? What are his plans for the future? What are his ambitions? What are his likes and dislikes? What are his habits of eating? sleeping? playing?

The worker will frequently be supplied with psychometric reports (findings of tests consisting of measurements of mental

---

[1] See FLOYD H. ALLPORT, *Social Psychology*, pp. 99–125, for a comprehensive discussion of personality traits.

[2] *Op. cit.*, p. 665.

traits and abilities) sent by the clinic.[1]   In cases of persons who
are members of a different language group or a different cultural
group it must be ascertained how much stress was laid in comput-
ing the intelligence quotient (I.Q.) on the child's knowledge of a
language other than his native tongue; his knowledge of facts,
customs, social life, other than those practiced by the client's
social group.   What is the score for the performance tests?
for the academic tests?

No tests have been devised to measure the intelligence, traits,
adaptability of children to their particular cultural and social
worlds.   There are no tests written in foreign languages which
would meet the needs of many children who are not thoroughly
conversant with the English language.   Neither are there tests
which would measure the reactions, biases, and prejudices arising
upon the encounter of persons coming from different worlds of
discourse, under a variety of social and personal handicaps.   A
reticent child, a child even mildly indisposed, or one temporarily
unable to concentrate will make a much lower score than he would
under usual conditions.

The findings of the psychometrist are very useful when related
to the general scheme of things under which the person lives.
The worker should, therefore, seek to learn to what extent the
tests have taken into consideration the unique circumstances of
the child at the time the test was performed.

Educational Situation.[2]—As Burt points out, much "grief
arises out of the incidents of school life."[3]   If there is school
unadjustment, how does it arise?   What are the person's reactions to the school, teachers, and schooling, past and present?
How much has he actually accomplished?   How much is he
capable of accomplishing?   What is his deportment?   What
studies does he most enjoy?   Which teachers have or have not
had the profoundest influence upon him?   If he left school, why?
if retarded, why? if truant, why?   What is the grade placement?
What should it be for the particular child?   What has the school
done to overcome truancy?[4]

[1] See *infra*, pp. 336, 410, 608–611.

[2] See White House Conference on Child Health and Protection, *The
Delinquent Child*, pp. 99–133; MARY B. SAYLES, *The Problem Child at School.*

[3] CYRIL BURT, *The Young Delinquent*, p. 466.

[4] See JOHN F. BENDER, *The Functions of the Court in Enforcing School
Attendance Laws;* also *A Study of 201 Truants in the New York City Schools*
(Albany, 1927).

"Truancy," Dr. Van Waters points out, "may be a misplaced virtue. It may be a biological protest against bad air, mental or physical defects, or healthy criticism of a course of study hopelessly dull, heavy, mechanical and uninteresting. Frequently it is an attempt to evade responsibility, to escape meeting an issue; again it is a mode of self-expression, or of taking revenge."[1]

The questions which the child is unable to answer should be secured from the school authorities. (See discussion of study of the school as a source of information, pp. 44–45, 83–84, 141, 425).

Recreational Situation.[2]—How does the person spend his leisure time? What forms of recreation does he seek and enjoy? within the family group? alone? with a gang? with members of the opposite sex? Does he seek and enjoy commercialized recreation? Does he form good and lasting associations within his play group? How much space is there for play in his own home? What are the chief recreational activities in which he engages? Does he have an allowance for recreational activities? What are his attitudes toward play and recreation? (see pp. 454–568).

Employment.[3]—In spite of child labor laws an astonishing number of minors work in industry, in domestic service, in agriculture,[4] in street trades,[5] as well as in hotels, restaurants, theaters, dance halls—without proper legislative safeguards. Those who are old enough to work are often subject to poor and improper conditions. The worker needs to learn whether the person is exploited by the employer, the parents, or the public. In the case of a theater usher, a waitress, a bellhop, and other children in similar pursuits, "it is mainly youth, beauty, charm and vivacity which sells their service. There is a perpetual demand on their power to please, soothe, flatter and interest tired adults."[6] They

---

[1] MIRIAM VAN WATERS, *Youth in Conflict*, p. 90; also E. K. WICKMAN, *Children's Behavior and Children's Attitudes.*

[2] See MARTIN H. and ESTHER S. NEUMEYER, *Leisure and Recreation*, pp. 56–57, 202–211; see also White House Conference on Child Health and Protection, *The Delinquent Child*, pp. 198–224; JESSE F. STEINER, "Recreation and Leisure Time Activities," in *Recent Social Trends*, pp. 912–957.

[3] U. S. Children's Bureau Publication, *Facts and Figures*, No. 197 (1930); see also FRANK, *op. cit.*, pp. 777–779.

[4] See NETTIE P. MCGILL, *Children in Agriculture*, U. S. Children's Bureau Publication, No. 187 (1929).

[5] See NETTIE P. MCGILL, *Child-workers on City Streets*, U. S. Children's Bureau Publication, No. 188 (1929); and *Children in Street Work*, U. S. Children's Bureau Publication, No. 183 (1928).

[6] VAN WATERS, *Youth in Conflict*, p. 117.

become wise to ways of the world at an early age with all its
artificiality and bigotry. They become accustomed to and
demand constant stimulation. Do home and school life then
become "tame and monotonous"?

The worker needs to learn whether the child has a work certificate. Does he work to the detriment of his health, personal
development, or school attendance? Why does he work? If
too young to work, what plans could be made for the family to
get along without his contributions? How many hours a day
does he work? under what conditions? How far from home is his
work? At what times does he get home? How much does he
earn? What does he do with his earnings? How does he like
his work? How does he get along with his superiors? with his
coworkers? What are his occupational attitudes? What degree
of social and personal independence does he derive from working
and earning? How much control do the parents still have over
him? Does he have any conflicts over his work? What are his
ambitions with regard to his work? How did he make the transition from school to work? (See also discussion of employers as
source of information, p. 84.)

Lack of Employment.[1]—When the boy or girl has graduated
from school or has left school, lack of employment is often a
disorganizing force. Idleness of itself is demoralizing. Lack of
employment may initiate a feeling of inferiority and a deepening
sense of failure and arouse defense mechanisms of various sorts.

It is important to know the relation between unemployment and
delinquency. (It is generally agreed that few delinquents steal
merely because of privation.[2]) Is misconduct an outlet for a
restless, defeated person? Is it a defense mechanism? What is
the parents' attitude toward their children's lack of employment?
Are they aggravated, grumbling, and uncongenial? What is the
attitude of associates? To what extent are plans and ambitions
frustrated?

Social Contacts.—How much does the person participate in
home life, routine, chores, family ceremonials? What is the
nature and extent of his associations with chums? gangs? clubs?
boys' or girls' organizations? How much do these contacts mean

[1] See MAXINE DAVIS, *The Lost Generation.*

[2] See BURT, *op. cit.*, pp. 62–90; also HEALY, *The Individual Delinquent,*
p. 292.

to him? How much would he miss them if deprived of them? Is he a leader? Is he accepted as a leader?

Social Conflicts[1] and Accommodations.—What social conflicts does the person develop as a result of his social contacts? What mental conflicts does he develop because of his social contacts or their absence? (Struggles between "one's desires and one's ethics or conventions, . . . when repressed, may then disturb the individual's existence in obscure ways, sometimes bringing about a psycho-neurotic condition."[2]) With whom does he conflict? over what? What conflicts have left a profound impression? Has he run away from home? school? why? What form do the conflicts assume? Have the social and mental conflicts brought him in conflict with the law? under what circumstances? What adjustments has he made? What accommodations? How?

Frequently the most useful starting point is to go back to the first conflict the child has experienced and to ask him to recall all he can remember about it, together with his own wants and grievances. Sometimes, however, it is necessary to start from the last conflict—if that is uppermost in his mind—and work backward rather than forward. Often a general question such as: "How is the world treating you?" or "Have you been happy lately?" or "What special worries do you have?" will start an uninhibited child to relating something about his inner self.

THE SIGNIFICANCE OF STUDYING THE UNDERLYING AND CONTRIBUTING FACTORS

While a discussion of underlying factors, pathological processes, etiology, and so on, properly belongs in the chapter on social diagnosis (see pp. 114–136) these issues must also be kept in mind during the exploration of the case. The worker encountering many problem situations—in various combinations—with delinquents and their families must be able to explore the process of unadjustment.

Thievery, burglary, begging, immorality, drunkenness, running away, vagrancy, gambling, idleness, parental rejection are but a

---

[1] See various papers in the *Proceedings of the National Conference of Social Work* (1927) on "Environmental Conflicts in the Family and Social Life of the Modern Child," by HENRY C. SCHUMACHER, pp. 281–286; by MARGARET H. WATSON, pp. 287–290; by LILLIAN S. COWAN, pp. 291–294.

[2] See S. L. and L. C. PRESSEY, *Mental Abnormalities and Deficiency.*

few examples of the complex variety of difficulties presented by and to problem children and juvenile delinquents. However, these must be regarded as mere symptoms of more far-reaching and serious unadjustments than the overt acts and external conditions indicate. Marilyn's truancy and running away and Marvin Levkowitz's running away are but symptoms of more deep-rooted problems (see pp. 33–52, *infra*).

Every social and personal problem or unadjustment has its starting points, its natural history, its roots and contributing factors, which are often very difficult to uncover. Yet, without the knowledge of the factors and forces which produced the unadjustment little or no insight into the situation can be gained and no effective plan for attacking it can be devised. We should be in the same position as the physician who tries to relieve a headache without attempting to learn what conditions contributed to the headache. Obviously different individuals suffer from different types of headaches arising out of different situations. A headache associated with eyestrain has to be relieved by different means than a headache associated with a tumor on the brain, or with ulcers of the stomach, or with worry over money matters, or with a mother-in-law. The headache itself is only a symptom of a more serious physical or mental defect which is not going to disappear with the treatment of symptoms. When the contributing factors are removed the symptoms—all other things being equal—disappear as well.

Assume a case of truancy, or stealing, or lying, or any other problem. We need to learn the kind of truancy, stealing, lying, and so on, that is, what are the underlying factors of these symptoms and with what are they associated? Stealing, for example, may be associated with the tradition in one's gang, with need, with neurotic factors, with revenge, with desire for new experience, bravado, etc., or any combination of these. Unless the worker learns through the social study the contributing factors, the treatment may be concentrated on the symptom and the person might be scolded, threatened, lectured, given demerits or awards without effect.

Of course, it is difficult to single out these factors because of their complexity. A person does not steal simply because his gang leader orders him to do so, or simply because he is in need. There are generally other circumstances and individual traits which have laid their groundwork for such behavior patterns.

Pathological Process.—Once a social problem gains momentum it brings in its wake other problems and pathological situations. For example, unemployment of the breadwinner may create tensions which will express themselves in incompatibility, wandering, drunkenness, marital discord, loss of respect by wife and children, loss of authority over children, individualization, and delinquency. Delinquency to begin with may be only a symptom in a long pathological process, but eventually it becomes a habit and becomes associated with numerous other pathological conditions and processes. The various steps and complexities of a process are often difficult to trace but a clear understanding of its development is essential for diagnosis and treatment of a case. The worker should inquire into what processes and problems were associated with the origin of misconduct. How did they affect the original situation? What were the results of each additional problem?

Briefly, the worker is concerned with the entire social and cultural setting of the person, his personality traits, his inner life, his tensions, the natural history and development of his behavior patterns, pathological processes, including symptoms, underlying and contributing factors, and crises.

Plan of the Family.—What does the child know of the parents' attempts to deal with his problems? What were these attempts? How does he or did he react to them? When interviewing the parents, and often older boys and girls who have some insight into their situations, the question may be asked regarding specific attempts made, their degree of success or failure in controlling the problems, the obstacles encountered. What resources have they already tapped or should be tapped? and what persons should cooperate in their plan?

Obviously these questions should be asked only after as much as possible has been learned about the offender and his family. The very inquiry into their plans may stimulate at least some families to plan for themselves, but the worker needs to know their attempts, desires, and intentions in order to coordinate his efforts with their efforts and capabilities.

(To be concluded)

CHAPTER IV

THE COMPREHENSIVE EXPLORATION OF A CASE
(Concluded)

THE STUDY OF THE FAMILY GROUP
AND OF THE COMMUNITY

STUDY OF THE FAMILY GROUP

The unique circumstances of each case frequently decide whether the family or the offender should be studied first and how intensive the study of each should be. A knowledge of family life, social setting, and background throws light on and provides many clues regarding the offender.[1] A knowledge of the offender and his reactions will often focus attention on the more difficult and subtle problems of family and community life. In actual practice, and particularly in the more serious offenses, the study of the family group and of the offender is often carried on simultaneously. Whatever the order of study the worker should keep in mind the constant interplay and close interrelation between the person and the group.[2]

If the child offender is interviewed first, undoubtedly most essential data regarding the family will be already at hand. The child should not, however, be questioned beyond the most obvious facts about the life and circumstances of his family group, particularly if they present serious problems. Children should not be put into a position where they must pass judgment on their parents.

[1] See E. W. BURGESS, "The Family as a Unity of Interacting Personalities," *The Family*, VII (March, 1926), 3–9; MIRIAM VAN WATERS, *Parents on Probation;* ELEANOR WEMBRIDGE, *Other People's Daughters;* CHASE GOING WOODHOUSE, "A Study of 250 Successful Families," *Social Forces*, VIII (June, 1930), 511–532; The White House Conference on Child Health and Protection, *The Delinquent Child*, pp. 79–96; JOHN SLAWSON, *The Delinquent Boy*, pp. 350–441.

[2] See WILLIAM HEALY, "The Psychology of the Situation," in *The Child, The Court and the Clinic* (a symposium), pp. 37–52.

Reactions to the Offense.—Frequently when a child has been arrested and detained or released to the parents in custody of the probation officer the parents expect and are ready to discuss the offense with the worker immediately upon his arrival at their home. Such a discussion will relieve their tensions; however, the worker should guard carefully against making any promises or undertaking any treatment before the investigation is complete and the situation adequately understood.

Since the parents are generally under severe tensions when their child is taken in custody, the worker should not attempt to evaluate their make-up until the strain is relieved. At best it is difficult to learn—except after considerable observation and study—whether the parents are well balanced, self-controlled, tolerant, or mature in judgment. These facts are essential but should be weighed carefully during the entire process of study. All attempts should be avoided at formulating hasty judgments upon unfounded impressions after a short period of conversation with a person.

When given an opportunity to talk the parents generally will relate their side of the story. The worker should discover what the parents know of the present offense and any previous offenses. What is their reaction to the offense and the offender? Such knowledge will enable the worker to judge whether or not and to what degree the parents' attitudes will need changing before adjustment can be brought about in the child.

It is also essential to know how the parents account for the child's delinquent behavior. If the information is not volunteered, the question may be asked: "How do you explain John's (or Mary's) conduct?" If the parents have no insight into their children's conduct, the worker must later undertake a long process of educating the parents regarding the contributing factors in their child's misconduct. It is believed that once they become sensitive to the sources and causal factors they may be able to prevent further misbehavior in the offender as well as in the other children. When did they first notice any signs of misconduct? With what occurrences or experiences can they associate the beginning and the continuance of the misconduct? Frequently the misconduct itself is of far less significance than the surrounding circumstances. The fear of punishment will lead a child to lying, running away, truancy; or jealousy concerning another child or person will lead to stealing, revenge, running away, etc. These factors then must be ascertained before any intelligent plan of treatment can be undertaken.

The Social History of the Child's Development in the Family Circle.—Each child evokes with its appearance in the family circle certain reactions and attitudes toward himself and toward other members in the group, who in turn reflect their attitudes toward him. If the child is wanted by his parents, welcomed by the other children, his developmental career will be different than if he is not wanted and welcomed or is simply taken for granted. What we need to learn in addition to the usual chronological history of birth, labor, instrumentation, breast feeding, dentition, walking, talking, etc., is the effect of these events upon the parents and the child as personalities. What emotional complexes and social attitudes were built up during pregnancy, normal or abnormal? What does the mother remember about the conditions of the birth of the child and what were her reactions to it which may have been carried over until this day? What role did the child play in the family circle? What are the aftereffects of the early diseases? What are the habits of eating, sleeping, and general behavior, and the reactions to them? Does the child suffer from enuresis? Is he teased about it? What is his reaction to it? his parents' reaction? What methods have been tried to overcome it? What is the nature of the child's sex curiosity? How has it been satisfied? What is the history of the adolescent behavior and accompanying habits? What is the attitude of the parents toward the adolescent? What outstanding personal and social traits has the child developed? What has been the reaction to them?

It is generally recognized that wrong trends usually show up early in life, and that, figuratively speaking, the tree will grow as the twigs are bent. A child's complexes, behavior patterns, and attitude can often be traced to outstanding elements in his early childhood and to the unique reactions of the family group toward him. At times the parents adopt too severe or too protective an attitude toward him. He never has an opportunity to develop self-reliance, or to think for himself, or to do those things for himself which would develop his personality and increase his vision. Children who are overly protected and have few opportunities to develop their powers and to find self-expression may develop a social world apart from their parents, and despite their solicitude the parents and the children may develop great social distances.

Dr. Van Waters observes: "The first impression we receive is that the antagonism is based on what we might call nothing at all! Not the child shivering on the worst bed in the house, discriminated against, eating what is left, getting blows, reprimands, and injuries is the one most likely to fall victim to the insidious disease of antagonism; on the contrary, we find it more frequently among children who seem well off from the skin out and who are hard put to find any tangible ills to complain of."[1]

Relation of Siblings (brothers and sisters).—Much information can be gathered about the siblings. The important information as far as the subject of study is concerned pertains to: the attitudes of the siblings toward the delinquent; the relationships and ties maintained between them; evidence of discrimination by parents or of invidious comparisons; activities, accomplishments, possessions, recognition of siblings, etc., which might serve as bases for discontentment or complexes on the part of the delinquent.

Family Status.—In addition to an account of whether or not the parents are alive, separated, or divorced it is important to learn what effect the family status has upon the child. What is the degree of solidarity among the various members? What are the family objectives, ideals, and sentiments?

A home may be broken by separation, divorce, death, desertion as well as by incompatibility, strife, lack of solidarity and of common interests between parents and children. Tensions and conflicts, lack of morale and *esprit de corps*, reflect themselves in the behavior patterns and attitudes of the youthful members. Tensions in family life produce tensions in children; lack of *esprit de corps* and of common interests tends to produce feelings of inferiority, strain, neglect, and "don't-belong."

Mobility of Family.[2]—Modern life, fast and cheap means of transportation, good roads, precarious conditions of work are often conducive to changes in residence and to the uprooting

---

[1] *Op. cit.*, p. 172.

[2] See E. W. Burgess, "Tentative Social Case History Outline of a Family" (mimeographed) or in Pauline V. Young, *Interviewing in Social Work*, pp. 106–107.

even of old-established households.   Even where the change is
beneficial to both young and old, a certain degree of readjustment
is required by all members to the new conditions of living.   The
stability of the various members may be impaired permanently
or temporarily as associations are broken.

The worker should interest himself in the reasons for the
wanderings.   What are the effects of such wanderings upon the
general life organization of the family?   On the individual
members?   What are the effects on home ownership?   Has the
family taken root in the new community?   Is the family responsive to any institutions of social control (church, community,
neighborhood) in the new environment?   Do the children find
sufficient security under the changed conditions of life?

Family Economy.[1]—How has the family economy influenced
the child's physical and social development?   Who is the breadwinner in the family?   What are the business or occupation, the
earning capacity, and the occupational attitudes of the breadwinner?   What are the effects of these?   If the mother works,
what are the effects on the children?

What is the division of labor between the various members of
the family?   What arrangements are made for support of the
family when the breadwinner is unemployed?   What are the
effects of unemployment?   How does the family manage on its
income?   For what are the largest expenditures made?   Do the
children receive a sufficient and well-balanced diet?[2]

Family Background.—The exploration of the past life of an
individual or a family is both a difficult and a long process.   What
elements in the complex background should be explored?   Psychiatrists and psychologists maintain that the hidden, the suppressed, and the subconscious often play a far more significant
role than the obvious and external behavior.   That there is a
direct and vital relationship between the past experiences, conditioning, emotional complexes, and present behavior patterns is
accepted by all competent students of human conduct.   The
investigator who is not limited in time will seek to learn as much of
the background as the family is able to provide, and he will
plumb the depths as thoroughly as his training, education, and

[1] *Ibid.*, p. 107.

[2] See FLORENCE NESBITT, *Chicago Standard Budget for Dependent Families*
(4th rev. ed.); see also ALICE BRADLEY, *Menu-Cook-Book;* see *infra*, p. 398.

understanding of the problem, the confidence established, and his interviewing skill will permit. It should be stressed again, however, that the worker is not interested in a mere account of past events and experiences but in their significant role in the present situation.

As a result of his experiences and social situations in childhood, adolescence, youth, and later life, what attitudes and values has the individual developed? What ambitions does he maintain for himself and his children? How does his background compare with that of his mate? of his associates? What conflicts result because of insistence upon adherence to them? What personal and social traits were developed in or carried over from the early cultural complex? What role does the family name play? family lore and traditions? What role does tradition play in the lives of the family group? Do the parents adhere to Old World traditions and customs? Do they insist on the adherence to them by their children? Do conflicts result because of differences in the cultural background of the old and the young? To what extent do they live in the same world of discourse? What is the effect of culture conflicts upon the behavior of the young? What is the education of the parents? What is their ambition for their children? Do any conflicts arise because of differences in educational levels or ambitions of the various members?

Health of the Family.—The worker is interested in an account and medical reports of the offender's family only in so far as they will throw light upon the behavior and on the health and tendencies of the offender himself. Is there a record of institutional care? prolonged hospital or clinical care? What are the sources or dangers of infections, if any? It must also be ascertained to what extent the poor health of the parents causes neglect in the care of the child. To what extent does poor health of the parents cause fears and complexes in the child regarding his own condition or that of his parents? How much of the family income is drained off for doctors' bills and medicine? Have the children been placed away from home because of ill-health of parents? What have the effects been of being away from home?

Family Organization and Control.—The organization of family life has a profound influence upon the members of the family group. The degree of close associations, of fusion of individuals in a common whole, of unity of purpose and interests, of a "we-feeling" is largely dependent upon the existing organization and control of the family. However, even where the family is bound by close ties of unity and solidarity there is always "self-assertion and various appropriative passions." These must not be regarded as manifestations of hostility as long as they are "socialized by sympathy and come or tend to come under the discipline of a common spirit. The individual will be ambitious, but the chief object of his ambition will be some desired place in the thought of the others, and he will feel allegiance to common standards of service and fair play."[1]

The worker should learn what the relation is of the members to the family group and to each other. What binds them together: "we-feeling"? religious principles? common interests? autocratic rule by elders? What role does the child play in the organization of the family group?

What form of discipline and of social control does the family use: physical punishment? appeal to self-respect or pride? appeal to conscience? to the family name? to social ideals?[2] Obviously such appeals can be made only to older and intelligent children. In each instance should be learned their effects on the child, not outwardly, but inwardly. Often a child will respond or obey in order to avoid further conflict or "preaching" but he may rebel and become moody or irritable.

Family events, reunions, picnics, holidays, birthdays, etc.,[3] are important means of drawing the young together and creating a "we-feeling." What is the degree of participation by the young in these events? What stress do the parents lay upon them? What is the degree of family solidarity? of family morale? What effect do family crises (births, marriages, deaths, accidents, financial reverses) have upon the young? How much do they know of the actual situation? To what extent do they share in the parents' sense of success or defeat in life? What status is accorded the child in the home? Frequently when children begin to earn money and to contribute to the family exchequer they feel not only an economic independence but a social independence and are inclined to control their parents or to become emancipated from their control. What is the situation in the home under consideration?

[1] CHARLES H. COOLEY, *Social Organization.* pp. 23–24.
[2] BURGESS, *op. cit.*
[3] *Ibid.*

Fixations and Emancipation.—Occasionally children prolong unduly their natural dependency upon their parents. There is a normal natural process by which the emotional ties of childhood are severed and individual emancipation effected. Failure to begin and carry on this essential transformation, by which the child will eventually become an adult, leads to serious unadjustments.[1]

Have there been overprotective attitudes on the part of the parent? Are the affectional relations of parent and child normal or extreme? Any emotional fixations? Any indication that the child is a "sissy" or "mama's boy"? Is the parent seeking undue control over the child's future? over occupation? over marriage? Does this represent a "projection" upon the child of the frustration of the parent?[2]

Religious Affiliations.[3]—It is not enough to learn whether the family or the children attend church or Sunday school, and what kind, but also what meaning the church has in their lives. What do they get out of the church connection? What are their reactions to religion? What conflicts do they have regarding religion? Does the church have or can it have any influence over them? If not, why not? Will they profit by a visit from the pastor?

If no religious affiliations are maintained, will they profit by attendance or by joining a church because of the religious instruction? or because of a satisfying attachment to a social and religious institution? Do the children have religious instruction at home? In case the mother and father belong to different churches, what conflicts arise over the condition? How much of the conflict is shared by the children?

STUDY OF THE COMMUNITY[4]

The worker should be interested not only in the physical aspects of the community, its type of streets, dwellings, presence of local

---

[1] See ERNEST R. GROVES and PHYLLIS BLANCHARD, *Readings in Mental Hygiene*, Chap. V.

[2] See MEYER F. NIMKOFF, *The Family*, Chaps. IX, X.

[3] See SHAILER MATHEWS, *New Faith for Old;* see White House Conference on Child Health and Protection, *The Delinquent Child*, pp. 137–164.

[4] See New York State Crime Commission, "A Study of Delinquency in a District of Kings County," pp. 17–18, 46–49; White House Conference on Child Health and Protection, *The Delinquent Child*, pp. 230–245; also R. E. PARK and E. W. BURGESS, *The City*.

industries, but also in (*a*) the variety and effectiveness of the social institutions—churches, schools, playgrounds, social centers, places of amusement, business and industrial enterprises; (*b*) traditions and standards of the group and their effectiveness; (*c*) group opinion and its effectiveness; (*d*) the methods of social control over the young and their effectiveness; and (*e*) outstanding persons in the community to whom the young respond.

This information is difficult to secure not only by a single worker but by an agency. Special types of studies and prolonged research are often carried on to learn of the forces and influences a given community exerts over its youth. At times the council of social agencies, or the local social center, or public school, or university may supply the pertinent information. At times old residents are valuable sources. Some reliable and scientific, as well as some literary, studies have been published on a number of foreign communities in America—the Mexican,[1] the Russian,[2] the Jewish,[3] the Polish,[4] the Negro,[5] and others. It is well to know not only the foreign community but the native American community as well.[6]

Frequently the argument is advanced that the same forces and surroundings which are apparently responsible for the disorganization of certain individuals have proved to be stabilizing and organizing forces for other individuals. That argument holds true with respect to all physical and social settings. Apparently the same environment will affect different persons with varied temperaments, constitutions, mental associations differently. As far as they are individually concerned the environment is different and they should be dealt with on that basis. That is, the worker should learn the unique reactions of each case to the particular environment.

[1] E. S. BOGARDUS, *The Mexicans in the United States;* see also JOSEPH HENRY JACKSON, *Mexican Interlude.*

[2] PAULINE V. YOUNG, *Pilgrims of Russian-Town.*

[3] LOUIS WRITH, *The Ghetto.*

[4] W. I. THOMAS and F. ZNANIECKI, *The Polish Peasant in Europe and America;* see also R. E. PARK and H. A. MILLER, *Old World Traits Transplanted.*

[5] The Chicago Commission on Race Relations, *The Negro in Chicago;* B. SCHRIECKE, *Alien Americans.*

[6] For example, HARVEY ZORBAUGH, *The Gold Coast and the Slum.*

It is essential to learn from the offender himself his reactions to the standard of living of the community, to the types of occupations in which the various members engage. What are his reactions to the type of community in which he must live—slum, ghetto, transitional, industrial area, residential district, and so on? What uses does he make of the places of amusement? of the social and religious organizations? What does he know of their status in the neighborhood? What are his reactions to group traditions and culture? Does he identify himself with the group culture, with its social institutions, its language? Does he have any conflicts with or concerning them?

Group life undoubtedly provides the widest bases for conduct. Through and from the group the individual gets his conception of the role he plays in life; the group supplies the cultural pattern; the social wishes assume significance and get a means of satisfaction through and in the group; social conflict is born and maintained in group life, and adjustment is achieved through the group. Man is the most social of animals. All the thoughts, actions, desires, and passions are aroused in and satisfied through groups. In order to understand the individual we must understand the group and vice versa.

Community surroundings, circumstances, and group life are always a part of the total social situation. The person forms his mental associations, derives the basis for his behavior patterns from the group.

What is the status of the family in the community? Is it respected? disregarded? ostracized? indifferent? How much does the child know of this status and what are his reactions? Frequently children form complexes because their parents are not accepted or respected by friends, neighbors, or relatives.

Housing Conditions.—Inadequacy of quarters, poor sanitation, poor arrangement, lack of privacy, poor housekeeping habits and household management are problems of vital concern to the worker, when the child under his care is expected to eat, sleep, and spend his leisure and after-school hours at home. Housing problems may not only interfere with the proper physical, mental, and moral developments of the child but may hinder the maintenance of his status among his associates. It is of importance to learn the child's reactions to the physical as well as to the social aspects of his home. Does he feel free to invite his friends into the home? If not, why not? Is he sensitive because of inadequacy of space? of poor or inadequate housekeeping and household management? of interference by elders or by younger children? In the case of girls this situation should be carefully studied.

If the girl does not bring her friends into the home, where do they meet? Does she feel disgraced or suppressed because of her inability to entertain them at home? What does she know of the reactions of her friends toward her home conditions?

How are the children aiding in improving the conditions of the home? How much responsibility do they assume for the care of the home? How can the existing conditions be improved?

Let it not be assumed, however, that a knowledge of the cultural pattern of the group will always tend to explain the mode of conduct of its members. Only some members pattern their conduct after the group. Those who are in conflict with the group may so widely deviate from its accepted standards and norms as to become total strangers. Therefore, in learning the individual's reactions to his community it is imperative to learn the extent and nature of conflict with it; the duration of conflict and its fundamental causes; the precise degree of participation in the group life and the role played in the community.

STUDY OF OTHER SOURCES OF INFORMATION

The worker should consider the following persons as further sources of information which may throw light on the behavior of the offender: the arresting officer, the complainant, witnesses, the school, the employer, the clergyman, and relatives. In each case the worker needs to be concerned not only with the data on the child which these persons may be able to supply but also to be sensitive to all clues indicative of their special interest in the case, their competency as witnesses, their role in the situation leading up to the offense.

The Arresting Officer.—The officer generally submits a written report to the court regarding the circumstances under which the offense was committed, the number of associates, the place and the time of arrest, and whatever identifying information he was able to secure from the offender. If the officer knows the offender well from previous contacts with him and his family, it is well to arrange for an interview and to secure the information outlined by Lieutenant Lester (see pp. 264–265).

The Complainant.—Occasionally the complainant is unbiased and impersonal and can supply helpful information regarding the offender: the offender's attitude toward the offense, arrest, damage done, and so on. How many times and in what ways was the complainant molested or injured? How many associates were there in the offense? What is known about the offender's family? The complainant's account should be carefully weighed with regard to his own interests involved in the matter, his intelligence, his personal standing in the community, and with full regard for the defendant's story.

The School Authorities.—The principal, the teachers, the school nurse, and the attendance officer can supply information concerning various aspects of the child's life in school. What is his grade placement? Is he behind or ahead in view of his age, intelligence, and possible accomplishment? Have any tests been given? What are their results? Under what circumstances were they given? Are his interests known to the school and is self-expression provided for? What is his academic record? if low, why? What is his attendance record? if irregular, why? What has the school done or is it capable of doing to improve these records? What outstanding personality traits and behavior patterns have the teachers noticed? Have they attempted to do something about these? What adjustments has the child made to his schoolmates of both sexes? Is he popular? well liked? friendly? sociable?

What does the school know about the child's parents? about their relation to each other? about the effects of the economic situation in the home?

Has the school considered the child's overt as well as his covert behavior? Frequently a child who is mischievous in school, though a serious problem to the teacher, needs less therapeutic care than the one who is a model child but is extremely introverted, daydreaming, and unusually reticent and submissive. How much does the school know of the child's inner life? What is the child's health record at school?

The worker needs also to become sufficiently familiar with the school itself, to formulate a judgment regarding the adequacy of the school in question to deal not only with the problem of the given delinquent but with children generally. Are there serious inadequacies in equipment, personnel, program, management to which delinquency may be regarded as a normal, or at least an expected natural response?

The Employer.—In the case of those offenders who are old enough to work—the age varying from state to state—or those who have graduated from high school before their legal working age, and all those who hold a work certificate for good reasons and who are known to their employer, it is generally considered inadvisable to consult the employer for fear of jeopardizing the chances for employment. The employer may become suspicious, afraid, desirous of protecting the name of the firm and the status of other employees when an officer or a worker from a social agency calls.

If there are any grounds for justifying the employer's attitude the worker has an obligation to him, his firm, and the other employees as well as to the offender. However, no inquiry should be made of the employer until it is ascertained that the offender is a source of danger and compromise to his employer. Occasionally employers give their full cooperation—knowing all the circumstances of the case—and assume the responsibility of a big brother as well as a job giver.

In dealing with employers the worker needs always to remember that children in industry are frequently exploited and that the hazards of industry are unusually great for children. The data which the employer can give concerning the child need to be reflected against the conditions under which the child works, the personnel practices of the employer, the character of the employer himself and of the fellow workmen, the moral atmosphere of the industry. The worker must be sensitive to every demoralizing influence which may be operating in the child's workaday world.

THE FACE SHEET[1]

The face sheet or card is "a blank form for registering a small range of outstanding facts which are in most constant use . . . which identify each case and present its basic facts in a way that enables the reader to get a skeleton outline of the social situation at a glance."[2] Experienced and well-trained workers rarely fill out a face sheet in the presence of a client. They maintain that a large amount of the data essential for the face sheet is secured indirectly during the course of the social study. What-

[1] See ADA E. SHEFFIELD, *The Social Case History*, pp. 42–50.
[2] *Ibid.*, pp. 42–43.

JUVENILE
FACE SHEET
Record No. ......

Probation Department of..............

Name	Address		Tel.	Color	Sex

Parents	Address	Birth		Verifi-cation	Death date	Reli-gion	U. S. citizen	Marriage		Occupation School grade
		Date	Place					Date	Place	
Father Maiden name Mother										
Stepfather										
Stepmother										
Children (chronologically, including subject)										
Others in home	Relationship									
Agencies and others interested	Address	Relationship or interest								

Court Hearings					
Date	Reason for referral	Docket no.	Disposition	Probation officer	

National Probation Association, 50 West 50th Street, New York City ever items are not thus secured should be asked for indirectly at the appropriate occasion or at the close of the interview. Some workers argue that the client "expects to be questioned" and has no hesitancy in supplying the needed information while the interviewer fills out the face sheet. This is undoubtedly true but the client cannot foresee the degree of his distraction while answering, watching, and thinking of possible consequences of "a record." The worker should explain, of course, to the mature clients that records are kept but he need not inhibit him by the actual evidence of such records.

The National Probation Association, New York, has devised a series of face sheets[1] of which we present only the forms for juvenile court cases, which lend themselves to ready use because of their simplicity. On the mechanical side they are commendable because they are spaced right for the typewriter and have distinctive colors. The data are logically arranged.

Only the relatively important information and the data having historical value are included. It is a form the use of which can be readily standardized.

Generally the face sheets used by probation departments are too full, crowded, and improperly spaced and attempt to put the whole history on a face sheet, which procedure tends to hinder a worker from developing a proper interviewing technique and from gaining insight into the situation and perspective of the case.

THE SOCIAL STUDY AND THE COURT

Agnes C. Sullivan in an address before the National Probation Association in 1936, on "Principles and Values in Case Recording,"[2] lists the following purposes of preliminary study and the following factors as influencing the social study of a court case:

The purpose of the preliminary investigation is twofold:

It puts the court in a position to make a disposition based on actual knowledge of the particular needs of the offender in relation to his situation and place in the community, a disposition which will best serve the interests of all parties concerned.

For the probation officer, the preliminary investigation provides the data which serve as a basis for initiating probation treatment, and which furnish the clues to further exploration and more complete understand-

---

[1] Reproduced by permission of the Association.

[2] Quoted by permission from manuscript subsequently published with modifications in *Yearbook of the National Probation Association* (1936). pp. 240–252.

ing of the probationer as the relationship develops. The preliminary investigation is primarily concerned with the social and personal history of the offender, a knowledge of which is basic to the formulation of any treatment program.

The quality of the preliminary social study is conditioned by a variety of factors. Listed in ascending importance, these are:

1. *The Amount of Time Allowed for Its Completion.*—To make an adequate preliminary social study a minimum period of from one to two weeks should be allowed when the probation officer carries a regular case load. The time varies, according to the size of the community, the case load of the probation officer, and the nature of the problem. In some instances an adequate study will be made within a few days, while in others more than two weeks will be required. A hurried and inadequate investigation is an injustice to the offender, to the court and the community. . . . Certainly, the more time that is allowed for collecting, correlating and interpreting available social data, the more adequate and, therefore, the more useful will be the preliminary study.

2. *The Circumstances and Setting of the Interviews.*—The place of the interviews and the circumstances under which they are conducted condition to a large extent the success of the study. Privacy is essential. The dangers of interviewing an offender in jail are obvious. The very atmosphere precludes free discussion, and tends to increase tension. Not infrequently fellow inmates coach the offender in a ready-made story that throws no light on his real situation. Incarceration of a potential probationer between trial and disposition should be avoided whenever possible. Its dangers far outweigh any benefits. Since a major purpose of the preliminary study is the discovery of the real problems and potentialities of the offender in order that treatment based on his actual needs may be planned, the offender should be studied wherever possible, in his natural surroundings. When we realize that the starting point in any social treatment must be the client's own evaluation of his problem, which generally begins with his own account of the problem, and that any individual who attempts to treat another individual must first know the attitude and interpretation which the individual to be helped has toward his problem, it becomes obvious that the offender must have an opportunity to tell his story fully without fears and tensions and tell it in his own way at his own pace.

The probationer may exaggerate or minimize his situation, or he may have an interpretation or explanation of it which is at variance with other findings, but he gives his explanation either as he sees it, or as he wants the probation officer to see it. It is *his* story and he better than anyone else is equipped to tell it. Whether his interpretation or analysis is accurate is of secondary importance at this stage. The important thing is that through the story as it comes from the probationer, the probation officer gets his most significant clues to the attitudes, values, and feelings of the individual whom he is responsible for helping, and who will only be helped as the attitudes, values, and feelings which motivate his behavior are understood. . . .

3. *The Use Made of the Study by the Court.*—The uncertainty as to how the preliminary study report will be used by the court has handicapped probation officers in getting adequate data both from offenders, and from social agencies who, in the past, have had their own relationship with clients jeopardized, when confidential information was thus divulged. Each magistrate or judge varies in his use of the investigation record. Some read the entire report, and make their disposition on the basis of its contents. Other judges do not read the report but merely ask the probation officers for a verbal summary. Still others read the report, but disregard its content or recommendations. . . .

It is important for both the court and the probation officer to realize that the study is not made "for the court." Rather it is made for the *offender*, in order that those charged with his rehabilitation may be in a position intelligently to carry out their responsibility. The court happens to be the first agency to use the information but many other agencies; particularly the probation department, the institution, the parole department, and other public or private welfare societies who may later be called upon to give specialized services, need and have a right to the preliminary study as a guide in their treatment programs. With this in mind it is essential that the preliminary study be broad in scope, specific in character, and directed toward those factors and incidents in the life of the offender, which will throw the greatest possible light on his problem, and provide clues or leads for helping in his rehabilitation by whichever agency is designated. . . .

Many judges who regard the investigations as being made solely for the court have attempted to limit them to a meager outline of data relative to the offense. Such investigations contain little more information than was divulged at the hearing and not only are useless as a guide to the treatment worker, but actually give the court no additional insight into the offender. Investigations of this nature are worthless and are an extravagance which no community can afford.

The probation officer has a responsibility to interpret to the court the various purposes which the preliminary investigation serves. An intelligent judge, conscientious about the responsibilities of his office, will value and use with discretion a well-recorded investigation. The small minority of judges who find their own "intuition" sufficient to explore and evaluate offenders' problems will have to be dealt with on an individual basis. It is recommended that judges of the latter type be given but extracts of the preliminary investigation—extracts limited to such material as they will use with discretion, or the divulgence of which will do little harm. In such instances the ordinary preliminary investigation should be made and recorded by the probation officer to be available for use by him, the institution or agency designated by the court to deal with the offender.

Perhaps no factor has tended more to retard the development and achievements of probation than the lack of understanding on the part of some judges who have within their power the opportunity to exert such significant and far-reaching influence.

4. *The Training of the Probation Officer.*—Finally, the quality, content and methodology of the preliminary study is determined by the competence, skill and vision of the probation officer who undertakes it. A preliminary study properly made and adequately recorded requires on the part of the investigating officer technical training in the study of personality and behavior problems, a knowledge of, and the skill to apply with scientific precision modern case work methods of interviewing; an appreciation of the dignity of the human personality even when convicted of an offense against the law, the ability to express clearly, concisely, and objectively in writing the results of the investigation so that they may be available for practical use.

Selected Bibliography

1. ALLEN, FREDERICK H.: "Psychic Factors in Juvenile Delinquency," *Mental Hygiene*, II (October, 1927), 764–774.
2. BURGESS, E. W.: "The Study of the Delinquent as a Person," *American Journal of Sociology*, XXVIII (May, 1923), 657–680.
3. ———: "The Family as a Unity of Interacting Personalities," *The Family*, VII (March, 1926), 3–9.
4. COOLEY, EDWIN J.: *Probation and Delinquency*, Catholic Charities of the Archdiocese of New York, 1927.
5. FERRIS, RALPH HALL: "The Case History in Probation Service," in Sheldon Glueck (Editor), *Probation and Criminal Justice*, pp. 135–164, The Macmillan Company, 1933.
6. GROVES, ERNEST R.: *Social Problems of the Family*, J. B. Lippincott Company, 1927.
7. ———: *The Drifting Home*, Houghton Mifflin Company, 1926.
8. HUGHES, ELIZABETH A., and FRANCELIA STUENKEL: *The Social Service Exchange in Chicago*, University of Chicago Press, 1929.
9. JUDGE BAKER FOUNDATION: *Case Studies*, Judge Baker Foundation, 1922.
10. NIMKOFF, MEYER F.: *The Family*, Houghton Mifflin Company, 1934.
11. REUTER, E. B., and JESSIE R. RUNNER: *The Family*, Source Material for the Study of Family and Personality, McGraw-Hill Book Company, Inc., 1931.
12. RICHMOND. MARY: *What is Social Case Work?* Russell Sage Foundation, 1922.

13. ———: *Social Diagnosis*, Russell Sage Foundation, 1917.

14. SHAW, CLIFFORD R.: *The Jack-Roller*, University of Chicago Press, 1930.

15. SHEFFIELD, ADA E.: *The Social Case History*, Russell Sage Foundation, 1920.

16. THOMAS, DOROTHY SWAINE, and OTHERS: *Some Techniques for Studying Social Behavior*, Child Development Monographs, No. 1, New York Bureau of Publications, Columbia University, Teachers College, 1929.

17. VAN WATERS, MIRIAM: *Parents on Probation*, New Republic, Inc., 1927 (Bibliography).

18. WHITE HOUSE CONFERENCE ON CHILD HEALTH AND PROTECTION, *The Delinquent Child*, esp. pp. 19–92, The Century Company, 1932.

19. YOUNG, PAULINE V.: *Interviewing in Social Work*, McGraw-Hill Book Company, Inc., 1935.

Suggestions for Further Study

1. Why is the term "social study" or "social exploration" better than "social investigation?" What other terms would you suggest?

2. Write a comparative critique of the approach to the cases of Marilyn Smith and Marvin Levkowitz.

3. Summarize these cases in accordance with the standards of your own agency.

4. Why are these cases suitable for discussion of case work techniques?

5. What is the difference in the technique between the study of the offender and the study of the offense? the offender and his world? the offender and the social forces surrounding him? his world and the general community standards and mores?

6. What is your philosophy of juvenile delinquency? of crime? of social disorganization? What is their relation to each other?

7. What is the importance of the study of social attitudes? How can they be studied?

8. What are the essential steps prior to the study of the case?

9. What is the value of citing the case of Albert and Richard Richardson? Is this case adequately presented? Why or why not?

10. What should be included in the list of social traits of an offender? of his family?

11. How can contributing factors to delinquency be adequately studied? What is their significance?

12. What is the sociological approach to the study of delinquency? the psychological? the psychiatric? the social work approach? How can these approaches be combined?

13. What is meant by the sociology of the family? What is meant by the sociology of the community? What is the sociological approach to the study of the community? What other approaches are there?

14. Since the case worker, using case work techniques, cannot modify the conditions in a given community, of what value is a study of the community in relation to delinquency?

15. What approaches might be used in the study of the school situation? of employment? of health?

16. What are your interviewing techniques in each of these fields?

17. What is the value of the face-sheet form presented here? the limitations?

18. To what extent can the court, the probation department, a child welfare agency, utilize the methods of social study discussed here? What are the limitations of these methods?

19. What is meant by psychology of delinquency? What are the psychological methods of studying delinquency? delinquents? What are the advantages of this method of study? the limitations?

20. How can the various methods be successfully combined?

21. What practical suggestions did you get from the discussion of the cases presented in Chapter II?

22. What effective and critical methods of study have you discovered in recent writings on the subject of comprehensive studies of delinquents?

CHAPTER V

SKELETON GUIDES IN THE SOCIAL STUDY OF A CASE

"Life doesn't want to be schematized. Life doesn't want to be put in outline form. But I think that we shall find it easier to understand these individual lives with which we work if for a little while we do rather schematize their problems."—Dr. James S. Plant, *"Understanding Sex Delinquency,"* Year Book, National Probation Association (1932–1933), p. 204.

Comprehensive outlines for study of individual cases have been developed in recent years by child guidance clinics, family welfare workers, sociologists, probation departments, and others, as an aid in bringing into focus the essential data to be secured in the study of an individual or family group. A case history outline should be regarded only as an aid to the worker in visualizing the scope of data which are essential in a comprehensive study of a case. These guides should offer an orientation in the subject rather than in the technique. It is needless to stress again that the study in the hands of a competent worker will not become mechanistic or stereotyped if he uses it as a suggestive starting point and as an aid in rounding out the total picture of the case.

It is the experience of executives and of case workers that in many specific instances the worker, with a vision of the objectives to be obtained, develops leads which carry him farther than anything that an outline can suggest abstractly. Outlines are most useful when digested and rearranged by each worker to suit his particular needs. It goes without saying that no outline form should ever be taken into the home of a family, nor should it be in evidence during an office interview.

One of the more comprehensive outlines for the social history is to be found in the volume by Porter R. Lee and Marion E. Kenworthy, *Mental Hygiene and Social Work* (pp. 290–309). These authors too desire not only "the concrete factors of family

92

and hereditary forebears but the dynamic and more potent influences of attitudes, interests, prejudices, and personality patterns of all of the family members including the first, second, and third generations."[1]

From a sociological standpoint Clifford Shaw, head of the Department of Research Sociology, Institute for Juvenile Research, Chicago, has demonstrated a successful approach to securing the history of behavior difficulties. His illuminating volume, *The Jack-Roller*, is a life record of a delinquent's own account of his experiences written as an autobiography and supplemented by a series of searching interviews. Shaw stresses "(1) the point of view of the delinquent; (2) the social and cultural situation to which the delinquent is responsible; and (3) the sequence of past experiences and situations in the life of the delinquent."[2]

History taking in dealing with delinquent and problem children has its beginnings in the work of Drs. William Healy and Augusta Bronner, pioneers in case studies and individualized treatment of children in trouble. A recent outline used by the Judge Baker Foundation Clinic in gathering family and personal history of the offender appears in the volume published by Sheldon and Eleanor Glueck, *One Thousand Juvenile Delinquents* (pp. 287–293). This stresses detailed knowledge of the problem; causes for misbehavior from the standpoint of the child, parents, and investigator; the circumstances of the arrest; standards of home and family life, social and cultural background of parents; antenatal, natal, and postnatal history of offender; his habits of eating, sleeping, drinking, smoking, masturbation, enuresis, nervous habits; interests and personality traits as shown at school, work, home, with companions, changes in personality, reactions to various phases of social and physical environment; family and neighborhood resources. Each child studied at the clinic is given a thorough physical examination, several psychological and psychometric tests, as well as a psychiatric examination.

Healy has long ago pointed out that, since nothing happens without a cause, motivation for conduct—which is frequently hidden and difficult to unearth—must be carefully explored;

[1] *Op. cit.*, p. 294.
[2] P. 3; see also Chaps. I–III.

and since each child is essentially different he must be understood in terms of his own social, mental, and physical surroundings.[1] Such a study requires careful accumulation of a great deal of detailed information.

The White House Conference on Child Health and Protection[2] further stresses the exploration of the basic needs. The old-time investigation comprising an inventory of the household and its inhabitants has given way to a study of the nature of relationships of members, their respective feelings and attitudes, the needs of each, their visions, cravings, and thwartings. "To know the delinquent we must know his family, not because it surrounds him, but because the lives of its members germinate, color, and shape his life."[3]

Hans Weiss, in a stimulating article, "The Social Worker's Technique and Probation," concludes that after many sources of information have been tapped the inquiry "should give a comprehensive picture of the individual's own world: of his personality, his relationship to others, his immediate environment as seen in relation to him. We should know something of his likes and dislikes, his desires and hopes, his disappointments and failures, his ambitions and plans, his shortcomings and disabilities, his qualities and assets, and above all, the possibilities of getting him on his feet."[4]

At times views are expressed that social case histories are given an overrated importance, that much of the data gathered are not actually used. One wonders what is meant by "used"? Can we understand the total problematic situation without sufficient data? Is it possible to forecast in advance when a situation will be understood with only a minimum of data at hand? The view is also expressed that if we accept the fact that "in the dynamics of human relationships, as worker or therapist to patient, inheres whatever is of value and of harm for the other person, we no longer need vast quantities of data."[5] This approach assumes that social therapy is based primarily upon a

[1] See *The Individual Delinquent*, Chaps. I–V; also HEALY and BRONNER, *New Light on Delinquency and Its Treatment.*

[2] *The Delinquent Child*, pp. 262–264.

[3] *Ibid.*, p. 263.

[4] In SHELDON GLUECK (Editor), *Probation and Criminal Justice*, p. 180.

[5] FORREST N. ANDERSON, "Some New Points of View in Child Guidance," *Social Work Technique*, I (July–August, 1936), 120.

relationship technique. Therapy is too complex a process to be based on one single factor. A satisfactory relationship is indispensable in any form of treatment but it cannot assume the sole role. Clients in trouble, once they discover that the therapist accepts just them, will deliberately seek his advice, relying upon his dispassionate attitude and his experience and training. Whether the task of the therapist is to give advice directly or to reinterpret the situation to the clients, he cannot do so adequately unless he is thoroughly acquainted with their personality traits, their ability to utilize advice, to reconstruct the past, to "reexperience the feeling of past events that have been inadequately assimilated and to which have been attached the anxiety and fear which have created the turmoil of the present."[1]

It would follow that a study of comprehensive social history assumes that, while it is possible to establish a satisfactory relationship with the client without becoming thoroughly acquainted with his life, it is doubtful whether such a relation will be of lasting value; furthermore that it is not possible to redirect problematic behavior without an intimate knowledge of a person's life and that it is impossible to release fear and anxiety without sufficient facts as to their origin, their surrounding circumstances, their relation to the life complexes and social setting in which the individual lives and their relation to the personal and social traits of the individual.

A Guide from the Probation Officer's Point of View.—Ralph Hall Ferris, formerly of the Domestic Relations Division, Recorder's Court, Detroit, Michigan, says that in general an adequate social examination will be concerned with the following groups of items, each being developed according to need:[2]

a. The offender's family history, with names, dates, residences, occupations, finances, diseases, etc., of siblings, parents, parental siblings, and grandparents, as well as reactions to them, and reasons for leaving home;

b. Schooling, including age of commencement and termination, studies enjoyed, reactions to school and teachers, reasons for leaving school, and desire for further schooling;

[1] FREDERICK H. ALLEN, *Presidential Address* at the meeting of the American Orthopsychiatric Association, 1934.

[2] "The Case History in Probation Service," in Glueck, *op. cit.*, pp. 142–143. Reprinted by permission of The Macmillan Company.

c. Account of offender's migrations, various environments, past and present associates and reactions to them;

d. Work record, including names of employers, dates of employment, reasons for change of employment, kind of employment preferred, wages, nature and periods of unemployment, and ambitions relative to employment;

e. Economic status, past and present, covering income and expenditures, debts, reasons therefor, and plans for liquidation, property (house, car, investments, luxuries), and insurance, and attitude toward these matters;

f. Health, including history of diseases, physical condition, past and present, physical disabilities, and attitude toward health matters such as personal hygiene, etc.;

g. Moral and recreational habits, such as use of tobacco, alcohol, of drugs, resort to prostitutes, homosexual or autoerotic practices, reading, including the type and number of books and magazines read, resort to poolrooms, dancing, bowling, theater attendance, and outdoor sports whether social as baseball or solitary as hunting;

h. Affiliations, fraternal and religious, and attitude toward them;

i. Marital history, if any, and reactions to sex life, marriage and children;

j. Delinquency record, juvenile and adult, and reactions to the same; and

k. In general ambitions, tendencies, aptitudes, hobbies, dislikes and obsessions, as the offender sees them.

It is significant to observe that Mr. Ferris lays considerable stress on reactions, interests, ambitions, attitudes, likes, and dislikes of the offender as well as reasons for his actions. He adds that "the social examination should contain an exact description of the offender's behavior during the interview and his reactions to the interviewer, the interview and the subject matter of the interview . . . any peculiar phraseology or action."[1] Such practice would be highly desirable were it not for the concern of many agencies that "space is too scarce" and that "records cannot become voluminous." No thoroughgoing studies have been made between the relation of inadequate recording and consequent inability to diagnose the case properly and the degree of recidivism. There are students who agree that some attempts to economize on the recording of a single interview tend in many instances to prolong the contacts with a client and thus no space

[1] *Ibid.*, p. 143.

is saved in the long run. Space as such should be of least concern in the record of adjustment of a human life. However, since no studies have been made, it may be argued that the above assumptions are little more than speculation. There are points on both sides. (See Chapters VI and XXI on "Recording.")

A Guide from the Sociologist's Point of View.—E. S. Bogardus prepared a social history outline for the study of a problem boy which is equally applicable to a delinquent boy or girl. He limits the social history to conflicts and accommodations within home, school, neighborhood, church, play and occupational activities, in terms of the resulting problems as the individual sees them. This outline is from the standpoint of a social psychologist taking into account one's social world, social relations, and the role one conceives himself to play in a given social group.

1. *Heritage.*—What was the boy's social heritage? What were the traditions of his parents? Their attitude toward religion, toward racial and national values, toward education, toward industrial activities? What is their type of family life? What was their equipment for training boys, including their handicaps and advantages? What difficulties occurred within the home in matters of adjustments between parents? What were their hopes and ambitions for this particular boy? What brothers and sisters did he have? What have been their outstanding traits? Their influences upon his life? What musical and artistic tendencies has he? His age, birthplace, race?

2. *Early Life.*—What was the nature of his earliest distinctive tendencies? The trend of his earliest interests and habits? His earliest conflicts? The first handicaps that he brought on himself? What were the earliest fears that he can recall, and his earliest joys? How were his earliest conflicts settled?

3. *Social Contacts.*—Which parent seems to understand him best? Which parent is he most like? What routine work does he do at home? How far do he and his parents associate in their amusements? If he lost his parents what would he do? What books, outside of schoolbooks, did he read? What magazines? What did he read that he liked most?

Who are his chums? Describe their likes and dislikes. Has any of them gotten into trouble and in what ways? Does he bring his "pals" into the home?

How often does he go to motion picture shows, to public dance halls, and to pool halls?

What girls has he known well? How intimate has been his friendship with them? What are his parents' attitudes toward the one or ones he likes best? What are their likes and dislikes? What does he do in his leisure time; how much leisure does he have and during what hours of the day? With whom does he come in contact at these times?

To what organizations, such as a boys' club, a gang, a church club or class has he belonged? What was the nature of the activities of each? Has he been a member of a Sunday School, of the Boy Scouts, of any similar organizations? Has he dropped out of any of these? Under what conditions? Does he smoke cigarettes? Why? or why not? His parents' attitude?

In what ways does he get along well at school? In what ways poorly? His parents' attitudes?

Has he been a leader in any of these clubs? In what ways did he lead well, and in what did he fail, and for what reasons?

4. *Conflicts and Accommodations.*—What difficulties has he had in the home, with either parent, of long-standing nature? What conflicts has he had with other members of his family and what has happened?

What outstanding difficulties has he had with his playmates? Any fights he remembers. Have him describe the history of any boyhood feud that he was a part of for any length of time.

Did he have any difficulties with the older people of the neighborhood? With the parents of other children?

Under what conditions does he remember most distinctly being punished? What activities does he seem to conceal from his parents? Is the home atmosphere one of peace or conflict? Of economic pressure?

What conflicts has he had at school, with any teachers, principals, truant officers, or with other boys at school?

Did he run away ever from home or school? Why and what were the reactions?

Has he a car? Any problems? His parents' attitude toward his use of it? What picture shows does he like best? Least?

Did he ever "swipe" anything, and if so under what conditions? Did he ever get "pinched"? His experiences in this connection? Ever been in jail? Experiences? Ever been on probation, either in school or in connection with the Juvenile Court? Experiences?

Has there been any breaking off of love affairs? What daydreams has he had? Has he had any troublesome dreams? Has he ever had imaginary companions?

In what ways does he feel that he has been treated most unjustly? Has he ever felt hampered, and wanted to upset things generally? What important questions does he decide for himself? How does he get increased independence?

In what ways does he feel that he has been most misunderstood? By whom, and under what conditions? Any disagreements with his parents regarding money, clothes, the automobile, girls, chums? What things does he ask permission to do?

Under what conditions has he experienced "pangs of conscience"? Does he remember feeling distinctly sorry for something?

Has he ever had any religious problems or conflicts or "been converted"?

Has he ever worked for wages? Has he ever wanted money and couldn't get it? Has he ever saved and why? What kinds of work does he like best, and what least?

5. *Philosophy of Life.*—What was his first or earliest choice of a vocation, and what changes have occurred along this line? What are his greatest ambitions today? His occupational expectations? Does he have any money-making ambitions, and what are his reactions to making money and becoming rich? What is his life aim? Do parents agree with it?

What are his religious beliefs? Does he believe that one political party is better than another? Does he believe in racial equality? Is he interested in more than one race or nation? What does he consider to be the leading public questions of the day? Does he have any ideas of social responsibility and social service and if so, how did they arise?

If he could have one wish above all others granted, what would it be?[1]

While Bogardus seems to lay stress on the child's account of his life experiences from his particular point of view, the data included in the outline take into account the experiences, attitudes, and reactions of other members of the group of which the child is a part. This outline omits specific discussion of health, housing, social-economic, family status, etc., which is included in the previous outline worked out by Ferris. Obviously, the worker could profit by a combination of the two points of view and sets of data, which are highly complementary to each other.

A Guide from the Mental Hygienist's Point of View.—The Louisville Mental Hygiene Clinic (Dr. Spafford Ackerly,[2] Medical Director) recommends the use of the following outline for the complete study of a child referred by another agency. Attention is called to the fact that complete data are required for a nondelinquent member of the family as well as the delinquent.

Part I
Outline of Family Tree

Date:

Names, ages. If dead, state same and give age at time of death. Indicate father, mother, delinquent and nondelinquent by capitals underlined.

Example

Paternal Grandparents   Maternal Grandparents

_____ Died 61, _____ 80   _____ 70, _____ 62.

[1] E. S. BOGARDUS, *The New Social Research*, pp. 165–168.

[2] Outline in use by the Louisville Mental Hygiene Clinic (July, 1936), mimeographed. Reprinted by permission of Dr. Ackerly.

Paternal Uncles and Aunts   Maternal Aunts and Uncles.

_____ died 24   _____ 34 _____ 31

_____ 38

Father: Thomas Dole, 36 **Mother:** Mary Brown Dole, 36 **Siblings**
_____ 15. Delinquency: John Dole, 13–6. Nondelinquency: Joseph
Dole, 12. Miscarriage. Names of others in family, relatives, boarders, etc.

Part II
Identification Data

Date: Referral date: By whom referred and how delinquent
came to be referred: Present court action:
Date of court appearance: Name of judge presiding and persons
present. Brief statement of what took place in courtroom. Final disposition, that is, dismissal, parole, suspended sentence, or commitment.
Date of termination of parole or suspended sentence.   Name of
probation officer and person or persons to whom delinquent is expected to
report.   Where?   How often?
Past court action of delinquent and other members of the family.
If reports to court or other agencies are requested, dates and nature of
reports. Delinquent's reaction to court appearance. Attitude of delinquent and his parents toward the clinic. Why case was accepted. State
criteria of acceptance.

Part III
Work of Other Agencies

Part IV
Sources of Information

Date: Description of informants.   Nature of their interest
in the case. Estimation of the reliability of data given, with special emphasis upon personal biases.   Number of interviews with each informant.   List future sources for investigation.   Where inconsistent factual material has been obtained or observed from one or more
sources state sources or refer to page in the record where source can be
verified. Throughout the summary the sources of important data should
be stated preferably by a mere name in brackets.

Part V
Problems

Date: Only problems of immediate family will be dealt with in this
section; *cf.* under *Personal Histories* for problems of grandparents, aunts,
uncles, etc.
     I. **Delinquent:** Delinquency as reported by others; as reported by himself. Personality and behavior problems other than delinquencies. Other
problems, physical, etc.

II. Nondelinquent: Personality and behavior problems; other problems, physical, etc.

III. Family Problems: Delinquency of mother, father, and other siblings. Personality and behavior problems of mother, father, and other siblings. Physical problems. Statement of marital, economic, social problems.

Part VI

Social History

Date: Unless some other scheme is more desirable, entries should begin with the paternal grandparents, finishing up with the father. The same order should be followed for the maternal side. The siblings should come next, putting the delinquent and nondelinquent at the bottom. Under *Personal Histories* should be placed material ordinarily described under the headings heredity and family background.

Date of birth, place of birth, years in United States, citizenship, general health, occupation, cause of death, age at death. Brief personality studies of grandparents, uncles, and aunts, including outstanding economic, social, educational failure or success, criminal tendencies, mental and physical abnormalities, alcoholism, drug addiction, chronic diseases.

Only the more important facts in the personal histories of the siblings need be mentioned, that is, facts that seem to have a special bearing upon the delinquent or nondelinquent.

For delinquent and nondelinquent complete prenatal, parturitional, developmental, and health histories should be stated. Dates of illnesses, doctors attending, all diseases and injuries to the central nervous system should be carefully gone into. Actions and attitudes of parents during these illnesses should be noted.

Some estimate of the delinquent and nondelinquent personalities during the preschool period should be made and the interplay of affection with each parent noted.[1]

A year-by-year statement of the important happenings in the lives of the delinquent and nondelinquent from birth to present age is desirable. Such facts as the following could be mentioned along with others—illnesses, accidents, births and deaths in the family, school changes, success or failure in promotion, changes of residence, names of new companions, clubs and gangs joined, play interests, enterprises, travel, camp, all sexual interest, fluctuations of interest from one parent to another, change of policies on part of the parents, severe punishments, etc. On the left-hand side of the page could be listed events given by informants. On the right-hand side the meaning of these events to the subject could be put down or references to the page in the record where such material could be found. The same could be done for the nondelinquent. At any rate, a chronological story of significant events is usually in the record and could be summarized here.

---

[1] Other data easily obtainable from institutional records which are very complete.

Part VII
Home Conditions

Date: Physical description of home and surroundings.
Social ideals, practices of the family; recreations, festivities, atmosphere of
the home. Economic status. Estimation of capital in cash or property,
past and present holdings, and earnings.

Part VIII
Physical Examinations

Date: Family health status. Delinquent, including neurological
and psychophysical.[1] Nondelinquent, including same. Special studies,
endocrine, etc. The psychophysical can be carried out in two stages, one
before the boy undresses, when he is asked about his health history, that is,
operations, injuries, illnesses, and detailed regional questions—head, eyes,
etc., the four systems, cardiorespiratory, gastrointestinal, genitourinary,
and neuromuscular; habits, etc. Leads found during this time can be
followed up during the physical examination.

Part IX
Psychological, Educational, and Vocational

Date: General intellectual, educational, and vocational levels of
the immediate family, father, mother, and other side.
Delinquent: Psychological tests.   School achievement. Vocational: positions held, names of employers, how much earned, and estimate
of boy's initiative and resourcefulness in such matters.
Nondelinquent: Same as delinquent.

Part X
Family Interrelationships

Date:
Paternal Grandparents: How they react to each other. How they react
to the father and mother. How the father and mother react to them. How
father and mother react to paternal uncles and aunts.
Maternal Grandparents: How they react to each other. How they react
to father and mother. How father and mother react to maternal uncles and
aunts. How father and mother react to them.
Parents: How they react to each other, before and after marriage. How
they react to their children. How children react to parents.
Delinquent's Reaction to: Grandparents, uncles, and aunts, on both sides,
if important. Father—father's reaction to delinquent. Mother—mother's
reaction to delinquent. Siblings—Siblings' reaction to delinquent.
Nondelinquent: Same as delinquent.

[1] Note: Reactions to real or fancied physical inferiorities or superiorities.

Selected Bibliography

1. BOGARDUS, E. S.: *The New Social Research*, pp. 145–179, University of Southern California Press, 1926.
2. BRINKER, DOROTHY: *Social History Outline* (Bulletin No. 1, New Series), State of California, Department of Institutions, Bureau of Juvenile Research (December, 1929).
3. FERRIS, RALPH HALL: "The Case History in Probation Service," in Sheldon Glueck (Editor), *Probation and Criminal Justice*, pp. 135–164, The Macmillan Company, 1933.
4. GLUECK, SHELDON, and ELEANOR GLUECK: *One Thousand Juvenile Delinquents*, pp. 287–293, Harvard University Press, 1934.
*5. HEALY, WILLIAM: *The Individual Delinquent*, particularly Chaps. I–V.
6. ———, and AUGUSTA F. BRONNER, *New Light on Delinquency and Its Treatment*, Yale University Press, 1936.
7. LEE, PORTER R., and MARION KENWORTHY: *Mental Hygiene and Social Work*, pp. 290–309, The Commonwealth Fund, 1929.
*8. RICHMOND, MARY, *Social Diagnosis*, pp. 373–448.

Suggestions for Further Study

1. What is the value of a skeleton guide? the limitations? What precautions should be observed in the use of such a guide?

2. What are the essential differences in the guides outlined by Ferris, Bogardus, Lee and Kenworthy, the Gluecks, and Dr. Ackerly?

3. What guides have you found most useful?

4. How should these guides be modified for the use by a probation department in a rural district? in a large urban, industrial center? by a child guidance clinic? by a court clinic?

5. What guide might have been employed to advantage in the study of Marilyn Smith? Marvin Levkowitz?

6. In view of the changing techniques in social case work is it advisable to use a general guide?

7. In view of the changing social philosophy in the work with families, children, communities, is it advisable to follow any definite techniques? Why or why not?

8. Work out a guide, which might be a combination of any of the above, for your particular needs.

* Note that * means that reference has been mentioned in a previous chapter and may be traced through the index.

CHAPTER VI

RECORDING OF THE SOCIAL STUDY OF AN OFFENDER[1]

The social study of an offender, as of any person or family, has for its primary purpose the understanding of his problems and behavior patterns in relation to his total social situation. On the basis of the findings of the social study a social diagnosis of the case is made and a course of action is outlined, in accordance with the offender's particular needs, capacities, and limitations. The facts supplied by the offender and by his family and associates serve also as the basis for orienting him to and supplying insight into his own situation. For these reasons the data should be recorded fully and accurately. Furthermore, the record constitutes the permanent body of data and the common property of the case worker, the judge, the teacher, the psychiatrist, the psychologist, the physician, and others. Although record means different things to each scientist, practitioner, or theorist, each can extract sufficient data for his own purposes if adequate information is supplied.

The worker cannot and should not rely on his memory for the pertinent facts of a case. To begin with, the worker's own note-book, and not a well worked-out record, frequently constitutes the basis upon which the report to the court is written. Often he dashes out to the family at the last moment for the missing information required for the report to the court. Hastily gathered material suffers from many obvious defects and tends to destroy the offenders' confidence in the worker. He makes little use of the record beyond constructing a report to the court. The supervisor or the district director, as well as the field worker,

---

[1] The most thought-provoking treatise on the social case history and methods of recording was written by Ada E. Sheffield, *The Social Case History*. The reader is urged to familiarize himself with this little volume. A more recent contribution was made by Gordon Hamilton, *Social Case Recording;* see also Family Welfare Association of America, *Report* of Recording Committee (September, 1934), and Margaret Cochran Bristol, *Handbook on Social Case Recording*.

should have time to go over the data before the report to the court is made and recommendations for the disposition of the offender suggested to the judge. The case record is the "map of the road," so to speak, and an aid in critical thinking about the case.

The problem of space which detailed records occupy and the element of time involved in reading a long record are both serious considerations for a busy and crowded office. Miss Agnes C. Sullivan, Probation Examiner, of the Division of Probation, Department of Correction, State of New York, maintains that "it is poor economy to skimp either in the making or recording of the preliminary investigation. . . . Hastily made, poorly recorded investigations result often in unwise dispositions by the court and the subsequent referral of wholly untreatable cases to the probation department. Such unsuitable material may consume so large a portion of the probation officer's time and effort that the really treatable cases are neglected."[1]

Perhaps while we are temporarily economizing on time and space, in the long run we are wasting a great deal of time and space if the offenders continue their delinquent careers because of inadequate, uncritical work and treatment when they first appeared in court. In reading several hundred probation records the writer observed that the cases on which the poorest work was done and which contained the most meager information were the most frequent and, at times, also the most serious recidivists. Their case history folders contained several different petitions, filed at various periods of time, several court orders, instruction sheets, filings from the crime-prevention divisions, reports to the court, brief clinical findings, inconsequential letters and telegrams, special-incident reports, and other official and semiofficial reports. The chronological history was very brief and from it it was often difficult to determine whether the offender committed rape, stole a bicycle, was truant from school, or burglarized a store. It was equally difficult to determine whether he was being "treated" for sex delinquency, or truancy, or petty larceny.

It is realized that the records of Marilyn Smith and Marvin Levkowitz[2] (see pp. 34-50) are presented in too great detail

---

[1] An address before the National Probation Association (1936). Subsequently published in the *Yearbook*, 1936, pp. 245-246.

[2] See MARY A. CLARK, *Recording and Reporting for Child Guidance Clinics*.

and that their form is unsuitable for the average court worker and other child welfare agencies. These records are presented for study purposes only, to indicate the scope rather than the quantity of the data desired for the understanding of a case situation. The case history of Peter Smith (see pp. 407–421) is perhaps a better illustration of a type of recording which is more suitable for the purposes of a court worker. The case history of Harold Crane (see pp. 440–449) is, on the other hand, a poor illustration and is an exhibit of how not to record.

The adequate recording of a case depends largely on the adequacy of the social study made of the case. The trite saying that one writes effectively and intelligently when one has something to write about a subject which he thoroughly understands applies also to case recording. Good case recording is closely associated with good case work and with ability to use English adequately. It is not the recording which is difficult but the mastery of the principles of case work[1] and control over vocabulary and grammar.

There are few forms or rules by which a vast variety of case records dealing with complex human situations can be governed. As Gordon Hamilton points out, "records should be written to suit the case, not the case geared to a theoretical pattern."[2]

Organization of the Data of the Social Study.[3]—There can be no definite order or organization of data relating to a vast variety of human experience. Each worker must organize the material to suit the particular needs of the case and the particular demands of his organization. It is clear that some type of organization should be adopted. The various outlines presented in Chap. V will provide some choice or a basis for creating a new form of recording. It should be stressed again that the value of the recorded data does not lie in a mere account of the happenings and incidents but also in an account of the reactions and attitudes toward these events in the life of the person.

The social study of a case, presenting a life process and a total social situation, can best be recorded topically and as a unit rather than chronologically. The treatment records lend themselves more easily to chronological entries, although there are some objections to that.

[1] See GORDON HAMILTON, *op. cit.*
[2] *Op. cit.*, p. 4.
[3] See SHEFFIELD, *op. cit.*, pp. 124–143.

What Should a Record Include?—It should include the face sheet (see pp. 84–86), which—since it provides the latest identifying data—should be kept up to date in every detail and all changes noted; a different kind of ink would at a glance set off the changes which have occurred. The record should indicate an account of all important home calls and of the data secured and of all important office and telephone calls and of the data secured. Notations should be made of contacts with other agencies which have or could provide material on the subject of study. As the Gluecks point out, one of the greatest weaknesses of all courts is a failure to keep adequate records. Without this it is idle to speak of scientific techniques in the treatment of offenders. (For further points see our pp. 249–250.) Rarely does one find letters of inquiry sent to other agencies or institutions which have records of the case under study (see p. 59). These are often of vital importance. The record should include reports, if any, of police records, court orders and hearings, institutional records, financial records, and so on. The major and most important part of the record is undoubtedly the complete written account of every contact, action, and decision taken during the investigation, diagnosis, and treatment of the case.[1]

Some kind of medical, psychiatric, psychological reports and other special reports have become almost routine matters in the larger probation departments and other child welfare agencies, but often these reports are difficult to find in a mass of other reports and official forms. Different colors for the various reports would be advantageous and practical.

Incoming letters and postal cards and copies of outgoing letters[2] should be filed separately in the folder or interleafed at the appropriate place in the special case history. In either case a separate entry should be made in the narrative when a letter was received or sent out, with a brief account of the nature of the letter. For example, 2–1–37: Letter received from Mrs. Smith regarding Marilyn's inability to attend school due to illness.

[1] For methods of recording diagnosis and treatment see pp. 133–134

[2] For a discussion of the essentials to be observed in writing a summary letter see SHEFFIELD, *op. cit.*, pp. 94–100; also HAMILTON, *op. cit.*, pp. 13–14, 74–86; for letters transferring a case to another agency see *Social Work Technique*, III (May–June, 1936), p. 109.

1-2-37: Letter sent to C.P.A. requesting report on their contacts with Mrs. Smith.

Correspondence which adds no information to the case should be omitted (Christmas and Easter cards, greeting cards, etc.).

The Division of Probation, Department of Correction, New York State,[1] recommends the following minimum records to be kept by all probation officers and standard procedures in handling them (quoted from manuscript by permission):

An investigation [*sheet*], for recording data obtained from the preliminary or social investigation.

Probation history [*sheet*], for recording all important events in the history of the case.   In all cases each probation officer shall keep a case history of each of his probationers and shall note on the case history form the plan of treatment, the conduct and progress during probation, the work performed by the probation officer, and the final results achieved.

An index card, and a chronological book or its equivalent for ready reference to the names and principal facts in a probation case.

Probation card, for written notification to the probationer of the terms of probation, to be given to the probationer when he is placed on probation.

Financial records, including a cash book, ledger, and receipts.

Statistical records for the monthly reports to the Division of Probation.

All reports and records made or kept by the probation officers are private and confidential records and shall be guarded against inspection by persons not entitled to inspect them.

No probation records shall be removed from the probation office, provided however, that any probation officer may temporarily remove the records from the files whenever necessary in the performance of his duties.

Probation records shall contain such information and be kept in such form as to meet the approval of the Division of Probation.

Miss Agnes C. Sullivan,[2] previously referred to, defines the social case history and analyzes the method of recording as follows:

The probation case history is the complete written account of every contact, direct or indirect, with and in behalf of the probationer, from the moment he has been referred to the probation department for investigation until the termination of probation, if probation be granted, or the court's disposition otherwise, if probation is not granted.   The

[1] *Report of* 1935, pp. 11–12.
[2] *Op. cit.,* pp. 243–252.

case history includes a written account of all interviews, decisions and actions taken by the probation officer in reference to the probationer. The written reports of any physical, psychological or psychiatric examinations are likewise part of the case history. This and any other data related to the offender or the offense assembled in one folder constitute the case record.

The social case history has two major divisions: (*a*) the preliminary or predisposition investigation which is oriented to such information as will provide a basis for understanding the nature and implications of the problems presented by the offender; and (*b*) the supervision or treatment history which is an account of the probation experience subsequent to disposition. . . .

Methods of Recording.—The method of block recording is generally used for the preliminary study, with the data synthesized, correlated and interpreted under topical headings for ready reference. This method of record has been found practical in the use of the investigation by the court. It has certain disadvantages for the probation officer or treatment worker who is concerned with broader implications than just findings. In block recording, social processes, the dynamics of the interview and the sequence of events in the development of relationships are difficult to record, yet for true understanding of the personality, motivation and values of the probationer they are basic. Emphasis in the preliminary investigation should be on motivation and reactions rather than on purely factual data or experiences per se.

What an individual does can be properly evaluated only when we know his reason for doing it, and his reaction to the act. Many individuals have identical experiences, yet their personalities differ, and the effect or interpretation of the same experience differs with each individual. In this difference of reaction and interpretation lie the most potent clues to the understanding of behavior, motivation and values, a knowledge of which are indispensable to intelligent treatment.

The preliminary investigation should be recorded with a view to its practical use, and with consideration for the weight which it carries, both in determining disposition, and as a guide in initiating treatment. Accuracy, honesty, objectivity and clarity characterize the well-recorded preliminary investigation.

The accounts of both the investigation and the supervision processes are part and parcel of the same case history and should be filed together in chronological order.

Inasmuch as study (investigation) and treatment (supervision) are not separate and isolated phases, but are rather interlocking and even concurrent steps in the same process it is essential that a practical type of record be developed which will facilitate the probation process.

The unit case record seems to meet this need better than any type so far suggested. In the unit record all data relative to one offender is filed chronologically in one folder for ready reference. . . .

The case record provides the most tangible yardstick available for probation to measure its own achievements. In reality, the case record is the mirror through which probation sees itself as it really functions. Without recorded, concrete evidence, probation is but another hopeful theory which yet remains to be demonstrated. (Quoted from manuscript.)

Style in Recording.[1]—A simple, direct, lucid style is the most effective. Short sentences and short paragraphs are clear and sustain the interest of the reader. It should be remembered that as a permanent record many workers with various backgrounds and purposes will undoubtedly read it. It is well to ask oneself: "Have I made the record so clear that a person not familiar with the case will without undue effort understand the circumstances?"

Writing is a psychological enterprise. It must arouse attention and hold interest. H. A. Overstreet suggests that it is best to ask: "What does the reader require of me?" rather than "What does the art of writing require of me?"

Evaluative entries should be avoided such as: "She is a poor disciplinarian," "the home is very crowded," "the boy is vicious," "there is a good deal of sickness in the family," "the man makes a good living." Instead concrete data should be given and it should be specifically stated what makes the mother a poor disciplinarian or the boy vicious; where the home is crowded indicate the number of rooms and the number of people occupying these; and so on. Other people may not agree with the worker's evaluations. Furthermore, there is nothing concrete to work on, and no treatment can be based on a worker's subjective evaluations. If it is known what makes the mother a poor disciplinarian, the situation can be interpreted to her specifically. If one knows the type and duration of the sickness in the family, proper arrangements can be made for needed medical care.

Impressions should be distinctly labeled as such and included preferably at the beginning or end of the case entry but should not be interspersed throughout the entire record.

As the Fowler brothers[2] point out "slang is meant to be spoken and not written." When quoting a client only those slang expres-

---

[1] See SHEFFIELD, *op. cit.*, pp. 113–123; also HAMILTON, *op. cit.*, pp. 114–137.
[2] See H. W. and F. T. FOWLER, *The King's English.*

sions should be repeated which reveal his attitude. An interview with a gangster will undoubtedly be interlaced with many quotations. "Here good taste and sense of what is significant must be the control."[1]

It is better to record Mr. A. or Mrs. A. than "man" or "woman," but when speaking of them in relation to their children they should be designated as father and mother.

Since the worker is the agency's representative he should refer to himself as "we" ("We shall make the arrangements," and not "I shall," or "The arrangements will be made").

Foreign words and phrases borrowed from other disciplines and languages should be briefly explained in the record or used only when they have been universally adopted by social workers.[2]

Considerable discussion arises from time to time whether the case records should be written in the first or third person.[3] The offender's own statement should be given in the first person while the rest of the record can be a combination of first and third (see the case of Marilyn Smith). Undoubtedly the verbatim record is valuable for the unbiased picture it presents of the client's mind, as far as he revealed himself, of the precise expressions which he used, but limitations of time and space generally preclude such practices in a probation department. When the client's own words cannot be adequately summarized, they should be quoted verbatim and interlaced with the worker's statement of the facts.

Care should be taken not to repeat "Mrs. Brown stated, Mrs. Brown further stated, Mrs. Brown stated again." The worker will be astonished at the number of times he repeats the word "stated" or "maintained" in a single write-up. These monotonous and superfluous repetitions can be avoided by adopting at the outset, if necessary, the statement: "According to Mrs. Brown . . . " which may be underscored, or capitalized or typed in red, in order to make it conspicuous if necessary.

---

[1] HAMILTON, *op. cit.*, pp. 132 and 115–137.

[2] For definitions of the most frequently occurring words see *The Social Workers' Dictionary*, edited by Erle F. Young, B. A. McClenahan, and Pauline V. Young.

[3] See articles by E. W. Burgess, Frank Bruno, T. D. Eliot, Linton B. Swift, and others in *Social Forces*, VI (June, 1928).

Details of interest only to the worker should be omitted. For example: "Called on Mrs. Smith. Found the door locked. Inquired at the neighbor's and learned that she went downtown for the day. Called later in the afternoon and found her just returning from a shopping tour. Waited while she changed the baby's clothes." Ada Sheffield calls these "behold-me-busy-details,"[1] which have no place in any record.

Selected Bibliography

1. BRISTOL, MARGARET COCHRAN: *Handbook on Social Case Recording*, University of Chicago Press, 1936.
2. BURGESS, E. W.: "What Social Case Records Should Contain to Be Useful for Sociological Interpretation," *Social Forces*, VI (June, 1928), 524–532.
3. CABOT, RICHARD C.: *Social Work*, Houghton Mifflin Company, 1919. (See statements on recording.)
4. CLARK, MARY A.: *Recording and Reporting for Child Guidance Clinics*, The Commonwealth Fund, 1930.
5. Family Welfare Association of America: *Report of Recording Committee*, Milwaukee (September, 1934).
*6. FERRIS, RALPH HALL: "The Case History in Probation Service," in Sheldon Glueck (Editor), *Probation and Criminal Justice*, pp. 135–164.
7. FOWLER, H. W., and F. T. FOWLER: *The King's English*, Clarendon Press, 1922.
8. HAMILTON, GORDON: *Social Case Recording*, bibliography, Columbia University Press, 1936.
9. SHEFFIELD, ADA E.: *The Social Case History*, Russell Sage Foundation, 1920.
10. *Social Forces*, VI (June, 1928), articles by Burgess, Bruno, Eliot, Swift, and others.
11. SULLIVAN, AGNES C.: "Principles and Values in Case Recording," *Yearbook, National Probation Association* (1936), pp. 240–252.

Suggestions for Further Study

1. Why do child guidance clinics favor a comprehensive record of a case? Why do family welfare agencies stress brevity of records?
2. How can accuracy and comprehensiveness be preserved in a brief, compact record?
3. What are the advantages and limitations of extensive and brief records?
4. What is the value of "the own story"?   (See Shaw's studies.)
5. What essential facts should a record include as a minimum?

[1] *The Social Case History*, p. 82.

* Note that * means that reference was previously used and can be traced through index.

6. Write a brief critique of Bristol's and Hamilton's books. What is the contribution of each?

7. What is the relation between adequate recording and adequate social study of a case? between ability to write effectively and ability to record?

8. What should be the bases for recording cases?

9. Analyze your methods and principles of recording in the light of Gordon Hamilton's discussion.

10. What recent contributions have been made to the literature on case recording?

11. What should the format and structure of a record be? (See Hamilton, *op. cit.*, Chap. II.)

12. What suggestions can you offer regarding writing of letters? of summary reports?

For recording of the social diagnosis and social treatment of case see pp. 133–134 and 459–466.

CHAPTER VII

DIFFERENTIAL SOCIAL DIAGNOSIS

The art of social case exploration is now sufficiently perfected to provide comprehensive studies of individuals and their families from various standpoints. Some social agencies now have excellent records of both the inner and the outer lives of their clients and of their particular social settings. Almost invariably, however, these records are a mere collection of data—invaluable for many purposes as such data are—with little or no attempt made to classify and to interpret these data, that is, to diagnose the cases. Under such circumstances social therapy can only be a hit-or-miss and haphazard affair and cannot be based on a systematic plan.

At one time there was a threat to take it [probation] away from us. The reason why probation was attacked was because it was a therapeutic procedure being used without diagnosis. It was often an emotional affair. . . .
The best way to treat a [delinquent], or any other sort of social problem, is first of all to make an adequate diagnosis, such diagnosis depending quite largely upon an adequate case history. This case history should be as complete as it is possible to make it. . . . We must not go ahead with plans for treatment until we have spent more time on the diagnostic side. . . . We must not give way to our tendency to doctor people until we have more data upon which to base our procedure. This is not an easy program to popularize, even though we have had prison riots and fires. The immediate effect of using it would be to cut down the criminal group.[1]

Classification of social data is a difficult process. Medical men have profited greatly by such works as Richard Cabot's *Differential Diagnosis*. Social workers need similar treatises on differential social diagnosis. The title of Mary Richmond's volume, *Social Diagnosis*, is from present points of view something of a

[1] ALBERT WARREN STERNS, "The Vision of the Future," *Proceedings of the National Conference of Social Work* (1930), pp. 99–101.

misnomer, since she deals for the most part with social investigation, devoting more than three-fourths of her book to evidence, sources of information, references, questionnaires of various types, letter writing, and so on. She uses some diagnostic concepts, but in general her book—a monumental piece of work which will remain a classic for a long time—is of comparatively little use to workers interested in methods of diagnosis, although the material she discusses is essential to diagnosis. Little else of significance has been written on the subject to orient the worker in the problems of social diagnosis.[1] There are several treatises[2] which imply diagnosis but do not treat it at any appreciable length. Certain psychologists[3] have tried their hand at psychological diagnosis but unfortunately they have so far—with few exceptions—concerned themselves chiefly with a discussion and classification of mental abilities and mental processes of individuals, ignoring for the most part the social-economic and cultural milieu in which the subject lives.

In spite of the fact that it is generally agreed that no sound plan of treatment can be worked out in a particular case without first diagnosing it,[4] social case workers in almost every field of social work often plunge into treatment with little or no actual diagnosis of the social situation. (For a discussion of the relationship phase of treatment which begins with the first contact, see pp. 318–327.)

The subject of social diagnosis in social case work is an uncharted field; therefore, the present attempts to discuss a few factors and considerations bearing on this subject must be regarded as *highly tentative*. The material is presented with considerable hesitation; one of its purposes is to provoke discus-

---

[1] See Augusta F. Bronner's book on *Psychology of Special Abilities and Disabilities*.

[2] See Susan Burlingham, Grace Marcus, Florence Day, and Bertha Reynolds, *Diagnostic and Treatment Processes in Family Social Work*.

[3] See particularly the recent books of Percival M. Symonds, *Psychological Diagnosis in Social Adjustment*, and Harry J. Baker and Virginia Traphagen, *The Diagnosis and Treatment of Behavior Problem Children*.

[4] In the field of court procedure see particularly Miriam Van Waters, "Juvenile-court Procedure as a Factor in Diagnosis," *Publications of the American Sociological Society*, XIV (1921), 209–217; also Frank J. O'Brien, "Adjusting Treatment to Diagnosis," *Year Book, National Probation Association* (1928), pp. 186–201.

sion which may ultimately lead to fruitful contributions to the solution of this problem, from both theorists and practitioners in social work.

An Attempt at a Tentative Definition of Social Diagnosis.—In medicine diagnosis—in its narrowest sense—means bestowing a name, from the symptoms presented by the case, upon a certain ill or pathological process.[1] The physician determines from the symptoms described by the patient and those observed during the examination whether the patient is suffering, for instance, from scarlet fever, or tuberculosis, or encephalitis, and so on, or from some combination of ills.[2]

Social diagnosis—also in its narrowest sense—has come to mean bestowing a name, from the various symptoms described by the client and those observed and studied by the worker, upon the social and personal problems and social pathological processes. These may be named or diagnosed, for instance, as sexual incompatability, marital discord, adolescent tensions, culture conflict, social isolation, amorality, and so on.

In its broader sense social diagnosis means more than naming a problem or a problem complex. It means classification and subclassification of the numerous factors and painstaking individualization of the particular pathological conditions in relation to those social forces, social settings, personality traits, and so on, which produce personal and social unadjustment. These conditions in turn depend upon the nature and the effects of age, occupation, habits, background, heredity, and so on. Thus we at once see that diagnosing a case is a very complex process and furthermore highly tentative since many of these factors may change with greater or less rapidity even during the course of study. A man may get a different job, move into a different environment, lose a member of his family, which may affect his personality as well as the larger social situation.

The Complexity of the Process of Social Diagnosis.—When the social diagnosis of a case is attempted by a worker, it is frequently oversimplified. When he finds, for example, delinquent children whose mothers are employed during the day, or who live in a neighborhood lacking recreational facilities, he concludes the

[1] GLENTWORTH R. BUTLER, *The Diagnostics of Internal Medicine* (2d ed.), p. 1.
[2] EVERETT C. BEACH, M.D., manuscript.

cause of their delinquencies is "a working mother," or "lack of supervision or of proper play facilities." Undoubtedly in many situations these conditions are contributing factors, but it cannot be said with such simple certainty that one is the cause of the other. Social life is seldom so simple as to consist of an isolated situation directly producing an isolated social problem. A worker who makes so simple a diagnosis ignores the fact that he has "isolated but one factor out of a mass of entangled influences and assigned primary importance to that factor."[1] In reality the mother's employment may be only one in a series of highly interwoven factors, such as extreme irritability or even neuroticism which appears when she must attend to disliked household chores, fear of insecurity, overprotection and oversolicitation, culture conflicts, personal conflicts between child and parents, and many others, all of which may mean that the mother's absence from the home may be an advantage—a stabilizing factor in the child's life. If these conditions do not affect his life adversely a host of others may be held accountable: ill-health, inferiority feelings, school unadjustment, disorganizing community influences, and many others of the tangled skein of social influences.

If the worker by chance or deliberate plan "wisely pulls on the thread he will soon drag other 'causes' into view, and may even find that he got hold of the end or broken middle of the cord instead of the beginning."[2] Furthermore, a classification into problems of ill-health, inferiority feelings, school unadjustment, culture conflicts, and so on, whether viewed one at a time or combined, is highly artificial since these may spring from common or from diverse sources, they may be highly interrelated with each other and with other problems which have not yet come to the surface, and they may highly influence each other, yet classification is only too apt to stress a single aspect of the situation, or at best a combination of a few factors.

The Gestalt psychologists[3] have done much to sensitize us to the "togetherness" of social processes, to the intricate relation

[1] CLIFFORD R. SHAW, "Housing and Delinquency," in John M. Gries and James Ford (Editors), *Housing and the Community-home Repair and Remodeling*, p. 13.

[2] *Ibid.*, p. 14.

[3] See particularly W. Köhler, *Gestalt Psychology*, and for an excellent brief summary of this school of thought see Gladys C. Schwesinger, *Heredity and Environment*, pp. 393–402.

between external and inner experiences. "There is something over and above summation of parts which makes up the whole; there is the attachment and integration of parts one with another. By breaking a thing up into elements, one destroys the concepts one is trying to explain. . . . [An analogy to chemistry may clarify the point.] Potatoes may be made of starch, sugar, water, ash, etc., but put these together in appropriate quantities and you do not get a potato!"[1]

While we fully comprehend the importance of this integration, yet we have no escape from the necessity for classification when we attempt to present a complex, interrelated totality orally, in writing, or even graphically. We simply lack the means to express the Gestalt adequately. Though we must for the time being resort to an artificial isolation of social processes and their component parts, that is, when we are classifying case problems, we need to keep in mind not a series or list of disjointed problems and isolated social conditions, but the inherent interrelated wholeness of a complicated pattern of life, a configuration—a Gestalt, which is at one and the same time "a historical and experiential continuum."

Let us consider certain aspects of a specific though very brief case.

The Case of Henry Harrison

Henry Harrison, fourteen years of age, was arrested by a police officer for vagrancy. He was found roaming the streets of San Y. late at night. The arresting officer recognized Henry as a previous offender. The record shows that Henry was detained for a few days in Juvenile Hall upon his first offense about six months ago, but, upon being duly admonished, he was returned to his parents and the case was dismissed.

The parents state that the boy has been running away persistently and staying away from home two days to two weeks at a time. He returns home only when he is desperately in need of food or clothing, or when he is ill. The last time, however, when apprehended by the police officer he was in possession of new pants and small change for which the parents could give no account. He has grown thin and appears seriously undernourished. He also suffers from a painful "skin eruption."

Henry states that he ran away the first time because he was afraid of his father who came home drunk, beat up his mother, and kicked his brother. "I was arrested, but why wasn't Pop? They talked to me about staying home but I was afraid of being kicked in the stomach, like Alex was. Why didn't they give him a talking-to?"

The study of the family, made after Henry's first offense, is very brief. Mr. Harrison is thirty-nine years old. Mrs. Harrison is thirty-five. Henry

---

[1] *Ibid.*, p. 393.

is fourteen, and Alex is twelve years of age. They live in a five-room bungalow, well furnished, in a nice residential section of the city.

Mr. Harrison drinks heavily and is therefore unable to hold a job. When working, as certified public accountant, he earns $75.00 a week. Has been out of steady work for nearly three years, during which time Mrs. Harrison's mother aided. There has been considerable conflict in the home, nagging and quarreling, and displays of temper, since Mr. H.'s loss of employment. Once Mr. H. came home so drunk that Mrs. H. had to run in the middle of the night to her mother's taking Alex with her. Henry had already run away from home.

Both Mr. and Mrs. H. are in good health; both had had two years of college work; they come from "good homes," got along well until "the depression set in." Now they are in constant conflict. The house is ill-kept and the children are neglected.

Mr. H. was baptized Catholic, but has not attended church for five years. Mrs. H. was born and reared a Baptist, but was married in the Catholic Church. She has no church affiliations. Henry was born in Grand Rapids, Alex in Fresno. The family came to San Y. in 1931, stayed a year, left for M., but after six months returned to San Y.

There are no savings, no negotiable securities, no automobile. The family is in need of food. Two attempts were made to reach Mr. H., but he was not found at home. He has no relatives in San Y.[1]

It is exceedingly dangerous to undertake a diagnosis of the Harrison family on the basis of the meager information at hand. We shall, for the sake of illustration only, indicate some of the outstanding problems. But how should this be done? To indicate one problem, then another, means thus creating the artificiality which we are trying to avoid. Perhaps the following classification of the problems involved in the case is more satisfactory in visualizing the interrelationship than a mere listing in serial order:

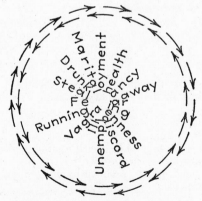

[1] From the files of M. County Probation Department.

Though the above presentation of the problems of the Harrison case is more satisfactory than a serial listing of these problems, yet it suffers from several inadequacies.   It does not assign relative *weights*[1] to the different problems which constitute the pathological situation.   Undoubtedly some of these problems are not so serious as others in their influence and effect.   Furthermore, this presentation does not indicate the order of appearance of some of the discernible elements of the problems.   For example, fear and running away appeared first and then the boy started to steal and became ill.

This presentation does not distinguish between symptoms and fundamental underlying causative factors, to say nothing of the lack of consideration of the role of the personal and social traits of the people who present these problems.

Clifford Shaw[2] in his discussion of the "vicious circle"[3] concept indicates the difficulties involved in assigning primacy to any element in the causative complex:

X is in prison for burglary.   On examination it is found that he is also a "constitutionally inferior psychopathic personality" and an habitual alcoholic.   Further inquiry discloses that X and his [parents] have been long in dire poverty and residing in the vilest tenement house in a "delinquency area."   Has X's criminality been "caused" by his drunkenness, or have both the alcoholism and the misconduct been "caused" by his constitutional inadequacy, or did X's habitual imbibing of alcohol aggravate his original weak inhibitory capacity?   Did X become a drunkard because he couldn't stand his family's miserable economic situation, or was the drunkenness the cause of that unhealthy economic status?   All these sequences may have occurred at different times in the life of X, in a series of vicious "action-reaction" mechanisms.   But even by close scrutiny of X's developmental history it would be difficult to assign *primacy* to any of the factors involved.

The great difficulty lies in determining what is "primary."   Some would naturally be inclined to place the constitutional inadequacy first; but it is conceivable that that defect alone would not have caused X to become a criminal, or that without his having lived in a deteriorated

[1] See SHAW, *op. cit.*, p. 15.

[2] *Ibid.*, pp. 15–16.

[3] "Vicious circle is the process by which a primary disorder provokes a reaction which aggravates such disorder," J. B. Hurry, *Poverty and Its Vicious Circles*, London, p. xi.   Adapted by J. Ford, *Social Problems and Social Policy*, pp. 581 *et seq.*

neighborhood containing many "speak-easies" X never would have become a chronic alcoholic, or that even if his inebriety preceded his criminality he never would have lapsed into crime, and had economic situation been adequate, etc.

Complexity of Symptoms and Causative Factors in Delinquency. From the definition of diagnosis given above (see pp. 116–117) it appears that the diagnosis is made from the symptoms, that is, from the more easily observable, recognizable, and specific evidence upon which is based a judgment of the nature of the underlying problems. The symptoms of marital incompatibility, for example, may appear as abuse, drinking, immorality, nagging, quarreling, jealousy, bad housekeeping, etc. The symptoms of adolescent tensions, as another example, may be spells of weeping, bashfulness, timidity, diffidence, moodiness, daydreaming, oversensitiveness, clash of personalities, etc.

When the symptoms are known and recognizable through empirical knowledge, diagnosis of a certain pathology may be possible. But in cases in which the symptoms are difficult to learn and difficult to recognize, or are missing altogether, diagnosis is exceedingly difficult if not well-nigh impossible. The worker should, therefore, make as thorough an investigation as possible and secure a complete statement as to the manifestations, origin, history, circumstances, sources, etc., of all problematic behavior. He also needs to become acquainted with the symptoms—arrived at both theoretically and empirically—of as many pathologies as are available to him, allowing, however, for wide deviations in different cases. The test of the diagnostician's power occurs, of course, when two basically different pathologies present similar symptoms.

Dr. Healy's discussion[1] and diagram illustrating at three levels—the offense (symptom), the offender (mental status), and the antecedent conditions (underlying causative factors)—further show the intricacy of causation in child unadjustment:[2]

We show in this at three levels the delinquency, the offender as a member of some general class, and the causal antecedents back of his

[1] WILLIAM HEALY, *The Individual Delinquent*, pp. 164–165. Reprinted by permission of Little, Brown & Company; see also HEALY and BRONNER, *New Light on Delinquency and Its Treatment*, pp. 4–5.

[2] See also SHELDON GLUECK, "On the Causes of Crime," *American Mercury*, XXIX (August, 1933), 430 *ff*.

tendency to delinquency. The combinations are made from only a few of the ascertained facts and types and could, of course, by the addition of facts, be made definitely more complex. The combining lines represent either sequence or conjunction of the portrayed elements.

We observe from the diagram that classification on any level tells little of what is of practical importance on other levels. For example, petty thieving may be committed by any one of the types of offenders on our diagram, who may in turn have been influenced by any of a number of different remotely antecedent or immediately inciting factors. As an instance, the feebleminded individual, the least difficult of all to group, may be with his deficiency the result of several possible causes, may be directly incited towards crime by inward or outward influences apart from his defect, and may commit any of the diagramed offenses.

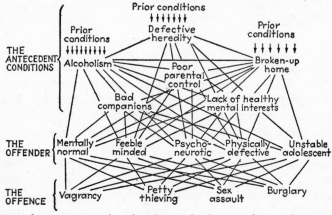

Diagram of sequence or conjunction of some simple antecedents and consequents.

The [delinquent] is not in himself to be grouped according to any logical system, and mere classification of either the antecedent or the consequent of his tendency leads only a short distance along the path of scientific and practical aims. This is the first lesson to be learned from the diagram. The second is, that each nucleus of fact cannot, in any fair-minded way, be interpreted as being or having a sole antecedent or a sole consequent. The diagram is worth pondering over with this in mind, before spending time on the estimation of the responsibility of alleged main causes, or the values of even partial panaceas.

Dr. Healy adds a statement to which we wish to call particular attention, since it shows the value and relative advantage of diagnostic diagrams after the disadvantages have been taken account of: "When it comes to the particular case, we find the greatest help from this articulating and viewing the facts. It leads to evaluation of causes by which adjustments become actually possible that otherwise would be blunderingly missed."[1] Cyril Burt,[2] after extensive research in the field of unadjusted youth, observes:

When we glance back through page after page and turn in succession to table after table, one striking fact leaps out in bold relief—the fact of multiple determination. Crime is assignable to no single universal source, nor yet to two or three: it springs from a wide variety, and usually from a multiplicity, of alternative and converging influences. So violent a reaction, as may easily be conceived, is almost everywhere the outcome of a concurrence of subversive factors: it needs many coats of pitch to paint a thing thoroughly black. The natures of these factors and of their varying combinations differ greatly from one individual to another, and juvenile offenders, as is amply clear, are far from constituting a homogenous class.

The foregoing discussion of the complexity of causation will, it is hoped, discourage any tendency to simple, unilateral classification of problems and will result in more deep-searching and painstaking efforts to recognize the multiplicity of the converging influences and forces operating variously in the lives of various individuals.

The assigning of the position of the "cart" or the "horse" to any given factor which is associated with another in the problem complex may be slightly facilitated, though not definitely established, when we trace the problems to their origin and establish their "sequence."[3] Did drinking appear first and then marital incompatability and then unemployment and then running away of the children, etc., or vice versa? It is essential to know whether when drinking is stopped through some alcoholic cure, for instance, marital discord will be softened or eliminated, and whether the children will fear to stay in the home of their father, or whether, on the other hand, we should deal with the juvenile problems directly as basic problems.

The importance of differentiating basic process from symptom is illustrated in the case of Henry H. Apparently in the treat-

[1] *Op. cit.*, p. 165.

[2] *Op. cit.*, pp. 574–575. Reprinted by permission of D. Appleton-Century Company, Inc.

[3] SHAW, *op. cit.*, p. 15.

ment of this case the running away of Henry was considered by the worker the paramount issue. But upon subsequent study Henry states that "fear of Pop" induced him to run away. When arrested and detained for running away, he developed further fears and he joined forces with a gang to gain a certain security. The gang accorded him some status; he found also thrill and adventure. Running away became a habit. While to begin with running away was only a symptom in a series of problems facing the home, after wrong diagnosis and treatment it became itself a *pathological process.* That is, running away in the first instance was incidental—"first-time-running-away"—while later it became "habitual-running-away," an entirely different thing when we examine the motivation. It is of prime importance to distinguish carefully these two varieties of running away. Undoubtedly other factors contributed to Henry's creating a habit of running away, but concentration on the wrong aspects of the problem by the worker gave new force to the disorganizing factors in his life.

A knowledge of the symptoms, their origin, their course, and characteristics—which with careful study of the case may be secured—will in many instances save much time and aid in preventing further disorganization.

Following are some of the more fundamental sources of child unadjustment, observed notably by the authors of the *Child in America,*[1] which may help the worker not only in gaining command of certain diagnostic concepts but also in using these in the process of elimination when considering certain types of his own cases.

William I. and Dorthy S. Thomas ascribe the wide variety of unadjustments to conflicts between child and parent, child and social codes, child and society, and to "organic peculiarities of the individual (physical, mental, emotional endowments and deficiencies) and the learning process, the acquisition of habits and attitudes."[2]

Emotional tensions, mental conflicts give rise to reprehensible forms of behavior, fixations, obsessions, incorrigibility, sex delinquency, temper tantrums.

---

[1] WILLIAM I. THOMAS and DOROTHY S. THOMAS, Chap. I.
[2] *Ibid.,* p. 94.

The enumeration of cases of mental disability, emotional instability, mental conflict, post-encephalitic disorders, specifications of stealing, truancy, adolescent flare-ups, family spoilings, etc., give the impression that we have located the sources of misbehavior—that it is like a sickness, that "something is the matter" with the child physiologically, mentally or emotionally, or that it is spoiled. But there is in addition a prevalent state of mind in the young—a determination to repudiate the way of life of the older generation and the conventional standards. Conformity, moral code, approved behavior, means that there have been established general and usual behavior reactions through definitions of situations. The "don't" of the family and the "shalt not" of the commandments, and the legal code represent such definitions. The family, the school, the church, the court, are representatives of these definitions, of the social, moral and legal codes. But the codes and definitions are themselves at present evolving, vague and unstable. There are rival definitions of situation. Literature and the moving pictures and the show girls may define the situation quite differently from the parent, minister or teacher. The difference in ideals and ways of life between the generations is consequently now very striking. Children may differ from their parents, or at least from their grandparents, in this respect as greatly as races and nationalities differ among themselves. There is thus a disharmony as to ideals and values, connected with the unstabilizing of society.[1]

Frequently children are unable to conform to social patterns of behavior because of mental deficiency; lack of proper distribution of abilities in a way which would enable them to meet the requirements of a school curriculum; failure to form certain important habit patterns because of lack of opportunity to come in contact with such patterns in an intimate and continuous way.

Overpowering desire for adventure, response, and recognition lead to predatory behavior, particularly when associated with gang activities.

A sense of social misplacement and personal inadequacy lead to frustrations, inferiority feelings, subterfuges, pathological lying, stealing, running away, sexual promiscuity, and so on.

Frequently children are old enough to respond to and to take on conventional behavior patterns but resist social patterning in a diplomatic manner and carry on amiable conflicts with society.

[1] *Ibid.*, p. 90. Reprinted by permission of Alfred A. Knopf, Inc.

Poverty is often urged as "a primary cause," but as Mr. Gold-stein[1] observes:

There are more poor than rich and so it is only natural that the delinquent children brought to the Children's Court should be recruited chiefly from the ranks of the poor.

With the rich, governesses often take the place of probation officers and military schools substitute for correctional institutions. With the rich, delinquencies of children are often "squared" by parents paying for the damage done and for the injuries inflicted, thus removing the cause that prompts complainants to petition the Children's Court for the arraignment of juvenile delinquents.

Even from this brief discussion we note that there is no general cause of delinquency. While such terms as "cause," "causation," "causal factors," "why," are used frequently it should be realized that it is exceedingly difficult to arrive at a determination of cause or etiologic factors and at an explanation of why a certain situation occurred in such and such form, time, circumstance, and so on. Many thinkers believe that "why" is a purely philosophical question, and even though we know many of the circumstances we are not in a position to trace the result or the effect to its cause.

The case worker is not concerned with ultimate or final causes, as is the philosopher, and does not seek for a final answer to the question "why." On the other hand he is concerned with the immediate causes, the antecedent conditioning viewed as links in a sequence of events which he thinks of as related to each other as cause and effect.

Motive[2] as Causal Factor in Delinquency.—We have so far mentioned only casually the inner life and motives of a delinquent child. Let us refer once more to the case of Henry Harrison and his brother, Alex, who were both subjected to the same treatment at the hands of a drunken father, to conditions following marital incompatability in the home, to conflict and deprivation. Why did not Alex run away? Or examine any of the situations in the cases cited in this volume and question the behavior of the problematic and delinquent child with the con-

[1] JONAH J. GOLDSTEIN, *The Family in Court*, p. 87.
[2] The concept "motive" in the above connection has been previously used by Dr. Bernard Glueck.

trasting behavior of his or her nondelinquent brother or sister. Why are "bad" environmental influences a stimulus to legitimate, socially acceptable behavior to one person and to illegitimate, socially unacceptable behavior in another? In some cases poverty, or fear, or conflict, etc., as Shaw says, is not only "a *situation* in the environment but a *motive* in the life of the individuals involved. Since the situational forces were similar, the difference in outcome in the two cases can only be attributed to the dissimilarity in the *persons* involved or to accidental factors of an unknown nature."[1] Shaw clarifies this argument by citing the following case:

A, a God-fearing, law abiding bank clerk, has never before even thought of stealing, needs money badly because of the illness of his wife or children, or in the dread of impending unemployment. He embezzles funds. Is the *situation* necessarily the "cause" of his criminality? The situation is, to be sure, the immediate determining factor; yet if A had been B he would not have stolen, even in the situation described. He would have sought some other solution of his acute and extraordinary situation, such as borrowing funds, or appealing to relatives, or letting his family go without their needs. In other words, the pressing situation would not have become a motive to misconduct. Here we see that, even in cases where the situation is the immediately precipitating stimulus, the make-up of the person (constitutional and conditioned) is still the factor that makes the real difference.[2]

According to Shaw the above illustration suggests two useful concepts in problematic and delinquent behavior-causation studies:

(1) A "factor," whether personal or situational, does not become a "cause" unless and until it becomes a "motive" and whether it will become a motive for one form of behavior or another depends upon the constitutional and acquired make-up of the individual. (2) Every person has his individual resistance-limit. It is difficult for all members of any society to lead a socially acceptable existence which involves a submergence of the ego desires to the supposed common weal. But most persons are capable of sufficient resistance and inhibition (natively and through education) to meet the ordinary requirements of the legal standard of the age and place in which they live. If society raises the demands somewhat, or, through social stress, such as continued unem-

[1] *Op. cit.*, pp. 16–17.
[2] *Ibid.*, p. 17.

ployments, etc., makes it more difficult to adhere to them, more persons will violate the law than before, because it thereby taps the level of those whose resistance-capacity is at present stretched almost to the breaking point.   If it raises the social taboos still higher or extends them or renders it more difficult to observe them, it further increases the number of violators of the socio-legal standard by tapping the tier of persons whose resistance-capacity is somewhat stronger than the prior group, etc.[1]   The [delinquent] act occurring at any one time is the outcome of constitutional and acquired, personal and situational forces, when the power of resistance has been overbalanced by the strength of the other circumstances.   Hence, some men would be [delinquents] (*i.e.* would violate the social conventions) in almost any society however rudimentary or complex, and in almost any "situation" in life, however ordinary or unique; others would be [delinquents] in extraordinary emergency though not in ordinary situations; still others would be [delinquent] only in an extremely complex society and in an unusually provocative situation.   [Delinquency] is thus shown to be relative to the time, place, and occasion on the one hand and the constitutional and conditioned make-up of the individual on the other.[2]

Still another question is in order: "Within a given complex social situation, with certain personality traits and critical incidents, why does a person respond by stealing or drinking? Or by any other behavior pattern?   It is assumed that he has a tendency or a susceptibility or a habit of body and mind which predisposes him to the adoption of certain behavior patterns and attitudes.   This predisposition to problematic behavior is called a *pathological diathesis*.   Pathological diathesis is akin to hereditary transmission but differs in that the characteristics or the condition itself are not transmitted but merely a tendency or a weakness is transmitted.

August Aichhorn's[3] statement throws further light on this matter:

[1] A similar theory may be advanced from a psychological point of view in connection with "regressions" to infantile levels.   The psychoneurotic soldier who, under the stress of battle, suddenly exhibits childish emotional and physical symptoms, has reached his particular regression point.   Other soldiers require a more severe fear-arousing stimulus before they will begin to react by regression as a means of "escape from reality." [P. V. Y.]

[2] SHAW, *op. cit.*, pp. 17–18.

[3] *Wayward Youth*, pp. 39–41.   Reprinted by permission of The Viking Press, Inc.

This conception of behavior as dynamically determined enables us to correct another common mistake. When I *ask parents how they account for the dissocial behaviour of their children*, I usually receive the answer that it is a result of bad company and running around on the streets. To a certain extent this is true, but thousands of other children grow up under the same unfavourable circumstances and still are not delinquent. There must be something in the child himself which the environment brings out in the form of delinquency. If for the moment we call this unknown something a predisposition to delinquency, we have the factor without which an unfavourable environment can have no power over the child.

We like to think that this predisposition is inherited. Psychoanalysis has shown us that heredity cannot explain everything, that the first experiences of childhood are important in determining later development. The predisposition to delinquency is not a finished product at birth but is determined by the emotional relationships, that is, by the first experiences which the environment forces upon the child. This does not mean that every child so predisposed will become delinquent. Bad company, street influences, and the like, factors which are not the underlying causes of delinquency but the direct or indirect provocation, also play a part. . . . When we realize that the provocation to delinquency is confused with its cause, that symptoms are mistaken for the disease, we understand why there are so many false conceptions of what should be done with the delinquent child, and we wonder no longer that treatment often fails. Without the discovery of the deep underlying causes of delinquency, any cure is accidental.

While we do not wish to stress the terms "cause" and "cure" as Aichhorn does, his statements regarding confusion of symptoms with contributing factors are nevertheless quite pertinent and clear.

The Crisis Situation.—There is at least one other aspect of diagnosis which needs emphasis. It should be clear by this time that a child's delinquency may be due to a multiplicity of causative factors, each springing from diverse social and personal situations, that his psychological make-up and social and personal traits effect and are effected by complex processes, but we may ask: "With the same complex processes and the same personality traits yesterday, or last week, drinking, or conflict, or poverty was not associated with misbehavior. Why should it be today?" Undoubtedly there was a long "build-up," but what precipitated the crisis today? Clifford Shaw would say, perhaps, that the "resistance-capacity" was stretched to the breaking point by some sudden pressure or stress, and delinquency emerged. William I. Thomas accounts for unpredictable behavior in terms of *crisis*—a situation in which a decision must be made and which demands focusing of attention.[1] Again we cite from the experience of Cyril Burt:[2]

> In any given case, amid all the tangle of accessory factors, some single circumstance not infrequently stands out as the most prominent or the most influential. Often, as we have seen, it can be definitely established that the child in question showed no delinquent tendencies until the year of some unfortunate event. An illness, a new demoralizing friendship, the death or the remarriage of a parent, the emergence within the growing child himself of some fresh interest or instinct—some dated crisis of this kind has often ascertainably preceded, and perhaps has plainly precipitated, his first violation of the law.

The precipitating crisis situation plays an important role both in the diagnosis and in the treatment and should, of course, be related to the total complex problem. At times it may be possible to prevent disorganization by preventing the occurrence of the crisis situation, or by removing the person from the situation.

Assets.—In spite of the intricate network of problems presented by a case, it is possible to list also certain assets. Assets are those positive, organizing factors in the family and individual which aid in reconstruction of the offender and in furthering the plan of treatment. "Nothing, however small, that might serve as an asset in the course of treatment and help to carry out plans toward a successful issue can possibly be insignificant. Whether this be an affection for a small dog, an ambition to play an accordion, or a lost or mislaid loyalty, the social physician must be able to use, and he must be able to recognize in order to use, such tools as these lie ready to his hand."[3]

Each family and each individual has a different set of assets according to its particular circumstances. Assets may include, all other things being equal, such factors as:

Strength of family cohesion.
Emotional ties of the family group.

[1] *Source Book for Social Origins*, pp. 13–26.
[2] *Op. cit.*, pp. 575–576. Reprinted by permission of D. Appleton-Century Company, Inc.
[3] Mary Richmond, *Social Diagnosis*, pp. 157–158.

Capacity for further training.
Capacity for energetic endeavor, for social development.
Intelligence, education, and training, good school record.
Health and vigor.
Possession of or desire to learn a trade.
Steady work of the head of the family.
Financial security.
Home ownership in a desirable community.
Intelligent insight into own problems.
Presence of good community resources, etc.

Such stocktaking of the available positive forces, when not undertaken in a purely routine manner, is exceedingly useful not only as clarifying the situation through the use of diagnostic concepts but since it leads the worker and the family to build on a solid foundation of constructive forces and also leads the family and the worker both to realize that they have "something to work with," something to rely on, something to save in their own lives. Thus they acquire a new dignity, new social status, and increased emotional stability, all of which are necessary elements in their readjustment.

Liabilities.—Liabilities are the negative and disorganizing factors which tend to frustrate the efforts of the worker and to hinder the plan of treatment. The number of liabilities is legion and as varied as the life circumstances facing each individual. Liabilities would include such factors as:

Broken home.
Economic insecurity of family.
Poor work habits.
Unfavorable heredity.
Defective mentality.
Poor housekeeping and management.
Poor health.
Lack of training and of ability to become trained.
Lack of education and of ability or opportunity to acquire it.
Emotional instability.
Religious conflicts or lack of capacity for religious training and affiliation, etc.

Prognosis.—Prognosis is the forecasting of the outcome of a case in view of the diagnosis. We have seen that social diagnosis is a difficult and complicated process. It stands to reason that prognosis, forecasting the future, is eminently more difficult.

Even the most careful and experienced workers, whose ability to make a differential diagnosis and whose accumulated knowledge of the outcome of a variety of cases serve them in good stead, often err in the forecast or prognosis of the case.

The worker must view carefully and intelligently the complex of causal factors and the pathological processes in terms of possible amelioration in a given social milieu, with a given set of personal traits, with given assets and liabilities inherent in the given situation. The limiting factors operating against the progress of the case and the positive factors suggesting potentialities for active treatment response which overbalance the liabilities, must, as far as possible, be seen and weighed.

When making a prognosis of a case, the limitations of the particular agency handling the case must be considered. An overburdened staff, or few community facilities, or inadequate equipment and untrained workers cannot contribute much to the favorable outcome of a case, although frequently cases adjust in spite of the activities of the agency rather than because of them. That is, in making a prognosis the worker needs to take full account of the "natural processes" which are operating for or against change in the situation and be careful not to overestimate the effects of treatment in controlling these natural processes.

The Value of Social Diagnosis.—A case carefully diagnosed often means it is more than half treated. If the diagnosis is competently arrived at on the basis of sufficient data secured with a minimum of bias or prejudice, and accurately recorded, it serves to indicate the outstanding or predominating social problems presented by the case. Such a diagnosis tends to eliminate guesswork; it tends to show where attention should be focused; it helps to decide what specialists, if any, should assume responsibility for study and treatment of the problems. Medical problems as soon as discovered are referred to medical authorities, educational problems to the schools, economic problems to the employment agency, social security board, relief agency, etc. The case worker, of course, has to see all these problems in relation to the whole situation and their effect upon personality. He further has to see the effects of the study and treatment of the various problems by specialists upon the person under consideration.

The following is tentatively offered as a summary[1] of elements which enter into a social diagnosis of a case:

Presenting situation (the situation as it appears; behavior viewed as symptomatic): running away; quarreling; drinking; etc.

The complex of basic problems: ill-health; marital discord; culture conflicts; etc.

Contributing underlying factors: to ill-health as determined by a physician; to marital discord; unemployment; sex incompatibility; mother-in-law-ism; drinking; etc.

Personality and social traits.[2]

Precipitating incident or crisis.

Assets upon which to build.

Liabilities to overcome.

Prognosis.

SUMMARY OF TENTATIVE SOCIAL DIAGNOSIS OF THE CASE OF MARILYN SMITH

(See *supra*, pp. 33–43, and *infra*, pp. 296–315.)

Presenting situations: running away, truancy, emotional attachment to a man nearly twice her age.

The complex of basic problems and their contributing factors: social isolation of and lack of common interests between parents and girl. Girl craves companionship and response but both parents are preoccupied with own interests. Lack of parents' participation in girl's recreation. High degree of native intelligence, wide reading, and numerous social contacts contribute to girl's maturity, which is not recognized by parents. Parental protection and overindulgence in girl as a young child and later inconsistent discipline which provoked confusion and impulsive behavior.[3] Lack of girl's participation in family affairs causes

---

[1] For other aspects of such a summary see Hamilton, *op. cit.*, pp. 43–64.

[2] See Chap. III or use any sociopsychological classification.

[3] Ernest R. Groves and Phyllis Blanchard observe that an "abnormal display of fondness for the child hurts him by giving him a grossly exaggerated idea of his own importance, at the same time that it prevents the turning of his affection toward winning more difficult but more wholesome rewards in the group outside the family. . . . It is unfair to force it upon the child suddenly by a complete change in the policy of the parents, by which without adequate preparation or sympathetic interpretation, the child is made to depend entirely upon his own guidance," *Introduction to Mental Hygiene* pp. 108–110.

further estrangement and social isolation. Lack of ethical standards of conduct of friends and relatives, also

Religious hybridism and lack of religious affiliation.
Lack of challenging activities in school.
Unwholesome employment.

Precipitating incidents or crises: newly found economic freedom. Meeting a man who showed interest and attachment.

Assets upon which to build.

Girl's craving for affection.
Devotion of parents to girl and to each other as well as to the entire family.
Intelligence and good health of entire family.
Girl's wholesome interests and desire for career.
Girl's cautious attitude toward sex matters.
Parents' high ambitions for girl.
Four well-adjusted and devoted sons.
A feeling of accomplishment and success in ability to raise the sons.
Happy and harmonious home background of both parents.

Liabilities operating against successful plan of treatment: parent-child conflicts are of long standing and are deeply colored emotionally and extend into many phases of their relationships.

Mother's popularity with a wide circle of friends and relatives is difficult to set aside in favor of closer relations with daughter.
Girl's transference of affection to an interested and satisfying male.
Lack of early training in assumption of duties and responsibilities.
Mother's conviction in unchangeable innate traits of selfishness, isolation, and individualization of girl.
Parents' lack of understanding of basic problems in girl's behavior and overemphasis they lay on symptomatic behavior.
Ready access to and easy success in blind-alley occupation which provides many stimulating but promiscuous contacts.

Prognosis: it may be argued that in view of the fact that the emotional conflicts are of long standing and are deeply rooted in almost every relationship between the girl, her parents, and brothers, and every phase of her life, such as work, recreation, religion, choice of mate, social attitudes and values, the prognosis is only fair. On the other hand, the devotion of the parents to the girl and the girl's craving for parental attachment, her intelligence, wholesome interests, happy and harmonious home background are strong indicators of a favorable outcome of the case. (For social treatment of case see pp. 296–315.)

Selected Bibliography

1. BAKER, HARRY J., and VIRGINIA TRAPHAGEN: *The Diagnosis and Treatment of Behavior-Problem Children*, The Macmillan Company, 1935.
2. BRONNER, AUGUSTA F.: *The Psychology of Special Abilities and Disabilities*, Little, Brown and Company, 1916. See particularly Chaps. I–III, "The Problem," "Method and Diagnosis," "Differential Diagnosis," pp. 1–39.
3. BROWN, L. GUY: "Social Causes and Cures for Delinquency," *Year Book, National Probation Association* (1930), pp. 9–30.
4. BURLINGHAM, SUSAN, GRACE MARCUS, FLORENCE DAY, and BERTHA REYNOLDS: *Diagnostic and Treatment Processes in Family Case Work* (pamphlet), Family Welfare Association, 1935.
5. BUTLER, GLENTWORTH R. (M.D.): *The Diagnostics of Internal Medicine*, D. Appleton-Century Company, Inc., 1906 (2d ed.). See particularly the chapter on the definition and method of diagnosis.
6. GLUECK, SHELDON: "On the Causes of Crime," *American Mercury*, XXIX (August, 1933), 430 *ff.*
7. HEALY, WILLIAM: *The Individual Delinquent*, Chap. IX.
8. O'BRIEN, FRANK J.: "Adjusting Treatment to Diagnosis," *Year Book, National Probation Association* (1928), pp. 186–201.
9. RICHMOND, MARY: *Social Diagnosis*. Russell Sage Foundation, 1917.
10. SHAW, CLIFFORD R.: "Housing and Delinquency," in John M. Gries and James Ford (Editors), *Housing and the Community-home Repair and Remodeling*, The President's Conference on Home Building and Home Ownership, 1932, pp. 13–49.
11. SYMONDS, PERCIVAL M.: *Psychological Diagnosis in Social Adjustment*, American Book Company, New York, 1934. See Chap. I, "Diagnosis of Criminal Tendencies."
*12. THOMAS, WILLIAM I., and DOROTHY S. THOMAS: *The Child in America*, Chap. I, "Varieties of Maladjustment."
13. VAN WATERS, MIRIAM: "Juvenile-court Procedure as a Factor in Diagnosis," *Publications of the American Sociological Society* (1921), pp. 209–217.

SUGGESTIONS FOR FURTHER STUDY

1. Prepare your own definition of social case diagnosis. Indicate the assumptions on which this definition rests.
2. Why is social case diagnosis an intricate and uncertain process?
3. Prepare your own terminology useful in the diagnosis of your cases.
4. What treatises on social diagnosis have you found most useful?
5. How does Miss Burlingham define social diagnosis? Miss Richmond? Dr. Cabot? Clifford Shaw?
6. What are the bases on which Healy established his system of case diagnosis?
7. On what does adequate social case diagnosis depend?

8. Who should make the social diagnosis of a case? the worker, the judge or the case supervisor? Why?

9. What is the relation between social case diagnosis and individualization of justice?

10. What is the relation between case diagnosis and case study? case recording?

11. What other concepts do you find useful in the diagnosis of your cases?

12. How can a busy worker diagnose a case carefully? How practical is the foregoing discussion to an overburdened worker?

13. Are there any short cuts to accurate diagnosis and treatment of a case?

14. What is the logic of social case diagnosis?

15. What contributions have you noted in the recent literature on social case diagnosis?

16. What is the difference between case diagnosis and case analysis?

PART II

LEGAL ASPECTS OF PROBATION

INDIVIDUALIZATION OF JUSTICE
SOCIALIZATION OF COURT PROCEDURE

Edited by Shelden D. Elliott
Director of the Southern California Legal Aid Clinic
Los Angeles, California

*Law is a living social institution and . . . it should
keep pace with the progress of the modern social sciences
and incorporate and utilize the ideas, the methods, and the
morals developed therein.*—H. H. LOU

CHAPTER VIII

THE REPORT TO THE COURT

After the various aspects of the offender's life and social relations have been studied, and the facts reviewed and diagnosed, a report[1] to the court may be drawn up. This report should be concise and clear. It should furnish the court with a complete picture of the offender and the offense, stressing the contributing factors and their bearing upon the present and future conduct of the offender. Many reports also specify recommendations as to the disposition of the case, whether the offender is to be placed on probation or to be committed to a reformatory or custodial institution or sent to a forestry camp.

THE CASE OF JOHN MACFARLAND

The reports to the court in the cases of John McFarland[2] and Amy Stewart[3] which follow are good illustrations of a comprehensive report on the investigation and findings of the more formal aspects of cases involving sex delinquency. No attempt is made here to discuss these cases from other angles:

IN THE SUPERIOR COURT OF THE STATE OF CALIFORNIA IN AND FOR THE COUNTY OF LOS ANGELES SITTING AS A JUVENILE COURT

IN RE JOHN McFARLAND
No. 00006 } Tuesday, December 10, 1935.
a person under the age of twenty-one years)
To the Honorable Superior Court:
I hereby respectfully report as follows in the above entitled Matter:
Boy in custody of Sheriff, County Jail

[1] See Chap. VI, "Recording of The Social Study of an Offender."

[2] Case study made and recorded by Patrick L. Palace, Court Investigator, Los Angeles County Probation Department. Quoted by permission of the Court. Boy's Americanized name further disguised.

[3] Case study made and recorded by Bess Hancock, Deputy Probation Officer, Los Angeles County Probation Department. Quoted by permission of the Court.

Reason for Hearing.—This matter comes to the attention of the Court on transfer from Superior Court[1] case no. 00055, petition having been filed by W. J., under Sub. 13, Sec. 1, Juvenile Court Law, alleging three counts of rape.

Remarks.—According to court investigator, boy is Oriental, having had sexual intercourse on three occasions with one Amy Stewart, a white girl, age sixteen years. Victim is reported to be pregnant. Probation officer feels this boy needs the supervision and training he will receive at forestry camp.

At the time this report is dictated a medical report has not been received from Dr. Blank, county jail physician, regarding the physical fitness of this boy to perform manual labor. This report has been requested and it should be available at time of court hearing.

Boy's Statement.—"I have known Amy about two years. I met her at James White High School, when they were giving out our Annuals. After a couple of months I started going with her. I would meet her over at the park and we would play tennis and sit around and talk, on occasions. Then later, on Tuesdays and Friday nights, I would see her over at the library. I had known her about five months when I had my first intercourse with her in Exposition Park. She was willing and I didn't use any force. I did use a contraceptive, though. Since then I had intercourse with her four or five times and about three of these times I completed the act in her without contraceptives. She was willing on all occasions. If she is going to have a baby I feel that it is mine. I love her and she loves me and although I know we can't get married in California, that doesn't mean we shouldn't get married. I can't see that race has anything to do with it. I think she ought to keep the baby but if she can't, my brother-in-law will adopt it."

Statement of Amy Stewart (As given to her probation officer).—She states that about a year and a half ago she met this Oriental boy, who was a star athlete at James White High School. States she in company with another girl used to go over and hang around the tennis courts where he would be playing and that this other girl got crazy about this McFarland boy and then she treated him rotten and so she felt sorry for him. She states: "I did not want to fall in love with him, but I just did . . . and now "I would give anything if it hadn't happened. Beginning about last April, I began sneaking out with him at night, telling my folks I was going to the library or a show. He used to sneak out, also, as his folks were strict about his going out and we used to meet in the park. We had sex relations about six times. I want to marry him and I would be willing to leave my folks and go live with his folks and if my folks wanted to disown me it would be O.K., because I love him and I want to keep my baby and marry him and raise my child. I do not want anything to happen to John McFarland because it is as much my fault as it is his."

[1] [The case was first heard in the Municipal Court and the defendant was later bound over to the Criminal Division of the Superior Court, but since he is a person under twenty-one years of age, the case was transferred to the Juvenile Court.]

The following facts relative to the girl's case, including her physical examination at Juvenile Hall, are respectfully submitted to the court. The girl was filed on under Subs. 2 and 11, by the Police Juvenile Bureau because of her association with this boy. The girl's family are active on the SRA, and according to the report of the girl's probation officer, the girl has advised her that she has taken castor oil and quinine in order to induce an abortion and that this boy gave her $5.00 to have an abortion performed by a doctor; that the school authorities took charge of the case before she could carry out her plans. It is also stated that her cousin had given her a pint of whisky to induce abortion. The girl's examination at Juvenile Hall, under date of Nov. 23, 1935, shows her to be three and one-half or four months pregnant.

Statement of Boy's Mother.—"John has never given me any reason to believe he was associating with this white girl. I was totally ignorant of what was going on, although since he has been arrested I have learned that my daughter and my neighbors knew this girl was calling at the house while I was away at work but they never told me. John is not a bad boy but this last year he has been leaving home to go to the library every night and then he would not come home until 11 o'clock or so. I used to tell him the library was not open until that time and used to scold him, but he would tell me that he was with a boy friend. I have since found out that the coach of the school knew that my boy and this girl were going together for a year or more and I cannot understand why they didn't say something to me about it. I am awfully sorry this happened and don't excuse John, but I feel that if you would read some of the letters she has written him, you will see that she is really crazy about the boy and wants to marry him and he tells me that he loves her. I don't know what to do—I know they can't get married."

Statement of Coach (of James White High School).—"This boy is not a criminal in any sense of the word. He is a high-class Oriental boy, who has developed a superiority complex by reason of his athletic ability and popularity at school. Then this girl began chasing him and would not let him alone. I talked to both of them and forbid them seeing each other around school or at the tennis court. Yet, I understand she used to wait for him elsewhere. The boy has told me he has tried to stay away from her. You see, we have a problem in this community of a preacher who has preached to those people every Sunday that they are on the same social scale as the white people and this developed a problem between all boys of colored races and white girls and it took a lot of work to break it up. Since this boy's being placed in jail, this problem has diminished, as it has taken a good effect. I do not believe he should be returned to this school because of the effect it would have upon the others and the possibility of placing him in the category of a martyr."

Previous Court History.—This boy first appeared before the court on Jan. 17, 1934, on a petition charging battery. This charge was not sustained after investigation and on Jan. 31, 1934, the petition was dismissed. He has no other delinquent record.

Home Conditions.—This boy comes from a home broken by the death of his father when he was quite small. Since then he has been in the home with his mother. She has placed a great deal of trust in him, resulting in a laxness of supervision. His hours have been late this past year and the boy has been able to take advantage of his mother's trust by deceit. The family has had a hard time financially this past two-year period, and the county has given aid to the family this last year until the older brother was given work in the SERA. The mother has been away from home during the day, earning a small salary. The older brother is now employed in the WPA. The home is very neatly kept, very well furnished, and the family is renting it for $16.00 per month, unfurnished. It is situated in a locality known to consist of the higher class people.

Family History and Background.—This boy's father is William McFarland. He died from tuberculosis. About three years ago an older brother, Fred, was granted four years' probation and ordered to serve eighteen months on the road camp, which he did, for a theft charge. He ultimately made good on probation and his case was dismissed. Aside from this there have been no other delinquencies in the family. Mr. and Mrs. McFarland married in 1901 in Arizona, came to the State of California in 1918. This boy is nineteen years of age, born Sept. 3, 1916, in Arizona. This birth date coincides with the date given by the school authorities. Aside from this boy there are two other children, one fourteen and the other thirty-two years of age.

School Report.—This boy at the time of his arrest was a senior in high school and expected to graduate in February. He states he liked school and was active in athletics, being a star in the track and tennis teams. He was taking an Industrial Art Shop course. School authorities show that from 1933 to the last semester, the boy's demerit record increased until last semester he had twenty demerits, most of them for cutting classes and being late. The date of birth as given by the school authorities is Sept. 3, 1916; intelligence quotient, 96, on a Terman-B test given in March, 1932. The boy has earned his letters in track and tennis, and according to his junior high-school record, he was very active in high jumping, and football, baseball, and a member of the band. At school the boy was known to have associated himself a great deal with the white group and according to the school authorities he was openly accepted by them.

School Activities and Recreation.—This boy does not smoke or drink. This is corroborated by the school authorities and his mother. He was formerly a member of the Boy Scouts and attained a second-class rating. He attended the Y.M.C.A. for a while, also. He is of the Episcopal faith and claims he attends church regularly and belongs to the Young People's Union. The boy plays tennis daily and is supposed to be quite prominent in this field at school. He does not attend shows or dances, claiming he does not like them. He states this is the first girl he ever had relations with and before that practiced masturbation upon himself. He has been attending the public library every night to get his lessons because of the noise of the radio at home. The boy had no gang interests and has affiliated little in group activities, preferring one companion. At school he was known as popular and affiliated himself with the white girls and boys, whom he claims welcomed him into their group. The boy had not had an automobile. He has had little spending money and what he has had, he received by cutting lawns.

Remarks.—The charge for which this boy appears before the court at this time involves a rather unusual situation. We have a high-type Oriental boy, cooperative and frank in his statements relative to his delinquency, falling in love with a young white girl, who certainly has reciprocated and encouraged this intimacy by her passionate love letters and constant association with him. This association was brought about primarily by the boy's acceptance into the social surroundings and activities of the group of white students at the school, where he was popular as an athlete. This has developed a feeling in the mind of the boy that no difference in status exists socially or otherwise between him and this girl and for this reason he should be permitted to marry her.

It is also to be said that from facts received, this association was seemingly approved by their companions, also. The school authorities faced with a like problem amongst several of the white girls and Negro boys in the high school attempted to adjust this problem as a group problem, not being suspicious of the density of the individual problem presented here. The boy, I do not believe, is fully responsible for his present predicament but is the victim of his acceptance openly by this girl. I believe, however, that he should be made to realize the seriousness of a problem of this kind by assuming the obligation to pay for her maternity expense, as she is to be confined in the A.B. Maternity Home at the expense of $25.00 per month to the county for this care.

This case has gained a great deal of publicity in the James White High School and, it is quite evident, affects a great deal more people than this couple and the views of the school authorities relative to this boy returning to that institution have been voiced in the statement of the athletic coach. It is felt that aside from this, the boy for the present should be placed at the forestry camp for the purpose of paying something toward the expense of the girl's care. He has no other means of income to do this than employment. This will also separate this young couple for a while and give them an opportunity to think this problem out. The boy's relatives are willing to assume the responsibility of caring for it, should the girl desire to give the baby up. This they are willing to do to relieve any possible stigma from the girl's future by possession of this baby. Examination for the forestry camp has been made, but return report has not been received at the time of this dictation but will be submitted to the court at the time of the hearing. It is felt that due to the high type of family this boy comes from, and his good past record, that he should be granted the concession of being relieved of the stigma of a felony by prosecution in the criminal court and given an opportunity under the Juvenile Court Act, which it is believed the boy will be amenable to. For that reason,

Recommendation.—It is respectfully recommended the boy be declared a ward of the court under Sub. 13, Sec. 1, that he be committed to the School of Industry during minority; being granted a stay of execution of commitment; be released to the custody of the probation officer for placement at forestry camp; monies earned there to be held in trust and to be paid toward the expenses of maternity of one Amy Stewart, now confined in the A.B. Maternity Home under court order by the Juvenile Court of this county; that this case be continued for a period of thirteen weeks for probation officer's report.

Respectfully submitted,
Probation Officer,
By _____
Court Investigator.

THE CASE OF AMY STEWART

The most vital information secured in the case of Amy Stewart—dealt with by a woman deputy probation officer—is already incorporated in the report on the case of John McFarland and needs not to be repeated here. (Note that the two probation officers, who because of the nature of the case must deal separately with the two families and the boy and the girl involved, conferred on the case and worked out a joint report.) The clinical report on Amy, the family history of the Stewarts, and the recommendations by the probation officer might throw further light on the case.

Report from Juvenile Hall Detention Home Clinic (Dec. 9, 1935).

Name	Age	Date Admitted	Time Admitted
Stewart, Amy	16 years	Oct. 21, 1935	Once

Physical examination, by Dr. Flora White: Oct. 21, 1935:

Well developed, well nourished. Hymen ruptured and relaxed—not recent. Uterus large, size of three and a half or four months pregnancy. Slight mucous discharge. Puberty established at 11 years—last menstrual period 6–4–35 (girl's statement). Wassermann negative. Smears negative. Two injections of toxoid for diphtheria immunization have been given, 10–21–35 and 11–4–35.

Recommendations: Prenatal care.

Psychological examination:

Test has not yet been given.

Psychiatric examination:

Superficial examination was given and no abnormalities were noted. No social history has been received and no request made for complete study.

Behavior report: Ten days' observation. Girl was quiet, polite, and helpful with small children while she was being admitted. The second day she was here she became ill and faint, and so was permitted to remain in bed mornings. She is worried; only rarely does she emerge from her distress to become interested in her surroundings. The last few days girl has shown some interest in school and group activities, and is apparently making an effort to accept her situation. She is courageous.

JUVENILE HALL CLINIC,
Medical Director.

Family History.—The father came to California in August, 1905, and to Los Angeles in September, 1905, and the couple were married May 31, 1918, in Los Angeles. The father, until recent years, has made a living as an electrician, having a business of his own. There is one other child, Florentia, age eight, a beautiful girl, who is in the B-3 grade. The parents state they have had no trouble with Amy; she has made good grades at school and is in her senior year, expecting to graduate in 1936. The parents state they agree and have always got along harmoniously, have had some little disagreements over the discipline of Amy, but not serious.

Paternal Relatives.—Paternal grandfather died in 1928 and the grandmother in 1916; two paternal uncles and two paternal aunts remain. One aunt living in _____, Calif., and one in _____. One uncle's whereabouts is unknown.

Maternal Relatives.—The maternal relatives live in and about Los Angeles. The maternal uncles and aunts having been ordered by the court to support the maternal grandparents after they had applied for an old-age pension. According to the parents they were exempt from contributing to the support of the grandparents because the father being out of work and himself dependent on the SERA.

Both parents were born in Alabama but have lived in California since 1905 and they do not have the race prejudice which might be expected from southern-born people. Indeed their attitude is unexpectedly tolerant toward this young man, John McFarland, stating that they have no doubt it was as much Amy's fault as his. However, they are brokenhearted and shocked and seem to be unable to make a plan for Amy at this time.

Observations and Suggestions.—It is the opinion of the probation officer that because this case has received so much publicity in school and because there is a situation in the neighborhood which involves more than this particular case, it would be advisable to have Amy placed in a maternity home rather than return to her own home. According to the parents, the cousin who offered to take Amy into her home is very little older than Amy and is lacking in judgment and the probation officer feels that this placement would not be advisable.

The court is respectfully referred to the report and recommendations of the Financial Department with reference to reimbursement in this case.

Recommendation.—It is respectfully recommended that Amy Stewart be declared a ward of the Juvenile Court, under Subs. 2 and 11; that she remain in the custody and under the supervision of the probation officer in Juvenile Hall, until released by the District Attorney in the case of John McFarland; that she be permitted to go to the A.B. Maternity Home; that a county order be made in favor of the A.B. Maternity Home at the rate of

$25.00 per month from date of admission to July 1, 1936, and the matter be continued four weeks for probation officer's report; the father to reimburse at the rate of $10.00 per month.

> Respectfully submitted,
> Probation Officer,
> By _____
> Deputy Probation officer.

These two reports to the court are more complete than is usually the case in many probation departments. These reports more nearly approximate the standards set by the Committee on Juvenile Court Standards (see pp. 1–10).[1]   Judges or referees as well as probation officers are enabled to make intelligent decisions on their cases when they have the facts before them.   Note that the report to the court includes offender's own statement, statements by parents, previous court history, an account of home conditions, of family background, of school history and activities, of social activities and recreation, religious affiliations.   Subsequent contacts with the offender should reveal more of the interests, motives, inner life of the offender and social life of his group.

The Los Angeles County Probation Department finds the following outline useful in writing the report to the court; it covers the major aspects of most cases (a more elaborate type of outline is used by other courts, notably by the Court of General Sessions, New York City):

REPORT TO THE COURT[2]

I. (a) Name and number of case.   (b) Time of hearing and date.   (c) Whereabouts of minor—in what places detained and how long. For example: one week in City Jail; in Juvenile Hall since Sept. 15, etc.

II. Reason for the hearing.   (a) Petition.   (b) Police report or petitioner's statement.   (c) Witness' statement.

III. (a) Child's statement.   (b) Parents' statements.

IV. The child.   (a) Previous court history.   (b) Home conditions.   (c) Family history and background.   (d) School record.   (e) Other social agencies.   (f) Community activities and recreation.   (g) "Confidential to the court."   (h) Clinical report.   (i) Financial status (if county order involved).   (j) Remarks and conclusion.

V. Diagnosis and present problem.   (Consider *only* such of the following headings as appear to be applicable to the case under consideration.)

[1] U. S. Children's Bureau Publication, No. 121, *Juvenile Court Standards.*

[2] Adapted from Bulletin No. 45, Los Angeles County Probation Department.

(*a*) Personal; physical defects, ill-health, mental conflict, social conflict, cultural conflicts. (*b*) Mentality; subnormal, unstable, deranged. (*c*) Unfit home; broken home, orphan, bad economic condition, immoral parents, etc. (*d*) Neighborhood conditions; lack of recreational facilities, poor associations, etc. (*e*) School conditions; poor school adjustment, need of specialized instruction. (*f*) Employment conditions. (*g*) Religious, or lack of, affiliation.

VI. Plan of adjustment. (*a*) By the school (change of school program; transferred to different type of school, etc.). (*b*) By clinics (dental treatment; orthopedic treatment, medical treatment, glandular treatment, psychiatric study, etc.). (*c*) By the family (more careful supervision by parents; change of environment, etc.). (*d*) By the community agencies (employment; spiritual and character development; recreation, etc.).

VII. Recommendation. Recommendation is to include the specific orders which the probation officer believes the court should give to the child, for example: not to drive a car; keep up medical treatments; renew Sunday school attendance; save a part of earnings; be home before nine o'clock; attend part-time school; contact with certain community agencies, etc. In other words, the specific instructions to the child which will enable the probation officer to follow out the adjustment plan outlined in paragraph VI.

The report should include all the major points considered in the social, psychological, medical, and psychiatric studies of the offender, his family, and community. Such a report is very valuable and, ideally speaking, should be the basis for all legal action and disposition of major offenses.

Some probation departments, according to the job-analysis study made by Miss Williamson,[1] instruct their officers to list in the record factors which in their opinion may prove "assets"[2] or "liabilities"[3] in the treatment of a given case.

The form of the report varies greatly within various jurisdictions, probation departments, and juvenile courts. Some judges wish the data summarized; some wish recommendations by the probation officer or supervisor; others do not permit or request them. Some judges require the report a day or two before the case is heard, others wish a brief oral statement by the probation officer or supervisor just before the case is heard.[4]

[1] MARGARETTA WILLIAMSON, *The Social Worker in the Prevention and Treatment of Delinquency*, p. 25.

[2] See *supra*, pp. 130–131.

[3] See *supra*, p. 131.

[4] See WILLIAMSON. *op. cit.*, pp. 25–26.

In most jurisdictions the report of the probation officer, together with the findings of medical, psychological, and psychiatric examiners, is sent to the superintendent of the reformative or custodial institution if the offender is committed.

Whatever the wishes of the judge and the practices of the court and probation department, the writer of the report should remember that his report serves as a basis for the court's decision involving not only the child but his family, the persons implicated in the offense, and frequently the community in which the offender will continue to live or from which he will be removed. The responsibility of the investigator as well as of the report writer is not small and every precaution should be taken to present such facts as will enable the judge to understand the salient points and to plan intelligently for the welfare of those concerned as well as to protect the interests of the community.

The technique of writing a report to the court is in many respects undoubtedly similar to that of writing a report on any problematic case in a variety of social service agencies. The report writer should carefully review and organize the material before attempting the actual writing or dictating of the report. This should be an accurate and succinct summary of the fruitful findings of the study, omitting what Ada Sheffield calls "behold-me-busy" details of interest only to the investigator, and facts of only temporary value.[1] The report should be uniform and orderly and should be topically arranged according to a form used by the particular probation department.

Selected Bibliography

*1. COOLEY, EDWIN J.: *Probation and Delinquency.*

2. Court of General Sessions, New York City: "The Report to the Court" (mimeographed), 1931 (see pp. 15–26).

*3. FERRIS, RALPH HALL: "The Social Case History in Probation Service," in Sheldon Glueck (Editor), *Probation and Criminal Justice,* pp. 153–160.

4. LOU, H. H.: *Juvenile Courts in the United States,* University of North Carolina Press, 1927 (see pp. 94–97).

5. U. S. Children's Bureau Publication, No. 121, *Juvenile Court Standards* (rev. ed.), 1934.

6. WILLIAMSON, MARGARETTA: *The Social Worker in the Prevention and Treatment of Delinquency,* published for the American Association of Social Workers by Columbia University Press, 1935.

[1] *The Social Case History,* pp. 82–94.

Suggestions for Further Study

1. On what facts should the report to the court be based?

2. What should be included in a report to the court?

3. How should such a report be written?

4. What factors, legal and social, should be taken into account in the preparation of such a report?

5. What are the advantages and disadvantages of a long report? of a short report?

6. What form is used in the criminal court when an offender is considered for probation?

7. Write a brief critique of the report on the case of John McFarland. Is enough information included to give the judge an adequate understanding of the situation?

8. What is the relation of the social study and diagnosis of a case to the report to the court?

9. What standards are advocated for writing a report to the court?

10. What is the relation of the court record to the report to the court? to record writing?

11. What effect did the establishment of juvenile courts have on reports regarding child offenders? adult offenders?

CHAPTER IX

THE JUVENILE COURT HEARING[1]

After the preliminary steps[2] in juvenile court procedure are completed, that is, after the offender has been taken into custody, the complaint has been filed, or the petition has been approved by the chief probation officer, the citation has been served or the summons or the warrants issued, and after an informal adjustment seemed inadvisable or impossible, the case is formally heard in juvenile court. At this time the petition together with the probation officer's report (discussed in Chap. VIII) and all other findings, including clinic reports, are considered by the court. In some cases the probation officer reviews or supplements orally this report just before or during the hearing. We present two transcripts of juvenile court hearings and one of a hearing in municipal court[3] (a preliminary hearing) for comparisons:

THE CASE OF AMY STEWART (Continued)[4]
IN THE JUVENILE COURT OF THE COUNTY OF LOS ANGELES, STATE OF CALIFORNIA

In the Matter of	
Amy Stewart	**PETITION**
A Person under the age of twenty-one years.	

TO THE HONORABLE JUVENILE COURT OF THE COUNTY OF LOS ANGLES, STATE OF CALIFORNIA:

YOUR PETITIONER_____A. L. D._____respectfully represents that the above named person is residing within said county and is

[1] See *infra*, pp. 185–190 and pp. 202–205.
[2] See *supra*, pp. 3–5, also *infra*, pp. 207–209.
[3] Quoted by permission of the court.
[4] The hearing was held before Referee Margaret Pratt, Los Angeles County Juvenile Court.

a person under the age of twenty-one years, to-wit, of the age of ___sixteen___ years, on or about the ___3rd___ day of ___September___, 193_5_, and is a person defined in subdivisions ___2 and 11___ of Section One, within the meaning of the Act of the Legislature of said State, known as the "Juvenile Court Law," approved June 5th, 1915, and Acts amendatory thereto. In that said person ___Amy Stewart___, who has no parent or guardian; or who has no parent or guardian willing to exercise or capable of exercising proper parental control; or who has no parent or guardian actually exercising such proper parental control and who is in need of such control, in that the parents have been unable to keep this girl from associating with undesirable companions.

In that said person, ___Amy Stewart___ who is leading, or from cause is in danger of leading an idle, dissolute, lewd or immoral life in that for the past year and a half this girl has been associating with one, ___John McFarland___, 19 years of age (Oriental), living at _____. Girl admits being pregnant and admits having sexual relations with ___John McFarland___.

As provided in Section 3, Juvenile Court Law, the Probation Officer of Los Angeles County has made an investigation of the facts herein alleged and has approved the filing of this petition.

That the said person is now in the custody and control of ___Juvenile Hall___ That your petitioner is the ___Policewoman___ of said person, and is entitled to the custody thereof. That the names and residences of the relatives of said person living in the said County are as follows: Parents: That in order to secure the attendance of said person at the hearing of said matter, it will not be necessary that a warrant be issued for the arrest of said person, ___Amy Stewart___.

WHEREFORE, your petitioner prays that this Honorable Court inquire into such matter and declare said person a ward of the Juvenile Court and deal with said person as provided in the above entitled Act of the Legislature, and make such order in the premises as to this Honorable Court may seem meet and proper, to which order your petitioner now consents.

A. L. D.

Petitioner.

Address _____

STATE OF CALIFORNIA, } ss.
County of Los Angeles,

_____A. L. D._____, the petitioner above named, being duly sworn, says that _she_ has read the foregoing petition, and knows the contents thereof, and that the same is true of ___her___ own knowledge, except as to the matters which are therein stated on _____ information or belief, and as to those matters that _she_ believes it to be true.

A. L. D.

Subscribed and sworn to before me this ___5th___ day of ___November___, 193_5_

L. E. LAMPTON, County Clerk.

by _____, Deputy.

Hearing in the Juvenile Court

This matter coming on regularly to be heard on Friday, this fifteenth day of November, 1935, at 10 A.M.

Amy was present together with the following witnesses and parties: Mr. and Mrs. Paul Stewart, parents; Mrs. H., probation officer.

The following proceeding was had:

Court. Will you all stand and raise your right hands to be sworn? (Witnesses sworn, including Amy Stewart.)

Court. What is your name? **Girl.** Amy Stewart.

Q. How old are you? A. Sixteen, on Sept. 3. Born in 1919.

Q. Where were you born? A. Los Angeles.

Q. What grade are you in in school? A. B-12.

Q. Do you go to church or Sunday school? A. Not very regularly; once in a while.

Q. What is your name? **Mother.** Florentia Stewart.

Q. Mother of Amy, are you? A. Yes.

Court. Your name? **Father.** Paul Stewart.

Q. Father of Amy? A. Yes, ma'am.

Q. What is your occupation, Mr. Stewart? A. Electrician.

Q. Where are you employed? A. WPA.

Q. Where were you employed before you had to get work through that agency? A. B. Department Store.

Q. Where? B.? Were you employed there a long time? A. Well, I was there off and on for the last seven years as an extra.

Q. Are you employed? **Mother.** No.

Q. Do you stay at home and take care of your children? A. I do.

Q. Amy, will you tell me what brings you to Juvenile Court? **Amy.** I am pregnant.

Q. Are you married? A. No.

Q. And who is responsible for your pregnancy? A. John McFarland.

Q. Who is John McFarland? A. A boy I have been going with.

Q. With your mother's permission? A. No.

Q. With your father's permission? A. No.

Q. And why are you going with any boys without your parents' permission? A. (No answer.)

Q. Amy? A. Because I knew they wouldn't give it if they knew.

Q. Did you expect to marry this young man? A. I did when I was old enough.

Q. You did. Whether your parents would give permission or not? A. Yes, ma'am.

Q. Mrs. H., will you tell us what the situation is in this case?

Mrs. H. This petition was filed by the [Police] Juvenile Bureau. I never have got just exactly clear how it came to their attention. It says an anonymous report. Amy—it had become known at school that she was pregnant and she had been going with this John McFarland, who is part Oriental, a senior at high school. Amy was also a senior. The boy is nineteen. Amy is sixteen. She, Amy, told me that she has been permitted to go to the library and to a show, slipping out and going with him, meeting him in the park nights where these acts took place. She says that she started this affair through chumming with another girl; they used to hang around when the boys were playing tennis and practiced their athletics and that the other girl made this boy fond of her and then she threw him over and treated him very badly, and Amy felt sorry for him.

Q. Was the other girl an Oriental girl? **Amy.** No.

Mrs. H. A white girl. The father, I think, feels that the school has failed in not reporting the matter to them, and of course, I think it should have been. However, as I see it from the school angle, it was not a particular problem in the case of these two young people, but a group of young people.

Q. I still agree with the father that the parents were the first ones who should have been advised of the situation. **A.** I think so too.

Q. Did you have sexual relations with any other boys than the Oriental boy? **Amy.** One other about two years ago.

Q. How many times within the past year? **A.** None.

Court. Amy, you may wait in the other room. (Exit.)

Q. Mr. Stewart, are you making any effort to secure regular employment? **Father.** Yes, ma'am.

Q. What is your opinion about this situation? **A.** Well, of course, it is a very serious situation and the way I look at it, of course I don't know—in what way do you mean?

Q. Well, your sixteen-year-old daughter having these ideas about her friendships. **A.** Well of course if we had had any idea at all that there was anything of that kind going on, why we would have prevented it, but not knowing of course, I had no idea such a thing—now as to her going to the library and so on and into the park, I had told her that she could only go to the library in the daytime. Well—the situation is that we get sixteen-year-old girls who get an idea that parents and other adults are old-fashioned, and old fogies in their ideas and that the young people are modern, have different ideas and only their ideas are right and I presume Amy thinks that they have outlived the age of white people feeling as they have toward other races. As far as—this is the first time we knew—she couldn't get our consent to go with him and she promised me and her mother both she would never go with any boy until he came and met us first. I told her if she wants to go out with a boy if he would come to the house and let me meet him and have a talk with him, then if I saw fit, I would let her go with him.

Q. Mrs. Stewart, what do you think about it? **Mother.** It is just too big a problem for me. I don't know.

Q. You have been a good mother to Amy, have you? **A.** Well you can ask Amy as to that.

Q. I say do you think you have? **A.** I think I have.

Q. Have you tried to teach her to be self-respecting and a good citizen? **A.** Yes.

Q. Have you? **A.** I have. (Pause.)

Court. Let's have Amy again.   (Entrance.)

Q. Amy, you have a sister.   Does she associate with boys as you have?
Amy. No, she doesn't.

Q. Do you think she should?   **A.** No.

Q. Then why did you think it is right for you?   **A.** I don't say that it is
right.

Q. Did you tell your parents that you wanted to marry this young man?
A. Yes.

Q. Where do you think you could go to get married?   **A.** Mexico, for one
place.

Q. You know that isn't recognized as legal in this state.   The law and the
courts have the opinion that people who go out of the state to evade the
laws of the state are not legally married when they go to another country for
the sole purpose of evading the laws. . . . Well, Mr. and Mrs. Stewart, of
course you will have to begin to think of this responsibility that you will have
to assume.   The care of your daughter and your little grandchild that she is
bringing into the world.   It will need care for many years.   Children are
minors until they are twenty-one in this state.   Under the circumstances,
there won't be anything else except for the family to take care of this little
baby.

Mother. Well, we understood that this boy's mother would adopt the
baby.

Q. That won't be considered.   This is Amy's baby.   We will have to
wait until after it is born and begin to see what is best for it later on. . . .
Mrs. H., will you ask for a psychiatric examination?   **Mrs. H.** All right.

Q. What is your recommendation for Amy?   **A.** I recommend that she
go to A.B. Maternity Home for maternity care.

Q. Is this man in jail?   **A.** Yes.   I recommend that she remain in Juvenile Hall until after the District Attorney is through.   The day the preliminary hearing was set, Amy was unable to attend as she was in quaran-
tine here in the Hall and I don't know when the next hearing of his will be.

Q. Who is investigating this situation in that school?   **Mrs. H.** Well,
the police were investigating the case of the other girls.   I don't know what
they found out.   Of course, I myself had a long talk with the principal and
she feels terribly about it and I think they really have met the problem
there.

Q. Well, I want to know what is being done about it.   **A.** All right.

Q. I want it followed up.   Bring us a report from the Police Department.
Father. I want—what I would like is, won't there be something done why
they don't notify the parents.   They admit it has been going on for about a
year and a half.   They didn't see fit to notify us at all.

Q. They knew Amy had been associating with this boy for a year and a
half?   **A.** Yes.

Mother. They said she quit for a while.

Father. They said she quit for a while and started in again.   I asked the
vice-principal why I had not been notified and she said Amy asked them not
to notify us.   That would have been all the more reason why they should

notify us and at that time we were living there within less than a block of the school and there was no reason that I can see whatsoever why we weren't notified.

Recommendation.—I recommend that Amy Stewart be declared a ward of the Juvenile Court under subdivisions 2 and 11, and be placed in the custody of and under supervision of the probation officer, to remain in Juvenile Hall until no longer needed as a witness by the District Attorney's Office in the case of John McFarland, and that she be placed in the care of A.B. Maternity Home . . . that a county order at the rate of $25.00 a month be made in favor of the A.B. Maternity Home from date of placement . . . and this matter be continued four weeks on the oral calendar for further report. These findings and recommendations to be presented to the Judge of the Juvenile Court in not more than ten days, nor less than five days from this date, to wit, Nov. 25, 1935, at 2 P.M. . . .

Amy. I thought that I would be allowed to go to my cousin.

Q. You need hospital care, Amy, and you need protection and you need to be away from everybody for a while. **A.** Don't you think it would be better for me to be happy and contented?

Q. You are going to be very happy in A.B. Home. It is very quiet and a very beautiful place to be and your mother and father will be very happy to know it is possible for you to be there and have hospital care and nursing care which you need. It means much to know that you are going to get through this and have good health afterwards. . . .

Mother. You don't think it would be advisable then to take her home for a few months?

Q. No. **A.** If we move away?

Q. She wants to get away from everything that would remind her of this experience. **A.** We would move out of the neighborhood.

Q. I want the psychiatric examination to be finished first so we know, if anybody can tell us, what the trouble is; and she has to stay here anyway until the District Attorney has completed his case against this man. That may take some time, and by that time it will be nearer the time for her confinement; and you can go to A.B. Home today if you want to and see it for yourselves and know just exactly why we are placing her there. We are doing it for her welfare.

Father. Sure, well, I think so myself. I think it is the best thing for her care.

Q. I think, to get away from any chance of neighbors' reminding her of this situation, is best. We are going to ask for an investigation of the situation in the school and it would be better for her to be away.

A. I think there should be something done in that school. If what I found out is true. . . .

Court. Amy, I know you feel badly, but I am telling you that we are doing the thing we think will make you happiest in the end. You are going to enjoy A.B. Home. Wait until you get over there.

Girl. It wouldn't make me happy to be away from my mother.

Q. What can we do about it now? **A.** Nothing, I guess.

The Petition.[1]—As far as the petition which initiates the court hearing is concerned we are at once struck with several outstanding features in this case which are not common to the apprehension, arrest, and detention of adults. We note that a petition was filed, giving name, age, residence of the girl and parents and stating briefly the facts which brought the girl within the provisions of the law. This petition is not an indictment or accusation of criminal behavior, and therefore no formal prosecution is in order. The filing of the petition is a means of informing the court of the problematic situation which the police officer (or probation officer, or parent, or any interested person) alleges to exist regarding the offender. The filing of the petition is essential to establish legal jurisdiction.[2]

Amy Stewart was detained in a juvenile detention home which provides temporary institutional care, clinical and hospital facilities, and a school for girls under eighteen years of age. This home is an observation agency for minors and is in no way to be regarded as a punitive institution.

The Hearing.[3]—Amy, as a delinquent girl, was regarded by the court as misdirected and misguided and needing aid, encouragement, and assistance, as it has been expressed in many statutes.[4] In accordance with the best practices of juvenile courts, the case of Amy was heard separately from adults and in a small courtroom,[5] simply furnished and devoid of any formal symbols with the exception of the court reporter and the clerk. The offender and the parents and the probation officer sat closely together as if in personal conference. In accordance with established practice, the public and newspaper reporters, had they tried to gain admittance, would have been excluded from the room. The publication of court proceedings in the newspapers is not allowed, and the court record is withheld from indiscriminate public inspection.

The court proceedings under chancery or equity practice[6] were informal, though dignified, devoid of technicalities and of strict legal formalities, though not arbitrary and irregular in character.

---

[1] For a more complete statement, see *infra*, pp. 207–209.

[2] See case of Weber *v.* Doust, 81 Washington, 668 (1914).

[3] See *infra*, p. 204.

[4] H. H. Lou, *Juvenile Courts in the United States*, p. 129, also pp. 129–142.

[5] See CHARLES A. GATES, "What Should a Juvenile Court Room Look Like?" *Year Book, National Probation Association* (1931), pp. 1–5.

[6] See *infra*, pp. 202–203.

The parents and the witnesses were sworn in by the clerk of the court. Generally a minor is not sworn in, but since Amy had to give testimony regarding the man implicated in her delinquency she was also asked to be sworn in. The court had the complete social history, including the results of the physical and of the brief psychiatric examinations given to Amy by the clinical staff of the detention home. Before the court was also the petition alleging that Amy came within the definition of the juvenile court law. The probation officer substantiated that the girl did violate a law of the state. The offender admitted in court the alleged offense. Therefore, the necessity of asking the question by the referee: What brings the girl to juvenile court? No charge was read to her and no entering of plea of guilty or not guilty was required of her, as was the case of her cooffender in the municipal court. While Amy's delinquency was established according to the rules of evidence[1] no strict application—as that which is in order in criminal proceedings—was adhered to in this case. Had it been a matter of establishing facts by evidence, only a preponderance of evidence[2] would have been required.

The offender's interests were represented by the probation officer and not by an attorney.[3] The court, filled with the spirit and welfare of *parens patriae,* is regarded as defender as well as protector. Though the child is entitled to representation by counsel his appearance is discouraged in the child's interests. The court acts as the "medium of the State's performance of its sovereign duties as *parens patriae* and promoter of its general welfare," to use the words of Judge Edward F. Waite.[4]

The primary function of the court was not to prove that Amy was guilty of an offense but to secure sufficient social data to enable it to decide on an intelligent plan of treatment. The hearing was held in a sincere friendly manner, conversing briefly with the minor about personal details and gradually leading up to the offense. There was not the slightest cross-examination, intimidation, or embarrassment. The procedure was intended to approximate the conduct of a wise and tender parent dealing

[1] See *infra,* pp. 187–189.

[2] See *infra,* pp. 206–207.

[3] See *infra,* p. 187.

[4] *Proceedings of the Conference on Juvenile Court Standards,* U. S. Children's Bureau Publication, No. 97 (1922), p. 55; see also *infra,* pp. 185–186.

with a wayward child.[1]   When the court questioned the parents
or outlined the responsibilities to them the girl was excused from
the courtroom and allowed to sit in the general waiting room, which
is under supervision of a matron.   However, the court did not get
a chance to get acquainted with Amy on that first day, to learn of
her motives, interests, and attitudes.   There were many other
cases waiting to be heard that day.   The court had to rely on the
social history prepared by the probation officer for a study of the
delinquent girl.   At no time, however, does a party in the juvenile court become merely a number on the court calendar.   He or
she is a human being and is not lost sight of when reduced to the
common denominator of "defendant" and "respondent," as
Jonah J. Goldstein puts it.[2]

The hearing in Amy's case can be considered more than a socio-
legal procedure.   The court had initiated a plan of treatment, and
some attempts were made to create insight in the girl into her
own problems.   The questions regarding the associations of
Amy's younger sister were particularly appropriate.   Also, Amy
was led to see that the court's plan of sending her to a maternity
home was for her best interests.   Thus, when the girl arrives
there she will have fewer inhibitions and defenses to break down.

The court did not consider Amy's case an individual problem.
A special investigation of the school was ordered.   Throughout
the hearing the court was concerned with the social implications of
Amy's delinquencies: the social control and discipline by the
parents, their attitudes and ability to understand and cope with
modern youth, Amy's confidence in them, the bonds of solidarity
existing between parents and girl; the economic status of the
home, the influence of the church in the life of Amy.   Since the
home had actually little to offer to Amy it was deemed best to
send her to a maternity home for care and "to get away from
everything for a while."   While both parents and Amy were
impressed with their degree of responsibility, there was no scolding, no antagonism, and no ordering-and-forbidding.   The case
was continued two weeks for further report.   Amy appeared
in court once before she was transferred to the A.B. Home,
once after the clinical reports were completed, and once after the

---

[1] See JUDGE CHARLES L. BROWN, *The Child and the Court*, An Address
before the Civics Teachers, Philadelphia Public Schools (1921), p. 9.

[2] *The Family in Court*, p. 25.

birth of her baby. Space forbids in this chapter to present more than a summary of this hearing. Amy was eager to keep her baby but her father refused to allow her to return home with it. Amy felt that under those circumstances she was being forced to give up her baby, but the court ordered her placed in a foster home until she as well as her parents could have more time to decide on a plan under lesser tensions. In August, 1936, the parents moved from the neighborhood, and Amy and baby returned home. Amy hopes to marry the father of the child when he leaves the Industrial School, provided the court gives permission. Thus the court continues to hear these cases until some satisfactory plan is made, considering the circumstances, or until the "probationer makes good and the petition can be dismissed."

The Hearing in the Criminal Court.—While the following is a transcript of a preliminary hearing in the Municipal Court—which in the State of California may hear the preliminary examination of a defendant and of witnesses in a criminal case—and while there was no jury trial, no counsel for the defendant, and no contest of charges, we observe that the hearing is much more formal than in the juvenile court.

CASE OF JOHN MCFARLAND (*Continued*)

In the Municipal Court, City of Los Angeles
County of Los Angeles, State of California

Division No. 005		HON. J. R., Judge
The People of the State of California,	Plaintiff,	No. 0052
v.		RAPE, 3 counts.
John McFarland,	Defendant	

Los Angeles, California, Nov. 18, 1935.

At 10 o'clock A.M., this case was called for preliminary examination before the Hon. J. R., Judge of the Municipal Court, City of Los Angeles, County of Los Angeles, State of California. The defendant appeared in court in person, without counsel. The People being represented by Mr. B., Deputy District Attorney of Los Angeles County.

The defendant had previously appeared, at which time he was duly arraigned, the complaint was read to him, and he was informed of his legal rights, *viz.*, the right to a speedy preliminary examination, to have the presence of counsel at his own expense at all stages of the proceedings, to have the process of the court issue to compel the attendance of any witnesses he may desire to appear and testify in his behalf, to be confronted by the witnesses testifying against him in the presence of the court, and to admission to bail, at which time said defendant gave his true name to be John McFarland.

With the consent of the defendant his preliminary examination was set down for Dec. 11, at the hour of 10 A.M., thereof.

E. E. was appointed as shorthand reporter to report the testimony and proceedings in this case in shorthand and to transcribe the same if the court should so order.

At this 10 o'clock A.M., the foregoing parties to the case duly appearing and announcing themselves ready to proceed, the following proceedings were had, to-wit:

The Court. People *v.* John McFarland. Is that your name? **The Defendant.** Yes.

The Court. Are you ready for examination now? **The Defendant.** What examination?

The Court. The proceedings in this court is a preliminary examination. It is not a trial. Are you ready to proceed with the examination? **The Defendant.** Yes.

Mr. B. Dr. White. Flora White, called as a witness on behalf of the People, being first duly sworn, was examined and testified as follows.

The Clerk. Please state your name.

The Witness. Flora White.

Direct Examination

By Mr. B.

Q. You are a physician and surgeon, licensed to practice in the State of California? **A.** I am.

Q. You are the examining physician for Juvenile Detention Home in this city? **A.** I am.

Q. Did you examine Amy Stewart? **A.** Yes, I did. I examined her on the twenty-first day of October, 1935.

Q. Tell us the result of your examination. **A.** I found the hymen ruptured and relaxed, which was not recent. The womb was the size of a three and a half to four months' pregnancy. There was no disease.

Mr. B. That is all.

The Court. Do you want to ask the witness any questions? **The Defendant.** No, sir.

Amy Stewart, called as a witness on behalf of the People, being first duly sworn testified as follows:

The Clerk. Please state your name. **The Witness.** Amy Stewart.

The Court. Speak loud enough so the defendant can hear you.

Direct Examination

By Mr. B.

Q. Where do you live? **A.** 0042 James Street.

Q. Have you a telephone there? **A.** No, we have none.

Q. Do you go to school? A. No.

Q. Are you the Amy Stewart who was examined by Dr. Flora White, the witness just off the witness stand? A. Yes, sir.

Q. Do you know the defendant, this man over here? A. Yes.

Q. Is he your husband? A. No.

Q. How old are you? A. Sixteen.

Q. When were you sixteen? A. September 3d.

Q. Have you ever had sexual intercourse with the defendant, John McFarland? A. Yes.

Q. Did you have sexual intercourse with him on or about the fifth day of March? A. Yes.

Q. His private parts penetrated your private parts? A. Yes.

Q. Did you have intercourse with him on or about March 10? A. I don't know for sure.

Q. When was the next time after the fifth of March when you did have intercourse with him? A. I couldn't say for sure.

The Court.

Q. Can you give us approximately the date? A. No, I can't.

Q. Did you have intercourse with him again? A. Yes.

Q. Approximately how many days was it after March 5? A. I don't know, it might have been a week or two weeks.

By Mr. B.

Q. Did you have intercourse with him about the middle of July? A. Yes.

Q. This happened in the County of Los Angeles? A. Yes.

Mr. B. That is all.

The Court. Do you want to ask this witness any questions? **The Defendant.** No.

Florentia Stewart, called as a witness on behalf of the People, being first duly sworn, was examined and testified as follows:

The Clerk. Please state your name. **The Witness.** Florentia Stewart.

Direct Examination

By Mr. B.

Q. Where do you live, Mrs. Stewart? A. At 0042 James St.

Q. Do you have a telephone there? A. No, sir.

Q. What is your occupation? A. A housewife.

Q. Amy Stewart, the girl who was just on the stand, is your daughter? A. She is.

Q. How old is she? A. Sixteen.

Q. When was she sixteen? A. September 3d.

Mr. B. That is all.

The Court. Do you want to ask the witness any questions? **The Defendant.** No, sir.

A. D., called as a witness on behalf of the People, being first duly sworn, was examined and testified as follows:

The Clerk. Please state your name. **The Witness.** A. D.

Direct Examination

By Mr. B.

Q. You are a policewoman of the City of Los Angeles?   **A.** Yes, sir.

Q. Attached to what station?   **A.** 032d Street.

Q. That is, the Juvenile Prevention Bureau?   **A.** Yes, sir.

Q. Did you have a conversation with the defendant?   **A.** Yes, sir.

Q. When did that take place?   **A.** On the twenty-eighth of last month.

Q. Where did it take place?   **A.** In the office of the Juvenile Bureau.

Q. Who was present besides you and him?   **A.** Amy Stewart, and another officer, I don't remember just who.

Q. What time did it take place?   **A.** I don't know, sometime on the twenty-eighth or twenty-ninth.

Q. Did you or any other officer use any force or threat of force against this defendant?   **A.** No.

Q. Or offer him any reward or promise him immunity?   **A.** No, sir.

Q. Relate the conversation.   **A.** I asked him if he had had any sexual relations with the girl, and he said he had; and I asked him how many times, and he indicated he didn't remember.

Mr. B.   That is all.

The Court.   Do you want to ask this witness any questions?   **The Defendant.**   No, sir.

Mr. B.   That is the People's case.

The Court.   Do you want to offer any testimony at this time?

The Defendant.   No, sir.

Mr. B.   The officer who is in charge of the case expresses the opinion now that $3,000 bail or a lesser bail than the amount recommended would be sufficient to hold the defendant, although we have no evidence that he can make any bail—we don't know.

The Court.   It appearing to me that the offenses charged in the complaint herein, to-wit: rape, a felony, charged in Counts 1, 2, and 3, have been committed, and there is sufficient cause to believe the defendant, John McFarland, guilty thereof, I order that he be held to answer to the same, and that he be admitted to bail in the sum of $3,000, and be committed to the custody of the Sheriff of Los Angeles County until he give such bail. The defendant will be required to appear for arraignment in Department 04 of the Superior Court at 9:30 A.M. on the second day of December.   Witnesses will not be required to appear at that time unless further notified.

In this court the case is considered as a matter of the state—which becomes the plaintiff—versus defendant who is charged with a crime.   There is a formal direct examination of witnesses in order to establish positive proof of guilt.   There is no inquiry into the social, economic, educational, religious, or other factors which might have influenced the offender.   There is no inquiry into the reasons for the offense nor into the plans to be made for the offender. The court is concerned with the offense and not with the offender. There is no attempt made at individualization of justice. If the defendant is proved guilty the nature and degree of punishment will be prescribed according to statutory provisions. There are other and more sharp distinctions in the procedure and the philosophy between the juvenile and the municipal and criminal courts which will be considered later (see pp. 181–185). Here we wish to point out that the judge and the referee of the juvenile court follow a socialized procedure, which is a greater aid to the minor and to the work of the probation officer.

However, not all juvenile court cases are dealt with in the manner and spirit displayed in the case of Amy Stewart. The following transcript of a court hearing in the Juvenile Court of S. County presents a sharp contrast and serves as an illustration of the need of a more socialized point of view, more training on the part of the judge in psychology, sociology, and social work, and also serves as an illustration of the problems such a judge presents to the probation officer when the offender and his family are compromised, insulted, and antagonized.

THE CASE OF NORA NORMAN (*Continued*) (See pp. 3–6.)
Hearing before the Judge

This matter coming on regularly to be heard on Wednesday, this fourth day of March, 1936, at 2:00 P.M.

Nora was present with the following witnesses and parties: Mr. A., the store detective, Mr. B., a store clerk, Miss C., the saleslady who waited on Nora, Police Officer Riley, Tom and Dick Dickson, Mr. and Mrs. Dickson, Mr. and Mrs. Norman, Mrs. Alden, the "aunt," and the probation officer. The following procedure was had.

Court. Will you all stand, except the boys, and raise your right hands to be sworn? (Witnesses sworn, including Nora.)

Court. What is your name? A. Nora Norman.

Q. How old are you? A. I was sixteen on Aug. 3. I was born in 1919 in ——.

Summary of Hearing.—The probation officer briefly reviewed the facts regarding Nora's act of petty theft (see Chap. I). The court was chiefly concerned with the degree of loss or damage of goods. Since no loss or damage was incurred the store witnesses were excused. Arrangements were made to hear the case of the boys later, and they and their parents were asked to wait in the lobby.

Court. Nora, what else brings you here today? (No reply.) (Question repeated twice, no reply.)

Q. Nora, why should you come up before a Juvenile Court? (Nora swiftly glanced at two rows of witnesses but did not reply.)

Q. Who is responsible for your pregnancy? A. John.

Q. John who? A. I won't give his name. It is as much my fault as it is his. I don't want to make any trouble for him. He left the state.

Court (To Mr. Norman). Are you the father of this girl? A. Yes, sir.

Q. And you are unable to control her? A. No, sir.

Q. Have you tried? A. Yes, sir.

Q. What's the matter? Are you afraid of her? A. No.

Q. How much do you try to really control her? A. I had tried everything I know.

Q. Parents should never bring children into this world if they can't train them. A. She was the first baby. I didn't know then . . . Well, what am I going to do?

Q. What can you do? A. I can't do anything with her. We live in a small town. She has no mother. I have remarried. Why can't she go where there are people who know how to handle her?

Court. Are you the stepmother? A. (Nod.)

Q. Can't you take care of her? A. I have troubles of my own. He drinks himself silly. I wouldn't stay with him if I didn't have to.

Q. The situation is this: the girl is not a public charge nor a public responsibility. She is yours. How much are you making a month, Mr. Norman?

A. Don't know exactly. Just started to work last week. Will probably make ninety dollars a month. (Wife interrupting: If he stays sober long enough.)

Q. How many are there in the family? Three, without Nora? A. Yes, sir. I don't like to have her gone, but I can't wreck the other girl's life. Decent girls won't have much to do with her.

Q. Well, that is not the court's concern in the matter. We cannot change her companionship very much. Is there any reason why you can't pay $20 per month for her support in a maternity home, if there are only three of you? A. It will be hard.

Q. You brought this girl into the world and she is a burden on somebody. It is up to you to make a sacrifice and to do your duty in this matter as long as you are unable to do your duties of parenthood; you will have to handle the financial end of it. The responsibility rests where nature put it. A. I was gassed in the war. I fought for this country and lost my health and soul. I am not the same man that I was a few years ago. I don't know what you mean by responsibility rests where nature placed it?

Q. I can't go into that here. But you are not doing your duty. A. (Nod.)

Court. Well, Nora will be declared a ward of the court and placed in the custody of the probation officer, to be maintained in a home of her choosing. It will be further ordered that the parents of the girl pay the sum of $20 a month for her support and maintenance in said home, and that the County of S. supplement not more than $10 a month. The parents are to make a payment to the probation officer on the first of each month, beginning Apr. 1, 1936, and to continue until the further order of the court. The girl is to remain in Juvenile Detention Home until no longer needed by the District Attorney's office. Now, Nora, you may wait outside.

Court. Nora won't talk here, although her report does not sound like it. Who is responsible for her pregnancy? **Father.** She won't tell.

Probation Officer. I can't find out. She is afraid that it will spoil her chances of marriage if she gives the name.

Court. You learn his name. Use the right approach. We can't let the man go free. What will she do with the baby? **A.** Has not decided.

Court. You get the name of that man. **A.** I'll try your honor, but I don't know if . . . **Court.** You try.

THE SOCIAL VALUE OF THE COURT HEARING

Nora's case, a case of sex delinquency and pregnancy, was heard before a male judge. Such a situation is inevitable in counties not large enough to maintain a referee, who generally is a woman. Undoubtedly Nora was embarrassed and hesitated to tell a man the circumstances that brought her into court. But, since the juvenile court is a court of record, facts must be established and recorded, particularly when adults contributing to the delinquency of minors are involved. Otherwise it would have been advisable to talk to Nora privately.

While the hearing in Nora's case was informal in character it was in some respects held from the legalistic point of view. No inquiry was made into the social, educational, religious, and other aspects of the case which were considered in the case of Amy Stewart. The court did not initiate a course of treatment, and Nora was not enabled to place her confidence in the court and to share her plans and thoughts with it. Legally Nora is under the jurisdiction of this court, but personally she did not accept it, and she virtually remained without natural parents and without *parens patriae*, which is the chief function of the juvenile court. Thus Nora's case was disposed of. Courts frequently assume that a girl is "sufficiently jolted" by arrest, detention, court hearing, commitment, pregnancy, facing the parents, and an empty future "to keep away from trouble." But does a young girl, if the sex experience has been satisfying to her, find "the jolt" a substitution for sex expression? The probation officer needs to remember that these young girls need absorbing work, physical exercise, congenial home atmosphere, sex instruction, religious affiliation, and whatever idealization and sublimation processes are suited to the circumstances and temperament of the girl.

It is apparent that there is considerable dissension in Nora's home, that there are no bonds of affection, of sympathy, or of common interests. Nora senses her homelessness and realizes that John is her only escape. Yet John is guilty of statutory rape, and he might involve other girls in pregnancy. The court's concern must, of course, be the welfare of the many instead of that of the single individual.

Under the present juvenile court organization the probation officer has little control over the nature of the court hearing in a particular case. He should, however, note all turns of the hearing, the effects on the offender and the family, and decide accordingly in what manner to follow up the case. He needs to be sensitive to the reactions and interactions resulting from the examination. He should not feel that the court is doing the work and that he can sit back and rest. The court hearing is one of the crucial moments upon which the officer can build his plan of treatment. Frequently he may have to undo much, particularly after such an encounter with a judge as was exemplified in Nora's case.

Tom and Dick and their parents appeared in court on the same day as Nora. The boys were remonstrated with, were ordered to "go directly home after school," and "to mind their parents." Both of them vociferously promised "to be good." Suddenly the judge asked the question: "And what made you do these things?" The boys looked at each other in confusion. The question was repeated. One boy mumbled in utter bewilderment: "I dunno." "But you must have a mind of your own and not allow others to mislead you." Again the boys promised, but somewhat less emphatically. And there the matter ended in court. The boys and parents were dismissed. Now the question may be raised: How can the court expect these little boys to keep their pledge, no matter how emphatically made, when so little is known about their ability to avoid future temptations or to resist them when encountered? Cyril Burt advocates to the child adviser to "draw from his young client what aims he has in view, how he thinks he can still satisfy his strongest interests without running counter to the law, and, with some well-framed policy of life will induce him to fortify himself against failure in the future."[1]

The judge, however, will make an outcry against this obvious real truth. He works overtime as it is. He is obliged to hear and to pass on ten, fifteen, twenty, and more cases daily. When can he follow this wise counsel? And after all is it his duty to assume the long process of reeducation of the wrongdoer? The probation officer, however, may be depending on the rascal getting his "jolt" in court to "reawaken him to his right senses." The appearance in court and the hearing are calculated, in some subtle way or otherwise, to be at one and the same time a critical and impressive moment in the offender's life. Only too frequently, however, does the child leave the courtroom bewildered and unable to carry out the promise which he made in all sincerity, since no practical ways and means were pointed out to him which would actually enable him to keep the promise.

Juvenile court authorities would agree that the procedure involving children's cases needs to be much more socialized than has hitherto been attained in most juvenile courts. On the other hand, we should not forget the real progress made in handling children's cases. Flexner, Oppenheimer, and Lenroot cite two typical hypothetical cases, before and after the establishment of juvenile courts, which indicate the far-reaching nature of the change due to the new procedure:

In the middle of the nineteenth century a boy thirteen or fourteen years old set fire to a stable. He was indicted by the grand jury, and because he could not give bail he was sent to jail until he was tried before a petit jury in a crowded courtroom. The State's attorney presented his evidence, consisting of proof that the boy committed the act with which he was charged and that he was old enough to know what he was doing. The boy's attorney offered evidence to the contrary. The judge ruled on questions of evidence. Hearsay evidence was not admissible. No one thought of offering testimony as to the boy's surroundings. He was convicted and sent to the penitentiary in which he served his sentence in the company of the usual hardened convicts in a penal institution.

That boy's grandson to-day sets fire to a garage in a jurisdiction that has a modern juvenile court. Complaint is made. The boy is brought in and sent to a juvenile detention home in which are no adults except

[1] *The Young Delinquent*, p. 552.

the persons in charge.   There he is examined physically and mentally.
In the meantime a court probation officer investigates the boy and his
environment.   He finds that the boy's grandfather was sent to prison,
that his family is poor, that they have moved from state to state, that
he has had little schooling, and that he has been associating with
vicious companions.   A plan is made for the boy's care and training.
His case is heard in a room informally arranged in which there are no
spectators except those immediately concerned in the case and no lawyer
except the judge.   The judge hears the complaint and reads the reports
of the physician, the psychiatrist and the probation officer.   The boy
admits the act complained of.   (If he had not admitted it the judge
would have heard the testimony and decided the question of fact.)   The
judge talks to the boy and to his parents and places him on probation.
The cooperation of social agencies is enlisted and a better job is found
for the boy's father.   The probation officer consults the school authorities and arranges for the boy to have school work that will hold his
interest.   He puts the boy in touch with recreational activities that will
occupy his spare time in a wholesome way.   The boy comes to the
probation officer regularly to report progress and to talk over his problems.   The probation officer visits the boy and his family at frequent
intervals and endeavors to bring the mother and father to a better
understanding of their son and his needs.   Finally, the boy is discharged from probation, or, if he continues in his old ways, he may be
committed to a training school for boys.[1]

In the second case cited we note that the probation officer
enlists the cooperation of the social agencies in finding a better
job for the father; the interests of the school and of the recreational authorities are secured in behalf of the boy.   Undoubtedly
much more was done for the boy and his family than this brief
report indicates.   It is apparent, however, that the executive[2]
and routine phases of social treatment predominated.   Chiefly
external aspects of the boy's behavior were considered.   Motives,
attitudes, emotional reactions, and the whole complex of the inner
life of the child are not mentioned.   This hypothetical case
is typical, as the authors maintain, of a large number of cases
handled by many probation departments.   If one may be allowed
to read into a case, it may be stated that the recorder of this case

[1] BERNARD FLEXNER, REUBEN OPPENHEIMER, and KATHERINE F.
LENROOT, *The Child, the Family, and the Court*, U. S. Children's Bureau
Publication, No. 193 (1933), pp. 18–19.
   [2] See *infra*, pp. 316–318.

had the premonition that not all was well with the handling of this boy when he indicates that "if he continues in his old way, he may be committed to a training school for boys," as, indeed, a large proportion of delinquents do persist in their old delinquent patterns, if treated in the above manner.[1]

As the procedure is being carried on at present, what is the law doing in the hearing of children's cases? To cite again the authorities on juvenile court law—Flexner, Oppenheimer, and Lenroot—the situation may be summarized as follows:

First, generally, as in cases of contract and property, it [the law] is determining an event. It determines whether or not the boy set fire to the garage, as it might determine whether a deed was actually signed or whether a seller failed to deliver an order. Second, it is determining a condition—the boy's health, mentality, and environment—again the factual question. Third, it is treating the event in the light of the condition, just as it may weigh considerations of public policy against considerations of individual interest in deciding whether a noise from a factory constitutes a public nuisance and should be enjoined. Fourth, it gives the case continued treatment, as it continues to supervise the administration of a trust in equity.[2]

The court hearing, ideally conceived, is in effect a conference at which all interested parties are able to secure an interpretation of the facts of the given case as well as the bearing of public policy, morals, and customs upon them. At such a conference issues are clarified and a decision is reached. The delinquent and his parents are thus able to get new definitions of the social situation, even though these may not be explicitly stated at the hearing. New conceptions of communal relations, of social controls, and of the role the offender plays in the group are bound to come out if the court hearing is planned to reorient him socially.

Selected Bibliography

1. BELDEN, EVELINA: *Courts in the United States Hearing Children's Cases,* U. S. Children's Bureau Publication, No. 65 (1920).
2. *The Child, the Court, and the Clinic* (a group of papers by leading authorities), New Republic, Inc., 1925, Part III, "The Court."
3. COCHRAN, HERBERT G.: "Juvenile and Domestic Relations Court," *Social Work Year Book* (1935), pp. 222–228.

[1] See SHELDON and ELEANOR GLUECK, *One Thousand Juvenile Delinquents,* pp. 159–184.

[2] *Op. cit.,* p. 19.

4. FLEXNER, BERNARD, REUBEN OPPENHEIMER, and KATHERINE F. LENROOT: *The Child, the Family, and the Court,* U. S. Children's Bureau Publication, No. 193 (1933).

5. GATES, CHARLES A.: "What Should a Juvenile Court Room Look Like?" *Year Book, National Probation Association* (1931), pp. 1–5.

*6. LOU, H. H.: *Juvenile Courts in the United States,* pp. 129–142.

Suggestions for Further Study

1. What effect did the establishment of juvenile courts have on court hearings regarding child offenders?

2. What form of hearings prevail in federal courts handling child offenders (see pp. 191–197)?

3. What is the difference between a court hearing before a referee and before a judge of the juvenile court? a commissioner?

4. What is meant by socialization of procedure in juvenile court hearings?

5. What are the legal aspects of a juvenile court hearing? the social? the psychological?

6. To what extent should the juvenile court hearing be a matter of establishing evidence? a matter of verifying the facts of social case history? a matter of social treatment?

7. How private are private hearings in the juvenile court? What is meant by the statement that the juvenile court is a court of record?

8. What should be the training of the judge, referee, or commissioner who hears children's cases?

9. Write a brief critique of the hearing in Nora's case, Amy's case, and John McFarland's. What are the outstanding differences in the hearing of each?

10. What suggestions can you offer for the improvement in court hearings?

CHAPTER X

THE JUVENILE COURT FROM THE POINT OF VIEW OF ADMINISTRATIVE LAW

"Important as are laws, the state of mind and social viewpoint of those enforcing them are of equal significance. Physical and psychiatric examinations and social diagnosis and treatment are meaningless if those enforcing the law lack a sympathic point of view [toward scientific procedure]." Jonah J. Goldstein, The Family in Court, p. 45.

Brief History of the Juvenile Court.[1]—Until the latter part of the nineteenth century the legal procedure followed in the case of a child over seven years of age was essentially the same as that of an adult, that is, punishment was meted out in accordance with the nature of the offense, which in some instances of children was the death penalty,[2] and in others, life imprisonment or very long terms of incarceration. There are instances of children who were committed to prison at the age of twelve and who were released at the age of forty or fifty years and older.

About 1890 the public was much outraged over certain verdicts returned against children and began a vigorous campaign for the establishment of juvenile courts. The year 1899 saw the first juvenile court laws being enacted in Illinois[3] and Colorado[4]

[1] The discussion which follows is intended to give the practical worker a basis for understanding the court and its functions. It deals with principles and practices only so far as they illustrate the development of the court and probation. Details of operation of specific courts will need to be learned by the worker during an in-service training period.

For a discussion of the background of juvenile court legislation see H. H. Lou, *Juvenile Courts in the United States*, pp. 13–23; Katherine F. Lenroot, "The Evolution of the Juvenile Court," *Annals of the American Academy of Political and Social Science*, CV (January, 1923), 213–223; Julian W. Mack, "The Juvenile Court," *Harvard Law Review*, XXIII (December, 1909), 104–122.

[2] Lou, *op. cit.*, p. 14.

[3] See *Smith-Hurd Revised Statutes of Illinois*, 1933, Chap. 23, Secs. 190–193, 199, 204, 212–214; see also *Laws of Illinois*, 1899, p. 131; and T. D. Hurley, *Origin of the Illinois Juvenile Court Law*.

[4] See *Laws of Colorado*, 1899, Chap. 136, p. 342; see also Judge Ben. Lindsey, "The Law and the Court," *The Problem of Children and How the*

under which the first real juvenile courts in the United States came into being in Chicago and Denver. However, prior to that year Massachusetts (in 1872)[1] and New York (in 1879)[2] and several other American states had statutes providing for separate hearings of children's cases.[3] We quote a brief summary from the well-known publication by the U. S. Children's Bureau, *Courts in the United States Hearing Children's Cases*, by Evelina Belden:[4]

[In 1899] the Illinois Legislature passed a law authorizing the establishment of a special kind of court for the hearing and disposition of children's cases.[5] This law, in accordance with which a juvenile court was established in the city of Chicago, in July, 1899, marked the beginning of the juvenile court movement in this country. Previous to that time certain states, following the lead of Massachusetts, had provided for the hearing of children's cases apart from those of adults and had made some progress in developing other special features. But the Illinois law was the first attempt at a serious modification of court procedure so far as it related to children. In 1901 the system under which the Denver Juvenile Court operates was established, in part under the authority of the school law of 1899.[6] In 1903 the Colorado Legislature passed a special juvenile court law.[7] Since then a great body of legislation affecting children who come before the courts has been enacted, and in communities representing every section of the country special courts have been created or special divisions have been established, and new methods have been introduced for the treatment of children's cases under existing court systems.

There is some dispute as to the country of origin of the juvenile court. H. H. Lou[8] believes that "it is a generally accepted fact that the first juvenile court, not only in the United States, but in

---

State of Colorado Cares for Them: A Report of the Juvenile Court of Denver (1904), pp. 28–29, 36.

[1] For the early provisions and modifications of court procedure in children's cases in Massachusetts, see Lou, *op. cit.*, pp. 16–17; also *Laws of Massachusetts*, 1869, Chap. 453.

[2] See *Laws of New York*, 1877, Chap. 428.

[3] See BERNARD FLEXNER and ROGER N. BALDWIN, *Juvenile Courts and Probation*.

[4] Publication No. 65 (1920), p. 7.

[5] Laws 1899, p. 131. Approved Apr. 21, 1899; in force July 1, 1899.

[6] Session Laws, 1899, C. 136, p. 342. Approved Apr. 12, 1899. Lindsey, *loc. cit.*

[7] Session Laws, 1903, C. 85, p. 178. Approved Mar. 7, 1903.

[8] *Op. cit.*, p. 19.

the world, began in 1899 with the establishment of the Chicago Juvenile Court, technically called the Juvenile Court of Cook County." Bernard Flexner, Reuben Oppenheimer, and Katherine Lenroot seem to imply that juvenile courts were not an American creation: "As early as 1890 children's courts were introduced in South Australia by ministerial order, and they were subsequently legalized under a State Act in 1895."[1]

The juvenile court movement rapidly spread not only in America but all over the world.[2] Great Britain and Canada organized juvenile courts in 1908; Switzerland in 1910; Belgium and Hungary in 1913; Argentina in 1919; India in 1920; Holland and Japan in 1922; Germany and Brazil in 1923; Spain, South Africa, New Zealand, and other countries have followed suit. Until 1932 Russia maintained a juvenile court but after that year the question of juvenile delinquency had been turned over to the education authorities, creating a special branch of social education.[3]

The movement for a juvenile court in the United States was not an isolated attempt to free children from severe criminal procedure, but was connected with the work in behalf of disadvantaged children in general, concentrating on factory inspection, child labor legislation, and separation of the young offenders from hardened adult criminals while incarcerated. This movement is identified with "a body of socially-minded women and lawyers, who had given earnest study to the problem of juvenile delinquency, and who had agitated for some kind of a court for children."[4] The following men and women are generally associated with the pioneer stage of the juvenile court work: Judge Ben B. Lindsey,[5] Harvey W. Hurd, Julian W. Mack, George Stubbs

---

[1] *The Child, the Family and the Court*, U. S. Children's Bureau Publication, No. 193 (1933), p. 12.

[2] For comprehensive discussion on the juvenile courts in England, France, and Germany, see articles by William Clarke Hall, Henri Rollet, Paul Cornil, Hans V. Hentig, respectively, in Sheldon Glueck (Editor), *Probation and Criminal Justice*, pp. 277–333; also T. W. TROUGHT, *Probation in Europe;* HERBERT FRANCKE, "Juvenile Courts in Germany," *Sociology and Social Research*, XVI (May–June, 1932), 403–416.

[3] M. S. CALLCOTT, *Russian Justice*, pp. 204–219.

[4] LOU, *op. cit.*, p. 21.

[5] Judge Lindsey was very active in the inauguration of a school law in Colorado which was the forerunner of the Colorado Juvenile Court Law. See *Laws of Colorado*, 1899, Chap. 136, and 1903, Chap. 85.

and Harvey Humphrey Baker, Mrs. Lucy L. Flower, Miss Julia C. Lathrop, Dr. Hastings Hart, Bernard Flexner, Henry W. Thorston, Homer Folks, and many others.[1]

The significant features of the new juvenile courts were: the age below which a child could not be regarded as capable of being a criminal was advanced from seven to sixteen years, and in some states to eighteen years; provision was made for classifying offending children under the milder term "delinquents"; the work of the courts was placed under chancery[2] or equity jurisdiction—a procedure based on mercy and natural justice followed for several centuries in matters relating to dependent and neglected children. The juvenile courts in America are based on English chancery proceedings, and the theory, both here and abroad, that "children," as Judge MacGill of Vancouver, Canada, observes, "who offend against the law should be more mercifully treated than adults is as old as the reign of Athelstane and the days of the Saxons. But it was a mere expression of a sentiment on the statutes and of no effect practically."[3] With the inauguration of the juvenile court law the delinquent child was to receive practically the same care, custody, and training which were accorded the dependent children. Thus the early juvenile court law may be regarded as an extension of the principles of guardianship by an equity court to all children who needed care and protection, including the wayward and delinquent.[4] Not punishment for crime, but treatment for a wrongdoer was the keynote, and not a strict legalistic procedure was to be followed but a scientific examination of the social facts by a socially minded judge assisted by a social worker, called a probation officer.

After the establishment of the juvenile court in Chicago, the movement developed rapidly. It had fired the enthusiasm of leaders, the general public, and the press.

At present every American state in the Union, except Maine[5] and Wyoming (although these two states have some of the

---

[1] LOU, *op. cit.*, p. 21.

[2] For a discussion of the chancery origin of the court, see Lou, *op. cit.*, pp. 2–12; see also Roscoe Pound, *The Spirit of the Common Law* and *Interpretations of Legal History*.

[3] HELEN GREGORY MACGILL, "Juvenile Courts and Their Work in Canada," Reprint from *Revue internationale de l'enfant*, VI (October, 1928), 1.

[4] EDWIN H. SUTHERLAND, *Principles of Criminology*, p. 271.

[5] In 1931 Maine passed a law extending the jurisdiction of municipal courts over offenses committed by children under fifteen years of age and providing

juvenile court methods), have adopted legislation providing special court organization for dealing with children's cases. Every American city with a population of over 100,000 has a court especially organized for children's work.[1] "The Federal Government has a juvenile court in the District of Columbia, but no other federal juvenile court."[2] Not all the cases of minors are heard in juvenile courts or tried by juvenile court procedure. "Announcement was made early in 1933 that all juvenile cases would be transferred by the Federal courts to the local juvenile courts. Nevertheless, 2,100 juvenile cases were heard in Federal courts in 1933, and final disposition was made there in more than three-fourths of these cases."[3]

Brief History of Juvenile Probation.[4]—Juvenile probation is the non-institutional social service phase of the work of the juvenile court. Probation, as we have seen, consists of a disciplinary and educative process which attempts to adjust the behavior of the offender in his own home or in a suitable home of a guardian, and at the same time it safeguards the interests of society. Contrary to a common belief, the probation method did not originate in the juvenile court, although the development and status of probation have been much enhanced since the formation of the juvenile court.

Probation as a method was first used in connection with adult offenders and was later adopted in the work with juveniles. The public strongly protested against the inhuman methods of punishment that the prison system used. There have been times and places when punishment has been meted out by beating, beheading, burning, cutting asunder, crucifixion, drowning, destruction by wild beasts, hanging, impaling, throwing from a height, stoning, strangling, smothering, drawing and quarter-

---

certain special procedure in these cases. (Act of Apr. 3, 1931, Laws of 1931, Chap. 241, p. 273.)

[1] See KATHERINE F. LENROOT and EMMA O. LUNDBERG, *Juvenile Courts at Work*, U. S. Children's Bureau Publication, No. 141 (1925).

[2] SUTHERLAND, *op. cit.*, p. 271.

[3] *Ibid.*, p. 271.

[4] For a more detailed discussion of the history of probation see Charles L. Chute, "The Development of Probation in the United States," in Sheldon Glueck (Editor), *Probation and Criminal Justice*, pp. 225–249; William Ballentine Henley, *The Development and Status of Probation Law in the United States* (Master's Thesis, The University of Southern California, 1935).

ing.[1] These methods were intended to deter others from wrong-doing. After the Quakers' attempt to abolish capital and bodily punishment in 1786 methods of punishment were limited to imprisonment, hard labor, flogging, fines, and forfeitures.

The relaxation of the rigidity of the criminal law first occurred in the treatment of juvenile offenders. The story of the experiment by John Augustus is famous to all interested in probation activities. John Augustus was a cobbler in Boston, in 1841, who had released to him certain boys who were accused of crime and sentenced to jail. The cobbler stood surety on the boys' bonds, and thus there developed a type of probation known as "bail-bonding." In the course of seventeen years John Augustus acted as surety for 253 men and 149 women and not one is reported to have violated the conditions of the release.[2]

Many children's organizations and volunteer societies kept vigilant watch over the activities in relation to children who were then tried in criminal courts. The following excerpt, also from William Ballentine Henley,[3] summarizes the bases of probation legislation and development of probation.

The first work was unofficial and was concerned chiefly with the placing of children in homes or special institutions. In 1869, Massachusetts adopted a law creating a visiting agent of the State Board of Charities to investigate cases and to be present at children's hearings. This agent was empowered to receive the child for placement if the court so ordered.[4] In 1873, the State of Michigan created a public officer, known as "the county agent" for each county in the state, who was to investigate, to place out, and to visit delinquent children. With the establishment of the juvenile court as a part of the legal system, the principles of probation were recognized. A foundation was thus laid for further work in their application in adult cases. . . .

A similar modification of treatment was going forward in dealing with adult offenders, based largely upon an extension of the principles of judicial discretion. Legal devices for mediating and for avoiding rigid and severe punishment for crime had developed even under the common law of England. The suspension of the sentence or the post-

---

[1] See HARRY ELMER BARNES, *The Story of Punishment: A Record of Man's Inhumanity to Man.*

[2] HENLEY, *op. cit.*, p. 21; RAYMOND MOLEY, *Our Criminal Courts*, pp. 159–160.

[3] *Op. cit.*, p. 35. Quoted by permission.

[4] GRACE ABBOTT, "History of the Juvenile Court Movement throughout the World," *The Child, the Clinic, and the Court*, p. 271.

poning by the court frequently was used, as was release of the offender
on good behavior. Under the common law system, the court could
suspend the sentence temporarily for various reasons. Convicts were
permitted to remain at large on good behavior from an early date. Sir
Walter Raleigh was executed under a sentence pronounced against him
fifteen years before, after having been put, in the interim, at the head of
a fleet and an army. Early America knew this instrument as "binding
to good behavior." Many of the States in America have upheld the
power of the court to suspend a sentence indefinitely. . . .

The legal system as such began in Massachusetts with the passing
of the Massachusetts law of 1878, providing for a paid probation officer
for the criminal courts of Boston. Massachusetts courts, however,
long had practiced what was known as "bailing on probation." By
this procedure the case was adjourned before sentence was imposed and
the defendant was released on bail. Under this system the probation
officer became the surety and was charged with the duty of bringing
the probationer back to the court at the end of a specified period. The
court could discharge the defendant at the time of adjournment or
otherwise dispose of his case.[1] The Massachusetts system soon became
state-wide. The appointment of probation officers was transferred to
the court in 1891, and was made mandatory in all district, municipal
and police courts. The Superior Court was given power to appoint
probation officers in 1898.

It was twenty years before another State followed the example of
Massachusetts. In 1889, Vermont enacted a state-wide law requiring
the appointment of a probation officer by a county judge of each
county.[2] . . . Since then forty-six States, as well as Alaska, Puerto-
Rico, Hawaii and the District of Columbia, have made provisions for
probation in their juvenile court laws. Adult or general probation laws
are provided for in thirty-two States and the District of Columbia.
Probation in juvenile cases only is provided in sixteen states, Alaska,
Puerto-Rico, Hawaii and the Philippine Islands.

Probation assumes different meanings in different states
depending upon the legislative provisions, quality of personnel,
methods of selection used in placing offenders on probation, and
so on. The theory behind probation administration is to save
the offender from the degrading effects of imprisonment and of

[1] CHARLES L. CHUTE, "Progress of Probation and Social Treatment in the
Courts," *Journal of Criminal Law and Criminology*, XXIV, No. 1 (May–June,
1933), 60–73.

[2] JUSTIN MILLER, "History of Adult Probation," Christopher Ruess
(Editor), in *Adult Probation*, p. 2.

institutional commitment, but in some jurisdictions probation, to repeat Glueck's statement, "is a farcical game of chance."[1] The disorganizing effects of mere surveillance (see the case of Harold Crane, pp. 440–449) and the fear of possible contamination of others in the community and the household have tended to place probation in disrepute.   Charles Chute[2] writes with respect to the "struggle for standards":

Thoroughgoing social investigation and supervision and qualified personnel are necessary.   In developing probation in connection with our system of punitive justice, there have been many difficulties to contend with.   Much of the probation work that has grown up has been of an inferior brand, without adequate investigation and with untrained, inadequate staffs.   The Courts and the public are only beginning to understand probation as scientific investigation and individual case treatment.   Probation work must be that or it is nothing but a form of leniency.   It requires standards, technique, and above all, trained, qualified practitioners.

Surveying the field, we can truly say that encouraging progress is being made, not only in bringing about a realization of the needs for standards, but here and there all over the country, in bringing them to pass. . . .

All those who have thought constructively about probation appreciate the need for a selected, trained personnel, but only in recent years has the demand become insistent for divorcing politics and "pull" from the appointment of these vital officers, for training candidates, and for continued education and adequate supervision of the workers, especially the neophytes.   I have referred to the now generally admitted need for adequate, qualifying examinations, whether by the civil service method or other competent examination plan.

The need for a satisfactory system of graded salaries and the employment of enough officers, so that the case-working probation officer shall never supervise more than fifty persons, and the probation officer giving his whole time to preliminary investigations shall not attempt to report on more than fifteen to twenty cases a month, are today accepted standards in the few well-equipped probation departments.

PHILOSOPHY OF THE JUVENILE COURT

Strictly speaking, much of the data presented in earlier chapters of this volume dealt by implication with the underlying philos-

[1] *Probation and Criminal Justice*, p. 4.

[2] "Probation in the United States," in Glueck (Editor), *Probation and Criminal Justice*, pp. 237–240.   Reprinted by permission of The Macmillan Company.

ophy, the processes, and the techniques of the work with delinquent and problem youth. It remains, however, to deal explicitly with the underlying philosophy, characteristics, and standards of the juvenile court in order to understand more fully the social service aspects of its work with juveniles.

As evident from the foregoing brief discussion, the traditional administration of criminal justice—prosecuting machinery, courts, bar, and penal procedure—is based on theories of retribution, on deterrence, and upon a specific body of rigid laws which govern in advance the decisions to be rendered regarding specified violations committed under various circumstances. Justice is characterized as impartial and impersonal in rendering decisions regarding acts which have been committed; but as Professor George H. Mead points out with keen insight, it makes no provisions of principles for the prevention of criminal acts, for returning the wrongdoer into a normal community maintaining normal social relations, nor for "stating the transgressed rights and institutions in terms of their positive social functions."[1] These theories are "the causes of many absurdities and distortions in the criminal law. They accomplish neither legal justice nor social good. This is why the traditional administration of criminal justice . . . spectacularly fails in the repression and suppression of crime."[2]

Roscoe Pound, perhaps more than any other man, has turned the attention of jurists toward the view that "law can no longer be regarded as a self-centered, self-sufficing science, isolated from other social sciences," but is an integral part of all social sciences of which law is but one phase. In an article on "The Scope and Purpose of Sociological Jurisprudence," he maintains that "the new conception of law points toward social justice which takes into account social causes, social effects in relation to prevailing social conditions."[3] But the sociological school of jurisprudence has had slow growth in the criminal courts.

The creators of the juvenile court responded to the spirit of modern social justice and have regarded law as a living,

[1] "The Psychology of Punitive Justice," *American Journal of Sociology*, XXIII (March, 1918), 590.

[2] Lou, *op. cit.*, p. 1.

[3] *Harvard Law Review*, XXV (December, 1911), 140–168; (April, 1912), 489–516.

progressing social institution subject to modification in accordance with the changing conditions of life and scientific thought. Medicine, psychology, and sociology were thought of as direct aids in deciding on an adequate course of treatment. Justice in the juvenile court is not only impersonal and impartial but objective, scientific, and dispassionate. The goddess of justice, figuratively speaking, has taken off her blindfold in the cases of juveniles and looked at the sordid social conditions, crime-infested areas, social and biological disease, child labor, ignorance, a civilization in transition producing personal, social, and institutional disorganization. The goddess, with full vision restored, has decided that law unaided by other social sciences is not competent to decide on a course of treatment for unfortunate, wayward, and delinquent children who are victims of circumstances and untoward social conditions.

The accepted philosophy of the juvenile court, that is, the total rational conception of what is involved in a given situation and the general ideas upon which we are to proceed, is based on the following assumptions: that every "normal" child has numerous possibilities for adjustment to society if properly trained and guided; that a child grows, develops, and thrives in and gains social consciousness through wholesome group participation; that a child's conduct is a response to his conditioning environment and therefore punishment as such is futile since the act which he committed was beyond his physical, mental, moral, and social control. Dr. Van Waters[1] points out that "studies of the integrative action of the nervous system indicate the adjustments necessary to full responsibility are impossible to the normal individual until after adult body-size and weight are reached and the more subtle phases of neurological growth are completed. Whereas some individuals may attain 'years of discretion' at eighteen or twenty-one, other normal individuals may require a longer period."

It is recognized that setting the age of eighteen or twenty-one as the age of discretion in the case of modern precocious youth may be nothing short of legal fiction, as far as a particular act of delinquency is concerned, but it must be remembered that the total situation producing the act is beyond the control and

[1] See MIRIAM VAN WATERS, "Juvenile Delinquency and Juvenile Courts," in *The Encyclopaedia of the Social Sciences*, Vol. VIII, p. 529.

comprehension of youth. To borrow Dean Pound's term of sociological jurisprudence and social justice, we need not rely to any great extent on any arbitrary date on the calendar, but we should remember that a child is the product of his social world. Nothing grows in a vacuum. Everything has its antecedent conditions, and the child's actions are a response to his conditioning social environment. For these reasons the juvenile court requires a social study of *the offender*, in all of his concomitant circumstances, as well as a study of the *offense*.

As repeatedly stated by the White House Conference report on *The Delinquent Child*, the primary function of juvenile courts "hinges on the fact that they are looking outwardly at the delinquent act, but, scrutinizing it as a symptom, are looking forward to what the child is to become." The vital question facing the court is not of leniency and mercy alone, but of fully understanding *why* the particular child is delinquent, "and, on the basis of this understanding to attempt intelligent treatment for proper adjustment toward responsible future living."[1]

The philosophy of juvenile court procedure is also based on the idea that every child has a right to a proper training, and where parents do not or cannot give such training the court must assume the duties of the *parens patriae*, or superparent. Furthermore, the court assumes that a child is not a fit subject for correction in a penal institution, since during his impressionable years he learns the habits of the underworld easily and uncritically, and that the atmosphere of a penal institution stunts his growth and development; that he learns best in the absence of fear and punishment and in the presence of encouragement, love, security, and recognition. It is assumed that the proper social environment of an offender is his own "normal" community life and his own home. When such conditions are lacking or are too disorganized to be of benefit to him, other conditions should be provided as a substitute.

COMPARISON OF CRIMINAL COURT AND JUVENILE COURT PROCEDURE

A direct comparison between these two legal tribunals is not only difficult but dangerous because of the great variations in procedure and administration in each court. The comparison[2]

---

[1] *Facts about Juvenile Delinquency; Its Prevention and Treatment*, U. S. Children's Bureau Publication, No. 215 (rev. 1935), p. 29.

[2] See also SUTHERLAND, *op. cit.*, p. 272.

is offered only to indicate the modifications which the procedure and treatment of juveniles have undergone since the development of special courts for children. However, it may be argued that the comparison is made on the basis of the procedure in a traditional criminal court with that of an ideal juvenile court. To some extent that is correct because, in general, juvenile court procedure has not been completely divorced from its criminal court antecedents.

CRIMINAL COURT

1. Person is *accused* of commission of a specific *crime* and a charge is lodged *against him.*

2. The purpose of the *trial* is to present sufficient evidence to prove the commission of the crime with a view of *punishing* the offender according to the seriousness and nature of the crime. "Trial is characterized by contentiousness, two partisan groups in conflict."[1]

3. The criminal law rests upon the theory that for the protection of society the offender must be punished.

4. The social and economic factors which may constitute the background for the

JUVENILE COURT

1. Person is alleged to have committed an *offense* and a petition is filed in *his behalf.*

2. The purpose of the *hearing* is to ascertain *why* the offense was committed and to determine through scientific methods of investigation regarding the nature, character, and general social conditions on a course of *treatment*, correction, care, *protection*, prevention. Every child is regarded as a potential asset to the community if properly guided. The state assumes a responsibility for him.

3. The juvenile court assumes that the child has done wrong but he was "sinned" against and, therefore, needs protection and guidance.

4. The social factors involved in the commission of an offense receive great stress

[1] *Ibid.*

commission of a crime are excluded as *irrelevant*.

5. *Public trials* are conducted in an open courtroom.

6. The criminal court is concerned with questions of *motive* and intent and regards the offender as a free moral agent who knew what was right but willed to do wrong.

7. Trials deal with questions of the *specific* criminal *act* only.

8. No previous investigation of the life history of the individual is made.

9. No reports are required by court from private or public institutions or agencies knowing the offender (except in cases where insanity is suspected).

10. Jury trials are used unless waived by individuals.

11. I n d i v i d u a l rights are guarded by providing the accused a counsel for his defense.

12. There are no specially designated judges for trials.

and are considered as the *underlying* factors in a child's conduct.

5. *Private hearings* are held in special closed chambers.

6. The juvenile court is not so concerned with motive and intent as the child is not regarded as a free moral agent or as capable of making decisions and therefore cannot be punished for his acts.

7. Hearings are concerned with *personality* and *total* social situation.

8. Hearings are based on life histories of offenders secured by probation officer as part of his duty.

9. Reports are required from private or public institutions and agencies knowing offender.

10. Offender is entitled to a jury if desired but no jury is generally used (see pp. 189, 195).

11. The necessity of counsel for defense is minimized. Should parent desire to hire a lawyer he can do so. Probation officer is the counsel for the child.

12. Special judges are designated for hearings.

13. Persons are held in custody or released on bail before and during trial.

13. Provisions are made to allow the child (for exceptions, see p. 178) to remain in his own home or be detained in a juvenile detention home or other suitable home subject to visitation by probation officer. Child is not put under bail.

14. Criminal court does not act on its own initiative to examine the behavior of offender.

14. Juvenile court does act on its own initiative and sends out its own agents to investigate in favor of the child's care.

15. Punishment follows conviction.

15. P r o t e c t i o n , education, training, and guardianship, if existing conditions show need, are used.

16. Criminal court handles matters of high judicial import and depends upon legal precedent to render a decision on a case.

16. Juvenile court does not handle matters of high judicial import, but rather matters of pedagogy, psychology, case work. The social and biological sciences join hands with legal procedure to work out a plan of treatment.

17. "Treatment in a specific case [is] determined not by the needs of the particular individual but by the legislature, in advance for all who violate the law in question, with reference primarily to other actual or potential delinquents."[1]

17. "Treatment in a specific case [is] determined by the needs of the particular individual without reference to other actual or potential delinquents."[1]

[1] *Ibid.*   [1] *Ibid.*

18. No board of visitation is appointed by court to concern itself with the conditions in prisons and penitentiaries.

18. Board of visitation is appointed by court to concern itself with conditions in child-caring institutions (for exceptions in California Court Law, see Section 17*B*).

19. Criminal court procedure is based on old *penal* theories, laws, and procedures of a purely legal nature.

19. Juvenile court procedure is based on *chancery*, summary, informal procedures, and on modern theories of social justice.

SOCIALIZATION OF COURT PROCEDURE

Judge Edward F. Waite, in an article on "How Far Can Court Procedure Be Socialized without Impairing Individual Rights?"[1] raises not only the question of socialization of court procedure but summarizes—and incidentally supplements our discussion which follows—the essential characteristics of juvenile court procedure:

What do we mean by "socializing" court procedure? Measuring time by standards appropriate to the development of human institutions, it may be said that until very recently the courts were concerned almost wholly with the adjustment of conflicting claims of individuals and groups against each other, and procedure was meticulously guarded to prevent unjust advantage for precisely the same reasons that dictated the details of the *code duello*. The modern tendency toward what is termed the socialization of the courts has produced new tribunals and evolved new functions of older ones, in which the aim is not so much the adjudication of private rights as the performance of what are conceived to be community obligations. This tendency chiefly interests the lawyer as it has enlarged the use of the police power to secure the general welfare. It interests the social worker chiefly as it brings directly and conveniently to his aid the judicial machinery through which alone, according to the tradition of free peoples, the State may exercise its ultimate authority in time of peace.

The working out of this tendency toward broader functions and a more human emphasis and aim has involved a more liberal procedure or method of transacting the business of the courts—or at least of certain

[1] *Journal of Criminal Law and Criminology*, XII (November, 1921), **339–347**.

courts in which the socializing process has made substantial headway. When a court is acting, not as an arbiter of private strife but as the medium of the State's performance of its sovereign duties as *parens patriae* and promoter of the general welfare, it is natural that some of the safeguards of judicial contests should be laid aside. This corollary to the main tendency to which we have referred may be fitly styled the socialization of court procedure.

I assume that by "individual rights" in our subject is meant those personal rights recognized by the common law as adopted in the United States and established by constitutions, National and State.

On the basis of these definitions, let us consider nine subdivisions of the general subject: (1) Exclusion of public, (2) representation by attorneys, (3) swearing of witnesses, (4) methods of taking testimony and conformity with rules of evidence, (5) weight of evidence, (6) jury trials, (7) investigation into circumstances of offense, (8) testimony of probation officers, and (9) use of referee in girls' cases.

The discussion will relate solely to so-called juvenile courts, and my contribution . . . must be untechnical, summary, and suggestive.

1. *Exclusion of Public.*—One who is accused of crime has a constitutional right to a public trial. As to what a public trial is, the courts have differed. If a juvenile court is organized as a criminal court for children, any child who comes before it charged with an offense is entitled to a public trial. If the Court that deals with him is exercising chancery jurisdiction, no such constitutional right exists, and for the purpose of this discussion noncriminal courts with purely statutory jurisdiction over children will be classed, though not with technical exactness, as courts of chancery jurisdiction. To a mind "not warped," as somebody had said, "by study and practice of the law" it may seem absurd that the hearing in the case of Johnny Jones must be public if he is charged in a criminal court with stealing and need not be so if he is charged in a noncriminal court with being delinquent because he stole. I shall not now defend this seeming inconsistency. If it is constitutional law, it is binding on the courts and legislatures, and it can be changed only by constitutional amendments.

There is no constitutional right to a public hearing when dependency or neglect is the issue; and the court has no right to deny it in cases of "contributing," since here it acts always as a criminal court, whether or not it has also chancery jurisdiction.

Even when the right to a public trial exists, much discretion is allowed the judge in the matter of excluding idle onlookers, in the interest of public decency or the good order of the court proceedings. Probably no reasonable exercise of this discretion would ever be questioned by or on behalf of a juvenile delinquent, for the protection of whose sensibilities and reputation it is commonly exercised. Indeed, all doubtful questions that have arisen in my own experience have had reference to inclusion rather than exclusion. I have sometimes found it puzzling to know how far it was just to children and their parents to permit their troubles to be heard even by qualified social observers who wished to use the clinical opportunities afforded by court sessions. The smaller the courtroom, by the way, the simpler the problem both ways.

2. *Representation by Attorneys.*—Here also the nature of the proceedings is the proper basis for distinctions. In prosecutions for crime, even of children, representation by counsel is a constitutional right. In noncriminal proceedings, however, courts of conciliation and small claims have made us familiar with the idea that legal rights are not necessarily violated by the elimination of attorneys. But is it not a moot question? Is not the experience of other judges like my own—that in most cases it is easily possible to make the lawyer who comes into the juvenile court an ally of the court and interest him in securing the real welfare of those for whom he appears? The absence of antagonistic claims of personal rights makes this the more feasible. I refer, of course, to cases immediately involving children. In "contributing" cases appearance of counsel must be permitted, and in my judgment should be encouraged.

3. *Swearing of Witnesses.*—I fancy most judges exercise wide discretion in this regard and are not conscious of any danger to personal rights. I can hardly conceive that if desired by the parties concerned all witnesses would not be sworn. Sometimes essential facts are within the knowledge of a child so young that to put him on oath would seem unreasonable. An obvious corollary to this situation would be the conclusion that his testimony would be unreliable. This would be true in general; and yet skillful questioning by an impartial judge might elicit important and well-accredited truth. The discretion to determine the competency of a child to testify has always lain with the court. Would it be any violation of rights for the judge to determine also whether or not to administer the oath? I think not. The greater discretion includes the less.

4. *Methods of Taking Testimony and Conformity with Rules of Evidence.* There can be no question of impairing rights in determining whether to receive testimony from the witness stand or the floor in front of the judge's table; or whether and to what extent the judge himself shall interrogate witnesses. Those and others of like sort are questions of taste and convenience, and the preference of any person fit to act as judge ought to be a safe reliance. As between criminal and noncriminal proceedings interrogation by the court is much more limited in the former, according to usage in the United States.

More serious questions arise in respect to conformity with the rules of evidence. Speaking generally, rules of evidence throughout the United States are the rules of the English common law, variously modified by local statutes, and uniform in their application to all courts deriving authority from the same source—the State or the Nation. I do not happen to know of any legislative rule of evidence peculiar to juvenile courts, except a Minnesota statute permitting findings upon the written reports of official investigators with like effect as upon testimony received in open court, in "county allowance," or "mother's pension" cases. Rules of ancient origin, approved or at least tolerated by the community for generations, encountered by the citizen whenever he resorts to other legal forums to assert, or defend his rights, should be not lightly set aside in juvenile courts. The only safe practice is to observe them. If hearsay, for example, has not been found justly admissible in civil disputes and criminal trials, it is no better in juvenile court proceedings. Exceptions should be made when appropriate, and informal short cuts will often be found agreeable to all concerned; but the exception should always be recognized as an exception. No judge on any bench has need to be more thoroughly grounded in the principles of evidence and more constantly mindful of them than the judge of a juvenile court. The boy against whom it is supposed to make an official record of misconduct, involving possible curtailment of his freedom at the behest of strangers, has the right to be found delinquent only according to law. The father, however unworthy, who faces a judicial proceeding, the event of which may be to say to him, "This child of your loins is henceforth not your child; the State takes him from you as finally as though by the hand of death"—that father may rightfully demand that the tie of blood shall be cut only by the sword of constitutional justice. Surely, these substantial rules of evidence which would protect the boy if the State called its interference "punishment," instead of "protection," and would safeguard the father in the possession of his boy, should apply the same issues which may involve the right of the boy to liberty within the family relationships and the right of the father to his child. The greater the conceded discretion of the judge, the freer he is from the vigilance of lawyers, the less likely he is to have his mistakes corrected on appeal, so much the more careful should he be to base every judicial conclusion on evidence proper to be received in any court of justice. Otherwise, the State's parental power which he embodies is prostituted; the interpreter of the law degenerates into the oriental *kadi*, and the juvenile court falls into suspicion and disrepute.

5. *Weight of Evidence.*—Shall the standard be preponderance of evidence or proof beyond a reasonable doubt? The latter, surely, whenever the proceeding is a criminal one; the former—technically, at least—in dependency and neglect cases. I say "technically," for while a jury would be so instructed, it is certain that the average juror, regardless of instruction, will require something more than a mere tipping of the balance before he will agree to a verdict that may separate

protesting parents from their child. And when, as in most cases, the duty to pass upon disputed facts falls to the fallible intelligence of a single person, any judge who realizes his responsibility will insist upon clear proof.

When delinquency cases are heard in noncriminal courts I suppose the true rule to be preponderance of evidence. But here I, at least, must plead guilty to judicial legislation, and I suspect I am not alone in this. When we have minimized the stigma of an adjudication of delinquency in every way that kindly ingenuity may devise, it remains true that in the mind of the child, his family, and his acquaintances who know about it, it is practically equivalent to conviction of a criminal offense. In the face of this fact legal theory should give way, and no less evidence should be required than if the hearing were a criminal trial. In the rare instances when I have juries in the juvenile court I instruct them to this effect, and I apply the same test to my own mind in reaching judicial conclusions.

6. *Jury Trials.*—It appears to be well settled that in none of the cases heard in noncriminal juvenile courts is there a constitutional right to trial by jury. In Minnesota, where juvenile court functions are exercised by the district court, which is the court of general jurisdiction, a jury trial may be demanded. This, however, is a privilege granted, rather than a right confirmed by the legislature and the privilege is rarely claimed. Doubtless this situation is typical. When, however, the court is so organized that a child is prosecuted for a criminal violation of a State law, I think it is generally understood that a jury must be called unless specifically waived. The same is true in "contributing" cases, especially when, as in Minnesota, the act or omission is made a misdemeanor.

7. *Investigation into Circumstances of Offense.*—If there is a question here it must be as to the use to be made of information obtained rather than as to the propriety of a preliminary investigation through agents of the court. The value of such an investigation in suggesting inquiry at the hearing is obvious. But when there are issues of fact to be tried it seems to me equally plain that statements made to an investigator out of court should have no standing as evidence when they are disputed by parties in interest, who by the implication of their denial demand the same right to be confronted with the witnesses against them that is freely recognized in other judicial proceedings. Without attempting a discussion of "due process of law," considerations of public policy seem conclusive. The undisciplined minds of the juveniles and most of the parents who come before the court cannot make clear distinctions between proceedings that are really friendly and paternal and those that are hostile, when the results may be alike in depriving them of liberty of action, which they had before they came into court and are

unwilling to surrender. Public opinion, too, looks askance upon any abandonment of traditional barriers against governmental interference with the citizen. However wise the judge and kind his purpose, he must have regard for both the individual and the community sense of justice; and Americans have an ingrained conviction that nothing, however well meant, ought to be forced upon them on the basis of information obtained behind their backs.

Let it be observed that I am now discussing policy rather than constitutional rights. As respects noncriminal proceedings, I am not prepared to set limits to the power of the legislature to enlarge and adapt to modern condition the ancient methods of official inquisition. Prof. Wigmore speaks of an increasing need "for the more liberal recognition of an authority such as would make admissible various sorts of reports dealing with matters seldom disputable and only provable otherwise at disproportion to inconvenience and cost." "This policy," he says, "when judiciously employed, greatly facilitates the production of evidence without introducing loose methods."[1]

It is probable that as socialization of the courts proceeds the tendency toward the use of this form of evidence will grow stronger, but popular prejudices must be reckoned with, and procedural convenience will be dearly bought if the cost be impairment of the general confidence in the administration of justice.

When, however, the adjudication is made the situation changes. It has been lawfully determined that the facts warrant the interference of the court. The nature and extent of that interference is discretionary with the judge within the limits set by the law. In exercising his discretion he may rely upon anything that brings conviction to his mind, and the parties concerned have no legal right to question the sources of his information. Here official investigation is a proper and valuable aid, whether made before or after the adjudication.

8. *Testimony of Probation Officers.*—No legal right seems to be involved; the question is rather one of expediency. In my judgment the probation officer should not appear as a hostile factor in court proceedings. The friendly relations with child and family that are essential to his corrective and constructive work would thus be jeopardized in advance. Should adverse information after probation is ordered be disclosed to the court? By all means, if it is important. No confidences should be received on condition of concealment. The probation officer is the eyes and ears of the court. What he sees and hears is a part of the court's knowledge of the case, and ought to be so regarded by all concerned.

9. *Use of Referee in Girls' Cases.*—Once more a distinction must be made between criminal and noncriminal proceedings. . . . In non-

---

[1] J. H. WIGMORE on *Evidence*, Vol. III, sec. 1672.

criminal matters, masters in chancery and statutory referees have familiarized us with the idea of delegation by the court of some part of its judicial authority. I think there is no constitutional reason why a court exercising chancery powers as a juvenile court may not be authorized to appoint a referee, not only to examine and recommend but to hear and determine. Masters of discipline in Colorado, juvenile commissioners in North Dakota, and referees in California and New Mexico are instances where statutes have expressly authorized such procedure. Other examples are referees in girls' cases. I have never heard a suggestion that rights were thus violated. On the contrary, girls and their parents are likely to deem it an advantage to have both inquiry and action in a woman's hands. Doubtless it is the experience of every man who acts as judge in cases of sex delinquency on the part of girls, that even if he has not the assistance of an official referee, a woman probation officer relieves him of embarrassing investigation and virtually determines the appropriate action.

If our discussion has any value, we may state three general conclusions:

1. In criminal proceedings the child has before conviction all the legal rights of the adult. Here the field of socialization is practically limited to treatment of the child after conviction.

2. In noncriminal proceedings there may be either with or without express legislative authorization, according to the nature of the court, the broad latitude customarily exercised by courts of chancery jurisdiction, this being appropriate and necessary to the full use of parental functions. Here no constitutional provisions relating to criminal prosecutions apply, and socialization of procedure may have wide scope. There are limits, however, of which the judge should be never unmindful.

3. In adopting this broader practice, courts should have regard to the popular sense of justice, even when it is not supported by established principles of constitutional law.

(To be continued)

CHAPTER XI

THE JUVENILE COURT FROM THE
POINT OF VIEW OF ADMINISTRATIVE LAW (*Continued*)

CHARACTERISTICS OF THE JUVENILE COURT

Jurisdiction over Delinquent and Dependent Children.—The Standard Juvenile Court Law drafted by a committee of the National Probation Association provides a "blanket" definition of delinquency and dependency.

The words "delinquent child" include: (*a*) A child who has violated any law of the state or any ordinance or regulation of a subdivision of the state. (*b*) A child who by reason of being wayward or habitually disobedient is uncontrolled by his parents, guardian or custodian. (*c*) A child who is habitually truant from school or home. (*d*) A child who habitually so deports himself as to injure or endanger the morals or health of himself or others.[1]

"It was no oversight that the juvenile court was given jurisdiction over both delinquent and dependent or neglected children and uses essentially the same procedure for both," remarks Sutherland,[2] as the purpose in both cases is essentially the same, that is, to determine the nature of the care, protection, and training to be provided by the state. The state provides parental control and reserves the right to their custody[3] in all cases where there is no parent or guardian actually exercising proper parental control, or willing or capable of exercising such control, and the children are in need of such control.[4] It is in regard to the delinquent children that the juvenile court movement introduced a new legal concept:

[1] Article I, Section 3; see *Proceedings of National Probation Association* (1925), p. 198.

[2] *Principles of Criminology*, pp. 273–274; reprinted by permission of J. B. Lippincott Company.

[3] See notes on "Rights of Parents to Custody of Children," *Columbia Law Review*, VI (June, 1906), 454–456.

[4] See *A Standard Juvenile Court Law*, Article I, Section 3, and *California Juvenile Court Law*, Section 1, Sub. 2–5.

The delinquent child is not to be proceeded against as one who has committed an offense against the State for which the State must mete out punishment, but is a subject for the State's special protection, care and guardianship in exactly the same degree as the child who is neglected or homeless. The power of the court to extend this protection to the delinquent child is the same power which the courts in England and in the United States have long exercised in respect to destitute or neglected children and is derived from the capacity of the State to act as the ultimate parent of its children.[1]

Age Limitations.[2]—Every juvenile court law defines the chronological age of a juvenile. The age limit under which the court may obtain jurisdiction in children's cases varies from state to state, from sixteen to twenty-one years of age. In 1933 the maximum age for boys in juvenile courts in thirteen states was sixteen years; in twelve states it was seventeen years; in nineteen states it was eighteen years; while in only two states—California and Arkansas—it was twenty-one years of age, the highest age limit maintained by a juvenile court in the Union.[3] The maximum age for girls varied still more widely in various courts. The Committee on Juvenile Court Standards had recommended eighteen years as the lower age limit for both boys and girls. If a child is declared a ward of the court just before it is eighteen it often remains under court's jurisdiction until it attains majority. In California a ward may even attain the age of nearly twenty-three years if the court assumed jurisdiction over him before he was twenty-one years.[4]

In many states, if a female ward marries with the consent of the court, the court withdraws its jurisdiction.

[1] EVELINA BELDEN, *Courts in the United States Hearing Children's Cases*, U. S. Children's Bureau Publication, No. 65 (1920), p. 10. See also JULIAN W. MACK, "Legal Problems Involved in the Establishment of the Juvenile Court," in Sophonisba P. Breckenridge and Edith Abbott, *The Delinquent Child and the Home*, Charities Publication Committee (1912), pp. 181–188; and BERNARD FLEXNER and ROGER M. BALDWIN, *Juvenile Courts and Probation*, pp. 7–9.

[2] For a fuller discussion of the subject see H. H. Lou, *Juvenile Courts in the United States*, pp. 47–52, and *Juvenile Court Statistics and Federal Juvenile Offenders*, U. S. Children's Bureau Publication, No. 232 (1933), pp. 11–14.

[3] Maine and Wyoming, which have no juvenile court laws, provide special procedure in cases of persons under seventeen and twenty-one years respectively. See *Juvenile Court Statistics and Federal Juvenile Offenders*, U. S. Children's Bureau Publication, No. 232 (1936), p. 100.

[4] See *California Juvenile Court Law*, Section 12 (1934).

The Chicago courts, believing boys over seventeen years and under twenty-one years are not fit subjects for either the juvenile or the criminal courts, organized a special Boys' Court, which is a branch of the municipal court. This court is not a juvenile court but a regular criminal court with certain modifications in legal procedure.[1]

Chancery Jurisdiction.—Chancery jurisdiction in cases of juveniles, as seen before, stresses not the offense but the offender, not the legal technicalities but the social facts, the child's physical and mental make-up and his social world, not the punishment but education, guardianship, and protection. But many of the courts have not been given full equity powers.[2] They have adopted in practice some of the features of the equity courts: informal, separate hearings, separate records, study of the social facts, but in the eyes of the law, the children coming into those courts are criminals.[3] Miss Evelina Belden[4] remarks:

Since the fundamental purpose of juvenile court procedure is not to determine whether or not a child has committed a specific offense, but to discover whether he is in a condition requiring the special care of the State, it follows that the chancery or civil, rather than the criminal, procedure is best adapted to the end in view. Under the criminal procedure—with apprehension by warrant and arrest, trial on specific charges, strict application of the rules of evidence, conviction, and sentence—the punitive aspects of the process are repeatedly emphasized. The judgment must depend upon the technical evidence presented, and the vital social facts of home and environmental conditions and the child's physical and mental make-up can be given, at best, limited consideration. In contrast to this complicated legal machine is the simple chancery procedure, under which the judge in an informal hearing can utilize all the information that has been obtained from the child and his family, decide whether or not the child is in a condition of delinquency or neglect, and apply the remedies best suited to the correction of the condition.

In some jurisdictions the essential features of the juvenile court have been developed under a procedure which remains criminal in form but which is in substance a chancery proceeding, the strict limitations of the

---

[1] See SUTHERLAND, *op. cit.*, p. 277.

[2] See KATHERINE F. LENROOT and EMMA O. LUNDBERG, *Juvenile Courts at Work*, U. S. Children's Bureau Publication, No. 141 (1925), pp. 8–9.

[3] These courts are in New Orleans and the District of Columbia.

[4] *Op. cit.*, p. 11.

criminal process having been relaxed. Most authorities agree, however, that the true chancery proceeding is preferable.

Even the courts which have full equity jurisdiction still have vestiges of criminal procedure, which, as Sutherland says, are right to trial by jury if parents or guardians so demand; the definition of delinquency though stated in general terms, still follows some specific terminology and technicalities in imitation of the criminal law; classification of offenses is in terms of criminal law, grand larcency, petty larceny, burglary, etc. Some judges still use short terms of imprisonment for children; some courts still cling to judicial and legalistic forms of questioning, retain the court paraphernalia, and allow police officers to deal with a large number of delinquents.[1]

The specific powers over children's cases in various courts of the country run a wide gamut from exclusive original jurisdiction and independence of any other court to highly limited jurisdiction and restricted powers over children's cases. These variations exist not only in various states in the Union, but often in various counties within one state.[2]

By 1929 independent juvenile courts had been created in nineteen states and the District of Columbia, but in fifteen of these states the juvenile court was independent only in certain counties. Consequently the juvenile court is usually a specialized branch of some other court, generally a county court or a probate court. In thirty-seven of the states and the District of Columbia and in parts of another state the court which hears juvenile cases has exclusive jurisdiction over children's cases, with certain exceptions. In the other states the delinquent child may be taken either to the juvenile court or to a branch of the criminal court. In 1929 in eleven states and parts of another, the juvenile court did not have any jurisdiction over juveniles charged with offenses which, if committed by adults, would be punishable by death or by life imprisonment, and similar limitations were made in a few other states for other serious offenses. Good reasons exist for the opinion that the juvenile court should have original, exclusive, and complete jurisdiction over all cases of delinquency of children.

The county seems to be the best territorial unit for a juvenile court system, at present.[3]

[1] *Ibid.*, p. 277.

[2] See LENROOT and LUNDBERG, *op. cit.*, p. 6.

[3] SUTHERLAND, *op. cit.*, p. 274. Reprinted by permission of J. B. Lippincott Company.

Separate and Private Hearings.[1]—The special modifications which court methods and court procedure have undergone in the development of the juvenile court are grouped by Miss Belden under three main headings: (1) methods of hearing and detention; (2) evidence; (3) judgment and disposition. With regard to these modifications she remarks:

The first step in the special organization of courts for hearing children's cases was the provision that hearings for children should be separate from those for adults. As before stated, this measure preceded in some States the enactment of more complete laws for the protection of children before the courts. In modern juvenile court procedure of the best type children are given the advantage not only of separate hearings but also of hearings from which persons not having a legitimate interest are excluded. Proceedings in chancery, including the use of petition and summons; a method of detention separate from adults for such children as cannot remain in their own homes pending the disposition of their cases; and special attention to cases of delinquent girls; these are essential to the fullest realization of the protective ideal of the court.[2]

Technicalities of procedure have been largely discarded by most juvenile courts. In the true spirit of the juvenile court law only informal and summary hearings can be consistent. The purpose of the hearings is a study of the offender as a person in a social group, and not a rigorous examination and trial regarding the offense; a conference in order to interpret to all interested parties the bearing of public policy, morals, and customs upon them, and not for the purpose of pronouncing a verdict.

Social Study of Cases.—The juvenile court is primarily concerned with such questions as: Who is the offender? Why did he commit the offense? What circumstances led up to it? What is his social environment? How can he best be readjusted? These are some of the questions which are of greatest importance in the consideration of cases of juveniles. The investigations—or, better, social studies—are made by probation officers who are the agents of the court. In the larger courts to which clinics are attached, medical, psychological, and at times psychiatric examinations are a part of the social study of the offender. Every juvenile court with chancery jurisdiction is required by law

[1] See *supra*, pp. 150–169.
[2] Belden, *op. cit.*, pp. 8–9.

to make these investigations before the court hearing. What these investigations involve is set forth in detail in Chaps. III and IV of this text.

Some courts have set aside certain probation officers to carry on the investigation and make the social study and, when this is completed, turn the case over to another probation officer who concerns himself with its social treatment and supervision. This plan has several advantages, namely, that there are many officers who do much better investigative work than supervisory or therapeutic; that specialization of service is useful; that the neglect in either branch of the work is avoided or minimized. Some disadvantages may be cited, namely, that children or families should not be expected to deal with and adjust themselves to several different officers in a relatively short period of time. Moreover, that it is almost impossible to begin treatment without getting personally acquainted with the personal traits, situation, and turns and peculiarities of mind—which generally are not included in the files of a case record. Furthermore, diagnosis is after all a tentative matter, investigation is never complete, and treatment is involved in the very process of investigation. In short, the separation of the case work process into such steps as investigation, diagnosis, planning, and treatment is highly arbitrary and does not correspond closely to any actual easily identifiable steps in the relation of the officer to the child. This is also true if we merely regard the division of work into its before-hearing and after-hearing stages. While there are certain changes in the psychology and sociology of the relation of the child to the corrective process, it does not follow that this change should be correlated with a change in officers.

Constitutionality of Juvenile Court Laws.—Juvenile court acts were met with vigorous objections on constitutional grounds;[1] they were charged with deprivation of liberty without due process of law, denial of the right of trial by jury, and violation of the guaranty of a public trial. But the acts and statutes have been upheld by the courts against these constitutional objections.[2] Miss Belden observes:[3]

[1] See MACK, *op. cit.*, pp. 181–201.
[2] *Supplement to Annual Report of the Attorney General of the United States* for the year 1914, pp. 23–55.
[3] *Op. cit.*, p. 10.

The fundamental principles of the juvenile court, as expressed in the first juvenile court law, have been sustained by a large number of judicial decisions. That proceedings instituted under juvenile court acts and similar statutes are not criminal in their nature has frequently been affirmed by the courts.[1] In an Illinois decision the court said:[2]

"Our statute and those of a similar character treat children coming within their provisions as wards of the State, to be protected, rather than as criminals to be punished, and their purpose is to save them from the possible effects of delinquency and neglect liable to result in their leading a criminal career."

In a Utah case[3] it was held that:

"Such laws are most salutary, and are in no sense criminal and not intended as punishment, but are calculated to save the child from becoming a criminal. The whole and only object of such laws is to provide the child with an environment such as will save him to the State and society as a useful and law-abiding citizen, and to give him the educational requirements necessary to attain that end."

The Supreme Court of Pennsylvania[4] has stated:

"The act is not for the trial of a child charged with crime, but is mercifully to save it from an ordeal, with the prison or penitentiary in its wake, if the child's own good and the best interests of the State justify such salvation. Whether the child deserves to be saved by the State is no more a question for a jury than whether the father, if able to save it, ought to save it. The act is but an exercise by the State of its supreme power over the welfare of its children."

Social Evidence.—The observance of the strict technicalities of procedure has been regarded, as stated before, as not essential in hearings of children's cases, but "rules protecting the essential rights, such as regular process of law provided to produce evidence and to aid courts in testing and weighing, will not be scrapped because the proceeding is a summary one."[5] Cases involving institutional commitment, or deprivation of parents of the child's custody, or removal of the child from the home temporarily should be carefully studied and evidence admitted regarding the fitness of parents, or delinquency of their children, so that the juvenile court will not be regarded as tyrannical. For this reason, Judge

[1] *Supplement to Annual Report of the Attorney General of the United States* for the year 1914, pp. 17–18.

[2] Lindsay *v.* Lindsay, 257 Ill., 328–333.

[3] Mill *v.* Brown, 31 Utah, 473–481.

[4] Commonwealth *v.* Fisher, 213 Pa. St. 48, 54.

[5] Lou, *op. cit.*, p. 129.

E. F. Waite believes that "no judge on any bench has need to be more thoroughly grounded in the principles of evidence and more constantly mindful of them than the judge of the juvenile court."[1] However, the juvenile court need not concern itself with "proof beyond reasonable doubt" but with "preponderance of evidence."[2]   Relative to evidence Dr. Van Waters says:[3]

> In a socialized procedure no useful evidence should be excluded from the court.   Each relevant fact should be admissible, but we should adhere closely to the body of the rules of evidence that applies a test of truth.   Hearsay, incompetent evidence, opinion, gossip, bias, prejudice, trends of hostile neighborhood feeling—all these sources of error should be ruled out of the juvenile court as rigidly as from any other court. . . . The test of truth in the juvenile court should be definite, scientific, carefully scrutinized.

The judge must concern himself with the offender, or as Judge Julian Mack[4] has put it: "How has he become what he is, and what should best be done in his interest and in the interest of the State to save him from a downward career?"   Thus formal evidence must be accompanied by social evidence based on a thorough-going study of all the social and familial conditions, personal history, and characteristics.[5]

Use of Petitions.—Most juvenile court laws provide the use of petitions in order for the court to obtain formally the jurisdiction over a minor.   These petitions (see pp. 150–151) may be filed by any reputable person who has the knowledge of the attendant conditions of the offense and the offender's circumstances. Petitions are most frequently filed by police officers and probation officers but at times by parents, and even by the children themselves.   Petitions allege briefly the facts responsible for bringing the child to the attention of the court and within the provisions of the law.   They include statements as to name, age, place of abode of the offender and his parents or guardian.

The information contained in the petition is generally of a social nature and not in the nature of an indictment, except in a few

[1] *Proceedings of the Conference on Juvenile Court Standards*, U. S. Children's Bureau Publication, No. 97 (1921), p. 59.

[2] *Ibid.*, p. 59.

[3] *Ibid.*, p. 67.

[4] *Op. cit.*, p. 198.

[5] *Cf.* BELDEN, *op. cit.*, p. 9.

jurisdictions in this country, where a child is still subject to criminal court procedure. Lou says:[1]

If the petition is not an indictment, the petitioner is not a prosecutor and is not required to make good his case or to prepare evidence, but he may base his action merely upon information and belief. The filing of a petition is merely a method whereby the people and the court may be informed of the situation which the petitioner alleges to exist, and the people become the real party complainant and must prosecute the proceedings. The filing of the petition is, however, essential to jurisdiction.[2]

When a petition has been formally filed, the case must be heard by the court, no matter what is the result of the investigation. In order to eliminate from the docket cases that have really no basis of fact or that could be easily adjusted without court action, the "complaint," or "information" system is provided in most statutes or adopted, in practice, by most courts. It does not signify the initiation of formal court action but merely the formal report by any person to the court of a condition that in his opinion or belief needs investigation. A petition is authorized to be filed formally only when a preliminary inquiry and investigation show that conditions warrant court action.

A petition may be filed by the person who makes complaint, by a probation officer, or, in a few instances, by a district attorney or a deputy district attorney. Though the filing of petitions by probation officers is a common practice it is undesirable, except for violation of probation or when no other person is willing to file, for it may be confused with prosecution in criminal cases and may, therefore, hamper the work of probation officers. The filing of petitions by district attorneys, of course, savors too much of a prosecution and is practised as an expedient only in small or rural communities. If possible petitions should be filed by parents or qualified social agencies.

The receiving of and passing upon complaints are of great importance, for they give the first impression of the spirit of the juvenile court to the child, the parents, and the public. Officers of the court receiving complaints may be the clerk of the court, the complaint clerk, or the clerk of the probation office. The judge or the officer designated by him examines and passes upon all complaints and, usually after a preliminary investigation of the case, determines whether the case should be dismissed, whether further investigation of the case is necessary, whether the case should be dealt with informally, whether a petition

[1] Lou, *op. cit.*, pp. 99–101. Reprinted by permission of the University of North Carolina Press.

[2] Weber *v.* Doust, 81 Wash. 668 (1914).

should be filed, or whether some other formal action should be taken. The judge usually delegates the power of passing upon complaints to the chief probation officer and, in some cases, to the clerk of the court, the superintendent of the detention home, or some other member of the probation staff. Generally, if any person is aggrieved by the investigation or the decision of persons other than the judge, he can insist upon filing a petition and the case must be heard.

Use of Citations, Summonses, and Warrants.[1]—When the necessary processes are completed and the date set for the hearing in court, the offender and his parents are notified of the hearing through a notice, or summons, or, as in the California courts, through a citation. (See *California Juvenile Court Law*, Sections 4, 4a, 4b.) The service of summons or citation is less formal than a warrant and does not constitute nor imply arrest, but failure to obey it usually constitutes contempt of court.[2] Generally the juvenile court laws specify that these notices must be served a given number of days prior to the hearing. If the notice, summons, or citation does not suffice, warrants are issued to compel the child's parents' attendance in court. Witnesses are served with subpoenas, which are the writs by which they are commanded to appear in court under penalty for failure to do so.

The issuance and service of a summons upon the person having custody of the child is held essential to jurisdiction of children,[3] [but] appearance at the hearing or waiver of notice will give the court jurisdiction even though notice has not been given. On the other hand, some courts hold that while a parent who did not have notice is not bound by a decree depriving him of custody of the child, that part of the decree which declares the child delinquent or dependent is nevertheless valid.[4]

Special Court and Probation Records.[5]—Most juvenile court laws make some provision regarding keeping the records of the cases heard in the juvenile court. Frequently these records,

---

[1] See LENROOT and LUNDBERG, *op. cit.*, p. 201.

[2] That a juvenile court has the inherent right to punish violations of its orders as contempt has been upheld in the United States *v.* Latimer, 44 App. D.C., 91 (1915).

[3] Cited by LOU, *op. cit.*, p. 103, on the basis of Karrib *v.* Baily, 212 Michigan 502 (1921).

[4] Cited by LOU, *op. cit.*, p. 104, on the basis of People *v.* N. Y. Nursery and Child's Hospital, 230 N. Y. 119 (1920).

[5] See *supra*, pp. 139–149.

especially the social case histories, are, by statutory provision, not open to inspection by the public except by special court order.

Juvenile records are of two kinds: legal records and social records.

The legal records consist usually of the petition or complaint, the summons, and warrant, orders of dispositions, the court docket, the daily calendars, and other miscellaneous records. All these legal records, kept by the clerk of the court, are important, for they show that the procedure required by law has been complied with and furnish the basis for statistics on the volume of work, the charges, and the dispositions made. They should be carefully indexed, filed, and kept in such a way that reference to them can readily be made.

The social records of the court, including the social evidence of each case—the investigator's report, the physical and mental diagnosis, the children's probation history, and detention home records—are of vital importance as a part of the equipment of the court for service to children. They are documents which picture the individual human being in his own social setting, describe what he actually did to bring him before the court, and relate his experience in the hands of the probation officer or judge. These records are usually kept by the probation department and are considered confidential.

The amount of information[1] called for on various social records varies in different courts and in different types of cases in the same court. . . . Other records commonly in use, such as the card notifying the child of the conditions of probation or notifying the parents that the child has been placed on probation, school reports, parents' reports, the recommendation for parole or discharge, and reports of violation of probation, are self-explanatory.

In most courts social records are quite inadequate. There is lack of uniformity and a wide difference in definitions, both in laws and in court usages.[2]

For the actual content of court records see the case of Sam Fineberg (pp. 421*ff.*). The obtaining of a comprehensive case history and the recording of the data secured depend on the training of the worker, the case load he carries, the requirements of his department as well as on the nature of the case. (For details of case investigation see pp. 53–91 and for methods of recording, pp. 104–113.)

[1] See *supra*, pp. 107–110, see also pp. 95–96.

[2] Lou, *op. cit.*, pp. 95–96. Reprinted by permission of the University of North Carolina Press.

Jurisdiction over Adults Contributing to Delinquency and Dependency of Minors.—Juvenile court officials early recognized that they must have some jurisdiction over those adults, parents and others, whose "wrongful acts, active encouragement, indifference, or indulgence" are factors in the wrongdoings of children. All states except Iowa have "contributing" laws. These laws provide that contributing to delinquency or dependency on the part of adults is a crime, usually a misdemeanor, punishable by a fine or imprisonment or both, and these adults are to be prosecuted through the usual processes of criminal procedure.[1]

Not all the statutes specify what acts on the part of adults, parents and others, are to be regarded as contributing to delinquency and dependency of children.[2] Contributing generally means desertion or failure to provide for the support of juveniles, violations of child labor law, failure to comply with the compulsory school law, aiding a child to escape from an institution, selling liquor to minors, providing tobacco to inmates of child-caring institutions, enticing minors to and maintaining them in houses of prostitution, permitting minors to remain in gambling houses, pool halls, committing acts of sexual intercourse or lewd and illicit acts, with or without the consent of the minor (a minor cannot legally give consent to such conduct).[3]

When the judge of the juvenile court hears contributing cases he sits as a judge of the criminal court and has all the powers and jurisdiction thereof. The justification offered for extending jurisdiction to adults is based on the fact that such procedure makes it possible to keep children, even as witnesses, away from the criminal court, and that it is easier to deal with the problem as a whole and by one judge rather than to divide the responsibility.[4]

In the Moreland case,[5] the United States Supreme Court held unconstitutional[6] a proceeding instituted against an adult in the juvenile

---

[1] *Ibid.*, p. 56.

[2] See S. P. BRECKENRIDGE and HELEN R. JETER, *A Summary of Juvenile Court Legislation in the United States*, U. S. Children's Bureau Publication, No. 70 (1920), pp. 21–24, 84–85.

[3] See LENROOT and LUNDBERG, *op. cit.*, pp. 8–15.

[4] See SUTHERLAND, *op. cit.*, p. 277.

[5] United States *v.* Moreland, 258 U. S. 433, 42 Sup. Ct. 368 (1922).

[6] See J. H. WIGMORE, "Obstructing the Efficiency of the Juvenile Courts," *Journal of Criminal Law and Criminology*, XIII (August, 1922), 165–167.

court under the statute of the District of Columbia imposing a penalty of imprisonment at hard labor for the crime of failure to provide for a minor child. The fifth amendment of the United States Constitution provides that "no person shall be held to answer for a capital, or other infamous crime, unless on a presentment or indictment of a grand jury." The court held the offense in question, because of the punishment provided, would be an "infamous crime" and therefore the proceeding could be instituted only in the manner prescribed in the Constitution. The practical effect of the decision was to deprive the District of Columbia Juvenile Court of jurisdiction over adults in this type of cases.[1]

However, this decision did not affect the procedure in the various states.[2] "The adult contributing laws vary in scope and efficacy. The jurisdiction of the juvenile court over contributing cases is exclusive in some States and concurrent in others."[3] There are many disagreements as to whether a person who by omission or commission of certain acts generally detrimental to children should be prosecuted without actual proof that such acts or omissions have resulted in a child's delinquency or dependency. Lou regards this as one of the most significant legal questions in contributing cases and concludes that the "weight of opinion seems to be that an adult's guilt of contributing to delinquency should not depend on the child's becoming delinquent,"[4] if these statutes are to be regarded in the spirit of prevention of delinquency as well as punishing the adult offender against the child. He maintains:[5]

Although adult contributory laws have been in force in many states for a number of years and have been uniformly approved, it can be stated with reasonable accuracy that, with the exception of a few places, these laws have not been generally enforced and have not produced the results anticipated. The enforcement of these laws, like the enforcement of any other law, depends largely upon the facilities of the court, the zeal of the officers, and the sentiment of the community. The increasing number of contributing cases in recent years shows a new vigor in enforcing these laws, but these cases deal mainly with cases of

[1] Comment by Shelden D. Elliott, editor of this section.
[2] See REUBEN OPPENHEIMER, "Infamous Crimes and the Moreland Case," *Harvard Law Review*, XXXVI (January, 1923), 299–320.
[3] LOU, *op. cit.*, p. 56.
[4] *Ibid.*, p. 59.
[5] *Ibid.*, p. 59. Quoted by permission of the University of North Carolina Press.

offenses against these children, especially sex offenses, punishable by other statutes in the jurisdiction. They are in reality preferred charges. These laws remain to be enforced more vigorously in those cases for which they are mainly intended. In order to handle this class of cases properly, one and the same court—a juvenile court—must have both criminal and chancery jurisdiction, including the power to suspend sentence and to use probationary supervision, so that proper treatment may be given.

Many court workers maintain that "behind many delinquencies committed by minors there is always an adult who can be held responsible for these acts." Obviously if juvenile delinquency is to be attacked at its roots, such an attack should include not only enforcement of adult contributory laws but also social study, treatment, and education of these adults in their responsibilities to children and their communities.[1]

DETENTION OF JUVENILES IN SPECIAL HALLS

Most juvenile court laws make some provision for the temporary custody and care of children during the interval between apprehension and the disposition of the case. These laws prohibit detaining children under sixteen years of age in jails and police stations, but in actuality such practice is far too common.[2] Such practices are used because of the lack of more suitable facilities or because of the belief that detention of certain types of boys in jail is safer than among children in a detention home. Girls are seldom detained in jails or police stations. Many county jails have special juvenile "tanks" for boys over sixteen years.

Generally, however, the child is allowed to remain in his own home with instructions to appear for the hearing, or a citation or summons is served on the parents or guardian to bring him to court for the hearing. Detention homes are sometimes used for other purposes, such as housing lost children, homeless children, foundlings, children awaiting admission to institutions, children on probation who do not have suitable homes, feeble-minded

---

[1] See Chaps. XVIII–XX.

[2] See *Dependent and Delinquent Children in Georgia*, U. S. Children's Bureau Publication, No. 161 (1926), pp. 10–14; see also KATHERINE F. LENROOT, "Progressive Methods of Care of Children Pending Juvenile Court Hearings," *Proceedings of the National Probation Association* (1926), p. 216.

children, and mothers with illegitimate babies. Many of these practices depend upon local conditions and local needs. It may be said in general that such a mixed lot of inmates might result in a complex institution very difficult to administer.[1]

Florence M. Warner,[2] who has made a comprehensive study of juvenile detention service in the United States, says:

In determining whether a particular child should be released or detained many factors are to be considered. Runaways, older children, federal offenders, and delinquents whose offenses are serious are most likely to be held. Children apprehended at night are also held as a general rule, and material witnesses are detained in many places, frequently without adequate justification. The distance of the detention home from the place of apprehension sometimes is a factor in the decision. . . .

Detention is also affected by social factors. Children from families of known good standing, in which the parents have money enough to pay the bills for damage done, are not likely to be held. An investigator was told about four boys who broke into a house in process of construction, damaging it to the extent of more than two thousand dollars. In this city it is the rule that all children apprehended by the police are taken to the detention home, but in the case of these boys this was not done, nor were they even brought into the juvenile court. The police took them to their parents and private arrangements were made for payment of the damage. Children from poorer neighborhoods in this same city are detained when their offenses involve only a few dollars of property damage.

Court policy in regard to dependency and neglect cases varies according to the resources of the community. Sometimes, as in the Boston Juvenile Court, the private or public children's agencies have the entire case-work responsibility for dependent and neglected children, the court functioning simply in legal decision and disposition. Detention in such circumstances rests on agencies other than the court. When responsibility for investigation and supervision of dependency cases is in the hands of the court, the public detention home is extensively used, but this does not preclude use of other institutions, public or private, for special cases. A policy agreement or a tacit understanding between the court and these other agencies frequently permits them to enter children in the detention home or to secure their release without recourse to court order. . . .

[1] Lou, *op. cit.*, p. 107.
[2] *Juvenile Detention in the United States*, pp. 21–22, 146–147. Reprinted by permission of the University of Chicago Press.

Detention is usually presumed to be the care of children pending disposition by the court. It is the method of caring for children which was inaugurated when children were taken out from under the old criminal law and given into the jurisdiction of the juvenile court with chancery proceedings. . . .

While detention is presumed to be a method of caring for children for the court, yet it appears that many children held in detention never have formal court hearings. In some communities the detention home has degenerated into a sort of "parking station" for children, and almost any person can bring a child to the detention home and leave him until called for. A plan not involving formal court hearing is more probable for girls than for boys, and for white than for Negro children. It is evident that the probation officers have more facilities for treatment for certain groups than for others.

Boys predominate in all types of detention facilities, except in private orphanages or homes, where girls slightly outnumber them. The ratio of boys to girls in jails and police stations is four to one, and in public detention homes, seven to three.

Negro children appear to be detained more frequently than white children. Whether they actually commit more offenses than do white children in the same economic group and living in the same type of neighborhood is not known. All that can be said is that the Negro children are detained away from their homes two and a half times their proportion in the general population. Especially in the jails is the percentage of Negro children high, for approximately one-half of the children detained in jails are Negro children. It was also found that there is a much larger proportionate use of northern detention facilities for Negro children than of southern.

In the larger juvenile courts clinical and laboratory study facilities are a part of the detention home. (For a more detailed discussion see pp. 596–625.) Often it is inadvisable to detain a child for clinical examination, since he could remain at home and be brought to the clinic at an appointed time for these examinations. When clinical observations are necessary the child, of course, should remain in detention. In spite of the fact that some children gain weight and respond to the discipline in the detention home, they should be detained only when no other provision can or should be made. A child should be detained only for the period of the clinical examination.

The length of detention in each case should be as short as possible. This may be accomplished through frequent court hearings, prompt investigation of cases, a sufficient court staff to expedite the movement of cases, adequate facilities for institutional care, and adequate means for ascertaining promptly the home conditions and the possibilities of care by the parents.[1]

If we apply Frank Tannenbaum's belief regarding penitentiary imprisonment to juvenile detention, we must realize that detention is the worst form of treatment which could be given to some types of offenders because it has the effect of focusing their attention on the fact which caused them to be prisoners.

Idle words and chance happenings have little meaning in the lives of people and are generally soon forgotten, but if you emphasize a situation and say that because of that situation they are to be [detained] . . . then their attention is focused on that particular situation.[2]

William I. and Dorothy S. Thomas observe:[3]

The conception of a juvenile detention home contained a fundamental misapprehension as to the effect of the congregation of young boys who had shown bad behavior tendencies. As adults we have a naive way of thinking of influence as transmitted from the older generation to the younger, and we appreciate the point that it is a horrible practice to place young children with old criminals, while influences seem to spread more rapidly laterally, as between members of a younger generation, than vertically, as between members of different generations. The congregation, therefore, of bad boys in juvenile homes and reformatories has had unexpectedly bad consequences. A preadaptation to influence, a somewhat correspondent stage of maturation and of situation have to be present or the influence is not transmitted. Thus, the influence of the example of a hardened and coarse woman might be revolting to the young girl, while the wild behavior of another young girl might serve as a stimulus and example. Similarly, young boys seem to be influenced toward bad behavior more positively by the tough boys under sixteen in the detention homes than by the old criminals in jails.

In his life history, Stanley of the *Jack-Roller*[4] calls the detention home "the baby band-house." His accounts of the experiences and contacts in juvenile detention homes are indicative of the moral atmosphere, nature, and effect of discipline, and the attitudes of the inmates of many detention homes.

[1] Lou, *op. cit.*, p. 106.

[2] Quoted by JUSTIN MILLER, "The Law and Probation," *Year Book of the National Probation Association* (1931), p. 86.

[3] *The Child in America*, p. 96.

[4] By Clifford Shaw, pp. 57, 68.

The detention home at first seemed like a palace to me. It was clean and in order. The very first night I took a nice bath (the first one I ever had), had a change of clothes, and a good meal. I felt like I'd never want to go back to that "old hole" (home) with my stepmother. I went to bed in a clean white bed, and I thought, "Well, is this jail? Who ever thought it was so nice?" But alas! my childish impressions were soon to be rudely shattered.

Inside the Detention Home I found a motley crowd of aspiring young crooks—young aspirants to the "hall of fame of crookdom." In their own minds they had already achieved fame in the world of crime, and proceeded to impress that fact upon the other boys. The whole thing seemed to be a lively contest, among young crooks, to see who was the biggest and bravest crook. . . .

The institution had too much discipline. I was very scared and frightened, and put into submission from the first till I was released. Physically I was a slave, but mentally I was free, and I took advantage of this freedom and dreamed. . . . I got lonely and sullen and full of fear, but my dreams kept me alive, and I dreamed every day. There I started to be a dreamer of dreams. . . . I wanted a chance to make good for I had the ambition, but who would monkey with a little mite like me?

Improvement of Detention Policy.—Florence Warner makes the following observations regarding the improvement of detention policy:[1]

The number of escapes from detention is large when consideration is given to the attempts made to hold the children by physical means, such as locks and bars. Some of the children take serious risks in their breaks for freedom. Many of them are held in the upper floors of buildings, and in attempts to escape there is grave danger of accident. The method of keeping the children occupied with a rich program, adequate supervision, and a competent personnel is the best safeguard against escapes.

A thoughtful consideration of the problem of detention strengthens the conviction that much of the difficulty could be obviated by competent workers to handle the problems of the children, dependent and delinquent. Much detention could be entirely avoided if family agencies were staffed with skillful, trained social workers, with sufficient funds to meet the needs of the family. Additional trained probation officers are greatly needed in many of the juvenile and other courts

[1] *Op. cit.*, pp. 148–150. Reprinted by permission of the University of Chicago Press.

handling children's cases. Children are too frequently sidetracked in the detention home by busy probation officers and workers in the agencies. Much recidivism could be prevented by good case work, which requires trained social workers with a moderate case load. The large number of children who come back again and again to the detention home and to the court shows a definite lack of wisdom in treating their problems. There is also a great need for trained workers in the detention home itself. If the admitting officer were a case-worker with authority to refuse to accept children, and with a knowledge of community resources so that she could refer them to the proper agency to care for their needs, the children's problems would be more ably treated. This same person might well be charged with the duty of speeding the departure of children from the detention home. Furthermore, if the detention home is to be used for purposes of observation, then worthwhile results can only be accomplished if the attendants are able to make observations of value.

Competent social workers in the social agencies and in the probation office, coupled with a socially minded judge of the juvenile court, will go far toward solving the problems of detention. Such a corps of workers for children will see that juveniles are not detained in jails or almshouses. Such a group will stir up the general public to see that there are funds for foster placement and other treatment resources for the care of the children who need such services. Such a group of workers will bring pressure to bear so that the juvenile court, the probation office, and the detention home are kept free from politics. The crying need is for trained social workers and for socially minded juvenile court judges.

Of course, detention practices and policies differ in various parts of the country. Juvenile Hall in Los Angeles is regarded as having one of the most up-to-date plants. On the whole, it should be the aim of any agency to avoid congregating and segregating children on the basis of their delinquencies. It is of importance to know that the juvenile court of Boston has avoided any detention home. It has used carefully selected and supervised boarding homes instead, "thus avoiding at the outset any institutional experience, and has placed the largest possible number of cases in foster homes."[1] It goes without saying that these homes should be under the supervision of a Department of Public Welfare and should be carefully selected on the basis of the fitness of boarding home parents to care for problem children and to insure their presence in court for the hearing.

[1] THOMAS and THOMAS, *op. cit.*, pp. 125–126.

COOPERATION OF THE JUVENILE COURT WITH PRIVATE AGENCIES

The juvenile court dealing with child welfare and family problems has seen from the earliest inception the necessity of cooperating with private agencies in the field of child welfare. We have already discussed the court's use of the social service exchange (see pp. 58–59), and the consultation with the various agencies reported by the exchange as having a record of the case (see pp. 59–61).

The Juvenile Protective Association, or, as it is in some cities called, the Children's Protective Association, generally works in close cooperation with the court. Helen R. Jeter[1] in a comprehensive study of the *Chicago Juvenile Court* (applicable to most juvenile courts) points out the relation of the juvenile court to the Juvenile Protective Association and to other private agencies:

The Juvenile Protective Association confines its attention to cases of a less serious nature, in which it is thought court action will prove to be unnecessary. Cases that seem to call for court action are referred directly to the court without preliminary investigation by the association. The Association also does work that the court does not feel it can undertake, such as the investigation of anonymous complaints and work of a detective nature. All such work that comes to the attention of the court is turned over to this association. In turning over cases that seem too trivial to require court action, the court uses its own discretion. If the situation is such that action, but not necessarily court action, appears to be required at once, the case is ordinarily referred to the association. If, on the other hand, this does not become evident until the officers of the court have made a partial or complete investigation, it is often thought better for the court, which is familiar with the facts and through its officers has established relations with the family, to continue the work. This is especially true if it seems at all probable that court action may be necessary later. . . .

The Jewish agencies maintain in relation to the court the same policy that they hold with reference to most organizations, namely, that Jewish families can be dealt with more intelligently by Jewish workers and Jewish organizations and that these organizations alone should work with them. The court has acquiesced in this policy to a large extent, and at the present time the great majority of Jewish cases are handled by Jewish agencies with the power and authority of the court

[1] U. S. Children's Bureau Publication, No. 104 (1922), pp. 100–104.

behind them.[1] All complaints that are received regarding Jewish families are turned over to the Jewish Social Service Bureau for investigation. This agency investigates and keeps a record of its work in its own office; it does not, however, report to the court the details of the inquiry or what action it has taken. If it is thought that court action is necessary, a conference is held of representatives of the three Jewish agencies . . . if the court orders probation or appoints a guardian, a representative of the Jewish agencies is always named as the probation officer or guardian. If the order is "guardianship with the right to place in a home," the agency makes no further report to the court. If, on the other hand, the order is probation, the representative of the agency is nominally at least under the supervision of the head of the family-supervision division and submits written reports to the court in accordance with rules covering reports on probation cases.

The court comes in constant contact with the United Charities since many cases, both dependent and delinquent, have at some time been known to that agency. No formal plan of cooperation now exists. At one time the society maintained an officer at the court, and recently one visitor of the society was assigned to all cases involving action in any court. These plans, however, have at the present time been abandoned. The probation officers are invited by the United Charities to attend district case conferences but rarely find themselves able to accept this invitation.

Successful cooperation often depends, of course, upon the willingness of other social agencies, both public and private, to carry through plans initiated by officers of the court. The work of the court can be rendered futile by the failure of the agency on which it must rely for special service.

---

[1] Miss Irene Kawin, Chief Deputy Probation Officer, Juvenile Court of Cook County, comments on this point:

"It is true that we generally refer complaints on Jewish cases to the Jewish Social Service Bureau. If the complainants refuse to go there, we, of course, must accept the complaint; however, that Agency does not act 'with the power and authority of the court behind' it. If that Agency finds that such power and authority are needed, the case is then referred to the court and our own officer makes the investigation. We work cooperatively with the Jewish Social Service Bureau and utilize material from their records. Where a Jewish child is placed on probation, our own officer takes charge. When children are committed to the guardianship of the Jewish Home Finding Society, that Organization is expected to make a semiannual report to the court. Some years ago the Jewish Social Service Bureau had a worker assigned to the court as a probation officer, but that is not the situation at present." (Personal Communication, Sept. 3, 1936.)

FEDERAL JUVENILE OFFENDERS

Offenders, whether juvenile or adult, who violate laws dealing with liquor, immigration, motor-vehicle thefts, mail robbery, kidnapping, smuggling, interstate commerce, white slavery, and so on come under the jurisdiction of the federal criminal courts.

The federal courts until 1931 followed the traditional criminal procedure in dealing with juvenile offenders. There are many cases on record[1] of children under the age of sixteen years who were dealt with in the federal courts according to strict criminal procedure, as illustrated by the following typical case.[2]

Two brothers, fifteen and sixteen years of age, were indicted in February, 1919, on the same charge, that of stealing mail from hall letterboxes. The first boy had been arrested prior to indictment, but his brother was not arrested until May. The parents were dead. One boy lived with his maternal grandparents; the other, and his sister, had been living with the paternal grandparents, but had been turned out of the home and at the time of the trouble was living with an uncle. Both of the boys had been before the juvenile court for previous offenses, one having been dismissed by that court and the other having been placed under suspended sentence to the state industrial school. Subsequent to the federal cases, the probation officer of the juvenile court reported that the boy had left his uncle's home and had not returned. Court procedure was as follows:

Feb. 4. First boy arrested; placed in jail.

Feb. 6. Removed from one county jail to another.

Feb. 14. Released from jail.

Feb. 27. Both boys indicted and bench warrant issued for the one not arrested. Bond set for first boy $1,500.

Mar. 6. Plea of not guilty entered by first boy.

May 9. Cause continued for trial to May 16.

May 12. Bench warrants issued.

May 14. Cause continued for trial to May 16.

May 16. Second boy arrested.

May 17. First boy, pleas of "not guilty" withdrawn and plea of "guilty" entered.

May 17. Second boy, plea of "guilty" entered.

May 17. Trial of both boys proceeds.

May 19. Motion of new trial entered. Cause continued for hearing to June 2.

June 2. Motion for new trial. Cause continued to June 7.

[1] See MIRIAM VAN WATERS, *The Child Offender in the Federal System of Justice*, The National Commission on Law Observance and Enforcement, 1931.

[2] *The Federal Courts and the Delinquent Child*, U. S. Children's Bureau Publication, No. 103 (1922), pp. 61–63.

June 7.   Motion for new trial.   Cause continued for sentence to Sept. 15.
Order entered canceling bond of first boy.   Defendant released on own
recognizance.
Sept. 15.   Cause continued to Nov. 17.
Nov. 17.   Both boys fined $5.00 and no costs.
Dec. 20.   Fine paid.

The above situation has greatly changed in recent years,
particularly since Dr. Van Waters' study for the National Commission on Law Observance and Enforcement on the *Child
Offender in the Federal System of Justice*, in 1931.   The U. S.
Children's Bureau Publication, *Facts about Juvenile Delinquency*,[1]
brings the situation up to date:

Boys and girls come into conflict with certain Federal laws as well as
with the State laws.   The problem of providing satisfactory care for
children who have violated Federal laws is complicated by a dual
judicial system whereby children are subject to both State and Federal
laws.   Except in Federal territory the Federal Government has never
made provision for special treatment of juvenile offenders in courts.
They are subject to arrest, jail detention, and public trial in accordance
with criminal procedure, just as though they were adults.   The Federal
Government maintains the national training school for boys and girls
in the District of Columbia and vicinity to receive delinquent children
committed by Federal courts throughout the country and from the
District of Columbia Juvenile Court.   Arrangements are made with
certain State and local institutions by the Federal Government for the
care of juvenile offenders.   It was not until 1925 that Federal courts
had authority to place children or adults on probation, and it was not
until 1930 that definite steps were taken to provide sufficient probation
officers even to begin to meet the demands made upon them.
A comprehensive study of methods of dealing with juvenile Federal
offenders was made by Dr. Miriam Van Waters, for the National Commission on Law Observance and Enforcement, under the joint auspices
of that organization and the White House Conference.   The principal
recommendation was as follows:
"It is recommended that the Federal Government recognize the
concept of juvenile delinquency and withdraw the child offender from
the ordinary operation of Federal penal justice save in cases in which
the local processes for dealing with delinquent children prove to be
or plainly are inadequate.   The precise nature of legislation required

[1] Publication No. 215 (1935), pp. 33–35; see also Publication No. 232,
op. cit., pp. 78–114.

to accomplish this result will have to be determined by expert legal research. The Federal law should have the same opportunity for the protection of childhood that States have achieved."

A circular issued by the Attorney General, August 14, 1931, to all United States attorneys, commissioners, marshals, bureau of investigation agents in charge, and prohibition administrators, stated that the policy established "is that, wherever practicable and consistent with the due enforcement of Federal statutes, juvenile delinquents who come into Federal custody will promptly be returned to the communities from which they come, for care and supervision or punishment by the State authorities." "You are requested," the circular states, "to execute this policy in dealing with cases coming under your supervision until legislation is passed authorizing it." A short time before the issuance of this circular the Attorney General requested the Children's Bureau to cooperate with the Bureau of Prisons of the Department of Justice in developing a program of State and local cooperation with Federal authorities in the treatment of juvenile cases. With the approval of the Secretary of Labor, this work was undertaken by the Children's Bureau. Through the cooperation of the two bureaus, steps have been taken to develop a Federal-State working relation that will increase utilization of local resources and special provisions for Federal offenders in the areas in which adequate local care cannot be secured.

On June 11, 1932, President Hoover issued [a] statement at the White House . . . [authorizing] the United States attorney of the district in which any person under twenty-one years of age has been arrested for a Federal offense to forego prosecution in a Federal court and to surrender him to State jurisdiction under the following conditions: (1) If after investigation by the Department of Justice it appears that he has committed a criminal offense or is a delinquent under the laws of any State that can and will assume jurisdiction over him and will take him into custody and deal with him according to its laws, and (2) if such surrender will be to the best interest of the United States and of the juvenile offender. The bill further provides that the juvenile offender must signify his willingness to be returned or his return must be demanded by the executive authority of the State. Expenses incident to the transportation are to be paid from the appropriations for salaries, fees, and expenses of United States marshals.

It soon became apparent, however—particularly through the work of the Children's Bureau in the evaluation of local resources—that the problem of the federal juvenile offender could not be dealt with according to the policy originally announced, that is, of turning these juveniles back to their own states.   Carl B. Hyatt, Special Attorney, United States Department of Justice, writes:[1]

For the calendar year 1935, there were 2,106 cases of Federal juvenile offenders.   In 1,573 of the 2,106 cases in which age was reported the offender was over the juvenile-court age of his state, while in 528 cases he was within juvenile-court age.   Theoretically then, 75 per cent of the cases were a Federal responsibility, while 25 per cent should have been handled through some State agency.   Actually this division cannot be made.   Three hundred and twenty-one of the 528 offenders of juvenile-court age came from 14 states, mostly southern states, in which the juvenile courts or institutions, or both, are generally inadequate, while only 189 came from the remainder of the United States.   Eighteen came from Alaska.   In other words, 14 states and Alaska contributed 64 per cent of the offenders of juvenile-court age, while 34 states contributed only 36 per cent.   The probable explanation of this is that a large proportion of the juveniles who violate Federal laws in the 34 states do not appear in the statistics, because they are diverted at the source, as they should be, to local resources. . . . There are almost 50 State systems of juvenile courts and laws in the United States, each system containing various types of social practice.   In fact, there are almost as many different juvenile court systems as there are juvenile courts, each highly local in nature, each more or less a law unto itself, and each possessing the strength or weakness of the particular locality or leadership.   Some are expressive of the most forward looking thought, and others represent the worst of the past.   It is recognized that the treatment afforded by many State juvenile courts and local agencies is constructive.   These courts and agencies should be utilized to the fullest extent.   It is also recognized that, because of the uneven development of State juvenile courts and agencies and the widely varying jurisdictions, the Department of Justice must retain custody of, and assume responsibility for developing constructive treatment for, many juveniles.   Carrying out this responsibility involves:

1. Continuing instruction of Federal officials in policies with regard to social investigation and proper detention care pending hearing.   In view of the harmful effects of jail detention, specific instructions have been issued that so far as possible such detention is to be avoided.   United States probation officers are also specifically instructed to make prompt and thorough investigation into the cases of juveniles charged with the violation of Federal laws and to afford intensive socialized treatment to those placed on probation.

[1] Quoted by permission from manuscript subsequently published with modifications as "New Treatment for the Federal Juvenile Offender," *Yearbook, National Probation Association* (1936), pp. 292–297.

2. Individualized study of cases of all juveniles committed to institutions, prior to designation of specific institutions by the Attorney General. When institutional treatment is determined upon by the Federal court, the court sentences the juvenile to an institution to be designated by the Attorney General. The designation of an institution best fitted to meet the needs of the juvenile is then made, following study of comprehensive reports submitted by the United States probation officer of the district from which he was sentenced.

In undertaking this work the Department of Justice is necessarily interested in the general problem of juvenile delinquency and its treatment and not merely in the program for the Federal juvenile offender. The solution of the problem of the latter lies not in the legal transfer, not in the changing of jurisdiction at one stroke of the pen, but in the raising of standards and the level of their achievement throughout the land, so that juvenile courts can deal more adequately with all offenders. The problem of the child is common to all juvenile courts, and all must prepare themselves for the common task. Needless differences in law and procedure must be faced and eventually eliminated. A youthful offender must not be regarded as a child in one jurisdiction and as a man in another. His socialized treatment must not depend upon whether he lives in the North, South, East, or West, nor upon whether he is a State or a Federal offender.

The Department of Justice recognizes that the care of the juvenile offender is primarily a task for the juvenile court. But in a broader sense, the local responsibility, which it thus recognizes, embraces the community of social forces dealing with child welfare, of which the juvenile court is only a part. Unless there is a mutual helpfulness between the court and outside agencies there is little left for the law except physical force. Unquestionably many social forces in the community have not as yet been harnessed and coordinated effectively against delinquency. Prevention and treatment do not depend upon the strength of the court within itself nor upon any one agency but upon the strength and power of combined efforts. Real advancement in solving social problems involving delinquency will be made in the future, not through the courts alone but through those activities that condition, train and readjust the individual.

The Children's Bureau, in close cooperation with the Bureau of Prisons, remains active in visiting state and local institutions in order to ascertain plans, programs, and facilities for the care and treatment of federal juvenile offenders and to acquaint the state and local officials with the policies of and plans for cooperation with the Department of Justice with regard to these offenders. As Carl B. Hyatt ably pointed out the program for these offenders can be effective only when local officials recognize the value of and utilize all of the social forces and agencies working in behalf of children. Officials also need to become more intimately acquainted with modern scientific procedures not only in regard to the physical care of the offender and administrative policies of institutions but with regard to the social treatment of the individual offender.

STATE SUPERVISION OF JUVENILE PROBATION

John Plover,[1] Supervisor of Probation, State of California, says that "state supervision of probation is, and must continue increasingly to be, a most necessary part of this modern plan of treating certain types of individuals who have violated laws." He continues:

Adult probation and its administration are not a local function. Generally the offender violates a State law and the tribunal hearing his case is established in conformity with State law and is in part supported by State funds.

In case incarceration of the offender is necessary, commitment is usually made to an institution directed and maintained by the State. In these days, when the cost of institutional care is so very high, the State should be interested in the support of a plan which will not only turn offenders away from a life of crime but will also materially reduce the cost of caring for those who have defied the law.

So, too, in the realm of Juvenile probation. The Juvenile Court Law is a State law, administered by a State court and using for the care of certain juveniles the facilities of institutions and schools established and maintained by the State.

The advantage and economy of a well-developed program of probation administration are well known to those actively engaged in the furtherance of this program, but there still remains a very large group of the general public ignorant of the real purpose and progress of the probation plan.

The State has a definite responsibility in the education of the average citizen to a better understanding of probation, in order that necessary moral and financial support may be forthcoming.

The State has an obligation in knowing that any person, adult or juvenile, who violates a law of the State shall have that treatment which will guarantee scientific and adequate consideration to the offender as well as proper protection to society.

Citizens of the State should be interested in the success and development of all plans of treatment for problem individuals, and there should

[1] Paper especially prepared for this volume by John Plover, July 20, 1936.

be developed an adequate plan for the gathering on a State-wide scale of statistical information. This is achieved through reports from probation officers, which may be used to indicate the scope and the success of the probation scheme. Such information should be distributed in the form of annual reports containing figures regarding the efficiency and the financial cost of this governmental activity.

Probation, both Adult and Juvenile, is now in reality a judicial function, an enlarging of the court's authority, under a State law to administer treatment to the delinquent. Such being the case, there is absolute necessity of developing State-wide standards of probation, to the end that the program will be administered by properly trained officials whose salaries are adequate and whose case load is not excessive.

State supervision of probation should be instrumental in raising probation standards so that those engaged in this work shall be placed on a professional basis. Educational qualifications should be high, and stress should be laid upon raising general standards of this service. Progress is being made in this particular phase of probation work, and courts are requiring evidence of knowledge and experience from those applying for positions on the probation staff.

To those who have through the years followed the probation program, there has come the belief that the State should follow this program with enthusiasm, to the end that beneficial results may be obtained by proper administration in all of the courts of the State handling criminal cases.

In the development of proper administration, the State should offer to judges and probation officers assistance based on research and experience in the proper handling of the various types of problem cases.

It is possible for the State to arrange for regional and State conferences of probation officials, for the consideration of problem cases, interpretations of procedure, and general standards of administration. To these conferences may be brought outstanding individuals as consultants and instructors.

Crime is the problem of youth, and the State must be interested in a program looking to the prevention of delinquency. The State, under proper direction, can educate and direct courts and probation officials to the necessity of organizing their communities to a realization of responsibility in eliminating those local factors that make for improper social conditions, lawlessness and delinquency.

It is hoped that a program of State supervision of probation will, in addition to its services in the way of education, be able to materially assist in the raising of personal standards by providing for certain subsidies to local probation groups. This plan is in keeping with present tendencies in other fields of social work, and there would seem to be no objection to applying to probation administration the general principles of the Federal Security Law.

A well-organized plan of State supervision should include in addition to a central administrative body, these essentials:

1. Every court administering either Juvenile or Adult probation should be required to have a sufficient number of properly trained and competent probation officers who must meet the qualifications set by the State.

2. When a local government has met the standards as to the number of officers, their qualifications and their salaries, the State should assist in the cost of the probation service.

Twenty-one of the States in the Union provide for some State supervision of probation. This type of service ranges from that which is in five states entirely supported by State funds, to that which is purely formal and consists merely of routine reports from the local groups to the central State organization.

In Great Britain the Criminal Justice Act of 1925 made provision by which the support of the cost of probation is jointly borne by local and national governments.

Probation is one of the most effectual means of treating certain types of individuals who have transgressed the law, and the State must show more leadership if probation is to find its real place in our plan of criminal procedure.

Franklin D. Roosevelt, in his book *Looking Forward*[1] says:

"Every scrap of authentic information from those who have been waging war against crime and criminals, night and day, reveals that there is but one way to reduce crime. That is through a policy of prevention. . . .

"If the criminal's past history gives good reason to believe that he is not of the naturally criminal type, that he is capable of real reform and of becoming a useful citizen, there is no doubt that probation, viewed from the selfish standpoint of protection to society alone, is the most efficient method that we have. And yet it is the least understood, the least developed, the least appreciated of all our efforts to rid society of the criminal. . . . By its intelligent extension, crime can be decreased, the overcrowded conditions in our penal institutions greatly ameliorated, and the necessity for building more and more prisons, for needlessly and ineffectively spending huge prison budgets, reduced. . . .

"It is a state's affair and this whole matter of probation should be made the state's business and put under wise state control. . . . I hope that in all states we shall be continually decreasing the number of prison guards and wardens and increasing the number of our parole and probation officers."

(To be concluded)

[1] P. 209.

CHAPTER XII

THE JUVENILE COURT FROM THE POINT OF VIEW OF ADMINISTRATIVE LAW *(Concluded)*

Methods of Treatment by the Court.—The disposition of cases in a juvenile court is in theory never punitive, but protective and educative. The court prescribes methods of treatment on the basis of the particular needs of each individual case. The probation department, child-caring institutions, and other social agencies in the community are depended upon to provide training and supervision to children either in their homes or in family homes. There are four methods which judges generally use in disposing of children's cases: dismissals, probation, home placement, and commitment. These will be considered here only as to their legal aspects.

Dismissals.—If a case is adjusted informally, it may be dismissed by the court without a hearing. If the evidence is not substantiated or is insufficient or is of too trivial a nature, or if the age of a child or other circumstances which made a court adjudication action inadvisable, the case may be dismissed without a hearing, or often only a preliminary hearing. When cases are left to the court to be fully adjusted they are dismissed after the court is satisfied that the probationer has made good, which in some cases may require a period of several years and many court hearings.

Probation.[1]—Since so large a part of this volume has been devoted to methods and principles of probation we need to concern ourselves here only with certain aspects not mentioned before. Charles Chute maintains:[2]

Probation, together with its co-partner, parole, is the application of the methods of social case work to delinquent people, delinquent

---

[1] See Chaps. XIV, XV, XIX.
[2] CHARLES L. CHUTE, "Probation in a Community Welfare Program," *Proceedings of the National Conference of Social Work* (1933), pp. 136, 138–139, 142, 144–145.

families, and delinquent situations.   It is the most important branch of corrective treatment from the point of view of the social worker.   The police, the courts, the prisons, and reformatories operate on a different principle, if the truth is told.   They seek to protect society through the apprehension, prosecution, and punishment of offenders.   Probation, broadly conceived, is the substitution of individualized treatment for mass punishment, whether it is applied in the court, by the police, or through an institution.   More strictly, probation substitutes social investigation and treatment by a community agency attached to the court for the earlier repressive methods of handling crime prescribed by penal law.   In considering probation in a community social welfare program we are not dealing with an outside agency but with one of the integral factors in any well-rounded community welfare program today. . . .

Probation departments should: (1) Handle cases through the court as provided by law to the end that children should receive protection and adjustment, and that adult probationers be carefully selected and assisted toward rehabilitation.   (2) Take leadership in the field of prevention of delinquency by (*a*) arousing community responsibility toward early adjustment of behavior problems; (*b*) co-ordinating local facilities, bringing together for united action the individuals, agencies, and institutions interested in the prevention of delinquency. . . . (3) . . . "establish in the community a consciousness of juvenile problems so that it will come to accept its proper share of the responsibility." . . . (4) Do a good job for the court through investigation, analysis, advice, and supervision of probationers.   (5) By maintaining co-operative relations with public and private agencies, influencing removal of causative factors of delinquency.   (6) By proper publicity, win public approval to the cause of the new social jurisprudence.

Criteria for judging the success of a probation case:

a. Was the agency right in accepting the case for adjustment, either at the beginning or at a later date?   Would the case have been better off had the agency not accepted it?

b. Should the case have been closed sooner?

c. Was there quality and promptness in investigation, diagnosis, and plan of treatment?

d. Was there effective co-operation with other agencies?

e. Were the rules of probation well carried out?

f. Was the adjustment achieved?

A professor who has made many court studies would judge probation by "the social records of the court, the size of case loads per officer, the number of contacts in follow-up work, and the reduction of the recidivist rate."

Another by "higher regard on the part of the community for the 'treatment' of the offender; recognition of different classes among offenders as to their condition and the circumstances of their offending." Still another states that we must also judge probation by "the effectiveness with which it utilizes existing agencies and the progress made in the community toward preventing crime." . . .

Summing up, probation is the social worker's most important direct attack upon the problem of crime and delinquency. Not only should it furnish the court with social diagnosis and individual treatment, but it should take an active part in educating the courts and the public to a social and scientific attitude toward delinquency, and it should cooperate and often lead in preventive measures.

As yet a large majority of probation departments fall far short of accomplishing these objectives; very few embrace the opportunity for public education and preventive work.

The reasons enumerated for failures and shortcomings are many but may be summed up in the statement that the public as yet does not appreciate the importance and economy (using the term in its broadest sense) of well-equipped probation service for all courts and so has failed to establish and support it. Added to this is the inertia of the judicial establishment and its local control and the dangers of American politics. However, none of these handicaps is insuperable. Some departments are functioning successfully and others are making progress. The securing of a trained personnel is the *sine qua non* of probation today. Probation work must stand or fall on the results it obtains, but these are difficult to measure. There is need to develop criteria of judgment based on research and case studies.

Adequate machinery for evaluating probation work is lacking, but hopeful beginnings have been made by state bureaus, by universities, through research studies, by local and state committees, and by national organizations.

Probation departments must become self-critical, must analyze their own results. There is need for greater cooperation from social agencies and from other services whose interests are related to those of the probation officer. And, finally, the need is indicated for increased supervision, to improve personnel and develop standards, and for financial assistance from the state and national government. With the attainment of these objectives, probation service will increasingly take its important place in the community social welfare program.

The primary purposes of probation are to keep the offender in his own home and community, if the situations warrant it, to avoid the stigma and the disadvantages of institutional commitment, and to train and reeducate him in a "normal" environment and within "normal" social relations. However, probation is not for everyone. Selective methods (see pp. 621–622) must be adopted. Probation should be used only when the social study indicates that the offender can profit by it and that "the seed of probation will fall on fertile soil." Of course, the results of probation and supervision depend as much on the training, equipment, and the administrative facilities of the probation officer and the department as on the circumstances and character of the probationer. Probation is regarded as useful especially for young or first offenders. The results of probation have been severely criticized (see index); however, the criticism has not been directed against the principles and philosophy underlying probation but rather against fragmentary procedure, untrained personnel, and unwise selection of probationers.

Home Placement.[1]—The juvenile court laws of the various states assigning chancery jurisdiction over children have generally made some provisions for suitable home placement—when necessary—and have conferred this power upon the juvenile court. Lou writes:[2]

It implies the transfer of the custody of the child to an individual or an agency and has a distinct object in view, that is, to make the child a member of the family home in which he is placed. . . . The foster-family-home care is regarded as the best treatment for a child whose own home is unfit, since it gives the child a chance to live a normal life, saves him from the artificial life of an institution, and yet separates him from the degenerating influences of his former environment.

A child is placed in a family home either through the appointment of a legal guardian of his person with the right to place and sometimes the right to consent to adoption, or through commitment to a public or private child-placing agency, which becomes the legal guardian of the child with one or both of these rights, or through the court itself when the child remains a ward of the court with or without supervision. Orders appointing guardians and committing to child-placing agencies are infrequent as compared with orders of probation and orders of commitment to institutions. . . . Children placed in family homes by probation officers who are appointed guardians, are usually directly

[1] For a discussion of when a child should be removed from his home, see *infra*, pp. 377–388.

[2] *Juvenile Courts in the United States*, pp. 167–170. Reprinted by permission of the University of North Carolina Press.

supervised by them through reporting or visits. . . . In some places the court has no power to place a child in a family home or to commit him to an institution except through the medium of a public agency. The major part of placing-out work in most courts, however, is done by various private child-caring agencies, usually styled as children's aid societies. These agencies are incorporated under the state law and are usually supervised by a local or state department. They become legal guardians of the children, usually dependent or neglected, who are committed to them, and the care of the children passes to them from court officers, to whom these agencies are usually required to report. Children committed to these agencies are usually placed in family homes and supervised by agents of the societies. The child-placing work, including home-finding, investigation, and supervision, is a highly specialized task and is now fairly standardized.[1]

A distinction should be made between placing a child on probation by the court itself in a home other than his own and what is known as child-placing, described above; for children on probation may be placed in the homes of relatives or close friends designated by the court and the court may sometimes utilize child-placing agencies for the care of children on probation who need to be provided for away from their own homes. . . . The distinction between the two is a fine and technical one, but it is, nevertheless, significant. In the first place, commitment to child-placing agencies and appointing individuals as guardians from outsiders or from among court officers are usually special and distinct court orders, while placing a child on probation in a home other than his own is often an informal arrangement, usually made by the probation staff and the order is still that of probation. Children placed in a family home on probation are usually subject to the same kind of probationary supervision as children placed on probation in their homes, except that they may be subject more or less to the supervision of a child-placing agency, if they are placed by it. In the second place, the probation order is generally used to meet problems more temporary than those met by family-home placement. Orders appointing a guardian or committing to an agency are generally used in those cases in which it appears that the arrangement made must be of relatively long duration owing either to the unfitness of the home or to the death of one or both parents. In the third place, the placement of children in family homes necessarily implies the transfer of guardianship to an individual or agency, but

---

[1] For technical points in child-placing work see *Foster-home Care for Dependent Children*, U. S. Children's Bureau Publication, No. 136; W. H. Singerland, *Child-placing in Families*; E. J. Butler, "Standards of Child Placing and Supervision," in *Standards of Child Welfare*, U. S. Children's Bureau Publication, No. 60, pp. 356–360.

placement in family homes on probation does not necessarily have such a legal consequence.

The wisdom of ordering placement of children in family homes has not been questioned, but opinions differ as to whether the court itself through its officers should engage in placing-out activities. Some juvenile courts . . . have established well-equipped child-placing divisions or bureaus in their probation offices. Very few courts are engaged in child-placing to any considerable extent, but most of them occasionally place children in family homes. It is believed, however, that, as a rule, when other agencies, public or private, are able to undertake placing of children, it is better for the juvenile court not to assume the responsibility for this specialized task and that only where cooperating facilities for child-placing are relatively undeveloped and cannot be made available, may there be some justification for the court to engage in this administrative work as a temporary expedient.[1] As most juvenile courts are generally already overloaded with work, to take upon themselves the work of child-placing would usually mean that the work must be done hastily and unscientifically and often by officers unqualified or at least inexperienced in this branch of social service.

Commitment to Institutions.[2]—When probation and supervision in the offender's own home or in a foster home seem inadvisable or have proved valueless, the court resorts to commitment to institutions especially organized for boys and girls. The child is placed in the custody of the institution for the duration of its care over him. The value of the relatively inflexible regime which at times characterizes correctional institutions has been gravely questioned, but this phase of the court's work is beyond the scope of this volume.[3] Suffice it to indicate what Lou says:

Commitment to institutions is seldom made without a preliminary period of trial on probation by which the child is cared for in his own community. . . . The steps usually followed in the best equipped

---

[1] *Cf.* THOMAS D. ELIOT, *The Juvenile Court and the Community*, p. 104; also KATHERINE F. LENROOT and EMMA O. LUNDBERG, *Juvenile Courts at Work*, U. S. Children's Bureau Publication, No. 141 (1925), pp. 219–220.

[2] M. REEVES, *Training Schools for Delinquent Girls;* NORMAN FENTON, *The Delinquent Boy and the Correctional School;* ALIDA BOWLER and RUTH BLOODGOOD, *Institutional Treatment of Delinquent Boys*, U. S. Children's Bureau Publication, Nos. 228, 230 (1935, 1936).

[3] See WILLIAM I. THOMAS and DOROTHY S. THOMAS, *The Child in America*, pp. 95–128; see also CLIFFORD R. SHAW, *The Jack-Roller.*

courts are continuance or several continuances, probation at home, family-home care, commitment to intermediate institutions, that is, county, city, or private institutions, and, finally, commitment to a state institution. Of course, in few cases would all these steps be taken, but one or another plan would be adopted, if that seems from the beginning the only logical order that the court can make. . . .

In delinquency cases commitment may be made to state institutions, city or county institutions, or private institutions according to individual needs and the availability of such institutions.

The institutions receiving dependent and neglected children are more numerous than those receiving delinquents and most of them are under private management. Private institutions are ordinarily used for temporary purposes when the cases are continued without adjudication, when a short period of good institutional care is needed to prepare a child for placement in a family home, or when his home conditions may be improved in a short time and the child may be soon returned to his home. In a majority of states there is a failure to provide adequately for the separate care of delinquent and dependent or neglected children and dependent and neglected children are often committed to institutions intended primarily for the care of delinquents. The laws of some states definitely prohibit the commitment of children from both groups to the same institutions. . . . In some states where training schools for delinquents are not available, older delinquent children are sometimes committed to a state reformatory, a semi-penal state institution for young adults from sixteen or eighteen to twenty-five or thirty years of age. This practice, except in exceptional cases, is, of course, not to be commended.

In addition to these old designations, institutions for juveniles have developed into various types. Truant schools, now generally styled parental schools, are usually limited to the care of truant children, but they occasionally receive delinquents. Then there are state, city, and county institutions for the care of dependent or neglected boys or girls and women. Private institutions and agencies to which the courts in most states are authorized to commit dependent and neglected children are usually under the auspices of religious or fraternal organizations. Private institutions other than training schools are represented by various types, such as shelters, protectories, day nurseries, children's villages, industrial farms, the House of the Good Shepherd, the George Junior Republic, and so forth. Most institutions, public or private, receive only delinquents or only dependents and neglected, but some of them receive children from both groups, though their primary purpose may be for the one or the other. In some places there are special institutional facilities for the care of dependent crippled children, feeble-minded and epileptic children, children venereally infected, and unmarried mothers and their babies.[1]

Some probation departments advocate placement of a child released from an institution in a foster home before going directly to his own home.   The artificial conditions and relations in an institution often tend to inhibit, suppress, or develop certain traits in the boy or girl which make it inadvisable to put him in contact with his own parents, who previously were unable to cope with him, provided that they have not been reeducated in the meantime.   While the son or daughter is in an institution or foster home, care should be taken to prepare his or her own home, parents, and siblings for his or her return.   Case work with these parents is still a very sadly neglected method of treatment.   Karl Holton of the Los Angeles Probation Department maintains that when children leave an institution after a period of commitment and when they "give vent to their pent-up energies once more, they are in danger of committing another offense almost immediately after release.   These children face a crucial situation and the probation officer needs to concentrate on these cases perhaps more closely than on some of those who were never committed."

Commitment to Forestry Camp.—Los Angeles County[2] is the pioneer in the establishment of a forestry camp in order to provide appropriate facilities for the housing of wards of the juvenile court who are amenable to discipline other than in close confinement, to secure a better classification and segregation of such wards according to their capacities and interests and their responsiveness to control and responsibility, to reduce the necessity of expanding the existing grounds and housing facilities on such grounds for the confinement of such wards, and to give better opportunity for reform and encouragement of self-discipline in such wards. . . .

Kenyon J. Scudder writes of Los Angeles County Forestry Camp No. 10 (in *Annual Report,* 1936):

In 1931 thousands of transients were coming into Los Angeles County. A certain percentage were boys who found themselves in trouble. Formerly we sent these youngsters back home where they were a proper charge against their own counties.   But due to unsettled conditions many came back again to Southern California.   It was an easy way to

---

[1] H. Lou, *op. cit.,* pp. 171–173.   Reprinted by permission of the University of North Carolina Press.

[2] See California Statutes, 1935, Chap. 33.

get a free ride. If we required these boys to earn their transportation home perhaps they would not be so eager to return.

In February, 1932, Forestry Camp No. 10 was developed for this purpose.[1] Located in San Dimas Canyon about thirty miles from Los Angeles, this camp has filled an outstanding need. Here boys work eight hours a day with pick and shovel, building a motor highway to protect one of Los Angeles County's most important watersheds.

The first boys were vagrants who earned their way home at the rate of fifty cents per day. This was applied against the purchase of their railroad tickets. Now the Camp consists of local boys who have been in serious trouble. Granted a stay of commitment to the Preston School of Industry, these lads are given one more chance for adjustment and most of them take advantage of that opportunity.

Sent in for burglary, robbery, grand theft and many other offenses, these boys soon get over the fear of work and lay to with a will. Stripped to the waist their bodies quickly gather a California sun tan of which they are very proud.

Still paid fifty cents per day for their work, the wages go to pay for the damages done some individual, to make restitution, or help support their families on relief.

In spite of serious offenses the Camp is wide open, no locks on the doors, nor bars on the windows. There is no corporal punishment and no loss of food. The camp is located only three miles from Foothill Boulevard over which thousands of motorcars pass daily. Yet there are few runaways and the worst punishment that can be given a boy is to take him out of camp.

Forestry Camp No. 10 is a cooperative enterprise between two county departments. The Forestry Department is in charge of the work end of the Camp, providing the work project and supervising the work itself. The Probation Department is in charge of the boys and is responsible for their custody, discipline, supervision, education, recreation and spiritual needs.

Almost a thousand boys between the ages of sixteen and eighteen have been through this Camp. Their average stay is four months. If sent to an institution their stay would be between fourteen and eighteen months.

[1] [The County Board of Supervisors empowered by provisions of the County Charter authorized the establishment, administration, development of the forestry camp projects, payment of wages to boy and so on, in February, 1932. The State of California authorized the establishment of forestry camps and, in addition to the above program, authorized the establishment of school camps, camps for girls, in cooperation with other departments, and so on, according to Statutes of 1935, Chap. 33.—P.V.Y.]

Can a boy be adjusted in a short period of four months in camp as against eighteen months in an institution? The results from Camp 10 indicate that by far the majority of cases never reach the Preston School. By cashing in on that first impulse and determination to make good, we lead these boys into a wholesome, invigorating outdoor program, and their adjustment is a lasting one.

And what of the cost? This camp to date has cost the County $112,060.68. This total represents all expenditures from the very beginning when only a few boys were in camp up to January 1, 1936, with a population of sixty boys: Capital outlay, $11,177.66; wages and maintenance $76,613.77; wages to boys $24,269.25. If these boys had been sent to the State School the County would have paid the State of California approximately $400,000.00 for their care. This camp represents an actual saving of $287,939.32 to Los Angeles County.

In addition the County has six miles of well-built motor highway on a valuable watershed. Miles of firebreak have been cleared, erosion has been prevented and the back country opened up to fire fighting equipment, thus reducing fire hazard. The social values and the influences of the camp on the boys top all of these.

The Probation and Forestry staff in this Camp have been carefully selected. They are men who understand how to work with boys. The discipline problem is simple in spite of the records these lads bring to camp. They enjoy their work and do more than many work camps where the men are paid four dollars per day. When they leave camp few find themselves in further trouble. The adjustment seems to be lasting. Only eleven per cent go on later to the Preston School of Industry. Without this Camp they would all go.

This Camp has demonstrated that many boys can be handled without institutional care and that formerly these same types were committed because of the seriousness of the offense; camp facilities were not available.

It is our belief that camps of this nature should be developed by the larger counties and our state institutions then used as a last resort. Recent legislation makes this possible. Such a policy would make unnecessary any large-scale building program to increase institutional facilities in California.

These boys return to their homes with an entirely different attitude from those with institutional experience.

We have urged other communities to start similar camps of this sort. However, adequate personnel is of the utmost importance to the success of the program. Adequate personnel has been furnished us in Camp 10 and this is largely responsible for the successful adjustment made under this project.

The boys going to Camp 10 are carefully selected. Few of the boys have an institutional record. Experience shows that boys who have been to state schools, and who later violate their parole, generally do not make a very satisfactory adjustment to Camp 10. They are "institution-wise" and either cause a disturbance or else "slide by" the best way they can. Neither do the definitely feeble-minded boys get along well and really do not have a chance in camps of this sort. Homosexual cases do not fit in. It was found necessary to remove them all with one exception. These boys have too much of a handicap to be able to adjust in a program of this sort.

The boys in the Camp are those whose delinquencies do not extend over a long period of time—although they may have been in trouble several times previous to being sent to Camp—and do not need a long and elaborate training program such as provided by the state schools, but rather a swift jolt or awakening, to cause them to realize the seriousness of law violation.

A very stimulating educational and recreational program is carried on in Camp 10. We have been very fortunate in obtaining adequate facilities from the nearby High School. This has greatly cut down the cost of administering this Camp.

Camp 10 is a laboratory for the study and adjustment of boys. During their stay we endeavor to determine the best type of placement for them upon leaving. It would be useless to carry on a camp program unless the placement work was carefully developed and the boy given adequate supervision after his release. Besides the program in the Camp a probation officer is assigned to work out the home situation in each boy's case. This officer visits the home, contacts the parents and works out a placement program pending the day of the boy's release. In many instances some very fine home rehabilitation work is carried on in this way by changing the attitude of the parents toward the boy and his problem.

Restitution and Reparation.—Fines are generally done away with in the juvenile courts of this country, but restitution for property taken, or reparation for property destroyed, lost, or damaged is frequently ordered by the juvenile court (see case of James R.), in accordance with express provisions made for such orders by the juvenile court laws or at the discretion of the judge. The Committee on Juvenile Court Standards strongly objected to fines, since these imply punishment and are without educative value, but advocated that restitution or reparation may be required in cases where these will have an educative or disciplinary value or will instill respect for property rights. If the offender is working, he is generally expected to make restitution and reparation out of his own earnings or savings.

"New Light on Juvenile Courts and Probation."—The following excerpts from a challenging address by Frederick A. Moran before the National Conference of Social Work[1] will serve to summarize the problems juvenile courts and probation departments are facing and how these problems might be overcome:

The juvenile court is America's most notable contribution to the field of criminology and penology. It is responsible for the revolutionary changes not only in society's attitude toward children who have offended against the laws, but toward adults as well. It is responsible for the development of probation and for whatever progress has been made in socializing procedure in courts dealing with adult offenders. Today the vanguard of thought is recognizing that many of the principles of socialized treatment which the juvenile court inaugurated, such as the study of characteristics of the individual and the environment in which he lives, are applicable and should be extended gradually to the whole field of criminal justice.

Rumblings of discontent with the actual operations of juvenile courts, however, are being heard from all parts of the country and from all types of persons having contact with these courts. What is wrong with the juvenile courts, and why have these courts failed to keep pace with modern standards of social work are questions that are being frequently asked. It is the contention of many that the failure of so large a percentage of the courts to function effectively is due to a misconception, willful or otherwise, of the purposes of these courts not only on the part of laymen, but of lawyers and judges as well, and that the greatest part of the responsibility for the present condition of affairs rests with the legalists.

Social workers are critical,[2] not only regarding the formal, legalistic attitude of a number of judges of these courts, but of the failure of the courts to understand and treat the needs of the individual child. It is charged by many social workers and with considerable justice that these courts neither understand nor accept the fundamentals of social case work.

The psychiatrists are critical because in their opinion children's courts during the past thirty years have had an unparalleled opportunity to deal with a vast army of delinquent and neglected children and dis-

---

[1] "New Light on the Juvenile Courts and Probation," reprinted in the *Year Book, National Probation Association* (1930), pp. 66–75.

[2] Italics are ours.

turbed family relationships, and with few notable exceptions little has been added to the general knowledge of human behavior from the experience of these courts. They are critical because of the unintelligent approach to the whole field of behavior and human relationships. The more sympathetic psychiatrists, however, frankly state that the community expects an impossible task of a judge of a children's court in that it expects the judge to be a psychiatrist, a psychologist, a social worker and a lawyer. Because of their lack of knowledge of the complex problems which the courts are asked to solve, fiscal authorities are of the opinion that juvenile courts are unnecessary, and indicate their lack of sympathy and understanding by their niggardly appropriations.

The sentimental backing responsible for the creation of many of these courts has disappeared. Other panaceas for the salvation of children now occupy the attention of former leaders in the children's court movement. Evidently recalling Julia Lathrop's remark that a child's welfare is best served by keeping everything normal about him, keeping him a school child even if he diverges from the straight and narrow paths, in recent years there has been increasing emphasis upon the assumption by educational authorities of responsibility for treatment of problem children as essentially an educational and not a judicial function.

Juvenile courts are criticized because they are mainly city institutions and have failed to render service to the rural sections or communities. The staffs of the courts are flayed because of their general lack of educational qualifications and their failure to appreciate or accept modern standards of social work.

"The constant strain of self-criticism that arises from the vocal and more thinking part of the American people," Adams reminds us, "morbid as it may seem, indicates a deep dissatisfaction with life and is the hopeful sign for the future. . . . " Certainly this statement might be applied to the criticisms made regarding juvenile courts. If these diverse criticisms were carefully analyzed, it would be found that they do not fundamentally relate to the theories underlying the creation of these courts, but to their administration. . . .

It would, however, be futile, if not intellectually dishonest to give the impression that there is no reason for the critical attitude of many thoughtful people toward juvenile courts. There is little doubt that the criticisms made of juvenile courts are in a great measure justifiable. Unfortunately there still exist, strangely enough, a number of juvenile courts, in which practically every detail is contrary to the thought underlying the movement which created them; these courts continue to be mere criminal courts in which the primary inquiry is directed to the evidence bearing upon the commission of a crime. The social side of the inquiry which has for its object the consideration of the child's needs so as to make him a useful member of society is a secondary consideration. . . .

The legalistic attitude charged against the juvenile court is in a large measure due to false notions of economy.   As long as we expect judges of juvenile courts to act as judges of courts dealing with adult offenders where legal evidence is still of major importance, society cannot expect informal court procedure and individual treatment for the children appearing in court.   The juvenile court should be a separate and independent court and the judge of the court should be allowed to devote his full time to it.

It is in the actual treatment of the child that most juvenile courts have signally failed in their efforts to adjust the child to the normal forces in the community.   The factors responsible for this failure are many and complex.   If the judge of the juvenile court is well qualified through personality, training, and experience for his responsible task, he may, in his efforts to make wise decisions, have utilized all the facilities available to throw light on the conditions responsible for the child's appearance in court.   And yet the plan of treatment formulated may result in failure.   If the decision is to place the child on probation, the staff of the probation office may not only be inadequate in number but be made up of individuals whose previous experience has been gained as undertakers, installment collectors, insurance agents, court attendants, or sign painters. . . .

If a child needs institutional care, it is quite possible that the local community or the state lacks the type of institution needed.   When institutions are available, too frequently normal children are detained too long because the limited probation staffs attached to the courts have no opportunity to reconstruct the home, and children have to be returned to conditions similar to those from which they were removed.   If the child is feeble-minded and the decision is that for a period at least the child should receive care and intensive training in an institution for defective children, it is exceedingly likely that the judge will be informed that the institution is over-crowded and for this reason the child cannot be accepted for an indefinite period.   Frequently, communities lack social agencies with acceptable standards of work, or if they do exist, their lack of understanding of the proper functions of a juvenile court and the part the social agency should play in a program of treatment may result in conflict and failure of the social agency to render the necessary service and cooperation that the court has a legitimate right to expect from it. . . .

It is high time that it be realized that juvenile courts are not strange and mysterious institutions.   None of these courts possesses an Aladdin's

Lamp that can be rubbed to change children from delinquents into those presenting no behavior problems. Outside of actual commitments to institutions there are no functions that these courts perform that could not be performed as well if not better by any social case-working agency with acceptable standards of work. . . .

Over and over again the need for crime prevention is being stressed. Thousands of dollars are being spent each year studying the causes of crime, and millions of dollars are expended on bricks and mortar to confine adults in jails or prisons. It is high time that the states realized that with wisdom they might expend some money on preventive work—and the practical place to begin is with children appearing before the courts. If, as most juvenile court acts indicate, the state takes in particular cases the place of the parent, it might, if it is to assume the role of a wise parent, make it possible to secure enough probation officers to make intensive study, care, and treatment possible. If states do not, we simply have proud words that in reality mean nothing. . . .

Most juvenile courts are proud of their so-called unofficial work. It is not claimed that the unofficial disposition of cases is provided for under juvenile court laws. It is frankly admitted that there is no part of these laws that authorizes it. The practice is justified on the ground that it enables the court to perform a most valuable social function in accomplishing all that a proceeding in court could do and at the same time protect the child. But the bald fact remains that the juvenile courts are responsible for the mushroom development of unofficial work. The court in the future cannot be all things to all men.

Too many juvenile court judges and most probation officers have become literally fanatic regarding their unofficial work. Unofficial work has been overemphasized. If its quality measures up to the standards of good official work, juvenile courts can be justly proud of the quality of it, but the fact that it is recognized that these cases do not need judicial action should indicate that it could be better carried on under non-court auspices. Within a short time if every juvenile court judge attempted to analyze the intake of his court, he would realize that because of the trivial nature of the charges, children should be protected from undergoing a court experience. Issues that can be solved by voluntary adjustment obviously should not be brought to the attention of the court. . . .

It needs to be emphasized over and over again that the failure of communities to provide adequate budgets for juvenile courts is responsible for many of the existing defects of these courts. Sooner or later communities must face the fact that it will cost money to prevent crime. Enough studies have been made to indicate that delinquent careers begin in childhood, and if criminal careers are to be prevented intensive work must be done with the families as well as the children presenting behavior problems. By providing juvenile courts with trained investigators and supervising officers, society will make an intelligent approach to this outstanding social problem.

SPECIAL QUALIFICATIONS OF THE JUDGES OF THE JUVENILE COURT

In some counties and states the judge of the juvenile court is elected, in others he is appointed by the governor, and in the District of Columbia he is appointed by the President of the United States. In rural communities, where the juvenile court is a part of the county, circuit, or district court, the judge of such court acts ex officio as judge of the juvenile court.[1] Under such circumstances the training of the judge, in addition to his legal training, for the specialized work of the juvenile court varies greatly. The critics of the juvenile court and others interested in child welfare have raised the question as to the need for technical and specialized training in child psychology, sociology, and the rudiments of social case work for judges of the juvenile court. If such training is to be required, it is obvious that a qualified judge of the juvenile court should remain continuously on the bench for a period of years at least, and not be subject to rotation as is the case in some counties and cities in this country.

Some of the judges maintain that the function of the probation department is to do the rehabilitative work and its workers should be trained in the social sciences and social work; yet it is apparent that the approach to the child by the judge, the understanding essential for viewing a given case in its social, economic, and psychological complexes requires more than legal training and common sense. Jonah J. Goldstein remarks: "If a judge in a Children's Court had a youngster who was giving him trouble, the last person he would consult would be another lawyer— whether that lawyer was a judge in a Children's Court or not. He would consult a child guidance expert and psychiatrist. Why not do for children generally what he would do for his own?"[2]

There are judges in some juvenile courts who have remained on the bench for a number of years and have taken a keen interest in child welfare and community organization, and have supple-

[1] See LENROOT and LUNDBERG, *op. cit.*, pp. 19–22.
[2] *The Family in Court*, p. 61.

mented their experience by wide reading in the field of child care, but under present methods there is no way to make certain that other juvenile court judges will follow the path of these socially minded leaders. These judges have proved invaluable assets to children and to other social agencies in the community. They have set the pace for what is called socialization of the law.

Use of Referees.[1]—The juvenile courts with chancery jurisdiction, whenever the work is too heavy to be done under the supervision of one judge, have the power to appoint referees (men or women) with authority to hear cases of boys and girls and to make findings and orders, subject to approval by the judge. Some of the juvenile court laws make specific provisions for the appointment of women referees to hear girls' cases. Though referees have no power to make final decisions, their recommendations are rarely disregarded. Mary E. McChristie[2] remarks regarding the role of the woman referee in girls' cases involving sex delinquency:

Many farsighted juvenile-court judges appoint women referees to hear all delinquent girls' cases. This is a great advance from the time when girls' cases were assigned indiscriminately to either men or women officers; when the girl delinquents were compelled to confess to immorality before a careless mixed crowd where they were as conspicuous as Hester wearing a scarlet letter. No matter how detached and professional a man judge may be in his contacts, this girl sex delinquent is keenly conscious of his masculinity and the intimate nature of the questions he is forced to ask. . . . Essentially and distinctly this is a woman's work.

Referees, men or women, are also used in urban communities where the area of jurisdiction is too large for one judge to attend; they are used in the hearing of cases of juvenile traffic violations; they frequently assist in unofficial handling of cases of first offenders,[3] and thus make possible a less crowded schedule and court calendar. Each case can receive more attention in court, and in the long run this fact will tend to reduce recidivism.

[1] For the types of cases handled by women referees see Miriam Van Waters, *Youth in Conflict;* Eleanor Wembridge, *Other People's Daughters* and *Among the Lowbrows.*

[2] "Why They Tell," *Survey,* I (July 15, 1923), 446–448; see also the hearing of Nora Norman, *supra,* pp. 163–166.

[3] LOU, *op. cit.,* pp. 74–75.

JUVENILE COURT STANDARDS

The United States Children's Bureau and the National Probation Association have been vigorously promoting standardization of juvenile court work and probation service, which, as was indicated, varies widely in various parts of the country. Under their auspices a Committee Report on Juvenile Court Standards was drafted which is clear and embodies progressive principles of work with delinquent children—which have been largely discussed in our chapters on "The Juvenile Court from the Standpoint of Administrative Law." This report concerns itself with the extent of court jurisdiction, nature of proceedings, age limits, qualifications of juvenile court judges, use of referees, the relation between the court and the police, detention policy and methods, social study of cases, hearing of children's cases and adult contributory cases, disposition of children's cases, probation and supervision, and system of recording.[1]

Following the adoption of the above report, a Committee on Standard Juvenile Court Laws was appointed by the National Probation Association to draft a standard juvenile court law. In 1925 the Committee submitted a Standard Juvenile Court Law specifying the establishment of juvenile courts, defining their jurisdiction, powers, and duties and regulating procedure therein.[2]

The National Probation Association has conducted a number of surveys, held conferences, and disseminated information and literature in an attempt "to educate the public as to the needs for better organized social court work . . . to extend the probation system and to secure better standards of case work, more thorough organization in social courts, and needed legislation. The passage of the Federal Probation Law[3] in 1925 was due chiefly to the persistent efforts of this organization."[4]

[1] See *Juvenile Court Standards*, United States Children's Bureau Publication, No. 121 (reprinted 1934), a report by a conference held under the auspices of the Children's Bureau and the National Probation Association, Washington, May 18, 1923; pp. 1–10. See also EDWIN J. COOLEY, *Probation and Delinquency*, pp. 319–330; FRANCIS H. HILLER, *The Juvenile Court of Los Angeles County;* and pp. 192–232 of this text.

[2] For the bill with a brief in the form of commentaries see *Proceedings of the National Probation Association* (1925), pp. 192–292.

[3] See *Proceedings of the National Probation Association* (1925), pp. 226–230.

[4] H. H. LOU, *op. cit.*, p. 197.

FAMILY COURTS[1]

As noted in passing before (see p. 26), students of juvenile delinquency have for many years advocated and urged the establishment of a family court with a separate division for children's cases, based on the belief that if children come into conflict with the law, the family should be studied. Only a few cities and counties in the country have created such courts; notable among them are the Court of Domestic Relations in Hamilton County (Cincinnati), and other cities in Ohio and New York; Detroit, Michigan; Essex and Union Counties, New Jersey; Portland, Oregon; Norfolk, Virginia, and elsewhere. Regarding the well-known Court of Domestic Relations of Hamilton County, Professor E. E. Eubank,[2] of the University of Cincinnati, voices a typical attitude of all those who are in favor of such courts:

This court gives constant evidence of the advantages of a coordinating family court. Within this one organization are handled all problems relating to the family, including (1) petitions for divorce and separation, (2) mothers' pensions, (3) juvenile delinquency cases, (4) juvenile dependency cases.

Among the advantages, two stand out especially. The first is that of having all phases of domestic relations handled under a *unified policy*. There is not one theory or line of procedure concerning adults which is neutralized by another concerning juveniles, but each reinforces and strengthens the other.

A second outstanding advantage is the greater efficiency that comes through the *mechanics of centralization*. Whatever problem has previously come up touching the family is right at hand in the records of the same court, available for immediate utilization; whatever decision is made in a given case profits by the direct knowledge of what has been done in regard to, or the conditions that exist in, that same family; and the case workers assigned when the case comes up easily get in touch for consultation with their colleagues on the same court staff who have had previous knowledge of it.

[1] See CHARLES W. HOFFMAN, "The Court of Domestic Relations in a Program of Family Conservation," *Wisconsin State Conference of Charities and Correction* (1918), pp. 19–28; THOMAS D. ELIOT, *The Juvenile Court and the Community*, Chaps. XIII, XIV; GOLDSTEIN, *op. cit.;* F. E. WADE, "The Prosecution of Parents for the Delinquencies of Their Children," *National Conference of Charities and Correction* (1909), pp. 297–307.

[2] Personal communication, July 14, 1936.

To have all of these coordinated under the same judge enables him to work with an intelligence, economy, and unity which would not be possible if they were handled by different judges, in different courts, working under different policies.

It is the aim of these courts to have broad and concurrent jurisdictions in the juvenile court and family court and to use a coordinated bench and staff, but to hold separate sessions for various problems and for juvenile and adult cases.[1]

Judge Charles W. Hoffman of the Domestic Relations Court in Cincinnati, Ohio, a leader in the movement for their establishment, says that the aim of such a court is the provision

for the consideration of all matters relating to the family in one court of exclusive jurisdiction, in which the same methods of procedure shall prevail as in the juvenile court and in which it will be possible to consider social evidence as distinguished from legal evidence. In fact, providing for a family court is no more than increasing the jurisdiction of the juvenile court and designating it by the more comprehensive term of family court.[2]

Judge Hoffman submitted a report to the National Probation Association as early as 1917 discussing the functions of a family court:[3]

Heretofore the emphasis has been placed upon the child in court; with a wider conception of the law, it will in the future be placed on the family in court. In short, the court will undertake to deal more effectively with the family which produces the neglected or delinquent child, who is merely a chapter in the larger, more complicated problem. This change contemplates a legitimate extension of the present court's functions. It will be vested with both equitable and criminal jurisdiction and will deal with all charges against minors, with neglected children and with all cases such as divorce, adoption, etc., in which the custody of children is in question. It will likewise embrace within its jurisdiction all violations of law where children have been wronged, such as child labor laws and compulsory attendance. It follows, as a matter of course, that it will have jurisdiction over all cases of adults who contribute in any way to the conditions of delinquency or neglect in children.

---

[1] GOLDSTEIN, *op. cit.*, pp. 29–30.

[2] "Social Aspects of the Family Court," *Journal of Criminal Law and Criminology*, X (November, 1919), pp. 409–422.

[3] "Report of the Committee on the Courts of Domestic Relations," *Proceedings of the National Probation Association* (1917), pp. 82–83.

In conformity with the above report the National Probation Association in 1917 adopted the following resolutions:[1]

That the National Probation Association recommends the organization of Family Courts, the term "Family Court" to supersede the present courts known as Courts of Domestic Relations.

That the Family Courts be given jurisdiction in the following classes of cases: (*a*) cases of desertion and nonsupport; (*b*) paternity cases, known also as bastardy cases; (*c*) all matters arising under acts pertaining to the juvenile court known in some States as the Children's court, and all courts, however designated in the several States, having within their jurisdiction the care and treatment of delinquent and dependent children and the prosecution of adults responsible for such delinquency or dependency; (*d*) all matters pertaining to adoption and guardianship; (*e*) all divorce and alimony matters.

That these courts be under the direction of a single judge except in such jurisdictions where the work of the court is so great as to require more than one judge for the convenient and proper disposal of the matters coming before the court. That in these cases, the court have special divisions, to which are assigned certain classes of cases; the court as a whole to be under the supervision and direction of a presiding judge.

That such courts be provided with ample probation departments upon which shall be conferred power to make all necessary investigations, medical, pathological, social, psychological or otherwise, as shall be considered necessary, and that in pursuance of this work there be provided psychopathic laboratories sufficiently equipped to conduct the necessary scientific investigations.

That all cases involving children and intimate family relations be conducted as privately as is consistent with the law and the constitutional rights of the individual, and that publicity concerning abnormal family conditions be discouraged.

That the procedure in the Family Courts be informal and summary so far as it may be consistent with positive law, and that such civil as well as criminal jurisdiction be conferred on the courts as will enable them to deal with all cases so as to effect the adjustment of the individual and family conditions without legal formality and delay.

H. H. Lou,[2] who has made an exhaustive study of family and juvenile courts in the United States, corroborates the opinions

---

[1] *Proceedings of the National Probation Association* (1917), pp. 85–86.

[2] *Op. cit.*, p. 204; see also pp. 203–212; see also RALPH HALL FERRIS, "Some Social Factors in Family Problems," *Year Book, National Probation Association* (1932–1933), pp. 180–188.

expressed by R. H. Smith[1] and Mary E. McChristie[2] regarding
the desirability of a unified family court:

Viewed from the aspect of the efficiency of the court machinery, the
unification of jurisdiction in domestic relations and juvenile cases is a
very desirable step. If the family is dealt with as a unit, there will be
avoided much duplication of effort which results from handling family
problems by separate courts. As courts are now organized, each has a
slice of the whole jurisdiction over all family problems. There is
neither unification, nor specialization, nor even uniformity of methods.
The present system, as it exists in some places, of handling divorce
cases in one court, separation suits in another, non-support in a third,
and juvenile matters in a fourth, unquestionably tends to nullify the
power of each court for good and to rob the law of much of its possible
effectiveness.

Regarding the establishment of a Court of Domestic Relations
in New York and its provisions, Jonah J. Goldstein,[3] a city
magistrate of New York City, says:

Although the headquarters of the National Probation Association is
located in New York City, it took the Empire City of the Nation sixteen
years to carry out only in part the recommendations of the Association
looking toward a consolidated Family and Children's Court. . . .
The law creating the Domestic Relations Court in New York for the
first time makes definite provision for important social service that shall
be rendered: (1) emergency relief for food and shelter shall be secured
from the proper agencies; (2) the home shall be promptly visited; (3) an
accurate, impartial, written report shall be made and become part of the
case history; (4) social history of the family shall be investigated;
(5) The Social Service Exchange shall be used; (6) the names of agencies
having previous contacts with the family shall be ascertained, recorded
and used; (7) previous criminal records and Children's Court records
shall be investigated and recorded; (8) conferences shall be had with
agencies in touch with the family or who have had previous contact
with it; (9) discretion to supplement and check the work of the court's
investigators, by use of the service of coordinated private social service
agencies, is authorized; (10) care shall be taken not to disturb a man's
relations with his employer; (11) in all cases, efforts at conciliation

[1] *Justice and the Poor*, pp. 72–82.

[2] "The Development of Family Courts," *Proceedings of the National Probation Association* (1924), p. 169.

[3] *Op. cit.*, pp. 42–44. Reprinted by permission of Clark Boardman Company.

shall be made and a report rendered of such efforts—all to be made part of the case history; (12) before the court may make an order for support, all the circumstances of the case, as revealed by the investigations, shall be before the court.

(It is of interest to note in passing that all the provisions, with the exception of the first and fifth, laid down in the creation of the Domestic Relations Court in New York, are embodied or implied in the Juvenile Court Law of California.)

It should be remembered that nearly all juvenile courts in the United States have jurisdiction not only over children's cases but over certain types of adult cases (pp. 203–205). But there are distinct advantages of a family court. Judge Harry A. Fisher of Chicago further outlines the advantages as follows:

The advantages of having such a court are in the main the possibility of establishing a social-service department in connection with it, which is required to make investigation of cases and when possible to avoid bringing these matters before the court either by effecting reconciliations or by obtaining voluntary contributions for the support ordered for the families, and to look after a proper collection of the money ordered for the support of wife or child. A separate court for these matters also develops expertness on the part of the judge who is assigned to preside over it. It separates these cases from the other cases that are usually brought before the criminal branches of the court, and above all, it makes possible the treatment of these cases from a social point of view. The proceedings are less formal, and the court is not limited to the trial of bare issues of fact. It is in a position to call to its aid the numerous private social agencies which exist in the city and which are able to help solve many domestic problems. In fact, our court has become much more a great social agency than a court. The judicial power is resorted to only where coercion is necessary.[1]

THE VALUES OF THE JUVENILE COURT[2]

As indicated before, there are students of juvenile delinquency who suggest merging the juvenile court with the general family court or that the work of the juvenile court be transferred to the schools (see pp. 535–536). We need not repeat the discussion at this point except to point out that while both of the above

[1] Quoted by BERNARD FLEXNER, REUBEN OPPENHEIMER, KATHERINE F. LENROOT, *The Child, The Family and the Court,* U. S. Children's Bureau Publication, No. 193 (rev. ed., 1933), p. 14.

[2] See pp. 25–30.

suggestions have been followed by certain courts and many of the schools have developed some form of unofficial treatment of delinquent and problematic children, there are many legal problems which the schools cannot handle and for the solution of which they must ultimately resort to court action, as for example, commitment to institutions when parents or guardians object to such treatment.   The school would have no power to deal with adults contributing to delinquency of minors who in the absence of the juvenile court would have to serve as witnesses in criminal courts and be subjected to cross-examination and the open-court-room procedure of the criminal court.   However, that the schools and other agencies should deal with certain problems is recognized by many jurists as well as sociologists and social workers.   Superior Judge Robert H. Scott, of Los Angeles County Juvenile Court, expresses the attitude of many progressive thinkers:[1]

When the idea of a special court to handle juveniles was first developed about a third of a century ago, we found our citizens peculiarly responsive.   A widespread concern for the welfare of children had been seeking expression, and the proposal that their misdeeds should be considered by a special tribunal was well received.   The underlying reason for this acceptance was the firm place of our courts in the governmental structure of our country.

As soon as people began thinking of having a special court to try juvenile offenders, they began studying the possibilities of such a court as an agency for child welfare, and as a next logical step it was thought that such a court could well embrace family welfare and the problems of the home.   During the process of its development, a variety of problems have been brought to the juvenile court, not only questions of delinquency, but dependency, mother's pensions, and, in some states, divorce.

It is, however, possible for us to find in practically any human problem some aspect of it which affects children and which might serve as a justification for bringing it into the juvenile court, and we should determine at this time its correct standard and true purpose.   The tendency to allocate to a court all of these diverse functions has been due to the tremendous power of the court to coerce the action and compel the cooperation of persons who might otherwise be more or less reluctant.   Its ability as a court of equity jurisdiction to cut across legal red tape and act immediately has made it seem desirable as a ready tool with which to get results.   Nevertheless, it would appear that only

[1] From an unpublished manuscript (March, 1936), pp. 1–2, 7.

those cases should be made the responsibility of the court in which the coercive power of the court is necessary to safeguard the child or protect society. To bring to a judicial tribunal other miscellaneous administrative duties, is to defeat the good end which we seek to attain. We believe that dependency and state-aid cases and other matters which are purely of an administrative nature should be definitely handled entirely outside of the court.

In addition to this reduction in the possible court load, there are many other steps which may be, and in many cases are being, taken in the same direction. Cases of truancy and school incorrigibility should largely be handled by a welfare department of the schools without court intervention. If there is nothing wrong with a child except his failure to attend school, the curriculum should be analyzed and the child examined mentally and physically to make sure that it is a case in which nothing else will serve except court action. If a child absents himself from school merely because he has no clothes to wear, it is a matter for a relief agency. Where the problem presented is one of bad home conditions, a family welfare agency may just as well give all the help that is needed, save in the exceptional case where the family is unwilling to cooperate and receive it. Where a child is a runaway, the matter can often be adjusted by the Traveler's Aid. It is entirely consistent with the primary concept of the juvenile court for private social agencies to perform many of these functions which theoretically could be done by the court. Why should we keep extending the work of the court to embrace matters which can as effectively be dealt with by them?

Even when we survey the activities of official agencies, such as the police and sheriff departments, we see a most interesting departure from the traditional program of these authorities. Police juvenile bureaus have been established and are now functioning on the theory that their job is not merely to detect crime and arrest criminals, but that it is to prevent crime and to protect the child as well as the community. Police officials now admit responsibility as social workers.

By keeping the number of cases it handles within reasonable limits it is possible to give to every case which does come into court for hearing by the judge, or referee, sympathetic, patient, and dignified attention to all of the parties and witnesses, bearing in mind that a lifetime impression may be created in the minds of those concerned, and that the legal basis for judicial order must be carefully and firmly laid. Because of the broad powers of the court and the comparative helplessness of those who come before it, we must at all times be concerned, not only to protect the community against misconduct of children, but also to safeguard the legal rights and human values of those with whom we deal, knowing that in preserving the integrity of their personalities we shall be best protecting society for the future.

The most successful juvenile court is one which can arouse the dormant conscience of the parents and the community to their duty to provide for childhood that care and protection, that guidance and inspiration, that example and encouragement, which, by their very origin and nature, coming from them, must be better than the best that any juvenile court can provide.

Drs. Sheldon and Eleanor Glueck,[1] who have made an exhaustive study of the Boston Juvenile Court, point out the following values of the juvenile court and make the following recommendations for improvement in practices of the juvenile court—which are applicable with equal validity to most, if not all, juvenile courts irrespective of their location.

The Juvenile Court also contributes tangible but real values which justify its retention. Such as, for example, the intelligence, combined with kindliness and firmness, with which a progressive juvenile court judge approaches his task of attempting to understand the delinquent, the forces operative in his misadventures, and the possible means of rehabilitating him. A judge of an adult criminal court may, of course, also consider his cases in this spirit; but since the means at his command are less flexible, since he is consciously or unconsciously hedged about by traditional legal attitudes, since the entire procedure is oriented from the point of view of blameworthiness, guilt, punishment, and the like, he is much less likely to do so than the juvenile court judge. In other words, we must view the juvenile court as a step in the slowly moving, painful evolution of society's crime-treating institutions, from the stage of the talion and of mechanically administered justice to that of humanitarianism and scientifically administered justice. Greater humanitarianism in the treatment of wrongdoers, whose careers so often reflect the pressures and pulls of forces hardly within their control, is a social value not to be lightly abandoned. And greater attention to the individual case—with a view to studying the etiology of the misconduct and to applying treatment which is at least calculated to meet the problem involved, even if it as yet fails to do so—is another social value not to be lightly discarded.

Clinic and Court should be retained but improved. The upshot of our argument, then, is that despite the disappointingly small number of successful outcomes of cases as measured by this particular research, the path of progress does not seem to lie in the direction of abandonment of the juvenile Clinic and Court. But when this is said, there remains

[1] *One Thousand Juvenile Delinquents*, pp. 241–242, 244–245, 247–253. Reprinted by permission of the Harvard University Press.

the patent need of considerable improvement in the work of these institutions. Some suggestions in pursuit of this aim may now be offered. . . .

Improvement in Practices of the Juvenile Court

Problems Involved.—The problems of the Juvenile Court may be fruitfully considered from the points of view of (1) the need for a consistent and unified children's code, (2) the judicial attitude, (3) the court hearing, (4) the relationship of the judge to the delinquent and his family, (5) the work of the probation officer, and (6) the need for recording the Court's experience. These topics will be taken up in order.

1. *Need for Unified Code.*— . . . it is high time for a fundamental reexamination of all the legislation regarding children with a view to the drafting of a simple, straightforward children's code based on well-defined, consistent principles. . . . Some of the chief features of such a code will naturally depend upon the solution of certain fundamental questions of policy, such as, for example, whether there is to be a state-wide juvenile court with rotating judges; whether instead of a juvenile court, one or more family courts are preferable; what relationship the court shall bear to the institutions to which children are committed for care, education, or correction; whether appeals on the questions of disposition of the case after a finding of delinquency should be abolished, so that the juvenile (or family) court will have final authority in matters of treatment as opposed to the finding of the child's status; whether the complaint in delinquency cases is to retain the technical form imposed on it by complaints and indictments in criminal cases; whether the age jurisdiction of the court shall be raised; and like questions.

2. *The Judicial Attitude.*—Though most juvenile court judges have some idea of the attitude appropriate to their work, it is in fact extremely difficult to define what the point of view of the juvenile court judge ought to be. On the one hand he is supposed to be sympathetic to the "clinical approach," which stresses the problems of the *individual* delinquent; on the other, he is expected by society to safeguard the *general* security. . . .

One cannot of course dogmatically state that a juvenile court judge should in all cases do thus and so. That is a chief weakness of many writers on juvenile delinquency, who, in their zeal to justify the clinical point of view, too often ignore the need of taking the general as well as individual welfare into account, forgetting that judges, representing society as a whole, cannot avoid facing this issue. Despite the difficulty of laying down general rules, it would seem that certain principles are more in harmony than are others with the objectives of the juvenile court movement, as well as with the need for safeguarding the general security. For instance, it is of the essence of the juvenile approach for the judge to be, and to convince the delinquent and his family that he is, sympathetic and understanding; but this does not mean that he should not also be firm.   Sympathy and understanding are not equivalent to naive sentimentalism, which is too readily and calculatingly imposed upon. . . .

Our conclusion is, then, that the attitude of the judge should be one of understanding and kindliness, but should be stiffened by firmness and by insistence that the delinquents and their parents shall at least sincerely try to do their part in the reciprocal obligations.

What does this specifically imply?   In the first place, the original interview should impress the delinquent with the seriousness of his acts, not only from the point of view of his own future but from that of society.   The delinquent and his parents should be made to realize that certain behavior carries with it inevitable penalties, in partially depriving him, and possibly also them, of something they value—self-direction and self-assertion, whether behind walls or at large under the direction of a probation officer.   Secondly, serious violations of the conditions of probation should not be lightly passed over, but should be made the occasion for the further impressing upon the delinquent and his family that the consequences of misconduct must in some degree be borne by them, because to some extent (however unmeasurable it may be, and however different in each case) it must, for the practical consideration of the social welfare, be deemed his or their own doing. Finally, the Court must work out some general policies regarding the amount of time and effort that can fairly be spent on cases which fail to respond to treatment. . . .

3. *Court Hearings.*—Certain suggestions may be made as to the mechanics of the hearing in the . . . Court.   One of these is that the probation officer be present throughout.   All important occurrences in the courtroom, and actions on the part of the judge and others concerned, do not always come to the attention of the probation officer, who is required to run in and out of the courtroom while the hearing is in progress.   It is also suggested that, as an experiment at least, a stenographer be present in the courtroom in an inconspicuous place, to take down verbatim all that occurs.   Analysis of the data thus obtained might furnish fruitful hints as to improvement of the hearings.

4. *Relationship of the Judge to the Delinquent.*—Having impressed upon the delinquent and his family that despite the compelling pressure of some causes over which they have little control they are yet bound to try their utmost to assume responsibility for the future conduct of the delinquent, the judge can then offer the assistance of himself and staff in aid of the program of rehabilitation decided upon. . . .

5. *Work of the Probation Officer.*—An obvious weakness in the procedure of the Boston Juvenile Court in the past has been that probation

officers did not attend the conferences at the Clinic on the cases in their charge. In fact at present they do not always do so. Attendance at the Clinic is necessary so that the Court may determine the exact reasons why the clinicians have made certain recommendations and may in turn point out to the clinical staff why certain recommendations are not feasible or will have to be modified in practice. (See Chap. XXVII.)

As to the quality of the probation service, one of the important findings of our study, as already stated, is that an appreciably higher proportion of the cases of certain officers are more successful than those of others. . . . It is the better part of wisdom to employ only properly trained men and women, who possess the capacity for understanding and influencing children and parents. (See Chap. XXII.)

6. *Need for Recording Experience.*—One of the greatest weaknesses of most, if not all, juvenile (as well as adult) courts is a failure to record their experiences in relation to the sentencing and treatment processes. Without this, it is idle to speak of developing a scientific technique for treating offenders. We have noted one serious gap in the records of the Boston Juvenile Court, namely the failure to set down the reasons for modifying or not following the recommendations of the Clinic. In practice, this has resulted in the Clinic's continuing over many years to make certain recommendations that the Court could not or would not follow, while the Court has kept receiving these recommendations without making it clear to the Clinic why and how they should be modified. This is an unfortunate failure to profit from experience. Had the Court set down its reasons for non-compliance with the Clinic's suggestions, it would soon have had the solid basis for a thoroughgoing inquiry into the practical utility of the typical recommendations made by the Clinic; these recommendations might thereby have been modified to the mutual benefit of Court and Clinic. (See pp. 608–614.)

Another function which the Juvenile Court ordinarily fails to perform is to check the *results* of the various forms of treatment resorted to by it, as related to different types of offenders and situations. A Juvenile Court judge has hardly more treatment facilities at his disposal than has the judge of an adult criminal court; and the exact degree of effectiveness of these various "medicines" must be determined if progress is to be made in the treatment of delinquency. If the Judge of the . . . Juvenile Court could periodically look into the practical utility of the various forms of treatment recommended and adopted, ideas for improvement of existing treatment facilities, or additions to them, would grow out of his day-to-day work with individual delinquents. Moreover, such a check is the basis for a practicable system of prediction that both Clinic and Court might use to advantage.[1]

[1] See Chap. XI. See also note 8, p. 6 [of the Glueck's study], where the need of an objective appraisal is indicated.

In the light of these needs, it is urgently advised:

1. That henceforth the judge record the reasons that impel him to modify or reject the several clinical recommendations.

2. That the Juvenile Court keep careful records of the progress of its charges not only during supervision but after treatment has ceased; and

3. That these records be periodically consulted not only by the judge and probation officers but by the directors of the clinic, and taken into account in making future recommendations and experimenting with various treatment devices.

Finally, we may say that examination of the investigatory and supervisory reports of the Boston Juvenile Court shows room for improvement in comparison even with the records to be found in certain adult tribunals, such as the New York Court of General Sessions. The Juvenile Court records might well be made more intensive in respect to the family situation and personality characteristics of the delinquent as disclosed during supervision, and more specific in respect to the various steps in the treatment process, their results, and the reasons for their modification.

As it becomes more and more evident that the problems of juvenile delinquency call for administrative rather than judicial action, the tendency grows to restrict the field of action of the juvenile court. Furthermore, since the type of administrative functions involved are so largely educational—for both the children and their parents—the search goes on apace for an organization possessing educational philosophy, methods, and experience with these problems. It may well be that such an agency could be created under the leadership of therapists who have been assigned such incidental legal prerogatives as this work requires. This is a device much used in other fields of administrative law and is directly in line with current developments.

SELECTED BIBLIOGRAPHY

Juvenile Courts: History and Philosophy

1. ABBOTT, GRACE: "History of the Juvenile Court Movement throughout the World," *The Child, the Clinic and the Court*, New Republic, Inc., 1925, pp. 267–273.
2. ADDAMS, JANE: "Efforts to Humanize Justice," *Survey Graphic*, LXIII (Dec. 1, 1929), 275–278, 308–311, 313.
3. BAKER, HARVEY HUMPREY: *Upbuilder of the Juvenile Court*, Judge Baker Foundation, 1920.
4. BARNES, HARRY ELMER: *The Story of Punishment, a Record of Man's Inhumanity to Man*, The Stratford Company, 1930.

5. BOWEN, MRS. JOSEPH T.: "The Early Days of the Juvenile Court," *The Child, the Clinic and the Court,* New Republic, Inc., 1925, pp. 298–309.
6. CHUTE, CHARLES L.: "The Development of Probation in the United States," in Sheldon Glueck (Editor), *Probation and Criminal Justice,* pp. 225–249.
7. HENLEY, WILLIAM BALLENTINE: *The Development and Status of Probation Law in the United States,* Master's Thesis, The University of Southern California, 1935, Chap. II.
8. HOFFMAN, CHARLES W.: "The Court of Domestic Relations in a Program of Family Conservation," *Wisconsin State Conference of Charities and Correction* (1918), pp. 19–28.
9. LATHROP, JULIA C.: "The Background of the Juvenile Court in Illinois," *The Child, the Clinic and the Court,* pp. 290–297.
10. MACK, JULIAN W.: "The Juvenile Court," *Harvard Law Review,* XXIII (December, 1909), 104–123.
11. ———: "Legal Problems Involved in the Establishment of the Juvenile Court," in S. Breckenridge and Edith Abbott, *The Delinquent Child and the Home,* pp. 181–188.
12. MEAD, GEORGE H.: "The Psychology of Punitive Justice," *American Journal of Sociology,* XXIII (March, 1918), 577–602.

Juvenile Courts: Laws, Standards, Practices, Probation

13. ABBOTT, GRACE: "Juvenile Courts," *Survey,* LXXII (May 15, 1936), 131–133.
14. BATES, SANFORD: "The Status of Federal Probation," *Year Book, National Probation Association* (1930), pp. 137–139.
14a. BEARD, BELLE B.: *Juvenile Probation,* American Book Company, 1934.
*15. BELDEN, EVELINA: *Courts in the United States Hearing Children's Cases,* U. S. Children's Bureau Publication, No. 65 (1920).
16. BRECKENRIDGE, S. P.: "Reexamination of the Work of the Children's Courts," *Year Book, National Probation Assn.* (1930), pp. 53–65.
17. ———: *Social Work and the Courts,* University of Chicago Press, 1935, pp. 190–240, 453–478.
18. BRECKENRIDGE, S. P., and HELEN R. JETER: *A Summary of Juvenile Court Legislation in the United States,* U. S. Children's Bureau Publication, No. 70 (1920), pp. 21–24, 84–85.
19. CANTOR, N. F.: *Crime, Criminals and Criminal Justice,* Henry Holt and Company, 1932. (See Chaps. VI, VII, "Factors in Crime Careers.")
20. CHUTE, CHARLES L.: "Digest of Papers on Probation," *Journal of Criminal Law and Criminology,* XXVIII (January–February, 1933), pp. 833–838.
21. ———: *Probation in Children's Courts,* U. S. Children's Bureau Publication, No. 80 (1921).
22. ———: "Probation in a Community Social Welfare Program," *Proceedings of the National Conference of Social Work* (1933), pp. 136–145.

23. ELIOT, THOMAS D.: *The Juvenile Court and the Community*, The Macmillan Company, 1914.

24. ETTINGER, CLAYTON: *The Problem of Crime*, Ray Long and Richard R. Smith, 1932. (See Chap. XVI, "Procedure in the Juvenile Court.")

24a. *Facts About Juvenile Delinquency: Its Prevention and Treatment*, U. S. Children's Bureau Publication, No. 215 (rev. 1935).

25. FLEXNER, BERNARD, and ROGER N. BALDWIN: *Juvenile Courts and Probation*, Century Company, 1916.

26. FLEXNER, BERNARD, and REUBEN OPPENHEIMER: *The Legal Aspects of the Juvenile Court*, U. S. Children's Bureau Publication, No. 99 (1922).

27. FLEXNER, BERNARD, REUBEN OPPENHEIMER, and KATHERINE F. LENROOT: *The Child, the Family and the Court*, A Study of the Administration of Justice in the Field of Domestic Relations, U. S. Children's Bureau Publication, No. 193 (rev. 1933).

28. GLUECK, SHELDON (Editor): *Probation and Criminal Justice*, The Macmillan Company, New York.

29. ———: "Probation," *Social Work Year Book* (1935), pp. 341–345.

30. GLUECK, SHELDON, and ELEANOR GLUECK: *One Thousand Juvenile Delinquents*, Harvard University Press, 1933. (See particularly pp. 241–253.)

31. GOLDSTEIN, JONAH J.: *The Family in Court*, Clark Boardman Company, 1934.

32. HALL, JEROME: *Theft, Law and Society*, Little, Brown & Company, 1935.

33. HALL, WILLIAM CLARKE: "The Extent and Practice in Probation," in Sheldon Glueck (Editor), *Probation and Criminal Justice*, pp. 276–297.

34. HALPERIN, IRVING W.: "Practical Problems in Administering Probation," *Year Book*, National Probation Association (1931), pp. 105–116.

35. HULBERT, HENRY S.: "Probation," *The Child, the Clinic and the Court*, pp. 238–245.

36. JOHNSON, FRED R.: *Probation for Juveniles and Adults*, Century Company, 1928.

36a. KAWIN, IRENE: "Organization of a Juvenile Probation Department," *Social Work Technique*, I (March–April, 1936), 37–43.

37. LENROOT, KATHERINE F., and EMMA O. LUNDBERG: *Juvenile Courts at Work*, U. S. Children's Bureau Publication, No. 141 (1925).

38. LINDSEY, BEN B.: "Colorado's Contribution to the Juvenile Court," *The Child, the Clinic and the Court*, pp. 274–289.

39. LOU, H. H.: *Juvenile Courts in the United States*, University of North Carolina Press, 1927.

40. McSWEENEY, RICHARD B.: "Federal Probation," *Year Book*, National Probation Association (1930), pp. 140–145.

41. MEAD, B.: "Evaluating the Results of Probation," *Journal of Criminal Law and Criminology*, XXIII (November–December, 1932), 631–638.

42. MOLEY, DR. RAYMOND: "Our Criminal Courts," *Year Book, National Probation Association* (1930), pp. 47–51.

43. MORAN, FREDERICK A.: "New Light on Juvenile Courts and Probation," *Year Book, National Probation Association* (1930), pp. 66–75.

44. MORRIS, ALBERT: *Criminology*, pp. 303–315. Longmans, Green & Co., 1934. (See Chap. XV, "Probation and Its Administrators.")

45. National Commission on Law Observance and Enforcement, *Report of Penal Institutions, Probation, and Parole*, No. 9 (1931), "Probation," pp. 146–207.

46. National Commission on Law Observance and Enforcement, *Report on Prosecution*, No. 4 (1931).

47. OPPENHEIMER, REUBEN, and LULU L. ECKMAN: *Laws Relating to Sex Offenses against Children*, U. S. Children's Bureau Publication, No. 145 (1925).

48. PARSONS, P. A.: *Crime and the Criminal*, Alfred A. Knopf, Inc., 1926. (See Chap. XVIII, "Specialized Treatment of Youthful Offenders.")

49. POUND, ROSCOE: "Preventive Justice and Social Work," *National Conference of Social Work* (1923), pp. 152–163.

50. ———: "The Individualization of Justice," *Year Book, National Probation Association* (1930), pp. 104–112.

51. RILEY, RALPH J.: *A Working Manual for Juvenile Court Officers*, University of Chicago Press, 1932.

52. "A Standard Juvenile-court Law," Prepared by the Committee on Standard Juvenile Court Laws, *Proceedings of the National Probation Association* (1925; revised, 1933), pp. 192–222.

53. SUTHERLAND, EDWIN H.: *Principles of Criminology*, J. B. Lippincott Company, 1934. (See Chap. XIII, "Detention before Trial"; Chap. XIV, "The Criminal Court"; Chap. XV, "The Juvenile Court.")

54. VAN WATERS, MIRIAM: *Report on the Child Offender in the Federal System of Justice*, National Commission on Law Observance and Enforcement, No. 6, 1931. (Chap. II, pp. 25–31; Chap. VI, pp. 107–148.)

55. ———: "Criminal Treatment of Juvenile Offenders in the United States," *Year Book, National Probation Association* (1932–1933), pp. 14–19.

56. ———: "Socialization of Juvenile Court Procedure," *Journal of Criminal Law and Criminology*, XIII (May, 1922), 61–69.

57. WILLIAMSON, MARGARETTA: *The Social Worker in the Prevention and Treatment of Delinquency*, Columbia University Press, 1935.

Juvenile Courts in Foreign Countries

58. CALLCOTT, M. S.: *Russian Justice*, The Macmillan Company, 1935. (See pp. 204–219.)

59. CORNILL, PAUL: "Substitute for Imprisonment in Belgium," in SHELDON GLUECK (Editor), *Probation and Criminal Justice*, pp. 305–317.

60. FRANCKE, HERBERT: "Juvenile Courts in Germany," *Sociology and Social Research*, XVI (May–June, 1932), 403–416.

61. HENTING, HANS: "Protective Supervision of Offenders in the German Legal System," in Sheldon Glueck (Editor), *Probation and Criminal Justice*, pp. 318–334.

62. LEAGUE OF NATIONS: Child Welfare Committee, *Auxiliary Services of Juvenile Courts*, Geneva (Feb. 15, 1931).

63. LE MESURIER, MRS. L.: *A Handbook of Probation*, National Association of Probation Officers, London, 1935. (See particularly Chap. II, "Law and Administration.")

64. MACGILL, HELEN GREGORY: "Juvenile Courts and Their Work in Canada," Reprint from *Revue internationale de l'enfant*, VI (October, 1928; Geneva).

65. ROLLET, HENRI: "The Probation System in France," in Sheldon Glueck (Editor), *Probation and Criminal Justice*, pp. 301–303.

66. Scotland, Departmental Committee Appointed to Inquire into the Treatment of Young Offenders: Protection and Training, being the report of the committee. His Majesty's Stationery Office, Edinburgh (1928).

67. TROUGHT, J. P.: *Probation in Europe*, B. Blackwell, 1927.

Juvenile Detention and Institutional Placement

68. ADLER, HERMAN M.: "The Work of Institutions in the Prevention of Delinquency," *Journal of Juvenile Research*, XV (January, 1931), 18–27.

69. BISSELL, ELIZABETH: "The Effects of Foster Home Placement on the Personality of Children," *Proceedings of the National Conference of Social Work* (1928).

70. BLACK, JACK: "Human Nature under Authority," *National Conference of Social Work* (1929), pp. 191–199.

70a. BLADES, LESLIE B.: "Longview Farm: A Study Home for Problem Boys," in Sheldon and Eleanor Glueck (Editors), *Preventing Crime*, pp. 267–290, McGraw-Hill Book Company, Inc., 1936.

70b. BOWLER, ALIDA, and RUTH BLOODGOOD: *Institutional Treatment of Delinquent Boys*, U. S. Children's Bureau Publication, Nos. 228, 230 (1935, 1936).

71. BULLER, MARGARET: "Problems of Administration in the Juvenile Detention Home," *Proceedings of the California Conference of Social Work* (1924), pp. 20–26.

72. CABOT, FREDERICK P.: "The Detention of Children as Part of Treatment," *The Child, the Clinic and the Court*, pp. 246–254.

73. CHAMBERLAIN, H. E.: "When Should the Institution Be Prescribed for the Problem Child?" *Proceedings of the National Conference of Social Work* (1928), pp. 383–389.

74. DOBBS, HARRISON A.: "Institutional Care for Delinquent Children: A New Appraisal," *Annals of American Academy of Political and Social Science*, CLI (September, 1930), 173–179.

75. ———: "The Problem of Juvenile Detention," *Year Book, National Probation Association* (1930), pp. 125–130.

76. FENTON, NORMAN: *The Delinquent Boy and the Correctional School*, Progress-Bulletin, Pomona College, 1935.

77. HURBERT, H. S.: "The Principles of a Successful Detention Home in a Large City," *Proceedings of the National Probation Association* (1924), pp. 152–155.

78. KAWIN, IRENE: "Relationships of Probation to Detention and the Institution," *Year Book, National Probation Association* (1931), pp. 221–230.

79. LENROOT, KATHERINE F.: "Juvenile Detention Homes," *Proceedings of the National Probation Association* (1921), pp. 92–100.

80. ———: "Progressive Methods of Care of Children Pending Juvenile Court Hearing," *Proceedings of the National Conference of Social Work* (1926), pp. 135–141.

81. LUMPKIN, KATHERINE D.: "Factors in the Commitment of Correctional School Girls in Wisconsin," *American Journal of Sociology*, XXXVII (September, 1931), 222–230.

82. LUNDBERG, EMMA O.: "Detention in Small Cities and Rural Districts," *Proceedings of the National Probation Association* (1924), pp. 155–160.

83. MILLIS, SAVILLA: *The Juvenile Detention Home in Relation to Juvenile Court Policy; a Study of Intake in the Cook County Juvenile Detention Home*, Chicago Board of Commissioners of Cook County (1927).

83a. MINARD, GEORGE C.: "Educational Experimentation with Problem Boys at Children's Village," in Glueck and Glueck (Editors), *op. cit.*, 291–304.

*84. SHAW, CLIFFORD R.: *The Jack-Roller:* A Delinquent Boy's Own Story, University of Chicago Press, 1930.

85. ———: *The Natural History of a Delinquent Career*, University of Chicago Press, 1931.

86. STERN, LEON: "Detention Homes for Children," *Social Work Year Book* (1933), pp. 129–131.

86a. URQUHART, DONALD T.: "Crime Prevention Through Citizenship Training at the George Junior Republic," in Glueck and Glueck (Editors), *op. cit.*, pp. 305–330.

87. WARNER, FLORENCE M.: *Juvenile Detention in the United States*, University of Chicago Press, 1933.

88. WILLIAMS, R. R.: "The Effects on Personality of Institutional Placement," *Proceedings of the National Conference of Social Work* (1928).

89. WILLS, ARNOLD L.: "Juvenile Detention Home Standards," *Year Book, National Probation Association* (1931), pp. 231–234.

90. ———: "Newer Aspects of Detention Care," *Year Book, National Probation Association* (1934), pp. 167–174.

SUGGESTIONS FOR FURTHER STUDY

1. What is a juvenile court? a criminal court? a superior court? a municipal court? a civil court? a probate court? a court of domestic relations? What is the work and point of view of each?

2. What are the distinctions between penal law, civil law, and common law?

3. Compare the history of the juvenile court with the history of the criminal court.

4. What is the philosophy of juvenile court law? of criminal court law?

5. For purposes of our discussion how essential is research into the original cases on which decisions were established regarding juvenile court practice?

6. Who are the outstanding jurists in the juvenile court movement? the outstanding social workers?

7. How do the juvenile courts in Europe compare with those in the United States?

8. What is meant by *parens patriae?*

9. What does Jane Addams mean by "efforts to humanize justice" and Roscoe Pound by "the spirit of the common law"?

10. Read *A Standard Juvenile Court Law* prepared by the Committee on Standard Juvenile Court Laws (National Probation Association) and determine to what extent the juvenile court law of your state deviates from that standard. How do you account for the deviations? What vestiges of criminal court methods and philosophy, if any, can you find? What would you consider the essential features of a standard juvenile court law?

11. On what philosophy is the Juvenile Court Law in your state based?

12. On what philosophy is juvenile probation based? adult probation? social case work in the courts?

13. Are we living up to the philosophy of the juvenile court law in our work with delinquent children? Why, or why not?

14. What is an acceptable philosophy of work with delinquent children?

15. What should be the function of a juvenile court in a large industrial metropolitan center?

16. With what social agencies should a juvenile court cooperate? a probation department?

17. What should be the relation between the juvenile court and the probation department? the judge and the probation officer? the judge and the community? the judge and the offender's parents?

18. What should have been the procedure in the case of the federal offenders "charged with stealing mail"?

19. What should be the procedure in federal courts dealing with children?

20. What are the values of state supervision of probation?

21. Over what cases does the juvenile court in your state have jurisdiction? What are the age limitations?

22. What is meant by chancery procedure? How did it originate?

23. What are the outstanding characteristics of the juvenile court in your state?

24. What is meant by "social evidence"? by "legal evidence"? by "preponderance of evidence"? by "proof beyond reasonable doubt"?

25. What is a petition? What form of petitions do you use? Why does the juvenile court use petitions instead of indictments?

26. Why does a juvenile court judge have jurisdiction over adults contributing to delinquency or dependency of minors?

27. What are the objections to detaining children temporarily in jails and police stations?

28. What are the detention practices in Boston? What are they in your community?

29. What should be the staff of detention homes?

30. What are the methods of detention used in the United States?

31. What advantages does the "boarding-home plan of detention" have over the detention home?

32. What does Jack Black mean by "human nature under authority"?

33. Consult juvenile court law in your state, and observe the provisions made for "detention pending hearing," "after conviction," in "felony cases."

34. Consult juvenile court law in your state, and observe the provisions made by the law for the maintenance of a detention home.

35. For what purposes should juveniles be detained in special juvenile halls?

36. What are the advantages of juvenile detention? the limitations?

37. To what extent can detention be a method of treatment?

38. What forms of social treatment are used by the court? What is their relation to socialization of treatment? What other forms of treatment does the probation officer use?

39. Under what circumstances can the offender's appearance in the juvenile court have therapeutic value?

40. What are the relative advantages of commitment to state or county institutions and "reform schools" for the child? for the community? for the home?

41. What are the relative advantages and disadvantages of forestry camps? In what way are they superior to state or county institutions?

42. What types of children can be advantageously placed in foster homes? What is Boston's experience with finding suitable foster homes?

43. What is the value of restitution and reparation?

44. What does Moran mean by "new light on juvenile court and probation"?

45. In addition to legal what other training and experience does a juvenile court judge need for socialization of treatment and individualization of justice?

46. What are the relative values of family courts? Why does or why does not your community use family courts for juvenile offenders?

47. Who should deal with juvenile delinquents? What social agency has an acceptable philosophy of work with children? Which social agencies have already demonstrated adequate standards of work to justify their taking over the functions of the juvenile courts?

48. What do the Gluecks consider the values of the juvenile court? the limitations? Grace Abbott? (See *Survey*, May, 1936.)

49. What suggestions do you have for improvement of the juvenile court? On what factors do such improvements depend?

50. What is your reaction to neighborhood centers doing most of the work of the juvenile court? (See Chap. I.)

CHAPTER XIII

THE ROLE OF THE POLICE[1] IN THE WORK OF DELINQUENT YOUTH

Brief History of the Crime Prevention Movement.—Los Angeles and Seattle were among the first cities to establish (in 1909 and 1912, respectively) special juvenile bureaus to deal with minors who had been placed under arrest by any police officer or against whom reports were received from parents, schools, neighbors, or other citizens, whether as offenders or victims.

The following notes,[2] from the office of Justin Miller, Chairman of the Attorney General's Advisory Committee on Crime, prepared by Miss Helen Fuller, indicate the recent work of certain crime prevention bureaus in this country:

Police Departments in most cities engage in some type of preventive work, ranging from one officer assigned to juvenile duty to a well-organized Crime Prevention Bureau. One of the most popular types of programs has been an athletic team or a boys' club, under sponsorship of the police officers. Crime Prevention Bureaus have a wide range of activities including inspection and supervision of commercial amusements, case work with individual delinquents, building constructive forces into the life of the community, sponsoring Coordinating Councils and recreation projects, and developing friendly attitudes on the part of youth and the community toward the law and law enforcement agencies.

There are two distinct ideas which have been attached to the meaning of the term crime prevention in regard to police work; first, preventing criminals from operating, and second, removing temptations and situations provocative of crime and guarding the young against criminal

---

[1] For a comprehensive discussion of the police situation see AUGUST VOLLMER, and OTHERS: National Commission on Law Observance and Enforcement, *Report on Police*, No. 14, and *Recent Social Trends*, pp. 1139–1146.

RAYMOND FOSDICK, *American Police Systems*, MARY E. HAMILTON, *The Policewoman, Her Service and Ideals*.

KATHERINE F. LENROOT and EMMA O. LUNDBERG, *Juvenile Courts at Work*, U. S. Children's Bureau Publication, No. 141 (1925), pp. 43–51.

[2] Paper especially prepared for this volume, July 25, 1936.

influences and tendencies. This first phase of crime prevention has received greater attention than the second, and action arising from this concept has generally proved manageable through the existing administrative set-up. The second phase, in many cases, requires the more specialized handling of a division or bureau especially designed for such work. Since research has shown that a large percentage of criminals begin their careers as juvenile delinquents, most of these special divisions center their work on the prevention of such delinquency. Departments which are engaging in this work have found it necessary not only to secure properly trained personnel for the prevention division, but also to reeducate the whole force in their attitudes toward young offenders and toward the prime importance of crime prevention.

We have obtained reports from the following cities that are doing special work in the field of crime prevention.[1]

Berkeley, California—Crime Prevention Division.—This division was organized under the leadership of August Vollmer in 1925. One of the features of its work is the close cooperation between it and other community organizations. The policewoman in charge is a member of the Berkeley Coordinating Council, and through the Council often obtains follow-up contacts of school counselling, guidance clinic and health center attention for the child who has been under police surveillance. Many juvenile cases are disposed of in an unofficial manner, adopting something like a clinic procedure. The results of psychiatric and other investigations are made available to probation officers and the Detention Home.

San Francisco, California—Crime Prevention Bureau and Big Brother Bureau.—Police officers of the San Francisco Police Department were detailed to a special study of forty problem boys of the juvenile court, and out of their activities grew a Big Brother Movement. Chief Quinn is visualizing his policemen as future boy workers with personal contacts forming the basis of a crime prevention program.

Denver, Colorado—Crime Prevention Bureau (Founded 1931).—An outstanding feature of the work of this division is the emphasis which it places on the importance of cooperation with existing crime prevention agencies. Through its part in the Denver Coordinating Council, the Police Department has established close working relations with the Probation Department, private social agencies, the School Attendance Department, and the Bureau of Public Welfare, helping them to remove

---

[1] See also HENRIETTA ADDITON, "The Crime Prevention Bureau of New York City Police Department," in Sheldon and Eleanor Glueck (Editors), *Crime Prevention*, pp. 215–236, and ELIZABETH LOSSING "The Crime Prevention Work of the Berkeley Police Department," in Glueck and Glueck, *ibid.*, pp. 237–263.

influences which hinder their work. All juvenile cases handled by the Police Department are cleared through the Crime Prevention Bureau which works in connection with the juvenile court on these cases. A large program for community recreation has been begun under police auspices through FERA and WPA.

Washington, D. C.—Women's Bureau and Metropolitan Police Boys' Clubs.—Many athletic teams and recreation programs, as well as a band, are being sponsored through the Metropolitan Police Boys' Clubs. The Women's Bureau deals with conditions conducive to crime and delinquency, and by its patrol and inspection service seeks to improve these conditions in parks, places of commercial amusement, and near schools.

Chicago, Illinois—Crime Prevention Division.—All juvenile cases coming through the Police Department are referred to the Crime Prevention Division, and the personnel of the division includes juvenile officers, policewomen, motion picture censors, etc., who investigate all cases of juvenile delinquency and pay particular attention to places of public amusement where children may be found. The Division tries to develop cooperation with the schools, recreation centers, and other social agencies in the community which may facilitate their work.

Wichita, Kansas—Crime Prevention Division.—In addition to investigation and probation work on juvenile delinquency cases, the division sponsors a Boy Scout troop and a Junior Traffic Control, and attempts to better community conditions which may cause crime by encouraging individuals and organizations to act upon them through such mediums as visiting teachers and child guidance clinics.

Detroit, Michigan—Women's Division (Organized 1921).—All cases involving women and children are referred to this division of the Police Department. Cases are treated from two angles, that of the individual's needs and community conditions. Inspection of amusement places and similar activities consumes the time of about half the staff. The division tries to provide examination and treatment for many individuals who cannot be taken into court. The regular police officers approach the problem of prevention through work in boys' clubs and the sixteen scout troops sponsored by the department.

Saginaw, Michigan—Juvenile Division, Police Department.—This division identifies itself as a "citizenship clinic" for individual treatment of juvenile delinquents. Complete examinations are made and records kept on every case as regards the child and his environment, and progress reports of his development are submitted from time to time. Social adjustment work is done with those boys who have not yet committed any act of an officially delinquent nature, and close follow-up relations are maintained in all cases.

New York City—Juvenile Aid Bureau (Founded in 1930).—This division of the New York City Police Department assumes the same task of investigation of particular localities as has been described in relation to other large cities. In addition, this Bureau has assumed an important function in attempting to seek out the problem child prior to his becoming officially delinquent and offer constructive outlets to him as a means of crime prevention. This work is done with the cooperation of the schools and courts in providing the "trouble list" for the attention of the police officers. A third phase of the work in New York is concerned with creating recreational facilities and leisure-time activities through stimulating other agencies to act, or conducting programs by their own officers. Several hundred WPA workers supervise dozens of street and play center projects throughout the city, and many new community centers are to be provided during the winter. Activities of the Police Athletic League are also being expanded. Organization of 150 out of a contemplated 300 neighborhood Councils has been completed for the purpose of examining and improving community conditions detrimental to the proper development of youth.

Cincinnati, Ohio—Juvenile Registry and Friendly Service Bureau, Department of Safety.—Through the Juvenile Registry of this department, the delinquent child whose case does not warrant an arrest is handled by a social case work procedure. The Department of Safety is also cooperating in the establishing of Community Councils to consider the problems surrounding this delinquency. The Friendly Service Bureau deals with the problem of Negro crime in Cincinnati. The job of the Negroes employed in this division is to ferret out potential crime breeders in the Negro districts before crime develops, and to coordinate all the social and religious forces in this district with a view toward better citizenship. Another form of prevention undertaken by the department is the enlisting of public cooperation for care in the protection of property in order to prevent criminals from operating.

Columbus, Ohio—Friendly Service Bureau (Founded in 1925). The purpose of the Bureau is to assist the migrant and maladjusted to become adjusted to city life. During the lifetime of this division the number of arrests among Negroes in Columbus has decreased 60 per cent. The basis upon which the work proceeds is that of acquaintance and friendship between the families and groups in the problem areas and the social workers and the volunteers connected with the Bureau. Community surveys determine neighborhood conditions, and organizations, social agencies, and industries are called upon to assist in remedying them. The Big Brothers Council with fifty members copes with the problem of delinquency among these unadjusted families.

Philadelphia, Pennsylvania—Crime Prevention Division and Civilian Crime Prevention Unit.—The work of this division is with the "older boy" group between the ages of 16 and 21, and its aim is to get the boy off the street, on the job, and teach a useful trade and wholesome play. Officers work with parents, employers, and school and recreation authorities to effect these ends. Several thousand boys have been enrolled in supervised clubs, many of them organized by the police, and arrests among this group have steadily decreased since the beginning of the program. Lately, WPA and other relief agencies have provided a large group of workers known as the Civilian Crime Prevention Unit which has materially broadened the scope of the work. The division has a section devoted to social case work with the individuals and another devoted to contacts with the public in relation to community development.

Los Angeles, California—Juvenile Police Bureau.—Since the Los Angeles Juvenile Police Bureau is one of the most prominent we cite it as an illustration of this type of organization.   Lieutenant E. W. Lester,[1] the Director of Boys' Work in the Crime Prevention Division of the Los Angeles Police Department, writes:

The Crime Prevention Division of the Los Angeles Police Department had its beginning in 1909 when one officer was assigned to handle all children's cases originating in the Police Department.   In 1910 the first policewoman in the United States was appointed to serve with the Los Angeles Police Department. This distinction was accorded Alice Stebbins Wells who is still a member of this Division.

In 1913 the staff was increased and the name Juvenile Bureau first applied.   As the volume of work increased and the duties became more complex, personnel was added until 1924 when a reorganization of the work was effected.   At this time the Juvenile Bureau, the City Mother's Bureau, the Men's and Women's Municipal Probation Offices were united under one head and the name Crime Prevention Division applied.

The next noteworthy development was a specialization of the work effected by the establishment of separate units to handle case work. These units consisted of the Boys' Detail, the Girls' Detail, the Detective Detail and the Missing Persons Bureau.   In 1930 a decentralization plan was developed whereby juvenile officers, both men and women, were placed in outlying police divisions.   This made juvenile work much more effective, since the officers became well acquainted with neighborhood conditions and with the problem children of the district. Other units have been added from time to time as the work of the Division expanded.

In 1929 the Dancehall Detail was created, in 1930 the Juvenile Traffic Bureau was established, and in 1934 the Bicycle Registration Bureau was added.   The latest unit to be created was the Special Juvenile

[1] Paper especially prepared for this volume, July 14, 1936.

Night Patrol which was established in December, 1935. This was the most outstanding step yet undertaken by any police department in the field of crime prevention. . . . Thirty-two officers, under the supervision of a police lieutenant, have been assigned to this new detail. Two of these officers work in each police division at night, wearing civilian clothes and cruising the district in a radio car. Their . . . work is to discover children who are in danger of becoming delinquent, and to find and eliminate all moral hazards affecting the youth of the community. They will be especially persistent in their efforts to eliminate the sale of liquor to minors. . . .

Children arrested by officers of the new unit are handled in the customary manner by the juvenile officers of the division of arrest. It is to be expected that juvenile arrests will increase materially with the adoption of this plan. With thirty-two additional officers fresh from an inspirational, short course in their new duties intent upon reaching the very source of crime, it would be surprising indeed, if much delinquency was not disclosed—delinquency that might otherwise have remained undiscovered. . . .

A confidential file, which does not constitute a police record, is one of the most vital factors in the new set-up. Sufficient information is taken to clear with the Social Service Exchange and a history of police contacts, voluntary recreational programs, if any, and progress reports are entered briefly on the 5 by 8 card. . . .

The work of the Crime Prevention Division is predicated on the idea that prevention of crime is just as essential as prevention of physical disease and that waiting until a crime had been attempted or committed means shortsightedness which is very costly to the taxpayers. Regarding the underlying philosophy of the Juvenile Police Bureau, its unique functions, and methods of work, Lieutenant Lester writes:

The Underlying Philosophy of Juvenile Police Work.—Juvenile Police work is based on the premise that a special police technique is required in the proper handling of children's cases. The Police Department is usually the first agency that comes in contact with the juvenile delinquent. Many times this first experience is a deciding factor in the child's future conduct. First impressions under the stress attendant to arrest are likely to form indelible concepts in the plastic minds of youngsters. Therefore, it is extremely important to have such cases handled by an expert who is conscious of the part he may be playing in the lives of these children and through them, the lives of others who may be influenced by social contacts.

Juvenile police work is concerned with the social adjustment of the child and contemplates correction but is in no way punitive. On the other hand, social justice for adults is based on the theory that the person who violates the law should be punished. One theory being the exact antithesis of the other, it is readily understood that the police officers who become adept in applying the one theory might find it difficult to apply the other fairly and justly. Because of this underlying principle it is even more essential that juvenile work be more specialized than other phases of police work.

Unique Functions of the Juvenile Police Bureau.—The Crime Prevention Division of the Los Angeles Police Department[1] renders the following community services:

1. Twenty-four-hour emergency service in all matters of crime and dependency affecting children.

2. Complete investigation of all criminal phases of cases involving children.

3. Investigation and prosecution of all adults who have committed crimes against children.

4. Discovery and elimination of the causes of delinquency through investigation of individual cases and community conditions.

5. Detection of children in danger and the minimizing of these dangers by suggested supervised recreational and character-building activities.

6. Counseling with parents in matters of supervision of pre-delinquent and delinquent children.

7. Complete cooperation with the Detective Service in clearing crime reports and making application of *modus operandi*.

Specific Methods Used by Juvenile Police Bureau.—The Juvenile Police are required to make prompt and thorough investigations of all cases where crime has been committed by or against juveniles, followed immediately by a proper presentation of all facts to the Juvenile Court. In the conduct of such an investigation it is necessary to:

1. Secure all details from the offender and the victim and go over these matters carefully with the suspect in an effort to determine two things: Has an offense by or a crime against a juvenile been committed? Did the suspect commit the offense or the crime?

2. Weigh all evidence and determine the advisability of detention or release. (Less than 50 per cent of the boys and girls arrested by the Los Angeles Police Department are detained even as long as overnight.)

3. Go into full details with the parents or guardians and learn the answers to the following questions:

[1] Compare these functions with those discussed by Henrietta Additon, *op. cit.* and Elizabeth Lossing, *op. cit.*

a. Has the child been a problem in the home? If so, how?

b. What standards are used by the parents in reaching their conclusions?

c. Observe the parents and their attitudes—are they dependable? Do they alibi and offer excuses? Are they reasonable? Do they blame the school, associates—the police?

d. Are the parents in any way responsible for the offense? If they are incapable of controlling their child, can they be helped to overcome their weaknesses?

e. Are the parents capable of making an adjustment? Do they need help? Who can best give this help?

If it is necessary or advisable to take the child before the court, all facts brought out by the investigation must be presented. . . . If the juvenile officer's work is properly done, he is in a position to offer helpful suggestions in the matter of the court's disposition of the case.

The juvenile officer must know the objectives and facilities of all social agencies in the field of child welfare and in the conduct of his investigations must ask himself these questions: (1) Can any of these agencies be helpful? (2) Will they accept the case? (3) How can the greatest assistance be given to the agency that undertakes the follow-up work?

If the parents request voluntary supervision by the juvenile police officer, a supervised program should be arranged when it would occasion no conflict with the officer's duties as an investigator. The officer must determine the objectives of such a program and how they can best be realized. Will the child cooperate—voluntarily or through compulsion? Can the program be rearranged in the event of failure? When is supervision to be relaxed or withdrawn? What constitutes a satisfactory adjustment?

The juvenile officer must analyze many factors in the conduct of his investigations and must determine the answers to the following questions:

(1) What other facts has the investigation brought out? (2) Were other juveniles involved in the commission of the offense? If so, were they found and were their cases thoroughly investigated and proper dispositions made? (3) Were adults involved? If so, was evidence preserved and were apprehensions and prosecutions successful? (4) Were other crimes committed? (5) Was *modus operandi* carefully applied? (6) Was all property recovered and returned to the victims? (7) Were moral hazards affecting children in the community disclosed by the investigation? If so, were they successfully removed? If not, were all community facilities brought into play in an attempt to remove them?

In the determination of a proper disposition of a case a number of factors are important. Many times the offense is less important than such factors as previous record, school reputation, community reputation, social history, intelligence, physical condition and environment. . .

Since police work concerns itself primarily with investigation, the duties of police officers assigned to the juvenile branch differ little from those of the rest of the service. This is true even of the work of police units whose efforts are basically crime preventive. Here, however, the emphasis shifts from the individual and his conduct to the community and the moral hazards that endanger youth. . . .

It is the responsibility of the police to protect life and property and to preserve the peace. The fact that a juvenile is a suspected perpetrator of an offense does not lessen in any way the responsibility of the police. It is just as important to recover and return stolen property to the victim of the offense as in any other case. . . .

The methods employed by juvenile police officers investigating the criminal aspects of a case are of vital importance to the ultimate adjustment of the delinquent child. Juvenile officers in Los Angeles long ago realized that efforts to obtain truthful statements by inhuman treatment are seldom effective and never justified. The ineffectiveness of so-called "third-degree" methods is overshadowed only by the brutalizing effect upon both the accused and the person resorting to such measures. Mental torture is as much to be deplored as physical violence, and resort to either is an indictment to the intelligence, experience, and initiative of the officer who employs it. Brutality, long abhorred in relation to juvenile cases, is just as intolerable when applied to adults.

To be effective the police approach must be gentle but firm—must be with a sympathetic understanding but without condonement. The child's confidence must be gained but never violated. The wise and experienced officer does not bargain for the truth. His technique is such that the child finds it easy to make a complete, truthful statement. As a case in point I recall a fifteen year old boy who was charged with grand theft of an automobile, burglary, kidnapping and robbery. The detectives of two cities and special agents from a large public utilities corporation investigated the case for several days and although the boy was positively identified by two of the victims, he stoutly maintained his innocence. The importance of securing a truthful statement from this lad lay in the fact that he had said to each of his victims, "If I'm ever nabbed by the cops and you dare to identify me, it will be the last thing you ever do, because I'm a member of a gang and everyone of us has sworn to kill any person who puts the finger on any member of our mob." This boy was finally surrendered to us by a sister city and brought to our Bureau where, after hours of friendly, earnest conversation with a juvenile officer, he made a full statement of the facts and confessed more offenses than he was known to have committed.   When asked why he had been so stubborn and uncooperative, he said, "Well, I thought I was a big shot and it would look like weakness if I helped the cops any," but he admitted that the talk with the juvenile officer had changed his point of view and . . . he was no longer proud of the crimes he had committed and was ashamed of the tough attitude he had assumed throughout the investigation.

The success of interviews with a boy or girl suspected of an offense cannot be measured alone by the truthfulness of the statements made but is likewise dependent upon the mental attitude assumed by the child regarding his or her confession.   The child should never feel that he has been trapped into making admissions.   His self-respect should be heightened, not lowered, since it is the misconduct, not the admission, that should bring remorse. . . .

The various factors contributing to the cause of the individual delinquency are of greatest importance to the juvenile officer.   By a careful study of the cause a better understanding may be reached with the child and a ready solution sometimes offers itself.   At the same time invaluable information thus obtained makes possible a more comprehensive plan for crime prevention.   It is generally agreed by students of social problems that a complete knowledge of underlying causes of crime is essential with individual delinquents for the success of any preventive program.   Any deep sympathetic understanding is logically based on a thorough knowledge of the underlying causal factors of delinquency.

When the juvenile officer has the authority to decide what action should be proposed, it is important in cases that may be handled out of court, that the background as a whole be scrutinized and the disposition made in view of all the facts.   The attitude of parent and child, the previous record and social history, are often far more important than the offense in the consideration of proper disposition of the case. . . .

It is not essential that the juvenile officer investigate extraneous phases of the conduct of a child, such as the school record and home relationships in those cases where the very seriousness of the offense demands court action.   This work must be done by the probation officer and duplication and overlapping of work should be avoided whenever possible.   This is particularly applicable to that percentage of cases involving definite criminal tendencies to which the Juvenile Court must give proper recognition through clinical diagnosis and careful application of scientific methods, lest Dillingers and Hickmans unwittingly may be allowed to develop in our respective neighborhoods.

Possibly the greatest advantage in having juvenile police lies in the value of coordination of community effort to effect two things—a wholesome district in which to live and rear children, and the satisfactory adjustment of the unfortunate youngsters who find themselves in conflict with society. Complete cooperation is always dependent upon a full understanding and appreciation of the other fellow's viewpoint. Before the attitude of an agency can be understood, it is necessary to have an intimate knowledge, not only of its objectives but also its facilities. A close relationship between the juvenile officer and other agencies interested in the welfare of children makes it possible to formulate a program that encompasses the whole field of crime prevention.

From reports received from various parts of the country it is evident that the police work in behalf of juveniles as developed in California[1] has much to offer to other communities. In many communities most of the work is done by policewomen. Henrietta Additon[2] has done much toward the development of the Crime Prevention Bureau of the New York City Police Department, but this work has been greatly curtailed at present.

As Professor Sutherland maintains, "at the time when strenuous efforts are being made in several departments to build up the respect for the police and the morale of the police, it is rather ungracious"[3] to hurl any criticism against it, particularly since the police officers in the juvenile bureaus are more discriminately chosen and undoubtedly possess far higher qualifications than those in the regular police department. But in order to understand the situation with reference to crime prevention it is necessary to state some of the objections raised to this form of police work. There is the general criticism in the mind of the average citizen of inefficiency, lawlessness, brutality, lack of education[4] of the average police officer. It may also be added that the officers in police juvenile bureaus rarely have the educational background and training to carry on social investigations in the field of juvenile delinquency and to engage in social treatment of offenders and their families. The above criticisms have been directed rather indiscriminately to the patrolmen on the beat, local precinct officers, and those in specialized bureaus

[1] See ELIZABETH LOSSING, "Crime Prevention Work of the Berkeley Police Department," in Sheldon and Eleanor Glueck (Editors), *Preventing Crime*, Chap. XIII.

[2] *Ibid.*, Chap. XII.

[3] EDWIN H. SUTHERLAND, *Principles of Criminology*, p. 203; see also pp. 199–227.

[4] *Ibid.*, pp. 203–208.

dealing with children's problems. The more faithful and efficient officers and departments are rightly "smarting under this criticism."

Vollmer[1] and others have done much to indicate the responsibility of the public in the work of the police and have shown under what serious handicaps the police must work. The White House Conference on Child Health and Protection adds:

> Much of the criticism heaped upon the police for their failure to enforce the laws and preserve the peace successfully should be directed to other law enforcing agencies. The public often forgets that the police, daily, display a high degree of intelligence, bravery and devotion to duty. Not only would a more just attitude toward them raise the *esprit de corps* of the entire police personnel, but children also would respond to the same attitude, coming to look upon the policeman as a friend and protector.[2]

Sutherland maintains that the concept of preventive police work has not been clearly defined:

> It seems to include a great variety of methods, including "hounding the hoodlums," attacks on criminal hangouts, frequent patrolling, warning residents and business concerns to keep doors and windows locked, friendly acquaintance with the residents on the beat, friendly relations with boys' gangs, organization of recreational activities in areas where delinquency rates are high, concentrated and cooperative efforts to influence boys who are getting into trouble, and social service work with families or individuals in distress. . . .
>
> On the other hand, much of the preventive work of the police must be done by the regular male policemen, and must become a part of the regular police program. This preventive work by the regular staff has been well developed in Rochester, New York, and in Berkeley. Efforts are made to build up friendly relations with the schools,[3] and in case conferences with the various social agencies which are interested in programs for individuals who are inclined toward delinquency.

Jonah J. Goldstein[5] maintains, however, that a rather regrettable attitude prevails on the part of the Children's Court toward the Bureau of Crime Prevention in New York:

[1] AUGUST VOLLMER and OTHERS, National Commission on Law Observance and Enforcement, *Report on Police*, No. 14.

[2] *The Delinquent Child*, p. 249.

[3] See AUGUST VOLLMER, "Predelinquency," *Journal of Criminal Law and Criminology*, XIV (August, 1923), 282–283.

[5] *The Family in Court*, pp. 106–107.

The records of the Children's Court are a closed book to the Bureau of Crime Prevention. Not only have there been no conferences with the Bureau but its activities are resented.

The Children's Court judges have, in conferences with street railway officials, sought to prevent the turning over of youngsters who hitched on trolley cars to the Bureau of Crime Prevention and requested that they be brought to the Children's Court instead. Since when is hitching on a trolley car or a taxi-cab evidence of juvenile delinquency? What normal boy did not at some time or other steal a ride? For his own safety, stealing rides should be stopped, and can be stopped much more effectively in cooperation with the Bureau of Crime Prevention than by arrest, arraignment and adjudication as a juvenile delinquent in the Children's Court. . . .

Instead of seeking an increase of business for the Children's Court through conferences with the railroad companies, such conferences should be held with the Bureau of Crime Prevention. A social check-up on the intake would prevent this ridiculous spectacle.

Methods of Cooperation with Other Agencies.—Albert J. Sargent,[1] Chief probation officer, Municipal Court of Boston, points out how to secure police cooperation by the probation department and how each can be of service to the other in their close contacts which they make daily in their work. His observations regarding the possible resentment by the probationer against the scrutiny by both a police and a probation officer are of interest. Although the following statements are written chiefly from the point of view of the adult probationer, they apply with equal validity to the juvenile probationer:

The inevitable meeting of police and probation work at various points brings at the very outset of a case an opportunity for immediate mutual help between the police and probation systems. The arresting officers come to court in many instances possessed of information of valuable, preliminary interest. Arrests in certain types of crime do not occur until after close and continued observation by the police officer during which he has acquired a knowledge of the defendant which embraces the local activities or even more remote facts of marked significance to the probation officer, whose job it is to gather the essential social history if he can.

Intelligent police officers, experienced in their work and the performance of their duties, who are under proper supervision, are as a rule

[1] "Getting Police Cooperation," *Year Book, National Probation Association* (1930), pp. 245–247.

observant and logical. Frequently they see beyond the crime, and pursue their inquiries to the point where information is gathered which is of direct value to the probation officer. Their investigations in connection with the acquisition of evidence preparatory to prosecution of a case often bring them in touch with factors in general social history, which though in many cases inadmissible at trial, are of pointed interest in the disposition of the case and, therefore, of special interest to the officer in court. This information should not be lost through silence or apathy on the part of either the police officer or the probation officer. When brought to light at the earliest possible moment it may be developed to its full value through efficient investigation. The very details of the offense upon which the officer bases his complaint are occasionally illuminating and serve as a guide to the trained court worker.

The probation officer in court should not pass over with indifference or judge too lightly the impressions of the arresting officer when honestly given in an effort to be helpful. These opinions on the part of the police officer usually spring from observation and thought, and if in some particulars their value may be later disproved by investigation they are often an aid to a well-rounded study of the case under consideration. Not the least of the advantages derived from early conference with the police officer is the correction of false information given by defendants to the probation officer or the detection of evasiveness. A check-up by the probation officer with the police frequently reveals conflicting statements by the defendant and results in a more definite persuasion of the latter to a reasonable and truthful viewpoint, thus avoiding misdirected efforts in the early stages of investigation. . . .

The police officer's contact with the case in its initial stages generally makes him a source of helpfulness to the probation officer. The fullest cooperation between the two cannot fail to produce beneficial results.

The police can render most acceptable service to the supervisor in the field, as they are generally more aware of what is happening in the community than probation officers. Their personal knowledge of the activities of probationers living within their district and coming under their supervision should therefore be of considerable help to the supervisor.

An objection might be raised that a probationer would be stirred to resentment or repelled from full cooperation if he felt that he was the object of scrutiny by both police and the probation department and that therefore the real purpose of persuading him to a better mode of life might be seriously endangered. The assumption by the police officer of the clear-cut duties and responsibilities of the supervisor is not what is contemplated in the situation just described; it relates instead to the confidential, timely observation and notice made by the police officer which may enable the supervisor to exert prompt and effective guidance of the probationer. The average probation officer has a heavy load to carry, he is charged usually with the care of a large number of cases and is unable to meet all the demands upon his time and attention. It is in these circumstances especially that the police officer's help may prove opportune in stemming developments which might seriously affect the success of supervision.

James K. Watkins, recently Commissioner of Police, Detroit, is inclined to take a middle road in the preventive work among young people. He says:[1]

Insofar as police departments are concerned, there are those who take the position that the police should leave the problem almost entirely alone and should not attempt protective work with young people. The exponents of this theory assert that the police are trained for their main job and that to use them in the protective and preventive field will necessarily result in poor work. They say that this work should be done entirely by other agencies—probation officers, child-caring agencies, boy scout organizations and the like. On the other hand, there are those who advocate the development in a police department of a bureau working among the youth of both sexes, and developing a protective and preventive organization of broad scope even involving treatment work with the individual. My own view is that the proper function of the police lies between these two extremes. I think that they can properly go some distance beyond the older and narrower conception, but that there is a line which cannot, it is true, always be clearly defined, beyond which the police should not go. The development of crime preventive programs in police departments has been necessarily slow and is still largely in the experimental stages. . . .

The great question is just how far they should go in their work and I believe that the limits can be fairly well outlined. Let us assume that we have the organization suggested above, with a detail assigned to each precinct. The regular officer walking his beat should be competent to recognize that a problem exists, for example, in connection with a gang of boys making trouble in a neighborhood, but he is probably not trained either to diagnose the difficulty or to administer the treatment. If the proper spirit of cooperation within the department is developed, he will report the condition to his superior officer, who can then direct the juvenile detail to investigate the situation. A member of the detail can then make a careful investigation, and, if he is properly trained, can determine in a general way the causes of the trouble and the

[1] "The Police and the Prevention of Delinquency," *Year Book, National Probation Association* (1932–1933), pp. 43–48.

proper agency to deal with it. It may be that the whole trouble is due to the influence of one dominating leader among the group. It would be within the scope of the officer's duties to get full information regarding this individual. It might then be the proper thing for him to see that a complaint is made against the boy and that he is brought before the juvenile court. On the other hand, this might be entirely wrong and the officer should perhaps see that an agency dealing with boys is brought into contact with this individual and, through him, with the group.

This, it seems to me, is as far as the police should go. I do not believe that the officer should himself attempt treatment. In a very short time the case load would be altogether too great. Again, the officer on the beat should be qualified to judge whether the conditions surrounding a poolroom or a dancehall are good, or bad, but he will not ordinarily be in a position to do very much toward remedying them, if he feels that there is need for improvement. He should report the condition to his superior officer and the matter should be assigned to the juvenile division, and if it is a dancehall, both the juvenile and the women's detail. They, working in cooperation, can perhaps themselves remedy the situation. If there are individual cases, however, which need attention, then they should be referred to other agencies. The women's detail in a precinct may learn, either through their own investigation or through the report from a citizen or another officer, of a case of neglected children. The work of the detail should be to make a thorough investigation of the situation and determine the proper steps for correcting it. But, in general, it will not be possible for the detail itself to bring about the improvement. Again, the case load would become altogether too heavy. Our woman's division last year, for example, had personal contact with some nine thousand girls and young women. With thirty-three officers in the division it is obviously out of the question to expect detailed attention to the individual case. All they can do is to take such immediate action as may be essential and then see that the matter is brought to the attention of the proper agency, public or private, for individual treatment. . . .

Looking at the matter purely from a selfish police viewpoint, there are definite advantages to be gained from a juvenile division. Some of the boys with whom the officers come in contact are bound to go wrong and it will unquestionably be of help to the department to have the information gathered by the juvenile detail when, at a later date, the detective division is forced to handle a problem involving the individual or the gang. I feel quite certain that as time passes the detective bureau will receive invaluable assistance from reports of the juvenile detail, particularly in connection with the activities of certain gangs.

Should Police Officers Carry on Social Case Treatment?—It is apparent from the foregoing excerpts that the juvenile police officer is concerned with more than "the immediate needs of the child and of the general public security . . . and the enforcement of particular laws," functions ascribed to him by the White House Conference on Child Health and Protection.[1] Some of the juvenile police officers are also concerned with serious conditions of family maladjustment, conflict with the law and social norms.

The police officer—the patrolman, or the officer at the local precinct, or the specialized juvenile officer—as stated before, is generally the first representative of the law with whom a delinquent child or "a child in trouble" comes into personal contact. He is in the most strategic position of all. His conduct, his approach, his attitudes toward "law-breaking and law-breakers" are of utmost importance in the tense and emotional situations in which these children find themselves. He needs a comprehensive knowledge of child psychology, of human nature, and of the adolescent world in order to do justice by them. Furthermore, "the people" depend upon the police officer "to determine the fact of conflict between children and organized society and to exercise discretion as to whether it is sufficiently serious to merit arrest or court action."[2] Thus he is called upon again to make decisions which involve a knowledge of the prevailing social norms and legal precedent in relation to child welfare. Therefore, even though the officer should concern himself with nothing more than the immediate needs of the child and the safety of the community he needs training in the various fields applying to human nature and the social order. There is no more reason to believe that—with the above demands put upon a police officer— he should be exempt from training and from a knowledge of, at least, the fundamentals of social work, any more than the probation officer making a social investigation relative to the various petitions filed in the matter of child delinquency should be exempt.

But should the juvenile police officer concern himself with "serious problems of maladjustment and home visits" beyond the initial contact? The White House Conference on Child Health and Protection is very emphatic in its statement that

[1] *The Delinquent Child*, pp. 246–247.
[2] *Ibid.*, p. 247.

"the police should not undertake intensive and continuous direction or responsibility for a child."[1] Such responsibility should rest with the child guidance clinics, probation departments, and other child welfare agencies—according to the nature of the problem—which have been organized to deal with the intricate processes of therapy. It has been proved—by such authorities as Healy, Burt, Lenroot, Shaw, Burgess, Thomas, and others previously referred to—to be far more expedient to have the problematic child referred to competent specialists in social therapeutics at the earliest possible moment and without any missteps.

The average juvenile police officer is not equipped to approach child welfare problems from the specialist's standpoint, and even if he were in a position to do so he would be duplicating the work of other agencies specifically organized to perform these functions.

With the establishment of children's courts, the view has been widely accepted that only these courts, through their probation officers, should deal with children's problems, and that the police, by virtue of the nature of their work in suppressing crime and their past failures in dealing with social problems, are disqualified or unsuited to assist in the solution of children's problems. If we accept the present conventional police methods as something that cannot be changed, then we must agree that this therapy is correct. It is believed, however, that most police departments gladly will cooperate in any reasonable plan pointed out to them, for the welfare of children and the prevention of delinquency and crime. That this belief is well founded is indicated by the attitude and practice of many individual police officers.

Justice is a single operation, working through a number of agencies. While the police start the process, it is left to . . . courts and other agencies to complete it.[2]

William I. Thomas and Dorothy S. Thomas[3] are also of the opinion that all problems of retraining of the child should be referred to regular child welfare agencies:

There is no question that the police should be associated with social work, that women should be a part of the police and that the entrance of women into the activities of the police will facilitate the socialization

[1] *Ibid.*, p. 248.
[2] *Ibid.*, pp. 248–249.
[3] *The Child in America*, pp. 217–218. Reprinted by permission of Alfred A. Knopf, Inc.

of police work. The main problem relates to the division of function between the police and the other agencies doing social work. The visiting teacher work, the social aspects of the child clinics and child guidance institutes, the study and management of cases under investigation and on probation, are now largely in the hands of women. The case workers themselves are dependent on the psychologists, psychiatrists and sociologists, and their work is becoming progressively a study of behavior in connection with the treatment of the case. Bad behavior trends are often set up in infancy, mental deviations, disabilities and conflicts are involved, the case worker has always a problem of retraining, and under the best handling and during long years the result is frequently disappointing. The participation of the police will be a benefit to the whole situation and what the limitations of their functions are will be determined by experience, but "prevention and protection" as used in their programs is not a simple matter. It involves cooperation and integration of work between persons specialized in different ways.

In addition to the juvenile police officers, patrolmen on the beat and the safety patrol as well as neighborhood precinct officers come in numerous contacts with juveniles. "Not infrequently individual policemen show by their work that they have a fine perception and appreciation of social values, and for this reason are qualified by temperament, if not by training to work with children."[1] Talks by police officers at schools regarding safety precautions in traffic have helped in making "the cop" a friend.

It is of utmost importance that the attitude of the policeman on the beat be friendly and sympathetic toward the children. Fortunately one hears only occasionally of such police attitudes as expressed in the following quotation by Caroline Ware.[2]

My opinion of the people on this street is that from five years up to sixty they are all thieves. They are all born criminals; I wouldn't trust any of them over three years old. You try and do something for them! It's no use; you might as well work on that sewer over there. You see the tin water drains on the church there? Well, they were all copper once, but the kids stole them all, and when the priest tried to chase them, they threw stones and broke the church windows. In ten years they'll all be gunmen and gangsters. If I had it to say, I'd send

[1] The White House Conference on Child Health and Protection, *op. cit.*, p. 249.

[2] *Greenwich Village*, 1920–1930, p. 403.

them all to Sing Sing. I wouldn't build no playgrounds for them; that won't do any good. I've been on this beat for twenty years and I ain't seen no change yet!

Such attitudes promote constant hostility and aggravate an already aggravated situation. Such officers tend to use "third degree" methods in their dealings with minors, a situation which has aroused considerable public condemnation.[1] On the other hand:

Friendly advice and admonition will usually be accepted by the child in the spirit in which it is given, but threats of punishment (in terms of the criminal law), are both ineffectual and foolish, as the child usually knows when the officer is bluffing and if he does not, is likely to take a chance in order to find out. Nothing will produce confidence in and respect for an individual more than the knowledge that he is honest and sincere, that he keeps his word when given, and that he will not threaten to do something impossible.[2]

Police Field Work Cases.—Eleanor L. Hutzel, Deputy Commissioner of the Detroit Police Department, and Madeline L. Macgregor,[3] Chief of Social Service of the Grand Rapids Child Guidance Clinic, cite a number of interesting "field work cases," showing procedure and facts obtained by questioning, during patrol contacts.[4] However, no case treatment is attempted. Three of the twenty-four cases cited are reproduced here for purposes of illustrating a possible approach to girls by police officers, police procedure in difficult circumstances, the data obtained in a short interview, and the referral of cases:

CASE OF VIVIAN 16-W

Patrol Contact.—Policewomen observed young girl on street corner in downtown district at 3 A. M. At that hour in the morning policewomen on patrol question any unaccompanied young girl whom they observe on the street.

[1] See DOROTHY WILLIAMS BURKE, *Youth and Crime*, U. S. Children's Bureau Publication, No. 196 (1930), p. 47.

[2] The White House Conference on Child Health and Protection, *op. cit.*, pp. 250–251.

[3] *The Policewoman's Handbook.* Reprinted by permission of Columbia University Press.

[4] See also MARY E. HAMILTON, *The Policewoman, Her Service and Ideals*.

PROCEDURE	FACTS OBTAINED BY QUESTIONING
Police-women approached the girl. Identified themselves as police officials. Explained that because she was alone on the street at that hour they wished to be sure that she was properly protected.	Age—given as 17 years. Present address—recognized as that of a cheap hotel where young girls were admitted without question. Previous address—also recognized as questionable. Parents living in another state. Said she could show letters that they were satisfied to have her here. Unable to find letters from parents.
Accompanied girl to her room in hotel in order that she might show letters from her parents. Interview in hotel room.	Articles of masculine clothing observed in room which girl explained belonged to her husband.
At this point man entered from an adjoining room.	Girl noticeably disturbed, introduced man, named him, and hurriedly added facts about the date and place of marriage.
One policewoman asked man to step into hall where she questioned him.	Policewoman noted that the girl's introduction of man gave him facts which he would have known if they had been married.
The other policewoman continued questioning girl.	What was wife's maiden name? No answer. Where had they lived since marriage? No answer. Where did wife's parents live? No answer.
	Girl admitted that she was not married to man; that her home was in Detroit. Gave her correct name and address of parents—correct age as sixteen years.
Man and girl taken to office of Woman's Bureau.	
List of missing girls showed that girl had been reported as missing by the Juvenile Court.	
Man charged with contributing to the delinquency of a female minor. Held at First Precinct Station.	
Parents of girl notified that she was located.	
Girl held at Juvenile Detention Home as police witness and for Juvenile Court.	
Special report written and left for Supervisor.	

CASE OF PEARL 13-W

Patrol Contact.—Girl observed loitering along the street in the down-town business section at 11 P. M. Policewomen followed girl for several blocks. She made no attempt to attract men but her aimless sauntering and her youth influenced the policewomen to speak to her.

PROCEDURE

Policewomen approached the girl, identified themselves, and explained that they would like to ask her a few questions.

FACTS OBTAINED BY QUESTIONING

Where are you going? Am waiting for my girl friend. How old are you? Sixteen years. Where do you live? 1801 B Street. (Fair residential district.) What is your friend doing downtown at 11 P. M.? She works in a restaurant. Where is restaurant? Do not know.

Policewomen then explained to the girl that in order to protect her, they would remain until her friend arrived. It was evident that the girl did not want this but the policewomen continued friendly conversation which was so casual that girl did not realize she was giving information about herself. In a short time the policewomen learned that the girl was not waiting for anyone. They then offered to take her home. Her reaction to this offer was such that the policewomen appreciated that there was something wrong. Further questioning resulted in information that the girl was thirteen years old and had run away from home.

Girl taken to office of Woman's Bureau. No telephone at her home. Precinct asked to notify parents that girl was located. Mother refused to come for daughter.

Girl taken to Juvenile Detention Home. Special report written and left for Supervisor.

Precinct later reported that girl left home early in afternoon after a quarrel with mother.

CASE OF MARTHA 14-W AND VERA 15-W

Patrol Contact.—Policewomen observed girls coming from an all-night restaurant at 2 A. M. Girls looked young and were dressed and "made-up" in a way that attracted attention.

PROCEDURE

Usual approach. Followed customary procedure of questioning girls separately.

Girls were then told that policewomen would take them home in their automobile. As soon as girls were in car, officers compared facts which they had obtained. There was enough disagreement to arouse suspicion, and the policewomen, explaining this to the girls, asked permission to verify statements by inspecting apartment.

Took girls to their apartment in a building which was known to officers as one where management was lax. Upon entering apartment found two men there. Girls became frightened when the men were found in the apartment.

Girls taken to bedroom by one policewoman; the other remained to question the men.

Sent for manager of apartment. Explained situation.

Telephoned for policemen to take men prisoners to office of Woman's Bureau.

Girls taken to Woman's Bureau in policewomen's car.

Woman's Bureau card index checked. Both girls known to department.

Office interview with girls, after explaining that parents had reported them missing.

Girls held at Juvenile Detention Home as police witnesses and for medical examinations.

FACTS OBTAINED BY QUESTIONING

Ages—eighteen and nineteen years respectively . . . Living? In nearby apartment house. No relation. No friends. How long at apartment? Five weeks. Employment? None; living on money from home. Other questions about their recent living, their families, etc.

One man said that he was the husband of Vera, calling her "R," and that he could show their marriage certificate. Said other man was his friend who visited him occasionally. He was asked routine questions and contradicted statements made by the girls.

Girls gave their correct ages as fourteen and fifteen years; admitted they had come from Canada; Vera denied marriage.

Men charged with pandering. Held at First Precinct Station. Parents notified that girls were located.

Records showed both girls were Canadian, reported missing for two months.

Special report written and left for Supervisor. Policewomen, in report, called attention to the fact that the girls should be further questioned in regard to any criminal responsibility of apartment house manager.

Girls stated they came to Detroit immediately after they ran away. Met one of the men found in apartment soon after coming to city. He arranged to rent apartment and brought the other man. Girls had prostituted with customers brought to the apartment by these men. Men did not live there but were in and out with customers.

The police officer in referring cases needs to familiarize himself or herself with the existing native institutions and key people as well as with the major social agencies serving the particular community, the "character-building agencies," the schools, the child-caring agencies, the private protective agencies, the welfare agencies, health clinics, guidance clinics, and, needless to add, the probation department and the juvenile court. The newspaper reporter may at times prove an important asset, if he is cooperative in "printing items to which the Police Department desires to give publicity, but which have no particular news value."[1]

The Police Officer and Neighborhood Conditions.—Smith Bruce[2] points out that police schools—still relatively few in this country—"usually emphasize such necessary elements as marksmanship but give little attention to methods dealing with juvenile problems or maintaining clean community conditions."

The maintenance of clean community conditions is one of the most valuable contributions that the police can make, and if effectively performed, under able leadership, will not alone insure physical and moral safety for children but in the end will result in a material reduction

---

[1] *Ibid.*, p. 147. For a brief history of the woman police officer see Katherine B. Davis, "The Police Woman," *The Woman Citizen* (May 30, 1925); and Henrietta Additon, "The Policewomen," *Proceedings of the Tenth Annual Conference of the International Association of Policewomen* (1924), pp. 51–52; and Chloe Owings, *Women Police.*

[2] See "Municipal Police Administration," *Annals of the American Academy of Political and Social Science*, CXLVI (November, 1929), 1–27; see also his *Report on the Subcommission on Police* (Albany, 1927), p. 7, quoted by the White House Conference on Child Health and Protection, *op. cit.*, p. 251.

of crime.   This service should include street patrol, inspection of parks, playgrounds, theaters, dance halls and similar services.   Unattended children found in public at night should be taken to their homes and their parents warned that if such conduct recurs they will be prosecuted for contributing to the delinquency or neglect of their children.

Both the juvenile police officers and the regular officers in many communities concern themselves also in addition to the services cited above with the discovery of adults "polluting the morals of minors," with children at street trades, particularly at night, with sale of liquor and of salacious literature to minors, with "undercover operations," and other similar situations.

Hutzel and Macgregor in their *Policewoman's Handbook*[1] add the following services which already are performed in some localities or should be performed by policewomen: looking out for discouraged unemployed women or girls who may be led into sexual promiscuity; secluded automobiles "under suspicious circumstances," or "cruising cars" occupied by men attempting to pick up young girls, or cars driven recklessly by hilarious young people; gambling devices and places; terminal stations; suspicious rooming houses and hotels,[2] motion picture "palaces,"[3] overcrowded and unsanitary housing conditions, and others.

J. P. Trought's[4] description of the Children's Police in Amsterdam gives interesting additional functions which might be assumed:

Day and night officers supervise minors in the streets, railway stations, markets, cinemas, dancing saloons, public-houses, etc., for the prevention of mendicity, truancy, vagrancy, and for maintenance of those prohibitive regulations especially established in the interests of the child.   Their work is preventive, corrective and, where necessary, repressive; their prime object is to be counsellor, helper and protector to the minor brought before the court of first instance.   General police who come into touch with a juvenile offender give notice to the children's police.

The headquarters of this service is as unlike a police-station as it is possible to make it.   Here the harassed mother brings her obstreperous

---

[1] See pp. 20–54.

[2] See also NORMAN HAYNER, *Hotel Life*.

[3] See HERBERT BLUMER and PHILLIP M. HAUSER, *Movies, Delinquency and Crime;* and HERBERT BLUMER, *Movies and Conduct*.

[4] *Probation in Europe*, pp. 123–124.

son for guidance as to his management. Here the pre-trial investigations are prepared for the children's judge, and the arrangement for placing in an institution or under other guardianship carried out. The collection of data for research work is filed together with information concerning offenders.

Recommendations by the White House Conference.—The White House Conference on Child Health and Protection[1] offers the following recommendations in dealing with juvenile delinquents by police officers:

In most instances it is unnecessary to arrest child offenders. Only in exceptional circumstances, or for the purpose of identification, should a child be placed in detention. When the child's identity has been determined and his correct address ascertained, he should be returned to the care and custody of his parents, preferably at his home, and the parents informed of the nature of his misconduct and of the probable action of the police. Under no circumstances should a child be arrested in his own home, except on warrant issued by the court. . . .

When a child is apprehended committing an offense that will necessitate his being brought to the attention of the court, the case should be referred to the children's bureau or detail for preliminary investigation and disposition. Whenever possible, children should be interviewed in their homes, and not in police stations.

In case it is necessary to send a child to a place of detention, the patrol wagon should not be used. Most departments are provided with passenger cars which have no markings to distinguish them from privately owned automobiles and this type of car should be used. Under no circumstances should handcuffs be used. The procedure followed must depend upon the facts and circumstances in each case. No set rules can be adopted that will fit even two cases, let alone many. There is no reason why there should be a difference between day and night procedure in dealing with children's cases.

If it possibly can be avoided, children should not be taken to police stations, and when brought in should be sent immediately to their own homes or to the house of detention. It is inexcusable to place children in cells with adults. The period of time between the arrest and hearing should be reduced to a minimum. As indicated before, it is only in exceptional cases that it is necessary to detain the child pending hearing. It is unwise to book a child on the regular police blotter because of the publicity, but a modern card system should be installed for use in children's cases and a record made of every contact or observation by the department. Where a social service exchange is available, all

[1] *Op. cit.*, pp. 253–256.

cases should be registered with it. By this method the police will be brought into more intimate touch and cooperation with other agencies. When it is necessary to interview a child in a police station it should be done in private. Where a children's detail is maintained, all interviews should be conducted by members of this detail. Third degree methods never should be used. A girl should always be interviewed by a woman. In case a child is placed in detention the parents and the juvenile court should be notified immediately. There should be the highest degree of cooperation between the children's bureau or detail and the juvenile court and probation department. It is a distinct advantage to have these departments housed in the same building. . . .

Special effort should be made to secure the cooperation and coordination of police service with other agencies in the community, particularly the schools; education, health and welfare departments; boys' and girls' clubs; and all other agencies dealing with social problems affecting children. Berkeley, California, under the leadership of Police Chief August Vollmer, has established a coordinating council, composed of the executive heads of the several departments and meeting at frequent intervals for the discussion of common problems.

There can be no question but that the police have a definite place in dealing with children's problems which they cannot avoid entirely, even if they would, and which affords a real opportunity to make a liberal contribution to the care and protection of children, and the general improvement of social conditions surrounding them. It is not the province of the police to undertake social case work but rather to act as official observer and report to the agency, either public or private, best qualified to handle the particular problems. Neither should the police undertake intensive character rehabilitation as provided in the probation program. They must, of necessity, make contact with children and it is, therefore, highly important that the result of the contact be an asset and not a liability.

Situations often arise when it is not possible or advisable for a police officer to interview a child in his own home, particularly when neighbors become curious or other children listen in. It would also be unwise to take him to school or a social agency for an interview, since such procedure would violate the privacy with which the police like to handle the case, particularly before it is ascertained that the child is implicated in a delinquency. Also, it is often impossible to avoid arresting a child in his own home, particularly when the parents call the police in cases of assault, drunkenness, and other disorderly conduct on the part of their son or daughter. In felony cases, after having trailed a suspect for some time and he is finally located at home, he must be arrested there; or when he is implicated in a serious offense and he can supply the names of the associates, the police must arrest him wherever they find him for the best interests of the community. However, these cases are comparatively rare and the above recommendations can be adopted in most cases.

So far it has only been stressed that the police should cooperate with other social agencies. The reverse must also be emphasized, namely, that there is just as much opportunity for the family and child welfare agencies to cooperate with the police departments. With more and better trained officers in the field, the agencies should gain more confidence in their ability to deal with juvenile offenders. The agencies must refer all cases which the police should handle and should not attempt to do police or detective work any more than the police officer should try to do case work. Neither should the agencies, including the probation department and the court, compromise the officer in the presence of a child or his parents even though there is ground for disagreement as to the measures employed or necessity of arrest. Not until a unified front is presented and genuine cooperation is achieved can there be any progress in child welfare work.

SELECTED BIBLIOGRAPHY

1. ADDITON, HENRIETTA: "The Crime Prevention Bureau of the New York City Police Department," in Sheldon Glueck and Eleanor Glueck, *Preventing Crime*, pp. 215–236, McGraw-Hill Book Company, Inc., 1936.
1a. Citizen's Police Committee, *Chicago Police Problems*, 1931, Chap. VIII, "Crime Prevention."
2. FOSDICK, RAYMOND: *The American Police System*, Century Company, 1920.
3. GLUECK, SHELDON, and ELEANOR GLUECK: *Preventing Crime*, McGraw-Hill Book Company, Inc., 1936.
3a. HAMILTON, MARY E.: *The Policewoman, Her Service and Ideals*, Frederick A. Stokes Company, 1934.
4. HUTZEL, ELEANOR L., and MADELINE L. MACGREGOR: *The Policewoman's Handbook*, Columbia University Press, 1935.
5. MOSS, JOSEPH L.: "The Relationship of the Juvenile Court to the Police," *Proceedings of the National Probation Association* (1926), pp. 201–206.
6. OWINGS, CHLOE: *Women Police—A Study of the Development and Status of the Women Police Movement*, F. H. Hitchcock, 1925.
7. *Recent Social Trends*, "The Police," pp. 1139–1146, McGraw-Hill Book Company, Inc., 1934.

8. ROLLER, ANNE: "Vollmer and His College Cops," *Survey Graphic*, LXII (June 1, 1929), 304 *ff.*

9. SARGENT, ALBERT J.: "Getting Police Cooperation," *Year Book, National Probation Association* (1930), pp. 245–247.

10. VOLLMER, AUGUST, and OTHERS: National Commission on Law Observance and Enforcement, *Report on Police*, No. 14, Washington, 1931.

11. ———: "Predelinquency," *Journal of Criminal Law and Criminology*, XIV (1923–1924), 279 *ff.*; XIX (1928–1929), 196 *ff.*

12. ———: "Meet the Lady Cop," *Survey*, LXIII (Mar. 15, 1930), 702–703.

13. WATKINS, JAMES K.: "The Police and the Prevention of Delinquency," *Year Book, National Probation Association* (1932–1933), pp. 42–49.

14. WOODS, ARTHUR: *Crime Prevention*, Princeton University Press, 1918.

15. ———: *Policeman and Public*, Yale University Press, 1919.

SUGGESTIONS FOR FURTHER STUDY

1. What are the functions of a juvenile police officer in crime prevention? in treatment? in investigation?

2. What is meant by crime prevention? How does a juvenile police bureau prevent crime? What research has been done on the subject?

3. What are the social, economic, and educational factors in a crime prevention program?

4. What is the attitude of the public toward such a program?

5. What role does the press play in such a program?

6. What is meant by "a crime inflated press"? How can that situation be prevented?

7. What agencies and forces are most effective in preventing crime?

8. What unit of government is best fitted to carry on a crime prevention program? Why?

9. How can socialization of treatment be used in police work?

10. What qualifications and training should a police officer dealing with juveniles have?

11. What does a crime prevention program include?

12. What are the present limitations and handicaps of crime prevention programs? in your community?

13. What is the underlying philosophy of crime prevention? of police work?

14. What is the crime prevention program in New York City? What was it in the past? of Berkeley, of Los Angeles? of Chicago? of your community?

15. What are Vollmer's contributions to police work?

16. What is the role of the policewoman?

17. What is the value of the cases cited by Hutzel and Macgregor?

18. How practical are the recommendations made by the White House Conference regarding police work?

19. What is the Gluecks' contribution in their book, *Preventing Crime?* How critical are they of the programs discussed in their book? Compare this book with the one by W. I. Thomas and Dorothy S. Thomas, *The Child in America.*

PART III

DYNAMICS OF SOCIAL THERAPY IN WORK WITH UNADJUSTED YOUTH AND PARENTS

*In effect, what there is in the way of preventive justice
. . . is achieved not by legal but by extra-legal agencies.
It is done for the most part, not by the agencies of the law,
but by social workers. . . .*

*The preventive activities of social workers are likely to
be more effective than legal rules. But in the making and
applying legal rules we must turn to the results achieved
by social workers if we are to understand our legal problems
aright.—*ROSCOE POUND

CHAPTER XIV

SOCIAL CASE TREATMENT OF DELINQUENT AND PROBLEM YOUTH

ILLUSTRATIVE MATERIAL

It has been generally recognized by competent students in the field of delinquency that within recent years the older philosophy and methods of reconstruction of offenders have undergone much the same profound changes as those which have occurred in the more general fields of social work.[1]

This newer philosophy and methodology of the treatment of delinquents are based on the recognition that the total personality of the delinquent, his interests, attitudes, wishes, complexes, and habits must be redefined and modified, and at the same time the total social situation of which the delinquent is an integral part and which supplies the ideation, stimulates his desires and interests, motivates his attitudes and creates his complexes, must at the same time be redefined, modified, and, when need be, completely changed.

Not until the extensive sociological research of such scientists as E. W. Burgess,[2] Clifford Shaw,[3] Frederick Thrasher,[4] Elio Monachesi,[5] William I. and Dorothy S. Thomas[6] began to appear was delinquency dealt with as something more than a psychological concept stressing in particular the individual behavior

---

[1] See FRANK W. HAGERTY, "The Delinquent as a Case Problem," *Year Book, National Probation Association* (1935), pp. 48–60; see also HANS WEISS, "The Social Worker's Technique and Probation," in Sheldon Glueck (Editor), *Probation and Criminal Justice*, pp. 165–195.

[2] See "The Delinquent as a Person," *The American Journal of Sociology*, XXVIII (May, 1923), 657–680.

[3] See *Delinquency Areas*, the *Jack-Roller*, *The Natural History of a Delinquent Career*.

[4] *The Gang*.

[5] See *Prediction Factors in Delinquency*.

[6] *The Child in America;* see also PAULINE V. YOUNG, *Pilgrims of Russian-Town*.

patterns, mentality, temperament, mental conflicts, complexes, and dreams. While these phenomena are exceedingly important when considering the life of a delinquent, they become meaningless unless they are related to the social world in which the delinquent lives and from which he derives his basic motivation for acting and thinking.

The social treatment of a delinquent would involve, therefore, not only changes in his habits and reactions but changes in the social relations which he maintains with his family, school, and other groups, changes in the community and its institutions, changes in the family's. approach to the problem, changes in their form of discipline, of social control, and of family organization.

At present the major emphasis in the treatment of delinquency falls on the delinquent himself, assuming that, once the medical and mental adjustments are made, the child will be able to resist the disorganizing forces and demoralizing influences in his social environment. Comparatively little attention is paid to the rehabilitation of the home and parents and the community. The cry that the parents are too old, too ignorant, "too far gone" to do anything with, that it requires too much time and money to reconstruct a home or a community, has so seriously pervaded the ranks of social work and blocked the development of methods of social treatment that only a cursory and often careless and preconceived evaluation of homes, parents, communities, schools, etc., is made, and as a result there is little or no attempt to deal even with the more promising people and social institutions which exert constant influence over the young. As a matter of fact we have carried on no actual experiments and made no honest attempts to reach these forces and, therefore, should not neglect them and denounce them arbitrarily.

Not long ago a probation officer related to the writer that some twelve years ago the oldest boy, Fred, son of Mr. and Mrs. K., was under his supervision for a period of one year. He could do nothing with the boy since "he was not amenable to discipline," and was, therefore, committed to a state school. A year later he was committed to an industrial school for older boys, and at present he is serving a penitentiary sentence of five to fifteen years for burglary and assault. The second boy in the K. family, following the delinquency pattern of his older brother, has also "graduated" from the same state school into the industrial school, while his sister is a truancy problem but is still living at home, and the youngest lad, twelve years of age, has already violated the conditions of his probation twice and is under commitment to a twenty-four-hour school for boys.

The probation officer maintains that both parents are congenial, intelligent, healthy, and were at one time well off financially, but that "the mother knows next to nothing about raising children," and is "too easygoing," and adds: "but who has the time and the knowledge as to how to deal with such mothers?"

There is no assurance that had the probation officer thought in terms of reeducation of parents that the delinquency careers of the younger children would have been prevented. But in view of the parents' assets, such as intelligence, health, economic security, an attempt—even when very prolonged—to deal with ignorance in rearing children would have probably repaid more than a hundred fold, when the time is compared with the years served in penal and reform institutions, to say nothing of the waste of young human lives and the easily calculated economic costs.

Sheldon and Eleanor Glueck,[1] the former of the Harvard Law School, two of the most eminent students of delinquency and probation, maintain that much of the rehabilitative work with delinquents can be done only through and in cooperation with the primary social institutions—the home, the community, the play group—to which they are responsive.

Probation consists not in putting the child "on probation," but in having him under the guidance of a sympathetic, carefully trained officer, who will exercise considerable ingenuity in influencing the family as well as the delinquent himself, and who in the process will know how to marshall the community resources. . . .

Reorientation of a personality, substitution of wholesome for morbid attitudes and habits . . . is a long and delicate process, requiring frequent adaption of means to ends, ingenious changes of approach, the mutual cooperation and unflagging interest of probation officers, social workers, school teachers, parents, and companions of the delinquent, and, in a certain proportion of the cases, psychiatric therapy. Rehabilitation does not occur in the courtroom; it occurs if at all, in the home,

---

[1] See *One Thousand Juvenile Delinquents*, p. 261. Reprinted by permission of the Harvard University Press.

the school, the playground or boys' club, the place of work. Hence it is futile to look for single nostrums that will "cure" delinquency. We are dealing with a complex problem; the stage on which the drama of personality distortion and unwholesome behavior is enacted is as broad as society and as deep as human nature.

Social Therapy and Social Case Work.—It is far easier to indicate where reconstruction is needed than to outline an actual technique of reconstructing complex human behavior and the social order. The social and biological sciences have not progressed sufficiently to aid us in understanding adequately human personality, motivation, social life, mental conflicts, and the interplay between the social situation and the genetic constitution of the individual. As William I. and Dorothy S. Thomas point out:[1]

At any given moment capacity or present [social] status can be measured with great precision, but the parts contributed to this present status by innate predisposition and environmental influences cannot be separated, and studies of growth have thrown little light on the problem because of the impossibility of controlling the various environmental factors and the present lack of exact knowledge about them.

Sheldon and Eleanor Glueck attribute the present inability to reconstruct behavior to the limited knowledge of human nature by the various scientists who have conscientiously devoted their lives to the study of man.

The mental tester is handicapped in defining and measuring intelligence because mental capacity can be measured only indirectly[2] and because it is difficult to rule out the influences of education, of social and economic advantages on the tested qualities which are supposedly innate. Both the psychologist and the psychometrist have given little aid in understanding the role intelligence plays, even if it could be defined and measured precisely, in human motivation.

The emotional forces[3] which play a potent role in motivating behavior have not yet been clearly explained by the psychologists,

[1] *Op. cit.*, p. 331.
[2] For a full discussion of the psychometric approach see Thomas and Thomas, *op. cit.*, Chap. VIII.
[3] See JUNE DOWNEY, *The Will-temperament and Its Testing;* C. LANDIS, R. GULLETTE, and C. JACOBSEN, "Criteria of Emotionality," *Pedagogical*

psychiatrists, mental hygienists, nor by the so-called "depth analysts."[1]

Furthermore, as the Gluecks maintain:

A carefully planned and adequately controlled attack upon the problems of criminogenesis and therapy from the psychoanalytic point of view still remains to be made.

Without detracting from the recent brilliant laboratory work in the field of endocrinology,[2] it must be stated that the enthusiasts who have attempted to apply endocrinology to criminalistics have thus far too greatly indulged in unwarranted claims and questionable inferences. They cannot as yet be taken too seriously as contributors to a science and an art of criminology.

Nor have the sociologists yet built up a science of criminology. Their "situational approach" is a useful working concept; but when all is said and done it merely emphasizes something that has been known for a very long time, namely "that personality formation in its normal and abnormal aspects is a very complex matter, bound up with the whole environing social situation."[3]

As to an art of treating delinquency, the nearest to it is the so-called case-work approach, which is to be credited rather to social workers than to theoretical sociologists. And "social case-work" still has a good distance to travel before its effects can make themselves felt in the treatment of delinquency in a truly fundamental sense.[4]

Removal of the "Cause" of Misbehavior as a Goal in Treatment.—As has been already pointed out in another connection (see pp. 121–126) it is essential that the symptoms of delinquency be not confused with the real fundamental processes underlying the delinquent acts. When a boy appears in court, for example, for "drunken driving" it is not a matter of chastising him for driving while intoxicated, nor for being intoxicated, but of discovering and removing the factors which lead him to the use

Seminary, XXXI (1925), 213–231; MARK A. MAY, "The Present Status of the Will Temperament Tests," *Journal of Applied Psychology*, IX (1925), 39.

[1] See AUGUST AICHHORN, *Wayward Youth;* FRANZ ALEXANDER and WILLIAM HEALY, *Roots of Crime.*

[2] See L. BERMAN, *The Glands Regulating Personality;* M. G. SCHLAPP and E. H. SMITH, *The New Criminology;* L. E. GRIMBERG, *Emotion and Delinquency.*

[3] THOMAS and THOMAS, *op. cit.*, p. 466.

[4] GLUECK, *op. cit.*, pp. 283–284. Reprinted by permission of the Harvard University Press.

of intoxicating liquors. Only when the fundamental causal factors in delinquency are dealt with can the person's energies be directed intelligently toward new outlets for expression and toward finding a new social and psychological environment which does not generate inner conflicts.

Students of delinquency cite case after case in which the unsocial behavior could not be changed except by altering the forces which determined it.   We can no longer rest content with such statements that "the boy is unruly, got mad and ran away," or that "the girl indulges in sex relations with a sailor because she frequents questionable dance halls." Such generalizations are unintelligent, superficial, dangerous, but very prevalent. We like to repeat Aichhorn's conclusion:

When we realize that the provocation to delinquency is confused with its cause, that symptoms are mistaken for the disease, we understand why there are so many false conceptions of what should be done with the delinquent child and we wonder no longer that treatment often fails. Without the discovery of the deep underlying causes of delinquency, any cure is accidental.[1]

When only the symptoms are attacked, the unsocial behavior rarely, if ever, disappears; suppressed and denied expression it frequently seeks a new path of discharge, and a new form of delinquency results.

It is even possible that a nervous symptom will develop. More often, however, it appears as if the psychic energies had gathered new force. Following a period of socially acceptable behavior, the original signs of delinquency often reappear, more deeply anchored and more pronounced.[2]

This phenomenon is well illustrated by the following case:
Case Summary of Reuben Allport.—Reuben Allport, thirteen years of age, a runaway from home, was arrested for vagrancy. In the detention home he was "boisterous, unruly, and unamenable to discipline," which made him very unpopular with both boys in his ward and the administration. Reuben sought attention in devious ways but received only rebuffs. One of the attendants maintained that Reuben's uncooperative attitude and unruly behavior was due to the fact that he believed that "no one could

[1] AICHHORN, *op. cit.*, p. 41.
[2] *Ibid.*, p. 39.

touch him." The attendant upon being provoked at continuous disobedience which undermined his authority "went after the boy with a strap, even though he did not mean to use it, just to scare the rascal."

Reuben quieted down considerably, but that evening his tongue had to be treated for serious cuts incurred by his biting it when panicky and in despair.

The attendant's aim was to have the boy "conform to standards and rules of the house," to have him "behave like a normal human being." However, without determining the underlying cause for the boy's behavior there was no real goal in treatment as far as the boy was concerned. Conformity completely disorganized him. There are many cases which do not lead to tongue biting, but to masturbation, or daydreaming, or enuresis, or stuttering, or some other emotional unadjustment and social misconduct.

Reuben obeyed outwardly but rebelled inwardly. His tensions and conflicts were not reduced but increased. Negative restraints meant further antagonism. He was not freed from his inner conflicts and was not provided with means, satisfactory to him, for voluntary cooperation at the detention home.

The physician who treated him realized that Reuben's cooperation was indispensable. A lacerated tongue cannot be easily cured without self-discipline. By asking Reuben, "How did your trouble start?" the medical man secured not only an account—in spite of a sore tongue—of the physical ailment but of the social conflicts in the detention home and with his parents. The boy released much pent-up energy in telling his story; he secured considerable satisfaction by his ability to gain attention; but his bitterness softened under the doctor's sympathy. While the doctor did not fully explore Reuben's social problems, his goal was directed toward the fundamental underlying problems which sent the boy away from home in the first instance: He was an unwanted child, received little or no affection, which he craved, but had no adequate technique for securing it.

Later the boy was placed in a boarding home of a very fortunate choice, where he received intelligent attention and devotion, which is the natural right of children. His inner conflicts and his social conflicts disappeared in proportion as his ability developed to gain confidence and overcome fear of others.[1]

[1] Reported by a graduate student. Quoted by his permission.

It should be noted that in all the cases cited below whatever degree of success in treatment could be claimed was primarily due to the fact that the underlying fundamental contributing causes were discovered, as far as possible, and attempts were made to remove them rather than merely to deal with superficial and outward symptoms of misconduct.

The case of Marilyn Smith, presented in some detail, may serve as an illustration of certain methods of therapy and their relative degree of success from the point of view of the total social situation and as a resultant of interaction between a particularly constituted personality and a particular social environment.

THE CASE OF MARILYN SMITH[1] (*Concluded*)

An Illustration of the Processes and Methods of Social Treatment

(The plan of treatment followed in the case of Marilyn Smith has much in common with cases—whether they ever come to the attention of the court and probation department or not—in which problematic behavior is manifested either on the part of the child, or the parents, or both. Probation is a form of social case treatment. The probation officer, the court worker, and other child welfare workers will find this and other concrete case data herein discussed helpful only in so far as they can compare these complex situations with their own case experiences and to the extent that they can do some reflective thinking on methodology, underlying philosophy, case work processes, and the logic of treatment. A discussion of case treatment is a challenge to the reader as well as to the writer.)

It is possible that the social treatment processes in the case of Marilyn and her mother date back to the first contacts with them. In the first interview, since the worker had asked some questions, and allowed them to talk about their problems, their health, their background, their family, their wishes and conflicts, etc., they had begun to form a clearer picture of the course of their lives, and they began to orient themselves to their own potentialities. The worker made no conscious attempt to "work with the situation," or "to take hold of the problem." Both

---

[1] For the social study of this case see pp. 33–43 and 133–134. Quoted by permission of the parents. Case treatment by Pauline V. Young.

the parents and the girl were actively brought into the venture since the worker depended upon them to explain motivation, to search for hidden meanings, to account for the formation of their traits and behavior patterns. Even though the worker had been sought out by the Smiths, who believed themselves unable to get along without help, the recounting of their life, of their good health, of their success with the four sons, of their popularity with friends and relatives, of their economic and social status greatly minimized their sense of failure and of pain. They recognized in the worker a person who respected them and who could bring out their initiative and resourcefulness and share their experiences with them. Perhaps the entire process of social study may appropriately be called "exploratory treatment," to use Betsey Libbey's term, while "the case worker is feeling out what kind of help the client both wants and can take in the situation,"[1] and how the worker can function.

It is assumed that the worker has established confidence and rapport with the family. They seem to be convinced of the worker's professional attitude, her genuine interest in the situation, her friendliness toward all members of the group, her lack of moralizing and of attempting to dominate the situation. They understand that the worker is interested in having them work out their own methods of changing the situation. Throughout all contacts with the family the worker assumed the attitude—well expressed by Miss Neustaedter—that she is not there to manipulate the individuals but she is dealing with human beings who have many possibilities for growth. What they may become she does not know but she gives them the awareness that, in their relationship to her, they are free men.[2] Not until the proper relationships between the family and worker are established can she hope to have any influence and to lead them toward the essential changes of attitudes and circumstances.[3]

10–25–35. *In an interview with both parents* the worker gave them the assurance that—barring all unforeseen circumstances—they are eminently

[1] Quoted by Bertha Reynolds, *Between Client and Community*, Smith College Studies in Social Work, p. 100.

[2] ELEANOR NEUSTAEDTER, "The Role of the Case Worker in Treatment," *The Family*, XII (July, 1932), 155.

[3] In recording this case an attempt was made to include "the thinking behind the plan of treatment." While this type of recording lends itself to teaching purposes it is not an illustration of case recording.

in a position to handle the situation with considerable success, although it might take some time to change attitudes and circumstances, since these had a long incubation period. The assets in the case were carefully reviewed, each one in turn, and the parents were complimented upon their success with the four boys, which they seemed to appreciate highly.

"I know that both you and my husband do not agree with me that Marilyn is a different being and that she is by nature a selfish, resentful, and disobedient problem child," remarked the mother to the worker. It was evident that as long as the mother clung to a genetic interpretation of behavior she would not exert herself sufficiently to change her own reactions, attitudes, and behavior patterns and would not consider them as factors influencing the girl's conduct. However, no brief explanation would be sufficiently convincing that a state of nonconformity does not mean abnormality and that abnormality is not necessarily inherited. A list of books[1] was suggested which would aid the mother in arriving at a different conclusion while the long process of redefining the various social situations involving Marilyn and the family group was undertaken. Her husband believed that only as "the two women are thrown in closer contact will they develop any tolerance for each other."

Since Dr. Smith is a very busy man it is necessary for Mrs. Smith to assume as much of the responsibility of the treatment of Marilyn as possible. Since the correction of the physical defects would perhaps involve least of Mrs. Smith's "giving of herself" personally, a discussion of these was deemed advisable at this time. The findings of the physical examination of Marilyn by the school physician were discussed. "What plans do you have for correcting these minor difficulties, Dr. Smith?" He suggested making arrangements with the dentist and the oculist for immediate examination and treatment. "What of the flat feet?" The mother thought corrective gym would be advisable and planned a talk with the gym teacher and, if necessary, with a physician. "While at school, Mrs. Smith, would you think it advisable to take up the matter of a more challenging course of study for Marilyn?" The mother agreed and also deemed it expedient to buy a typewriter on which Marilyn could practice typing at home.

The mother planned to have Marilyn's old music teacher return, but since Marilyn felt resentment against classical music only and was in conflict with the teacher because of the regulation against the enjoyed duets with the brother, it was asked if it would not be more desirable to have a new teacher who could more successfully take into account Marilyn's interests and who could wisely combine popular and classical music? It was asked if a gradual reintroduction of music into Marilyn's life were not essential? Could the brother bring home some popular duets and invite his sister to play with him?

It was asked if Marilyn's lack of responsibility in the home was not partially responsible for her isolation and concentration on self? Common interests and bonds tend to grow as responsibility is shared. Appropriate

[1] PHYLLIS BLANCHARD, *The Adolescent Girl;* W. R. BOORMAN, *Personality in Its Teens;* GRACE L. ELLIOTT, *Understanding the Adolescent Girl.*

responsibilities tend to develop a "wider self" and a social consciousness. Activity in the home would also provide occasions for praise and for securing status in the family circle. Marilyn would learn to appreciate her weekly allowance more if it were earned, and activity in itself is useful and broadening.

Mrs. Smith raised the question of assigning certain kitchen tasks to Marilyn. It was pointed out that while such procedure was highly important it would be necessary for the mother to draw the girl closer to her before assigning tasks which the girl disliked. The ideal way was to have Marilyn assume some responsibilities of her own accord when some ties of affection had been established. Since she liked driving to market and doing the shopping and enjoyed driving her little brother for his organ lessons, she should be encouraged to take on these responsibilities regularly.

The mother planned to talk at once to Arthur and "have him understand that he cannot molest a little girl." Wouldn't the pair under those circumstances be driven under cover? Since Arthur is the girl's only emotional outlet she cannot be torn from him abruptly. Mrs. Smith mentioned her plan of sending the girl to a convent or to relatives in order to separate the pair. Since the mother believed that Marilyn is seclusive and secretive, would a long separation from the home tend to alienate the girl still further, particularly since the girl resents the idea of being sent away? The mother readily saw the point. By attempting to explain why she thought the plan inadvisable the mother fully convinced herself that it should not be considered.

It appeared that since many of the mother's suggestions had to be modified it would be necessary to leave her with something constructive to do for the girl. "What could you and your daughter do together which would give her the feeling that you do regard her as an adult and that you respect her judgment?" Mrs. Smith decided that it would be a good plan to drive to the city and do some family shopping. Marilyn's opinion would be solicited and followed as far as possible.

10–28–35. *Interviewed Marilyn alone at her home.* She was somewhat more composed than at the time of the first interview (10–19–35) and volunteered the information that "things are going a bit better at home because mother seems to have changed, but she still does not welcome Art."

"Marilyn, what can you do to make things pleasanter for your mother? You know, she and your father are beginning to look weary."

"I can't do anything for them. Why, my mother is so distant she would not want me around much. My father is worrying over finances and not over me. He has several patients who have not paid him in months."

"That's true, too, but he is taking your situation very much to heart. And your mother, Marilyn, is far more devoted to you than you will ever realize. She is not of a demonstrative nature but she loves you dearly just the same. There are many people who do not show their affection. She has been busy with friends and relatives who depend upon her and demand her time. It is just as difficult for her to give up her friends as it is for you to give up yours."

"But she has lived her life already, and I am just beginning. Why should she ask me to give up Arthur?"

"Of course, she believes that she is serving your own best interests since Arthur is not very well." (Girl sat in silence for two or three minutes. At this point it might have been asked if Arthur would be willing to go to a physician for a thorough checking over, but since the girl was depending upon the emotional attachments to him, it was not deemed advisable to disturb the relationship at this time.) "Marilyn, what can you do to make things easier for your mother?"

"We are driving to the city Saturday early in the morning. Mother asked me to help her with the shopping for the boys and for the house. I like to shop but I don't suppose I can please her. I really would like to remain in the city with my aunt."

It was discussed with Marilyn in some detail regarding the dependence of her happiness on that of her parents and others. Several anonymous cases were cited which stressed the importance of maintaining strong bonds of affection between parents and children. Marilyn asked if often these bonds have to be maintained by the daughter? It was pointed out that that would seem to be the conclusion, particularly if the daughter is capable of understanding her parents.

"You're the only daughter your mother has. She is no longer a young woman. You yourself will derive considerable pleasure by going out of your road to make her happy. You will develop character and will be admired by all when you try to create warmth and happiness for others." (Girl listened attentively and after a pause asked worker when she could meet some of her school chums. Arrangements were made at a later date.) Marilyn is participating in a debate which her class in economics is staging.

11–2–35. The mother reported in an interview held at home that Marilyn had been helping with the dishes and other chores, almost every night since the last interview. "She is much happier and things are going as well as might be expected but there is still lots to be done. She is still pretty selfish and isolated." The mother was asked what she thought was the effect on a girl whose parents provided her with comforts, gifts, and certain pleasures but who had for many years asked nothing in return and made no reasonable demands on the girl. The mother realized that Marilyn did not exert herself to provide any pleasures for her parents but it took considerable discussion before the mother reasoned it out herself that the distance between them grew greater because of their divergent interests, the girl's lack of early training to assume some responsibility in the home, and lack of bonds of affection. The mother began to realize, although she did not openly admit —an admission was not only not expected of her, but would have been avoided by the worker—that Marilyn's "selfishness" or absorption in self was logical. Such children do not develop a social consciousness and a "wider self."

The mother related that the trip to the city was not very successful. "We had some words in the car over driving and by the time we arrived at the store, she was pretty sullen." The next day the parents entertained out-of-town relatives but Marilyn was away practicing with the debating team and later visiting her girl friend until she was late for supper. Mrs. Smith was asked how Marilyn might participate in the entertainment of guests or relatives which would assign her some status and at the same time draw her into the family circle? Since the Smiths maintain numerous and strong family (or even clan) bonds they cannot be expected to sever them for the sake of one member of the group. Mrs. Smith believed that it would be best to curtail these entertainments to some extent and when three or four guests are present, and not on school nights, Marilyn could entertain them while the mother is getting dinner or the refreshments. She agreed that it will be necessary to limit the entertainment to those friends and relatives whom Marilyn could converse with and entertain. A more careful selection of guests was also necessary from the point of view of their interests and standards. Since it is difficult to limit one's social functions suddenly Mrs. Smith suggested a trip with Marilyn as soon as she graduates from high school, which would enable her friends to forget her a while and upon their return home the entertainments would be highly restricted.

Marilyn had a date with Arthur for the following evening. The mother was planning to receive him and sound out his plans very carefully and casually.

Marilyn was attending the dentist, who was filling several teeth. Her eyes were examined by Dr. C., who did not advise glasses but a more suitable reading lamp and no reading in bed. The gym teacher had not as yet arranged for the corrective exercises. Marilyn had enjoyed playing some "popular but silly duets with her brother." She did not spend so much time in her room but she was irritated by her brother's choice of music. It was suggested to allow Marilyn to choose her own music. She refused to continue with music lessons "as it is too much bother to practice."

In interview with the psychiatrist who examined Marilyn it was learned that he had not made a diagnosis of the case as he had seen her only twice, and since she was very resentful about his services he "was not able to do much with her nor about her." He did not explain to her the purpose of his services. Though "no diagnosis was made he considered her prognosis poor" and believed her to be of "unadjustable type." However, he advised "further psychiatric care."

11–5–35. *Worker met Marilyn at her home.* The girl was much disturbed because her mother antagonized Arthur when he visited the home. She plainly told him "to keep away from her little girl," that "he was a cripple and that he was contributing to the delinquency of a minor, which is a penitentiary offense." He vigorously denied that his conduct was in any way objectionable and that no one could accuse him of impropriety. He told the mother that for the girl's sake he had better not discontinue the contact suddenly. He admitted that he had no intentions of marrying her soon. "Now, why did she have to do that? I knew it was a mistake for him to call at the house. I just have to meet him at the shop or at the station and without her knowledge." It was explained that the mother had fully planned to welcome Arthur but in her anxiety for the girl's future she deemed it best to have an understanding. At this time Marilyn was asked how much she knew about her friend and why he had not married before the age of thirty-one? She knew very little of his background except that he was poor and not in good health. She did not believe that the difference in the economic level and in the standards of living, to which she is now accustomed and the one which she will have to maintain when living at her own home, would make any difference to her. Marilyn realized that she had been aggressive and perhaps forcing the issue of marriage when she knew too little about this man.

"Differences in age, in religion, in health, in economic and social status, in education might be overcome but they should be tested out first and over a long period of time." It was also pointed out that the clever modern girl becomes acquainted with several young men rather than deciding definitely on the first one who has shown interest in her. Also that men lose respect for girls who meet them on street corners or at the place of work. It is too embarrassing for them to explain to their friends that the girl cannot arrange to receive them at her own home. While they seemingly understand the situation they also feel that only that girl can make a good wife who can be a good daughter and help keep things smooth at home.

The question regarding a career was raised. Marilyn showed little interest. "A job is good enough," she said. Worker explained that while there was no way of predicting correctly it might be assumed with little doubt that Marilyn might later regret that she had thrown away her opportunity of going to college. "You are intelligent, Marilyn. You will not be satisfied clerking or doing some routine job. You are not taking advantage of your own opportunities and native abilities. Everybody should do what he is best fitted to do by nature, otherwise he eventually becomes unadjusted."

It should be noted that the interview with Marilyn is intended to widen her outlook upon life and to enlarge her social world. Introspective and introverted persons can best be adjusted gradually to a wider variety of social relations. It should also be noted that the worker, though not approving of the mother's attack upon Arthur, did not make that known to the girl directly; instead the mother's motives were explained and upheld. Any other procedure would tend to alienate the girl from the mother still further and to create a greater rift between them. While the worker is eager to maintain the confidence of Marilyn, she does not wish to do so if the mother's position would thereby be compromised.

11–12–35. *Interviewed Mrs. Smith in her home.* The doctor was present for the first few minutes but was called on a case. The worker reported on the conference with the psychiatrist and indicated his recommendation for further care, which was curtly declined by Dr. Smith. Asked him to consider the matter further, particularly with regard to care by another psychiatrist. "We will consider it if and when there is a need for it," he said, and excused himself.

Mrs. Smith said that she realized, from the reactions of Marilyn, that her approach had not been correct in Arthur's case. However, emotional and mental catharsis was achieved, and apparently without further conflict, she was much more at ease. Yesterday Marilyn invited two school chums to the house and they all had a good time. Marilyn's brothers helped to entertain them. They played baseball in the back yard and ate heartily at supper. "Marilyn seemed like a normal girl." Mrs. Smith said that she would encourage such friends and do all she can for them. She has not entertained anyone this week in the evening. She had a crowd out for early lunch but everybody was gone by three o'clock.

The importance of participating in the children's entertainment was discussed. The cinema presents a varied, rich, and intriguing life to the youth, which needs interpretation. Such interpretation also tends to create common interests and bond between parents and children. Laughing and playing and creating together also form lasting emotional attachments. When children attend the movies alone, live through a wealth of experience, or are stirred deeply and have no one with whom to talk the situation over, they tend toward daydreaming and isolation.

Mrs. Smith told of her constant attempts to bar liquor from the house. While no one has ever drunk to excess, she believed that it should not be served and particularly in the presence of the young people.

Marilyn had seen Arthur twice this week, but he stayed in the back yard both times with her. He avoided Mrs. Smith and declined an invitation to dinner. Marilyn is moody after his visits and goes to her room.

Her mother had met her twice this week after school and had taken her to the dentist. The new reading lamp was secured and the corrective gym exercises started. Mrs. Smith informed worker that she had written to her brother, whom her mother is visiting, about Marilyn's entire situation, and that she had realized that she had never given Marilyn enough of her personal attention to establish a strong tie between them. Since the grandmother had been away, fewer relatives had visited the Smiths. She asked her brother to extend an invitation to her mother to remain in the East several weeks longer. While she misses her mother and the relatives, she deems it advisable to spend the time with her daughter.

When Mrs. Smith expressed her satisfaction with the recent improvements and progress Marilyn has made, she was warned of the usual unforeseen complications and relapses. Adolescent girls are inclined to rapid changes of mood and toward emotional upheavals on slight provocation.

11–20–35. *Mrs. Smith phoned for an appointment,* which was granted. Marilyn has grown moody and irritable since Arthur has taken ill with flu. She still thinks a great deal about him. The mother was asked whether a strong emotional attachment can be broken down easily or rapidly and whether it should be expected to be broken down? The mother says she has not spoken unkindly of Arthur but has told the girl that she cannot understand what attracted her to him. He is not nice looking, he is not a success in life, he is not well. It was pointed out that the mother would have to look through the "love-eyes of Marilyn before she could appreciate Arthur." It is best not to minimize the traits of her friend if the mother is to keep the girl's confidence and respect. Mrs. Smith recalled that when she was a young girl she looked blindly at her boy friends. Reliving her youth and school days she gained somewhat more insight and sympathy into the girl's problems. She suggested that it would probably help Marilyn physically as well as serve to distract her if she joined a swimming class on Saturday at the Y. W. C. A. That was agreed upon as a very good plan.

Marilyn helps with the housework occasionally. She gets along with her brothers better and again takes a great deal of interest in her school work, but it is evident that the girl is troubled with something. The mother is distressed that Marilyn does not confide in her more since she has been staying home a great deal for Marilyn's sake. It was carefully explained that while the girl craves her mother's affection she has become accustomed to rely upon herself and that such habits are changed only gradually in an atmosphere of friendship and kindness. The mother derives considerable satisfaction from the companionship of her sons, who have remained unaffected by the changed relations with Marilyn. They, too, try to interest their sister in their activities and in their friends. Only occasionally does she pay any attention to them.

11–22–35. *Met Marilyn after school in her own home.* She had invited six or seven boys and girls to tea. These young people were well dressed, active, intelligent, not overly boisterous and not much different from most modern high-school pupils. Their conversation rambled from school subjects, faculty gossip, current events, entertainments, to passable jokes. They were articulate and did not seem to suffer from inhibitions. (The worker was most of the time on an adjoining screened porch.) Marilyn, however, seemed detached. She looks tired and worried over Arthur's illness. She went to see him once without her mother's knowledge. He is much improved by now. She plans to return to work. She misses the contacts at the "shop" a great deal. "We all have to work out our own destinies," she remarked. An appeal in behalf of her father's health and reputation moved her sufficiently to reconsider returning to work. The girl was asked whether she might be able to offer her services at the high-school office. She thought there would be something at the library, but she was not very enthusiastic about it.

She did not believe that she had any interest in any church or in young people's religious organizations. "Nobody in our home has gone to services in ages. I don't think I care to go now."

She spoke of her plans after graduation. She wants to take a business course in the summer, learn shorthand and typing, and take a job in the fall and save her money to attend college. She was greatly encouraged in her summer plans.

12–2–35. *Interviewed Mrs. Smith at her home.* She reported that most of the time things move smoothly. It was evident that her attitude toward the girl had changed considerably. She thought in terms of what she and Marilyn can do together. They discuss family matters, community happenings, and household problems and plan occasional entertainments for Marilyn's friends and relatives of the family. Marilyn invites her friends to the house, and Mrs. Smith welcomes them warmly. They attend the picture show once or twice a month.

Mrs. Smith told the worker that she tried to explain to Marilyn the danger of and the ease with which she might contract an infection "when around the man she goes with." The girl flew into a rage, saying that her mother does not trust her and that she still has a very low opinion of Arthur. Mrs. Smith asked the worker to talk to Marilyn about venereal disease. The worker stated that this information can best be imparted by a physician, from an educational standpoint, without referring to Arthur. It was evident that while Mrs. Smith felt the need of help from the worker she was becoming uneasy and perhaps somewhat jealous of the way in which Marilyn confides in the worker and the manner in which the girl responds to the conferences with her. It was explained to Mrs. Smith that just as her husband would not operate on his own child but would call in a colleague to do so, and furthermore if the operation required highly specialized skills he would call in a specialist, so it is advisable for professional workers who can view the situation dispassionately to cooperate in the readjustment of social problems.

Mrs. Smith pointed out, however, that she and her husband had read sufficiently of psychoanalysis to fear the use of transferrence of the daughter's affections upon the worker instead of upon the parents. It was explained to Mrs. Smith that a warm and friendly feeling must be established between her daughter and the worker in order to gain her confidence, but the worker's aim was to release the girl's emotions and to interpret certain situations which would improve the girl's relations with her parents.

(Every worker who deals with personal and intimate family or parent-child relations should watch for the opportunity of explaining her position with regard to the problem member who begins to form attachments to her. As soon as the parents become uneasy or jealous over such contacts, it is perhaps indicative of the fact that the parent is ready to assume more responsibility in the problematic situation. However, when no explanation is offered, the parent may become inhibited in the presence of the worker or bar the continuance of free associations with the child.)

12–5–35. *Marilyn came to the worker's office* of her own accord inquiring what arrangements to make regarding a work permit in order to return to the "shop" just over the Christmas vacation. She agreed to talk the matter over with her father and in case she felt that he no longer had any objections to her working at the "shop" they could work out a plan then. In case her father still felt strongly against her return to work she would like to visit an aunt in Nevada who had promised to take her to Boulder Dam.

Marilyn told the worker that her mother insulted her when she spoke to her on the subject of venereal disease; she felt like leaving home again but decided against it knowing that her "parents would worry too much. Mother has changed, I don't know, she talks differently to me, but we are still strangers." Again the girl was assured that her parents are deeply devoted to her.

Arthur is back at work now. He looks thin and pale. She will persuade him to take osteopathic treatments and to rest all he can. He had not called her for a week, but she did not expect him to under the circumstances.

Marilyn says that she has been thinking a great deal about the sexual side of marriage. She inquired about infection. The worker carefully discussed some of the material in A. A. Forrell, *The Sexual Question*. She enjoys Arthur's companionship. She wants to get married to be independent. However, she would like the worker to meet Arthur and to learn whether she herself is overestimating him. "I can't rely on mother's judgment since she was highly prejudiced from the start."

In order to remove any suspicion that the worker's judgment is purely personal, and to impress upon her mind that the whole social situation is considered on the basis of extensive experience, several cases were discussed with her objectively. Most young girls who have married men of different social, economic, educational, and age levels, of a different religious faith, and in poor health, had discovered only too late that they were not prepared to meet the many issues which such a marriage inevitably involved. Neither could they rely a great deal upon their families for support. At this point Marilyn stated that she believed her devotion to Arthur to be sufficiently strong to make the adjustment to him, in spite of the numerous difficulties, rather easily. "How can you tell what my expectations in marriage are?" she asked. The worker agreed that it was very difficult to foresee but that a knowledge of similar cases served as an indicator in her situation. Marilyn agreed that neither could she tell and that the wisest thing to do is to wait and to test herself out. Again it was suggested that she make a conscious effort to mingle more with young men only a few years older than herself and in good health.

"Only I would have to live with Arthur and no one else; why can't I suit myself?"

This question was carefully considered and Marilyn agreed that neither her family nor Arthur's could be expected to stand by them a great deal, and that the couple would be relatively isolated from friends and relatives. As time goes on both of them would crave the associations of the family groups. Life affords pleasures only to the extent that congenial relations with others are developed. It is necessary to win the parents over, to establish ties of affection and confidence before she could expect to gain their approval. She would have to make a conscious effort to chum more with her mother.

(Since these points were discussed with Marilyn once before and since she has turned those over in her mature mind on previous occasions, it was considered appropriate to allow her to project herself into the future, a practice not advisable with less mature young people.)

Her final remark was: "Well, I guess I have a good many things to consider before I do anything," which was agreed upon as being a very safe course to adopt in any situation.

12–19–35. Marilyn invited the worker to pay a visit to Arthur's mother, Mrs. L., living in ―――――, who was just recovering from a severe attack of bronchitis. She was very friendly to both guests, talked at length about her devotion to Arthur and his love and tender care of her. It was evident that she was afraid of Marilyn's interest in her son but was confident that her "son would stand by her." Marilyn understood that both she and the mother were definitely competing for the affections of one man. Worker stimulated Mrs. L. to talk about Arthur's thoughtfulness of her and her plans for the future. "If Arthur should decide to get married one of these times you would miss him a great deal." "But he never would leave me alone, that just isn't Arthur, you don't know him very much," she emphatically replied. This was hard on Marilyn, who remained in subdued silence.

The home was very poorly and meagerly furnished and Mrs. L. was poorly dressed. Both she and the home surroundings stood in sharp contrast to those in which Marilyn lives at present. Mrs. L. remarked several times that it must be nice to live in Marilyn's neighborhood.

Since Mrs. L. was weak and tired after her talk only a few conventional statements were exchanged before terminating the visit. Marilyn later remarked on the difficulties of adjusting to "a woman like that," but believed that if they did not have to live together it could be done. Marilyn was in a hurry to return home as she was leaving the following day to visit her aunt in Nevada.

12–22–35. *Mrs. Smith phoned* that Marilyn hurt her back, was at times in severe pain, and was unable to leave on the contemplated visit. She is taking care of Marilyn without any assistance and hopes that this contact with the girl will lead to greater companionship. Worker declined Mrs. Smith's invitation to visit Marilyn, explaining that the worker was leaving on a trip East.

1–27–36. *Mrs. Smith phoned* a day after worker's return from New York that Marilyn was back in school and working hard trying to catch up with her studies. Arthur had come out to see her several times, and she had written him very often. Marilyn has changed her plans for the summer, but the mother was at a loss to learn what the new plans were. She asked the worker to meet Marilyn some day after school. Worker indicated that since summer vacation is still a long way off it would be best not to press Marilyn with plans too much. The mother, however, seemed to urge the point and a conference with both parents was requested.

2–4–36. *Met Dr. and Mrs. Smith in the doctor's office.* Mrs. Smith seemed more upset than usual and indicated that she had worked hard to create "normal relations and affectionate ties with her daughter" but she was of the opinion that the girl would give up her home at any time for the "cripple." Mrs. Smith pointed out that she had given up her own pleasures, friends, and relatives just for the sake of one member of the family, that she missed these contacts a great deal, and would again plunge into a series of entertainments disregarding the needs of her daughter. Mrs. Smith was highly complimented for the numerous sacrifices which she had made and was asked to indicate the progress which she believed her daughter had made within the last few months. The recount helped her to visualize the many changes, which she called "blessings," that were brought about. However, she was urged to meet her friends and relatives if she felt a need for them, but to observe their relations with their daughters and the problems which they presented.

Dr. Smith was asked if there might be an opportunity for Marilyn to work in his office during the summer, chiefly along clerical lines, filing, letter writing, reporting on clinical tests, etc. He agreed that Marilyn could attend business college in the morning and work afternoons in the office, for which he would pay her sixty cents an hour. He will present the plan to Marilyn and his desire and need for her work with him.

2-10-36.   Met Marilyn in her own home after school.   She is still greatly absorbed in various school activities but appeared despondent over a contemplated plan by the radio station to transfer Arthur to Seattle, Washington.   It means an advantage for Arthur, and his mother and sister are eager to move there.   Marilyn feared that this change would mean her loss of Arthur.   Worker pointed out that she evidently had reasons to lose confidence in Arthur if she feared that a transfer to another city would make him give her up.   This transfer should be regarded as a test of his as well as her affections.

She could not keep her mind on the proposal for summer work which her father made to her and halfheartedly remarked that at this time she did not see any objections to it.

Her mother was planning a Valentine party, her brothers would invite several of their friends and she would ask Arthur and his sister to join them, as well as some friends at school.

2-18-36.   Mrs. Smith phoned that Arthur was unable to attend the Valentine party, but his sister came.   Marilyn was moody and took little interest in her guests.   The mother remarked: "I feel sorry for Marilyn, at times I feel that she is exceedingly fond of him and that we ought to let her have her way, if I could only be convinced that she would be happy with him."

Arthur left unexpectedly on the seventeenth of February, and his sister and mother will follow him in two weeks.   Marilyn is hurt because he did not take her more into his confidence.

3-2-36.   Mrs. Smith in worker's office.   Arthur writes occasionally to Marilyn.   It appears that the sympathy which Mrs. Smith showed Marilyn when she was suffering over Arthur's absence from the Valentine party has served to bring the mother and girl closer together.   Mrs. Smith has been attending luncheons and entertainments given by friends, but she no longer "enjoys them as she used to."

4-2-36.   Interviewed Mrs. Smith and Marilyn at their home.   Marilyn had just finished helping her mother set out some shrubs in the garden. Arthur was in town a few days ago and visited for over an hour at her home while other guests were present.   He was invited to tea, but his crude manners embarrassed Marilyn and he himself was ill at ease.   Marilyn said that she is surprised that she does not miss him as much as she thought she would. He told her that he is trying to arrange to return to San Bolero as the climate in Seattle does not agree with him.   He has been under almost constant medical care since his arrival in that city.   "I almost wish that he would not return here," remarked Marilyn when the mother was out of the room. The mother indicated that "love for Arthur is a thing of the past," and that only "good sense used in the arguments with Marilyn had served to talk her out of him."   She has been taking more interest in the family group and in friends at school.   She lost her temper a few days ago but got over it surprisingly quickly.   She seems to fit into the home far better than previously, although she is still subject to unwarranted moodiness.   She has become chummy with a neighbor girl who is greatly admired by the Smiths. She also chums with her brothers much more than she ever used to.   She has been very regular in her school attendance. The plans for the summer are still uncertain.

5–2–36. *Interviewed Dr. Smith at his office.* He reports that Marilyn has been very busy with various school functions and plans for graduation. She is participating in graduation exercises. "Everything is moving smoothly with Marilyn." Two weeks ago, Charles, the youngest son, was drowned while swimming in Santa Monica. The tragedy has deeply affected every member of the family. Mrs. Smith went on a short trip to one of her brothers. Marilyn is assuming some responsibility in the management of the household. She misses her mother.

5–30–36. *Interviewed Mrs. Smith at her home.* She and Marilyn are leaving a few days after graduation for a short trip. After their return Marilyn will help her father with his files and correspondence. Mrs. Smith says that "things are moving smoother than might be expected." She is still of the opinion that "Marilyn's love affair is all over." Arthur is back in town but Marilyn has not seen him. She has not considered inviting him to the graduation exercises. Explained that Mrs. Smith should be prepared for a sudden revival of interest in Arthur when school closes and there is a lull in the girl's activities. (Case continues active at mother's request.)

INTERPRETATIVE SUMMARY OF THE CASE OF MARILYN SMITH

It should be noted that the treatment of the mother and Marilyn was carefully planned on the basis of the diagnosis of the case, while the diagnosis was worked out on the basis of a careful study of the total personal and social situation.

It was recognized that while a study of Marilyn was undertaken because of the presenting problem of truancy, truancy was, nevertheless, only a symptom of far more deeply rooted maladjustments.

The major emphasis was placed on the mother. It was necessary to change her attitude toward Marilyn's conduct and toward her responsibility in the problems facing her daughter. One recalls the words of Miriam Van Waters:

> The doctrine of heredity is another stumbling block to parents. They observe . . . the radical differences between children in the same family, and they conclude that although the design may be somewhat worn by handling it, it was stamped on the coin from the beginning. Hence it is easy for parents to be fatalists. For them eugenics is the new Calvinism. It is also the least troublesome way out, for it furnishes excuses for bad behavior of children and places the blame upon undesirable relatives. . . . No first rate biologist is ready to say that we

inherit gloom, selfishness, temper, avarice, or stubbornness, although certain writers on eugenics tell us so.[1]

At no time, however, was it discussed with the mother that the girl's problems were a direct and natural result of the home situation, since such direct discussion would put the mother on the defensive.   Too much time and energy would be wasted in tearing down defenses.   The mother gradually arrived at the desired conclusion when she was asked to trace every one of Marilyn's behavior problems to their starting point and asked to account for the cause of such behavior.   To understand one's self is the first stage in treatment.   However, mere intellectual appreciation of what is involved in a given problem on the part of one who is not accustomed to plan specifically to remove the problematic situation is not sufficient.   Concrete ways and means need to be provided as an aid in the readjustment of the problem.   Thus, in order to establish ties and common grounds between mother and daughter, it is also necessary to find definite things which they might do together or singly for each other.

Marilyn is active, healthy, and of superior intelligence.[2] However, her intellectual capacity is not out of proportion to that of her parents and brothers.   She need not look greatly for intellectual stimulation outside her own home.   The work at school is too easy for her and she has lost interest, in spite of the fact that she is more than one year ahead of her grade.   It is important that more challenging, more stimulating, and additional work be supplied.   Children fall into bad habits of work, into daydreaming, when they "are bored to death" if their faculties are not occupied.   They do not take advantage of their keen intellect and frequently do not wish to continue with higher education.   There is a danger that they may match their wits with sharks and charlatans and exploit each other as well as others.

Marilyn's mind should be kept occupied with academic assignments as well as projects of her own choice and inclination.   She really belongs in an ungraded opportunity room for superior students but the high school she attends does not have one.

[1] *Parents on Probation*, p. 41.
[2] See LETA S. HOLLINGWORTH, "The Child of Very Superior Intelligence as a Special Problem in Social Adjustment," *Annals of the American Academy of Political and Social Science*, CXLIX, Part III (May, 1930), 151–159.

Study of languages, debating, music, extracurricular activities, typewriting, home responsibilities must serve this purpose.

It was recognized that the chief enemy of virtue is not vice but idleness, but on the other hand, as Burt maintains, "mechanical drudgery at abstract tasks or hated housework is not real activity for the volatile [youth]. If no interest is kindled, no enthusiasm stirred, the mind closes its eyes and droops into a sensuous dreaming. . . . Room must be found in the child's life for cultivating by hard but congenial work each natural proclivity."[1]

Since Marilyn and her mother were not ready at the start for any sudden cooperative efforts and intimate personal relations, it was deemed most advisable to have the mother start with the arrangements for medical and dental attention which Marilyn required. The mother worked out her own plans and followed them faithfully and consistently. It was often necessary to restrain her from attempting too vigorous or sudden changes, for which the girl was not emotionally ready. Every bit of therapy was weighed in the light of probable emotional reactions of the one who was executing it and the one who was receiving it. Marilyn, for instance, was not ready to help with unaccustomed housework duties until she had built up a stronger attachment toward home. The mother was not ready to deny herself the companionship of friends and relatives until she had found sufficient attachment and pleasure in her daughter.

The worker, in stimulating or encouraging a plan worked out by the parents, had to foresee the emotional consequence as well and to remember the significant words of Dr. William White that "no conflict could be solved at the level of conflict."

The mother is intelligent and has considerable initiative and imagination. Many of the plans suggested by her were sound. When she lacked insight into the problems, these were interpreted to her but no suggestions for treatment were made unless she no longer was capable of acting on her own initiative. The specific methods for carrying out the treatment were generally left to her.

When suggestions were offered not more than two or three were made at any one time. Already bewildered by problems a discussion of too many issues is frequently only further confusing. No suggestions were made which were not carefully considered in

[1] *The Young Delinquent*, p. 483.

the light of the parents' ability to carry them out.   No visits were made just to check on or receive a report on the girl's behavior. The visits were for the purpose of carrying the plan of treatment a step further.

In changing attitudes of the conflicting parties, care was taken not to pass judgment on either party but to interpret sympathetically one to the other and to bring them closer together.

An attempt was made to consider all the various aspects which have contributed to the problem: lack of satisfactory home relationships, physical defects, unwholesome employment, lack of proper recreational facilities, of challenging school activities, of religious affiliation, and of insufficient sex information.

At all times the problems were discussed from the point of view of Marilyn and her mother.   There was no inclination to impose standards upon them.   Suggestions were made when they were expected or solicited as people on an equal footing often do.   The worker tried to relive the various situations with them in order to penetrate more fully into their personalities, their desires, plans, and interests.   With Marilyn more so than with the mother, abstract discussions of cases were carried on.   She responded with eagerness and reflected upon fundamental ethical and moral questions.   An attempt was made not to experiment upon them but to share as far as humanly possible their experiences.   As Gordon Hamilton points out: "The ability of human beings to interpenetrate and yet to maintain awareness is the germ of the matter."[1]

The father was not seen nearly so often as the mother because he is an extremely busy man and would have had to give up some of his professional work to confer at length with the worker. It was not advisable to change the organization of the family life any more than absolutely necessary.   He had never been a very dominant factor in the rearing of the children and it could not be assumed that he would play a more dominant role without further complications, although his interest and responsibility were solicited and gained to some extent.

The brothers were seen in the house but were not approached as agents in the case treatment.   It was left to the mother to seek their cooperation and interest in Marilyn's development. The less the members of the family can be disturbed by outsiders

[1] "Sharing Experiences," *The Survey Graphic*, LIX (December, 1927), 317.

and the more the parents can be induced to handle the situation the more gratifying will be the results and the greater the tendency toward unifying the group.

There was no attempt made to interview relatives since nothing constructive could be gained through a contact with them which Mrs. Smith could not undertake. Since the family is large, it might be assumed that their reactions to Marilyn as "a case," "to social workers," "to trouble" will vary greatly and that considerable internal gossip might result. Care was taken, however, to have the mother handle the case of the relatives and to eliminate the necessity for interference by an outsider. Relatives should be interviewed only when the parents are incapable of supplying the needed information and when they cannot be motivated to carry out the necessary plan of treatment and must rely upon help from relatives.

Since Marilyn is mature, of superior intelligence, and is in the habit of projecting herself into the future, an attempt was made to have her realize that the amount of satisfaction and security obtained from social conformity outweighs any immediate satisfaction derived from impulses and pleasures of the moment. Life in the social group affords security, recognition, and response while her life in comparative isolation could not offer her these values. To put it in the words of August Aichhorn, an attempt was made to provide Marilyn with "incentives for the conquest of the pleasure principle in favor of the reality principle."[1] Or to use W. I. Thomas' concepts, hedonistic values need to be offset by utilitarian values. That is, the long-time values built up by the family provide for needs of the individual more effectively in the long run than the values which the individual achieves in impulsive reactions to immediately stimulating and satisfying pleasure values.

The problem of sex was discussed not stressing unduly the pathological aspects but the health and joy to be derived by normal and sanctioned relations.

Marilyn's infatuation with a man in poor physical condition and nearly twice her age is symptomatic of the lack of emotional attachments within the family circle. She wanted personal affection, generously given, and not distant devotion. She wanted companionship. When it was not forthcoming she

[1] *Op. cit.*, p. 193.

became introverted and depended at first upon herself for whatever pleasures life could afford her and later turned to Arthur, who provided recognition and response. According to Aichhorn, children brought up in such surroundings as those develop "a proportionately increased thirst for pleasure and for primitive forms of instinctual gratification. They . . . have a strong though distorted craving for affection."[1] The newly formed attachment to Arthur was very strong, and it could not be hoped that as soon as the parent-child situation was rectified and the conflicts removed that Marilyn would automatically sever her bond with this man. He was an important factor in her mental and emotional life, and this situation was treated as a major fact. On the surface it appeared that Arthur, being from a different social, economic, educational, and age level, of a different religious faith, and in poor health, would not be a desirable life companion for Marilyn, but she had shown many signs of genuine affection and devotion to him. To rule him out of her life either by arguments or by the ordering-and-forbidding technique would mean creating further mental and emotional conflicts difficult of solution. Friendships with other young men were strongly advised as a substitute and as an opportunity to broaden her emotional attachments and to give her a basis for comparison and decision.

It was recognized that while Marilyn had not indulged in sex relations, it was important to deal with the mental aspects of her sexual life. Mature and well developed, and in need of affectional response, her fundamental urges, instincts, and sexual ideation were undoubtedly intensified in the presence of a courting young man. Vigorous physical exercise and play, swimming, ball playing, hiking, and any other group activities were suggested as a means for releasing energy.

A frank, sympathetic discussion of sex problems convinced the girl that she could ask questions and receive unbiased information. She was also supplied with scientific and vivid information regarding the ease with which infections are contracted and their serious dangers. However, great care was taken to stress the health and joy of family life rather than the pathological aspects in order to prevent any possibility of forming complexes about sex, pain, and disease. The worker attempted to implant

[1] *Ibid.*, pp. 148–149.

a "proper realization of the sacred duty she owed her future in keeping mind and body sound." Dr. Wallin's statement comes to mind:

Children should be protected from the evils of ignorance, misinformation, baffled or unrequited sex curiosity . . . it is better that the child should be forewarned and protected by wholesome and reliable enlightenment than he should be deceived by concealment, misled by ignorance, and debauched as the result of studied observance of a policy of laissez-faire in matters of sex.[1]

[1] J. E. WALLACE WALLIN, *Personality Maladjustment and Mental Hygiene*, p. 453; see also GROVES and BLANCHARD, *Introduction to Mental Hygiene*, pp. 120–121.

(*To be continued*)

CHAPTER XV

SOCIAL CASE TREATMENT[1] OF DELINQUENT AND PROBLEM YOUTH (*Continued*)

THE EXECUTIVE PHASE OF TREATMENT IN THE EXECUTIVE-LEADERSHIP-INTERACTION PROCESS

In the general field of social case work, more than in the specialized field of probation, attempts have been made to develop a methodology of social therapy. Those probation officers who regard probation as a form of social treatment will find such methodology valuable. Porter Lee's[2] discussion of the *executive* and *leadership* aspects and Virginia Robinson's[3] and Jessie Taft's[4] discussions of the *relationship* technique of treatment are the most notable contributions. These three aspects of therapy, as we shall see, must be regarded as closely interrelated phases of one unified process of therapy, mutually complementing and supplementing each other. In a given case at a particular time one or the other aspect may seem to predominate over the rest. Though they are inseparable, yet limitations of thought and presentation require us to discuss only one at a time. Their mutual interdependence and inseparableness we shall not overlook. (Sociologists prefer the term social *interaction* to the term *relationship*.)

There are many routine activities carried on by a case worker in behalf of his clients which serve as therapeutic measures in that they help to curtail problematic and delinquent behavior. Such activities as drafting budgets, arrangements for wholesome diet, securing employment, provision of medical care, securing

---

[1] In the following discussion the terms treatment and therapy are used interchangeably to mean simply the administration of some plan designed to effect adjustment.

[2] "A Study of Social Treatment," *The Family*, IV (December, 1923), 191–199.

[3] *A Changing Psychology in Social Case Work.*

[4] *The Dynamics of Therapy in a Controlled Relationship.*

of pensions, state aid, financial relief and institutional placement, modification of school programs, provision of vocational and recreational activities and of suitable housing conditions, establishing the proper community contacts and utilizing the existing neighborhood and community resources, etc., are called by Porter Lee the executive aspects of treatment, since they involve chiefly the discovery of a particular resource and an arrangement for its use.[1] Mr. Lee further maintains that it is exactly in this phase of treatment that social workers have thus far achieved their most numerous successes and that it is the phase of treatment which is most effectively handled:

> With the rapid increase in the number of community facilities— medical clinics, psychiatric and psychological clinics, special classes in public schools, laws for the protection of [neglected and delinquent persons], facilities for recreation, and so on—it is possible now to organize programs of treatment for disorganized [persons], which include far more of these tangible benefits than was possible [at the beginning of the century which perhaps marked the origin of social case work].
>
> A reading of case records, however, leaves the feeling that even with respect to this aspect of treatment we do not take full advantage of the facilities which American communities offer. The quality of this executive side depends on the resourcefulness of the case workers themselves. It requires in the first place an alertness of the varied needs of a family. It is easy to think of treatment in terms of certain routine possibilities: insistence upon children's going to school, attention to obvious physical needs, housing conditions and so on. Beyond these rather obvious needs, which every case worker has schooled herself to look for, lie others which are only apparent to one who is alert and whose conception of treatment is as broad as human need and as specific as the entire range of community resources.[2]

Executive phases of treatment tend to remove not only certain objective difficulties in the way of self-help but they are often the *medium* by which stimulus, self-confidence, and hope may be imparted to clients. A wholesome diet, needed medical attention, regularity in eating and sleeping, etc., may give strength and energy; and increased vitality tends toward the development of a virile personality. Suitable employment in itself is often a therapeutic measure. Financial independence brings with it

[1] *Op. cit.*, p. 192.
[2] *Ibid.*, p. 193.

prestige, self-assurance, and social status, which in turn promote familial and social responsibility. Constructive recreation is not only a means for letting off steam but an opportunity for creating lasting and desirable associations, comradeship, and attitudes of sportsmanship.

Great skill and diagnostic ability, however, are required in determining how much the client can do for himself and how much responsibility he can assume for his dependents in discovering and utilizing resources of all kinds and in mobilizing his own abilities to meet specific problems. As it is stressed in case work today: "Do not play Providence and do not take the problem away from people, just assist them to mobilize their own capacities and to keep active as far as possible in their own behalf."

It must be remembered that disorganized families and particularly youths, ravaged by poverty, ill-health, social isolation, personal demoralization, crime and delinquency, subjected to the influences of unwholesome associates and of social and community surroundings, are apt to become so deeply involved in a mental, emotional, and social morass that they cannot easily extricate themselves unaided by personal service. Children and young people need more guidance, supervision, and personal service than their elders (although there may be some dispute on this point).[1]

Furthermore, there are some cases where neither employment, medical care, relief, nor new vocational, recreational, and educational activities are needed. Antisocial behavior seems to be an outgrowth not of the external elements of life but of rejection by parents, or fear of illegitimacy, of discrimination, or lack of self-confidence, bad habits, and so on. Other phases of treatment must predominate in such cases.

THE INTERACTION PHASE OF TREATMENT IN THE EXECUTIVE-LEADERSHIP-INTERACTION PROCESS

Before any direct and decisive approach can be made to a "person in trouble," confidence, rapport, and a sense of security must be established. To some extent the social agency of which the worker is a representative lays the foundation for such relations through its good work with clients and its favorable reputation in the community. The worker, however, carries the

---

[1] See MIRIAM VAN WATERS, *Parents on Probation, passim.*

greatest part of the responsibility in the establishment of such relations as will be conducive to ease, serenity, frankness, articulateness, which will promote a desire to launch unabashed into a mutual exploration of the circumstances surrounding "the trouble."

Interaction in the Treatment Process.—Much has been written in various fields on the high value of confidence and friendliness, long before social case work became a distinct technique. Tolstoy repeatedly pointed out that: "You may deal with things without love; you may cut down trees, make bricks, hammer iron, without love. But you cannot deal with men without it just as you cannot deal with bees without being careful. If you deal carelessly with bees, you will injure them and will yourself be injured. And so with men." "Not material aid, nor mere instruction, but one's self," warned Emerson. "Not alms but a friend," a statement uttered by Octavia Hill, still serves as a sound basis for contacts between worker and client. Mary Richmond's recognition of an intimate relationship between worker and client is expressed repeatedly in her book, *Friendly Visiting among the Poor*. "Friendly visiting means intimate and continuous knowledge of and sympathy with a poor family's joys, sorrows, opinions, feelings, and entire outlook on life. The visitor that has this is unlikely to blunder either about relief or any detail; without it he is almost certain, in any charitable relations with members of the family, to blunder seriously."[1] Elsewhere she continues, "To be really interested, to be able to convey this fact without protestations, to be sincere and direct and open-minded—these are the best keys to fruitful intercourse."[2] This natural, simple, human friendliness serves as the basis for the establishment of rapport and identification which gives the client sufficient security to release his impulses, to which fear, uncertainty, guilt, and confusion might be attached.[3]

In the writings of Eduard Lindeman[4] the concept of "participant observation," which is akin to the process of identification, is developed; Jean Piaget[5] speaks of "reciprocity"; Otto Rank[6]

[1] MARY RICHMOND, *Friendly Visiting among the Poor*, p. 180.

[2] *Ibid.*, p. 200.

[3] See JESSIE TAFT, "The Use of the Transfer within the Limits of the Office Interview," *The Family*, V (October, 1924), 145.

[4] See *Social Discovery*, pp. 190–200.

[5] See *The Child's Conception of the World*, pp. 196–197.

[6] See particularly *Technik der Psychoanalyse*.

expounds on a "dynamic interaction in social life"; Jessie Taft[1] was perhaps the first to introduce the term "transference" (direction of affectional feelings toward a new love object) into social work literature. Thomas' concept of "response" as a natural craving for personal attachments makes a distinct contribution: "The desire for response . . . is primarily related to the instinct of love, and shows itself in the tendency to seek and to give signs of appreciation in connection with other individuals."[2]

Undoubtedly one can find various shades of meaning in these concepts but there is considerable common ground in the thinking of these various writers. They are all aware that men seek to relate themselves to other men, to identify themselves in experience, thinking, and emotions with their fellow men. Man is the most sociable of animals and he craves a responsive friendliness which establishes, with those with whom he can associate, social proximity, appreciation of whatever he is, and a sympathetic understanding of what he has become, an *interaction*.

In interviewing a large number of boys and girls who faced various social and personal problems the present writer[3] discovered that several processes contributed to the establishment of a satisfactory relationship and rapport:

Leisurely methods of interviewing, beginning with common interests (sports, favorite school subject, vacation) not necessarily relating to the "heart of the trouble," as far as the children could see, gave them a sense of security and relaxation.

The exploration and discovery of common interests were extended into an exploration of unique interests, of their own life circumstances and personal problems. As these young people related about their home life, associates, school, interests, employment, and the like, questions were asked about their reactions to these situations. There was an attempt to understand, not to

---

[1] See particularly *op. cit.*, pp. 143–146.

[2] *The Unadjusted Girl*, p. 17.

[3] See PAULINE V. YOUNG, *Pilgrims of Russian-Town*, Chaps. VIII–X; "Getting at the Boy Himself: Through the Personal Interview," *Social Forces*, VI (March, 1928), 408–415; "Boy Scouts and Delinquency," unpublished manuscript; "Educational Problems of the Immigrant Child," *American Sociological Review*, I (June, 1936), 419–429; *The City Boy and His Problems*, study directed by Emory S. Bogardus; Pauline V. Young one of the research assistants.

moralize, not to criticize, not to pass judgment. There was an attempt made to search for deeper meanings of these situations and problems and not to gain a mere accounting of past and present events which happen to flicker across the memory at the moment.

The interviewer's questions served as her response to the information given by the interviewees and served also to aid the narrators to search for deeper meanings than those which they saw on the surface, and to acquire greater insight than had hitherto been attained. The net result was a more intimate and personal mutual exploration of the issues involved in a situation.

It had been noticed that in reviewing their life before a sympathetic listener, and frequently with hidden meanings brought to light, the children began to form slight emotional attachments to the listener because they felt the kinship which occurs only when people realize that they have been accorded the status of a friend. There was, however, no relationship akin to idolatry and worshiping which some psychiatrists ascribe to *transference*.[1] The net result was possibly the same, response, but this response was brought about not by the children's centering their affection upon the interviewer but centering their thought on their social situation, into which they gained new insight. They had come to accept themselves—as they were—in relation to the interviewer, because no attempt to censure, to disprove, to guide, or to impose standards was made. The interviewer listened because of sincere interest and desire to understand; occasional questions were asked in order to understand the situation and the forces and abilities of the individual; and this search for understanding soon became the goal of these children. Through insight into their own situations they began to grow. Thus instead of the emotionalism of transference, which often tends to obscure vision, insight was created, which tends to develop a person's own abilities and potentialities.

It might be said the children themselves talked themselves back to courage and common sense. The interviewer supplied

[1] See TAFT, *op. cit.*, pp. 143–146; WILLIAM C. MENNINGER, "The Mental Hygiene Movement of the Boy Scout Movement," *Mental Hygiene*, XIII (July, 1929), 501–502; MARION KENWORTHY, "Psychoanalytic Concepts in Mental Hygiene," *The Family*, VII (November, 1929), 213–223.

the sympathetic and understanding audience with occasional questions to clarify their thinking. Reorientation, awareness of interest of the interviewer, respect, and improved status brought about responsiveness in them. Under these conditions they readily accepted and followed whatever suggestions were seen wise to be made.

Friends have the ability to bring out the best that is in a person, and the awareness of being at one's best gives added prestige and protection. Having gained impetus, the process of right thinking, feeling, and acting accelerates. These youths were eager to maintain their status. There was a danger, however (which perhaps could be traced to faulty interviewing methods), that a few of these youngsters would fabricate and lie in order "to shine"; this occurred until they discovered that the interviewer accepted these statements as she did anything else they told her but was interested in why they had to defend themselves and sought to know their wishes and aspirations. When they discovered that the interviewer could not reconcile these fabricated statements with reality, they even helped to point out and explain the inconsistencies.

This drive for response may lead to a certain social security, or a sense of "belonging," when the child is accepted by some one person or group; it may lead to social status and recognition; it may produce very satisfying new experiences in contacts with others, and provide a friendly responsiveness through intimate associations. However, interaction may also lead to conflict, subordination, domination, inhibition, and force a withdrawal into one's own little world. We need constantly to remember that the basic drives are neither organizing nor disorganizing, neither good nor bad, in and of themselves. They take on such attributes only as they are related to the social situation in which the person is attempting to function.

(It may be well to note in passing that psychiatrists speak frequently of the role which a sense of security plays in the development of a child's personality, particularly security in the affections of his parents. This is not quite the same as security in the sense of W. I. Thomas,[1] but is rather response. The sharper differentiation of these concepts is not in point just here.)

---

[1] See *ibid.*, pp. 17–31.

The Approach to an Offender.—The statement of Hans Weiss,[1] a famous probation officer,[2] regarding the approach to a client is particularly pertinent:

When human beings meet, a sensitive interplay of forces begins to create situations which open or close the doors to constructive intercourse. If we like a person, we are willing to listen to suggestions and we feel the desire to reveal ourselves. The social worker, or anyone else who wishes to help, should know the art of making himself liked by his client. This should not be misunderstood to mean an effort at indulgence; dignity, sympathy and purposeful leadership are the qualities which attract. There are definite elements in methods of approach conducive to an attitude of response by the client. First of all, the worker should radiate a spirit of sympathetic understanding (we would like to call it love—if the word had not suffered so much abuse), an interest apt to create an undercurrent of well-being which will set the client free to speak frankly and which will lead him to disclose thoughts and actions of a more intimate nature. For it is information of this type which throws light on the mental processes of the individual. The worker should not try merely "to find out";—he should try to find out because he wants to help. This presupposes a willingness on the part of the worker to listen patiently and with real—not feigned— interest to whatever the client wishes to say. Through occasional questions if put skillfully, the worker may "steer" the conversation to some extent. But he should not press for information or force a point. Anyone who has been successful with "people in trouble," knows from experience that patient listening always pays, even when the person seems to drift far from the point. It is just the direction indicated by such drifting that very frequently is most illuminating on what is going on in a person's mind. In addition, the chance to talk and to be listened to, often has a liberating effect. It may relieve the client and, at the same time, may be the cornerstone for that relationship of confidence that is so essential to guidance.

Approach is not a thing to be learned or accepted easily. It is an outgrowth of a more fundamental attitude toward the work, an outgrowth of the worker's philosophy of life. If a social worker believes that Negroes are humanly inferior, she cannot help displaying this belief toward a colored client. If a probation officer speaks of "hope-

---

[1] "The Social Worker's Technique and Probation," in Sheldon Glueck (Editor), *Probation and Criminal Justice*, pp. 172–173. Reprinted by permission of The Macmillan Company.

[2] As this book goes to press a report is received that Mr. Weiss was killed on August 9, 1936, in an auto accident.

lessly lost girls," or of "tough girls" who need a "strong hand," she will rarely succeed in learning a single thing about the inner life of her charges. If a boys' worker wishes to work only with "good boys," he can never expect to be fair to a delinquent boy. An Americanization worker who considers the immigrant as an inferior being, will only be able to "Americanize" a poor type of immigrant; the more refined type with some education will shun him. Our personal ideas on questions of race, nationality, immigration, delinquency, ethics, economics and similar problems are bound to influence our attitudes toward clients. We cannot cherish private "pet-ideas" without having them color our thoughts and attitudes in our work. The broader and more unprejudiced the personal philosophy of a social worker or probation officer is, the more will he be able to develop an approach which opens people's ears and prepares them for accepting the leadership they need.

There is also a danger that a worker may become partisan, subjective, sentimental, through such intimate relations; but there is as much danger that without this intimate relationship to the client the worker may become prejudiced, distant, uninterested in the client's problems. The fault does not lie in the technique; the fault lies in the worker's lack of the needed skill to use the technique properly. The trained and skillful worker can be at one and the same time scientific and impartial, and also radiate confidence, warmth, and affection without becoming involved in the emotional morass in which the client may be struggling.

Yet there are workers who are afraid of entering into a personal relationship with their clients. They fear becoming involved or assuming responsibility for a relationship which will demand their personal effort and extra time since clients do not readily distinguish between professional friendliness and personal friendship, which they may crave to extend into their private lives. There are clients who, wishing to gain the good graces of their visitor, will attempt to arrange for personal contacts or who will pay personal visits to the office of the agency. Skillful, professional workers can gracefully decline such purely personal invitations, without setting up barriers and social distance, if they will indicate to the client the pressure under which they work. Whei there is none of the transference of affection of which Jessie Taft, Aichhorn, Rank, and others speak but rather a concentration on the clients' own abilities and potentialities, the likelihood of their seeking personal attachments is minimized.

"We cannot expect anyone to accept our leadership unless we have been able to develop a relationship of confidence which builds a bridge of common understanding and of joint effort between social worker and client."[1] It may be added that we cannot expect the client to reveal himself to us and to give us intimate, personal data about his life unless we have shown respect for his personality, a respect which, in turn, wins respect for the worker. "The most elementary concept for an ethical relationship rests upon a mutual respect for the integrity and the individuality of the other. Without this as a foundation the case work relationship is a travesty."[2]

Children as well as adults sense very readily not only the absence or presence of sincere interest, understanding, unfeigned warmth, and social proximity, but the degree to which these qualities are a part of the social worker's equipment. Without the client's conscious awareness of these attributes in the persons who come to guide his destiny, he responds with an emotional paralysis. Giving clothing, suggesting work, arranging for regular food orders, supervising the habits and routine of a child's life can turn out to be highly ineffective and damaging when the child is too hampered emotionally to make use of such services, because he feels insecure and unresponsive in the worker's presence.

Aichhorn adds:

The optimistic attitude of the counsellor toward life, the cheerfulness with which he works, create an atmosphere in which remedial work can be carried on without great effort. Thus the counsellors are able to approach their pupils in such a way that the latter have confidence in them and feel their understanding. Most of these young people have never had their infantile needs for affection satisfied. They have never experienced the happiness of a close relationship to the mother. They need love. This constitutes a great demand on the personality of the counsellor. He must be highly intuitive in order to know the right approach to the child. The science of education has nothing to offer him in this respect. It is not enough to comprehend what the child says and does; the worker must be able to "live" himself into the situation so that these experiences become his own. . . .

---

[1] *Ibid.*, p. 171.
[2] Robinson, *op. cit.*, p. 165.

We sacrificed none of our authority but we had taken away the children's fear of us and replaced it with their confidence. . . .[1]

The most cynical of men admit that they would perish altogether were it not for their awareness that they have friends and that they are loved by their family. One shudders at the thought of being suddenly stripped of friends and relatives who show confidence and friendship, traits which to a large extent distinguish us from the lower animals and ascribe to us the quality of being human.

The "person in trouble," frequently isolated from friends and relatives who could supply moral backing, requires of the case worker, as Virginia Robinson points out, "far more understanding and patience and self-discipline than one is ever called upon to exercise in the relationship of a friend."[2]

Obviously sympathy and friendliness are not enough. Sick patients may have confidence in a doctor, irrespective of the amount of sympathy he shows, if he has established the reputation of possessing competence and skill. Helen Keller's parents showed their afflicted child a great deal of sympathy and devotion and love, but it took the sympathetic understanding, skill, professional competence, and technical ability of Miss Sullivan to turn a violently impulsive, resentful child to a sweet, reasonable, responsive, and intelligent person.

Without a doubt the interaction technique is invaluable in social therapy as long as it is realized that it is only one phase of the therapeutic process, that it is only one factor in the dynamics of therapy. The proper relationship to the child may aid in the release of inhibitions and repressions, fear, and guilty feelings; it may give rise to self-expression, to release of potential energies and capacities essential for emotional growth and adjustment. There is a grave danger, however, of exaggerating the importance of interaction. There are numerous other ways in which the worker can aid a person or children facing problems, particularly when these problems are beyond the client's control and when they can be freed from them only by the proper contacts with community facilities and by intelligent training and judicious guidance and orientation.

[1] AUGUST AICHHORN, *Wayward Youth*, pp. 152–154. Reprinted by permission of The Viking Press, Inc.

[2] *Op. cit.*, p. 128; see also TAFT, *op. cit.*, pp. 143–146.

When one examines a large number of probation records and observes that the process of supervision of the delinquent frequently consists only of a firm handclasp, a hearty reception, and a friendly conversation, one begins to fear that real leadership has been overlooked.

In commenting on George Pratt's *Three Family Narratives for Use in Parent Education Groups*, Paul Popenoe observes that for the worker, the use of "relationship" is "too likely to become a mere escape from hard work and preparation . . . and may degenerate into a flight from reality on the part of a lazy ill-trained social worker. . . . [The average social worker should] guard himself carefully against expecting that some miraculous result will be produced, in a way not capable of precise description, from the creation of the auspicious emotional atmosphere!'"[1]

There is also the further danger that much that is called "relationship" therapy has as its goal simply the resolution of conflicts as such. The worker needs to realize, as William James and many sociologists have shown, that conflict is a very ancient human pattern and may have high social value. The individual who can be brought to fight through his difficulties, who can be given conflict techniques, may thereby win his battle. The conflict situation most to be avoided is the stalemate in which action has been slowed down and perhaps ceased in hopeless bewilderment. Reorientation, revivification, and a renewal of the struggle may be what are needed. Meeting the ups and downs of human life, vigorous contacts, rivalries, conflicts, modesty in success, resolution in defeat, and not a sweetly idyllic and lovely sympathetic "relationship" to others, with all misunderstandings, all bitterness, all hates eliminated, is neither the historical situation nor apparently the future destiny of humans. Creative effort, courage, high resolutions, character are quite as much products of conflict as of accommodations in human society.

THE LEADERSHIP PHASE OF TREATMENT IN THE EXECUTIVE-LEADERSHIP-INTERACTION PROCESS

To adopt another of Porter Lee's concepts, although not his earlier definition, we shall designate as the leadership phase of treatment those personal services which motivate and stimulate

[1] *Social Work Technique*, I (January–February, 1936), 28.

the client to adopt a new course of action, a new outlook on life, which define and redefine the social situations facing him, which lead him to orientation and the gaining of insight into his problems, which change his attitudes, motives, and philosophy of life.   In this course of treatment the case worker turns teacher and nurturer, interpreter, discussant, and participant in all activities and problems which need his aid.

Securing suitable employment, for instance, for a delinquent youth is in most instances not sufficient.   The worker cannot rely on all inexperienced persons to know how to conduct themselves on a particular job, or how to plan their activities, how to spend money wisely, and to what extent to share in family responsibilities.   Where parents are capable of exercising the proper controls and exerting the suitable influences the worker will do best to leave these tasks to them, but where such arrangements cannot be made and the youth himself is ignorant on this point, the worker should undertake to define the situation in terms of social relationships, or responsibilities, standards of conduct, thrift, and so on.

With the provision of recreational, vocational, educational activities, of medical care, of communal resources, the real task of the worker begins.   Youths are eager for adventure and new experience, for security, response, and recognition.[1]   They should be taught what constitutes wholesome adventure attainable within their means and environs; how to secure response and recognition through approved and socialized channels of conduct and by means of constructive activities and associations.   They must be taught how to make and keep friends in their environment, how to maintain a well-balanced program of school, work, and recreational activities, how to recognize and emulate high ideals of ethical conduct, what to read, how to control their desires, and so on and on through a complex variety of activities and problems which go to make up the variegated fabric of youth.

The leadership phase of treatment depends almost wholly on face-to-face relations and is predicated on the belief that it is possible to reconstruct human personality by affecting a change in the attitudes and goals of the individual.   This phase of treatment must be based on: (1) a thorough knowledge of the existing

---

[1] For a systematic discussion of the four wishes see Thomas, *op. cit.*, Chaps. I, II.

problems, attitudes, wants, interests of the delinquent and problem persons; (2) a complete understanding of the contributing factors, of the bases for the given delinquent and antisocial attitudes and interests; (3) a knowledge of the personality traits; (4) and a knowledge of the social setting in which these people most vitally live which either, as Lindeman says, "create the stimulating flush of loyalty"[1] or bring about rejection and social isolation. It is well-nigh impossible to lead persons to change their conduct and attitudes if little or nothing is known of their attitudes, and the origin and setting of these attitudes; it is impossible to lead and to recanalize people's activities and thoughts unless much is known of their powers to change and to comprehend. Since, in the words of Ada Sheffield, "all of any given person's significant habits form themselves within relationships between himself and environing persons, institutions and ideas, his personality is a web-like creation of a self interacting with other selves in a succession of situations."[2] The leader, under such circumstances, must know who else is responsible for the conduct of the single unit which he is trying to lead. The most effective leader is the one who knows his people most intimately.

Mr. Lee points out that in the field of human attitudes, in regard to the objectives of human life case workers are not recognized as authorities "for the very good reason that in this field every human being is his own authority." Neither does one easily "take advice of others with regard to conduct, attitudes and purposes because in this field the human being is traditionally his own master."[3] The person's status and dignity must, therefore, be preserved through a process of participation. Lee and Kenworthy say:

[By] leadership in this sense we mean that quality in human relationships which permits the exercise of personal influence over others without weakening their own initiative. . . . Leadership at its best in social case work accomplishes its purpose in two ways. First, it succeeds in giving to the patient the feeling of participating in the analysis of his own needs and the development of a program to meet them. We say "a feeling of participation" because we do not mean that leadership

[1] LINDEMAN, *op. cit.*, p. 117.
[2] *Case Study Possibilities: A Forecast*, p. 10.
[3] *Ibid.*, p. 199.

leaves the patient to his own devices to sink or swim. We take participation to mean that the patient has the feeling of being a party to a discussion of his situation to which the worker is also a party. Leadership does not mean achieving results with the worker kept in the background. It means achieving results by assigning equally responsible roles to worker and patient.

In the second place, leadership at its best accomplishes its purposes by refraining from pressing any step in social treatment which the client is not willing to accept as part of his own purpose.[1]

It should not be assumed that even children can be expected to follow advice readily and to accept the authority of the worker unquestioningly. They, too, should be given the feeling that they are in a measure masters of their own destinies. What the worker should aim to do is to explain and define situations, standards of conduct, ethical codes, in such a way as to provide independent bases for judgment and action. Offering advice and guidance often means that the worker does all or most of the thinking. A person cannot grow and develop while leaning on the moral and mental crutch of his counselor. A true leader motivates to action and stimulates to thinking but leaves the actual and specific processes of carrying out plans and activities to the persons concerned.

We have fallen into the way of over directing our clients, of managing too much, exhorting too much, playing the role of patron, lady bountiful, indulgent parents. We see more clearly that, in the emotional area as in the practical, the best case work occurs when the greatest possible activity is elicited from the client.[2]

The worker must recognize "the good of activity," to use Dewey's concept, the joy which comes from accomplishment, and the growth of personality which results when one's capacities are utilized and energies released. This utilization of creative energy is character building.

It requires genuine skill to abstain from advising, from persuading, and from commanding those who for various reasons have become disorganized and demoralized. Yet reorganization depends more on the ability to use one's own potentialities than

[1] PORTER R. LEE and MARION E. KENWORTHY, *Mental Hygiene and Social Work*, p. 247.

[2] GORDON HAMILTON, "Methods of Family Case Work," *Proceedings of the International Conference of Social Work*, II (July, 1932), 186.

on any other single factor. Social case work has for many decades been defined in terms of those social processes which develop powers of self-adjustment and self-direction. When the social worker assumes too dominant a role, he degenerates into a master-commander rather than becomes a leader.

Maud E. Watson points out that the objective of treatment becomes of great interest because it means not only assisting the child to adjust to his present environment but to "develop a philosophy which will enable him to interpret future new experiences and to adjust to them with a minimum of conflict and at the same time offer a constructive contribution of his own. Even very young children can understand simple explanations, appreciate adult frankness, and like the recognition and approval that comes from being allowed to assume some responsibility for their own particular problem."[1]

It has frequently been pointed out that what a person does for himself constructively counts far more toward an abundant and satisfying life and permanent well-being than anything that can be done for him.[2] This procedure, of course, assumes that the worker is quick to discern what is constructive and destructive in a given situation and is at all times ready to interpret and guide toward the desired goal rather than assume the reins.

"Influencing Human Behavior."—Harry Overstreet strikes a significant keynote in his discussion on "Influencing Human Behavior,"[3] in which the wider implications of these "new" approaches to the delinquent are set forth:

Formerly it seemed enough for a society to punish the social deviates. This, we now know, was like locking the stable door after the horse had been stolen. We now realize that punishment is only a last and very ineffective resort. As a matter of fact, it is an acknowledgment of our own defeat. Therefore, more and more, we are addressing ourselves to the problem of preventing life from becoming maladjusted, or of correcting maladjustments when first they make their presence known.

Thus the very central problem of life today is so to influence human behavior from the very beginning that the individual grows in the way that fine human life should grow.

What, fundamentally, are the ways in which we may do this?

[1] *Children and Their Parents*, p. 79.
[2] See particularly ROBINSON, *op. cit., passim.*
[3] *Year Book, National Probation Association* (1932–1933), pp. 10–13.

First of all, we are recognizing that domination and terror are the worst enemies of the good life. They are stupid because they are positively productive of the very types of life that we wish to prevent. Hence, in our newer attitude toward children—in the family and in the school particularly—we are learning to substitute techniques that bring out the wholesome qualities in young people.

What are these techniques? In the first place, they are those that aim at the establishment of confidence. The child, we know, must have his place in the sun. It must be a place in which he secures the respect and admiration which his basic life demands. If we do not help to give him that place in the sun, he will make a place for himself—by means of mischief, depredations and gang terrorizings.

How do we enable him to gain a fundamental confidence? We find that giving him friendly and pleasurable associations with others of his age is perhaps our chief means. Inasmuch as we are basically social creatures, we all are happiest when we are saved from isolation and enabled to function happily and effectively in a chosen group.

In the second place, we find that the individual has a fundamental drive to activity. If we do not make possible wholesome activity, unwholesome activity will take its place. But activity of some sort there must be.

Thus we are learning that the greatest way to salvation for any individual lies in his enlistment in a kind of occupation that absorbs his whole personality. We are gradually awakening to the fact that the schools have done immeasurable damage to our children because they have imposed activities that repelled rather than attracted the interest of our children. Hence, in large measure, education has been a process not of integrating the personality, but of splitting it up into antagonistic parts. We now realize that there is a kind of "occupational therapy" that is needed all along the line. To get a boy thoroughly absorbed in the doing of something that is worth while is better than a thousand preachments and certainly better than a thousand lessons learned under silent protest.

In the third place, we find that wholesome life requires a fairly continuous amount of triumphant achievement. The individual who is constantly being defeated develops bitterness and a sense of frustration that may easily turn into antisocial ways of life. To give an individual a chance to show what is in him and to make it possible for that which is in him to come to triumphant fruition is to help him gain not only his self-respect but the most genuine kind of happiness. With that happiness comes a confidence in life and a friendliness toward it that removes the individual from the danger of antisocial deviation.

Finally, we are discovering that there must be in every wholesome life a kind of magnet that draws that life to higher levels. We know the disintegrating and the demoralizing effect of bad companionship and evil literature. It is not enough to inveigh against these. It is only the better, really, which can drive out the worse. Hence we realize our profound obligation to place in the environment of the child that which inspires him with high admiration. Herein, of course, lies one of our most perplexing difficulties today. We live in a world of fairly low motivation. The child very quickly realizes that the system of life is largely activated by self-interest and by the wish to get something for as little as possible. To influence children greatly we must first influence ourselves greatly enough to transform our present rather low order of civilization into one of a more finely human type. While our children are surrounded by examples of vulgarity, commercial deceit, "getting by," law-breaking, and so forth we have little reason to hope they will rise above the level of their environment.

Unquestionably this is the most serious challenge to ourselves which we have to meet. We have done a great deal in illuminating the family relationships, in bettering the educational techniques, improving our attitudes toward the juvenile offender. But we have as yet done almost nothing to bring wholesomeness and high-mindedness into our business world.

Therein, I take it, lies our next step in the influencing of human behavior. We must develop motives in business, political and social life that will be as magnets which will draw our children upward instead of, as today, dragging them downward.

The most helpful sign of the times is that we are realizing as never before the profound obligation which we have to develop our children into fine men and women. As that realization grows in intensity and effectiveness, we may hope for the kind of society in which the nurture of life will be our most precious concern.

THE CASE OF JAMES R.[1]

The case of James R., which follows, supplies us with a detailed account of a case dealt with by the Court of General Sessions. This case illustrates a well-rounded plan of treatment based on an adequate diagnosis of the case, which in turn is based on an adequate study of the boy's behavior, social background, personal history, family relations, environmental influences. We quote the social study only in part since many of the data are included in Mr. Cooley's "Study of the Process of Adjustment." Our

[1] Reprinted by permission of Edwin J. Cooley, *Probation and Delinquency*, pp. 167–203.

interpretative summary of the case (see pp. 348–352) shows concretely the development of the executive, interaction, and leadership plans of treatment.

It should be noted that the case worker consulted a physician, psychiatrist, psychometrist, and psychologist. Their findings were carefully considered, in the formulation of a plan of adjustment. Throughout the study the probation officer was concerned not only with the boy's overt behavior and expressions but with his impressions, ideation, and attitudes; his reactions were carefully noted and even his gestures observed, and his activities and plans were considered in the light of his abilities and personality make-up.

Part I

A. **Legal History** (Summary).—James R., past eighteen years of age, was arraigned in the Court of General Sessions—with the codefendant, Peter M., charged with stealing a taxicab, breaking through a plate glass window of a sport shop, taking two revolvers and some cartridges. When a traffic officer attempted to stop them, the two boys drove off, sending several shots in his direction. James pleaded guilty. Peter M., who had a long criminal record, was sentenced to State Prison for from two and one-half to five years.

B. **Study of Background of James R.** *Father.*—Age forty-eight, born in New York City . . . received an elementary-school education. In earlier life he was a popular ballplayer, and even now pitches ball for a neighborhood club. His social life is limited to his home and a political club in the district. Mr. R. is still in vigorous health, and shows interest in the political news and plans for civic improvement. He lives in harmonious relations with his wife and children. Mr. R.'s parents emigrated to New York and Mr. R. was one of four, healthy, normal sons. He worked steadily as a chauffeur until about three years ago, when he resigned to work as a laborer, averaging $8.00 per day.

Mother.—Age forty-five, also born in New York City, and received an elementary-school education. She is in good health, and is interested in the affairs of the household. She is attentive and considerate toward the children and seems sincerely devoted to her husband. The mother's parents were immigrants, and Mrs. R. was one of five siblings, two of whom died of diphtheria in their preschool years. All the family are of average intelligence, and there are no evidences of psychopathic traits, mental disease, or defect.

Siblings.—James has three sisters living: Margaret, age twenty-five, Genevieve, twenty-two, and Ellen, sixteen years of age. Another sister died in infancy. Margaret is married, and out of the home. Genevieve left school at the age of sixteen and secured work in a factory, while Ellen works in the stockroom of a large mercantile company.

C. Developmental History of James (Summary).—His history shows no abnormality, although he was "a decidedly cranky child who made a good many demands for attention upon the other members of the family."

Home and Neighborhood Conditions and Influences.—James was born and has lived all of his life in the same neighborhood. The family lives in a tenement flat, adequately furnished, clean and well kept. James sleeps on a folding couch in the living room. There are a few books in the home, and a small collection of adventure-story magazines owned by James. The family have a moderate amount of social life, occasionally entertain friends in the home. While the parents are fond of James, they have been worried for some time about his increasingly disordered life, and have been admonishing and reproaching him. The sisters feel humiliation and chagrin at his arrest.

School History.—James completed seven grades during the ten years that he attended school. He repeated several half-year terms, principally because of indifference and poor conduct. James is remembered by his teachers as variously responsive and resentful, as cooperative and stubborn and well behaved and mischievous. He enrolled in continuation school for a few months, but his classes in mechanics and electricity were in no way related to his job.

Habits and Interests.—James was always active in outdoor games, especially ball playing and swimming. He had read such books of adventure as came to hand, and occasionally attended movies. He manifested an interest in mechanics. After leaving school he continued to participate in sports, and has attended motion pictures as well as a few house parties. He enjoys the sport pages of the newspapers and the family radio.

He has shown a moderate interest in girls, and had kept company with one for several months. He revealed that he had developed a feeling of animosity toward the codefendant in the offense herein, for he found that Peter had seduced the girl with whom both of the boys used to chum.

Although Peter absolved James completely in the responsibility for the robbery, James wept when his friend was sent to prison and he was allowed to go free. However, he later remarked that he did not owe Peter anything because of his conduct with the girl.

While James's habits had ordinarily been well controlled, he had begun to drink excessive amounts of alcohol in the few months prior to his arrest, and on the night of the offense he had become intoxicated.

Companions.—His immediate chums were well behaved and orderly, but he had made the acquaintance of a few disorderly and boisterous men at parties, clubs, or poolrooms. James had never belonged to any settlement houses or church clubs, but was a member of a billiard club, which had developed poor habits. While a considerable number of youths in the district had criminal records, these were not among James's closer friends, and he did not admire their reckless exploits.

Work History.—James had been working for fifteen months as a watchman for the Manhattan Railroad Company, at $15 a week. His duties were monotonous, consisting solely of riding a horse along the railroad track, waving a red flag to warn pedestrians of approaching trains.

Previous employment in a stockroom at \$12 a week had also been monotonous. His record showed punctuality, as well as steady employment. He always contributed his salary to his mother.

Religious Observance and Training.—James had received religious instruction at Sunday school during his school days, but had recently given up church attendance. While the family regularly attended, James had acquired the habit of idling on the street corners with other boys, during church time.

Contacts with Social Agencies.—Family had no previous contacts. James had no previous court record.

D. Study of the Individual (Summary). *Physical.*—James has a well-knit and sturdy frame. His gait and posture show well-developed musculature but physical and mental sluggishness. He is in good health.

Neurological.—The examination shows normal reflexes and no pathological condition.

Psychological.—Of border-line intelligence in the psychometric tests; failed the average adult series except the code test. Mental balance normal. Good emotional control.

Personality Traits.—He is undemonstrative, with a kindly, interested manner. His attractive appearance and expression make a good impression.

Psychiatric.—Here is a type easily influenced by the braggadocio of companions who arouse egotistical ideas in him. He is suggestible to flattery, and is the type of boy who, as a rule, would be chosen by gangsters as a tool. His associates often lacked the higher concept of morality and community service which he would have accepted with equal readiness.[1]

Part II.   The Process of Adjustment

A. Formulation of Plan. 1. EARLY CONTACTS. *First Interview with Probationer.*—James's first contact with the probation officer was at the bureau immediately after he had been conditionally released by the court. He was accompanied by his mother. The probation officer was conversant with James's background, and the personal interview afforded another opportunity for insight into his personality and for laying the foundations for the confidence and establishing the rapport with his client which must provide the basis for all progress.

James was instructed in the conditions of probation. The more obvious causes of his delinquency, bad companionship and abuse of intoxicating liquor, were pointed out to him and reluctantly admitted.

His sullenness but innate honesty was apparent. His dynamic qualities were negative. That his lethargy was constitutional was contradicted by well-developed musculature and occasional changes of expression which entirely banished his resentful appearance for a moment or two.

Personality characteristics of stubbornness and rebelliousness evidenced themselves in his discussion of his immediate needs. He was jobless and without funds. He said his parents would provide a home and he would get his own job. He was disgusted with small wages and was going to be a

---

[1] Part I summarized by Miss Eleanor Gay.

police worker. He thought they got bigger salaries. He did not desire the probation officer's help. He preferred probation to prison confinement, but if he felt any enthusiasm at being placed on probation, he was not going to let anyone know it. His good character traits of loyalty, developed according to gang traditions, were manifested in his brief reference to the codefendant. Toward his mother, who was emotionalized over her son's experience, he was kindly and responsive.

James's mental content, ideation, imagery, and impressions were revealed only slowly and as his confidence in and admiration for the probation officer came into being during the ensuing months.

James was directed to report to his probation officer regularly on Tuesday evenings. He would be received in a private office without undue waiting, thereby avoiding proximity with other probationers.

First Visits to Home and Other Places.—The probation officer visited James's home a few days after his first contact at the office. He interviewed both parents. The father, who worked in the vicinity, was at home for a noonday dinner. The intelligent cooperation of the parents was sought. James's personality, problems, reactions to his environment, his needs, and the conditions of his probation were made clear. The probation officer encouraged the parents to expect more of James and to indulge him and condone his shortcomings less, in order to stimulate him to greater efforts. This interview was illuminating to the probation officer as well as to the parents. Friendship, understanding, and mutual confidence, which were born on that visit, existed throughout the following months, when differences of opinion and conflicting viewpoints sometimes had to be reconciled.

The pastor of James's church was visited. He knew of James's situation from the family and also from the investigating officer of the bureau, who had called on him in the course of the diagnosis of the case. He promised to see the probationer as soon as possible and to influence him to attend church regularly and to live in harmony with its teachings. He was especially concerned over James's addiction to alcohol and desired to have him take a pledge to abstain from its use. He invited the probation officer to call on him whenever he could be of any service.

The police officer on the post was, of course, known to the probation officer, whose probationers all lived within the district. His discretion and social viewpoint had been tested and proved. He knew James and his associates, and the probation officer enlisted his cooperation in gaining knowledge of his client's activities and promoting his well-being. Through this impersonal source of information the probation officer was never in the position of making plans based upon inadequate information or incorrect premises.

The president of the Boys' Club of the church was seen, and his willingness to welcome James as a member if he should apply was ascertained. The president was a product of the neighborhood, the type of individual who is made, not hindered, by obstacles. Alert, ambitious, sympathetic, and stable emotionally, he was a local hero, whose helping hand was outstretched to aid his weaker neighbors. His friendship meant much to James, who, later on, was persuaded to join the club.

Economic and Social Status.—James was without a position as the result of his incarceration in the Tombs while awaiting trial, and a new position was difficult to obtain at a time of year when laboring positions were few. He lacked the skill to fill any other available job. The expense of his lawyers, time lost from work by other members of the family in order to attend court hearings, and James's own loss of wages aggregated a cost of several hundred dollars. He had caused his parents anxiety and had lost the esteem of some of his friends.

Creative Interpretation of the Facts.—James was reluctantly amenable to the disciplinary aspects of reporting and answering inquiries at the outset of his probation period. He was not ready to accept the probation officer as a friend nor to believe that probation could do anything for him.

His sullen disposition and resentful attitude were aggravated by his joblessness, lack of funds, and a sense of failure. The shock of his arrest and imprisonment had made him more serious but had not enlarged his horizon.

James's needs were carefully considered by the probation officer to the end of effecting his social adjustment and bringing about his personality development, keeping in mind what he would do and what he would be throughout the years to come when he would no longer be under probationary supervision.

At a difficult case conference, the probation officer presented James's case to a group including other supervision officers, the officer who investigated the case, a church visitor, a psychologist, and the case supervisor.

2. CASE ANALYSIS.—At the conference on James's case the following presentation of the problem, causal factors, and plan of treatment was drawn up:

a. Problem.—James's poor school work, due to his limited capacity for responding to academic education, has developed in him a feeling of inferiority which is reflected in his gait and manner and in his defensive reactions to his experience.

He lacks vocational training or any special skill. His earning capacity is low, and this has further tended to isolate him from the larger activities in which he could take his place if he had a better community standing and a larger income. The desire for new experiences, natural to a youth of eighteen years, has been blanketed by his monotonous employment, which taxed neither mental capacity nor physical strength nor agility.

Accustomed to giving most of his small wages to his family, James was unable, because of his inadequate allowances, to seek the company of the girls of the neighborhood, whose response might have compensated for his growing feeling of inadequacy.

He had tried to stifle this feeling through attending wild drinking parties. Deep-buried in his subconsciousness, his wish to be acclaimed for his prowess in some line was revealed when his inhibitions were released by alcohol. His desire to secure the recognition of his associates, schooled in crime, led him to follow for an hour a career of larceny, vandalism, burglary, shooting, disregard of traffic ordinances, and indifference to the orders of the police.

He is indulged at home and lacks intelligent and decisive supervision, due to his parents' anxiety about him, their inability to plan constructively for his needs, and a fear that he will leave home and fall in with evil associates.

b. Causal Factors.—James is of dull-normal intelligence (see psychologist's report). His tastes are mechanical and for active outdoor work, rather than for intellectual pursuits or a sedentary life. Receiving no encouragement nor understanding in this regard, bewildered, he has thought that as an office worker, a white-collar man, he could gain recognition and social standing. Lack of intelligent vocational guidance has thus been an important element in the development of his delinquency ideation.

His family "hope for the best" but in reality expect little from James, and he is aware of this attitude. He appears sullen and resentful and masks his sense of futility under a cloak of bravado.

His recreational facilities are limited to cheap commercial amusements and the social gatherings of a group which includes some disreputable and lawless individuals.

He has recently been indifferent in his church attendance and thus deprived himself of religious influence and incurred the displeasure of his family, which increased his sense of isolation.

He has never had a savings account, and this means for strengthening his appreciation of the property rights of others has never been a factor in his life.

He has developed a certain hopelessness and fatalism in the three years that have elapsed since he left school because of his stagnation, mentally, morally, physically, economically, and socially.

c. Plan of Treatment.—James will report to the probation officer each week. His home will be visited at least twice a month, and after he secures employment his place of employment will be visited monthly or oftener if necessary. By discipline, reeducation, and example, efforts will be made to strengthen his self-control and to bring about regularity and order in his mental life and in his habits and conduct.

The report of the detention prison psychiatrist described James as normal, rather dull mentally, negative neurologically, rather suggestible, but fairly well balanced emotionally. The more intensive psychological, psychiatric, and physical examination at the clinic indicated the need for close supervision and placement where he could learn a simple trade.

The plan for his industrial and economic advancement provides that for the present he shall be permitted to seek for employment, unaided, in accordance with his preferences. In view of his lack of equipment for office work, it is obvious that he cannot succeed in that field. After a period of gaining experience through trial and error, he will be more ready to accept the probation officer's offer of advice and assistance. He will then be encouraged to work at a vigorous out-of-doors job that will build his muscles and stimulate his latent energy. He will be entered in a class in automobile driving and elementary repair work. After a few months he will be aided to obtain a chauffeur's license. Employment in his brother-in-law's automobile repair shop and an opportunity to learn the business will be open to him if he evidences a desire to make good. His brother-in-law's earnings average $60 to $70 a week, and James can hope to earn this amount within a few years.

Necessary dental treatment will be arranged for. His strength and health will be built up by systematic exercise and proper diet. He will be given instruction in biology and hygiene. Constructive cooperation with other agencies will be effected and membership in a young men's club secured. The friendly contact with his parish priest will be developed. Regular church attendance and observance of the sacraments will be encouraged. A budget of expenses will be drafted and systematic savings begun.

The cooperation with the family will be maintained. James's limitations and capacities will be further discussed, and the moral support of his parents and sisters will be secured to the end that he may find in his home a refuge from the difficulties of life, understanding of his aims and plans, and an inspiration to do better things.

Continued study of James's personality and environment will be made to the end of gaining greater insight and leading him to a realization of himself as he is. Finer objectives and new visions and goals will be held out to him. His skill and strength of character will be developed, and adequate and stimulating social relationships will be established. His wishes will be determined and guided into constructive channels.

Every step in the process of adjustment will be taken with the end in view of securing James's permanent adjustment within himself and within the community. The plan of adjustment will be developed in cooperation with the probationer, and he must approve and accept it as his own before it is put into practice. Otherwise he will reject the plan when the supervision of the bureau is removed. The plan will be modified from time to time as the need arises.

B. Acceptance of Plan by Probationer. *Gaining Confidence and Respect.*— James had an indifference, amounting almost to prejudice, toward law and order and their representatives. To him the probation officer represented law and order. *Ipso facto*, James believed in not letting him know too much of his plans. Courtesy and civility were expedient. But friendship and regard were not ideas associated in his mind with a probation officer.

During the weeks that followed, James's interests were sounded. He was led into many conversations on sports and current events and matters of opinion, wherein he became almost enthusiastic, in contrast to his earlier phlegmatic unresponsiveness. Gradually he forgot the officer, in his better knowledge of the man. He began to draw on the probation officer's larger knowledge and experience, and his confidence in and respect for him slowly became established.

Arousing Admiration.—James began to turn to his probation officer as to an authority who knew or could find out everything, as a friend who always could be depended on, and as a "square guy" who kept his promises absolutely and was truthful. He admired him, too, because he represented nearly everything that James had more or less consciously desired to be. He was considerably taller than James, his physical development bespoke his athletic prowess, his friendly, interested manner of talking won friends readily. He became a hero to his youthful client, who began to imitate him in many ways.

Realization of Problems and Motives by Probationer.—James's frequent reports provided the probation officer with opportunities for gaining increased knowledge of his character and disposition. Through instruction in morality and in his relation to society, James began to consider himself and to see himself as he was. He saw himself as a problem and ceased to feel that most of the world, except himself, was out of step. He came to a realization of the motives, tendencies, and impulses that he must control and overcome if he were to become attuned to the desirable aspects of his environment, resist the undesirable elements, and live in harmony with the community.

Removal of Antisocial Attitudes.—At first James was constrained by motives of expediency to follow suggestions that he avoid his former associates and accustomed habits. Subjectively, his antisocial attitude persisted longer. His indifference, sullenness, and feeling of isolation were deeply ingrained. His disregard of good community standards was based on the unethical beliefs of his earlier associates.

Time and skill were required to bring about a change in James's mental beliefs. A growing regard for the probation officer helped his progress. New activities and the probation officer's revelations of new goals and his interpretations of life eventually brought a new outlook into existence.

New Visions and Goals.—False ideas and mental vacuity were replaced by sound concepts of life, new visions and goals. First he was educated in the knowledge of finer personal standards and acquainted with the high achievements of others, in individual and social attainment. Then the ideal of himself as a person who possessed the capacity for like attainments and could achieve them was held out. These were more satisfying, more flattering ideas than he had previously held. Here were ways by which he could win the good opinion of his family and himself. At first with reservations and eventually wholeheartedly James entered with a new spirit into plans for his spiritual growth.

Under direction, he was reeducated in the fundamentals of ethics. He was gradually brought to a new viewpoint, and his self-sufficiency was penetrated.

Transference of Objectives.—A transference of objectives was achieved by leading James constructively to sublimate his energies and change his negative, destructive, and indifferent outlook to a positive, constructive, and interested attitude. By encouragement, patience, and good example the probation officer was bringing James into line with the social thought and feeling of the community. In the light of James's increased knowledge and experience, the older and criminal characters, whom he had considered the heroes of the neighborhood, no longer appeared attractive. The probation officer's presentation and interpretation of the activities of burglars and bandits revealed them to James from the standpoint of the law-abiding citizen, and he began to see them as they appeared when divested of the glamour with which he had previously invested them. The antisocial, quasi-criminal element could never again hold James so completely in the grip of its influences and activities. The probation officer was gaining the position of wise philosopher, guide, and friend. James had absorbed his beliefs, his inner life had been modified thereby, and he was getting ready spiritually to put those beliefs into practice.

He still felt, however, that he was in a strange field of thought. It would take time to become familiar and on easy terms with the ideas he had accepted. He must get rid of his self-consciousness, of the fear that his new mode of behavior would be commented on by his family or jeered at by scoffers. He had adopted the concepts of the probation officer whom he admired and believed in. His own experience would have to prove whether they would be generally accepted by his associates.

Trial and Error Permitted.—For several weeks at the outset of his probation period, James insisted on finding his own job. He claimed that he did not require or desire any help from the probation officer. He repeatedly reported that he expected to obtain various positions. Some of those he had learned of through friends, others he had seen advertised in the newspapers. Tentative promises of future employment had been received from the personnel managers of some establishments where he had applied. However, the promised jobs failed to materialize. He had filed applications with several concerns. In one he had been given a physical examination, which he passed, and was placed on the waiting list. He had "shenangoed" on the docks for a few days, but his height and weight were not great enough to bring his services into much demand as a dock laborer. His mother had become impatient with his failures although she believed that he was making a conscientious effort to secure work.

James joined a social club in the neighborhood which he admitted included some boys whose habits did not coincide with his newborn ideas of what constituted desirable habits. He said he had to join, that the fellows kept after him, but that he did not go to the club often. But he would not admit the comparatively greater advantages of the church club, suggested by the probation officer.

He also postponed entering the automobile mechanics class on various pretexts. The summer nights were too warm for study, and he wanted to have steady employment first, so he could meet the tuition expense himself. He had occasional lapses in regard to his appearance and was not uniformly neat and well groomed.

James had to learn by his own experiences, and sometimes from his own mistakes, to make his choices wisely. Always the process was one of slow natural growth.

Acceptance of Plan by Probationer.—It was important that James's days should be filled with productive labor, alike for its psychological effect, physical benefit, and that he might be self-supporting. After many talks the probation officer brought him to see how unfitted he was for office work and that there could be no future in that field for one of his limited academic education, especially in view of his dislike for school work and his reluctance to pursue his studies further. His stubborn determination to accept only a clerical position was further weakened by the complaints of his family in regard to his idleness and the embarrassment of being confined to a very limited allowance. He became willing to work at anything available.

At this time an auto mechanics class was decided upon, and with new interest and energy James applied for admission. Wholeheartedly, he accepted the plan, once the entering wedge had been effected. He also joined the church club, after a talk with its president. The persuasions of his pastor and the probation officer, combined with his desire to please his mother and to live up to the standard he had adopted for himself, led him to take a pledge to refrain from using intoxicating liquors. His dress and manner also improved.

Through trial and error James had arrived at a willingness to consider and accept plans other than those he had initiated. The advantages of various forms of employment were talked over. The physical benefits accruing from outdoor activities and the relatively high wages paid by construction companies or subway builders made positions offered by these concerns seem more attractive in the light of his own recent failures, his greater knowledge of working conditions, his desire to contribute to the maintenance of the household, and his need for spending money. The opportunity to save, to repay the debts his parents had incurred in his behalf, also was an important consideration with him.

Before James could be placed in this type of position, which seemed to offer so much and to supply so many of his needs, his mother's objections must be overcome. She had halfheartedly promised her aid, but her leniency and coddling had done much to develop James's indifference toward manual labor. He had been assured of the comforts of home whether he worked or not. However, the appeal of the probation officer's arguments and James's own unsatisfactory experience in vainly seeking employment combined to produce a change of attitude in her. His mother's approval secured, with new enthusiasm he set out to obtain work as a subway excavator.

Part III.—The Process of Adjustment (*Continued*)

A. Social Adjustment. DEVELOPMENT OF SOCIAL RELATIONSHIPS. *Right Job.*—James secured the job. He worked in the open from eight A.M. to five P.M. assisting skilled workers. The position proved quite satisfactory; the association with industrious fellow workers was wholesome. The probation officer enlisted the interest and cooperation of the foreman, who was pleased with James's energy and dependability. He reported for work regularly, was always sober, and his associates were among the more desirable of his fellow workers. The probation officer maintained cooperation with his foreman by means of frequent visits, at least monthly, and was thus kept informed regarding James's progress.

Financial Independence: Budgeting and Thrift.—His weekly wage in his new position was $28 and his usual earnings, including overtime, aggregated $32.50. With James's new financial independence (he was earning exactly twice as much as he had ever earned in his life) came an appreciation of family responsibility and a thought of himself as a responsible economic unit.

With the probation officer's assistance he drafted a budget which provided for establishing and regularly adding to a savings account and for generous contributions to the support of the household. New clothes were bought, and he commenced repaying the money he owed his parents. He contributed regularly to church collections, and in the ensuing weeks he took out a small insurance policy and was able to pay dues and other expenses incidental to engaging in organized recreation. His developing social attitude and the wise direction of the probation officer prevented him from indulging in the extravagances and frivolous expenditures which would so readily have depleted the wages, which, by careful planning, were adequate to cover all his expenses and leave a margin.

Family Adjustment.—The probation officer had become a familiar and welcome visitor in the home. Many opportunities for understanding the family viewpoint and explaining James to his previously bewildered father, despairing mother, and impatient, resentful sisters had arisen. They readily conceded the futility of reproaching and labeling as a failure the son and brother whom they loved. Their fear that he would go the way of many of the neighbors' boys made them suspicious, doubting, and sharp of tongue.

James's efforts were shown to them. That his need of help and encouragement at this time was greater than during his period of detention and that their cooperation was essential to his progress was made apparent. However, their rational acceptance of this viewpoint and their intelligent appreciation of James's circumstances considerably preceded their ability to govern the expression of their attitude so as to manifest the kindliness, faith, and encouragement which he needed to receive.

The family began to display a new regard and consideration for the son and brother of whom they had been fond but a little ashamed and whom they had previously considered a liability and a burden. Gradually his restoration to a proper social status was recognized, and he now became a real partner in the family plans, difficulties, and achievements.

This deference and the appreciation of his opinion and efforts were flattering and stimulating. He had become a family asset. He began to hold his head higher, he became more alert and confident.

Constructive Recreation.—The probation officer, whose survey of his territory had familiarized him with its recreational resources, acquainted James with the advantages and opportunities offered by the clubs of the neighborhood. The type of association, the completeness of equipment, the athletic direction, the prowess in sports of its members, its accessibility, its approval by his family, and his desire to improve his social status led James to become a member of the social and athletic club under the auspices of his church. The club provided a gymnasium and billiard rooms and sponsored occasional boxing bouts, dances, and smokers, furnishing a full and wholesome program of recreation. James was enthusiastic in his attendance at the gymnasium. He lifted weights and ran and boxed in company with youths of good character. He was a quiet but interested attendant at all meetings. When he began to attend the dances, he could be found in the smoking room or in a corner with other nondancing youths. He was hesitant about displaying his limited accomplishments as a dancer. With the encouragement of the girls, who thought it a regrettable waste that such a presentable young man could not dance, he became in the course of several evenings sufficiently proficient to move about the floor without embarrassment.

Restoration of Social Status.—By reason of the better adjustment within himself, James was accepted naturally at his place of employment and in his other social contacts. Guided by the counsel of the probation officer, his family began to exhibit a new confidence in the boy, and this was most helpful. Neighbors and even the police noted that he was steadily employed and absent from his old haunts. But it was at his new places of recreation that he was most favorably received and accepted without any reference to his previous history or conduct.

All of this had a very stimulating effect upon James. His redirected energies, formerly absorbed in channels subversive of good conduct and right living, now found satisfying expression in physical activity, reading, and in his adequate and stimulating social relationships. The need of the speak-easy and the corner gang had been removed.

B. Personality Development. *Holding Up Ideal of Self.*—From the beginning the probation officer had held up to James an ideal of himself which appealed to his nature and awakened a growing response. He had been shown an ideal capable of realization. His finer personality traits, his only partly developed capacities, his self-control, ambition, and inhibitions, the sublimation of poorly directed expression—these were new forces, new tools with which to gain that strength and power which he had subconsciously desired for a long time.

Physical Rehabilitation.—After he was placed on probation and before he cooperated in plans for his rehabilitation, James had spent considerable time in idling, with resultant irregularity in eating and sleeping and diminution of his strength and energy. He was lazy and sluggish in body as well as in mind. The labor of his employment in the open and the play activities of the gymnasium now began to manifest themselves in the improved tone of his muscles, the clearness of his eyes, his more alert manner, increased vitality, and virile personality.

He had no physical disabilities, as shown by the clinic examination and confirmed by the examining physician for the insurance company and the examination at the club gymnasium. His carious teeth required attention. The probation officer accompanied him to a good dentist, who made a thorough examination and indicated cavities on a chart. Arrangements were made for weekly appointments and regular payments. The dental work, extending over several weeks, cost $67, all of which James paid for without neglecting his other obligations.

Character Building.—The frequent and continued contacts with James offered the probation officer ample opportunity to study him in relation to his character weaknesses and strengths and to carry out a plan of constructive development based on this knowledge. The underlying causations of his former intemperance, his indolence, and evasiveness were brought to light. The demoralizing influence of friends who were loose-lived, abandoned, and disorderly in their habits was evident. The most important phase of his personality development was the upbuilding of his character, and to this end the probation officer directed his efforts.

He taught James to see in retrospect how he had been swayed by asocial suggestions. He dwelt upon James's wish for response and his desire for recognition. He showed him how he would fail to achieve the friendship of worth-while people, the standing with his friends, and the economic goal that he sought if he did not build up within himself a strong character.

His antisocial behavior tendencies, his disorderly conduct, had been expression of cravings for new experience combined with a lack of knowledge of wholesome channels in which he might satisfy his desires.   Consequently, his energies were recanalized, and he grew in strength, morally and phys- ically, and in poise through following a well-balanced program of athletics, club work, job, and vocational education, according to the plan he had accepted.

James's desire for response, which had manifested itself through associa- tion with neighborhood ne'er-do-wells, was met by better adjustments at home and the wholesome companionship of his coworkers and fellow club members.

The wish for recognition, the desire to dramatize, displayed so conspicu- ously in the commission of the instant offense, was transformed into seeking acclaim for his good conduct, thrift, industry, and participation in club or church activities.

The probation officer held up before James high ideals of ethical conduct in all his relations with home, work, play, and associates.   His renewed religious practices gave added force to these ideals.   James absorbed them until they constituted the underlying basis and the motivating impulse of his moral concepts and codes of behavior.

The probation officer was afforded excellent opportunities to enter into a sympathetic and invigorating relationship with James on the occasions of his weekly reports at the bureau.   Here was the privacy which could not be attained in James's home or at his place of employment.   Here were dis- cussed the intimate problems which were perplexing him.   During these conversations, the probation officer obtained an understanding insight into James's character because he had, early in the course of their contacts, gained his full confidence and respect.   He was able, by means of advice and exhortation, to influence deeply James's beliefs, attitudes, and conduct. The sympathy and understanding and guidance of the probation officer were a great factor in James's progress.

Vocational Education.—The school year was well advanced when James was placed on probation.   It was coming to a close when he arrived at that feeling of respect and admiration for his probation officer and confidence in his guidance which brought ready acquiescence to his suggestions.   James's association of ideas with regular educational forces carried unpleasant memories; he had not liked school nor did he desire to be a part of further activities in a connection which would bring a feeling of inferiority and which he was convinced would teach him nothing.   For these reasons it did not seem desirable to overpersuade him to resume his interrupted elementary and school education by attendance at evening academic schools.   The opportunities provided by the club, the daily news, and the course of reading which he had been persuaded to undertake by the probation officer were expected to supply his academic educational deficiencies as far as possible.

He was willing, however, to enroll in a class where he received instruction in automobile driving and in elementary repair work. Several months later he passed the road test successfully and secured a chauffeur's license. The plan for his industrial career outlined in the case analysis was a goal toward which he steadily aimed and slowly progressed.

New Resources and Outlets.—James's youthful energies were now finding expression in satisfying activities. The impulsion to succeed and the desire for response and recognition were gratified as he increased in skill at work, in gymnasium, and in dancing, and met the approval of his family and the acclaim of his friends. He could drive an automobile and make some repairs. In the course of his mechanical training, he had gained knowledge which he was able to apply to the family radio when it got out of order. His increasing popularity in the club culminated in his election as assistant secretary—an honor which afforded him much pleasure. Life had become very full for James, and his bewilderment and lack of direction were memories of the past.

Regaining Self-respect.—The probation officer helped James in self-interpretation. Through his guidance James saw that it was the qualities and resources within him which were bringing social esteem. He gained a new self-respect and appreciation of himself.

Social Consciousness.—His consciousness of his place in the community expressed itself by his complete cooperation with the activities of his various sources of contact, his home, club, church, and job, into which he entered fully, where formerly he was at, and not of, the gathering.

He had developed a sense of oneness with his family. Their aims were his aims. The feeling of kinship with his own world—with fellow club members, coworkers, neighbors, the probation officer, and even the once avoided police officer—had become an impelling force in the development of considerate and altruistic conduct and made James's future as a law-abiding citizen reasonably predictable.

Appearance and Manner.—Under the impulsion of his new associates and his sense of what was fitting according to his new conception of himself, James began to wear better clothes and to take pride in his appearance. In contrast to many of the youths of his neighborhood, James, encouraged by the probation officer, did not scorn to wear a collar and tie on occasions, and his shoes were invariably well polished. The memory of a $67 dental bill, which he had paid out of his own savings, combined with the effect of the probation officer's example and the information which he received through pamphlets on personal hygiene, led James to an improved care of his teeth. The training at the gymnasium had improved his gait and posture. Proper diet and bathing gave him an air of cleanliness and freshness.

He developed a consciousness of the appearance of his hands and came to an appreciation of the fact that clean hands and nails were not nearly so much in the way as hands which needed attention.

His manner of withdrawing from participation in what was going on, his sulky reticence, and doggedness were no longer in evidence. They had been replaced by an affability and confidence that quite changed the attitude of others toward him.

Religious Development.—The probation officer maintained cooperation with James's pastor and the church visitor by visiting them at intervals. The pastor and visitor knew the family well but had become discouraged in regard to James because of his apparent indifference toward religion. Encouraged by the successes of the probation officer, new efforts to revivify James's interest were undertaken. He was visited and invited to call on the pastor and the visitor. His religious indifference was discussed, and, as a result, he resumed regular church attendance.

Throughout the efforts to develop James spiritually, the emphasis was on the positive rather than the negative side, on virtues and not on vices. He was encouraged to renewed efforts on a high plane or morality. James's dormant religious spirit became reenergized, and his behavior and point of view were unconsciously modified in every phase of his life.

His earlier feeling of isolation from the things of religion was removed. He kept the pledge that he had taken to abstain from intoxicants. He became a regular communicant and showed increased interest in church matters. He was reinforced by the spirit of religion, which influenced his conduct seven days a week.

Outlook for Future.—The outlook for James's future is apparently a favorable one. Although he needs close and continued supervision for a few years, there are no irremediable deficiencies which preclude the possibility of his carrying on without continued supervision. The effort is being made to develop within him such a strength of character, such a sense of the security of his position in the community, and such a belief in his own integrity that he will not readily turn to paths of evil but will be held to the high standards of conduct.

Through his development of self-control, his improved physical condition and healthier mental outlook, vocational equipment, broadened horizon, bettered employment, new prestige and standing with his family and friends, his industry, wholesome recreational contacts, strengthened religious affiliations, economic security, and an appreciation of what he may become, he has been led away from his position of uncertainty into safe channels of social and personality adjustment which give every promise of permanency.

INTERPRETATIVE SUMMARY OF THE CASE OF JAMES R.

The case of James R. is an illustration of what can be accomplished within a comparatively short period of time when a well-trained, experienced, and imaginative probation officer is able to devote a great deal of time to one case. It may also be inferred from this case that probation service, under the above working conditions, is a tremendous saving in terms of money, time, energy, and human life and happiness. It is probation at its best, if carried on consistently in other cases.

The probation officer shows unusual insight into the boy's capacities, his needs, and his struggles for lost status, his reactions to probation and to the probation officer, and his need for trial-and-error methods in the development of his personality.

With keen foresight the boy was led to accept and approve the plan of adjustment as his own before it was put into practice in order to eliminate the possibility of its being discarded after the probationary period was over.

The probation officer also shows remarkable appreciation of difficulties involved in carrying out an actual plan even though an intelligent understanding and acceptance of this plan had been attained. His considerate regard for these difficulties and patient waiting until all persons concerned were emotionally ready to act wins respect and confidence in his skill as a professional worker.

No time nor effort was spared in carrying out the plan of James's adjustment. Thorough knowledge of the case, careful diagnosis and planning, and continuous contacts with the probationer and his family are generally highly productive of good results. A well-balanced program of athletics, club work, suitable employment, vocational training, religious pursuits, and wholesome associates was put into operation almost simultaneously. A vigorous attempt was made to incorporate the boy into the family group and its activities.

The cumulative effect of these various activities achieved for James increased vitality, economic independence, prestige, a new self-respect, a new outlook on life, a oneness with his family, "affability and confidence which changed the attitude of others toward him." These assets broadened his horizon and provided a new zest for life.

It should be noted that once the process of adjustment starts and is accepted by the probationer it gains impetus rapidly. The person develops a social consciousness and an increased control over desires and actions. He becomes an accepted member in the group and does not dare to risk his status and prestige.

The specific techniques used in the treatment of James and his family were notably those of redefinition of the social situation, motivation toward a higher code of ethics and standards of conduct, orientation and gaining of insight into his own social situation, identification with interests of probationer, and mutual cooperative planning. At no time did the officer use the ordering-and-forbidding technique. He allowed the boy to try and err until he was ready to accept the officer's plan. Sympathetic insight is the keynote to success in this case.

The question may be raised, however, whether the probation officer had not robbed the parents and boy of an opportunity to become better acquainted with each other and to carry out some of the plans which the officer took upon himself. He even accompanied the boy to the dentist, made arrangements for recreational and athletic activities. The father's interest in sports might have been revived had he been induced to accompany his son to the gymnasium. It was the mother's place to accompany her son to the dentist and make the necessary financial arrangements. Overactivity on the part of the probation officer and interference with family functions may lead in many instances to failure in developing desirable family relations and the child's rejection of control by parents. Moreover, it is embarrassing to many probationers to have their associates and medical aides learn of their probation.

The father was interested in plans for civic improvement (see p. 334). Was the boy's interest in civic affairs and in the pursuits of his father promoted? He was the only son in a group of four sisters and the more the father and son could be brought together the more effective would have been the struggle to banish the social isolation of each.

The probation officer might have recommended some reading for James on sex hygiene, on sportsmanship, on character building, as well as on subjects calculated to supply his academic deficiencies.

The probation officer did not recommend moving from the district in order to escape the influence of "disorderly and boisterous character of associates." He depended on creating sufficient integrity of character in James to withstand any temptations which he might face no matter where he lived.

Perhaps the careful plan of treatment of this case can be brought into sharper focus if we indicate the accomplishments in the three major phases of social therapy (see pp. 316–331).

Executive Phase of Treatment.—Arrangements for dental care, systematic exercise, and wholesome balanced diet.

Provisions for instruction in biology and hygiene.

Cooperation with young men's clubs, gymnasium, and athletic opportunities.

Contact with parish priest.

Cooperation with police officer on post.

Cooperation with foreman and employer.

Provision of vocational, educational, and mechanical training.

Drafting of budget of expenses and plans for savings account and payment on insurance policy.

Interaction Phase of Treatment.—Development of plan of adjustment in cooperation with probationer's desires and experiences.

Stimulation of interests in and enthusiasm for sports and current events, thus providing an opportunity to get acquainted with officer as man to man.

Keeping promises scrupulously.

Friendly interested manner of talking.

Keen appreciation and warm sympathy for boy's feeling of isolation and indifference.

Steady confidence in boy's ability to make good and to achieve higher goals.

Constant encouragement, patience, good example of courtesy, truthfulness, patience, industry of probation officer.

The probation officer embodied "hero attitudes," and the boy developed emotional attachments to him.

Leadership Phase of Treatment.—Explanation of boy's role in and relationship and responsibility to society.

Interpretation of the motives, tendencies, and impulses which needed to be brought under control.

Acquaintance with achievements of others.

Holding out boy's innate capacity for personal and social attainment.

Education in the fundamentals of social ethics and familial solidarity.

Reinterpretation of criminal activities and influences.

Strengthening and redirecting boy's desire for response from association with local ne'er-do-wells to wholesome companionship with fellow workers and club members.

Transforming wish for recognition from a gang and by conspicuous commission of offenses into search for acclaim for good conduct.

Changing mother's attitude toward manual labor and show of too great leniency and coddling.

Interpretation of boy's need of the faith and love of the family group.

Changing family's attitude of resentment, fear, suspicion, and reproaching to tolerance, encouragement, kindliness, and confidence.

Development of self-assurance and prestige in own social world.

(To be continued)

CHAPTER XVI

SOCIAL CASE TREATMENT OF DELINQUENT AND PROBLEM YOUTH (*Continued*)

Methods of Changing Attitudes and Habits.—The most effective and lasting adjustments are achieved through a change of attitudes and habits. But these are difficult to change because they are frequently deeply rooted, have an emotional significance to the person, and have validity and reason for their existence. As Dewey points out:[1]

Habits are arts. They involve skill of sensory and motor organs, cunning or craft, and objective materials. They assimilate objective energies and eventuate in command of environment. They require order, discipline, and manifest technique. They have a beginning, middle and end. . . .

A bad habit suggests an inherent tendency to action and also a hold, command over us. It makes us do things we are ashamed of, things which we tell ourselves we prefer not to do. It overrides our formal resolutions, our conscious decisions. When we are honest with ourselves we acknowledge that a habit has this power because it is so intimately a part of ourselves. It has a hold upon us because we *are* the habit. . . . All habits are demands for certain kinds of activity; and they constitute the self. In any intelligible sense of the word will, they *are* will. They form our effective desires and they furnish us with our working capacities. They rule our thoughts, determining which shall appear and be strong and which shall pass from light into obscurity.

Recently a friend remarked to me that there was one superstition current among even cultivated persons. They suppose that if one is told what to do, if the right *end* is pointed to them, all that is required in order to bring about the right act is will or wish on the part of the one who is to act. He used as an illustration the matter of physical posture; the assumption is that if a man is told to stand up straight, all that is further needed is wish and effort on his part, and the deed is done. He pointed out that this belief is on a par with primitive magic in its neglect of attention to the means which are involved in reaching an end.

[1] JOHN DEWEY, *Human Nature and Conduct*, pp. 15–28, 34–35. Reprinted by permission of Henry Holt and Company.

To *reach* an end we must take our mind off from it and attend to the act which is next to be performed. We must make that the end. . . . The only way of accomplishing this discovery is through a flank movement. We must stop even thinking of standing up straight. To think of it is fatal, for it commits us to the operation and established habit of standing wrong. We must find an act within our power which is disconnected from any thought about standing. We must start to do another thing which on one side inhibits our falling into the customary bad position and on the other side is the beginning of a series of acts which may lead into the correct posture.[1] The hard drinker who keeps thinking of not drinking is doing what he can to initiate the acts which lead to drinking. He is starting with the stimulus to his habit. To succeed he must find some positive interest or line of action which will inhibit the drinking series and which by instituting another course of action will bring him to his desired end. In short, the man's true aim is to discover some course of action, having nothing to do with the habit of drink or standing erect, which will take him where he wants to go. The discovery of this other series is at once his means and his end. Until one takes intermediate acts seriously enough to treat them as ends, one wastes one's time in any effort at change of habits. Of the intermediate acts, the most important is the *next* one. The first or earliest means is the most important *end* to discover.

Change of attitudes is rarely achieved through scolding, admonition, punishment, but rather through the child's experiences and his desire for change when he is helped to understand the necessity for change. When the social situation is not defined, we resort to the crude and ineffectual method which Thomas calls "'ordering-and-forbidding'—that is, meeting a crisis by an arbitrary act of will decreeing the disappearance of the undesirable or the appearance of the desirable phenomena, and using arbitrary physical action to enforce the decree. This method corresponds exactly to the magical phase of natural technique."[2] On the subject of punishment, Healy and his associates observe that while no one can deny the value and the correct psychology of unpleasurable returns as a means of checking misbehavior, and while

---

[1] The technique of this process is stated in the book of Mr. Alexander . . . , and the theoretical statement given is borrowed from Mr. Alexander's analysis. [M. Alexander, *Man's Supreme Inheritance.*]

[2] W. I. Thomas and F. Znaniecki, *The Polish Peasant in Europe and America*, p. 3.

One can hardly advocate threats or holding "a big stick" over an offender's head; yet there can be no doubt that in exceptional cases, where the delinquent does not respond to constructive and kindly effort, a vigorous warning may be of great value. . . .

It is of much greater importance, however, that the more constructive but often neglected principle of reward and praise could be generously used to prevent delinquency. Reward and praise represent the positive aspect of treatment stimulus, the encouragement to right-doing rather than to mere repression of wrong-doing.[1]

Undoubtedly reward as a method in reeducation has its disadvantages, since the child may become discouraged over the remoteness of the reward and the losses suffered in relapses of behavior. Particularly dangerous is the feeling which may arise that every good deed needs to be compensated.[2]

In Aichhorn's opinion the most valuable method of changing attitudes of wayward youth is "talking together and aiding to understand the causes and effects of maladjustments and displaying an attitude of forgiveness toward even the worst offenses. This served us [as psychoanalyst in a house for wayward youth in Austria] well because we had the confidence of the children."[3] He cites the following case as an illustration of one method to be used in reeducation:

The Case of A.[4]—An eighteen-year-old boy, expelled from a military school for stealing from his comrades and who had stolen at home and elsewhere. After he had been with us for several months, I put him in charge of the tobacco shop. The employees each contributed a certain amount to buy their tobacco in common. I told the cashier to keep an eye on the boy without letting him know and to report to me when any money was missing. Four weeks later, he reported that about half the sum taken in weekly was missing. This seemed to be the right moment to expose the boy to an emotional shock in order to bring about catharsis, although I had no clear idea how I was going to do this. . . . I inquired how he was getting along and gradually we approached the topic of the tobacco shop. "How much do you take in each week?" He mentioned a certain sum. We continued to dust the books. After a pause, "Does the money always come out right?" A hesitating "Yes" of which I took no further notice.

[1] WILLIAM HEALY, AUGUSTA F. BRONNER, EDITH M. H. BAYLOR, J. PRENTICE MURPHY, *Reconstructing Behavior in Youth*, pp. 21–22.

[2] *Cf.* MARY ANTOINETTE CANNON and PHILIP KLEIN, *Social Case Work*, p. 193.

[3] AUGUST AICHHORN, *Wayward Youth*, p. 163.

[4] *Ibid.*, pp. 159–161. Reprinted by permission of The Viking Press, Inc.

After another pause, "When do you have the most trade?" "In the morning." Then still later, "I must look in on you some time and go over your cash drawer." The boy was getting more restless all the time but I ignored it, went on working and kept coming back to the tobacco shop. When I felt that I had intensified his uneasiness sufficiently I suddenly brought the crisis to a head. "Well, when we get through here I'll go and take a look at your cash." We had been working together for about an hour and a quarter. He stood with his back to me, took a book from the shelf, and suddenly let it fall. Then I took cognizance of his excitement. "What's the matter?" "Nothing." "*What's wrong with your cash?*" His face became distorted with anxiety, and he stammered out the sum. Without saying a word I gave him this amount. He looked at me with an indescribable expression on his face and was about to speak. I would not let him talk because I felt that my action must have time to take effect and so I sent him away with a friendly gesture. About ten minutes later, he came back and laid the money on the table, saying "Let them lock me up. I don't deserve your help—I'll only steal again." He was greatly excited and was sobbing bitterly. I let him sit down and I began to talk to him. I did not preach, but listened sympathetically to what he poured out, his thievery, his attitude toward his family and to life in general, and everything that troubled him. The emotion gradually receded, relieved by the weeping and talking. Finally I gave the money back to him, saying that I did not believe he would steal again; that he was worth that much to me. I said too, that it was not a present, that he could smoke less and pay it back gradually. So that no one should know about this, however, he had better put the money back in the cash drawer. I told the cashier that the amount had been returned and that he need take no notice of the affair. In the course of the next two months, the money was actually returned.

It is not improbable that the contrast in emotion from fear to relief brought about the solution. Practically the treatment was effective; in the short time he stayed with us, he conducted himself well. Later he was employed as a draughtsman in a furniture factory and acquitted himself creditably. In this case we had succeeded in arousing a strong emotion in him and in making use of it in his retraining. We must wait for further experience with this method to see in which cases it is applicable as a special technique.

The Case of Arline Watkins.[1]—The case of Arline Watkins is a good illustration of how a well-established habit of stealing was overcome in a girl through kindness, confidence, provision of attractive clothes, sweets, wholesome amusements, and particularly those things for which the child had a secret longing; through fostering a sense of responsibility, a feeling of being a grown-up, and by building stronger personality traits through

---

[1] Case study made and recorded by Aileen McHenry. Quoted by permission of the San Pedro Police Juvenile Bureau and of Miss McHenry.

encouragement, response, and recognition. Gaining a new name with its implication of new personality was a powerful motive.

In this case a girl who was well on the road to becoming a "wild child," homeless, living from moment to moment, responding to every possible impulse, sustaining few of the tensions which social living requires, was converted into a responsive, adjusted well-balanced child amenable to the requirements of family life.

Petition filed in August of 1935 by the San Pedro Police Department—Juvenile Bureau. The child had been known to the Bureau on more than five separate occasions, after having been apprehended for burglary, stealing suitcases, and money; and on the occasion of the last theft of $60, her partner, a boy, was also filed on. The parents have been inefficient and disinterested; although repeatedly warned against it, they have allowed the child to roam the streets at all hours; and she had been selling newspapers. She has been described by the San Pedro Police as a "regular bandit." The neighbors have made numerous complaints to the police, who feel that nothing further can be done by their department, as the child needs supervision which cannot be given in that home. She was brought to the attention of the police several times when her uncle reported her missing. The first time she was found at midnight by the soldiers at Fort McArthur, sleeping in a truck. Later, in the company of a boy, she took a suitcase and other articles valued at $31; on the occasion of the $60 theft, she and the boy had seen a ring on a dresser through a bedroom window. He helped her open the screen, and she went in, found a wallet in the top drawer of the dresser, and took it, but did not take the ring. The boy took the wallet from her, and went to his own home. He later spent part of the money, but Arline spent none of it.

REPORT OF JUVENILE HALL CLINIC

Physical Examination.—General physical appearance good. Small denuded area on lower lip, probably a herpes (cold sore). Throat slightly inflamed. Temperature 100 degrees at 11 A.M. Hymen edges inflamed, but no evidences of gonorrhea. Hymen not ruptured. Wassermann negative. Smears U—negative.

Psychological Examination.—Stanford-Binet. Physical age 10:6; mental age 8:4. I.Q. 79. Border-line or dull normal. Reads fairly well, but too slowly to pass the ten-year test. Very poor memory. Unable to give the day, month, or year correctly. Fails ninth-year arithmetic problems badly. Poor comprehension, necessary to repeat most questions; follows directions poorly.

Behavior Report (from Juvenile Hall Hospital).—The patient is apparently an untrained child who has grown up without constructive influences, or any environmental advantages. She seems crude and somewhat sophisticated. Has an independent manner, and has no doubt been much "on her own" without supervision. From the child's manner and statements it is inferred that she runs about as she pleases, without supervision or plans for her leisure time. Has been associated with various stealing episodes, but has ready alibis or excuses which show her incidental connection with these escapades. She has in all probability felt much deprivation in the home, has lacked satisfactions, and has reacted to this by unconsciously seeking other compensations, which have proved socially unacceptable.

Social History and Home Conditions (mother's statement).—Arline and her oldest brother, Fred, are the woman's children by a former marriage. Their father died after an operation when Arline was two months old. Woman married not long afterwards, and there are three children by the second marriage. Mother's statement and Arline's agree on the stepfather's behavior. He is continuously drinking, and very often brings drunken men into the home; demands food at all hours for himself and his drunken friends; is very ugly toward woman and children; curses a great deal; is untidy about his person and about the house; is so rough and unreasonable with the children that they dread being at home when he is there. Woman's relatives come only when they do not expect him to be there. He is suspicious of woman and often accuses her of being immoral with other men, and threatening to take the children from her, though she cannot understand why he would want them, when he is so abusive toward them. Woman has several times left her husband, but comes back on promises of good behavior, which are never kept. She has had him before the San Pedro City Prosecutor on charges of nonsupport, but his contributions to the family's support have always been very irregular, despite his regular $75 per month income from work in the lumber yards. Spends much money on liquor, and some on other women. Mother feels helpless to cope with Arline's stealing and other bad habits.

In September, 1934, Arline was placed on probation in the home of her maternal grandmother in San Pedro, with her mother's home only a short distance away. In December, 1934, she, in company with a seven-year-old boy, entered the Richfield Warehouse, and took from the open safe $35, much of which was recovered. Further contact with all relatives showed none able to assume the responsibility. As the stepfather and mother were again living together, the child was returned to them after the hearing. In July, 1935, Arline was brought to court on a new petition. She had remained away from home the greater part of the night, in the company of three boys, aged twelve and thirteen years. The children had broken into a garage, stolen a rifle valued at $5; the same day they had broken into a store, and took canned goods valued at $5; they then went to a garage at the rear of a court, where they slept all night. However, no physical injury seems to have ever befallen the child at the hands of the boys with whom she played. She herself was more like a boy than a girl in mannerisms and behavior. When asked once if she wasn't afraid one of the boys would hurt her sometime, she replied that they wouldn't dare so much as lay a hand on her.

At the hearing that followed the last escapades, boarding home placement was recommended and she was placed with Mrs. Florence Jones of Long Beach. She is still there, and making a very remarkable adjustment.

She is happy, and shows signs of improvement in many ways. The school reports that the child is doing as well as she is mentally capable of. The only outstanding trouble has been bed-wetting and soiling clothes, which is gradually being corrected. There has been backsliding at times, but on the whole continuous progress. She still tells some stories, and is a bit careless about her person, but there is a marked improvement. Arline has adopted the name of her foster mother, and calls herself "Arline Jones," and arranged for the school records to be changed accordingly on the approval of Mrs. Jones and the probation officer. Her mother is a little hurt by this change of name, but it seems to have had an excellent effect on Arline. She thinks of herself now as a different person, and occasionally says, "Well, when I was Arline _____ I could do that, but since I am Arline Jones, I can't."

Interviewed Mrs. Jones, boarding mother; also Arline. Mrs. Jones states that she has had Arline with her since August, 1935, and has noticed improvement all along the line. At present, Mrs. Jones has only two girls with her, both aged thirteen years. During the past year, she has had also two older girls, but they were there only for a short time.

Only once since her arrival has Arline been known to take anything that did not belong to her. Shortly after her arrival, the girl was visiting Mrs. Jones's married daughter, who lives near by. On this occasion, the daughter was making a quilt of some very pretty material. A few days later, a square of the material was found among Arline's personal belongings in the bedroom. When questioned, she repeatedly denied knowing anything about the material, where it came from, and how it had got into the girls' bedroom. After the foster mother had failed to get any response but denials, Mr. Jones talked with her long and earnestly, telling her how much they were trying to help her, and the trouble that comes of stealing. She seemed to be touched by his kindly manner, and cried, but still did not admit the theft. Then Mrs. Jones said, "Now, Arline, we aren't going to say anything more about this mistake that you have made. Just take the cloth and go back to the place where you got it, and lay it down where you found it. You needn't say anything at all to the lady, and she will understand." The daughter reported to her mother that little Arline entered the house and laid the material on the sewing machine, where it had been on the day of the child's visit. The incident was never again mentioned to Arline.

The little girl has been several times taken into stores by Mr. and Mrs. Jones, turned loose and told to look around at things, but to keep her hands in her pockets, if necessary, to keep from picking up things. If she saw something that she felt she had to have, and couldn't get along without, to come to them and tell them about it. If they could possibly afford to get it for her, they would; if not, they would get her as good a substitute as they could afford. On several occasions, they have had to buy for her attractive clothes that had caught her eye in stores, but the urge to steal seems to have been conquered. Temptation is removed in many ways. Fruit and the wholesome candies and sweets are kept in the house at all times, and given in moderation to the children; ice cream is frequently bought. Other things that they desire may be had as rewards of good behavior and something to work for. The children go to shows once a week, but just recently have they been allowed to go alone in the afternoon. This they consider a great honor, and quite grown-up.

The girls' bedroom opens into the hall, and until a short time ago, it was always kept open. Now the door may be closed at night on good behavior. If they have misbehaved, it is a sign that they are still just children, and must be watched over at night, so the door is left open. They both feel the disgrace now if the door is left open some night because of what they have done that day. Washing dishes is a special privilege.

The most persistent habit of Arline's has been bed-wetting over the entire period of her stay. Although it has decreased considerably, it has not been stopped, despite the fact that almost everything imaginable has been tried. Her physical examination shows no particular weakness that would account for it, and when she is promised some very special privilege for not wetting the bed for an entire week, she seldom does. Mrs. Jones has tried to shame her, deprived her of privileges, and talked with her about the extra work that she made her boarding mother, who was already very busy. About two weeks before the visit, Mrs. Jones, wearied and discouraged, told Arline that she was tired of continually having to wash out clothing after a thirteen-year-old girl, and that hereafter all clothing soiled by Arline would have to be washed out by Arline, and that the girl would have to take money from her savings to buy her own soap. This was a bitter ordeal, and probably hurt the boarding mother more even than the girl, who cried long and loudly while washing the clothing. But this drastic measure seemed to make her realize the amount of work that bed-wetting did cause, and the soiling of clothing has since been almost nil.

Both children go by the name of "Jones" providing that they live up to the good name of that family. They are told that the Jones family is well known and respected in the community and the children that are known as theirs must be a credit to them. They are very proud of their new name.

Children who have stolen because of an acquisitive impulse—not too seriously complicated with other factors—should not be deprived of their pocket money, as is frequently done, since the deprivation often gives them an added incentive to steal. It may seem paradoxical to advocate that their allowance be increased. Burt observes that "the readiest way to cure the robber is to use him with unexpected generosity; give him, not only pennies to spend, but sixpences to save and a cash box of his own to lock them in. Ownership is the best school of responsibility and faithfulness."[1]

Older boys and girls may be given opportunities at home to earn more and more as their needs increase. If they work outside the home and earn, definite but reasonable arrangements should

---

[1] *The Young Delinquent*, p. 475.

be made to their satisfaction as to how much should be saved, how much should be contributed to the family exchequer, and how much retained for pocket money.

Sweets, toys, clothes, amusements, special coveted articles, should be provided by adults, as far as possible, in large enough amounts to overcome any impulse to acquire them illegitimately. Where financial circumstances do not allow purchases of articles not absolutely necessary for maintenance they can be made at home. Though crude in form they may have more meaning, when properly interpreted and made with the assistance of the young, than many ready-made articles.

When a child has made a genuine attempt to conquer his habit of stealing he should be generously rewarded for it. The reward is more than a material gain; it also means heightening his status and self-respect.

Methods of Dealing with Lies.—The act of lying is not the chief concern of the case worker. His real concern should be "Why did the person lie?" It is often a healthy thing to ask oneself: "What have I done to cause the offender to lie to me or to be afraid of me?" It seems almost too trite to repeat that the basis for lying, as for other unadjustments, can be traced to other more fundamental and deeper underlying causal factors. Few people lie simply for the sake of lying. At times, no lie is intended. The person may possess only partial knowledge of facts; he may have a tendency to generalize too broadly. His memory might have tricked him[1] or he may have made the wrong mental associations.[2]

If the worker is concerned chiefly with personalities, the products of psychological metabolism, he will be interested in the inconsistency of the account only in so far as it indicates that the offender has or has not fully revealed his attitudes. Professor Lindeman remarks:

Even if the answers are false, they may serve to define the ultimate conclusions. In fact, the psychiatrist who makes inquiries of his subject does not anticipate true replies, but he nevertheless makes use of such responses as he receives. . . . What is in a person's "mind" may or may not be true but it is the sum total of his rationalizations upon

[1] See HUGO MUENSTERBERG, *On the Witness Stand.*
[2] See HANS GROSS, *Criminal Psychology.*

which his life has proceeded.   If he acts upon the basis of these rationalizations, they are in so far significant in explaining his behavior.[1]

The interviewer must distinguish between (1) lies as defense
mechanisms; (2) pathoformic lies; (3) conventional lies or
so-called white lies; (4) lies due to mental conflict;[2] (5) seeming
lies which arise in differences in point of view regarding matters;
(6) accidental lies, due to tricks of memory, illusions; (7) lies due
to a desire to control the situation.   Professor Cooley says:

Even telling the truth does not result so much from a need of mental
accuracy, though this is strong in some minds, as from a sense of the
unfairness of deceiving people of our own sort, and of the shame of being
detected in so doing.   Consequently the maxim, "Truth for friends and
lies for enemies," is very generally followed, not only by savages and
children, but, more or less openly, by civilized people.   Most persons
feel reluctant to tell a lie in so many words, but few have any compunc-
tions in deceiving by manner, and the like, persons toward whom they
feel no obligation. . . .   "Conscience is born of love" in this as in many
matters.   A thoughtful observer will easily see that injustice and not
untruth is the essence of lying, as popularly conceived.[3]

Aichhorn states that no child is absolutely trustworthy, so
we must weigh his statements carefully:

We do not yet know whether he told the truth.   The statements of
delinquents should always be checked.   However, when we catch a child
in a lie, we should not shame him.   Expressions such as "You lie,"
"You must tell the truth," should always be avoided.   It is much more
efficacious to act as if the child had made a mistake.   We can say, for
example, "Are you sure you meant what you said?", "Now think a
minute," or "Take your time; tell me again," etc.[4]

Cyril Burt[5] has given a very comprehensive discussion of the
analysis of children's lies and their prevention:

The telling of untruths is a frequent reproach, not only against
habitual delinquents, but also against children not otherwise unprincipled.   "One of my pupils is an incorrigible story-teller.   What am I to
do with him?"   The appeal is a common one, and the first reply is

[1] EDUARD C. LINDEMAN, *Social Discovery*, pp. 187–188.
[2] See WILLIAM HEALY, *Mental Conflicts and Misconduct*.
[3] CHARLES H. COOLEY, *Human Nature and the Social Order*, pp. 388–389.
[4] AUGUST AICHHORN, *Wayward Youth*, p. 24.
[5] *The Young Delinquent*, pp. 361–366, 375–381.   Reprinted by permission
of D. Appleton-Century Company, Inc.

another question: "What kind of stories does he tell?" Children's falsehoods are of many forms, and the treatment differs with the type. . . . Here it is not with moral but with psychological distinctions that we have to do. Classed by their underlying causes, we may recognize at least six or seven varieties, all broadly distinguishable, yet running imperceptibly the one into the other. . . .

1. There is, first, what may be named the *playful lie.* Tiny children are full of make-believe: *"Let's pretend"* is their favorite game, and much of their amusement owes its charm to a passing or a partial self-deception. . . .

2. There is, secondly, the *lie of confusion.* Children are exceedingly suggestible. They see little disparity between a fact that is real and a fancy that is vivid. What they have genuinely witnessed gets easily jumbled in their minds with what they have simply imagined or what they have merely been told. . . . All such misstatements are to be dealt with for what they really are—accidental errors or illusions and not downright untruths. . . .

3. "The lie of vanity." Lies designed to attract self-notice. . . . Such lies may range all the way from the empty but straightforward boasting of the braggart boy, to the subtler and more highly colored romances of the self-centered semi-neurotic, sensation-mongering girl; they merge, at an older stage still, into the baseless complaints of persecution or illness made by the truly hysterical. They express wishes, not perceptions, and are frequently the impulsive utterance of fancies that have long been dwelt upon in daydreams. The most morbid form consists in false self-accusations, in the bogus confession of imaginary misdeeds that have been neither performed nor intended.

4. Graver still are lies where the object is not to extol or magnify one-self, but to belittle, annoy, or even endanger another—the *lie of malevolence and revenge.* Where a serious charge is falsely laid, the outcome may be tragical. Sometimes the persons so traduced are the very ones who have been nearest and dearest to the child. Sometimes, too, the statement—not infrequently an accusation of a sexual assault— seems so foreign to the thoughts of a healthy child and the childish denouncer herself seems so guileless, plausible, and innocent, that credence is given at once without inquiry. As a rule, after careful exploration, some analogous experience in the past, hidden or half-forgotten, can generally be brought to light, and may be shown to have provided a basis for the calumny, though the doings or sayings recollected have been fastened, for private and malignant motives, upon a person entirely guiltless.

5. In most of the foregoing examples, harmless and heinous alike, the child is often self-deceived as well as deceiving. In the *excusive or exculpatory lie,* the child is acutely conscious of deception. The pur-

pose is usually plain. There is something done or something left undone for which the dissembler is anticipating blame. Such lies, in the main, are not constructive fictions but negative disavowals or denials. Most thieves lie to cover up their wrongdoings, and nearly every offender will perjure himself over the offenses which with him are most habitual or for which he has been constantly condemned. But even among the honest and obedient, there are few who have not upon occasion proffered a false explanation for being late, for forgetting an errand, or for breaking a cherished vase. . . .

6. In the more hardened and unprincipled, the positive line is exploited no longer as a fear-stricken excuse, but as an audacious pretext—no longer to shirk punishment, for what is past, but to gain profit or pleasure in the near future. Cheating at games and at lessons is the commonest and perhaps the least objectionable form of what may be termed the *selfish lie*. Where the lie is deliberately manufactured as an instrument to some further offense, the practice becomes more reprehensible. "Mother says will you please lend her a penny for the gas meter," is a favorite ruse for fraudulently obtaining a coin. The begging tales of the young delinquent are, as we have noted, at times most elaborately woven, and the wiles of the juvenile swindler are often miracles of ingenuity. One curious feature, making it harder than ever to detect the lie and to visit justice upon the liar, is to be found in a result well recognized, namely, that the habitual imposter may lose all sense that he is simulating and grow to believe implicitly in the truth of his inventions. Frequently he is himself his own most perfect dupe.

7. *Lies of loyalty and convention* are not uncommon among older children. In the elementary school the spirit of a sportsmanlike comradeship which prevents one child betraying another to an elder is not so general as in the public school, and everywhere it seems rarer among girls than among boys and older youths. To keep up a joint or completed lie is much easier for male conspirators than for female. To girlish lips it is the lie courteous rather than the lie of allegiance that comes with greatest readiness. . . .

Conventions differ greatly in different social classes, and just as the poorer classes are sometimes shocked by what seem to them the shams and hypocrisies of their betters, so the so-called better classes regard as indefensible untruths and shameless falsehoods what are no more than traditional tactics—tactics quite justifiable in the eyes of the humble diplomats themselves, when they feel themselves confronted by an inquisitive stranger from an alien social sphere. . . .

Lying, then, takes countless shapes and has a thousand different motives. It may be employed to compensate for almost any form of intellectual weakness. It may be inspired by almost any emotion—by fear more than any other, but also by greed, anger, self-display, submissiveness, and even by mistaken loyalty and affection. . . .

1. *Differential Treatment.*—In dealing with a particular lie uttered by a particular child, the first step is to ascertain whether that lie is a single isolated lapse or one of a numerous series; if the latter, it becomes important to inquire what type of lies he generally tells and what may be their animating motive. One lie does not make a liar. All children tell occasional untruths, and many have fits and periods of dissembling. The sense of systematic truthfulness comes late.

Different forms of falsehood call for very different remedies. As a rule, what has to be attacked is not the lying, but some deeper trouble in the background, and this may vary from child to child. To treat the lie as a simple, self-subsistent mode of perversity, to scold and castigate the liar each time he is found out, will seldom purge him of his tricks; it will only teach him a sharper cunning for the future. Accordingly, the basis of every lie must be explored before the lie itself is dealt with. . . .

2. *Avoid Provocative Occasions.*—Both the incipient and the habitual liar must be protected from situations setting too great a tax on their intelligence and candor. A regular thief who has been as regularly punished for his thefts should never be questioned as the sole source of information and thus presented with a gratuitous chance to tell yet another untruth. So far as possible, all lies must be immediately detected; the first exculpatory falsehood that a child happens to palm off with success is often the starting point of a long series of deceptions, each cooler and more calculated than the last. Never let the child see you are uncertain whether he is speaking the truth or not. Rather throw the uncertainty to him; let the blusterer feel puzzled whether you may not be laughing at him in your heart for a bluff so silly and transparent. Equip yourself beforehand with conclusive evidence; never challenge him on the strength of pure suspicion, trusting, from a downcast head, a stammer or a blush, a shifting eye, or a brazen stare, to detect his consciousness of guilt. Should you, indeed, be doubtful allow him the doubt's benefit, accepting what he says with punctilious civility, just as you would accept the statements of an equal. Treat the deceiver just as though he were trustworthy and you may shame him out of his deceit. Grant him, therefore, the fullest credit for every particle of fact his fabrications may contain, with the dictum of the practiced charlatan always in mind. . . .

3. *Confession.*—No punishment should follow a confession. To extort an admission publicly, in the face of the whole class or in front of the injured party, is to make that admission insuperably hard and a shuffle irresistibly easy. As a means of eliciting facts, the practice of urging a clean breast of things should be abandoned.

It is amazing how almost every teacher and parent expect the most hardened little sinners still to tell the truth about their sins—as if a lie were the last and worst offense the child could fall to instead of the easiest and the first.   Should a child be bad enough to steal, he is almost certain to be bad enough to equivocate about his theft, when taxed with it outright.   And once he has begun to delude you, a barrier is set up and any free and friendly discussion about his general situation becomes all but impossible.   In the rare case of a frank or voluntary avowal, the outlook is most hopeful.   With the remainder, it should be almost an unbroken rule never to begin with a direct interrogation—"Did you or did you not take that sixpence?"   For thus asking the child to own to his undisclosed misdeeds, there is but one justification; it might be put to the culprit in such terms as these, though it is better expressed by an attitude than by an argument; "You and I have been friends hitherto.   We can remain friends no longer if you are conscious of misleading me and I am conscious of mistrusting you.   Let us each be unreserved and open, so that we may start afresh on the same happy basis as before.   I am asking you to tell the truth, not because I am too lazy or too stupid to get decisive proof myself, much less I am asking you to bear witness against yourself that I may then reproach and punish you.   My only motive is that I may understand you better.   Friends have no secrets from each other—not even shameful ones.   And if everybody lied to everybody else, society would be impossible and all intimacy poisoned."   At times in seeking a confidence it is wise to disarm a possible dread beforehand by saying, plainly and explicitly: "You need not answer if you do not wish . . . "

The utmost discretion must be used as to when to expect an acknowledgement of guilt.   Demand it too soon, and the agitated conscience, all eager to disown the misdeed even to itself, may be hustled into a lie it never for one moment meant to tell.   Defer it too long, and the child may feel that, after all, the blame has not been brought home to him, and in reply to some more hasty questioner, he may have committed himself to a denial already and may not think it too late to retract.

4. *The Encouragement of Confidence.*—With young children truthfulness is at first no more than loyalty to persons, a return of gratitude to those who are sympathetic and kind—to their mothers, to their favorite teachers, to their closest companions and friends.   Children, like savages, feel that frankness and candor are precious gifts, pledges of affection, to be bestowed upon near and understanding comrades, and that a stranger, or an elder, or a representative of authority, is a sort of impersonal or potential enemy, an alien and a spy, with no title to the free exchange of confidence, an inquisitor whose entrapping questions are rightly countered with an equal craft. . . .

Should any form of rebuke or punishment seem necessary the best measure is not to stigmatize the child to his face as a liar, nor yet to thrash him there and then, much less to expatiate on how he has pained you: it is rather to cur or cold-shoulder him (as you might any adult acquaintance whom you found dishonorable) until of his own accord he resolves to prove himself worthier of your trust and credence.

5. *Literary Instruction.*— . . . With the young fabulist who is telling himself or others extravagant romances because his own life is so limited and dull, the best course is to enlarge and enrich his range of actual experiences. Let him learn that truth may be more thrilling and more entrancing, as well as stranger, than fiction. Travel, school journeys, visits to places of interest, will give him authentic matter to relate. With older children the over-active imagination may be given its needful grist through good fiction, good poetry and good romance. . . .

6. *Scientific Instruction.*—Crude homilies on the sinfulness of lying are of small avail, and to cite the fate of Ananias may create more harm than holiness. The child should be led to understand what a baffling thing it is to formulate the precise and literal truth. The task of the truthteller is two-fold, first to know, and then to express. Each is a science in itself. . . .

To the youthful mind, an ounce of scientific instruction and of linguistic practice is far more helpful and wholesome than any quantity of high-flown narrative or of trite and tedious moralizing. . . .

7. *The Avoidance of Pious Figments.*—Finally, if you wish the child to tell no lies to you, have a scrupulous care to tell no fables to the child. Myths about Father Christmas, the all-seeing Eye, the origin of babies, and the riddle of the sex, should never be offered as facts to the young and sensitive inquirer. The strongest shock may ensue when the child finds out that those whom he thought impeccable have told him tales about the most solemn of mysteries, and it is no more than a natural reaction should he start fabricating lies and legends of his own.

Pathological Lying.—Both Healy and Burt maintain that pathological liars are rare.[1] Pathological lying, says Healy,[2]

is falsification entirely disproportionate to any discernible end in view, engaged in by a person who, at the time of observation, cannot definitely be declared insane, feeble-minded, or epileptic. Such lying rarely, if ever, centers about a single event; although exhibited in very occasional cases for a short time, it manifests itself most frequently by far over a

---

[1] See WILLIAM HEALY, *Pathological Lying, Accusation and Swindling,* particularly pp. 1–4, 9–10, 43–45, 250–253.

[2] *Ibid.,* p. 1.

period of years, or even a life time.   It represents a trait rather than an episode. . . .

At times workers will spend considerable time in checking and verifying information, or in attempts to change a person's attitude, in having him follow a particular course of action only to discover that they have been deceived at each step.   While persistent and pathological liars are comparatively rare, they present perplexing problems, which, if undetected, will cause much concern and loss of time.

There is little that the general worker can do with pathological liars.   They are subjects for psychiatrists and psychologists. However, he must be able to recognize the pathological liar and not waste time nor delay getting the patient into competent medical hands.

Redefinition of the Social Situation.—The cases of Milton M. and Dora J. are illustrations of successful treatment through rather striking redefinition of the social situation and vision of the workers handling the cases.

Case Study of Milton M.[1]—*Petition* filed in behalf of Milton, fourteen years of age, arrested in company with another boy his own age.   They admitted they had pulled a fire-alarm box at a given address on a certain date.   These boys also admitted breaking the glass in three other fire boxes in that vicinity recently.   The petition stated also that the Fire Department reported numerous false alarms coming in from that particular locality. The filing was made under Sub-division 13, of the Juvenile Court Law of California and charged specifically Malicious Mischief.   The boys were held in custody in Juvenile Hall.

Probation Officer's first call on Milton at Juvenile Hall found him readily admitting participation in this mischievous habit, telling of such activities covering a large area over a long period of time in the section of the city in which he lived.   He even boasted of being the leader of a gang that specialized in false alarms.

Family Cooperation.—Milton is an American-born Italian boy; his parents had been born in Italy.   A call on them found them ready and willing to cooperate in any manner of probation.   The parents believed that it was more than a year previous when their younger children had first come to them with the story of Milton's breaking the glass in a fire box.   They stated they had questioned him from time to time but the boy had always denied any wrongdoing.

The Juvenile Hall Clinic next reported that a physical examination showed the boy well developed, nutrition poor, twelve pounds underweight, jerking

[1] Case study made and recorded by Carroll A. Stewart, Los Angeles County Probation Department.   Quoted by their permission.

movements of muscles, tonsils large, especially left, pus in posterior naso-pharynx, adhesions of foreskin to gland, puberty pro, marked course tremor of finger; Wasserman negative. The psychological examination showed physical age of 14:6, mental age of 11:6, giving an I.Q. of 79, dull normal or borderline; just misses twelve-year vocabulary (Italian spoken at home); poor in linguistic (verbal) type of test; successful in arithmetic induction and reasoning (fourteen-year level); quiet, rather indifferent effort, gives up quickly with a shrug of shoulders. *The recommendation from the Clinic* was for a tonsillectomy and intensive feeding.

School Report.—Showed the boy to have a good attendance and by an Otis primary intelligence test given a year previous, the boy had received an I.Q. of 77; his marks for all twelve subjects he was studying at school were all twos and threes with the exception of spelling, in which he received a four; his behavior was reported as quick-tempered, sulky, inclined to "pass the buck"; was frequently reported for quarreling, impertinence, and failure to do his work; gives up easily when task is rather difficult. The school reported the parents as being cooperative.

Process of Treatment.—Milton was released from Juvenile Hall and taken home to await the hearing in court. At this time the father stated the boy practiced masturbation and that probably this was the cause for his trouble, and the mother added that Milton was a bed-wetter and she thought this might be the cause of his trouble. Just as probation officer was leaving the house a policeman came to the door to ask if he might come in and talk to Milton. There had been reports of two more false fire alarms having been turned in on the night previous in that district but Milton had been in Juvenile Hall. . . .

In court Milton's story was heard, and the boy was duly admonished. He was declared a ward of the court and was instructed as to just what would be expected of him in the future. It was further ordered that arrangements be made for an operation for tonsillectomy and circumcision. Those physical adjustments were made in due time but on account of the boy's great fear of doctors the final winning of Milton over to having the operations performed would make a story in itself.

Now started the period of supervision. In nine days Milton had pulled another box. He denied his guilt to the police but later admitted to the probation officer that it had been he. This particular box had been pulled at 10:30 P.M., the streets had been slippery from a rainy afternoon although the night was clear and I remembered having read a newspaper account of how a serious accident had been narrowly averted between a fire truck and a privately owned machine. It took three days to get the boy to admit his guilt, so on the evening of the third day Milton and myself were at the fire station for a confidential chat with the captain. Almost an hour was spent in telling the boy of the hazards of sending the fire department on "wild goose chases," of the many dangers to the traveling public when the big machines rolled out on a rainy night; the cost to the city for these extra runs; the wear and tear on the nervous systems of the firemen, getting up and dressing two and three times and sometimes more, a night, for no good reason at all. The boy had been very favorably impressed with this friendly chat. Two days later he had written in school what he remembered about the talk. He seemed to have remembered all the high points of the visit. One week later, however, Milton was caught by an alert policeman pulling another box while three of his companions looked on.

Again Milton was told what persistent antisocial conduct could lead to. Then it was proposed to him to become a fireman himself. Milton seemed to be interested in becoming a fireman, but was wondering how he was to become one, and when. Part of the next day was spent in telling the plan to the parents and getting their full cooperation. It was decided that the boy actually thought enough of his home so that the contemplated action would not cause him to run away. So, with everything ready, three nights later the cure began. The probation officer called at the home at 11:00 P.M. The father went with him to the boy's bed; he looked very comfortable and snug and in two minutes time he was out of bed and being hurried to a greater speed at dressing. Once outside he at last came to life and asked where we were going. "To a fire," was the casual answer, but when we got there it appeared the alarm had been false.

This period lasted for five and one-half weeks; an average of two calls a week were made. On four occasions two calls were made in one evening; on one particular good night we got in three calls. When more than one call was made in an evening, just enough time was given the boy to get nicely snuggled back under the warm covers between the first and second call. It might be said that extreme caution was always used not to expose the boy to any dangerous draft or otherwise harm his health. The boy never had to be forced out of the house after he was once up and dressed.

At the end of two weeks it was hoped that Milton might ask for a truce. However, he lasted the five and one-half weeks; the last night of the probation officer's call, Milton had established his sleeping quarters under the bed rather than upon the top under the covers. When he was under the bed he came out on his knees and with considerable emotion fervently begged to be discharged from the fire department; he would never molest another fire-alarm box, and he added that he would see to it personally that none of his gang ever did either. He further promised he would study at school; that he would obey at home and stay in nights.

These promises were all voluntary on Milton's part. It was then he announced with thanks and offered to me as an inducement to cease the treatment the fact that the many trips up at night had caused him to overcome the habit of bed-wetting.

Milton was taken at his word and evidently he meant what he said. At the end of the year his case was dismissed. He made good in much less than that time. He had likewise helped several others to make good. There has never been any further trouble with false fire alarms in that neighborhood.

A probation officer must have not only considerable imagination and power to win the parents' cooperation, but he must also be deeply in love with his job to undertake a series of nocturnal visitations to the home of a boy and wild-goose chases to reputed fires.

The Case of Dora J.,[1] eighteen years of age, senior in high school, has run away from home, secured work as mother's helper in a near-by town, enrolled in the local high school and refuses not only to see her mother and to return home, but to have her mother visit her.

Dora was legally adopted as a small child by Mrs. J., once a well-to-do woman. Dora knows of her adoption but says that she "has no feelings on the matter," but "is violently opposed to her mother because she would not let the girl out of her sight, insisted on sleeping with the girl in the same bed, interfered with all of her interests and activities." The girl accuses the mother of "cruelty to one husband who was driven away from home, and to another who was driven to his grave"; of making a "mess of her business affairs," and of ruining "her life as well as Dora's." She repeated that her mother was cruel, unethical, un-Christian.

The tensions and conflicts between the daughter, who had little opportunity to participate in normal situations, and an overanxious mother are intense and of long standing. Even in her new environment the girl was "unable to forget the treatment at the hands of that neurotic, un-Christian-like woman," and continued to be moody, hard to deal with, and at times even desperate when her mother tried to communicate with her. An interview with the mother substantiated all of the statements Dora made regarding her and convinced of the impossibility of any rapid or drastic changes in her.

Dora's health broke down, unable to stand the strain of the conflict and unaccustomed housework. It was necessary to remove her to a rest home, but she applied for relief rather than to accept any help from her mother. Relief was given pending investigation, and considerable attention was given to the medical aspects of the case.

The girl was hard to manage at the rest home because of her morbidity, threats to commit suicide, irregularity of eating. She changed rest homes every few weeks, which created additional irritations and seriously undermined her morale.

It is obvious that in order to work out any permanent plan for Dora a great deal more information must be secured regarding the adoptive parents, the real parents, Dora herself, her health, her relations with other people, and a host of other things. However, the immediate problem facing us calls for some immediate treatment to prevent complete demoralization and physical breakdown.

Dora found life too hard; her antagonism to the mother was at least partially justified, but the girl could not divorce herself from

[1] Case dealt with by Assistance League of Southern California. Quoted by permission of the League.

her past and could not create a different social environment even though she was separated from her mother. It was obvious that little could be expected of the older woman which the younger one would recognize as love for her own sake. It is necessary then to arouse, if not genuine affection, tolerance and Christian charity in the girl. A picture was painted of the mother's state of mind and emotions and of what was expected of an ideal daughter under such difficult circumstances.

Since Dora had rather well-formed conceptions of ethics and Christian principles, repeated appeals were made to her to aid her mother, who was unfortunate enough to be left all alone and unable to change her ways because of advancing age and undermined health. Dora's tendencies to self-pity were turned into constructive outgoing energy toward another human being, and the attention on self was converted into a relationship demanding sacrifice and charity. It was not planned for Dora to return home but in order to remove the mental conflict the girl had to acquire a different definition of the whole situation.

(To be concluded)

CHAPTER XVII

SOCIAL CASE TREATMENT OF DELINQUENT AND PROBLEM YOUTH (*Concluded*)

Enuresis as a Physical and Psychological Problem.[1]—Enuresis (bed-wetting) is the source of much conflict, unhappiness, and nervous and emotional upsets for both the family and the child afflicted with the habit. Regarding the case of Marvin Levkowitz, cited earlier (see pp. 43–52), the Child Guidance Clinic of Los Angeles provides the following interpretation and recommendations.

Case of Marvin Levkowitz.—(*Continued*). His bed-wetting, a source of discomfort and inferiority, probably rests on a physical basis. He presents just enough physical signs and symptoms to indicate that these are of an endocrine involvement. His build is suggestive of a hypergonad condition. His large nose and extremities indicate some pituitary involvement. His very active reflexes, trembling hands, and cyanotic extremities indicate an associated vasomotor condition. It is very important that he come into the care of a man like Dr. _____. The sooner this is done the better, since he is approaching an age when medical treatment may be of no avail. [Moreover other complicating factors appear.] He is the "ugly-ducking" and "Orphant Annie" of his family. The siblings are all superior to him in accomplishment and better looking. He is ugly, awkward, and has a large nose and fuzzy hair. The superior accomplishments of the siblings are always rubbed in and he is made the household drudge. He has to stand for the abuse and mockery of the older siblings. Even if this situation could be reversed overnight and all his experiences rendered ideal, it probably would be too late to lift him out of his depth of despair because in his ten or twelve years of conscious life he has internalized his experiences too much. Besides the mother is far from being a person who could change her attitude overnight and the other vigorous youngsters are beyond any such control. In other words the situation as it is is absolutely impossible, and there is nothing to do but to place Marvin in a

[1] See H. F. Scoe, University of Iowa Child Welfare Studies, V, No. 4 (1933); also The White House Conference on Child Health and Protection, *The Child and The Home.*

well-chosen boarding home. He should preferably be in one in which he is the sole child, if possible. Merely getting away from the hostile home will be of great help but if he can find a home in which he receives some affection and some degree of understanding and praise, his better adjustment will be hastened. He has the stuff in him to make good and is well worth any expenditure that would give him an opportunity. Failure to break into the vicious circle of circumstances now may make him a community liability later.

The school has given and still has much to give this boy. The friendliness, encouragement, and understanding of his counselors and teachers have made possible for him the nearest approach to a satisfying adjustment that he has had anywhere. If he can be placed where his out-of-school time also brings him constructive and satisfying experiences, the continued interest of his teachers should have even a greater influence on him. He has such excellent potentialities and such sterling character qualities that he is well worth working with.[1]

Many medical authorities have come to regard the problem of enuresis as endocrine or central nervous-system defects which must be treated by physicians and more particularly by endocrine specialists. Dr. Helen T. Wooley[2] writes on enuresis as a psychological problem as follows:

In considering the possible cause of enuresis in any child the first point to determine is whether or not there is any physical cause for the difficulty. A physician should be called in to give a complete and thorough physical examination. Often a series of laboratory tests is necessary before it can be determined whether or not a physical basis is present. If physical difficulties are present, the first step is obviously their treatment and cure. But most authorities agree that a large majority of cases reveal no physical cause for the trouble; many physicians put the proportion in which no physical cause is detectable as high as 90 per cent. The possibility, however, that physical difficulties, though as yet undiscovered, are playing a part in the result should always make one particularly gentle and careful in dealing with children suffering from this defect. Some recent studies suggest that endocrine disturbances which are as yet little understood, are a contributing cause.

Many pediatricians feel quite hopeless about cases of enuresis in which no physical difficulties are discoverable. They say quite frankly that

---

[1] Case dealt with by Child Guidance Clinic of Los Angeles, December, 1935. (The order of this report has been slightly rearranged by the present author.)

[2] "Enuresis as a Psychological Problem," *Mental Hygiene*, X (January, 1926), 38–53. Reprinted by permission of *Mental Hygiene*.

they have found no successful way of dealing with such cases and they frequently advise parents simply to wait for adolescence, when the trouble usually disappears.

In so far as enuresis has no physical cause, it must, of course, be regarded as primarily a problem of habit training and of the mental attitude of the child. . . .

The most common failures in developing correct habits about the use of the toilet have to do with the age at which training is undertaken, and with the emotional atmosphere that surrounds the training. They might be listed as follows: first, postponing the period of training beyond the natural time for it; second, conducting the training in such a spirit that the child's antagonism is aroused and he comes to desire to wet his clothes or his bed to annoy the adults and get his own way; third, making the bad habit the occasion for emotional scenes of an exciting kind, in which case the child may keep it up just for the satisfaction of being the center of the stage and the object of so much emotional solicitude; fourth, using such severe methods of training and surrounding the child with an atmosphere so repressive and unhopeful that he develops a fear of wetting which is in itself enough to make him do it. He gets obsessed with the idea of doing it instead of being filled with a faith that he can keep from doing it. A child who is anxious to please, and at the same time afraid when he cannot, is apt to be betrayed into this type of obsession. Fifth, there is the failure resulting from undue emotional dependence upon the mother; a vague desire to continue the period of infancy and enjoy the kind of maternal care given to infants may be the determining cause. No case is simple enough to display only one of the situations suggested above, but in most instances one or another of them seems to be outstanding. . . .

Suggestions for Treatment If No Physical Cause Is Present.—First, let me state the changes a parent most frequently needs to make: Stop all punishments; stop all arguing and rowing; stop all displays of intense emotional concern and substitute for them a matter-of-fact attitude; cultivate an optimistic spirit.

Second, let me state the changes that should be induced in the attitude of the child: Eliminate fear; build a faith that success can be attained; stimulate interest in success; develop a sense of responsibility on the part of the child for his own behavior.

The best method of developing a belief in the child that he can succeed is for the adult to cultivate in himself an atmosphere of optimism and confidence. Very frequently some outside source of stimulation and inspiration is necessary. The doctor or the psychologist may be able to build up the faith of both parent and child. Frequent reassurance and suggestions of success help. Getting the child to adopt the idea that he can learn to awaken himself at night when he needs the toilet is a

long step toward success. Some doctors have even gone the length of
pretending to perform an operation, with assurances to the child that
the operation would bring about a cure. Even though it may have
succeeded in certain instances the method is not one that can be recommended. A general anesthetic is too dangerous to be employed unnecessarily. Furthermore, a cure built upon a fundamental falsehood is a
house built upon sand. There are too many chances that the child will
discover the truth and feel that he has been duped. Complete honesty
of attitude should be the foundation of mental hygiene for young
children.

Interest in success and a desire to attain it may be promoted in many
ways. Here, again, a completely candid attitude on the part of the
adult is essential. Some doctors have adopted the plan of administering
a bad tasting but harmless medicine to the child every time he was discovered wet, with the assurance that the medicine would cure the
wetting. Margaret's mother tried the plan on her at one stage, but
Margaret was too keen to be taken in. She understood the entire
transaction, and retaliated by wetting both her clothes and her bed more
persistently than ever until the medicine was discontinued. She proved
to her mother that the medicine would not work. More legitimate
methods of arousing interest are to be found. Strong social approval
for success is one of the best. . . . [In the case of younger children a]
visible record of successes, in terms of a calendar marked with a star
for every dry night, often helps. A record should be kept to show to
some outside authority, such as the doctor, psychologist, or social
worker, and should be submitted at regular intervals—once a week for
children from three to six and as often at the start for older children,
though it is often possible to lengthen the interval for them later.
In keeping a calendar, the best policy is to mark successful days only
and leave the unsuccessful days blank. . . .

Often a new social situation furnishes a most vital kind of interest and
motive for controlling enuresis. . . . Going away to school [or to a
foster home] will often accomplish the result. The desire to stand well
with one's fellows constitutes a sufficiently strong motive. . . .

If enuresis has once set in there are certain measures that frequently
help in bringing about a cure. Very many children are unable to sleep
through the entire night without urination, but if they are able to awaken
themselves there is no difficulty. The child who has enuresis is not
able to do this and must be taught to accomplish the result. Frequently
children suffering from enuresis seem to sleep very soundly and prove to
be difficult to awaken. . . . A child should not be shaken and picked up;
he should be touched and spoken to a number of times and taught to
waken first at a touch or at the sound of a voice. The less stimulus
required for waking, the more probable it is that the child can waken

himself without any stimulus at all. When wakened, he must be led to feel that the adult is doing it merely to help to teach him to waken himself and does not expect to keep that responsibility permanently.

Dr. Esther Loring Richards, in her book on *Behavior Aspects of Child Conduct*,[1] says regarding enuresis:

Bed wetting up to five or six years of age may be due to causes other than biological instability. It may persist as a sort of stubborn rebellion against training, or it may be the result of inadequate training as one sometimes sees it in dependent children who have been handed about from one relative to another. Enuresis in children over five or six years must as a rule be taken as evidence of unstable endowment. (Of course it is taken for granted that urinary apparatus is in good condition.) It makes the child uncomfortable, it embarrasses him, it isolates him from many social contacts that he otherwise might have, such as going away for a visit, or going to summer camp. If he really could help getting out of this fix, I am sure he would if only for the sake of better mental and physical comfort. Medical science has tried in vain to devise some means of curing enuresis. Aside from elimination of fluids an hour before bedtime and seeing to it that the child is as free from strain as possible, I know of nothing that can be done to help this distressing condition except to wait for its disappearance in time. The suggestion of saying verse about the matter on retiring, the policy of making the child wash bedclothes every morning are in my opinion not only a waste of time, but a somewhat unintelligent and cruel procedure —unintelligent because they keep the child in a state of tension and uneasiness which tends to fix the habit, and cruel because they are associated with reactions of shame and embarrassment.

Foster Home and Institutional Placement.[2]—A complete discussion of this problem would require a separate volume. The

[1] Pp. 142–143; see also R. S. ADDIS, "Statistical Study of Nocturnal Enuresis," *Archives Diseases* of *Childhood*, X (June, 1935), 169–178; J. E. ANDERSON, *Happy Childhood*, Chap. V, "Control of Basic Habits," pp. 59–61.

W. E. BLATZ and H. BOTT, *Parents and the Pre-school Child*, "Habits of Elimination," pp. 91–102; J. GLASER, J. B. LANDAN, "Simple Mechanical Methods for Treatment of Enuresis in Male Children," *Journal of Pediatrics*, VIII (February, 1936), 197–199; H. F. SCOE, *Bladder Control in Infancy and Early Childhood*, University of Iowa, paper; A. H. STEELE, "Nocturnal Enuresis in Institutions for Children," *Proceedings of American Association of Mental Deficiency*, LIX (1935), 127–135; FOREST N. ANDERSON, "The Psychiatric Aspects of Enuresis," *American Journal of Diseases of Children*, XL (1930), 591–618.

[2] See ELIO D. MONACHESI and EDITH M. H. BAYLOR, *Children Transplanted*.

present brief statement is intended only to introduce the worker
to a type of treatment to which he must at times resort or recommend to the court.   It is hoped that the reader will turn for an
adequate analysis of this problem to the proper sources.[1]

Placement of Delinquents of Defective Intelligence.[2]—The mentally defective child, when so diagnosed by a competent psychologist, is not a fit subject for the average case worker, since he
can probably exert little or no influence.   Of course, there
are various types and grades of mentally defective.   The
"borderline" cases are difficult to deal with but may still be
within the control of a skillful, intelligent worker.   The children
who are of "very inferior" mentality tend to fall prey to exploitation and constitute poor risks on probation unless they live in a
very guarded and protected environment.

Burt maintains that it is essential to a just treatment of the
delinquent to deal with him not as a criminal but as a defective.[3]
It is beyond the scope of this volume to discuss the treatment of
defective delinquents.   Such a discussion should properly be
limited to psychologists and psychiatrists.   The works of William
Healy,[4] H. H. Goddard,[5] Cyril Burt,[6] A. F. Tredgold,[7] John
Slawson,[8] and others should be consulted on the subject.

[1] *The Social Work Year Book*, 1935, lists many references on foster care for
children, pp. 159–168; see also H. E. CHAMBERLAIN, "When Should the Institution be Prescribed for the Problem Child?" *Proceedings of the National
Conference of Social Work* (1928), pp. 383–389. HARRISON A. DOBBS,
"Institutional Care for Delinquent Children: A New Appraisal," *Annals
of the American Academy*, X (September, 1930), 173–179; CORNELIA HOP-
KINS and ALICE HAINES, "A Study of One Hundred Problem Children for
Whom Foster Home Care Was Advised," *American Journal of Orthopsychiatry*, I (January, 1931), 107–128.

[2] For a discussion of the interpretation of results of intelligence tests, see
Eunice M. Acheson, "Studies in Coordination of Effort Between Psychologist and Social Worker," *The Family*, XVI (November, 1935), 205–209.

[3] CYRIL BURT, *The Young Delinquent*, p. 298.

[4] *The Individual Delinquent*, pp. 446–589.

[5] *Juvenile Delinquency;* see also GODDARD and GIFFORD, *Defective Children
in the Juvenile Court.*

[6] *Op. cit.*, pp. 284–307.

[7] *Mental Deficiency*, pp. 174–200.

[8] *The Delinquent Boy*, pp. 270–349; see also LAWSON G. LOWREY, "The
Relationship between Feeblemindedness to Behavior Disorders," *Proceedings
of the American Association for the Study of the Feebleminded* (1928), pp. 96–
100; V. C. BRANHAM, "The Classification and Treatment of the Defective

Only in passing may it be remarked that special day schools and industrial schools, constant home supervision and knowledge of the child's whereabouts, colonies and institutions providing special care, and other placement under appropriate guardianship are more suitable provisions than probation. The average probation officer has neither the facilities at his disposal nor the technical skill required to deal with the mentally defective, and he should rarely undertake their supervision.

Educationally backward children should not be confused with the mentally defective. The former may be retarded in school but they may have good, average, or even superior native intelligence.

Placement of the Delinquent of "Normal" Intelligence.—Cyril Burt, after prolonged study, arrives at the conclusion that removal of a child of normal intelligence from his home should be a last or late resource. "After all, wherever it is feasible and wherever the child is himself not already beyond reform, to improve the child's own home forms a far better policy than to take the child away from it. If poverty is the main contributory factor, the aid of private or public charity can usually be invoked to relieve the stress of economic want."[1]

Groves and Blanchard also point out that "the history of children committed to the most efficient institutions reveals that they encounter even greater hazards [there] than in the home."[2] Antoinette Cannon, in a recent *Bulletin* of the New York School of Social Work, maintains that a child has a certain security with his own mother. Frequently where there is conflict between parent and child the element of security may be obscured by the struggle but "the experience of child placing agencies shows that

---

Delinquent: A Study of 135 Cases at the New York State Institution for Defective Delinquents," *Journal of Criminal Law and Criminology,* XVII (August, 1926), 183–217; STANLEY POWELL DAVIES, *Social Control of the Mentally Deficient,* pp. 78–93, 132–145, 169–180; FLORENCE BEAMAN, "The Value of Social Factors in the Training of the Defective Child," *American Journal of Sociology,* XXXVII (September, 1931), 240–246; JOHN SLAWSON, *The Delinquent Boy,* pp. 1–194.

[1] *Op. cit.,* p. 113.

[2] ERNEST R. GROVES and PHYLLIS BLANCHARD, *Introduction to Mental Hygiene,* p. 111–112; see also EDITH M. H. BAYLOR, "When Should the Foster Home Be Prescribed for the Problem Child?" *Proceedings of the National Conference of Social Work* (1928), pp. 377–383.

later instability may result from breaking in upon this first security of the child."[1]

The case of Marvin Levkowitz (see pp. 43–52) is a case in point. Marvin was attached to his parents. (The writer was present at the case conference held by the Child Guidance Clinic staff with the executive secretary and field worker of the Jewish Big Brothers. At the conference the examining psychiatrist revealed that the boy expressed his devotion to both parents and to his younger brother, although this information did not find its way into the report.) Placement in a foster home was recommended. Although the boy's enuresis made the finding of a suitable home difficult, the Jewish Orphans' Home to whom the case was referred for placement succeeded in locating one. At first Marvin accepted his living in a foster home wholeheartedly, but later his attitude changed to one of apathy and then to antipathy. The worker of the Jewish Big Brothers' Association believes "that the boy's attitude is due to the fact that his mother could not control her desire to see the plan effected. Whatever she urged he opposed, and this opposition progressed to the point that not only would the boy refuse to leave his home, but he also would not accede to endocrine treatment. Marvin continues to live at home."[2]

Should it be assumed that the boy finds sufficient response which he has always craved in the conflict[3] with his mother, and that living at home continues to provide more satisfaction than he believes he could find in a foster home? Too little is known of the developments after the conference to make an adequate analysis of the case. It is clear, nevertheless, from the social history that sufficient attachment existed between the boy and his mother to warrant his remaining at home, under the intelligent guidance of the agency. It may be argued that the mother was neurotic or even mildly psychopathic and no satisfactory adjustment was possible in the home. It may, on the other hand, be expected that such a mother would cause endless com-

[1] MARY ANTOINETTE CANNON, "An Experiment in Providing Instruction for Relief Workers," *Bulletin* of the New York School of Social Work (October, 1935), p. 29.

[2] From a letter from the worker on the subsequent history of Marvin, June 9, 1936.

[3] See Jessie Taft, *The Dynamics of Therapy in a Controlled Relationship,* Chap. I, for a discussion of ambivalent attitudes.

plications for the boy in a foster home. If the mother, though intelligent and able to get along well with three other children, "cannot be reasoned with," as has been the worker's experience, then the mother's attitude, the family relationships, and the boy's attitudes may be reinterpreted to him. The worker and the psychiatrist at the clinic have the boy's confidence and respect and, with sufficient time allowed for therapeutic conferences with the boy, it may be assumed that more could have been accomplished with the boy himself than with placement in a foster home. It is to be regretted that the service that the Child Guidance Clinic rendered in this case limited itself chiefly, according to the report, to the examination of the boy and recommendations to the referring agency. Undoubtedly the boy could profit much from psychiatric treatment.

The following case of Noble Morrell (fifteen years of age), from the files of Cook County Probation Department,[1] presents an entirely different situation from that of Marvin. The father, who conflicted with Noble, was very old, highly eccentric, and unable to get along with any of his children. Noble has rebelled against his father to the point of dangerous hatred. While the boy repents and excuses his father's treatment, the conflict is so serious that there is little opportunity for a change of attitudes and habits. No analysis of the case as a whole is undertaken here; it is presented simply to illustrate a home situation which is beyond the control of a probation officer, and, therefore, not a fit home for a boy in trouble.

THE CASE OF NOBLE MORRELL

10–16–35. Interviewed Noble at Juvenile Detention Home. Both parents were seen in an extended interview at their home.

Noble was reported to the Shakespeare Avenue Station by both parents. They state that he is beyond control and generally incorrigible. The parents report that he had threatened to kill his father on 10–6–35, the day of his apprehension. He recently stole a brace and bit from his home, and about a year ago stole $27 from a neighbor. The father suggests a mental examination as he believes the boy is a mental case.

Noble was examined by the Institute of Juvenile Research, No. 00105, on 4–12–33. An examination has been requested on the police history. Date of hearing is set for 10–21–35.

Noble completed the Moos School in June, 1935. He was to have started Crane, and gave his parents this impression. He failed to enter as stated.

---

[1] Quoted by permission of the Department.

He disclaims any difficulty at the Moos School and adds that he always liked school. A report has been requested. . . .

There is a very marked conflict between Noble and both parents, as well as discord between the parents themselves. Noble speaks of conflict with his father and places much of the family disorganization upon the father. Noble has little or no regard for his father's suggestions. He has been maintaining hours beyond midnight.

Active in all sports. Member of baseball team at Moos School. Member of basketball team at the Allendale Farm, where he vacationed through courtesy of the relief agency. Unable to swim. No club affiliations. Former member of the Y. M. C. A. Interested in airplane modeling. Enjoys working with tools. Reads considerably in aviation. Has a rather good stamp collection. Reads extensively—three to five hours daily. Sees a movie once monthly. Claims he is not much interested in movies because "they are not real—I go in and after I am out I don't know what I saw." Listens to stories over the radio. Had a girl friend until a month ago. Claimed she "turned dirty." "I don't care for these kind of girls." According to the parents, Noble is a smart dresser and is particular about his dress. Is interested in radio construction.

Pals chiefly with Joseph K., nineteen, who attends Continuation School. Also associates with M. K., sixteen, who also attends Moos. The parents accuse Noble of associating with the "wrong crowd."

Noble was entirely frank and complete in his statements. He is direct and most pleasant; not at all apprehensive and was not too anxious to speak against his parents, stating that possibly he "doesn't appreciate what they are trying to do" for him. Noble is quite talkative; displays considerable intelligence.

"My parents treat me pretty good. I think I treated them dirty. I took too much liberty. I made lots of errors which I since have realized. I see now they were trying to help and push me up. Things were disappearing about the house and they blamed me for all of them. Most of them were found. My father is getting old and is absent-minded and misplaces many of the things I later found for him. He gets mad and calls me a liar, a dog, a rat, a skunk." (Noble mentioned other names which indicate that the father has gone the limit in addressing his son.)

"My father makes us listen to lectures like Dr. B. and Father C. I didn't like this at first, but soon learned to like it. I didn't understand at first that he was doing it for our own good. He also made us go house to house selling needles, threads, etc. I would take money from the sales and stay away from home days at a time. He would tie my hands and beat my back with a belt and then rub pepper and vinegar in the sores—he would also duck my head under water until I nearly passed out—he learned this from a Sunday school teacher. It seemed like the more they done it the worse I got."

Noble claims he kept out of difficulty until he associated with a corner gang, some of them having court records. They used the Morrell front steps for their headquarters. He shot dice and played cards with them. Denies ever having gone on a "job" with them. Admits maintaining hours as late as midnight against his parents' wishes.

"I never could get along with my father. He would start an argument early in the morning. I couldn't iron my clothes on Sunday. I wanted a clean shirt for Sunday because there was no clean shirt in the house. My father would not let me iron. I said, 'If you can swear on Sunday I can iron.' My father picked up the iron and threw it at me. It missed me. I picked it up and went toward my father. My mother and sister managed to get it away from me. My father grabbed a stove poker—at this time I said, 'If you want to play that way I will kill you." I just talked that way as a bluff. I know I would never have killed him regardless of how much I hated him. I swung at him and hit him in the arm. (Noble denied ever having struck his father before.) He uses rough tactics when he punishes. He doesn't think before he does it. He's beat me up quite a bit. He shakes our heads against the wall by grabbing our ears. Every slang word I have ever used I learned from him. . . . (At this point Noble mentioned some very discreditable words which his father directed at the mother in the presence of the children.)

"We both have to change in our attitudes. I will leave it up to you. I will try to make peace in the home. My father has perhaps treated me better than most fathers but I haven't realized it. It takes a lot to boil me up. I am positive I can get along with my brothers and sisters and mother. I am willing to cooperate in any way you say."

The officer talked over two hours with both parents. They first impressed the officer as having a rather favorable relationship, quite intelligent, having common religious interests and a desire to give the most to their children. Both quoted scriptures, but were not fanatic. They were quite liberal in their interpretations. When questioned on their date of marriage they referred to the sin which they are unable to live down, having lived in common-law marriage four years. Mr. M. thought that the Lord had punished them by giving Noble his present incorrigible tendencies. . . .

Not until the officer questioned them on a possible "division of authority" within the home, and informed them that Noble's present behavior and apparent intelligence would indicate that this might be true, did Mrs. M. break down and very frankly admit a very deep-rooted conflict between the two. She discussed some very delicate matters, and Mr. M. in response would bring out other conflicting situations.

The parents verified all statements made by Noble. Mr. M. admitted that he observed the punishment methods indicated and also mentioned other "Elizabethan" methods of punishment, as tying their arms over their heads for hours at a time. Also stated that he had learned of the water-ducking method from a Sunday school teacher who claims he reads considerably about methods of correction in correctional institutions, and thought if they used these methods, they must know!

Mr. M. also admitted that he forced the boy to spend long hours Sunday mornings listening to sermons and lectures.

When questioned on the use of vile language Mr. M. responded: "No one has ever heard Austin Morrell use vile language unless in despair." Mrs. M. checked him on this and he admitted using the vilest of terms in addressing his wife and children. He claims he only used these words in "despair."

. . .

The officer frankly indicated that they could expect difficulty from the other children if they continued to carry out their present methods of training and discipline. Mr. M. seemed to have sufficient confidence in the officer to ask that he decide how each of them shall behave, and that he would follow out the suggestions. He admitted that the two had no acceptable standard to follow and that their differences in activity and interests were the probable causes of their difficulties. The officer tried to make clear to them that they were responsible for Noble's present personality maladjustments, that possibly they would have to make more concessions and greater adjustments than would Noble. The parents seemed to recognize this and accepted the remarks intelligently and in good faith. They admitted that their differences had been brewing over most of their marital life. . . .

The officer is of the impression that Mr. M. is the victim of circumstances which cannot be changed. He craves "attention" and feels deserted when Mrs. M. leaves the home. He is expecting entirely too much from her. He is apparently willing to do what is expected but is not able to make adjustments readily. Mrs. M. has "taken" a lot. She states that her marriage to Mr. M. had no other basis than actual love. She admitted to the officer when Mr. M. was out of the room that everything would be well were he out of the home. Yet she has withstood all of this wrangling for all these years. She impresses one as willing to carry out her original expression that her marriage was not a failure.

It is questionable whether Noble can change his attitude toward his father. It is also improbable that Mr. M. can make concessions in order to assist Noble. There may be much more discord than was evidenced during the interview. Mrs. M. may be unloyal to her husband. The officer is inclined to believe that Mrs. M. is more faithful to her husband and family than Mr. M. is ready to admit.

Just to what extent the parents will succeed in carrying out their promises to "start from scratch" in their own attitudes and behavior will be interesting to observe. The officer is of the opinion that Noble might benefit from foster home placement until the home situation is cleared. This is quite improbable. Should this situation continue, the other children will also have to be considered as dependents.

1–26–36 to 3–4–36. The boy was released to his parents under the guidance and supervision of the probation officer but the boy could not make the adjustment at home. Conditions remained unchanged and the conflict unabated. The boy was then placed in an institution.

Parents who themselves present such serious problems are, of course, in need of rehabilitation before much change can be hoped for in their children. Impulsive infantile behavior, as the overt expression of strong passions, is, unfortunately, only too common among adults. In this instance sexual unadjustment is clearly indicated with religious interests as compensations, and, to "keep their face," a carelessly worn mask of conventionality. How far such demoralized adults can be reconstructed is an unanswered problem. That in most cases they will produce problematic children is a foregone conclusion. Clearly the first step is to protect the children.

The particular form of discipline which Mr. Morrell adopted is not typical of the homes in which conflict rages between parents and children, but the home situation, the relations between husband and wife, between parents and children, the behavior patterns of the offender, and his unadjustment are typical of many cases for which placement away from home is to be considered.

In general it may be said that a child should be removed from the home when the parents are, for whatever reasons, unable to cooperate and unable to gain insight into their situation and that of their child. However, defective family relationships, defective discipline, parental alcoholism, and general lack of guidance and training are not the only indications to be used in deciding on removal of a child from a home. When the parents are unable, after repeated trials, to adjust themselves to their children and to change their habits, then removal is necessary. Removal is also essential when children lose respect for their parents, when they become disorganized because of the disorganization of their parents (see case of Harold Crane, pp. 440–446), when the children's health and discipline are neglected, when they can profit by a change of schools or of neighborhoods, and in order to break up gang associations.

Many probation departments have a separate child placement division whose purpose it is to study the case and the home or the institution and make appropriate placement. Every private foster home in which a child is placed by the court should be licensed by the state social welfare department and should be subject to inspection, to the rules and regulations by the department. Some probation officers feel that the child placement division, seeking a home for a child whom it knows only through the meager account of an inadequately kept probation record, errs frequently in the choice of a proper home. The probation officer who prepares the child for placement in a foster home should know the foster home and parents to whom the child will be entrusted. The preparation can then be made more intelligently and concretely.

Child placement presupposes formation of new habits and attitudes in the child which will enable him to cope with whatever conditions he still finds in the home on his return.   It further presupposes that the parents are not "trainable" or not able to cope with the child as he is.   As a matter of fact, many placements are made without a careful consideration of the possibilities of the parents, the adaptability of the child to a new environment, and the opportunities of the foster home.   Frequently the decision to place a child in a home or even in an institution is casual and arbitrary.   This situation may perhaps arise from the fact that the worker hesitates to deal with the parents, to "intrude upon the privacies of their home."

When the juvenile court assumes control of a child and becomes *parens patriae*, it may set the parents completely aside—if they are declared unfit—or it may limit the control and even bar visits by the parents while the child is in an institution or foster home. If the parents fail to comply with court orders they may be declared guilty of contempt of court. However, they may continue to exert an influence upon the child through letters, presents, and visits by their friends and relatives and thus constantly keep alive the attachment and memory of the forces and environment which the court wishes to eliminate.   The worker should keep in mind that psychological elements cannot be ruled out by law and should be dealt with as the situation arises both with the natural and foster parents and with the child after he is removed from the home.

Also, frequently other children remain in the home, who need guidance as much as the child removed from the home.   Therefore, a worker has a multiple responsibility when a child is placed away from home: supervision of the child, contact with the foster home, and reeducation of the child's parents and aiding in their preparation to receive the child upon his return.   If the parents are intelligent, devoted to their children, and have the facilities to improve the home conditions—social and physical—a child is undoubtedly better off when allowed to remain at home.

Since the real difficulties do not reside so much in the external defects of the home—poverty, neglect, lack of discipline—as in the inner complicated tangles of habit, attitudes, and reactions,[1] it may be assumed that they will persist even after the child is "reeducated" in a foster home and is ready to return to his own home.

[1] Burt, *op. cit.*, p. 119.

Burt found that

> To offer two or three words of abstract advice, to enunciate a few generalized maxims on household government, will be of little avail; more likely it will be resented. The instruction must be an instruction through concrete suggestions, as each new problem emerges; it will work better by example than by precept. Tell the mother outright that her boy wants sympathy, generosity, and fuller opportunities for amusement; and she will at once retort that he has all he can possibly deserve or expect. Quietly invite him to a tea party or the Zoo, speak to him with studied gentleness and courtesy, reward him with a penny or two when occasions afford, and she will probably be the first to emulate your own benevolent methods, and perhaps become wholesomely jealous lest you win greater trust and devotion than she herself has hitherto inspired. . . .
>
> Visiting the family at first almost daily, a kindly advisor, with . . . a wide experience, will thus be able to join in the domestic councils. She will be ready with acceptable proposals, and will do her best to see them carried into effect, leaving the general principles to take shape slowly by themselves. She will supply, as it were, a simple tutorial course on family management, not by the theoretical lecturing, but by practical demonstrations and cooperative help. When at last the leading members have grasped the underlying axioms of their own accord, then probably they will be able to cope with the situation without further assistance and without any occasion for grim and rigorous proceedings.[1]

Burt speaks of "passive expectancy" from children whose good sense may be trusted to work a spontaneous recovery. He believes that for the short, sharp, moral breakdowns of children whose mental constitutions are at bottom healthy and strong, the best plan is "to wait and hope," and one might add and "watch in surroundings conducive to recovery."[2]

Frequently the child is wrongly conditioned toward the institution to which he is sent to improve. Time and time again does the judge say to a delinquent: "Now, don't compel me to put you where you can't get into trouble; where you will be watched, and won't have the freedom to do as you like," or "I have no other choice; you had your chance, but you can't behave like a decent citizen, you have to be sent away where they can deal with your kind."

[1] *Ibid.*, pp. 121–122.
[2] *Ibid.*, pp. 341–342.

Frequently judges would be shocked if they were told that they instill suggestions in the young delinquent that he is wicked, sinful, irredeemable, a rebel against home, and an outcast from the group. Such judges may be well meaning but they do not reflect upon the interpretation the child may place upon their statements. Furthermore, these judges often destroy the opportunity for the court to become *parens patriae* in whom the child can confide and have respect.

Instead, the picture needs to be repainted. The delinquent must be reassured that he is trusted and can assume some responsibility, that he has many assets upon which he can build good habits. "Everywhere virtues should be viewed with a magnifying glass and faults with a blind eye. . . . Whatever happens . . . he should be inspired with hope, not with desperation. . . . In the most hardened miscreant there is always a better self. Never let him think this better self is dead."[1]

In summary it might be said that social treatment starts with the first contact and continues throughout the entire course of the agency's contacts with the case, and that it extends into the child's home, his foster home, and the institution and continues after the release from the institution.

One of the most effective methods of treatment is orientation to and self-control of one's wishes, desires, problems, causal factors, and one's entire "social stock in trade." If the worker is skillful and emotionally stable, he will actively bring his clients into a continued exploration of their possibilities for self-guidance.

Effective social therapy is not a haphazard plan. It requires constant and consistent service leading the individual to gain insight into his own problems and his own potentialities and leading him to intelligent use of the community resources which will redefine his role in the group.

"No matter how much of a 'chance' an individual in trouble is given, he will not ordinarily find his way out of the labyrinth of difficulties unless he is helped to understand the causes and effects of his own maladjustment."[2] Providing insight, or

---

[1] *Ibid.*, p. 553.

[2] Hans Weiss, "The Social Worker's Technique and Probation," in Sheldon Glueck (Editor), *Probation and Criminal Justice*, pp. 167–168.

orientation, is one of the most difficult tasks of the social worker. Before this process can be accomplished the social worker has to be most intimately acquainted with the stream of events which shaped the life or course of the maladjusted person. Without orientation there is no true therapy. It is an imposition of norms by an outsider and not a development within. There can be no self-motivation without adequate orientation. Without self-motivation treatment becomes a forceful pressure by an outside agent and not a part of the positive growth of a developing individual.

Effective social treatment must be *wanted*, and must be *satisfying*. The human mind finds numerous and varied means of defeating and avoiding imposed conformity and social pressures. But convinced of the desirability of the plan of treatment, adoption of it is more certain. The worker must make certain that the new plan presents possibilities acceptable to the client, and that it offers new satisfactions of the social wishes. It is well to ask: "From the client's point of view, what is there in the new plan which is desirable and to be wanted? If he is to accept it, what satisfactions will he find in it?" It is obvious that people and particularly youth are not inclined to accept a plan or new modes of action which will not yield a minimum of satisfaction. We all tend to seek pleasures and to avoid pain and unpleasantness. It is possible that our constitutions demand the development of a tendency to seek satisfying activities and not painful ones in order to survive and to thrive. Frequently the child will act impulsively and seek pleasures which are satisfying only momentarily. The reality has to be interpreted and the child must be taught to project himself into the larger present situations and into the future, which may hold out permanent satisfaction and reorganization of the social wishes. A child becomes oriented through experience and training.

Recounting of the problems frequently brings also an emotional release necessary for growth and assumption of responsibilities. A satisfactory relationship with the worker releases inhibitions and fears, assigns the client status, and lays the groundwork for a certain amount of self-motivation.

Effective social therapy requires ample time. Therapy can very seldom, if ever, be a thing of the moment. The worker needs time for study, for evaluation of his methods, for becoming acquainted with and accepted by the person in trouble, who is often inhibited, distrustful, fearful.

Delinquent children are brought to the worker and rarely come of their own free will. It takes time to penetrate behind the mask of such a child. The worker must not hastily conclude that he was accepted by the child when the latter agrees and promises to reform. That consent may be the easiest way out and the most diplomatic way of keeping peace in the family.

The child is under tension. It takes time to dissolve tensions. In these situations little can be accomplished. The child is not himself. He cannot concentrate on what is expected of him.

Changing of attitudes is a slow process. An abrupt change can rarely be expected by an intelligent worker, and sudden change will rarely be lasting. People's habits of acting and thinking cannot easily be modified under pressure. Like learning to speak French or Greek, or to dance, changing of habits and attitudes must run a definite course. Only rarely can we depend upon sudden changes or mutations[1] which will be lasting and effective. Aichhorn is right when he says: "I do not wish to alarm you, but simply to warn you, that unless we avoid haste and superficiality we are doomed to failure."[2]

Social treatment is a complex process. The services of many professionals and resources should be utilized.

Selected Bibliography

1. ABBOTT, GRACE: "Case Work Responsibility of Juvenile Courts," *Year Book, National Probation Association* (1929), pp. 85–93.
2. AICHHORN, AUGUST: *Wayward Youth*, The Viking Press, Inc., 1935.
3. ALLEN, FREDERICK: "Therapeutic Work with Children," *Journal of Orthopsychiatry*, IV (April, 1934), 193–202.
4. BAYLOR, EDITH M. H.: "When Should the Foster Home Be Prescribed for the Problem Child?" *Proceedings of the National Conference of Social Work* (1928), pp. 377–383.
5. BRANHAM, V. C.: "The Classification and Treatment of the Defective Delinquent: A Study of 135 Cases at the New York State Institution for Defective Delinquents," *Journal of Criminal Law and Criminology*, XVII (August, 1926), 183–217.
6. BURKE, DOROTHY WILLIAMS: *Youth and Crime: A Study of the Prevalence and Treatment of Delinquency among Boys over Juvenile Court Age*, U. S. Children's Bureau Publication, No. 196 (1930).
*7. BURT, CYRIL: *The Young Delinquent*.

[1] PAULINE V. YOUNG, *Interviewing in Social Work*, pp. 324–327.
[2] AUGUST AICHHORN, *Wayward Youth*, p. 64.

8. CANNON, MARY ANTOINETTE, and PHILIP KLEIN: *Social Case Work*, Columbia University Press, 1933.

9. CHUTE, CHARLES L.: "Progress of Probation and Social Treatment in Courts," *Journal of Criminal Law and Criminology*, LX (May–June, 1933), 73 *ff*.

*10. COOLEY, EDWIN J.: *Probation and Delinquency, The Study and Treatment of Individual Delinquents*.

11. ———: "Guideposts of Probation," *The Family*, VIII (January, 1928), 323–329.

12. DEWEY, JOHN: *Human Nature and Conduct*, Henry Holt and Company, 1922.

13. ELIOT, THOMAS D.: "The Project-problem Method as Applied in Indeterminate Sentence, Probation and Other Reeducational Treatment," *The Child, the Clinic and the Court*, pp. 102–107.

14. ———: "Should Courts Do Case Work?" *Survey*, LX (Sept. 15, 1928), 601–603. See also "Courts and Case Work: A Reply by Marjorie Bell," *Survey*, LXI (Oct. 15, 1928), 91–92.

15. FRANZ, ALEXANDER, and WILLIAM HEALY: *Roots of Crime*, Alfred A. Knopf, Inc., 1935.

16. GLUECK, SHELDON: "A Thousand Juvenile Delinquents," *Year Book, National Probation Association* (1934), pp. 63–75.

*17. GLUECK, SHELDON, and ELEANOR GLUECK: *A Thousand Juvenile Delinquents*, Harvard University Press, 1933.

18. GROSS, HANS: *Criminal Psychology*, Little, Brown & Company, 1911.

19. GROVES, ERNEST R., and PHYLLIS BLANCHARD: *Introduction to Mental Hygiene*, Henry Holt and Company, 1936.

20. HAMILTON, GORDON: "Methods of Family Case Work," *Proceedings of the International Conference of Social Work*, II (July, 1932), 178–186.

21. HEALY, WILLIAM: *Mental Conflict and Misconduct*, Little, Brown & Company, 1930.

*22. ———: *The Individual Delinquent*, pp. 49–67.

23. ——— and OTHERS: *Reconstructing Behavior in Youth*, Alfred A. Knopf, Inc., 1929.

23a. ——— and AUGUSTA BRONNER: *New Light on Delinquency and Its Treatment*, Yale University Press, 1936.

24. HILLER, FRANCIS H.: "The Juvenile Court as a Case Working Agency: Its Limitations and Its Possibilities," *National Conference of Social Work* (1926), pp. 142–148.

25. HOUSTON, JOHN W.: "The Right Selection of Probation Cases," *Journal of Criminal Law and Criminology*, XII (February, 1922), 577–581.

26. FRANK, LAWRENCE K.: "The Management of Tensions," *The American Journal of Sociology*, XXXIII (March, 1928), 705–736.

27. LEACOCK, STEPHEN: *Humor: Its Theory and Technique*, Dodd, Mead & Company, Inc., 1935.

28. LEE, PORTER R.: "A Study of Social Treatment," *The Family*, IV (December, 1923), 191–199.

29. LEE, PORTER R., and MARION E. KENWORTHY: *Mental Hygiene and Social Work*, The Commonwealth Fund, 1929.

30. MACBRAYNE, LEWIS E., and JAMES P. RAMSEY: *One More Chance*, Small, Maynard and Company, 1916.

30a. MONACHESI, ELIO D., and EDITH M. H. BAYLOR: *Children Transplanted*, Harper & Brothers, 1937.

31. NIMKOFF, MEYER F.: "Pioneering in Family Social Work," *The Family*, XII (January, 1931), 279–281.

32. O'BRIEN, FRANK J.: "Adjusting Treatment to Diagnosis," *Proceedings of the National Probation Association* (1928), pp. 186–201.

33. ODENCRANTZ, LOUISE: "The Social Worker," in *Family, Medical and Psychiatric Social Work*, Harper & Brothers, 1929, pp. 33–35, 136–139, 144.

34. OVERSTREET, HARRY A.: "Influencing Human Behavior," *Year Book, National Probation Association* (1932–1933), pp. 10–13.

35. PRATT, GEORGE K.: *Three Family Narratives—for Use in Parent Education Groups*, National Council of Parent Education, Inc., 1935.

36. RICHARDS, ESTHER LORING: *Behavior Aspects of Child Conduct*, The Macmillan Company, 1933.

*37. RICHMOND, MARY: *Social Diagnosis*.

37a. SAYLES, MARY B.: *Substitute Parents*, The Commonwealth Fund, 1936.

37b. STONE, WALTER L.: *Youth Education in a Changing World*, 1936 (mimeographed).

*38. TAFT, JESSIE: *The Dynamics of Therapy in a Controlled Relationship*.

39. THOMAS, WILLIAM I., and DOROTHY S. THOMAS: *The Child in America*, Alfred A. Knopf, Inc., 1928. See Chap. II, "The Treatment of Delinquency"; Chap. IV, "Community Organization."

40. VAN WATERS, MIRIAM: "The Delinquent Attitude: A Study of Juvenile Delinquency from the Standpoint of Human Relationship," *Proceedings of the National Conference of Social Work* (1924), pp. 160–165.

41. WALLIN, J. E. WALLACE: *Personality Maladjustment and Mental Hygiene*, McGraw-Hill Book Company, Inc., 1936.

42. WATSON, MAUD E.: *Children and Their Parents*, F. S. Crofts & Co., 1932.

43. WEISS, HANS: "The Social Worker's Technique and Probation," in Sheldon Glueck (Editor), *Probation and Criminal Justice*, The Macmillan Company, 1933, pp. 165–195.

44. WHITE, HELEN C.: "Activity in Case Work Relationship," *Proceedings of the National Conference of Social Work* (1933), pp. 280–286.

44a. WHITE HOUSE CONFERENCE ON CHILD HEALTH AND PROTECTION: *The Adolescent in the Family*, D. Appleton-Century Company, Inc., 1936.

45. WHITE, WILLIAM A.: *Mechanisms of Character Formation*, The Macmillan Company, 1924, pp. 62–75, 270–316.

46. WILLIAMSON, MARGARETTA: *The Social Worker in the Prevention and Treatment of Delinquency*, Columbia University Press, 1935.

47. YOUNG, PAULINE V.: *Interviewing in Social Work*, McGraw-Hill Book Company, Inc., 1935.
48. YOUNG, PAULINE V., and ERLE F. YOUNG: "Getting at the Boy Himself through the Personal Interview," *Social Forces* (March, 1928), 408–415.

Suggestions for Further Study

1. What is meant by social treatment? personal treatment, individual treatment? family treatment? community organization? organization of institutions? What is the relation of each to the other?

2. What is the value of a discussion of social treatment when "each case is different"? What do Cannon and Klein mean by their statement " 'every case is different' is the refuge of the unthinking who use it without realizing how true it is"?

3. What do Cannon and Klein (*Social Case Work*, p. 24) mean by "Discussion of case problems cannot take the place of meeting them at first hand in practice. But when a student has actually encountered a difficulty discussion can help to find him forms and meanings in it, and to realize his own total emotional reaction to it"?

4. What is meant by "ordering-and-forbidding technique"? What is its role in modern social case work procedure?

5. What is the value of the discussion of Marilyn Smith's case? of James R.?

6. What methods were used in these cases to change attitudes? to gain insight? to change the environment? to create a "wider self"?

7. What are Shaw's methods of social treatment (*The Jack-Roller*)? Jessie Taft's (*Dynamics of Therapy in a Controlled Relationship*)? Mary Sayles (*Three Problem Children* and others)? J. E. Wallace Wallin's (*Personality Maladjustment and Mental Hygiene*)? Luella Coles' (*Psychology of Adolescence*)? Ruth Baker's (*The Diagnosis and Treatment of Behavior Problem Children*)? William Healy and others (see index)? Pauline V. Young (*Interviewing in Social Work*, Chaps. XV, XVII)?

8. What biological, social, economic, familial, communal, educational, legal, political factors should be taken into account when considering a program of social treatment?

9. What is the relation of social treatment to social diagnosis? to the study of the case? to the court hearing? to the facilities of your office? of your community?

10. Why is social treatment a difficult process?

11. What is the relation of discipline, training, guidance, education, self-development to treatment?

12. What is the relation of treatment of the child to treatment of the home? the community?

13. What methods of social treatment were used in the case of Marilyn Smith?

14. What is the underlying philosophy of the treatment of this case?

15. How can the case worker utilize the sociologist's approach? the psychologist's? the psychiatrist's in the treatment of certain phases of social and behavior problems?

16. What is the value of the interpretative summary in the case of Marilyn Smith?

17. What is meant by the "executive," "leadership," "interaction" phases of treatment? What better terms can you provide? What is the value of "the executive-leadership-interaction" process?

18. What is meant by "transference"? What are its advantages and limitations?

19. What is meant by "assigning social status"? "providing response and recognition"?

20. What is the role of the social wishes in social treatment?

21. What is the role of mental catharsis? definition of the social situation? identification? (See Pauline V. Young, *Interviewing in Social Work*, pp. 294–358.) What are their values and limitations?

22. What use can a busy probation officer or other child welfare worker make of the above techniques?

23. How practical are these techniques in your particular cases?

24. What methods are used in changing attitudes?

25. What methods does Aichhorn advocate?

26. What are the methods of dealing with lies? pathological lies?

27. When should children be removed from their homes? What criteria should be used in the decision?

28. Write a brief critique of the approach to the parents of Noble Morrell, to Noble.

29. What is meant by the statement that "the plan of treatment should be wanted, satisfying, and understood"?

30. What guides and "principles" of social treatment can you formulate on the basis of your experience with delinquent children? on the basis of the above discussion?

CHAPTER XVIII

PARENTAL EDUCATION[1] AS A FACTOR IN THE ADJUSTMENT OF DELINQUENT AND PROBLEM YOUTH

Are Children or Parents or the Community on Probation?— From the discussion of cases cited so far it is apparent that unadjusted youth may be regarded, as Mary Sayles puts it, as "no more than a chip in the troubled sea of family life,"[2] and of community life, should be added. Perhaps it is too obvious to repeat that children's problems are very often traceable to the problems parents face in a modern social-economic order, to conflicts of the mother, or father, or both, which at times have remained unsolved since their own childhood. As Dr. Thom points out: "In our contact with maladjusted children we find that all too frequently we are dealing with problem environment and problem parents, rather than with problem children."[3]

Dr. Belle Boone Beard,[4] who has made an exhaustive study of 500 cases dealt with by the Judge Baker Guidance Clinic of Boston, says:

One might think, to read the list of factors contributing to juvenile delinquency that the parents of the children studied had memorized Dr. Miriam Van Waters' "nineteen ways of being a bad parent" and had tried them all.[5] Lack of parental control was considered responsible for the delinquency of almost one-half of the children (176 boys and 50 girls). School teachers, club leaders and social workers are often heard to say, "It is not the child but his parents who need treatment." What can the probation officer do to reform ignorant, lazy, immoral, cruel, selfish, or thoughtless parents? Can the parents be put on probation?

[1] See White House Conference on Child Health and Protection, *Education for Home and Family Life* (Section III), and *Parent Education: Types, Content and Method* (Section III).
[2] *The Problem Child at Home*, p. 148.
[3] DOUGLAS A. THOM, *Everyday Problems of the Everyday Child*, p. 11.
[4] *Juvenile Probation*, p. 51.
[5] *Parents on Probation*, Chap. IV.

It is necessary to realize that a child in the modern city represents many tensions, particularly since most parents are parents by accident rather than by choice. In a world increasingly devoid of traditions with regard to childbearing and rearing and largely freed from moral responsibilities, parents do not get satisfaction from a child, and raising it may become a serious problem. Raising a child in the city furthermore demands their constant attention, which is in sharp contrast to personal convenience and freedom enjoyed before the child arrives. Frequently the parents in their youth have never been associated with child raising, and they therefore find the emotional and physical adjustments difficult to make. Perhaps it would be more correct to refer to the problems parents face rather than to the problems parents present, since they themselves have to cope with the many perplexities of a rapidly changing social-economic order and of social institutions in a transitional state. It is strongly recommended that the reader familiarize himself with some of the general treatises on family relations, by Colcord,[1] Groves,[2] Mangold,[3] Mowrer,[4] Nimkoff,[5] Rich,[6] Van Waters,[7] Goldstein,[8] and others.

If the parents face serious personal problems the court and child welfare worker—under the present organization of work with children—may adopt one or more of the following approaches, depending upon the nature of the case and the facilities of the agency and of the community: He may refer the case to a family welfare agency for personal service as well as material aid when needed; he may enlist the interests of an institute of family relations which, in addition to the personal guidance of the family welfare agency, provides specialized medical, psychological, and psychiatric service; he may deal with the case himself if he has

[1] JOANNA C. COLCORD, *Broken Homes.*

[2] ERNEST R. GROVES, *Drifting Homes, Wholesome Parenthood,* and in collaboration with W. F. Ogburn, *American Marriage and Family Relationships.*

[3] GEORGE B. MANGOLD, *Problems of Child Welfare.*

[4] ERNEST R. MOWRER, *Family Disorganization.*

[5] MEYER F. NIMKOFF, *The Family, The Child.*

[6] MARGARET E. RICH (Editor), *Family Life Today.*

[7] MIRIAM VAN WATERS, *Parents on Probation.* See also various articles pertaining to family life in *Recent Social Trends.*

[8] JONAH B. GOLDSTEIN, *The Family in Court.* See particularly pp. 191–208.

special skill and training. Often also it is possible to secure the services of a visiting teacher, of well-organized parent education groups, etc., and in cases needing legal advice, the legal aid clinic may serve.[1]

The worker needs to regard the family as the primary "training station" of children, where they get their nature and nurture. What they get there, good or bad, profoundly affects their entire career,[2] or as Dr. Mangold states: "The forces of social heredity, comprising the ideals, moral and religious impulses, teaching, discipline, order, personal habit and superstitions of the parents overpower the child by their almost irresistible momentum."[3]

But parent-child relations and conflicts cannot be divorced from and dealt with in isolation from the problems parents are facing in their marital relations and in the rapidly changing social-economic and cultural worlds or from the host of emotional problems which result from a vicious circle of interrelated complexities which grow of their own momentum once "trouble sets in."[4]

When the child welfare worker undertakes to deal with some of the family problems he should aim to tap as many of the community's resources and facilities as possible. Many of the families are able to utilize these resources once they are informed about them and the values are interpreted to them.[5] It goes without saying that a worker should not do for a family what it can do for itself, but that does not mean that every family can be expected to learn of and to interpret the advantages of various agencies and activities once they are put at its disposal. Considerable time may be needed to educate and motivate the family to the proper use of the social forces in the community.

Housekeeping Service.[6]—Within the household itself the work

[1] See MARGUERITE R. GARIEPY, "How the Family Case Worker and the Legal Aid Society Cooperate," *Social Work Technique*, I (May–June, 1936), 77–81.

[2] ERNEST R. GROVES, *Problems of the Family*, p. 4.

[3] *Op. cit.* (1929 ed.), p. 403.

[4] For childhood origin of adult difficulties see Marion E. Kenworthy, "Parents and Children," *Child Study*, XI (May, 1934), 229–232, 256.

[5] See ELIZABETH PENDRY and HUGH HARTSHORNE, *Organizations for Youth.*

[6] SALOME S. C. BERNSTEIN, "Mothers by Proxy," *Survey*, LXII (Apr. 15, 1926), 81; RUTH BOWEN, "Visiting Housekeeping with the Jensens," *Journal of Home Economics*, March, 1919, 125; "Housekeeper Service Discussed,"

is quite varied and often complex.   Amey Watson, in her article
on "Reorganization of Household Work,"[1] lists some fifty separate tasks which need the combined attention of the family,
social worker, and community organizer.   It should be explained
to parents that the efficient management in the home with respect
to sanitation, orderliness, adequate budgeting, planning, etc.,
requires the division of labor and the participation and cooperation of all members in the household.   Parental negligence in
teaching children to participate and cooperate, and overprotective attitudes on the part of the parents not only rob the children
of their opportunity to become vital and integral parts of the
homes in which they live and to learn the skills which equip them
for living and to acquire a sense of a "wider social self," but also
interfere with the comfort, efficiency, and harmony of other
members.   Many families will need much more than mere
interpretation; some may have perhaps already sufficiently
interpreted the situation to themselves but they lack the actual
technique for efficient housekeeping.   Many of the social settlements and some of the family welfare agencies supply instruction
in the details of housekeeping.   The public schools offer courses
open to adults in the various arts of housekeeping and household
management.   There is a wealth of literature on housekeeping
service[2] and many useful pamphlets are supplied free of charge by
the United States Department of Agriculture and by the United
States Children's Bureau.   Families also need instruction in the
actual use of such literature, if it is not to be shelved and accumulate dust.

Family welfare workers, more so than child welfare workers,
have provided budgetary guidance to the poorer families, but
from the records of children's agencies this service is also needed
by families in upper economic levels.   If such guidance cannot be
secured from any other agency, the worker in the court and child

---

Bulletin, Child Welfare League of America, XIII (May, 1931); *Annual
Reports of Chicago Home for the Friendless*, 1931, 1932, 1933; JACOB KEPECS,
"Housekeeping Service," *Jewish Social Service Quarterly*, March–June,
1930; *idem*, "More about Housekeeping Service," *Child Welfare League
of America*, XI (September, 1929); LOTTIE MARCUSE, "Housekeeping
Service," *Bulletin, Child Welfare League of America*, XII (May, 1930).

[1] *The Annals of the American Academy of Political and Social Science*, CLX
(March, 1932), 165–178.

[2] See ALICE BRADLEY, *Menu-Cook-Book*.

welfare agency will do well himself to go into the intricacies of budgeting, dealing with both its financial aspect and its psychological implications.

Parent Education in Child Training.[1]—William Ogburn in his article on the "Family" in *Recent Social Trends* observes that "in earlier times, when life was much the same from generation to generation, rules for bringing up children were developed in detail and readily disseminated. But the new and changing perplexities of modern life require education for parenthood. . . . Education of parents is truly as broad as education for life, since it requires fundamentally the development of the total personality. But certain specific subjects may be taught. . . ."[2] "Being a parent is the biggest job on earth," points out Dr. Thom, and we might add Dr. Meyer's statement that parents need a good dose of preparedness in facing life for their children. The public schools are occasionally offering courses in parental education. The National Council of Parent Education, which at present has member organizations in many large cities, has been very active in promoting study groups on subjects of interest and value to parents.

Frequently it is necessary to arrange to have the more reticent parents especially invited by the organization or escorted by a member-friend, after the worker has discussed the function of the organization with the parent and interested him in attending.

LeRoy E. Bowman, Director, United Parents Association of New York City, Incorporated, strikes a significant note when he says that his organization attempts to lodge the leadership in the parent groups:

The general idea of the work in the United Parents Associations is included in the phrase education through organization. It means that we are trying to get real educative value out of everything that is done in committees or in any way by parents in parents associations. We, therefore, are not so much concerned with the perfection of our work as with the way we do it. The other main idea is that we are working with people in their neighborhood habitat and neighborhood complex rela-

[1] For a detailed evaluative discussion of the various programs of parental and preparental education see William I. Thomas and Dorothy S. Thomas, *The Child in America*, Chap. VII, "Parent Education," pp. 295–329.

[2] P. 705.

tions.   We do not use experts to tell parents what to do except as the experts act merely as resources for the lay people to refer to occasionally for facts or expert opinion.   Leadership, initiative, responsibility, these all are centered in the lay people.

This works out in very many ways.   First, of course, the study groups.   We have about 80 of them in our more than 200 associations led by lay leaders.   Each leader is being trained in the technique of discussion and in the method of analyzing problems as well as in the ways of finding out expert answers.   Hence each leader is helped by a resource secretary who makes contacts with people who know the facts and the procedures in very many realms in which parents are interested. There is a third leader in each study group who helps the parents to follow their individual problems. . . .   In general, our idea is in all our work: to start with experience of the individual; to get him to understand the implications back of his own appreciation of his problems; we offer no solutions but require responsibility and initiative on the part of parents.   Our general method is the discussion method and democratic organization.[1]

The Institute of Family Relations in Los Angeles.—The Institute of Family Relations . . . [has for its purpose the] bringing together in one place and making available to anyone interested as much as possible of the existing scientific information that will make for success in marriage and parenthood.

Counselling is offered on problems involving sex, heredity, marriage and parenthood through the Department of Personal Service. . . . The Department of Research has made numerous minor studies and is at present collaborating in the most extensive study yet undertaken of the factors that make for success or failure in marriage.   The Department of Education cooperates closely with other societies in related fields and with state and local boards of education, in offering lectures, conferences, and discussion groups.   It also offers a correspondence course in the technique of counselling, including a specially prepared handbook. . . .

Due to the wide variety of problems presented, there is little standardization of interviewing procedure.   The client is allowed to tell his story in his own way, and the interviewer then develops the history according to his own judgment.   Pre-marital causes may involve a study of the personal and family history, a study of the personality (through a battery of standard psychological tests), a physical examination, and special assistance in securing needed educational preparation, particularly in matters pertaining to sexual adjustment.   Liberal use is made of such instruments as the Humm-Wadsworth Temperament

[1] Personal communication, March 5, 1936.

Scale,[1] the Bernreuter Personality Inventory,[2] the Willoughby Emotional Maturity Scale,[3] and the Bernard Scale[4] for marital happiness. To save the time of the staff, the client is encouraged to read appropriate material available in public libraries. When his problem involves sexual maladjustment he is given a pamphlet specifically prepared by the Institute.[5] Clients with medical or legal problems are referred to their own physicians or lawyers, or if necessary to public or charitable agencies in those fields. [Most] cases extend through the preliminary interview and four counselling periods.

Clients are referred out of the office to collaborators in home economics when necessary, and the cooperation of many other professional persons, such as clergymen, recreation officials, and educators, is freely called upon when needed. The Institute has a particularly close working partnership with the Southern California Society of Mental Hygiene.

The average client belongs to the white collar class or to the upper levels of skilled labor; he has a high school education or better. Clients seeking premarital service are definitely highest in socio-economic status. Some clients are referred by charitable agencies, but the number of referrals accepted is limited, as the Institute has no endowment or regular financial support, and is dependent on its earnings from fees, sale of publications, payments for lectures, and the like. . . .

The general director of the Institute is a biologist who has specialized in heredity and eugenics; the educational director and research director are sociologists; the medical director is a gynecologist. The medical counsellors (whose function is mainly to counsel the staff, not to counsel the clients) include specialists in dermatology, obstetrics, genito-urinary diseases, and psychiatry. Family relations counsellors are trained in psychology as a background for specializing in the field of family relations. All the Institute's counsellors give their services on a part-time basis, the only full-time members of the force being the staff secretary and office manager.[6]

Some of the other professions have attempted to give advice on marital problems. The minister's interest is perhaps outstand-

[1] *The Humm-Wadsworth Temperament Scale*, by Doncaster G. Humm, and Guy W. Wadsworth, Jr., Published by Doncaster G. Humm.

[2] *The Personality Inventory*, by Robert G. Bernreuter, Published by Stanford University Press, Stanford University, California.

[3] *Willoughby Emotional Maturity Scale*, by Raymond R. Willoughby, Published by Stanford University Press, Stanford University, California.

[4] Jessie Bernard, *Rating Scale* (mimeographed).

[5] *Premarital Conference* (4th ed., revised 1935), Institute of Family Relations, Los Angeles, California.

[6] From statement by Dr. Popenoe, July 17, 1936.

ing, although the physician, teacher, lawyer may be included for their specialized services. John Oliver reports that life-adjustment clinics have been created in some of the Protestant congregations.[1]

The Reverend Oliver M. Butterfield, a Bachelor of Divinity and a Doctor of Philosophy, gave up the pulpit a few years ago to devote his time to the Family Guidance Service which he established in New York City. He says:

The Family Guidance Service is a private professional service organized to assist people in solving a wide variety of intimate, personal and family problems. All cases are strictly confidential and in no way connected with research or charitable organizations.

While such work is best done by a series of personal interviews, some cases can be successfully handled by correspondence. . . . Our cases cover the general field of family case work exclusive of economic relief. Our clients are mostly of middle class and well-to-do people who consult us on social and psychological problems just as they would physicians or lawyers for medical or legal advice.

Our work is fundamentally educational. We use medical and other specialists in diagnosis and treatment—several prominent experts being on our reference list. Most of the guidance work is done in personal interviews and we see as many of the persons concerned in a situation as it is possible to manage.

In child behavior problems we secure school, home, and recreational observation reports, so that we have no guess work. . . . The success and effectiveness of such a private professional service depends in part on the skill and personality of the consultants, and partly on the acceptance by the public of such work as a legitimate and useful service. This latter factor is slowly being achieved both locally and generally quite apart from our particular activities. Whether it ultimately proves to be a successful venture and becomes financially self-supporting remains to be seen.[3]

Dr. Butterfield lays great stress on prematrimonial work with couples contemplating marriage. He writes:[3]

An appalling number of husbands and wives are not really married but simply undivorced; they live in a sort of purgatory. Habits,

[1] *Psychiatry and Mental Health*, pp. 13–14.
[2] Personal communication, July 7, 1936.
[3] "To Live Happily Ever After," *Readers Digest*, XXVIII (May, 1936), 27, 30. See also his *Marriage and Sexual Harmony* and *Adolescent Love Problems*.

responsibilities to children, convention, opportunism hold them together, rather than the growing love that might have been their bond, had it not been for ignorance, immaturity, various missteps, and the wrong attitude toward their venture at the start.

To meet this situation there is growing up a group of marriage doctors —counselors skilled in the art of human relations, rendering professional service in the problems of family life. Today, after eighteen years in the ministry, I am spending full time as a consultant in such matters. Remedial work is regrettably necessary, but what is most acutely needed is to see that young people are acquainted with the realities of marriage before the ceremony is permitted. . . .

Sex is but one of the many satisfactions in married life, but unless this relationship is right, nothing else can be right. After a good deal of experience helping couples overcome sexual difficulties, and after many conferences with medical specialists, I am convinced that there are very few cases where marriage needs to fail because of sexual incompatibility. The human body is far more adjustable than the human mind when once the latter has been twisted through unfortunate experiences. I have helped couples find sexual satisfaction after years of blundering and that is why I try to start young people off right, so that they may not decide after a few months that they are hopelessly "mismated" and allow ignorance to break up what might otherwise have been a successful marriage.

The Jewish Social Service Bureau of Chicago has been the pioneer in establishing a Domestic-discord Consultation Service for maritally unadjusted families. Their consultant, Mrs. Harriet R. Mowrer, has done considerable research in this field.[1]

From *Recent Social Trends* we learn that a number of family clinics dealing with a variety of marital and sex factors have been planned during the past decade, but only three have been established. "Literature on the subject of birth control and the married sex life has shown a marked increase in recent years and is apparently less tabooed than formerly, although its distribution is somewhat hampered by existing laws."[2]

The parent-teacher associations—to be found in almost every large school in the English-speaking districts and in many schools in foreign communities—as organizations of parents and teachers, aim to study "reciprocal problems of the child, the home, and the school and the relation of each to the community and the

[1] See HARRIET R. MOWRER, *Personality Adjustment and Domestic Discord.*
[2] P. 707; see also GOLDSTEIN, *op. cit.*, pp. 182–190.

state in order that the whole national life may be strengthened by the making of better, healthier, more contented and more intelligent citizens."[1]

The main interest of the local associations is protection of children, involving regulations regarding health, better films, recreation, Americanization activities, welfare activities, physical development, etc. But these associations, as adult education in general, have not become "behavior-conscious," and thus are of little direct value in the adjustment of the most vital problems parents and children face. Furthermore, as Dr. Wooley points out, "the daily routine of earning a living and caring for babies and doing housework is too exacting . . . [for parents to present themselves for any instruction offered on a voluntary basis, and those who need it most fail to do so]."[2] H. A. Overstreet's remark is also pertinent:

A movement is taking shape now-a-days for adult education. This means that we are endeavoring to build up a new type of intellectual habits among adults. There are large handicaps to overcome—the weariness of workers; the enervating evening comforts of the "bourgeois"; the general indifference to learning; the competing attractions of the theatre, film, and radio. It is noticeable in most cases, however, that no effort is made to overcome these handicaps by establishing delightful association-constants. In Denmark, where the adult education movement has become powerful, every effort is made to link up the intellectual work with the surroundings and activities that give pleasure. The same is true in some of the adult education centers in Switzerland. In America, however, the older connotation of education as something severe, even repellently severe, is maintained. Ugly lecture rooms; hard seats; absence of pictures, music, social life—it must be a hardy adult intellectualist who can flourish under such conditions![2]

The worker should guard against the belief that once parents are participating or are members of some "study group" that they will be able to reorganize their lives and those of their children. The fact remains that these people will still need intelligent guidance in dealing with behavior difficulties of any member of their families.

[1] "Parent-Teacher Associations," University of Iowa, Extension Bulletin, No. 142 (Feb. 15, 1926).

[2] HELEN T. WOOLEY, "Vassar's Adventure as a Psychologist Sees It," *Vassar Quarterly*, X (1924), 27.

[3] H. A. OVERSTREET, *Influencing Human Behavior*, p. 166.

Many pertinent questions have been asked regarding the relative values of lectures, reading, discussion that prevail in adult education. How do people—with various social and educational backgrounds—learn and take on a point of view?[1] How can the problem of control and their relation of authority with their children be interpreted to them in these difficult transitional periods in which little or no balance has been struck between children's freedom and their self-expression on the one hand and transmission of the acquired culture on the other hand? When should the parents allow their child to use his selectiveness and free choice and when should he follow authoritative methods of the social institutions and groups of which he is a member? How can one teach parents, harassed by economic and financial straits, family tension, and emotional disorders, the elementary and basic principles of living expected of their child in a highly changeable moral, social-economic order?

Parental education should consider the tensions and problems parents face in urban industrial centers. It should concern itself —in addition to habit formation, methods of understanding the preschool child, the adolescent, and the child in his teens—with the adjustment a parent has to make to himself as a parent, as a parent in a world in transition. It should concern itself with schools which would prepare young people for the housekeeping and management arts in such a manner that they would not be considered a "daily drudgery." It is difficult to train for motherhood as that process generally involves too many adjustments and human emotions which do not mature until the child becomes a reality, but it is possible to teach young people to "see something beyond themselves" and to lift them to "an objective study of human emotions," as Dr. Van Waters expresses it.[2] Parental education should be related to the particular social conditions in which parents live and to the tempo and standards of our individualistic life.

The parents realize that in spite of prolonged care the child is not theirs in the same sense as it used to be; they also realize that "there is just as much control in the home as there always was, only it has changed hands," as one articulate father expressed

[1] The White House Conference on Child Health and Protection, *The Delinquent Child*, p. 93.

[2] *Youth in Conflict*, p. 269.

it for a goodly number of the less articulate ones in the same predicament. The loss of control also means loss of guidance, not a little of which can be traced to the schools and social agencies taking over much of the responsibility of the home, from nursery days on. Once the individual worker gains perspective of the parents' difficulties he will not be inclined to "blame them for stupidity, negligence, meanness," nor direct the charge against them which is implied in the following quotation: "It is not gin, jazz, nor modern pleasure that destroys young people, but parents. They do the most harm. They thwart and hamper their children, for what excuse? For their whims, based on nothing, not even tradition."[1]

[1] Quoted by Miriam Van Waters, *Parents on Probation*, p. 254.

(For Bibliography see end of Chap. XX)

CHAPTER XIX

SOCIAL CASE TREATMENT OF THE FAMILY GROUP

A series of cases, involving various problems and approaches, is here presented for illustrative purposes of the case work techniques and processes with certain family groups—as unities of interacting personalities.[1]

THE CASE OF PETER SMITH

The case of Peter Smith from Westchester County Department of Probation of New York State is a good illustration of probation work carried on in close cooperation with a wide variety of social work agencies and other community resources, and relatives, in an attempt to rehabilitate not only the offender, for whom the probation officer had a legal responsibility, but all the members of the family. The treatment is carefully planned after a diagnosis of the case is made. This case indicates that with concentrated and intelligent effort a variety of problems can be adjusted within a comparatively short time.

Preliminary Investigation.[2] 1. *Complaint Summarized.*—(a) Peter Smith (fourteen years of age) is charged with being a juvenile delinquent in that on the twenty-sixth day of April, 1931, at about 3:30 P.M. at 19 Blank Street in the City of Yonkers, he did unlawfully enter the Jones Grocery Store, located at the above address and did take $7.00 in cash.

(b) That he has been for the past two weeks unlawfully absent from school for a sum total of six days, on Apr. 14, 15, 16, 22, 23, and 24, 1931.

2. *Previous Record.*—No previous court record.

3. *Respondent's Explanation.*—Peter stated that there had been constant quarreling between his mother and father since his father had been out of work for the past six months. He heard nothing except "money-money" all day long until it had got on his nerves. He had been playing truant

---

[1] See E. W. Burgess, "The Family as a Unity of Interacting Personalities," *The Family*, VII (March, 1926), 3–9.

[2] Quoted by permission of the Westchester County Probation Department, White Plains, New York (mimeographed).

from school for the past two weeks because he did not have money which was to be collected for the school paper and the Athletic Association. He was ashamed to go to school in the clothes he had, and felt resentment against his father because he had been drinking lately.

On Sunday afternoon he was wandering around—had been to the golf course but could not get any caddying. He had gone by two moving picture shows wishing that he might go in, and had watched the other people. The previous week some fellows in his crowd had been talking about how easy it seemed to be for the "big shots" to get away with money in the papers. On the previous day he had run some errands for Mr. Jones and knew that there was money in the cash register at the closing hour. He began to think of what might be done with that money if he had it. It would pay up his school debts, buy him a baseball outfit which he wanted, and give the "kids at home" a little fun. When asked how he could spend it without his parents' knowledge, he said he hadn't thought that far. He wandered by the back door of the grocery store three or four times and when he discovered that there was no one in sight, he picked up a sharp piece of iron, which he found near by, and pried open the very shaky lock. He went in and took $7.00 from the cash register, leaving about $20.00, as he "liked Mr. Jones, and didn't want to swipe it all." He stated, "I spent $2.00 on the fellows for candy and ice cream and had $5.00 left when the cops pinched me."

4. *Motives and Underlying Causal Factors.*—(a) Father's unemployment causing constant quarreling in the family; (b) drinking by the father; (c) desire to appear well before his school companions; (d) effort to obtain money for movies and baseball outfit, as well as to make himself "solid" with the other children in the family.

5. *Attitude.*—At first resentful because of his feelings of guilt and his fear of punishment. After a friendly understanding feeling had been established by the probation officer, feelings of remorse and keen regret arose at having stolen and having brought the disgrace of court procedure on his mother.

6. *Family History.*—*Father*—Henry Smith, age forty-two years. Born in the United States. Religion—Roman Catholic, but does not attend church. Has always been a steady, hard worker until the past two years, when he has had irregular work as a plumber's assistant. Within the past six months he has been able to get only odd jobs. He has been drinking recently to excess and has been spending much of his time in a poolroom to escape his wife's constant nagging for money. He has little understanding of the children's problems; has never played with them, and has left the discipline to his wife except when he has happened to see some misconduct; he has on occasion beaten Peter.

Mother—Mollie Sullivan Smith, age forty years. Born in Ireland. Came to the United States at sixteen years. Married Henry Smith at eighteen, after a year's acquaintance. Religion—Roman Catholic, devoted to her church. Attends regularly and feels keenly her husband's lack of religion and tries to bring her children up in the church. She is a tall, thin, very nervous woman. Is a neat, clean housekeeper, and during the period when her husband was working regularly, she was able to keep a comfortable, happy home. She is in poor physical condition and has been advised by the

Visiting Nurse to attend the clinic for treatment, pending a possible operation. She has never cooperated with them.

Her attitude toward her children has been one of alternate overindulgence and impatience and nagging. She has been very anxious to have them go regularly to church but has received no cooperation in this matter from her husband, which has caused much dissension in the family. She feels very keenly the disgrace of Peter's stealing and, while one moment she shields him, the next she says that "he is a bad boy."

Siblings—John, age eighteen years. Born in the United States. Graduated from the grammar school. Worked for a time as errand boy. Caddies occasionally on the links. Has recently been hanging around a poolroom because of his long period of unemployment. Is sympathetic toward Peter —feels that "the kids will never have a chance." Is interested in mechanics, particularly airplanes, and has a great ambition to learn airplane mechanics.

Mary, age thirteen years. In the seventh grade at school with a good school record. Beginning to stay out late at night. Goes to church on Sunday and does not return for the entire day. Mother is distracted and is inclined to "want Mary put away so she won't get into trouble."

Herbert, age ten years. In the fifth grade in school. Is known at school as a bright, mischievous boy. In need of tonsillectomy which the family have been unable to pay for.

Sarah, age six years. In the first grade at school. No problem.

Betty, age two years. Apparently normal but somewhat undernourished child.

Interested relatives: Paternal grandparents, Mr. and Mrs. Harry Smith, living at 23 School Street, Yonkers. Mr. Smith, although sixty-six years old, still works and has been a thrifty, temperate man. Has helped the family from time to time.

Three paternal aunts, married, and living in distant cities; one in a small country town in Connecticut; all with children of their own.

Maternal relatives have a negative history. The man died of tuberculosis in Ireland and his wife is dependent upon other children in Ireland.

7. Respondent's History.

A. Education.—Principal of the school states that Peter has never been a conduct problem in school; that he has during the eighth grade been restless and inattentive and a daydreamer, but until his recent truancy has never caused the school any difficulty.

B. Religious Training.—Peter has attended the Catholic Church. Has been fairly regular in attendance but recently has been skipping Mass when sent by his mother. Feels that he does not understand the meaning of it all, but goes because his mother gets so "mad" when he does not go.

C. Moral Training.—The moral training has been negative rather than positive. Constant nagging and bickering in the home, with overindulgence on the part of the mother and occasional beatings from the father, have given the children little to depend upon.

D. Home Conditions.—The home is a five-room apartment on the fourth floor of a tenement. It is light and airy, fairly well furnished with furniture which has very evidently been of the cheap variety and badly in need of repair. The bedrooms are clean but threadbare. The mother and father and Betty sleep in one room, Sarah and Mary in another room, Herbert and Peter in the third bedroom, and John sleeps on a couch in the living room. The financial conditions have been so serious that the mother states they have often not had enough to eat, and that the Public Welfare Officer paid their rent for two months and that they are now three months in arrears and expecting to be dispossessed.

E. Neighborhood.—The neighborhood is a poor one. There is a candy store, and poolroom in the rear, on the first floor of the tenement. There are no playgrounds in the vicinity.

F. Associates.—According to Peter's brother John, Peter has recently "picked up with" a "smart alec gang" of the neighborhood, and is trying to live up to their standards.

G. Habits.—Peter has an evasive way of hanging his head when spoken to. Sleeps restlessly at night; has had nightmares. Acknowledges smoking for the past year. Has never had temper tantrums. Mother states that he is the most helpful of the children about the house and will willingly run errands. Claims never to have played craps although he has watched the other fellows often.

H. Employment.—Peter has been employed on the golf links but has never made very much money because the other fellows always get ahead of him.

8. *Physical Condition.*—Peter is generally considered to be in good health. There is a history of measles at three, and diphtheria at six years. No other serious illnesses. Examination shows him to be a fourteen-year-old boy, average height, slightly underweight, several carious teeth which should be cared for.

9. *Mental Condition.*—*Psychiatric examination* reports Peter is a shy, timid boy with a drive to identify himself with a group and anxious to have friends and to be well thought of. Subject is worried about the theft and shows great concern over his act.

Psychological Examination.—I.Q. 90. Mental age 13:2. He has a comparatively good memory and understanding of vocabulary. He adjusts readily and handles concrete material unusually well. Is able to use his hands with good manual dexterity.

10. *Miscellaneous Facts of Importance.*—Lack of cooperation with the nursing service shows much health work to be done with the family. Only one visit has been made on the part of the Attendance Officer. He reports cooperation from the family. The boys in school report that Peter is popular.

11. *Problems Presented, and Contributory Factors.*—(a) Incompatibility between mother and father aggravated by lack of financial security. (b) Lack of unity in family discipline and religious problems. (c) Poor physical condition of several members of the family. (d) Lower family living conditions because of economic strain. (e) Lack of supervised recreational program. (f) Neurotic traits in mother reflecting in the training of the children. (g) Drinking on the part of the father and lack of understanding of the children's problems. (h) No feeling of security on the part of boy among his friends or in his family. (i) Lack of opportunity to develop mechanical interests.

12. *Assets.*—(*a*) Fair physical condition. (*b*) Good normal intelligence. (*c*) Fair insight into family conditions and presenting problem. (*d*) Good vocational possibilities. (*e*) Attractive appearance. (*f*) Healthy interest in athletics and recreation. (*g*) Fair material in the family for rebuilding. (*h*) Unmarried paternal uncle whose interest may be solicited in two oldest boys. (*i*) Attachment to mother and siblings. (*j*) Interested teacher.

13. *Recommendations.*—Because of the following factors: good mentality, fair physical condition, good religious training, and the possibility of constructive work because of the boy's own attitude, it is recommended that Peter be placed on probation with the following:

Plan of Treatment.—(*a*) An effort be made to secure work for the father, possibly supplemented by immediate financial aid.

(*b*) That a family agency become interested in the physical condition of the mother and work out some plan for reconstruction of the family morale.

(*c*) That the School Nurses be given backing to help with the physical condition of the younger children.

(*d*) That the attention of the Big Sisters be called to the thirteen-year-old girl.

(*e*) That Peter be encouraged to finish the eighth grade with the promise of transfer to Saunders Trade School.

(*f*) That he become interested in some organized recreation.

(*g*) That a Big Brother be asked to further his interest in mechanics.

(*h*) That physical recommendations be carried out.

(*i*) That the interest of the young priest in the parish be enlisted in the boy and his religious problems.

5–4–31. *Initial Interview.*—Talked with Peter immediately after the judge had placed him on probation in order that he might understand the conditions of his probation. Peter was in a very receptive, earnest mood, a little fearful but feeling that the judge and probation officer were friendly toward him. Talked with Peter about his interest in athletics in order to help him to forget the immediate problem and establish a feeling of friendly cooperation. In a short time Peter was showing spontaneous interest in the possibility of playing on his school baseball team if some equipment could be obtained through his work.

Problem of school was discussed with Peter. He was ashamed to return to his classroom after the present court episode. The problem was presented to Peter of his possible transfer to another school and the making of new friends. It was explained to him that of course this was running away from the situation, and he was asked to decide whether he would rather go back and face his friends, determined to make a name for himself again, and with a great deal of pride he determined to do this, particularly because he had a feeling of respect for his schoolteacher, who had been very kind to him in the past.

P. O. went with Peter to the school, where he was received by the principal. The principal and P. O. discussed with Peter the possibilities of making good grades during the rest of the spring term pending his admission to Saunders Trade School in the fall. Asked Peter whether he wished to have P. O. go to his home in order to explain certain things to his family. Peter felt that he would rather not have "the kids in the neighborhood" see him coming home the first time with someone else, so Peter was allowed to remain at school and return home at the end of the session.   P. O. then told Peter that he would go alone to the home and try to explain the situation to the mother and father.

Called at 15 Green Street.   Found the mother and Betty home alone. Both mother and father had been present during the court hearing and knew that Peter had been placed on probation.   Explained to the mother that the probation officer was to act as a friend to the family, and although she felt so keenly disgraced by Peter's acts, Peter had excellent material in him, and P. O. needed the help and cooperation of the family.   Asked the mother if she would be willing to have a representative of the Catholic Charities come in and help her with her family problems, explaining that she would be able to arrange for treatments for the mother without expense to her.   She half-heartedly agreed to allow the visitor to come.

During the interview the father came in feeling very antagonistic toward the whole social system and inclined to blame his wife for Peter's delinquencies.   Considerable time was spent with the father before he was willing to concede that there might be a chance to ease some of the family's distress. He finally agreed to go to the Unemployment Relief Committee and accept other work than that of his plumber's trade, spending the other days a week looking for work in his own line.   The religious question was not discussed with him at this time because of his cynical attitude toward the situation.

Suggested that Mr. Smith accompany P. O. to the Public Welfare Officer and explain his present situation and ask for temporary relief until he could be placed at work.   He finally agreed to go with worker.

Asked that John come to the office at the Children's Court on the following evening so that some plan might be worked out with him.   Finally left a note for John explaining to him that his help was needed in making a plan for Peter as well as himself.

Financial Aid.—Accompanied Mr. Smith to the Public Welfare Officer where arrangements were made to supply the family with grocery orders until other plans could be worked out.   ABC:D (probation officer)

5–5–31.—Conference with the Catholic Charities, presenting the case and asking them to assume certain elements of the family situation.   They agreed to do this.

Letter to the Visiting Nurse explaining the court's interest in the case and offering our cooperation with regard to Herbert, who is in need of tonsillectomy.   (Copy on file.)

Letter to Catholic Big Brothers Association requesting a conference with the secretary regarding the type of Big Brother to be assigned at a little later date for Peter.   (Copy on file.)

Letter to Mr. Fred Smith, paternal uncle, asking him to come to the office the following Thursday evening, explaining to him that his interest was needed in the family and particularly in John's problem.   (Copy on file.)

Letter to the Catholic Big Sisters to ask for their interest in Mary, particularly explaining to her the need for new clothing and a recreational program. (Copy of letter on file.)

Interest of Priest.—Visited Catholic Church and discussed with the young priest the problems of the family and asked his interest particularly in Peter, but also his cooperation in trying to persuade the father to return to church. He agreed to take a special interest in Peter and to see him personally from time to time. ABC:D

5–6–31.—John came to the office. An effort was made to make John feel some responsibility for Peter and to get him occasionally to take Peter with him in some form of wholesome recreation. John stated that his uncle could get him work at least part time as errand boy, but that he had stated that he was "sick of the whole family" and would do nothing further for them because of the father's drinking. The conference resulted only in a feeling of cooperative interest on the part of John. ABC:D

5–7–31.—Called at 15 Green Street late in the afternoon and found all of the family at home with the exception of Mr. Smith. Peter reported that he was much happier at school; that the teacher had been "just swell" to him; but that the fellows had teased him about his experience. He is planning to caddy over the week end so that he may earn the fifty cents required each week toward the $2.00 restitution.

Mrs. Smith stated that her husband was working three days a week for the city to pay for the rent and food, but she expects that he will get the money somewhere and "go on a bat over the week end."

Visit of Catholic Charities.—Miss Clark, a representative of the Catholic Charities, had been to see Mrs. Smith earlier in the day and Mrs. Smith had agreed to attend the clinic with her. She had also given the family some clothing, which had helped to build up the family morale. ABC:D

5–12–31.—Letter received from Catholic Big Brothers suggesting Mr. Tom Reilly, a young college man who had played on the football team at Fordham and was now an automobile salesman, as a Big Brother for Peter.

Reply to the letter of Catholic Big Brothers, asking that an appointment be made with probation officer and Mr. Reilly at the Catholic Boys' Club on Thursday evening. (Copy on file.)

Telephone message from Visiting Nurse thanking court for their offer of cooperation and stating that plans were going ahead for physical care of the children. Mention was made that some of the children were undernourished and that there is need for more milk in the home.

Letter to the Visiting Nurse suggesting that an appeal be made to one of the service clubs for milk to be sent to the Smith family. (Copy on file.) ABC:D

5–14–31.—Mr. Fred Smith, paternal uncle, came to the office. His attitude was one of annoyance at being dragged into the Henry Smith family troubles. An appeal was made to him on the ground that it would be greatly to his credit if Peter and John could be helped to be useful citizens instead of becoming involved in further delinquencies. He responded to this appeal, but felt rather hopeless about the situation. When he was approached on the subject of a job for John, he stated that John wasn't much good and he did not want to be responsible for him. John's expressions of admiration and respect for the uncle were repeated to him and he finally agreed that he would do what he could to "help the kid" but he wanted worker to understand that he could not be constantly annoyed. He was to let worker know within a week's time the possibilities of a job for John. An athletic outfit for Peter was then approached. He finally gave the worker $5.00 to "give the kid a start" but made it very plain that nothing further was to be expected of him.

Contact with Big Brother.—Later in the evening called at the Catholic Boys' Club and met Mr. Reilly. He was very enthusiastic about becoming a Big Brother to Peter. Explained to Mr. Reilly that the family difficulties would take long and patient care, and that he must be prepared, if he undertook the work, to carry his enthusiasm over a period of time; that nothing was more dangerous to a boy than to have a young man interested in him and have his faith built up and then to have it dropped. After some consideration Mr. Reilly agreed to accept the problem. In discussing the family with him, worker suggested the possibility of a Boy Scout troop for Herbert and he agreed to undertake this contact as well.

Later Peter arrived and was introduced to Mr. Reilly. He was extremely ill at ease and after a short conference it was suggested that Peter and Mr. Reilly go to the movies. Mr. Reilly had agreed to this plan previously.

5–19–31.—While visiting an apartment house on the Salerno case, learned from the janitor's wife that her husband had been taken to the hospital that day seriously ill, and would have to give up his job. Asked her for the address of his employer. Immediately went to the realty corporation and talked with Mr. Blake. Explained to him the excellent work record that Mr. Smith had had previous to his unemployment, also the good qualities of the wife, and asked Mr. Blake to give Mr. Smith an interview for the janitor's place. Explained to him how valuable it would be to him to have a plumber and also that Mr. Smith was a good handiman. Mr. Blake agreed to interview Mr. Smith if he could be brought to his office immediately.

Called at 15 Green Street. Learned from Mrs. Smith that her husband had been doing better lately but had had one drinking spell. Mrs. Smith also reported that Peter had worked the previous week end on the golf links and had done very well. Gave worker $1 of his money toward the restitution ordered by the court.

Enlisted Mrs. Smith's cooperation in the possibility of the janitor's job. The job pays $60 per month and room rent in a very livable five-room apartment. Located Mr. Smith at a near-by poolroom. He agreed to go to apply for the job immediately but was not enthusiastic over the result; said he did not believe he could get it. Told him that he must absolutely stop drinking. He felt that he could do this as he had not been drunk at any time but had been drinking "to keep up his spirits." Sent him to Mr. Blake's office with instructions to report back later in the day if he secured work. ABC:D

5–20–31. Mr. Smith called at the office with the good report that Mr. Blake was going to give him a trial and full of promises to make good. ABC:D

5–26–31. Conference with Father Mahoney, who felt very much encouraged about his contacts with Peter. Said the boy had asked him very intelligent and very searching questions about religion. ABC:D

5–27–31. *Smoking Episode.*—Telephone call from the principal of the school stating that Peter had been found smoking in the basement, and that the principal was keeping Peter in his office. Worker called at the school and had a long talk with the principal and Peter. Peter explained his smoking by the fact that the boys had seen him talking with the priest the previous Sunday and had called him a sissy, so he had smoked just to prove to them that he was not. Explained to Peter how much harm this experience had done him in contrast to the possible fear of the boys' calling him names, and tried to get him to show them on the baseball field or through athletics that he is not a sissy. Peter agreed not to repeat the smoking. He asked not to be transferred to a new school, and the principal agreed to this. The principal stated that Peter's work had been fair and that he was disappointed to have to call in the probation officer because of the smoking episode.

Peter told worker that the family was moving at the end of the week to the apartment house where his father had a new job. He especially asked that Mr. Reilly not be told of his smoking, as Mr. Reilly was going to take him to the League game the following Saturday. Promised Peter not to tell Mr. Reilly, but suggested that Peter talk it over with him himself and get the viewpoint of an athlete on what smoking would do to a fourteen-year-old boy. Told Peter that worker would come to his new home on the following Tuesday afternoon and asked him to go directly home from school.

While at the school talked with the school nurse and called to her attention the doctor's report that Peter needed his teeth cared for. She promised to make an appointment with the clinic. ABC:D

6-2-31. Called at 20 Spruce Street, where Mr. Smith is janitor of the apartment, and talked with Mrs. Smith previous to Peter's coming home from school. She stated that they were very happy about their new home but she was constantly in fear that her husband would drink and spoil it all. Worker tried to build up some feeling of security and told her that she must not refer to this, and constantly believe that Mr. Smith would not lose his job. She stated that John had been able to secure a part-time job through his uncle, which was bringing in a little money. The uncle had been over to see them twice lately and had given her a little money.

Later the children came in from school, first Mary with the two younger children. Mary was very enthusiastic about a lawn party she had attended the previous week, given by the Big Sisters, and Mrs. Smith showed with some pride sewing which Mary had done at one of the sewing classes. Herbert has joined the Boy Scouts. Mrs. Smith is still worried about John's going to the poolroom at night and is afraid he will get into serious difficulty.

Peter came in at this point. More and more as visits are made to the home, the Smith family are accepting worker not as a representative of the court, but as a friend. Peter is enthusiastic about Mr. Reilly, who has sustained his interest and has been able to secure some new clothes for Peter. ABC:D

6-11-31. Call from the Catholic Charities explaining that Mrs. Smith has been taken ill and, because of her inability to respond to treatments, she will be taken to the hospital. Their plan is to send Sarah and Betty to the maternal aunt for a period and to solicit the help of the paternal grandmother. A visiting housekeeper will be sent in occasionally to help Mary, who will have to assume some of the housekeeping arrangements. As Mr.

Smith is at home much of the time, it is thought that the family can get along without additional supervision until Mrs. Smith returns.   ABC:D

6–12–31. Called at 20 Spruce Street in the evening. John seems to feel his mother's illness more keenly than some of the other children, and agrees to stay home more often in the evening and to help Mary with the housework when he is not at work. Mary's Big Sister has agreed to visit the family regularly and help wherever she can. Mr. Smith reported that Peter had been out very late two evenings recently.

Dental Care.—Peter reported that he had been attending the school dental clinic almost daily and that his teeth were practically all taken care of. He has been having good luck at the links lately. He says that he thinks he will graduate from school at the end of June. Peter asked if he might discuss with worker privately some things that were troubling him. Worker made an appointment with him at the Catholic Boys' Club, where Peter is now a member, to talk to him alone.   ABC:D

6–16–31. Met Peter in the afternoon at the Catholic Boys' Club. He was reticent about talking about his problems but after some time he told worker that he had never been able to talk to anyone about physical facts in life, and that he was concerned about himself; that he had heard stories from the boys in the street and that he was frightened and alarmed. Told Peter that there was nothing to be alarmed about but that worker felt that a doctor should answer his questions. Peter explained that he had been going with one of the older boys who had been telling him all sorts of tales. Told Peter that an appointment would be made with a doctor so that he might discuss quite freely with him whatever was troubling him.   ABC:D

6–19–31. Sent Peter a note telling him that Dr. Williams would see him on Monday afternoon at three o'clock and that worker would take him to his office.   ABC:D

6–22–31. Took Peter to Dr. Williams' office. At the close of his conference, Dr. Williams had a talk with both Peter and worker. On the way home Peter stated that he was very much clearer about things and felt that he was now in a position to listen to the older boys and make his own decisions.

Peter is to graduate from school on the twenty-sixth. He stated that his mother was coming home on the twenty-eighth but would not be able to go to his graduation. He said that he had been up to the hospital to see her several times. Peter has now been able to pay all of his restitution money so that this tie with the court procedure is now cleared up. Peter expressed his pleasure at that.   ABC:D

6–26–31. Attended Peter's graduation accompanied by Mr. Reilly. He had on a new suit which had been given to him by Mr. Reilly. Saw Peter for a few minutes after the exercises. Told him worker would come to his home next Tuesday to discuss summer plans. Discussed with Mr. Reilly plans for Peter's going away to camp, and he said he would see what could be done about it.   ABC:D

6–29–31. *Month at Camp.*—Talked with the head of Camp Sloane about the possibility of a vacancy for both Peter and Herbert for the month of July. Was able to secure places at the rate of $8.00 per week. Telephoned

Mr. Reilly, who said he would be able to secure the necessary amount to send the boys to camp for a month from his college club.   ABC:D

7–3–31.   Peter and Herbert went to Camp Sloane to remain for a month.   ABC:D

7–8–31.   Received an enthusiastic letter from Peter telling of the activities of the camp.   (Letter on file.)   ABC:D

7–10–31.   Replied to Peter's letter.   (Copy on file.)   ABC:D

7–22–31.   Letter from Peter full of enthusiasm for his life at the camp and expressing his regret that within ten days he would have to return home. (Letter on file.)

8–3–31.   Telephone call from Peter stating that he had returned home and wished to discuss further summer plans.   ABC:D

8–6–31.   While discussing another case with Father Mahoney, learned that he had been able to secure some cooperation on the part of Mr. Smith and that the latter had even gone to Mass on two previous Sundays. Father Mahoney said he was satisfied with Peter's response and promised to continue his interest   ABC:D

8–10–31.   *Further Recreation.*—Peter has returned to the golf links to caddy as there are no other jobs for fourteen-year-old boys this summer. Mr. Reilly continues his interest and has made it possible for Peter to have a membership in one of the swimming pools, where Peter is spending a good deal of his time.   ABC:D

8–13–31.   Called at 20 Spruce Street.   Mrs. Smith states that she is feeling much better and regrets that she did not have the operation long ago. The two youngest children are still with their aunt in the country.   Mrs. Smith's greatest problem is what to do with Herbert, who is running the streets and was found by the policeman on the beat playing craps.   He is still going to the Boy Scout meetings, but as these are held only once a week, it does not provide a program for all of his time.   He has been unwilling to go to the neighboring playgrounds because he says that there are so many kids there he doesn't have any fun.

Stopped at the neighborhood playground.   Enlisted the interest of the woman in charge, in Herbert, asking her to try to get him to be a marshal for her playground and see if something could be done to keep his interest there instead of on the street corners.   ABC:D

8–18–31.   Called at the Catholic Boys' Club and saw Peter.   Talked with him about Herbert and his responsibility toward helping Herbert keep out of difficulty.   Peter is making three or four dollars a week on the links, which he is giving his mother to save for clothing for the fall, as the Smiths are still heavily in debt.   Peter promised to do what he could to help Herbert and said maybe he would take him to the movies with him next time he went.   ABC:D

8–26–31.   *Trade School.*—Called at 20 Spruce Street and talked with Peter and Mrs. Smith about Peter's entering the Saunders Trade School. Peter is looking forward to this with much pleasure, and plans to go into the automobile mechanic division.   He has discussed it with Mr. Reilly, whom he has been seeing regularly and who has advised him to go into this line of work with a view possibly of becoming interested in airplane mechanics also.

John has been able to get work at one of the shops which has recently taken on more men. Mrs. Smith reports that she has not had any recent trouble with Herbert, but that Mary is now giving her some concern. Told her to discuss this with the Catholic Big Sister quite freely and she would help her with her problems. ABC:D

Three Months' Summary. Treatment Received.—(a) Employment secured for father; (b) cooperation of the Catholic Charities, Catholic Big Sisters, and Catholic Big Brothers, priest, and school nurse; (c) reestablishment in school resulting in graduation from grammar school; (d) transfer to Saunders Trade School; (e) period of time secured at camp through the Catholic Big Brother; (f) continued contact with the psychiatrist through conference on physical problems; (g) restitution made of $2.00.

Continued Problems.—(a) Continued encouragement of the father to stay away as much as possible from drink; (b) several outstanding bills to be paid; (c) encouragement of boy in trade school to be carried on to avoid lack of long-time interest; (d) further conferences with Big Brother to keep his constant interest in the friendship of the boy; (e) further contact with the church to help straighten out the father's religious problems; (f) constant encouragement of John in his interest in the younger boy in order to stabilize him; (g) constant contact with Peter to continue his interest in wholesome recreation. ABC:D

INTERPRETATIVE SUMMARY OF THE TREATMENT OF THE CASE OF PETER SMITH

Executive Phase of Treatment.—The probation officer at once realized the necessity of rehabilitating the family as a whole as well as Peter individually. Various community resources were utilized to improve economic, health, recreational, educational, and religious aspects of the Smith family group. The mother, ill and discouraged over finances and the alcoholism of her husband, burdened with a large family, and living in comparative social isolation, was not acquainted with the available community resources which her family could use effectively in the amelioration of some of the problems facing them. The probation officer made immediate use of various resources in behalf of different members of the family, although Peter alone was his legal concern.

The school and the principal were approached.

The Catholic Charities' interest was enlisted as a means of providing not only relief but medical care and personal service as well. Note that personal contacts were established and a conference held with the visitor of this agency.

The Unemployment Relief Committee was solicited as a means for securing a job for Mr. Smith.

The Visiting Nurses' Association was called upon for treatment.

The Catholic Big Sisters and Brothers were approached and a Big Brother for Peter was interviewed personally and continuous interest solicited. Contact was established with a physician to give Peter sex instructions and sex hygiene and to explain some "perplexing problems."

A Catholic priest of the local parish was interviewed, requesting his influence on moral and religious problems of the family.

Catholic Boys' Club and neighborhood playground were recommended for the boys.

Arrangements were made for summer camp for Peter and Herbert.

The paternal uncle's interest in his nephews and financial situation of the family was also secured.

The probation officer was on the alert to discover employment for Mr. Smith and better housing conditions for the family.

It takes an active imagination, alertness, and a thorough knowledge of community facilities to bring so many resources into the life of one family. Care should be taken, however, that the use of each resource is carefully explained to the parents and to the various members concerned, and that sufficient interest and enthusiasm is aroused in their utilization of these resources, so as not to cause confusion and bewilderment when a variety of strange agencies make their appearance and offer their services. The ideal procedure, of course, would have been to motivate the family to seek their own resources but perhaps that was too much to expect of the Smiths in their condition at the time.

Perhaps the probation officer dominated the situation too much when he undertook to accompany Mr. Smith to the Public Welfare office in order to secure a job. It might have been embarrassing enough for Mr. Smith to apply at this agency without the added compromise of appearing in the company of a probation officer. Furthermore, Mr. Smith's own initiative and ingenuity needed development.

Interaction Phase of Treatment.—The probation officer sought to establish himself as a friend of Peter as well as the family before he undertook to influence them in any way. He met Peter on his own level, talked with him about his interests in sports, respected his wishes, and solicited his opinions regarding the initial home visit and school adjustment; he allowed the boy to make his own decisions and met his needs in straightforward, friendly, and cooperative manner. He had the boy's interest strictly at heart and all his activities were directed to promote the welfare of the child. The probation officer's patience, keen interest, and unwavering faith in Peter's success won perhaps more than half the battle.

Leadership Phase of Treatment.—The probation officer changed the boy's attitude toward church, toward running away from his problems (at school and with his companions), toward smoking, toward his responsibility to his younger brother and to his parents. He built in the boy a picture of himself as he was and compared with this a more ideal picture of what he might be. He encouraged the boy to attain a higher status and provided an ideal through the Big Brother toward which to strive. He thus built character in Peter.

The probation officer did not attack directly Peter's offense of stealing. He assumed that with constructive recreation, spiritual development, improved economic and housing conditions, better social relationships with other members of the family, Peter's misconduct would disappear. To a large extent he was correct.

Undoubtedly Peter's stealing was symptomatic of the difficulties he found in the home, but greater recognition should be given the fact that in the process of his delinquencies Peter had already built up a certain ideational content and derived certain emotional satisfactions from "treating the kids." It is necessary to develop a sense of property rights, to give him a sufficient allowance, to provide directly or to substitute for the things which he craves and which he believes are essential for the maintenance of status and recognition, in order to remove any further temptations to steal.

With continued supervision and guidance the boy's conduct would further materially improve. Ideally, however, there is yet much to be done both for Peter and for all the younger children. We should aim to rehabilitate the parents themselves more adequately in order to prevent misbehavior in the younger children and recurrence of conflict and delinquent conduct in Peter. A more adequate understanding of the nature of the husband-wife conflicts should be attained.

The parents should be led to realize the effects of nagging, quarreling, dissension, drinking, and family discord on the minds and emotions of growing children and of consequent loss of control over them. An attempt should be made to teach the parents the value and the technique of fair and consistent discipline.

The introduction of a host of community resources in the lives of the children, particularly a much desired Big Brother and Sister, tends to diminish actual parental influence over children and thus family solidarity is indirectly undermined unless an attempt is made to develop greater family cooperative unity through an equitable division of labor, participation in common interests, activities, and amusements. The probation officer's dependence upon outside sources is probably too great and his reliance not great enough on family and home unity.

Peter stated that he felt a resentment toward his father, who drank. While drinking should not be justified an attempt should be made to explain the conduct of the father in terms of unemployment, discouragement, and lack of moral support from his children. Peter should be interpreted to his parents, but the parents need to be interpreted to the children in order to bring about more family solidarity and cooperation.

The world on the golf course needs also explanation in order to prevent any false identification with and idealization of the "big shots" for whom he is caddying. Without proper interpretation a child may readily build false ideals.

THE CASE OF SAM FINEBERG[1]

The case of Sam Fineberg (eight years of age), from the files of the Los Angeles County Probation Department, is another illustration of case work with the family in order to adjust the child's difficulties. This case involves changing of the parents' attitudes and therefore frequent visits to the home.

IN THE SUPERIOR COURT OF THE STATE OF CALIFORNIA IN AND FOR THE COUNTY OF LOS ANGELES SITTING AS A JUVENILE COURT

IN RE SAM FINEBERG
NO. 00019
a person under the age of twenty-one years

Friday–September 25, 1934.
A.M.

To the Honorable Superior Court:
I hereby respectfully report as follows in the above entitled Matter:
Sam is with his parents

[1] Case dealt with and recorded by Emily Heitman Sanson, deputy probation officer, Los Angeles County Probation Department. Quoted by permission of the Department.

The petition in his behalf was filed by the father under Subs. 2 and 9. Sept. 14, 1934.

Reason for Petition.—According to the father's complaint, Sam is a habitual runaway, appears to be a school problem, and refuses to obey at home.

Statement of Father.—"It's an old story, he's been like that since he was three or four years old. He's incorrigible, disobedient, and the last few weeks has taken things from a garage and a book from school. It's misery! He fights with other boys, runs away, tells lies—one after the other, and it's impossible to manage him. I was afraid he'd be arrested and I wanted to avoid that."

The father goes on to relate that when Sam is told to do certain things he will do just the opposite; for example, when sent on an errand the boy promises to be back in ten minutes but the father tells him not to hurry, to take twenty minutes or so, then no more is heard of Sam until three or four hours later when he comes home scratched and bleeding as the result of fighting. During the past year the teacher sent for the father several times because of stealing at school. Sam once cried to a stranger on the street, told of needing ten cents and having no money. The father declares the boy has everything he needs but no allowance. The father tried to give Sam a job selling papers but the boy claimed he had lost his money or other boys took it from him. Sam brings home half a dozen books at a time from the library, doesn't read them, simply spoils and tears them. When he owed thirty-six cents on overdue books and his library card was taken away, the boy took a book from the library without checking it out. During the past few weeks Sam has been spending practically all his time with nine-year-old Cornelius, who lives in the same block.

Mr. Fineberg states that for discipline he has put Sam to bed, made him go without food, whipped him, but all to no avail. The boy is ready with many promises but doesn't remember these from one day to another. When Sam was four years old the parents took him to the Child Guidance Clinic, where they were advised to place him in the Jewish Orphans' Home, but there were no vacancies at the time. Later the parents went to the Jewish Big Brothers for help but "the more they talked with nice words the worse Sam got."

Statement of Mother.—"Sam has always been disobedient, it's an old story, anything I ask him to do he does just the opposite. When sent on an errand he stays several hours, lies about where he has been. He wants to be on the go all the time and will not do anything to help at home; he will help if I keep right after him and talk and talk all the time. I tried to teach him early but he just will not help. Recently he took papers and envelopes from a near-by garage but I made him return them. The teachers say he is disobedient."

The mother states that when Sam was smaller she disciplined him by making him stand in the corner or sit on a chair for two hours, but that he would soon repeat the offense for which he had been punished. "Talking doesn't help, nor beating, but he ought to get a whipping a few times every day."

Sam's Statement.—"Sometimes I don't mind, then they tie my hands and feet and spank me with a strap, oh! maybe two or three times a day.

I took envelopes and I took a book from the library. They took away my card because I owed them thirty-six cents, so I just took a book out when they weren't looking. Sometimes I sneak away and go down to Cornelius' to play, we fight sometimes just for fun." Sam goes on to relate that he has no play space at home (true) and has only a wagon to play with and the father won't let him use that.

When asked how he liked his ten-months-old brother, Sam pretended to be in deep thought (an evasion he used several times during the interview) and didn't answer.

Family History.—Sam was born Jan. 28, 1926, in Los Angeles, of Polish-Jewish parents. The father was previously married but divorced from his first wife, had no children by this marriage. Sam has always lived at the present address, where the parents own their home, with the exception of about three two-weeks periods when he was placed in three different boarding homes, about three years ago. The mother states Sam couldn't get along when placed, while the father refers to him as a "victim" who was beat up by the other children. The father has always provided for the family by selling barber supplies, such as massage creams, hair tonic, etc. He states he used to make a good living a few years ago, but now makes about $40 a month. The father suffers from bronchitis while the mother has asthma. Sam has had no severe illnesses, had tonsillectomy about three years ago.

The family lives in a four-room side rear house, adjoining the store building which the father owns and for which he receives $50 per month rent. There is only a pavement surrounding the house, nothing that affords a place for play. The interior of the home was not seen as no one was there when a call was made.

Personality Traits, Interests, and Recreation.—Sam appears to be quite a likable youngster rather quiet and suppressed at first, seemed to feel he was in for reproof but after a time became quite at ease and talked about the things he likes to do, such as reading, play ball games, etc.

The mother states that nothing interests him for more than a few minutes; for instance, he will read a book for a minute or two and then put it away. Once he had many toys but was so destructive with them, would play with them for a while and then take them apart until the parents stopped buying toys for him. Now he has only his wagon. Cornelius is the only boy he plays with; he has a big porch and yard at his home and Sam likes to go there, has to be called home for meals. The mother adds that Sam is good-natured, promises to do anything, is not affectionate, has no affection for his home, doesn't appreciate anything, though the parents have tried to give him everything.

When questioned about Sam's good points the father reported he couldn't see any.

Plan.—The mother declares she would be only too happy to have Sam home but she is completely discouraged after suffering with him so many years. She fears "some big things will come up and then it will be too late to do anything for him." The father, too, said he feared the boy might be arrested some time and he wanted to avoid that.

Remarks.—Despite the parents' declaration that they are concerned about Sam's possible future difficulties, we cannot help but feel that they are

anxious to be relieved of their responsibility immediately.   When informed
that they would have to pay for the boy's care elsewhere the parents stated
that they cannot do this and that that is their reason for not placing Sam
before.   No doubt Sam would be much happier if placed outside his own
home, boy apparently is not allowed to have any or many wholesome small-
boy interests in his home.   We are inclined to believe the parents put great
faith in the maxim of children being seen and not heard.

School Report.—Sam attends L. K. Street School.   The reports from
there read: "Sam is an undisciplined child.   When he comes to school each
day he acts like a suppressed child who has been given his freedom.   Consequently he talks incessantly.   Many times he quarrels with his companions.   The main trouble seems to be that he does not know how to play
with other children.   He is not malicious or bad.   He seems to be rather
truthful.   The parents do not seem to know how to discipline Sam, they are
too strict and deprive him of play and companionship.   The child's attendance has been very regular."

Report from Other Agencies.—Unfortunately, at the time of dictating this
report there is no report to make of contact between this family and the
Child Guidance Clinic or the Jewish Big Brothers.   However, these reports
will be ready for court.

Recommendation.—I respectfully recommend that Sam be declared a
ward of the Juvenile Court, that he be placed in the custody and under the
supervision of the Probation Officer, that he remain in the home of his
parents; that this matter be continued to Feb. 26, 1935, for report in court.

> Respectfully submitted,
> Probation Officer
> by Deputy Probation Officer.

9–23–34.   Called at Child Guidance Clinic, as case was known to them.
Director of Social Work states Sam was referred to them for psychological
examination in June, 1929.   Father brought boy to clinic.   Complained
boy was a behavior problem, destructive, disobedient, had temper tantrums.
Psychological test as given 7–12–29 reads: C.A., 3:6, M.A., 2:10, I.Q. 81.
Is apparently retarded in mental development; just how much, it is difficult
to determine because of his poor attitude and interest.   Dull-normal or
border-line.   The clinic wrote Mr. B. of J. O. H. that a study (complete)
would be made if another agency was interested.   Mr. B., however, refused
to consider taking Sam.

10–13–34.   Met Mr. Feuer of the Jewish Big Brothers at the home by
appointment.   Mrs. Fineberg says Sam is worse than ever, but when
pinned down to specific complaints her only ones were that he didn't come
home from school promptly and twice had gone off to play when sent on an
errand and came home an hour late for supper.   Mr. Feuer and P. O. made a
list of things to go on chart by which Sam can check himself.   If he has a
satisfactory record he is to go to the show every Saturday afternoon.   The
mother does admit that Sam is very honest.   The boy himself says before
he goes to school every A.M. he scrubs the tub, etc., sweeps the bathroom,
dining room, and kitchen, and scrubs these floors on Saturday.   We told the

mother we felt Sam did very well to do that much but she complains he doesn't always get the corners clean. Told her she must not expect perfection, etc. Complimented Sam on the very nicely written letter P. O. had received from him that A.M. P. O. is to make chart and send to Sam. Mr. Feuer and P. O. to visit in the home on alternate weeks. Mr. F. to call next week. During last of interview Sam was asked to go outside for a time. When P. O. was ready to leave Sam was down the street a way with some children. Went down to tell him to go home at once; reminded him he'd promised to let his mother know whenever he left the house.

10–13–34. Letter received from Sam; very nicely written.

10–26–34. Phoned Mr. Feuer, of Jewish Big Brothers. Asked him to visit this week as P. O. will be out of town.

10–26–34. Mr. Feuer phoned. Situation unchanged. Says no matter what Sam does the parents continue to complain. Feels it is rather hopeless to continue keeping the boy in his home.

11–7–34. Mr. F. phoned. Told him P. O. would soon go out, but had not been out yet. Still feels Sam should be removed.

11–16–34. Mr. F. phoned. Told him P. O. would call at home this week. He will get school report.

11–24–34. Home call. Parents still insist they see no improvement in Sam and want him placed. Told them case would be on calendar soon.

11–30–34. Phoned Miss S. of Jewish Orphans' Home for prospective boarding home for Sam. She asks that we supply her with written history, but told her P. O. could not do that for several days.

12–1–34. During P. O.'s absence from office, Miss S. phoned suggesting home of Mrs. B., 0011 W. Avenue 40. In meantime P. O. was interviewing Mrs. Jessie Tecker. She can take boy.

12–2–34. Letter to Mr. Fineberg (long hand) in re hearing. Phoned Nursing Division in re Tecker home. Miss M., visitor, says Mrs. Tecker needs more equipment in the way of bedding, etc.

12–3–34. In court Mr. Fineberg asked for another chance with Sam at home. Court talked at length to Mr. Fineberg about his attitude toward Sam, but this made little impression apparently. One minute he would declare maybe it was all his fault, and the next he would say he was the most devoted father in the world. He was instructed by the court to get Sam some toys, as boy has only a wagon. The family do not observe Christmas, neither do they observe a similar Jewish holiday, which comes earlier. When the Court explained to Sam he was to go home for a while longer, the father turned to the boy and asked, "Now, will you be a good boy?" But the Court retorted, "Will you be a good father?"

12–4–34. Phoned Mrs. Tecker that Sam is not being placed at present.

12–9–34. Miss M. phoned. Mrs. Tecker has not yet secured the necessary equipment. Told her boy was not to be placed now, but hoped Mrs. Tecker's home would be available later if we need it. If not, Miss M. says she will be glad to recommend other homes.

12–16–34. Jewish Big Brothers Association phoned to inquire if P. O. had called at home; told them we would call early next week.

12–22–34. Home call. Took box with six puzzles for Christmas present for Sam. Mrs. Fineberg rather grudgingly said: "Oh, he's all right"; gives one the impression that she felt Sam might be taken away if she didn't give such a report. The parents did not buy Sam any toys for the Jewish holiday that comes just before Christmas, though the mother says she did buy him some trousers and a belt. Didn't talk much to Mrs. Fineberg, as she was doing her laundry and was so troubled with asthma that she could hardly breathe or talk. Talked with Sam. He says he has no more toys, though father has promised to get him new tires for his wagon.

12–23–34. Mr. Feuer phoned. Gave him above report. He will call next week.

12–30–34. Mr. Feuer phoned. Called at the home today and was politely told by Mr. Fineberg that he didn't want him (Mr. F.) to come around any more. The father further complained that he was nagged twice in court. Mr. F. had taken out an Erector set and another toy for Sam, but Mr. Fineberg wouldn't accept them and declared it was enough to have the P. O. come; that the Big Brothers had not helped in any way; in fact, Sam was worse since under their supervision, etc. Mr. F. took it all good-naturedly. Said they would close their case.

1–4–35. Home call. The parents made no reference to what had happened when Mr. F. called, though the father asked what the Big Brothers could do since they couldn't place children in homes or give material aid. We discussed a chart we had made for Sam. They will see that he checks it every day after they have all discussed the workings. The parents still complain that Sam does not come home on time and wanted suggestions. We suggested they buy him a dollar Ingersoll, teach him to tell time, and let him carry the watch with him all the time so that he will know when he is to come home. They agreed to do this. Mr. Fineberg displayed with a great deal of pride the skates and games he had bought for Sam. For once the parents actually smiled, and even laughed. They seemed to want advice, expressed appreciation, agreed it might be a good thing to have Sam go to Juvenile Hall for physical and psychological examination. They are planning to send him to a Jewish school that meets after the regular school; commended them for this. Mr. Fineberg touched on the financial side just to say he sends $15 a month to his blind sixty-year-old mother in the "old country."

1–11–35. Very nice letter received from Sam, giving an account of his activities.

1–18–35. Home call. Neither the parents nor Sam have put one mark on the chart. Told them it must be marked every day and that way we would know what his weak points are. They agreed to this, but seem to feel nothing should be put on the chart unless Sam is perfect. Said Sam did not go to a show last Saturday because he preferred going to the playground. Told them of the playground at R.L.S. Junior High, two blocks away, which is open to all ages. They said Sam might go there.

2–1–35. Made appointment for Sam to come to Juvenile Hall next Saturday for physical and psychiatric examination.

2–2–35. Called at L. Street School for recent report of Sam. Miss M., who had him last semester in B-4, says the only criticism she has to make was that Sam was "sneaky about whispering," lazy in arithmetic, and inclined to be "fisty" on the playground. Was never dishonest, seemed bright, up and coming, wide awake, liked to recite, a willing worker. Seemed to have a hurt feeling inside of him, a shifty gaze, seemed to expect criticism. Was one of the few boys in the room permitted to take sloyd. Seemed greatly pleased. Interviewed Miss S., present teacher, in A-4. Says she is quite pleased with Sam. Seems very nice, though he occasionally "cuts up a bit."

2–3–35. Letter received from Sam.

2–5–35. Sent copy of school report, first court report, etc., to J. H. with his recent school report; requested reports be returned. Especially want psychological examination for Child Guidance Clinic, where Sam got an I.Q. of 81 in July, 1932, while the school gives him 106.

2–8–35. Miss Nelson of Juvenile Hall phoned. Sam given I.Q. of 115. Can see psychiatrist next Saturday. J. H. requests he be there promptly at 8:30. First court report (already returned by J. H.) will be sufficient for psychiatrist.

Report from Juvenile Hall Clinic

Name	*Age*	*Date Admitted*	*Time Admitted*
Fineberg, Sam	9 years	2–13–35	Three

Summary of Social History Obtained from Probation Officer.—Patient referred as habitual runaway and school problem; disobedient in home. Father states boy has been incorrigible since age of three years. Fights constantly. Various forms of discipline used without effect. At six years taken to Child Guidance Clinic; advised to place him in Jewish Orphans' Home. Mother states child always does the opposite to what he is told and steals. Patient states he has no place to play at home and goes away and fights for fun. Born Jan. 28, 1926, Polish-Jewish. Distractible. One companion only. Not affectionate. Father says boy has no good points. Mother discouraged. Parents anxious to shift responsibility. Boy has no interests at home. School states he is undisciplined—does not know how to play with other children, attends irregularly.

Physical Examination.—Well developed, well nourished. Abnormal amount of fatty tissue over body and upper extremities. Yellowish areas of discoloration over left shoulder. Scar at outer end of left eyebrow. One small carious area in teeth. Tonsils not seen, probably out. Has been circumcised. Puberty pre. Wasserman negative.

Psychological Examination, 2–6–35.—Stanford Binet: physical age, 9:0; mental age, 10:4; I.Q. 115. Superior normal. Concentrates very well—prolonged attention span. Reads exceptionally well for his age. Ready associations. Very responsive—tries hard, eagerly. Works well with praise, encouragement. Alert to many stimuli around him—that is, his gaze follows gaze of examiner, turns quickly at opening of door, etc.

Psychiatric Examination, 2–13–35.—The fact that this child has always been regarded as a "bad boy" has fostered this ideal of himself and he has more or less lived up to it. Whether consciously or unconsciously he has been rejected by the parents and he has reacted against this in order to obtain compensation for his emotional deprivation. Early training was faulty and as a child of superior intellect he has "put it over on" the parents. Then when over-restrictiveness came he resorted to evasion mechanisms. The advent of the younger brother has further added to his sense of insecurity. He is a bright boy, very much interested in all about him, and responds eagerly to any indication of friendliness or praise. He is amenable to influence and under guidance of a kind, understanding person would no doubt adjust well.

Recommendations.—One of his chief needs is that of a sense of security and of belonging and being wanted. He must have interests that are really satisfying to him—outdoor activities that require some mental as well as physical effort. A small allowance with guidance in using this would remove cause for stealing and also help to develop in him a sense of responsibility. As he seems especially to like music and drawing some special work in these might be considered for him. His interest in geography could well be utilized in his home as well as school activities. He needs to have a few simple consistent rules to live up to, rules that must be adhered to if very definite unpleasant consequences are to be avoided. He has already felt so much deprivation that spankings and taking things away from him are ineffectual—they only add to his deprivation. He needs to be helped by kind, affectionate guidance to realize how much more happiness he can obtain through satisfactory behavior. Definite work with the parents is necessary; they need a change of attitude and regime. It would be well to place this boy in a suitable boarding home until adjustment is made in the home situation. As to school placement, A-4 or possibly A-5 is good for his ability. He should also have encouragement in pursuing hobbies, reading, sports. His responsibility should be developed by school duties, school projects, and possibly extracurricular work.

JUVENILE HALL CLINIC
Medical Director

3–3–35. Mr. Fineberg in office to learn results of examination. We discussed findings and recommendations with him. He was more ready to listen than ever before. Was especially pleased with the I.Q. (115) and commented several times he was glad there was nothing wrong. He said Sam spends all of his time drawing maps and various charts. Fears boy is behind in arithmetic. We promised to discuss this matter with his teacher at school. He tried to follow some of the instructions we were giving him regarding Sam and gave Mr. Fineberg a bit of praise of the effort he and his wife were making, suggested that perhaps they were too serious and needed a sense of humor more than anything. The father assured us of his interest, declared he cared a great deal for Sam, "my own flesh and blood." This is the nearest the father has ever come to showing affection for the child. He excused the mother on the grounds of ill-health, said she is apt to be irritable.

3–4–35. Called at L. Street School to see Miss S., Sam's teacher in A-4. Gave her J. H. report to read. She says Sam is getting the extra work in sloyd. Mentioned especially his splendid map work and showed several of his maps. The maps of the State of California, with counties, was made by all the class, and Sam's was the best by far. There were about two others that compared in any way with his. By way of extra work he is making a chart of California. Sam has about four lessons in arithmetic that he could do as outside work. Miss S. will send arithmetic work home with him, and he agrees to do this every evening before drawing his maps.

3–19–35. Called at the Bureau of Vital Statistics and verified the birth record of Sam.

4–12–35. Called at L. Street School. Miss S. says Sam was sent home Friday because of a rash that looked like the beginning of measles, but has been seen by some of the children at the library. Miss S. says Sam has not been so good lately, restless, whispers, wanders about the room; also behind in his arithmetic. Miss S. says she cannot tell him to take work home. P. O. suggested father might call at the school for home work.

Called at home; saw mother and boy; mother called the doctor, who said the rash was caused by something the boy had eaten; prescribed some medicine which is proving effective. Boy shows a great deal of pride in the homework he has been doing in arithmetic; is through Lesson 82 and says that is further than the class has gone; his work is unusually neat; he made an attractive cover in Indian design in which to keep his work; this was entirely his own idea; is especially interested in drawing and painting. Told Mrs. Fineberg of the lovely maps he had made at school; she seemed somewhat interested but had no word of praise for his neat work in arithmetic. We learned he had sloyd every Thursday at 1 P.M. Sam asked P. O. to visit the school at that time some day and for the first time the mother expressed interest in going too. She will send Sam back to school as soon as possible. Sam turned in chart he had filled out. Had negative reports in re work at home, coming home from school on time, and when playing away from home. All in all the attitude toward Sam seems improved.

5–11–35. Home call. The mother was quite concerned because recently when she sent Sam to the store he brought home a 5-cent candy bar which he later admitted taking. She showed it for evidence, will not let him have it; is not putting candy in his school lunch this week, but will not hear any suggestion that Sam be made to return the candy, as she feels so disgraced about it; does not want anyone to know; requested we say nothing to the teacher. Again recently Sam was sent to the store on Saturday morning to get vegetables for the baby's lunch; had time for this before going to the 10 o'clock story hour at the library. When he did not return the mother went to the library, found he was not there. He came home after 12 o'clock; said he was at the library, but the mother finally secured the true story from him; then told him she had been to the library. Commended her for the way she had checked on him and let him know she was "on the job." Told her P. O. would call on Sam at school and then come out in another week. Called at L. Street School, talked with Sam, who made many promises. We discussed the fact that most of his troubles came because he is sent to the store and that the thing for him to do is to make a game of seeing how quickly he can go on an errand. Talked with Miss S., his teacher, who says

Sam has not been so good in school lately; restless, talkative, etc. **He is** now up with the class in arithmetic.

5–17–35. Home Call. Mr. Fineberg there and Sam came in soon after, 3:45, when he is supposed to be home at 3:15. He explained he stayed to see the track meet at school though he had not secured permission from home to do this, but felt it was quite all right because "his school won, anyway." We told him he must let his parents know about special events like that. Explained to Sam the new chart we had made for him. Beginning today through June 1, he is to mark down the time he returns home from school, when he is sent on an errand, when he returns, and what his home duties include. The father says there has been no difficulty about Sam taking things.

6–22–35. Home call. Sam there, not feeling very well. The mother says he perspires so easily and thinks his present condition is the result of working in the heat a few days ago. Sam has decided to sell magazines (*Woman's Home Companion* and *Collier's*) this summer. Mrs. Fineberg doesn't like the idea because it takes him away from home and also because she feels he gets too warm walking and is consequently ill. Saw his report card. Final grades for the semester were 3's in Citizenship, except for 2 in Cleanliness; 3's in Writing, Arithmetic, Art, and Physical Education; 2's in Effort, Music, and Nature Study; 1's in Reading, Language, Spelling, Geography, and History. Complimented him on this, especially since most of the grades were better than he had received earlier in the semester. The parents had nothing to say by way of praise. Received from Sam the chart we had given him some time ago. During sixteen days he returned home from school three times about 4 o'clock, when sent on errands his time away varied from ten minutes to one hour and fifteen minutes, average about a half hour. When we complimented him on this the mother commented she seldom sent him on errands; the father generally goes since he is not working. Mr. Fineberg most grateful for our information that the summer recreation center at R. Avenue School is to be open from 12 to 6 daily. He will take Sam there for enrollment at once. Mr. Fineberg has just painted his house; looks very fine. Both the father and mother are much more pleasant and cooperative than at first, not so ready to criticize Sam all the time.

7–8–35. Met Mrs. Fineberg on Whittier Blvd. while en route to her home. Was on the way to the market; had sent Sam on two errands today and on each occasion he had more than overstayed his time. Is quite discouraged. Declares he is *very* bad. Probation Officer promised to call some day soon when Sam could be seen.

7–26–35. Home call. Sam away with his father for the day. Mrs. Fineberg says, "He's the same Sam." Her special complaint was that the day we met her on the street she had sent him for the plumber that morning and he had not returned until 2:00 P.M. She took the baby and walked quite a distance to the market. Sent him again on an errand in the P.M. and he did not return until 9:00 P.M. Hadn't had a thing to eat all day. They scolded him for this and the father decided Sam would have to sleep on the floor. The mother was so concerned that she got up about 2:00 A.M. and put Sam to bed without the father wakening. However, he felt she should have left him on the floor all night, but as it was, the boy was quite stiff the next day. Suggested that if Sam stays away too long again she have him undress and go to bed. The only difficulty is the house is so small he could hardly be placed in seclusion. Mrs. Fineberg asked if we had other cases as bad as Sam. We briefly sketched for her some of the worst small boy cases we had had. She said it was a frequent subject of discussion in their family whether or not other parents brought their children to the court, asking for help; assured that many of them did. She was quite relieved at this, said a worker from another agency had made them feel they were quite incompetent if they had to ask the court's assistance. Declared when we were leaving that she felt quite encouraged.

8–9–35. Home call. Sam not there. Parents more optimistic than usual. They have made arrangements to have him tutored by boy in neighborhood.

8–19–35. Mr. Fineberg in office to ask if P. O. will tutor Sam in arithmetic since we had previously offered to do this. Arrangements made for Sam to come to the office every Monday and Thursday at 10:00 A.M. The father is certain boy can come alone. Mr. Fineberg had no complaints to make, instead seemed to be in a pleasant mood.

8–24–35. Called.

Sam was out with his father. Mother said Sam sits in the shade and reads while the father canvasses a block. Danny, the twenty-two-months-old brother, was very much in evidence. The mother proudly told of all he can say, seems to take special pride in this because Sam was so backward, and feels more optimistic about Danny's future. Assured her many bright children were late in learning to talk. She began discussing her affection for the two children, declared that she believes she loves Sam more because he has given so much trouble and she has been so concerned about him. Showed new suit they had recently bought for Sam.

Mrs. Fineberg seems more pleasant every time we meet her. Instead of complaining about Sam she talked a great deal about her brother, who is a doctor in New York City. She is very proud of him.

9–6–35. Home call. The parents very pleasant but still somewhat discouraged about Sam, although they can give little explicit information. Sam had just left for the home of the boy who is tutoring him in arithmetic; the parents felt certain he had returned there on the pretext of looking for a lost paper. We commended the father for all he had done in taking Sam with him occasionally on his daily rounds this summer.

9–28–35. Home call. Mrs. Fineberg suffering with toothache, but very pleasant in spite of that. She reports that the first day of school Sam came home at 5:00 P.M., the father switched him a little, then made him sit in the corner for two hours; since then he has come home promptly. She doesn't object if he goes to the library but wants him to report home first. Sam told her the B-5's were divided into *A* and *B* sections, the former division consisting of students who can advance faster, that he was with the

A group. Asks that we verify this. When we remarked that he could certainly do the work with the *A* section, the mother showed the library books Sam is reading. *Famous Men of Modern Times* and *Household Stories from the Bros. Grimm.* He selected these books alone at the library. We commented very favorably on his choice; the mother says the trouble is Sam likes to read too much but we assured her we felt that was no cause to worry as long as he selected such books. She also asked that we request the teacher to provide Sam with some homework every night. Showed some arithmetic problems the father had given him. Called at L. Street School. Mr. Smith, Principal, directed us first to Mrs. W., who was then having the B-5's in music. Sam was the first and only one to raise his hand to answer a question pertaining to the lesson. She has them three times a week. Suggested we see Mrs. H., his home-room teacher in Room. 15. She has Sam in the social studies and arithmetic. She verified his placement in the *A* group, and said the line between the two was difficult to draw, but Sam did especially well in reading with only two receiving higher marks. Is satisfactory in arithmetic, doesn't need special tutoring, though Mrs. W. will be glad to give him homework every day. Saw Sam for a moment, commended him for his promptness in returning home from school. He wanted to know if his mother had shown us his letter from Fred Harvey. Sam is evidently very proud of this. Had written Mr. Harvey in re an Indian collection his grade is making and in return had the letter and promise of a contribution to the collection.

10–20–35. Home call, after school, but Sam not there. The parents explained he attends a Jewish school for about two hours every day after regular school, goes and returns by the school bus. The parents have no complaint to make; in fact, Mr. Fineberg asked if the petition might be dismissed. Said he felt Sam was doing so well now and that they could manage him.

11–5–35. Met the family by chance at the entrance to the Brack Shops. They were looking for a place to have their pictures taken since Mrs. Fineberg's mother had requested a picture.

12–13–35. Home call. Sam in school. The parents continue to give a favorable report of the boy. Told them the case would again come before the court in February, that we would let the matter of dismissal go until then. Satisfactory to them.

2–14–36. With parents, Mr. and Mrs. Irving Fineberg. Present situation: Sam is getting along very well. Some time ago the parents requested the case be dismissed. Recommendation: Continue four weeks on regular calendar with view to dismissal.

3–4–36. Home call. Both Sam and the mother there. She felt the case may be dismissed soon, though she felt a bit discouraged about the boy's report card. He had two 3's in citizenship—mother saw only those—the grades for scholarship ranging from 3 to 1. Sam has again been permitted to have his violin after it had been put away for some time since he would not practice. He wants to take lessons again and the parents want him to have them, but cannot afford a regular teacher. Told them we would inquire about the Music Settlement.

3–9–36. Boy continues to do well in school and at home. **Petition dismissed.** (See petition, Mar. 9, 1936.)

IN THE SUPERIOR COURT OF THE STATE OF CALIFORNIA IN AND FOR THE COUNTY OF LOS ANGELES SITTING AS A JUVENILE COURT

IN RE SAM FINEBERG ⎱ Thursday, March 9, 1936
       NO. 00019   P.M.
  a person under the age of twenty-one years ⎰

    To the Honorable Superior Court:

    I hereby respectfully report as follows in the above entitled Matter:

        Sam is in the home of his parents

The case was continued to this date from February 9, with view to dismissal.

Résumé.—Sam was brought to the attention of the Court in September, 1934, by the father, who complained that the boy was beyond his control and he felt certain "there was something wrong with Sam's head."

The parent's complaint was chiefly that Sam did not return home promptly from school, or when he was sent on errands; that he liked to spend a great deal of this time with a neighbor boy (he has a large back yard and many playthings).

We took Sam to Juvenile Hall for the routine examination and when the parents learned how well Sam did in his psychological test they began to take an interest in him. Gradually, bit by bit, they have overcome their pessimistic attitude of regarding Sam as "a bad boy," are less inclined to be so critical of him, especially when we could report that the school made no complaint of Sam, rather commented on the fact he was an outstanding student, especially in geography and subjects that interested him particularly. He has done some truly remarkable map work in geography.

We feel that the parents have been an even greater problem than Sam in this case but it has been encouraging to see them change toward the boy. They were at one time concerned that they had failed as parents because they asked the assistance of the court, but when told that many parents came seeking help they seemed to realize other parents might have difficulties, too. We felt rewarded for any assistance we might have given on the case when about two months ago the parents asked for dismissal stating that Sam no longer needed court supervision. The parents as a reward to Sam permitted him to have his violin again, which they had put away two years ago because he wasn't interested in practicing. Now they are making arrangements for lessons; we attempted to assist them through the Music Settlement, but they decided to make arrangements for someone to come to the home to give the lessons.

In addition to his regular school Sam has been attending a Jewish school every day.

While Mr. and Mrs. Fineberg are still a bit inclined to expect perfection from Sam, they do seem to realize what a fine boy they have. The parents have been most cooperative always and we feel a great deal of credit is due them.

Recommendation.—I respectfully recommend that Sam remain with his parents and that this petition be dismissed, no further need for court supervision.

Respectfully submitted,
Probation Officer
By Deputy Probation Officer.

Since a similar case (Peter Smith) has been discussed in this chapter it is perhaps opportune to ask a few questions which would enable the student to discuss, diagnose, and analyze the case from his own angle of approach.

Is this a case for the juvenile court and probation department to deal with?

What other agency might have dealt with the boy and the family?

What is the fundamental difficulty in Sam's behavior?

What might have prevented the parents' resentment against the work of the Big Brothers Association?

What is the effect on the boy of receiving presents from the probation officer?

How do you explain the parents' failure to take an interest in the chart?

What is your reaction to the statement by probation officer (1–18–35) "told them it must be marked every day"?

How do you explain the differences in the I.Q. given the boy by the school and by the clinics (on 2–5–35 and 7–12–32)?

What methods has the worker used to change the parents' attitude toward Sam?

What further information from Sam's activities is needed in order to understand his interests?

What other community resources should have been called to the attention of the parents?

Write a brief critique of the method of recording the chronological history and the closing entry. What other form of recording would be suitable? See Gordon Hamilton, *Social Case Recording*, and write your critique in the light of her discussion (pp. 17–41). (See also pp. 104–113 and 459–466 in this volume.)

What social processes were utilized in the leadership and relationship aspects of treatment? What steps were taken in the executive plan of treatment? What processes would you have followed if you were the worker in this case?

Jewish family life is ordinarily culturally rich, with many rituals and common activities in which all members participate. The cultural barrenness of the home life of this family is particularly striking. There is simply nothing in the home for the small boy. The conventional attitudes which the parents take toward the boy fail wholly to meet his needs. Disappearing down the street is a normal small-boy response to such a situation. He has discovered a larger free world in which satisfactions are readily available. When, however, he follows these natural impulses, he immediately earns the name "bad boy." The great social distance between adults and children is well illustrated. Whatever may be the deeper lying attitude of these parents toward their child, their overt behavior is to deal with him as an abstraction and thus to initiate an age-youth conflict at a very early age.

Fortunately the probation officer was sensitive to this situation and set about correcting it by dealing through the parents. The technique used is precisely that which any well-trained competent child welfare worker or family case worker uses and may raise the question: Should not such cases more properly be dealt with by a noncourt organization? However, in this particular case the family declined the services of a private, noncourt agency and voluntarily followed the plan of the court.

(To be concluded)

CHAPTER XX

SOCIAL CASE TREATMENT OF THE FAMILY GROUP

(*Concluded*)

The cases discussed so far in this volume—while not representative of the general run of cases and of methods of treatment used by probation departments and other child welfare agencies—have served to illustrate some sound principles of case procedure based on an acceptable philosophy of work. The first case cited below brings into focus the necessity for the proper approach to the family, the second the disastrous results of unplanned procedure, of probation merely as surveillance, of a bewildered and confused worker who lacks not only a philosophy of child welfare and probation work but also case-work skill in understanding and dealing with problems of the parents and their children.

Summary of an Interview with Mrs. Jordan.[1]—The following summary of an interview during a home visit with Mrs. Jordan is an illustration of what the agency on the case called "an unfortunate approach."

Father.—Norman Jordan, thirty-four years, born and reared in California, one of two children. Came from a broken home and shifted for himself a good deal after the age of seven years. Father's mother was erratic, periodically deserted. Mr. J. completed the eighth grade at fourteen years, herded sheep, worked in a garage, joined the navy at eighteen; married at twenty; secured work as _____ for interurban railway at about $130 a month, and has continued to work there. Main interest is his work; also he has always wanted to buy a home.

Mother.—Lillian, thirty-seven, one of a family of eight, born on a farm in the Middle West, reared in California after her fourth year. Completed high school, worked in an office for a short time, then remained at home, where she was indulged because of a heart condition (this later cleared up entirely) until her marriage at the age of twenty-three. Was secretary of a small club of employees where she was employed, enjoyed music, dancing, and sewing. Marriage was successful until the death of Mrs. J.'s mother several years ago, and Mrs. J. was put entirely on her own responsibility. The situation recently reached a crisis, due to Mrs. J.'s pregnancy.

[1] Case dealt with and recorded by Mrs. X. of Y. Child Welfare Agency of Z. Quoted by permission of the agency.

Children.—Marie, eleven; Norma, seven; each had a slight attack of infantile paralysis a year ago, which resulted in shortening and lack of growth in one leg in each child.

2–13–34. A visit was made on Mrs. Jordan in response to a call from her stating she cannot bear her situation any longer. She feels badly due to her pregnancy; both children are sick in bed; Mr. Jordan leaves her alone evenings and is cruel and abusive when he is at home.

The house itself is in good condition, has a large sunny location, no near neighbors, plenty of air space, and is large enough for sufficient privacy for individual members of the family. The atmosphere inside is wretched, however. There is practically no furniture, no rugs, and no curtains. Everything is in great disorder and does not appear to have been cleaned for days. Marie (eleven years) has been sick with bronchitis but is now well enough to call her mother every few minutes and Mrs. Jordan went to her every time the child called, although she wanted nothing after her mother arrived. When Mrs. Jordan did not go, Marie started to scream. *Worker finally closed* the door, leaving Marie by herself. At this she cried all the harder out of sheer anger. Norma (seven years) also had bronchitis, according to Mrs. Jordan, and should be in bed but is so restless and stubborn that Mrs. Jordan has been unable to keep her there. Norma is a very spoiled child who is constantly trying to get attention, and when her behavior does not bring the desired result, she gets pouty and defiant, starts slamming doors and kicking the furniture. Mrs. Jordan was in a complaining frame of mind and several times started to cry, saying that after the years of unhappiness she has given up all hope and is utterly discouraged. She resents having to stay home all the time while Mr. Jordan can leave every evening.

Mrs. Jordan is approached regarding the children and it is suggested that they should have some responsibility in the home instead of being waited on all day. Although Mrs. Jordan does not mind it now in a few years the children's behavior will no longer be "cute" and by that time Mrs. Jordan will have difficulty in controlling them. Mrs. Jordan realizes this but she has nothing to do all day but spoil the children; also they are the only thing she has to cling to in her wretchedness; she is not willing to give up this last consolation. She is *told* that the children will not be much consolation to her if they are not better trained, as they will not respect her. This will mean that they will be inconsiderate of her just as her husband is and she realizes how unhappy she is over the latter. Also, the children will not be able to get along either in their studies or with other children at school unless they have been taught fair play, habits of obedience, and attentiveness. Since Mrs. Jordan loves her children so much and more than anything else wishes to prevent unhappiness for them, she must not lose further time. Mrs. J. had not thought of the matter from this angle before and now *feels worried* about it. Worker promised to introduce her to a parent-education class at the school to help her work out habit charts, etc. Mrs. Jordan accepted the idea happily as it will give her a new interest.

The problem of clinic care for Mrs. Jordan was discussed. At first she refused to go, saying she can neither take the children nor leave them alone.

She is told to go on the day the girls go to the hospital for their treatments. Her next objection is that she has no clothes to wear. Worker suggests working out a family budget so that the family can be better clothed, and offered to give Mrs. Jordan some clothes to bridge the gap until the budget can be made to function. Mrs. Jordan then said that she had a fear of doctors and hospitals; that her mother had the same fear. Mrs. Jordan was reminded of how pleased she has been with the care and service recently given her children at the Children's Hospital. She stated that they are being treated for a definite disease while she is merely going to have a baby and cannot see the need for medical care. The worker reminded Mrs. Jordan that she had been complaining ever since Norma was born that she was not feeling well and another birth without medical attention may make her condition worse. She gets exasperated at all her husband's complaints and she is putting herself in the same position, if she will not try to remedy her situation. It is explained that she has always been very conscious of her bad teeth; that unless she takes care of herself now, her teeth may get worse and in addition the coming baby will have a poor start. Mrs. Jordan thinks it would be embarrassing to have a medical examination. She was *told* she will gain self-confidence by being one of so many expectant mothers at the clinic. If her health is improved, she will have more vitality and consequently be able to meet her present problems better; also, she will be more attractive in looks and personality and can start to win back her husband's affection. Only recently in speaking of their early married happiness Mr. Jordan spoke of how vivacious and sweet-looking his wife had been. If Mrs. Jordan will compare herself now with six years ago, she can see that perhaps all her unhappiness has not been her husband's fault, as she has neither cared for herself nor her house. It follows that Mr. Jordan has nothing pleasant to stay home for in the evenings. In addition to the physical appearance of herself and the house, and the children's lack of training, Mrs. Jordan is in an unhappy frame of mind and goads her husband into ill-temper. Mrs. Jordan can "get farther" with honey than with vinegar. This platitude appeals to Mrs. Jordan immensely, and as she is anxious to make peace with her husband, she agrees to go to the clinic on February 16 and says she would like to make a better home but has nothing to work with. The household equipment is gone over and it is found that Mrs. Jordan is much in need of equipment of every kind. She becomes enthusiastic during this inspection and enthusiastic about the budget idea, on the basis that there is sufficient income in the family if it were properly managed. Mrs. Jordan will have a chance to prove herself, should her husband accuse her of wasting all the money (the chief family trouble), and worker is certain Mr. Jordan will agree to this and he can readily understand how impossible it would be for him to do his own work without tools.

Mrs. Jordan will spend the next week figuring out the family "bills" so that we can have definite data for working out the budget at the next call, and worker will explain the matter to Mr. Jordan in the meantime.

We shall discuss only some of the more obvious transgressions of good case work procedure and rules of common courtesy and proper social relations. (No attempt is made here to discuss the shortcomings in the social study of the case, chiefly because it is only a summary.) The worker did not act as a visitor in the home when she "closed the door and left Marie alone by herself." This act was a reflection on the mother's discipline and an unwise procedure in the presence of the child.[1] Such acts create subtle or open conflict between worker and client and result frequently in the necessity of "closing the case because the client did not cooperate." The client's failure to cooperate is often a reflection upon the worker's inability to secure cooperation.

"Mrs. Jordan is *told* . . . " It is difficult to project oneself into the thinking and past activities of a worker who perhaps does himself injustice by summary recording of a case, but the reader has only the written account by which to judge. Perhaps also the very force of the worker's dignified personality and proper tone of voice eliminate much of the sting of *being told* by an agency representative what one should or should not do (even though what the worker does tell is constructive). We need not elaborate on this point here since it is dealt with in another connection (see pp. 327*ff*.). We may only raise the question regarding the relative effectiveness of *being told* as against *being led to believe* as accomplished through a discussion of the problems involved and questions raised which would oblige the mother to think the situation through for herself. (For example: Mrs. Jordan was asked what the probable effect of her waiting on the children will be on them as they grow older.) The worker through her behavior succeeded in angering the child and worrying Mrs. Jordan. It is evident that little rapport was established since the client was not free to discuss her problems with the worker and gave one alibi after another, avoiding the main issue. The worker may also have laid too much responsibility on Mrs. Jordan for the rift in the home, without taking into consideration the possible contributory factors by Mr. Jordan's behavior. While it is necessary to talk to Mr. Jordan in order to understand the total situation, the worker should avoid "explaining matters" which the wife can or should be able to explain to her own husband. Many women nurse an undercurrent of resentment at the intimation that another woman can manage her man better

[1] See White House Conference on Child Health and Protection, *The Young Child in the Home.*

than she. On the other hand, a client, inclined to self-pity and complaint was brought out of her mood. It should be observed that the worker not only recognized the major issues contributing to Mrs. Jordan's unhappiness, but in many instances effectively interpreted them to the client. The worker also attempted to utilize some available community resources which would provide instruction for child training, prenatal care, and dental service. Some form of recreation should have been suggested for the family.

THE CASE OF HAROLD CRANE[1]

In the record of Harold Crane, which follows, both the family and the boy presented serious problems but the probation officer failed to deal with either. He worked under difficult conditions, which explain in considerable measure the character of the treatment administered—probation as surveillance.

The Boy.—Harold Crane. Born in Montana, Dec. 23, 1916. He is in the seventh grade, attending Crescent Special School. Is reported to be in good physical condition and of normal mentality. He has never been a behavior problem in his home. Is not interested in school. Has few associates. Attends Sunday school regularly.

The Complaint. 2–26–32.—Police Officer P. E. Jones arrested Harold Crane and James Emerson, Edward Stone, and Earl Andrews for stealing a Chrysler sedan of Howard Smith's and abandoning it after driving it to V. and back.

Boy's Statement. 3–16–32.—Boy at home. "The gang and I was coming out Sixteenth Street; saw a car parked over across the street and James said, 'Let's get in it' so we went in there and got it. We drove around until about 9:00 A.M. and parked the car on Twentieth Street and left it there. On our way to the beach, some boys asked us for a ride and we gave them a ride to the beach. From there we went to V. and later returned, intending to park the car where we found it."

The Mother.—Born in C., Texas, 1892; has high-school education. Works as a trained nurse. Married Arthur Crane in C., Texas; divorced in 1922. She married Willie O., 8–22–24; divorced after twenty-one months. Assumed her maiden name of Williams. "Harold is always good and never gives us any trouble." Mother belongs to Eastern Star.

The Father.—Arthur C., born 1888 in C., Texas. Eighth-grade education. Cook employed by himself. Remarried; belongs to Masons.

Brother.—John, twenty-three, musician, married.

Sister.—Mary E., twenty-one, married.

[1] From the files of K. County Probation Department. Quoted by permission of the department.

Home Conditions.—Family lives in an eight-room frame house at C. Street. Household consists of the boy's mother, his brother, his brother's wife, his sister, her husband, another sister, and her daughter. All are employed and contribute to the support of the home. It is orderly, well kept, and well furnished. It is, however, in the midst of a deteriorated neighborhood and not far away from two families whose boys have appeared before the court on several occasions.

Finances.—The earnings of the children, $125; mother $60. Family owns car, piano, and phonograph.

School.—Harold attends Crescent Special School regularly and seems to be getting along fairly well.

Community Activities.—Harold belongs to no special organizations; attends the Baptist Sunday school.

Remarks.—There is a crowded condition in the home and a laxity of supervision. The boy states he did not know the seriousness of his offense other than that it was wrong. Promises never to steal again.

Recommendation.—Since this is the boy's first offense it is respectfully recommended that the boy be released to his mother in the custody of the probation officer. It is further recommended that the boy be reprimanded and admonished, forbidden to ride or drive any car without the permission of his mother; he is to return immediately to school; to keep away from his associates who exert an evil influence upon him; and to remain under strict supervision by the probation officer.

History

3–18–32.   Boy interviewed; attending school regularly; in early; good conduct.

3–24–32.   Not at home.

3–25–32.   Interviewed mother at home; good report.

3–31–32.   Interviewed boy at home; getting along nicely.

4–15–32.   Boy and mother at home; doing well in school and living up to terms of his probation.

4–25–32.   Not at home.

5–17–32.   Interviewed boy and mother at home; boy had participated in a track meet at school and had won first place in the fifty-yard dash, first in relay, and second in seventy-five yard dash; good report.

5–25–32.   Boy interviewed on Twenty-second Street Playground, which he attends; good report.

6–9–32.   Mother in office; states boy has a sore throat; good report.

6–30–32.   Boy at home; doing well and living up to his obligations.

7–21–32.   Interviewed mother at home; states boy stays at home, helps, and is congenial and no complaint.

9–26–32.   Interviewed mother; she is trying to arrange for a transfer to regular school; she has gone to the Board of Education and made quite a fuss.

10–24–32.   Talked to mother and Board of Education regarding transfer of boy to regular school. It was agreed that the boy should be transferred at the end of the semester, if he makes good.

11–22–32. Interviewed mother at home; states boy is now sixteen years old, has auto license; drives mother's car; good report.

1–27–33. Mother at home; boy attends Crescent Special School regularly; states he believes the teachers discriminate against him. The boy was asked to come to the office on 1–28–33 for explanation by probation officer.

2–11–33. Boy was promoted to B-8; transferred to Jordan Junior High School; appears to have a changed attitude toward school; prospects look good for the coming year; good report.

3–21–33. Mother at home; states boy seems to have better attitude since being transferred; attends school regularly and goes to show once a week.

4–4–33. Interviewed mother at home; boy does not seem to be progressing as fast as he should; attends school regularly; congenial at home; good report.

5–6–33. Probation officer called; family moved; left no address.

5–9–33. Interviewed Principal of Crescent Special School, who states "Jordan had kicked him out." This boy does not seem to adjust in school.

5–23–33. Interviewed Principal of Jordan School, "The great trouble with this boy is his attitude toward school; does not like to be told things." No behavior problem; absent.

(Mother had controversy with the Board of Education; boy transferred to Jordan School, absent three or four times a week. Family moved and did not notify the probation officer. Family and boy do not cooperate.)

5–29–33. Interviewed R. W. Forrest of Newton Police Station; states Harold Crane and Kenneth F. stole a jack from a truck on Central Avenue.

5–31–33. Interviewed boy in jail; admits charge; admits being out of school and that mother did not know he was out of school; spent his lunch money to go to shows (see report).

5–31–33. Later: Mother at home; family moved to 0035 East Twenty-first Street; mother thought boy was attending school; there had been no trouble at home. Mother ill of heart trouble; states she told boy to notify probation officer of new address.

6–6–33. Boy in jail; states he is tired of jail; we believe he will profit by his experience; "another boy kicked him in the eye and he thinks differently about himself."

6–8–33. [The case brought into court. Probation officer's report summarized the case to date and made the following analysis and suggestions for treatment.]

Diagnosis and Present Problem.—(1) Poor association; (2) poor school adjustment; (3) lack of religious affiliation; (4) lack of interest, obstinacy, and heedlessness.

Plan of Adjustment.—(1) More careful supervision by parents; (2) return directly home from school; (3) choose better associates; (4) read more good books and magazines; (5) join the Y. M. C. A.

Recommendation.—It is, therefore, respectfully recommended due to the fact that the property was returned to the owner in this case and that the boy has had a chance to learn by experience of confinement in this matter the duty he owes to the law, that he has promised to follow any course of instruction mapped out for him and that we will never have an occasion to bring him into court again, it is our opinion that it is worth while to give this boy a chance to exercise his diligence in carrying out these promises made. Therefore, we recommend that this boy be released to the custody of the probation officer to return to his home and enter school, and that a rigid plan of supervision be made; that the case be continued two weeks for submission of plan.

6–9–33. Interviewed boy and mother at home; boy attending Crescent Special; he is docile since being in jail; mother's attitude toward probation is changing.

6–14–33. Boy and mother at home; attending Crescent Special School regularly; plan of supervision talked over with mother and boy.

6–16–33. Interviewed boy; attending Crescent Special School and expects to go to Lake Elsinore with the mother on vacation; good report.

7–24–33. Interviewed boy and mother at home; boy seems to be living up to the terms of his probation; home influences do not appear conducive to the highest moral good.

8–12–33. Letter requesting boy to come to office 8–18–33.

8–18–33. Boy in office; states he stays at home most of the time; plays on the piano; does not care for athletics; worried; noncommunicative.

Later: Mrs. B., police officer, brought Mrs. Crane, Mrs. Jones, and May Jones—neighbors—to office to report that May is pregnant and to file a petition in behalf of May. Harold admits responsibility; both mothers are willing for children to be married.

8–26–33. Home call; boy not at home; several men were in the room, one appeared to be intoxicated. Mother asked to be excused to talk to probation officer. The home has an atmosphere of immorality. Mother not convinced that the boy should marry.

8–30–33. [Case again in court. The probation officer's report reviewed the case. He added the following recommendations.]

Although the parents of the girl are anxious for the girl to be married to Harold, so that the coming child might have a name, and further that the boy's mother might be induced to give her consent, the probation officer feels that such a step would not serve the best interest of the boy, girl, nor their obligation to society. The girl is the product of parents of retarded mentality and of a home in which there have been behavior problems, in that her sister was once a ward of the court as an unwed mother, and at the present time, her younger brother, John, is a ward of the court, all of which would indicate poor supervision of the children in that home. On the other hand, Harold, the boy in the case, has not been amenable to discipline, nor to the social forces which would develop good citizenship in him. He has been tried on probation and has violated his trust, and by his most recent acts shows that he is devoid of supervision in his home. It is respectfully recommended that this ward be detained in Juvenile Hall Clinic for medical and psychiatric examination, that the case be continued two weeks for further report and recommendation.

8–31–33. Boy sent to clinic; later talked with aunt, Mrs. C., and grandmother, also Mrs. C., at East 13th Street; both believe they should be married.

9–6–33. [Case again in court. The probation officer now recommends as follows.]

It appears from further investigation made by the probation officer into the possible financial affairs of both families, that the boy's mother is probably in a better position than the Jones Family to assist the young couple. The records show that once before, an older daughter of Mr. Jones was an unwed mother, and at that time he agreed to take her into his home and to provide for her. Later, he applied to the court for aid for his daughter and became indignant because he was refused.

Several conversations with the boy since the last hearing brought out the fact that Harold and May had been sweethearts since childhood days in Montana and have been practically reared together. They seem to be deeply in love with each other and both are very anxious to be married. By their own statement, they plan to continue school, Harold going to part-time and she going to full-time school after her baby is old enough to be left with someone for the day.

It is respectfully recommended that in view of the attitude of both families toward the young couple, their love and devotion for the children, and their apparently sincere promise of protection and financial aid, that the boy be permitted to marry May Jones. It is further recommended that Harold be instructed by the court to avail himself of such program of training and attendance at classes as will instruct him in the duties of a father and a husband and to carry out such program as the probation officer might outline for him from time to time; that the case be continued two weeks for presentation of plan.

9–8–33. Telephoned Harold and May; asked them to come to office; accompanied them to license bureau for marriage license; both extremely jubilant; Mrs. Jones present to give consent.[1]

9–15–33. Called at home; boy married 9–12–33 by Rev. Robinson in old courthouse; he seems very happy over solution to his problem; wife and sister sewing on baby clothes; the family was disappointed by Mr. Jones's insistence on the immediate performance of the marriage; they wanted the ceremony at home with friends and flowers; boy is frank and communicative; wants to transfer to part-time school and look for work. Mother plans to make arrangements for May's confinement at hospital next week. Boy does not drive car; family does not possess one now.

9–25–33. Checked marriage with County Recorder, Vital Statistics, Book 1173, Page 7, Marriage Records.

9–29–33. Mr. Olson of Crescent Special states boy came to school one week, stated he was going to be married and left school; he was not properly checked out.

10–5–33. Message from Children's Protective Association that they will continue work with May.

10–9–33. Called at request of mother, who states that boy is unruly, refuses to go to school since married; saw another drunk at the house; boy promised to reenter school immediately.

---

[1] See ARTHUR W. TOWNE, "Young-girl Marriages in Criminal and Juvenile Courts," *Journal of Social Hygiene*, VIII (July, 1922), 287–305.

10–11–33. Phoned Mr. Olson; states boy returned to school.

10–21–33. May had a Caesarean operation; baby well; mother fair; Harold excited; out of school all week.

10–23–33. Mother phoned; Harold's wife died at the hospital at 3 A.M. today; boy is stricken with grief.

10–24–33. Mr. Jones shopped among undertakers for a cheap funeral; called at 4 P.M. to claim the body. Infant was named Barbara.

Later: Home visit; boy went for a walk with his father-in-law; arrangements for the funeral had been made for the following day. Mother states May was taken to the hospital very ill. Father refused operation at first until the following afternoon. Harold and others gave blood; Mr. Jones gave only a little; there were five transfusions; she died at 3 A.M. next morning.

10–26–33. Home visit; boy playing jazz on the piano; boy has transferred his interest to the baby; May was buried in Paradise Memorial Cemetery.

10–28–33. This home with its loud, electric, slot-machine phonograph and loud voices, and secrecy is still a puzzle. Mother asked aid for infant.

10–30–33. Mrs. White of C. Welfare Department on phone states that mother of boy applied for aid for child of son and she believes she is trying to get aid for all of the family; the attitude is that the child is a public responsibility.

11–2–33. Mrs. White on phone states mother will keep child without aid. A case will be opened.

11–10–33. A headline article regarding the police breaking in and beating the mother and her eldest daughter without cause or warrant, appeared in the East Side Star. A suit has been filed against the officers and the city. An attorney has taken the case.

11–30–33. Boy at home; it is his birthday; he has been out of school for two weeks and seems indifferent to it and wishes to go to work and support the baby.

1–19–34. Called at home; boy away; mother and sister cleaning house; phonograph has been removed; boy not attending school; thinks he will go to Montana and visit father for a while; baby had pneumonia at Christmas, had to be taken to the hospital but is improved.

2–1–34. Boy in office; promises to return to school; plans to apply for enrollment in CCC; mother no longer has lodgers; plans to move to a smaller house; older sister convalescing from operation for tumor; baby is doing well; boy is anxious to buy a car.

2–7–34. Principal reports boy out of school fifty days; asks cooperation.

2–13–34. Letter asking boy to report.

2–20–34. Boy not in school.

3–13–34. Principal reports boy out of school again; he refuses to work when he does attend.

Later: Called at home; boy expressed a dislike for Crescent Special; family not in sympathy with his refusal to attend school; mother and two sisters living at home; aided by Welfare Department as mother has no income; boy stays around home most of the time; goes to show once or twice a week; at times is disobedient.

3–14–34. Principal of Crescent School is considering filing a petition for nonattendance.

3–21–34. Supervision of Attendance of City Schools on phone; boy is to be expelled for nonattendance.

3–24–34. Home call; boy away; mother and sister at home; believe family sells whisky; not much to work with in this family.

4–20–34. Boy is not living up to court order; recommend change of plan.

5–7–34. Called at home; boy and mother sign new plan; boy likes it; boy promises to get work in a week or two.

5–14–34. Boy and mother at home; Harold lives a happy, carefree existence; boy wants to perfect his piano technique; family no longer has a piano; infant happy and well cared for.

5–24–34. Called at home; Harold does not seem to take life seriously; has made little effort to secure employment to support child; family in poor financial circumstances.

6–2–34. Boy in office; his plans for immediate future are indefinite; has only one ambition, that is, dismissal from probation.

6–15–34. Family seems to enjoy enforced leisure; Harold plans another attempt to enroll in CCC; baby well; boy carrying out all instruction, except going to school.

7–12–34. Call; boy at home; not making much headway at employment; wants driver's license to secure job as chauffeur; but it is believed that he just wants to drive for pleasure.

8–6–34. Boy takes life easily; does not care about present obligations or future security.

8–14–34. Harold on playground; not working and not going to school.

10–11–34. Call at home; boy's only desire is to be free from supervision.

1–6–35. Boy seen in car.

Later: Call at home; states the car belonged to a relative and he had permission from his mother.

The work carried on in the case of Harold Crane is typical of the work of the overburdened and untrained probation officer. He is responsible not only for the high rate of recidivism and rapid increase of the case load but also of the continued demoralization of the offenders, who tend to implicate others in the mire.

The probation officer was aware that Harold lived "in the midst of a deteriorated neighborhood and not far away from families whose boys were before the court on several occasions," and that these boys "exert an evil influence upon him." Assuming that this evaluation is correct, it might have been a good plan to induce the family to move from the district. A change of residence and removal from demoralizing associates, a change of school, properly chosen, is frequently desirable.

"To reprimand, to admonish, to forbid" and "to order" to keep away from evil associates means adoption of a negative course and leaving the boy with nothing constructive to fall back on, or, as Cyril Burt points out:

To lecture the misguided weakling and then do no more, to appeal to him to "give up those who do him no good" without removing him from their dominance, or simply to shut him up indoors during out-of-school hours and so deprive him of all recreation, good as well as harmful— such a course, though often the sole refuge . . . is usually unavailing and frequently unfair. The child himself has his own loyalty to his comrades; they in turn, with jeers and solicitations, will make it hard for him to throw them over; and any curtailment of his liberty by prohibition or confinement is likely to provoke deceit, resentment, and even forcible flight. The only effective step, therefore, may be to take the child where his old confederates . . . can neither expect nor oblige him to renew their perilous acquaintance.[1]

The probation officer's chief concern seemed to be the boy's regular attendance at Crescent Special School. What did this school offer the boy from an educational standpoint and from the standpoint of the satisfaction of his wishes? No medical, psychological, nor psychiatric examinations were made. There was no plan of treatment followed. The boy was interviewed at very irregular intervals from one to nine weeks apart.

One wonders what is meant by "good report," "getting along nicely," "doing well and living up to his obligations," and so on, when in the midst of these reports the boy becomes implicated in more and more serious offenses.

It is known to the writer that this probation officer carried a case load of 150 cases, an administrative difficulty over which an individual probation officer has little control. Under such circumstances there can be little more than a monthly visit and a history of the type which is described in this record. Note, however, that the delinquencies of this boy continued over a period of nearly three years, from February 27, 1932, to January 6, 1935. What is the financial cost of supervision, court hearings, of arrests, and further supervision over a period of three years? What is the financial cost to the community of several petty and grand thefts? What is the social and human cost to Harold, to his mother, to May, his wife, to their orphaned infant, to May's

[1] CYRIL BURT, *The Young Delinquent*, pp. 189–190.

parents, and to the community? Obviously these questions imply that had the boy received adequate supervision and social therapy, in accordance with a well-ordered, systematic plan, the financial, social, and human costs would have been greatly minimized. One can expect nothing else, if he is to retain his faith and confidence in a system of probation. If probation is to be maintained at all it should be well ordered and systematic. "A child who is amenable for evil is often equally amenable for good; and it may prove as easy for a sensible friend to guide him right as for a corrupt acquaintance to lead him astray."[1]

On the basis of the meager information contained in the record it is difficult to suggest a plan of treatment. It is, however, evident that the probation officer might have at least appealed to the Eastern Star or Masons to contribute their financial and moral support to this family. A Big Brother might have been secured for the boy under the supervision of the worker. A contact might have been made with a trade school and the boy's interests enlisted. The personal services of a family welfare agency and those of other community resources might have been secured.

Judging from the description of the home circumstances, of the mother's associates, and of the guidance afforded the boy, he should have been removed from his home. The officer recognized the fact that the home was unfit but he made no attempt to remove the boy from it nor to reconstruct it. There was no attempt made to orient the mother to the source of the boy's problems. The social problems multiplied as the boy continued his probationary period.

We need, of course, to remember that Harold lived in a home and community which supplied very little, if any, moral support for an adequate probation plan. Failure is "normal," perhaps, under these conditions even with the best of case work. While it is true that organized persons can and do live in disorderly homes and communities the chances are so heavily weighted against it that had Harold been energetic, wholesome, efficient, orderly, it would have been very difficult to explain that situation. In no case, however, could we expect a radical reform, such as occurred in the case of James R. (see p. 333), even though intimate relations had developed between officer and boy. It seems

[1] *Ibid.*, p. 188.

highly probable, moreover, that the family itself is not prepared to swim against the social currents in which their lives are being lived. This was a case for foster home placement for the boy, change of residence for the family, and a consistent and enduring guidance for the family during Harold's absence from the home and after his return into it. Perhaps this form of concentrated service might have prevented the initiation of disorganizing forces into the third generation, which will undoubtedly continue to exact a heavy social and financial cost.

Edwin J. Cooley, formerly Chief Probation Officer, Catholic Charities Probation Bureau in the Court of General Sessions, New York County, gives us the benefit of his study of almost fifty thousand home visits made by probation officers in the homes of their probationers:[1]

THE HOME VISIT

During the period of its supervisory work, the Bureau constantly endeavored to keep in mind that the family and not the individual must be the unit of treatment. Little social improvement could be expected of the delinquent unless his father, mother, brothers and sisters, and other relatives could be persuaded to forget their resentments and disappointments regarding the offender who had brought disgrace to their good name. Inharmonious relationships and undesirable conditions had to be removed as a first step in this process. The methods and services of the modern family welfare organizations in the adjustment of family relations was made an integral part of the case work of the Bureau.

The greater proportion of the probationers lived with their families . . . one of the most frequent problems was: How could the parents exercise effective supervision and control over the children? With the assistance of the officer, many such problems of discipline were successfully solved. Health problems, involving tuberculosis, undernourishment, or mental defect, which required diagnosis, treatment, or possibly institutional care of the afflicted members of the family, were frequently met with and attended to by the officer.

In adjusting important problems involving the mistress of the home, such as excessive burden of work, necessity for managing on an insufficient income, the efficient and economic purchase of good food and clothing, proper diet and cleanliness, the assistance of home educators of cooperating social agencies was enlisted.

[1] Edwin J. Cooley, *Probation and Delinquency*, pp. 125–128.

Family plans for home ownership, purchasing new furniture, establishing the father and son in business, and securing safe financial investments were worked out in collaboration with the probation officer. Each member of the family was also encouraged to contribute his quota to the maintenance and to the upbuilding of the household.

Job analysis and vocational guidance were not limited solely to the probationer, but included the whole family, especially the younger members, who were aided in obtaining positions which afforded congenial employment, and possessed possibilities for advancement and adequate remuneration.

The brothers and sisters of school age were encouraged to complete their education in elementary or high school or, when employment seemed more advisable, to pursue courses in night and continuation schools. The parents, wherever necessary, were persuaded to attend Americanization schools.

Recreation outlets for the family were studied, and the resources of the community were ascertained. Such outlets included club and library membership, affiliation with neighborhood activities, and the attendance at lectures and public meetings. The main objective was that of developing and exercising the play spirit of the family as a group, rather than as separate individuals.

The establishment and the maintenance of a spirit of friendliness and harmony in the home involved the solution of a great number of problems of human relationship. To reduce the friction and resentment between the reputable family and the delinquent member, to solve the problem of the over-stern or over-indulgent parents, or to eliminate the nagging of brothers and sisters, the assistance of the psychiatrist and the psychologist was sometimes required.

Where it was not possible nor desirable to keep the family together, the question of child-placing or of finding a home for older members of the family sometimes arose. Where the breaking up of the family was of a temporary nature due to the illness of the mother and the presence of young children in the home, the counsel and the sympathetic oversight of the officers of the Bureau were valuable and often resulted in such arrangements for the care of the members of the household as were calculated to facilitate the family reunion as expeditiously as possible.

In this work of adjusting the family within itself and within the community, the various social agencies and community resources were utilized, particularly the Church, the school, neighborhood forces, and the employer. To increase the sense of family solidarity, to regenerate and build up its spiritual life, and to strengthen and augment the wholesomeness of the influence of the home constituted the aims of the Bureau. That the family might not remain in a static condition of negative non-delinquency, constantly balancing itself precariously on the border line of disreputability and dependence, but that it might constructively direct its efforts towards social and economic stability, which would be maintained without assistance after the conclusion of the probationary period, was the objective kept in mind by the probation officer.

How Do We Rate as Parents?—The Los Angeles County Probation Department has found very useful the following extract from Goodwin Watson's "Scale for Rating Home Contribution to Personality Development of Children,"[1] in discussing the type of home which destroys character and the one which builds character.

How Do We Rate as Parents?

What do our children think of us?   Apply this scale to *your* home.
Compare each item in First Column with Same Number in Second Column

THIS TYPE OF HOME DESTROYS CHARACTER

1. Child feels that both parents hate him, he is a nuisance, a "nut," an expense, one of the world's worst liabilities.

2. Parents constantly quarreling, threats of separation, each tries to prejudice the child against the other.

3. Jealousies and favoritisms in family. Intimacy and tenderness between child and parent of opposite sex, antagonisms to other. Emotionally unweaned.

4. Child's every whim must be satisfied. No sacrifice too great, anywhere, by anyone, if the child wishes it. At the slightest sign of reluctance, the child fusses, and is given his way at once.

5. Parent's every whim must be satisfied. Any resistance on the part of the child met with extreme severity, or with whining protests of ingratitude, pleas for sympathy.

6. *Variable* discipline, conduct laughed at today, is met with blows

THIS TYPE OF HOME BUILDS CHARACTER

1. Child feels that both parents wholeheartedly want him, love him, *appreciate* him.

2. Parents wholeheartedly love each other, and all happy together, considerate of each other, trusting each other completely.

3. Wholesome enjoyment by each person of understanding relationships with each other in the family.

4. Child is expected to consider others as they consider him. Many things good for adults are not good for children. Many disappointments can't be helped. Make the best of things. Co-operate in best solution.

5. Child is treated with intimate courtesy. Parents ready to make adjustments and sacrifices, where helpful, without pretense, or demand for appreciation.

6. Consistent attitudes. Once a working solution has been decided

[1] Reprinted by permission of author.

This Type of Home Destroys Character	This Type of Home Builds Character
tomorrow if parent is more irritable.	upon, it is pursued steadily until consciously, thoughtfully modified.
7. Discipline all negative. Blows, nagging, sarcasm, mean remarks, contempt.	7. Comments on child's behavior largely praise, appreciation. Any criticism points in matter of fact fashion to more helpful response. Emphasis on consequences.
8. Child ignored in family planning. Expected merely to submit. Seen and not heard. Domination by one member of family.	8. Democratic family. Wishes of each taken into account. Plans for choice of apartments, room decorations, meals, budget, vacations, time schedules, use of equipment, made co-operatively.
9. Obedience to an arbitrary person. "Do as you are told."	9. Understanding recognition of unchangeable features of situations, and co-operation in group agreements.
10. Child is center of stage. Much ado over physical and other development.	10. Child is one of group. Most situations met with take it or leave it objective attitude.
11. Child's achievements constantly evaluated in comparison with those of brothers, sisters, playmates, or classmates.	11. Child's achievements recognized on intrinsic basis. Do because worth doing. Improve own record where important to do so. Do well.
12. Much argument, pleading, teasing, bribing, coaxing in connection with routine duties. Flurries of hurry.	12. Routine accepted as a matter of course. Practically invariable. *Comfortable allowances of time.*
13. Parents expect child to be genius, president, artist, high marks, etc., (to compensate for parental inferiority feelings).	13. Parents well satisfied, serene and zestful in own living. Will co-operate with child in working out any plans which promise satisfaction for child. Child's ambitions well within his possibilities.
14. Child led to believe he is different from others, better behaved, higher ideals, more sensitive, or no chance, hopeless, especially cared for, especially neglected, in a special class.	14. Child recognizes kinship with all castes and classes, thinks of human nature realistically, regardless of sex, race, creed, street address, school attended, etc.
15. Parents extremely fearful of injury to child, much bundling up, doctors on every pain, constant round of specialists, parents go everywhere to protect child. Recreation strictly supervised.	15. Parents recognize that children live through all kinds of things. Reasonable provisions against infection, provision for diet, sleep, play in good neighborhood, mutual confidence, then faith in child's resources.

THIS TYPE OF HOME DESTROYS CHARACTER	THIS TYPE OF HOME BUILDS CHARACTER
16. Complete dependence. Child unable to decide anything by himself. Unable to meet new situations; or, anxious, worried, with sense of world on his shoulders.	16. Growing independence of child. Increasing opportunity to make choices and enjoy or suffer consequences. Developing technique for deciding.

Dr. Van Waters lays down certain maxims for parents, which in reality must become the responsibility of the worker to interpret and to teach, wherever necessary. A brief summary of the major points made by Dr. Van Waters[1]—and a few references to recent literature added by the present author, which will help to orient parents (with an inclination to read books) to some of the wider implications of the serious business of being a parent— would include the following:

1. Parents must learn to evaluate social resources to be tapped for the development of their children. (See *Organizations for Youth* by Elizabeth Pendry and Hugh Hartshorne.)

2. Parents must thread their way through a maze of scientific theories and religious dogma. (Shailer Mathews, *New Faith for Old;* Archibald Black, *Opening Roads;* James H. Gilkey, *Getting Help from Religion.*)

3. Learn from their experience that behavior can be modified and that parental patterns are the explanation of many traits which children exhibit. (Miriam Van Waters, *Youth in Conflict;* Eleanor Wembridge, *Other People's Daughters;* Miriam Van Waters, *Parents on Probation.*)

4. Parents must know the world in which the child lives. (*The Child and Society*, by Phyllis Blanchard; *Children at the Cross Roads*, by Agnes E. Benedict; *Understanding the Adolescent Girl*, by Grace L. Elliott.)

5. Parents need to realize that children must have security, steady love, and the unshaken faith of stable parents, and an assurance that nothing is too much trouble for their development. (*Tuning In with Our Children*, by J. L. Lacy; *Wholesome Parenthood*, by Ernest R. Groves.)

6. Parents must know that children should learn the meaning of sex in early childhood. (*Growing Up*, by Karl de Schweinitz;

[1] MIRIAM VAN WATERS, *Parents on Probation*, pp. 31–56.

Sex Education of Children, by Mary W. Dennett; *So Youth May Know,* by Roy E. Dickerson.)

7. Parents should learn that children must pursue their own spontaneous interests and be initiated into the delights of sustained activity. (*The Modern Parent; Building Personality in Children,* by G. C. Meyers.)

8. Parents must learn that children should have cooperative living and shared responsibility as well as an opportunity for being alone. (*That Problem Called the Modern Boy,* by Jerald O'Neil; *Fathers and Sons,* by E. B. Castle.)

It is not to be assumed that reading of books will solve the difficulties of the parents or their children. But they provide facts and may create an inquiring attitude of mind; they may orient the reader to the existing problems and provide a basis for discussion with an intelligent counselor. It must be remembered that at best families will have difficulty in concentrating on any program of child welfare as long as the home continues to suffer from financial straits, unemployment, neighborhood and community demoralization, urbanization, mobility, and a host of other problems besetting the family in the modern city.

Selected Bibliography

1. ADLER, HERMAN: "Home Made Failures," in *Why Men Fail,* Maurice Fishbein and William White (Editors), Century Company, 1928.
2. BRECKENRIDGE, SOPHONISBA P., and EDITH ABBOTT: *The Delinquent Child and the Home,* Russell Sage Foundation, 1912.
3. BRIDGMAN, RALPH R.: "Parent Education," *Social Work Year Book* (1935), pp. 310–315.
4. ———: "Guidance for Marriage and Family Life," *Annals of the American Academy of Political and Social Science,* CLX (March, 1930), 144–164.
5. BURGESS, ERNEST W.: "The Family as a Unity of Interacting Personalities," *The Family,* VII (March, 1926), 3–9.
6. BURNHAM, WILLIAM H.: *Intelligent Parenthood,* Chicago Association for Child Study and Parent Education, 1928.
7. BUSHONG, EUGENE M.: "Family Estrangement and Juvenile Delinquency," *Social Forces,* V (September, 1926), 79–83.
7a. BUTTERFIELD, OLIVER M.: *Love Problems of Adolescents* (in press).
8. DE SCHWEINITZ, KARL: "Social Work as It Contributes to the Strengthening of Family Life," *Proceedings of the National Conference of Social Work* (1923), pp. 294–299.
9. ELLIS, HAVELOCK: *Little Essays of Love and Virtue,* George H. Doran Company, 1922, Chap. I, "Parents and Children."

10. FERRIS, ROBERT H.: "Some Social Factors in Family Problems," *Year Book, National Probation Association* (1932–1933), pp. 180–188.
11. GROVES, ERNEST R., and GLADYS H. GROVES: *Wholesome Parenthood*, Houghton Mifflin Company, 1929.
12. HART, HORNEL, and ELLA B. HART: *Personality and the Family*, D. C. Heath & Company, 1935.
13. KILLICK, VICTOR W.: "Suggestions for Parental Administration Calculated to Reduce Juvenile Delinquency," *Journal of Delinquency*, II (September, 1927), 194–205.
14. FRANK, LAWRENCE K.: "The Management of Tensions," *The American Journal of Sociology*, XXXIII (March, 1928), 705–735.
14a. MEAD, MARGARET: *Growing Up in New Guinea; Coming of Age in Samoa*, William Morrow & Company, Inc., 1930, 1928.
15. MOWRER, E. R.: *Domestic Discord*, University of Chicago Press, 1928.
16. MOWRER, HARRIET R.: *Personality Adjustment and Domestic Discord*, American Book Company, 1935.
17. NEUMAN, FREDERIKA: "The Effects on the Child of an Unstable Home Situation," *Proceedings of the National Conference of Social Work* (1928), pp. 346–353.
18. POPENOE, PAUL: "A Family Consultation," *Journal of Social Hygiene*, XVII (June, 1931), 309–322.
19. PRATT, GEORGE K.: "Doctors in Matrimony," *Survey Graphic*, LXVII (January, 1932), 359–360.
20. RICHARDS, ESTHER LORING, "Practical Aspects of Parental Love," *Mental Hygiene*, X (April, 1926), 225–241.
21. SAYLES, MARY B.: *The Problem Child at Home*, The Commonwealth Fund, 1928.
22. SCHUMACHER, H. C.: "Environmental Conflicts in the Family and Social Life of the Modern Child," *Hospital Social Service*, XVI (October, 1927), 299.
23. SCHMIEDELER, EDGAR, and M. ROSA MCDONOUGH: *Parent and Child*, D. Appleton-Century Company, Inc., 1934, Chap. VIII, "Discipline"; Chap. IX, "Disciplinary Devices"; Chap. XVI, "The Personality of the Child."
24. SMITH, JEANETTE A., and CAROLINE DENTON: "An Experiment in Case Work with a Group of Parents," *The Family*, XVI (December, 1935), 242–247.
25. TAFT, JESSIE: "The Effect of an Unsatisfactory Mother-daughter Relationship upon the Development of a Personality," *The Family*, March, 1926, 10–17.
26. TOWNE, ARTHUR J.: "Young-girl Marriages in Criminal and Juvenile Courts," *Journal of Social Hygiene*, VIII (July, 1922), 287–305.
27. WEMBRIDGE, ELEANOR R.: *Other People's Daughters*, Houghton Mifflin Company, 1926.
28. WHITE, EDNA NOBLE: "Experiments in Family Consultation Centers," *Social Forces*, XII (May, 1934), 557–562.
29. WHITE, WILLIAM ALLEN: *Mechanisms of Character Formation*, The Macmillan Company, 1924.

30. White House Conference on Child Health and Protection: *The Young Child in the Home*, D. Appleton-Century Company, Inc., 1936.
31. ———: *Education for Home and Family Life*, D. Appleton-Century Company, Inc., 1932.
32. ———: *The Adolescent in the Family*, D. Appleton-Century Company, Inc., 1932.
33. ———: *Parent Education*, D. Appleton-Century Company, Inc., 1932.
34. WOODHOUSE, CHASE GOING: "A Study of 250 Successful Families," *Social Forces*, VIII (June, 1930), 511–532.

Suggestions for Further Study

1. What constitutes parental education? How is it best accomplished?
2. What are the values and limitations of a program of parental education in family life of today?
3. What is the philosophy of parental education?
4. What are the methods of parental education?
5. What are the values of study circles? of discussion groups? of adult education? of family clinics?
6. What social, economic, biological, and psychological factors should be taken into account in programs of parental education?
7. What is the relation between parental education and community education?
8. What agency should sponsor a program of parental education?
9. When should parental education begin?
10. What is the program of parental education in primitive tribes? (See Margaret Mead, *Growing Up in New Guinea*.)
11. What are the difficulties to intelligent parenthood in modern urban life?
12. What are the effects on children of unstable home situations?
13. What constitutes a "successful family"?
14. What aids did you receive from the discussion of the case of Peter Smith? of Marilyn Smith?
15. Write a brief critique of the approaches to the Smith and Fineberg families; of probation supervision; of case work techniques.
16. What is the difference between probation supervision and surveillance? Write a critique of methods of work used in the case of Harold Crane. Under what difficulties did the probation officer work? What important facts are missing for an understanding of the case? What would have been your approach to such a case?
17. What is Professor Overstreet's philosophy of punishment, of treatment, of "influencing human behavior" by the family? the court?
18. How do Overstreet and Dewey agree or disagree regarding the fundamental principles of human nature?
19. What is Mr. Cooley's philosophy of social treatment?
20. What elements does Mr. Cooley discuss in the process of adjustment of a probationer? What processes of adjustment are seen in the case of James R.?

21. Why is the formulation of a plan of treatment essential? How rigidly should it be adhered to? What relation should it have to the plan by the family?

22. What is involved in the formulation of a plan of treatment by the family? the probation officer?

23. What is meant by the "acceptance of a plan by probationer"? Why is this acceptance essential? To what extent was the plan accepted by James R.? by Harold Crane? by Sam Fineberg?

24. What does Karl de Schweinitz advocate regarding the plan of the client?

25. What are the methods of gaining insight into a problem by the supervising officer, by the probationer? by the family? How was this situation accomplished in the cases cited?

26. How do these methods differ in the case of a juvenile offender and an adult criminal?

27. How are antisocial attitudes removed? How were they removed in the cases cited?

28. When may the "trial-and-error" method be used? What are its dangers?

29. How are social relationships developed? How were they developed in the cases cited?

30. What is involved in the adjustment of a family? How was the family of James R. adjusted? of Sam Fineberg? of Harold Crane? of Marilyn Smith?

31. What is E. R. Mowrer's approach by "domestic discord," "family disorganization"? How do these influence the probationer? How may they be overcome?

32. What is Harriet Mowrer's approach to the problem of family conflicts?

33. What is the aim of the "home visit"? What was accomplished during the home visits in the cases cited?

34. What social forces contribute to the disorganization of a family? to family conflicts?

35. What is the role of the supervision officer in bringing about family adjustment?

36. What role does the supervision officer play in bringing about: neighborhood improvement? financial independence? suitable employment? proper philosophy of life? restoration of social status?

37. What is the role of the following in the adjustment of the probationer and how may they be attained: constructive recreation? vocational education? emotional stability? social consciousness? religious development? How were these attained in the cases cited?

38. How are "discipline" and "self-control" brought about? How were they brought about in the cases cited?

39. What is meant by "character building"? How is character built? What are W. I. Thomas' theories regarding building of character? Hugh Hartshorne and Mack A. May's?

40. What elements are involved in building character? How was character built in the cases cited?

41. What does Dr. White mean by "character formation"?   How does his approach differ from that of Mr. Cooley? of W. I. Thomas?

42. What is Dr. White's account of the "Adlerian point of view" with respect to conflict?

43. What are the mechanisms in the resolution of conflict situations?

44. Give specific illustrations of application of psychoanalytic theories in your daily practice.

45. What methods of treatment does Mr. Lou suggest?   (*Juvenile Courts in the United States*, pp. 143–178.)

46. What is the value of restitution? of money penalties?   When should these be imposed?

47. Indicate some social forces which influence human behavior.

48. Which of these forces are the most potent?   Why?

49. What is the role of the family in shaping the child's conduct?

50. What competing forces does the family encounter in influencing the young?

51. What is meant by the statement that "each probationer is a part of a unit, and that unit is the family"?   Of what other units is the probationer a part in the modern city?   What is the relation of these units to the family?

52. What other material do we need to consider for a complete understanding of the home in relation to probation?

53. Why is there so much more material on the investigation of the home than the treatment of the home?

54. Read: Sheldon and Eleanor Glueck, *One Thousand Juvenile Delinquents*, pp. 63–83.   What are the Gluecks' conclusions regarding the family background of one thousand delinquents studied by the Judge Baker Foundation of Boston?   How do you account for the large percentage of delinquent boys coming from immigrant families?

CHAPTER XXI

THE TECHNIQUE OF RECORDING TREATMENT PROCESSES AND PLANS

The Department of Probation of the County of Westchester provides the following outline to aid probation officers in their summary or block recording of case treatment. (For a discussion of the technique of recording the social study see pp. 104–113, and for the diagnostic summary see pp. 133–134.)[1]

THE SUMMARY

I. Home Situation. Give names of persons interviewed, relationship and interest.
   a. Description of changes in home situation
      1. The present as compared with that noted in last summary.
      2. If new address, how does new home and neighborhood compare with former, and reasons for moving, rental paid.
      3. Note changes in composition of household group, new boarders, births, deaths, marriages.
      4. Health problems newly developed and Probation Officer's efforts to solve them.
      5. Economic problems newly developed and Probation Officer's efforts to solve them; total family income.
      6. Agencies interested, nature and extent of their current interest; relief bureau, crime prevention bureau, religious organizations, clinics, etc.
   b. Other changes
      1. Changes in attitude of family members toward each other.
      2. Changes in attitude of family members toward probationer.
      3. Changes in attitude of family members toward Probation Officer.
II. Personal Situation
   1. Regularity of reports with explanation of deviations.
   2. Changes in personal appearance.
   3. Citizenship.
   4. Employment visits and verification. In recording this, note persons interviewed, character of fellow employees, conditions of

[1] See also E. FRED SWEET, "Report of the Committee on Case Records," *Yearbook of the National Probation Association* (1936), pp. 413–417.

work, adjustment to job; wages, how verified.   Changes in school
attitude and program.

5. If unemployed, his job seeking technique, mental attitude,
   dependence, Probation Officer's efforts on his behalf and the
   probationer's response.
6. Health—current problems; if physical, what the probationer or
   Probation Officer's efforts have been on his behalf, and probationer's response.
7. Thrift—how probationer or family manages his fiscal affairs,
   budgeting of income and expenditures, instalment purchases,
   extravagance, regularity and amount of savings, insurance, benefit
   society, property accumulation.   Describe Probation Officer's
   efforts and probationer's and his family's response.
8. Leisure time—how occupied and Probation Officer's estimate of
   the value to probationer.   Describe Probation Officer's efforts to
   effect a more desirable change in activities and associations;
   plans suggested or organized, outlets, schools, etc., contacted,
   and probationer's response.
9. Other changes—note changes in probationer's development of
   better understanding of his responsibilities and his efforts to
   shoulder them.

III. General Problems.—Probation Officer should denote the degree of
   progress and success achieved in resolving the probationer's general
   problems and reason.

IV. In Summary *Underline*
1. Significant changes in civil status such as new home or employment address, birth, marriages, etc.
2. Significant *factual* items in social status, as earnings, hospital
   contact, family welfare contacts, savings, etc.

Underlining is most efficiently used when used most sparingly.   Devote
separate paragraph to family support and restitution status—preferably at
end of summary.

This outline is merely suggestive of the scope of material to be
included in the record.   Each worker must use discretion in
using any outline and not attempt to fit unique experiences and
particular situations into a definite mold.

Ethel N. Cherry, Supervisor of Case Work of the Probation
Department of the County of Westchester, writes:

A committee of the probation officers representing each type of
education, worked on an outline for summary or block recording.   We
have used it now for a period of over a year and with few exceptions
find that it keeps the work up to date, that it is simpler for the probation
officer but far more important in that he puts some diagnostic thinking
into his work in addition to simply factual recording.   In order to combine a month's work and put in all the important things, the probation

officer finds that he must think through exactly what has happened and this calls to his attention what still needs to be done for the case.[1]

Summaries can be arranged under appropriate headings, suggested in the foregoing outline, or any other headings suited to the particular character of the case. Miss Cherry supplies the following sample of block recording.[2]

Summary for Nov. 15 to Dec. 16: HV: Nov. 20, Dec. 12; SV: 3; OC: 2; L: 3; R: Nov. 15, 29, Dec. 6. (Explanation: R: reports. These are done at a Y. M. C. A. clubhouse, in only occasional cases at the court building. HV: Home visit. SV: School visit. OC: Other contacts. L. Letter.)[3]

During this period the family moved to a new six-room apartment at 6 *Blank Street, White Plains.* Mrs. Esposito with the help of Mrs. J., a more Americanized neighbor, has put up new curtains, and there is now a room which may be used for a common family meeting place. The bedrooms are lighter and airier and the house was in much better order. The mother's whole morale has been helped by this change and was very much pleased by P. O.'s approval. They pay $30 a month rent, which is partially paid by the Public Welfare Department, who are supplementing the earnings of Mr. Esposito and the two oldest boys. The location of the home is nearer the clubhouse and the mother with great pride told the P. O. that she would be able sometime now to go over "and straighten up the club."

Tony's health continues to be a matter of concern although the mother states that he is taking his cod-liver oil and eating better at meals. She is concerned about the father, feeling that he is growing thinner and coughs some at night. The father was interviewed on the second home visit. He is still opposed to having a physician examine him, but is not so belligerent and accepts the suggestion with better feeling.

The school reports show the boy's effort has improved. Copies of these are filed. Vito's promptness at school has improved. At a recent meeting of the club, when the school reports were discussed, Vito told this with a great deal of pride.

The boy has continued to go swimming at the Y.M.C.A. each night. There was only one thing of concern that happened during this period.

[1] Personal communication, June 20, 1936.

[2] Quoted by permission of the department.

[3] Perhaps a somewhat clearer form may be gained from the following arrangement:

HV: Nov. 20
    Dec. 12
SV: Dec. 3
OC: Dec. 3 } (Report should follow.)
 L: Dec. 3
 R: Nov. 15
    Nov. 29
    Dec. 6 [P.V.Y.]

Both boys failed to appear at home one night until eleven o'clock, when they were supposed to have been attending a workshop. The mother was quite terrified. The P. O. had learned from the instructor that a substitute had been placed on that night and because of the boys' intense interest had neglected to close the class at the 9:30 hour. It took a great deal of time on the part of the P. O. to convince the mother that the boys were not hanging around the streets. The old-world attitude of distrust of any deviation, while commendatory in checking on the boys' whereabouts, caused some difficulty. The boys have gotten to the place where they both resented the fact that their story was not believed. The family's attitude was interpreted to the boys, which they finally accepted. Both tried to understand each other's view points in the future.

Tony and Vito are planning with the other club members for the Christmas celebration. A Christmas basket of food which is to be paid for by their two cents a week dues is to be given to some needy family. The boys earn this money by running errands on Saturday.   AWT:eg

This form of recording may be compared with the diary or chronological entries (see case of Sam Fineberg, pp. 421–434). Perhaps the record on Sam Fineberg's case would have lent itself more readily to block recording. It is agreed that chronological entries[1] are useful when the case is known only a short time, when the worker does not think in diagnostic terms, or when he is extremely busy and carries an excessive case load and cannot remember the clients sufficiently to summarize the case work processes in these particular cases. (Note that the case of Marilyn Smith is purposely recorded in diary form since this record is reproduced primarily to indicate in detail the thinking behind the worker's procedure and not as a model for case recording.) The following case progress record, which is in reality a case work organizer, is found by many to be of great service in keeping up with the mechanical details incidental in all case work procedure. Erle F. Young,[2] who designed the case progress record sheet, writes as follows:

Certainty and speed of action are two prime considerations in efficient social case work. The case worker must be at once a leader—able to discover and develop the hidden resources of family and community— and a skilled case work mechanician. The mechanics of case work are a sore burden to many case workers; frequently they require so much energy that the quality of the work is impaired. With a heavy case

[1] See GORDON HAMILTON, *Social Case Recording*, pp. 17–41.

[2] "The Organization of Case Work Routines," *Social Work Technique*, I (May–June, 1936), 94–96.

Smith, John & Mary
FAMILY NAME

A 4321
CASE NO

CASE PROGRESS RECORD
A Casework Organizer designed by
ERLE FISKE YOUNG, Ph. D., Professor of Sociology and Social Work
School of Social Work, University of Southern California

INSTRUCTIONS: Note on this sheet all decisions on the case made by the worker, the supervisor; or in case conference. Make separate entry for each action, such as visits to be made, letters to be written, verifications needed, etc. Only specific operations should be listed.

DATE OF DECISION RE ACTION	BY WHOM	PERSON OR AGENCY TO BE CONTACTED	LETTER PHONE VISIT	REGARDING WHAT?	TO BE DONE BY WHEN?	DATE COMPLETED	REMARKS RE CHANGE OF PLAN FOLLOW-UP REQUIRED, ETC
1936			SOME SAMPLE ENTRIES SHOWING THE USE OF THE FORM				
3/6	JS	Amer Red X, SF	L	Their rec of Fam	3/8	3/7	Rep due 3/13 R
3/6	JS	Hammond Lbr Co	L	Emp Rec of Man	3/8	3/7	Rep due 3/12
3/6	JS	J P A	P	Arr case conf	3/6	3/7	Set for 3/9
3/6	JS	Mem Disp	P	Clinic Rep on woman	3/6	3/7	Will mail
3/6	JS	Family	V	Immediate needs	3/8	3/8	
3/6	co	Juv Ct Com	V	Filing on Jim	3/10	3/10	
3/14	RB	Hammond Lbr Co	L	Follow-up on 3/6	3/15	3/15	Rep due 3/21 R

EXPLANATION

The above entries show the method of using the form. Of course, the sheet would probably be pasted on the inside of the front of the case-folder and the entries would be handwritten. Note the free use of abbreviations. The second line, for example, reads: On March 6, 1936, JS (the case worker) decided to write a letter to the Hammond Lumber Company asking for the employment record of John Smith. This letter was to be gotten out on or before March 8, and was actually sent March 7. The reply was expected on March 12. When it had not been received on March 14, RB (the district supervisor), see the last line entries, asked that a follow-up letter be sent on or before March 15. This letter was gotten out on the 15th. A reply was expected by the 21st and was received on or before that date.

Do not enter on this form: general plans for case, policy decisions, or general directions which are standard for all cases, such as, clearing the case, making first visits, and the like.

load there is constant danger that decisions will be forgotten, promises unfulfilled, letter-writing needlessly delayed, and many important treatment details lost sight of. The usual hastily scribbled notations which the supervisor attaches to case records are lost or forgotten, and there is no regular method for checking up on the performance of operations agreed upon in case conferences or in consultation with the individual case worker. Oral instructions are even more apt to result in failure to perform or in misunderstandings.

During the early stages of intensive work on a case—the first interviews, verifications, and so on—when special attention is focused upon the case—there is relatively little likelihood of serious oversights. The trouble begins after the first diagnosis has been made and a plan determined upon. Then attention is apt to shift to the investigation of new cases which require intensive work.

A natural result is that the investigational and diagnostic phases of case work frequently secure relatively more attention than case strategy (planning) and case administration (the execution of the plan). Needless delays in the execution of plans result in a too low case turnover and a consequent piling up of the case load. The drain on the financial and personnel resources of the agency becomes excessive and the quality of work drops. This situation causes loss of public confidence in the agency and makes adequate financing difficult.

Many devices have been developed to set standards of performance and insure thorough investigation and proper social diagnosis. However, there are few facilitating devices to assure workers and executives that action will be certainly and speedily taken.

The Case Progress Record (see illustration) is a simple device which is designed to reduce to a minimum delays in treatment and follow-up and to make certain that instructions, decisions, promises, and so on, are not unnecessarily overlooked or delayed.

The Case Progress Record is designed to supplement rather than displace existing record-keeping devices. Well organized records are already provided with face sheets, budget sheets, case diagnostic sheets, treatment-plan sheets, and so on.

In using the Case Progress Record the executive will find it advantageous to follow certain procedures:

1. The form should be presented and explained fully in staff conference. Be certain that everyone understands how to use it.

2. Emphasize the help which this device affords the individual worker. Do not present it as an executive control device, though from the executive's point of view it serves that purpose also. The wholehearted cooperation of case workers is best secured when they appreciate fully its usefulness to themselves in doing good work particularly when under a heavy burden.

3. Note the method suggested for dealing with letters.

4. Entries should be made in the first six columns at the time each decision is made. The last two columns are used to check results.

5. Supervisors should *not* be encouraged to forego necessary individual conferences with workers by using this as an instruction sheet. Rather they should use it to make notations of instructions given *during* such conferences.

A treatment evaluation summary,[1] particularly in cases extending over a long period of time, would be useful if recorded in brief summary form periodically (and not only when closing the case), indicating what has been attempted but failed of results, what has been successfully accomplished (for teaching purposes it would be valuable to know the method of such accomplishment and the reasons for success or failure), and further plan of treatment by client, by agency, through the use of community resources, etc. Miss Hamilton[2] shows some of the wider implications and complexities of recording in the following statement:

The notion of recording a plan is particularly relevant if "executive treatment," or service, is contemplated or if environmental factors are to be manipulated or if habit training or other similar education is to be attempted. Planning is less easy to state if methods of progressive education are to be employed and the client is to learn from experience in a dynamic situation. A formal plan seems less relevant in so-called relationship treatment or attitude therapy. The ideas of treatability, planning, controls and outcome instead of plan are, however, inherent in all methods of treatment and not the least in relationship therapy. If the worker has a definite plan it is probably wise to state it; if the plan is one offered by the client and agreed upon with the agency, it is wise to state it; if no plan is contemplated, it is impossible to state it. Workers of certain training and approach would prefer to think of "movement" rather than activity, and when the stress is on the client's use of the worker, rather than on the leadership of the worker, the planning process is fluid and difficult to formalize in any ordinary sense.

Evaluation lies close to diagnosis, but we think of it more in connection with treatment. What has proved better or worse, more or less constructive in the progressive handling? The norms in evaluation are social and personal. Mores shift from generation to generation and from country to country, and people may differ or deviate markedly from the mores without necessarily feeling unadjusted. The case

[1] See HAMILTON, *op. cit.*, pp. 35–41.

[2] *Ibid.*, pp. 57–58, 72–73. Reprinted by permission of Columbia University Press, New York.

worker has to resist alike the temptation to arbitrary over-simplification and useless qualification. "This seems apparently, in a manner of speaking, to be approximately something or other." All diagnostic effort or treatment evaluation is extraordinarily complicated, tentative, and flexible, and is understood as such by the well-trained reader or writer of records. The difficulty is not in recording clearly but in learning to think clearly, and no record can be said to be professional until our fragmentary and imperfect diagnostic thinking is included. The patient exposed to the full battery of scientific method was right in complaining that he wished just for once he could be treated for what ailed him.

The closing entry should stress the outstanding problems at the time the case was referred, those developed subsequently, the course of treatment followed successfully, and of that attempted without success, the results of treatment obtained, and the reason for closing.

"A closing entry need not in simple cases be longer than a paragraph or so, and a narrative style . . . seems to be the most satisfactory."[1]

Attention is called to the final petition (March 9, 1936) in the case of Sam Fineberg, which is illustrative of a concise summary report on a case active in the agency for eighteen months. Undoubtedly this summary could be abbreviated, but it shows the essential points to be included in the summary.

For Bibliography See Chapter VI (p. 112)

Suggestions for Further Study

1. Read Ralph Hall Ferris, "The Case History in Probation Service," in Sheldon Glueck (Editor), *Probation and Criminal Justice*, pp. 153–159. What constitutes a supervision record? a treatment record? How should such a record be kept? How should all the subtle phases of probation supervision be recorded? of child welfare work in general? How can a record serve as a "map of the road" to another probation officer or judge? or other worker? Should the treatment record be written in the first person? Why, or why not?

2. Read Ada E. Sheffield, *The Social Case History*, pp. 60–69, "The Summary." What does Mrs. Sheffield include in the summary of a social case history of a family? What should be included in the summary of a probation case? of a problem child case?

3. Read Gordon Hamilton, *Social Case Recording*, and indicate her method of recording case summaries, transfer summaries, closing summaries.

4. What does Erle F. Young mean by a case work organizer?

[1] *Ibid.*, p. 33.

CHAPTER XXII

THE WORKER WITH DELINQUENT AND PROBLEM YOUTH

It is difficult to discuss the personal and social traits and the educational equipment needed by the worker with delinquent and problem children in view of the variety of circumstances that he is called upon to meet and the variety of techniques he uses. Whether the child welfare worker is attached to a probation department, police department, family welfare association, child-caring agency, children's protective association, child guidance clinic, a school, or some other agency directing its efforts in behalf of children, there are certain common qualifications which these workers are generally expected to possess. It is often said that "probation is what the officer makes it." This is true only to a certain extent. The work depends also upon judges with a socialized point of view who do not put on probation persons who are poor risks, on the available community resources, on the intelligence and personality traits of the offender, the case load, the equipment and administrative facilities of the agency, and numerous other factors. However, since the worker on any case is the explorer, diagnostician, prognostician, chief coordinator, motivator, educator, and therapist, a large share of responsibility falls upon his shoulders.[1] (The training and qualifications of child welfare workers in other than probation departments are generally recognized to be higher than those of probation officers. It will be necessary, therefore, to limit some, though not all, of the discussion to probation officers, a restriction which it has been possible in general to avoid in other sections of our discussion.)

[1] For a discussion of the role of the probation officer see Bernard J. Fagan, "Selection and Training of Probation Officers," in Sheldon Glueck (Editor), *Probation and Criminal Justice*, pp. 70–94; also Dorothy S. Kahn, "Professional Standards in Social Work," *The Compass*, XVI (June, 1935), 1–5; James E. Hagerty, *The Training of Social Workers*.

Some Types of Probation Officers.—Hans Weiss[1] lists several distir ct types of probation officers which are also useful in classifying other social workers:

The embryo stage we find exemplified by the probation officer who is only a card index, or clerk, busying himself with filling out simple record cards and doing similar clerical duties. His vocabulary is primitive and his vision limited. He talks to the boy, he tells him to be "good" and to leave things alone that belong to somebody else. I have seen probation officers of this type who never had a real conversation with their probationers. A few perfunctory questions are asked about school or work. Once a week the boys line up and their probation cards are marked. A probation officer of this type depends in his judgment of the child solely on the offense and the uninvestigated remarks made by police officers and parents. If the boy or girl is not arrested again during the probation period and if the parents do not take the trouble of making complaints to the probation officer in court, the case is filed when the "term is up"—and the "probationer" is judged a success. This sounds unbelievably primitive. From what I have seen of the probation work carried on in some of the courts, I am forced to think that this type of probation officer is far more frequent than we like to admit. . . . [2]

Another type of officer is the one who assumes the role of a "parson." His lectures are long and exhaustive but boringly monotonous. Threats in veiled or open form flow in abundance. I know a probation officer of this type who makes practically the same speech to every boy no matter what his offense or problem may be. . . .

Neither of these probation officers is a good listener. The child has no chance to tell his story. The court experience is a mere incident in his life which gains importance only if he gets caught again, as he may be "sent away." Both of these probation officers never leave the courthouse. If any information is brought to them in their office before closing hours, they may use it in court. Their discretion in this matter is unlimited.

The third group consists of probation officers with a touch of technique. They know something about social investigation, and they attempt to supervise by means of house calls and consultations with the attendance officer or even occasionally with the child's teacher. But it is a haphazard affair and lacks the discipline of mind required to build up a diagnosis and plan of treatment.

[1] "The Child on Probation," *Year Book, National Probation Association* (1929), pp. 105–108; see also "Our Relationship with the Child," *Yearbook of the National Probation Association* (1936), pp. 193–208.

[2] See the case of Harold Crane, pp. 440–449.

Next, we meet the "supervisor,"—the probation officer who is conscientious enough to follow the child's conduct in the community but expects him to wage a lone struggle for reconstruction. This probation officer stands aloof and has no relationship with the child. He is eager to be the "watchful eye of the court," but he lacks the vision to recognize his opportunity for constructive work. He is an official with a conscience but no imagination.

On a considerably higher plane moves the social technician. This probation officer knows social case work and practices it so far as his time permits. He views his problems in terms of cases, he is efficient, he diagnoses and plans—but he too, fails to build a relationship with his ward which is the basis of true leadership. He dictates rather than guides. This type is rare. However, we are on the way of increasing the number if we follow the course which social work has taken in so many places. There is a large number of social workers who are efficient and well trained case workers but are lacking in vision, independent judgment, humility, real sympathy and a sense of humor, all of which should permeate their work. Social workers of this type never achieve the kind of understanding which is the essence of any worthwhile human relationship. The emphasis placed on technique by some of our schools of social work is largely responsible for this situation. . . .

The highest type we meet is the probation officer who is a leader in the work with maladjusted boys or girls. His idea of probation work will move along lines of constructive social case work. If he exists at all, it still remains to be seen how near he comes to the requirements set forth. "It takes unusual insight and imagination to realize the human forces with which the probation officer deals. He has the two-fold task of discovering human forces and of directing them into the conquest of delinquency. Probation officers should have the requisite education, training and experience. There is no excuse for their not knowing the elements of biology, psychology, sociology and the facts of mental hygiene. They should be social physicians. Their attitude should be that of the social worker who builds up social relationships. They should have respect for the worth, dignity and integrity of human personality. They should use knowledge, not force, in the solution of their problems. They should believe in miracles. Daily miracles of the reconstruction of broken human lives."[1]

Probation is being increasingly criticized by the public. It is commonly considered a merciful gesture of a benevolent judge who "gives the poor kid a chance"—to go on. What a fair, real chance means in an individual case, neither the judge nor parents seem concerned with.

[1] Quoted from Dr. Miriam Van Waters: "Knowledge versus Force," *Proceedings of the National Probation Association*, 1923.

The public is right if court and probation officers fail to do a real piece of work. As it is—how can the layman conceive that probation does not run against the interests of a civilized community, but expresses its highest ideals?—how can the man of the street be made to see that probation is the most hopeful way out of delinquency and crime? If we care to safeguard this most modern of methods in criminology, it is our duty to condemn unhesitatingly the work of the large majority of probation officers of today who are merely holding jobs in public office. Their presence is directly and indirectly harmful to the work with the individual child as well as to the progress of the work in general. Unless we take a firm stand in this matter, we shall never see the day when probation work as we understand it will be carried out on a large scale in this country. Not until then shall we be able to evaluate the extent of our success in aiding delinquents to adjust themselves in the community without submitting to the hazards of institutional training.

Function of the Probation Officer.[1]—The probation officer is the most important factor in the probation system. He makes investigations and reports to the court, before sentence, the facts of character, past record, home and social conditions and other important individual and social factors. He also has the supervision of offenders under the terms imposed by the court. He keeps informed as to their conduct by home visits and in other ways, and, by friendly and helpful means, aids them to improve their habits and circumstances. By gradually changing their associations and manner of life, and by securing the cooperation of their families and of other persons, the probation officer brings about results that punishment rarely produces. This assistance has come to be the most important part of probation. . . .

The work of the probation officer is of the most varied character. His task is the reformation of the offender, and he can accomplish it in any way he finds possible without forcibly controlling his actions. This inability to control the activity of the offender, as is done in a correctional institution, determines the first work which a probation officer must do in each case. He must find out and decide whether the individual is suitable for probation. Many delinquent persons are not adapted for such methods of treatment, but require constant oversight and discipline. "Stability of residence and of family connection, a reasonably favorable previous record of behavior, in the case of adults a work record which does not suggest well-developed antisocial tendencies, and a measurable degree of emotional control are among the tests most frequently applied."[2]

[1] Adapted from Fred E. Haynes, *Criminology*, pp. 425–427. Reprinted by permission of McGraw-Hill Book Company, Inc.

[2] FRED R. JOHNSON, *Probation for Juveniles and Adults*, p. 4.

Once the offender has been placed on probation, the second phase of the work of the probation officer begins. The problem is to change the attitude of the probationer—to help change his point of view so that he will look at life in a different way. A scientific technique for the modification of attitudes has not yet been developed. A great deal of information of this sort is in the minds of experienced probation officers, but it has not been definitely formulated for use. Such statements as "by gaining the confidence and friendship of the young man," "through friendly admonition and encouragement," and "by stimulating the probationer's self-respect, ambition and thrift," do not help very much in the making of plans to assist a particular individual to regain the place in a community he has lost, or to reeducate the young person who has had little chance to form character because of unfavorable environment.

The attitude of the individual is largely a product of social contacts. The technique of reformation consists chiefly in changing or enlarging the group relations of the probationer. Either the probation officer, or a Big Brother or Big Sister, or a club, settlement, or church must make the probationer feel that he has intimate friends who are interested in him, and that these new friends are more worth while to him than his old associates who led him into trouble. Such a result cannot be brought about by preaching, or threatening, or ordering. Only as one friend helps another in intangible ways can social attitudes be fundamentally altered. The essence of probation is "constructive friendship." The probation officer must cultivate all that is good in the individual and attempt to get rid of the qualities which have gotten him into trouble. Furthermore, he must be familiar with the home environment of his charge. One probation officer said: "When you undertake to make over the average delinquent your work will be one-fourth reforming him and three-fourths reforming his family."

It is evident that the work of the probation officer is personal in its character. Mass probation, like mass education, cannot produce good results. A teacher may lecture to large numbers and a minister may preach to large numbers, but effective teaching and preaching are not accomplished in such ways. Personality must touch personality and numbers dilute the contagious influence that one person can exert upon another. The larger the number of probationers assigned to a single officer the more he must depend upon purely mechanical means, such as formal reports at his office once or twice a month in place of frequent social contacts that would make formal reports unnecessary. No exact limitation of numbers can be estimated, but, on an average, forty or fifty are enough for a single officer. . . . Overloading is only too common. In spite of the saving to the community by the use of probation, it is difficult to get sufficient funds for the support of an adequate staff. An inadequate staff means fewer contacts with probationers. How much can a weekly visit do in outweighing the evil influences which are exerting their forces on the individual day in and day out? The average of a visit a week is probably better than is actually maintained in most places. Is it any wonder that probation fails so frequently? Real probation has very rarely been tried.[1]

Viewing the serious responsibility of workers with youth in our modern life, no prescription for their qualifications can be too long or too exacting. If the prescription does not seem practical at the time or at a given agency limited by funds, legal restrictions, community backwardness, and other restraining forces, it must be remembered that the ideal itself and the process of hitching one's wagon to a star are of value in the formulation of goals. If the prescription seems too weak to some, it must be remembered that in some sections of the country probation is so superficial and inadequate that only a gradual application of rigorous and vitalizing forces can strengthen it. Sheldon Glueck remarks:[2]

We are still in the stage of "extensive agriculture" in the field of probation. Our procedure is still too often wasteful. In too many places, probation work is superficially conducted instead of intensively cultivated. Let us see if we are right in this conclusion.

If we take up *personnel*, it is an indisputable fact that in a good many courts of the United States, probation officers are appointed who have not the slightest technical equipment for their tasks. The fact that a man has a strong urge to help his fellow men is an important qualification for probation work; but it is not the most important. Probation work should consist essentially not of "letting the offender off easy" or of "giving him another chance," but of taking definite steps to help him to avoid misconduct in the future. This means that obstacles in the way of his physical or personality development, or his family situation, or his means of earning an honest living must, if possible, be removed. Now, while we are still far from having evolved a first-rate technique for this work, certain arts have developed that must be utilized by the probation officer if he is to remove the obstacles mentioned. Psychology and mental hygiene have something to contribute, social case work has much to offer, adult education may have a role to

---

[1] EDWIN H. SUTHERLAND, *Criminology*, pp. 573, 576–577; LOUIS N. ROBINSON, *Penology in the United States*, pp. 200–204.

[2] *Probation and Criminal Justice*, pp. 13–15. Reprinted by permission of The Macmillan Company.

play. What these arts have to give in the work of rehabilitation of the offender cannot be ignored; nor is a probation officer born knowing such subjects, however bright and earnest he may be in his work. At the same time, the practical experience with life that some untrained probation officers bring to the job is too valuable to be ignored. Obviously, then, what is needed is a combination of scientific training and maturity of outlook on the problems of life. How can this be brought about?

A sound recommendation seems to be that the probation officers of a metropolitan district, under the guidance of the board of probation or a similar body, arrange for courses in social case work, psychology, and criminology, to be taken by probation officers on two or three afternoons and evenings a week. Training in such subjects should be considered as part of the work of probation officers and additional officers should be appointed to make this possible. Moreover, future candidates for probation work should be required to have had training in these fields, in addition to whatever other pertinent experience they may bring to the work. Only in some such way can probation work be raised to the dignity of a profession. . . .

Provision for such training, and the raising of salaries to a plane commensurate with the dignity and social importance of probation work, are absolutely indispensable if probation is to be stirred out of the stagnation into which it has fallen in many courts of this country. Not careless, thoughtless, wasteful "farmers" are needed in the probation field, but scientific "agriculturists," adequately equipped to do intensive work in the rehabilitation and reeducation of offenders.

"Personality" Plus Education.—We need not concern ourselves here with the question of whether a good social worker is made or born. We assume that an indispensable minimum of desirable personal traits is needed. But the desirable personality traits alone, if training, experience, and education are omitted, are ineffectual in professional work. There should no longer be a question of personality or education. The standard should be personality plus education. Only under these circumstances perhaps can we avoid the indictment that probation fails not only because of lack of understanding on the part of the public, inadequate number of probation officers, unwise selection of probationers, and other factors, but also because the probation staff is "made up of individuals who previously have been undertakers, installment collectors, insurance agents, court attendants, or sign painters,"[1] who bring these varied personali-

[1] FREDERICK A. MORAN, "New Light on the Juvenile Court and Probation," *Year Book, National Probation Association* (1930), p. 70.

ties into the work with problem children but little or no other training and education in technical and scientific fields. In the writer's experience a worker's failure to gain a sound understanding of the total complex situation with all its social implications, leads to more faulty, blundering procedure, hit-or-miss methods of treatment, domineering—at times mannerly disguised as "gentle pressure"—conflict politely suppressed, and a general condition of confusion for both the worker and the client than any other single factor. The medical profession, in setting standards for medical education and practice, would have no conflict of choice between "personality" and "education," as far as the biological physician is concerned. Whether a social or biological physician, he must have professional competence which cannot be attained without considerable education and training. Furthermore, sympathetic insight, an essential quality in the worker, cannot be attained without experience and education. "The work of the probation officer is as important as that of other professions. To be trained for constructive work with offenders against the law requires long and difficult preparation."[1]

An adequately trained personnel is the crying need of most probation departments. Perhaps to some extent this deplorable situation is due to the fact that both executives and workers have for so long relied on "personality" that they have overlooked the other essentials, that is, ability to make a comprehensive social study of the total complex situation involving the offender or problematic child, his family, social setting, community resources; to make a careful diagnosis of the problematic behavior; to carry on a consistent, carefully worked out plan of treatment; and to coordinate his efforts with those of others, whether technicians, social engineers, community organizers, or others.

Someone remarked that "a good probation officer ought to have the skill of a scientist, the devotion of a missionary, and the stomach and health of a Missouri mule," to which might be added: "and the feet and humor of an Irishman."

Some Personal and Social Traits of Child Welfare Workers.— In general the following may be regarded as "desirable" personal and social traits of workers with children: expert knowledge of child nature and child nurture, of the social world in which he lives, and of the larger economic, communal, political, and social

---

[1] CLAYTON J. ETTINGER, *The Problem of Crime*, p. 491.

forces which shape that world and determine to a great extent his destiny; ability to attract people, which depends essentially on the ability to be genuinely interested in their problems, experiences, interests, and desires; ability to see objectively the situation from the other person's standpoint without any prejudice and emotional coloring; ability to carry on teamwork with one's clients and coworkers; cordiality; intellectual honesty; detachment from own problems and resolution of own conflicts.[1] Again we refer to Dr. White's statement that conflict cannot be resolved at the point of conflict.

A child welfare worker needs infinite faith in the favorable outcome of the case once he has decided to enter the situation. Here is a case in point.

Edwin Edwinson, seventeen years of age, intelligent, attached to his parents and parents attached to him, has a serious handicap (palsy). The doctors have told him that he may never be better. He has been operated on several times without results. The boy's attitude is: "I am a burden to myself, parents, and society. Why shouldn't I commit suicide?" The probation officer—who to all appearances has some unsolved problems of his own— agrees that "the best thing is to have the boy dead" and he adds: "But I can't very well encourage him to commit suicide."

A worker must realize that it is not for him to decide on whether such a boy should live or die. The discouragement of the worker is promptly transferred to the boy, even though he is not openly encouraged to suicide. The worker had failed to make a contact with the State Rehabilitation Department, which frequently has some form of occupational therapy and vocational education as well as reeducational devices for various types of handicaps. He had failed to look into such books as The White House Conference on Child Health and Protection, which has a comprehensive report on the physically and mentally handicapped, *The Handicapped Child*, or Marion Hathway, *The Young Cripple and His Job*.

The worker regarded this boy solely as an economic problem. He had overlooked the fact that there was devotion between the parents and the boy. The words of Robert E. Park are in point here: "The community, including the family, with its wider

[1] *Cf.* Pauline V. Young, *Interviewing in Social Work*, p. 255; see also pp. 256–260.

interests, its larger purposes, and its deliberate aims, surrounds us, encloses us, and compels us to conform; not by mere pressure from without, not by the fear of censure merely, but . . . by a sense of responsibility to certain interests not our own."[1]

He had overlooked the fact that new experiments, new inventions, and discoveries are constantly challenging scientific endeavor. He had overlooked the fact that many crippled boys whose conditions in childhood were no more propitious than those of Edwin had been taught to compensate and to accept their handicaps as a challenge and have risen to the fame of Steinmetz, the physicist, Noguchi, the bacteriologist, Michael Dowling, a famous Minneapolis banker (both feet amputated), Estes Snedacor, former president of Rotary International, who has climbed on crutches to Mount Hood.[2] It should be noted that these people were handicapped from childhood and came from homes of modest circumstances.

In other instances workers have frequently displayed this attitude: "What is the use of appealing to the boy's religious beliefs, or asking him to go to church? He is too intelligent to have faith in religion." (For contrary attitudes see pp. 495ff.) The worker can decide for himself whether he wants to follow any religious belief or whether he can or cannot have faith, but he cannot arbitrarily decide such things for children. He must assume that they can be appealed to and if he could only talk convincingly he would impart a significance of spiritual values to them. He cannot perhaps assume the role of spiritual leader but he can arouse interest.

Dr. Van Waters[3] makes the following statement regarding the dignity of probation and the qualities of the probation officer:

The probation officer is dealing with forces and materials as any other scientist or artist deals with them. Only these human forces are difficult to discover because they are so commonplace, so abundant, so deceptively simple that it takes rare human ability to discover the beauty of personality, or to gather scientific data from the everyday stream of life. The probation officer has the two-fold task of discovering human forces and of directing them in the conquest of delinquency. No profession

[1] "Community Organization and Juvenile Delinquency," in ROBERT E. PARK and E. W. BURGESS, *The City*, p. 104.

[2] Statement from Missouri Society for Crippled Children, July 20, 1936.

[3] *Proceedings of the National Probation Association* (1923), pp. 156, 164.

today is more searching or more glorious, for the probation officer is translating the knowledge of experts in human life, the physicians, psychologists, psychiatrists, into action. He is working with the sensitive bodies and minds of individuals. He is the courteous and comprehending friend to whom all may be told without offense and from whom might be expected complete understanding and the wisdom and strength of ideal parenthood.

Dr. E. W. Burgess maintains that the primary requisite of the social investigator is:

a sense for the dramatic in all human life, a sympathy broad enough to encompass the manifold diverse manifestations of human nature, even those that are commonly regarded as shocking or even outrageous.[1]

By a sense of the dramatic, Dr. Burgess means the true artist's ability to assume the role of beggar and king, magnate and ditchdigger, brokenhearted lover, or hermit, or child, and so completely plunge into the life of another that for the time being he *is* the other in imagination if not in body. Complete identification need not mar the intellectual alertness and detachment essential in noting all turns in the situation of another person. Elsewhere Dr. Burgess remarks of the ability to approach children by *empathy* which enables a worker to see their life as they conceive it, rather than as an adult might imagine it. "Empathy means entering into the experience of another person by the human and democratic method of sharing experiences."[2]

Empathy presupposes actual or vicarious experience. If a worker finds limitations of age, race, health, or social level too great to use this human and democratic method of sharing experiences of others, of viewing the child as a child and not as a miniature adult, he should realize that such an inability is a sign that he must either revitalize himself or leave this type of work.

A worker must have a sense of humor, a joy of living, and a "controlled enthusiasm for a demanding task."

William J. Harper,[3] Westchester County Probation Department, lists the following as "desirable qualities, in addition to

---

[1] "Statistics and Case Studies as Methods of Sociological Research," *Sociology and Social Research*, XII (November–December, 1927), 118.

[2] "Discussion," in CLIFFORD R. SHAW, *The Jack-Roller*, pp. 194–195

[3] Mimeographed.

training and experience," in probation officers but these qualities are equally applicable to other kinds of social workers:

a. Probation Officer should be in good physical health.

b. Probation Officer should maintain an impersonal attitude. He must be sympathetic, tolerant and try to understand the delinquent's needs and capacities, but must not let his personal prejudices and beliefs come into play.

c. Probation Officer should be a keen observer.

d. According to E. J. Cooley, the good probation officer must

   1. Avoid too close supervision; must not "hound the probationer."

   2. Avoid impatience with relapses. Allow certain amount of trial and error in the difficult process of adjustment.

   3. Avoid subtle antagonisms. Must not let inability to make progress cause him to be antagonistic to his charge.

   4. Avoid mere objective case work. The probation officer shall not be satisfied with mere objective, external improvement of employment, home life, etc. He should "tap the central springs"— effect an adjustment from within that will be permanent.

e. Good probation officer must divest himself of the acquiescent attitude toward commercialized amusements, unhealthy living conditions and other forces which work toward predisposition to delinquency and adverse behavior patterns.

f. Arouse interest of the public in probation, its aims, purposes, and accomplishments and thus enlist their aid and support.

g. He shall consider himself a *Social Worker* and aim toward cooperation with other public and private organizations and societies in the effort to bring all the resources to the offender.

h. He shall realize that every case requires exhaustive, careful diagnosis and plan of probationary treatment, sufficiently individualized to needs and capacities of the offender.

i. By attending lectures, conferences of difficult cases, etc., probation officer shall keep abreast of the times and be fully aware of present doings, the contributions of the various sciences as psychology, criminology, penology and other sciences that have a bearing—direct or indirect—on probation work.

Problems of Probation Officers.—There are many problems which the probation officer faces which preclude his maintenance of such standards as outlined above: his case load is too heavy; he has too many responsibilities—clerical, preprobation, and others—which consume a great deal of his time; he loses many hours each week while waiting for his cases to be heard; his efforts are vitiated by the decisions of a judge who is not a case worker, who is unacquainted with the roots of social knowledge, and who carries over into the juvenile court punitive theories of justice.[1] There is lack of adequate cooperation between social agencies; "probation has had a slow growth because of hostile public opinion"; the court is held up to the child as "a stick" and he is threatened with an "officer of the law," which destroys confidence and rapport; the judge is either too lenient or too strict and creates conflicts between parents and children and the officer; the officer is also overworked and underpaid and cannot take advantage of professional courses and of "keeping up to date with new literature in the field." Such problems are of a difficult administrative nature and are beyond the scope of a treatise on case work. This additional suggestion may, however, be offered to the overburdened worker, that is to say, one who carries more than fifty or sixty cases: select one or two or three of the most serious cases each week which need careful attention and supervision and do a thoroughgoing piece of work on those while the others are carried as adequately and conscientiously as possible. Many workers in several counties in California have tried this procedure and found that they were able to expedite matters on the most serious cases and not delay study or treatment on the rest of the cases. In the long run they were able to dismiss the more serious cases, which received intensive attention, much sooner than others, and thus slowly lightened their load. This procedure needs, however, more study before positive results can be claimed for it.

WHAT CONSTITUTES ADEQUATE CASE PROCEDURE?

This question is one of the most difficult to answer and yet it is one of the most frequently asked by both case worker and case supervisor. The difficulty lies in the fact that case work procedure is intimately associated with case work processes, which are related to complex life processes, and these do not lend themselves easily to analysis and to testing. Furthermore, we have

[1] *Cf.* Francis H. Hiller, "The Juvenile Court as a Case Working Agency," *Proceedings of the National Conference of Social Work* (1926), p. 143; see also Charles L. Chute, "Probation in a Community Welfare Program," *Proceedings of the National Conference of Social Work* (1933), pp. 136–145.

devised as yet no satisfactory criteria for testing the adequacy of case work. Too little research has been done on "what works" and "what doesn't work" and "why" and "why not" under varying conditions of life and varying circumstances of case work. Miss Richmond observed a long time ago that "interviews which have covered every item of past history and present situation with accuracy and care can be total failures."[1]

The following is from a *Report of the Committee on Case Recording* on some "Tests to Be Applied to Case Histories":[2]

a. First Interview
1. Is the family's confidence gained?
2. Are the family needs definitely indicated?
3. Are further sources of information given? (Relatives, employers, schools, doctors, public records, other agencies, previous addresses, etc.)
4. Is the family's own plan and point of view secured?

b. Collateral Investigation
1. Have all clues indicated in the first interview been followed?
2. Have other sources of information been revealed?
3. What is the net result of each interview with the further sources?
4. Was full and satisfactory information secured?

c. Problems
1. What are the problems or the opportunities for service indicated by the complete investigation?

d. Plan
1. What is the plan outlined to meet these problems? Is adequate provision made for family's (a) budget, (b) health, (c) religious life, (d) recreation, (e) friendly association, (f) supervision?

e. Cooperation
1. Was the case cleared with the confidential exchange?
2. Were all other agencies on it consulted in the formulation of the plan?
3. Was co-operation secured from (a) family, (b) other sources—relatives, employers, etc.?

In addition to the above the following is offered tentatively as a test of case work procedure:

a. What opportunities have been created for understanding of problem?

b. What concrete ways and means have been developed for change, elimination, or adjustment of problem?

c. What opportunities have been provided by worker for understanding of problem by client?

[1] MARY RICHMOND, *Social Diagnosis*, p. 130.
[2] Adapted from *Report of Committee on Case Recording*, p. 30.

d. What use has been made of community resources, of other social agencies?

e. What changes have occurred in outlook of client since contact with agency? (Not only an account of the actual state of affairs but also the reaction that counts.)

f. What has case worker done to create or restore self-respect in client?

g. What has case worker done to change attitude of various members of family toward each other?

h. How has case worker provided for "spiritual" growth and development of a social consciousness in client?

i. How has case worker changed client's attitude toward others, the community, the agency?

j. How workable is the plan of treatment?

The Work of the Case Supervisor.—At the present stage of development of the work with delinquent and problem youth it is not advisable to go beyond the enumeration of some of the aids or skills in the mechanics of social case work with children.[1] E. A. Francis of the Los Angeles County Probation Department[2] states that in reviewing cases under supervision by a probation officer, the director of supervision checks whether the following instruments and papers are included in the case histories: (*a*) the petition setting forth the reason for bringing the juvenile before the court; (*b*) police report giving detailed facts concerning the offense committed; (*c*) clinical reports; (*d*) probation officer's report; (*e*) chronological history of the case; (*f*) records of court orders; (*g*) miscellaneous records, such as birth certificates, school reports, letter reports, interagency correspondence, and so on.

In reading the case history carefully the director of supervision tries to ascertain whether the alleged reasons which bring the child before the court have been not only recorded but understood by the worker; whether the family background, the present home, school, and work situations have received sufficient attention; whether the worker is carrying out the plan recommended by the clinic, and if not, why not.

[1] See *Supervision: Philosophy and Method; Worker and Supervisor*, reprints of articles from *The Family*.

[2] Excerpts from manuscript especially prepared for this volume (June, 1936).

Regarding the specific orders of the court the following should be checked, says Mr. Francis:

Are court orders being followed?

a. Is the juvenile in the custody of the person as ordered by the court?

b. Is he complying with instructions given him by the court and the probation officer?

c. Is he making restitution to the victim as ordered?

d. Is he attending Traffic School, if ordered to do so?

e. Are special orders such as obtaining membership in character-building organizations, etc., being carried out?

Relative to the supervision given by the worker the following should be checked: Are regular contacts with the juvenile being made by the officer? Is a written report made by the supervising officer on all cases under his supervision at regular intervals? Are the suggestions of the director of supervision carried out; if not, why not? When the boy is placed in a foster home, is he being visited at regular intervals by the worker?

A statement on the work of the girls' supervisor by Miss Helen Stover, of the Los Angeles County Probation Department,[1] supplements the above statement:

The worker makes a plan for each girl on the basis of her particular need and the problem which brought her to Court. This is presented to the Court. The court suggests corrective measures and gives definite orders as to treatment. These orders embrace physical care, recreation, school placement, companions, environment, etc. The family also receives definite instruction. The worker is to help the child and the family to carry out these orders or instructions and to make periodic reports to the Court on the progress or failure of these plans. In the relationship built up between the worker and the entire family comes the breaking down of antagonisms, the changing of attitudes, the gradual building up of a family and the fitting of a child into her home, school and community—this is the case work aim of the Probation Department. The worker is supposed to make a record of her contacts with the family, and the success or failure of the plan for the child, etc. This is what is known as the record of supervision.

The supervisor checks all cases, reviewing the physical, social and mental findings. She checks the Court orders and plans and reads the worker's supervision record to see if the orders have been carried out,

[1] Excerpts from manuscript especially prepared for this volume (June, 1936).

if the plan as outlined at the time of the Court hearing is working satisfactorily, and what progress has been made in adjustment. If matters are not progressing she suggests substitute plans. Finding out just what has been accomplished by the worker is often the particular problem with which the reviewer is faced, as the worker sometimes fails to record her work and the change in family attitudes or does it so sketchily that little can be gathered from it. During the time of review a running commentary is made on the Ediphone by the case supervisor to each district supervisor, calling attention to the Court orders unfulfilled, plans not adhered to, asking questions regarding family situations, etc., suggesting new plans, termination of cases, etc. The district supervisor takes up each point commented upon by the reviewer with the worker handling the case, and tries to see that the suggestions are carried out, and the omissions corrected. The district supervisor in turn replies to the reviewer on each point mentioned. In many cases a conference is held with the case supervisor, the district supervisor and the worker. Difficult cases are talked over in conference before the Court hearing, by the worker, district supervisor and reviewer, and the case supervisor helps in formulating a general plan. All cases in which boarding home or institutional placement is indicated are talked over with the case supervisor before the Court hearing.

Where children are removed from their own homes and placed in boarding homes or institutions, the problem becomes one of rebuilding the home to receive the child and adjusting the child in a new environment, and at the same time being careful not to sever completely the parent-child relationship. In placement cases, the Court orders are usually quite specific, in regard to the family, the locating of a parent or relatives. In such cases the reviewer has to remember to check on the adjustment and growth of the child in its new setting, the progress of the family toward a rehabilitation that will again admit the child into its own home and the specific Court orders regarding other possible placements. These cases require more frequent conferences and reviews and constitute two-thirds of the case supervisor's work.

The case supervisor also reads the new petitions as they are filed and gets a brief picture of the case before it ever reaches the worker. This is for the purpose of being familiar with the child's name and problem as given by the petitioner and able to answer questions from the agencies, parents and relatives regarding detention, Court hearing, etc. All such inquiries go over the case supervisor's desk when the worker is out. This also gives the case supervisor a more comprehensive idea of the problem when the worker arrives to confer with her on it. As a matter of interest it is surprising to note the difference in the problems many times as revealed by the investigation of the worker and that stated by the petitioner. The case supervisor also checks the Court's rough

PERSONNEL RATING CARD—SOCIAL CASE WORKER

Form A—For analyzing and rating caseworker's ability. (Rate by checking in one of the three groups for each question.)
Designed by Erle Fiske Young, Ph. D., School of Social Work, University of Southern California

Name of Worker...
Agency or District...
Date of Rating...

	Low	Med.	High			Low	Med.	High
I. Skill in Social Case Work					*b.* Make diagnosis at earliest feasible time..			
A. Skill in investigation:								
1. To what extent does the worker—					*c.* Make new diagnosis when necessary.......			
a. Secure information essential to accurate diagnosis............					2. To what extent does the worker—			
b. Use the best available sources of information					*a.* Use diagnostic concepts accurately......			
c. Make all necessary verifications..........					*b.* Entertain wide range of hypotheses........			
d. "Follow through" investigations promptly					*c.* Differentiate individuals, families, and communities accurately...			
2. In dealing with persons to what extent does the worker—					*d.* Use scientific findings in case work........			
a. Gain their confidence.					3. In the application of case logic, to what extent does the worker—			
b. Get their point of view								
c. Discover their plans and purposes........					*a.* Grasp causal connections of data........			
d. Deal tactfully with difficult situations and personalities........					*b.* Recognize critical points in the case.....			
3. To what extent does the worker anticipate probable future conditions...					*c.* Grasp the significance of clues and symptoms			
B. Skill in case diagnosis and prognosis:					4. Does the worker correctly evaluate own bias and prejudice..........			
1. To what extent does the worker—					5. Does the worker have a grasp of general principles of case work.......			
a. Defer judgment until data necessary for accurate diagnosis are secured.............								

Personnel Rating Card—Social Case Worker.—(*Continued*)

	Low	Med.	High		Low	Med.	High
C. Skill in planning treatment:				(1) Inspire self-confidence in them.....			
1. In formulating a plan, to what extent do the plans —				(2) "Sell" the plan to them............			
a. Grow out of the nature of the case..........				(3) Secure their co-operation..........			
b. Take account of the potentialities of the individual or family and the resources of the community..........				(4) Develop their powers..............			
c. Anticipate the probable future of the case..				b. Effectively organize the community resources—			
2. In fitting the plan to the case, to what extent does the worker—				(1) Secure the co-operation of relatives and family friends			
a. Formulate definite procedure for each case...				(2) Use the local or neighborhood forces...........			
b. Change plans as the situation demands....				(3) Make proper use of legal remedies..			
c. Make alternate plans.				(4) Enlist the services of other social agencies, private and public........			
D. Skill in administering case treatment:				(5) Develop new resources..........			
1. To what extent does the worker—				(6) Use each resource to best advantage.			
a. Vary the treatment to suit the case........							
b. Maintain consistent policies in dealing with case problems........				Summary Rating..........			
c. Sense the success or failure of plans.......					Low	Med.	High
d. Follow cases through to the end...........				II. Skill in the Mechanics of Case Work			
e. Close the case at the proper time..........				A. Skill in interviewing:			
2. To what extent does the worker—				1. To what extent does the worker—			
a. Effectively organize the resources of the family or the individual treated—				a. Approach persons to be interviewed naturally..............			
				b. Control the course of the interview........			

PERSONNEL RATING CARD—SOCIAL CASE WORKER.—(*Continued*)

	Low	Med.	High		Low	Med.	High
c. Release any inhibitions of the persons interviewed..........				*b.* Write readable, informing reports......			
d. Vary interviewing methods to suit situation.................				*c.* Use local color properly			
				d. Organize the case history..............			
e. Prepare the way for continued contact....				*e.* Use facilitating devices correctly.......			
B. Observational skill:				*f.* Keep records up-to-date...............			
1. To what extent does the worker—				F. Skill in organization work:			
a. Make accurate observations...........				1. To what extent does the worker—			
b. Develop a retentive memory for case data.				*a.* Systematize his work.			
c. React readily to case clues................				*b.* Master details of work			
C. Skill in the use of documents:				*c.* Devise work methods.			
1. To what extent does the worker—				*d.* Correctly apportion his time............			
a. Use the public and private records consistently.............				*e.* Maintain a steady output of work.........			
b. Correctly use personal documents and letters				Summary Rating..........			
c. Get accurate impressions from written material.............					Low	Med.	High
D. Skill in correspondence:							
1. To what extent does the worker—				III. Maintaining Professional Attitudes			
a. Write clear, concise letters...............				A. Team-work abilities:			
b. Write readable, interesting, effective letters				1. To what extent does the worker—			
c. Observe courtesies in correspondence.......				*a.* Contribute to the "esprit de corps" of the agency..........			
E. Skill in report writing:				*b.* Maintain loyalty to the purposes of the agency..............			
1. To what extent does the worker—				*c.* Submit to the discipline of the agency...			
a. Write clear, concise English..............				*d.* Maintain cordial and generous attitudes towards colleagues and helpers..............			
				e. Observe professional confidences.........			

PERSONNEL RATING CARD—SOCIAL CASE WORKER.—(*Continued*)

	Low	Med.	High
f. Participate in the life of the community....			
g. Assume responsibilities willingly.........			
B. Ability to grow and keep up-to-date:			
1. To what extent does the worker—			
a. Enter into professional conferences..........			
b. Maintain contact with the development of the underlying sciences...			
c. Profit by own experience and that of others			
d. Take part in the development of the field			
e. Sustain interest in case work...............			
f. Keep in contact with changing social conditions in the field......			
g. Acquire new methods of work.............			
h. Maintain interest in other fields.........			
C. Ability to maintain professional bearing:			
1. To what extent does the worker—			
a. Work successfully under stress.........			
b. Control personal conduct according to professional standards...			
c. Place a proper value upon social case work in relation to other professional work.....			
Summary Rating.........			

	Low	Med.	High
IV. Acquiring and Using Professional Equipment			
To what extent does the worker—			
1. Use English effectively..			
2. Use necessary foreign languages.............			
3. Deal effectively with legal aspects of case work			
4. Deal effectively with health problems........			
5. Teach when the work requires................			
6. Successfully handle recreational problems.....			
7. Adapt methods to local conditions............			
8. Adapt methods to the social background of families and persons....			
9. Undertake only those tasks for which he is the best qualified available person...............			
Summary Rating.........			

	Low	Med.	High
V. Personal and Social Qualities			
To what extent does the worker—			
1. Maintain high personal standards.............			
2. Recognize the importance of neatness in dress and personal appearance			
3. Display "fine-grained" attitudes (*i.e.*, be sensitive to social proprieties).................			
4. Act tactfully in dealing with colleagues and patrons................			

PERSONNEL RATING CARD—SOCIAL CASE WORKER.—(*Continued*)

	Low	Med.	High		Low	Med.	High
5. Act effectively aggressive in conversation and conference				7. Show courage and enthusiasm..............			
				8. Maintain an effective personal and social philosophy.............			
6. Attract people (*i.e.*, be interested primarily in what others are doing)..				Summary Rating.........			

minutes as they come each day, thus catching at once the Court order and asking for a post-Court conference on any matter which had previously been discussed. In short, the case supervisor tries to keep a finger on the pulse of every girl's case that comes into the department and in so doing has a close contact with the worker and district supervisor.

Since adequate case work depends so largely upon the adequacy of the case worker it is in point to examine his abilities and qualities in this connection. Erle F. Young's "Personnel Rating Card—Social Case Worker" is an aid in analyzing and rating case workers' ability.

The above rating card (pages 484–488) is not to be self-administered. Experience shows that the conscientious worker tends to underrate himself, while others tend to overrate themselves. The director who knows the workers well can use these cards to best advantage.

SUMMARY OF CERTAIN PRINCIPLES IN INTERVIEWING[1]

Skillful interviewing does not depend upon rules and maxims, but a knowledge of certain principles found helpful by a large number of interviewers may provide some suggestions which can be utilized in a large number of cases:

I. Preparation for the Interview:
    1. Understand why the interview is held.
    2. Be prepared to be viewed by the interviewee and to answer any questions he may wish to ask.
    3. Gather all possible clues and concentrate on each one to see which might be best utilized toward a successful approach to the interviewee.

[1] YOUNG, *op. cit.*, pp. 86–89. Reprinted by permission of McGraw-Hill Book Company, Inc. See also Chaps. III, IV.

4. If time is limited and problems are pressing formulate tentative objectives for your interview or chart its course as far as possible.

5. Keep in mind the unique problems of each case and relate them to the total social situation in which the interviewee finds himself, as far as is possible under the circumstances.

6. "Size up" your interviewee from whatever clues you may possess, but keep your mind flexible when you are in contact with the interviewee.

7. Make appointments whenever possible, thus showing respect for the client's time.

8. Provide privacy, comfort, and agreeable surroundings.

9. Be modestly and suitably dressed for each occasion.

10. Introduce yourself to the interviewee, explain the function of the agency you represent, and state briefly the purpose of visit.

11. Extend cordial greetings.

12. Observe conventionalities of the interviewee's home and social group.

II. The Interview Proper:

13. Show interest in everything the interviewee wishes to tell you. Make the interview "his moment."

14. Be at ease with the interviewee, thus helping him to be at ease with you.

15. Adopt a leisurely pace to give the interviewee the feeling that you consider his situation seriously.

16. Allow sufficient time to learn the facts which will enable you to understand the problems involved.

17. View all problems confronting the interviewee from his point of view.

18. Make suitable allowances for your preconceived notions about his problems, for your biases and prejudices.

19. Meet the interviewee on his own terms.

20. Gain, keep, and deserve the interviewee's confidence.

21. Identify yourself with the interviewee through similar experiences, points of view, mutual likes or dislikes.

22. Gain sympathetic insight into problems confronting the interviewee.

23. Assign social status to the interviewee, remembering that status is one of his most priceless possessions.

24. Ask only questions which you would not resent answering about yourself under similar circumstances.

25. Ask questions which are easily understood.

26. Ask questions which do not imply their answers.

27. Take care not to sound insinuating or impertinent.
28. In asking questions be frank and straightforward rather than cunning.
29. Avoid "getting around" the interviewee or extracting information against his will or knowledge.
30. Allow the interviewee to tell his story in his own way and to take his time in telling it.
31. Allow the interviewee to think for himself and give him time to think his situation through.
32. "Make your minds meet"; that is, be sure that you understand what the interviewee says, what he wants and what his culture complexes are and he yours.
33. Listen with interest.
34. Follow up every important clue of interest to the interviewee.
35. Seek to understand source, cultural setting, and development of the interviewee's behavior patterns.
36. Meet objections in a way which is satisfying to the interviewee.
37. Avoid ordering-and-forbidding techniques.
38. Allow for face-saving.
39. Lessen tensions by assigning status, by soliciting help, by complimenting good performance, etc.

III. Controlling the Interview:

40. Check story in your own mind to see if there are any inconsistencies.
41. Deal with inconsistencies as misunderstandings.
42. Remember the saying that the truth is told to friends and lies to enemies.
43. Eliminate opportunities which an interviewee might seize upon to deceive you.
44. If you sense that an interviewee is going to falsify start out by stating the facts of the case as far as they are known to you.

IV. Closing the Interview:

45. Close the interview before you have worn out your welcome.
46. Close the interview when the interviewee is at ease emotionally.
47. Close the interview when the interviewee has caught the desire to manage his own affairs.
48. If subsequent interviews are necessary close when you still have something important to talk about.
49. At the close of the interview ask if there is anything else the interviewee wishes to talk about. "What else would you care to tell me?" "What didn't we touch on?"
50. Test the success of your interviews.

Selected Bibliography

1. ELIOT, THOMAS D.: "Welfare Agencies, Special Education, and the Courts," *American Journal of Sociology*, XXX (July, 1925), 58–78.
2. HAGERTY, JAMES E.: *The Training of Social Workers*, McGraw-Hill Book Company, Inc., 1931.
3. KAHN, DOROTHY S.: "Professional Standards in Social Work," *The Compass*, XVI (June, 1935), 1–5.
4. KARPF, M. J.: *The Scientific Basis of Social Work*, Part IV, Columbia University Press, 1931.
5. NORTON, PARKER L.: "A Probation Officer Comes Up for Air," *Survey*, LXIX (June, 1933), 215–216.
6. TUFTS, JAMES H.: *Education and Training for Social Work*, Russell Sage Foundation, 1923.
7. WALKER, SYDNOR H.: *Social Work and Training of Social Workers*, University of North Carolina Press, 1928.
8. WEISS, HANS: "The Child on Probation," *Year Book, National Probation Association* (1929), pp. 105–108.
9. YOUNG, ERLE F.: *Personnel Rating Card*, Western Educational Service, 1927.
*10. YOUNG, PAULINE V.: *Interviewing in Social Work*, "Personality Traits of Interviewers," pp. 255–260.

Suggestions for Further Study

1. Write a brief critique of Mr. Weiss's discussion of types of probation officers. Make your own classification of probation officers.

2. What are the difficulties in the development of "higher types" of officers? What is a "high type"? What is the relation between the type of officers and the nature and equipment of probation departments?

3. Why does not "personality" alone suffice? "training" alone?

4. Make a list of personal and social traits of probation officers and other child welfare workers which would be of greatest value in your community; in your agency.

5. What are the problems of child welfare workers in your community?

6. What constitutes adequate case procedure in your community?

7. What should the standards be?

8. Is it advisable to develop tests to be applied to case histories? to interviews?

9. What is the work of a supervisor in a private child welfare agency? in public nonlegal agency? in a probation department?

10. What is the relation between case supervision and case study? case diagnosis and treatment?

11. Read Parker Norton's article, "A Probation Officer Comes Up for Air," *Survey*, LXIX (June, 1933), 215–216. How do you account for his statement?

12. What are the bases for the selection of probation officers?

13. What are the methods of appointment of probation officers?

14. In what sense is "probation what the officer makes it"?

15. Read Grace Abbott, "Case Work Responsibility of Juvenile Courts," *Proceedings of the National Conference of Social Work* (1929), pp. 153–162, and indicate why and what is the case work responsibility of juvenile courts? What philosophy underlies Miss Abbott's thinking on this subject? How has her philosophy changed (see *Survey*, May 15, 1936, 131–133)?

16. What is meant by the statement that "it is pathetic to witness the childlike simplicity that most of us still have in the enactment of laws to solve social problems"? How does the presence or the absence of this "simplicity" affect the probation officer? (See Frederick A. Moran, "New Light on the Juvenile Court and Probation," *Year Book, National Probation Association* [1930], p. 73.)

17. What is meant by "the legalistic attitude"? How does it affect the probation officer? the child?

18. Compare the problems faced by the juvenile court discussed by Mr. Moran with those existing in the court of your community.

19. Read Francis H. Hiller, "The Juvenile Court as a Case Working Agency: Its limitations and Its Possibilities," *Proceeding of the National Conference of Social Work* (1926), pp. 142–148. What limitations hinder the juvenile court from becoming a case working agency? To what extent are these limitations true of any public agency?

20. What constitutes the trial judge's dilemma, according to Professor Sellin? to Judge Ulman? In what respects do these views differ? See Sheldon Glueck (Editor), *Probation and Criminal Justice*, pp. 99–132.

PART IV

UTILIZATION OF COMMUNITY RESOURCES IN THE WORK WITH UNADJUSTED YOUTH AND PARENTS

. . . the trained man understands how little the mind of any individual may grasp, and how many must cooperate in order to [accomplish] . . . things.—HANS GROSS

CHAPTER XXIII

THE ROLE OF ORGANIZED RELIGION IN THE ADJUSTMENT OF DELINQUENT AND PROBLEM YOUTH

Social case workers—because of the nature of their work with separate units—largely emphasize the role which the individual and familial factors play in unadjustment. It is these factors over which they have exhibited some degree of control. One can "take hold of a boy" or his parents, bring them to court, work out plans for or with them, hold them accountable for what happens, write up reports on their situations and their behavior. There is, therefore, a constant tendency to forget that the unadjustment with which we are dealing is a lack of adjustment involving both a person and a community and that either or both may be unadjusted. We have already noted on several occasions that delinquent behavior of the child may be a natural, that is, an expected, response to the social environment in which he lives. That environment may itself be so badly disorganized that delinquency in a given community has become almost universal—a folkway of long standing. Erle F. Young writes:[1]

The worker needs, therefore, to give full weight to such phenomena as the moral atmosphere of the neighborhood and of its institutions, of the social class and occupational group to which the family belongs, the permitted and expected personal behavior in the status-conferring groups of which the child and his family are members or into which they are seeking to secure admission. The worker should also remember that frequently the child's apprehension as a delinquent can be explained as simply the spasmodic working of formalized controls which themselves do not represent the spirit of the times. Delinquency under these conditions of social chaos is symptomatic, not of personal, but of social and communal disorganization.

Case work in such times loses its bearing. Since its primary function is to adjust personalities to the communities and groups in which they live, that function becomes an abstraction when the social order itself

[1] Manuscript.

comes into a state of flux and ceases to be an adequate frame of reference for personal organization. Under these circumstances before case work could be effective it would be under the necessity of setting the community in order—but that is community organization and not case work—or it would need to develop in its clients new personalities capable of taking critical attitudes toward the society in which they live and motivated and trained to undertake its reorganization—but that is the function of education and not of social case work.

In short, case workers must need be cognizant of the limitations of their techniques. They must frankly face the fact that they cannot correct by case work a considerable number of the cases of delinquency which come to their hands.

If case workers are not to provide mere amelioratives, custodial care or other purely symptomatic treatment, they must canvass thoroughly and understand the possibilities and limitations of the various communal resources and social institutions capable of exerting a wholesome influence on the young and their homes. But the case worker can also not only enlist the intelligent cooperation of the church, school, playground, industry, coordinating council, governmental agencies in his work with unadjusted youth, but he can supply them with the concrete data of the effects of the breakdown of these organizations or their negligence in dealing with the problems of the community which contribute to delinquency.

THE CHURCH AND DELINQUENCY

Few studies have been made on the effect of religious training on offenders. John Miner, in his study of "Church Membership and Commitment to Prisons,"[1] indicates that fewer people who maintain membership in churches are committed to prison than those who are not members. E. W. Burgess reports that the Committee on the Workings of the Indeterminate-Sentence Law and Parole in Illinois found that "only a small fraction of the inmates had been regular in attendance prior to commitment. . . . " The Reverend J. H. Ryan, the Protestant chaplain at Pontiac, in an interesting and detailed study, found that of a group of 1,000 youths questioned only 90 had been attending religious services, 689 had at one time attended but had left the

[1] *Human Biology*, III (September, 1931), 429–436.

church, and that the others, numbering 146, had been very irregular in attendance, while 75 had never attended any services.[1]

The question may be raised as to the proportion of youths in the general population who are attending church regularly, irregularly, or not at all. Control groups are needed in making such comparisons. Elio D. Monachesi, in his exhaustive study of *Prediction Factors in Probation* (see p. 620), found that "individuals who do not attend church are poor probation risks. In this day very little influence is ascribed to the church in determining conduct. Perhaps this may be an under-estimation and religion may be a significant factor in the lives of a great number of people."[2]

Sutherland observes with regard to adult offenders:

In America the Baptists and the Catholics have the highest rate of commitment to those prisons which report religious affiliations. This is apparently explained by the fact that most of the Negroes are Baptists and most of the families of recent immigrants are Catholics. Similarly, an intensive analysis of the differences in crime rate of the several denominations in Hungary resulted in the conclusions that these differences were due not to the differences in the creeds, but to the differences in the economic, educational, and family status of the members, to the differences in places of residence, and to the differences in age and sex.[3]

The question may also be raised as to the activities of the church in relation to delinquents who have no religious affiliation or who, though affiliated, are not "touched by religion" at all. Have the nonchurchgoing delinquents and the church parted ways[4] until the former find their way into correctional institutions where "church attendance is compulsory"? Of course, it should be clear that a religious organization cannot "poke religion down their throats," if they do not desire its teaching. But again the question arises why has religion—a most potent force in the life

[1] "Factors Making for Success or Failure on Parole," *Parole and the Indeterminate Sentence*, p. 233.

[2] P. 40.

[3] ERVIN HACKER, *Der Einfluss der Konfession auf die Kriminalität in Ungarn*, quoted from Edwin H. Sutherland, *Principles of Criminology*, pp. 176–177.

[4] See FRANCIS D. McCABE, "Church Participation in a Probation Program," *Year Book, National Probation Association* (1935), p. 189.

of our fathers and forefathers—ceased to have influence on so large a proportion of young people?

Dr. Van Waters[1] shows keen insight into the problems of youth in their relation to the church:

Today the some two hundred thousand delinquent boys and girls in correctional schools, hundreds of thousands before courts and social agencies, know little about religion, art, and science. The young people in dance-halls, cabarets, resorts, millions who throng city streets in a ceaseless, unhappy quest for "something to do" have certainly not been reached by any valid adventure of the spirit.

The social worker hesitates to criticize the church, but viewing prisons, hospitals, reformatories and courts, with one's ears echoing stories of drab lives, unlit by warmth of any genuine religious experience, children whose hearts have never beat faster for the mystic presence of any spiritual being, youths by hundreds who believe in nothing, know nothing of the feeling of an enlarged, creative power except that which may somehow come to them from their luck charms, "hunches," and innumerable modern idols and fetishes; the social worker seeing all this and knowing that to these half-starved, bewildered young spirits the least drop of living water would be as a miracle, questions whether it is essential for churchmen to busy themselves with talk of Fundamentalism versus Modernism. If clergymen cannot awaken youth to faith, humility, and gratitude, or quicken his enthusiasm for life beyond himself, the church cannot cope with delinquency. Doubtless the modern church is reaching many young people with its classes, organizations, brotherhoods and sisterhoods; one cannot praise too highly the work of some of its protective bureaus and committees.

This proves that the church is concerned for the welfare of erring youth, but it is church turned social worker. Social activities within the church do not fulfill the whole need, nor supply authentic spiritual leadership. In spite of friendly visitors, campaigns, drives and educational movies in churches, it is evident that lives of the young delinquents have been left singularly untouched by religion. Not only are juvenile court boys and girls ignorant for the most part of the history of religion, its dogmas, creeds and ritual, but its literature, festivals, its great personalities, its warm and vivid experiences are unknown. If you ask: "What saying of a clergyman has most impressed you?" the average young delinquent stares and is blankly unable to answer anything at all. Nor is this state of affairs due to callousness, or stupidity on the part of youth. The fact is they have not heard anything from

[1] *Youth in Conflict*, pp. 140–141. Reprinted by permission of New Republic, Inc.

the church that is memorable, moving, soul-stirring or liberating in all their lives. The social worker does not question that there exist religious personalities today who are capable of uttering truths precious to youth; the pity is that the vocabulary is either too technical, or the isolation too complete. They fail to make connection with ideas and emotions of the young who are to become delinquent.

Religion does not flow from the church into the community in which the young delinquent moves, hence the church has no authoritative voice in those social standards which are today most powerfully in conflict with the moral code.

Dr. Francis D. McCabe, Director of Probation, State of Indiana, has made a searching study into "Church Participation in a Probation Program,"[1] and brings together findings from the existing literature on the subject from addresses by leaders and churchmen, and from his own probation staff. We quote his critical statement in part:[2]

The modern Nathans who have the courage to say to the modern Davids, "Thou art the man," are so few in number that they are a negligible quantity. Please understand me, I am not bringing an indictment against the clergy. No finer, nobler, more honest, intelligent, consecrated men can be found in any profession. The indictment is against the system that enables the well-to-do sinners in the pew to circumscribe the work of the prophet of God with a threat to cut off support, if he offend them in the slightest degree.

The failure of the churches, generally, to cooperate in delinquency prevention programs is so widespread that Katherine F. Lenroot, Chief of the United States Children's Bureau, took cognizance of it, in a recent address when she said, "Instances in which probation officers have been definitely handicapped in attempting to work out a program for a child who has been before a juvenile court, or in an institution for juvenile delinquents, because of a narrow or prejudiced attitude of the Church itself toward such children, might be cited. The primary function of the Church is to assist people in developing a sound spiritual and philosophical basis for life and a sense of security with reference to their place in the universe." Marjorie Bell, assistant director of the National Probation Association, blames the, "We don't want people like that in our church," attitude for their failure to cooperate. Eleanor Glueck, co-author with Sheldon Glueck of *Five Hundred Delinquent Women*, declares that, "A large proportion of children who later become delin-

[1] *Year Book, National Probation Association* (1935), pp. 188–199.
[2] *Ibid.*, pp. 191–192, 195–196, 198–199.

quent attend church regularly or irregularly during childhood. There is a considerable falling off in such attendance during the adolescent age. This seems of great significance to the programs of the churches. If the Church loses its interest and hold on young people in the adolescent years, there is something radically wrong. Whether the churches feel that this particular problem is theirs or not, I do not know. We have not found that the Church, except in rare instances, reaches out into the community to bring in ex-offenders." . . .

Recently, I sent a questionnaire to our ninety-five probation officers seeking an expression from them as to what part religion had played in the lives of their probationers. Of the fifty replies, all stated that religion had played a very minor part. One officer who handles juvenile cases only, said, "The movies interest most of them more than Sunday School. One boy told me very frankly that he did not understand the Sunday School lessons. They were not explained to him sufficiently." Another stated that 80 per cent of her boys and girls have had no contacts with the church. An adult officer replied, "In those cases where the probationer received early religious training but has lost contact with the church, he has a foundation on which to build character."

The next question was, "Do the clergy cooperate with you in your plan of treatment of probationers? If so, to what extent." The majority of answers to the question indicated a rather indifferent attitude on the part of most clergymen. One probation officer said, "I have never found any clergyman unwilling to help a parishioner. But they do not seem to want in their church strangers who are on probation." The officers working in rural communities appear to secure better cooperation than those in urban centers, doubtless due to the fact that the city clergyman's time is preempted with other matters pertaining to the welfare of his church. . . .

The editor of *The Churchman* recently drew attention to a paragraph in Russell Henry Stafford's book, *Religion Meets the Modern Mind*, in which he declares, "We must remind ourselves that human relations are as much the concern of religion as are relations with God. Vice flourishes where clean amusement is frowned upon. Many a country community has a thin coating of non-social pietism over a veritable cesspool of morbid preoccupation with sex, which would be cleaned out overnight if the local churchmen and churchwomen would see it as a part of their Christian duty to provide normal and attractive outlets for the high spirits of the neighborhood. Religion is not contaminated when a place is made in its expressional activities for innocent gaiety. It is redeemed from the contempt of its critics by showing itself wholesomely human as well as hypothetically divine." Mr. Shipler, commenting on this paragraph wrote, "To induce a parish to tear itself loose from conservatism and launch a social program is almost like trying to turn a cave inside out. But, unless the Church is to surrender to the world, the flesh and Mr. Mephistopheles, all alluring to young men and young women through their appeal to social camaraderie, it must show an increasing regard for social and pleasurable pursuit." . . . When the Church is fully aroused to a sense of the need, it will sound the note which will usher in a new day for probation, as well as all other professional social service.

Too many workers see only the fact that "parents and their children are at fault because they quit going to church." Workers need also to ask: "What has the church to offer them? Why could not the church keep their interest?" Burt cites some extreme cases:[1]

. . . child responds best to an imaginative appeal; . . . is swayed more by ideals of austere renunciation and self-sacrifice; . . . is moved most by a personal presentment. . . .

It is perhaps with the sensuous adolescent girl that the spell of religion is most potent. The effect is not always so lasting. At times to substitute religious feeling for sexual feeling is merely to displace one gush of sentiment by another; and the temporary conversion is so hollow at the core, so hypocritical in its nature, so ruinous in its swift collapse, that the final outcome may be far worse than the first state of unsophisticated sin.

With the boy a corporate form of worship and a public form of service—a band of a hundred singing hymns together with a Salvation Army gusto—this is the spirit that comes home to him best. Heart-to-heart talks and the language of the Bible class he takes as an insult to his manly years. And any exhortation to a private devotional life can but convince the needy offender that "religion" (to borrow the phrase of one of them) "is not his line." "How," he will ask, "can he pray and meditate in a twelve-foot bedroom, surrounded by four rowdy occupants?"

Fortunately this does not represent the general situation among the boys and girls who have had the opportunity to come in contact with competent religious leaders.[2]

The social worker in dealing with delinquents in relation to religion can only ascertain the facts regarding church attendance, religious beliefs, interests, conflicts, etc., and can strive to under-

[1] CYRIL BURT, *The Young Delinquent*, p. 236.

[2] See ARCHIBALD BLACK, *Opening Roads: Addresses for Young People;* SHAILER MATHEWS, *New Faith for Old;* JAMES GORDON GILKEY, *Getting Help from Religion.*

stand why religion has failed to exert an influence on the given family or child. He can recommend attendance or certain affiliations if the situation warrants it. Actual religious training must, of course, be left to the religious leaders. There is dearth of material on the role of the church in the adjustment of delinquents who are not churchgoers. It is revealing to note how little space is devoted to the church and religion by writers on delinquency, and those who do devote space to it frequently do so in order to bring serious indictments against the church. Perhaps such criticism is too severe in view of the problems which the church faces and is too indiscriminate in view of the numerous churches and clergymen who have given much time and serious consideration to the problems of wayward youth. Undoubtedly much more competent religious guidance is being carried on in this field by certain religious leaders than has found its way into present writings.

There are many special provisions for religious instruction for children who attend the church, thus providing a basis for ethical conduct. The Religious Education Association[1] and the International Council on Religious Education have made several studies and have published material as guides for effective curricula with a view to integrating religion into the everyday life of persons. Catholic churches have special children's masses and sermons suitable to their age. Sabbath and Sunday schools are held by many churches, and day schools for general instruction which relate religion to everyday life are open to children of many sectarian groups. But there are many gaps and much unevenness as the churches attempt to enlarge their activities and inaugurate programs to meet the complexities of modern life.[2]

Furtherance of Religious Development of the Child.—Edwin J. Cooley,[3] formerly of the Catholic Charities Probation Bureau in the New York Court of General Sessions, writes as follows regarding religious development:

Since the aim of the Bureau was to bring about not merely objective evidence of good conduct, but to effect a sincere and lasting reform from

---

[1] See *The White House Conference on Child Health and Protection*, pp. 142–148.

[2] See *The Development of a Curriculum of Religious Education*.

[3] *Probation and Delinquency*, pp. 156–158. Reprinted by permission of author.

within, close attention was paid to the furtherence of the religious development of the probationer. Frequently a complete re-education in spiritual values and moral standards was essential.

After the supervision officer had gained the confidence of his charge, it was possible for him to talk over his religious practices, the religious training he had received, and the other influences which might have determined his spiritual outlook. A sympathetic insight and understanding based on their common allegiance to the same faith then made it possible for the officer to develop an individualized plan for bringing his client into vital contact with religious influences. Attendance at Church was required of all probationers. They were also counselled to receive the Sacraments regularly. A more intimate acquaintance with his pastor, affiliation with Church societies, and the use of the social and recreational facilities of the parish were encouraged with the idea that, through the constant contact with these wholesome and attractive associations, the probationer's attitude, point of view, and behavior gradually would be modified to conform with the ideals of the Church.

In many of the steps which we have enumerated for the upbuilding of personality, the influence of religion was found to be potent. Often the remoulding of the probationer's ideal of himself was promoted by recalling to him the religious experiences of his early life, and the good example given him by a father or a mother, now dead, but still watching over him. Men who had become discouraged by their own failures were reminded of the forgiveness and help which God has promised to those who mingle their sorrow for the past with a sincere determination for the future. Magdalen and Peter still move the souls of men. . . .

The resumption of the simple practice of night prayers, where it could be secured, not only awakened wholesome memories, but provided a daily personal checkup on progress and reminded the probationer of his continuing dependence on and accountability to God. The reception of the Eucharist after months of neglect was a visable sign of his reinstatement in the Divine favor. Frequently the probationer was rescued from a spirit of loneliness and weakness when he was brought to realize that a loving, all-powerful Father was always near him to strengthen and to guide.

The resources of the Catholic Charities of the Archdiocese of New York, organized to cope with the spiritual and social needs of the neglected, dependent and delinquent members of the Church, were drawn upon to develop the personalities of the probationers and their families.

Cooperation and support were freely given by the Divisions of Families, Children, Health, Protective Care, and Social Action of Catholic Charities, and by the many special works under Catholic auspices such as probation schools, special educational activities, parish clubs, day nurseries, hospitals, convalescent homes, Big Brother and Big Sister organizations, and institutions for the dependent, delinquent, aged and infirm.

The Religious Fanatic.—Contrary to the parents and childern who show no or little interest in religion, the worker has many cases of religious fanaticism which should be called to the attention of religious leaders. Here are, briefly summarized, three cases in point:

Case of Paul Paulton.[1]—Paul, thirteen, found begging, told the worker, after many interviews with him, that his father induced him to leave home with him, as his mother was possessed of the devil since she would not accept their faith of the Truest Gospel. The father worked out unique dietary rules, conduct canons, prayers, ceremonials, and so on. He joined a group of "old faithfuls" whose beliefs were similar to his, but he was unable to reconcile himself to their leadership. He persuaded the boy, apparently with little difficulty, to leave school because the school nurse had insisted on some medical treatments for a skin disease, which was rapidly spreading over the boy's body. The disease was denied and the treatment staunchly refused. When pressure was used by the school—in order to protect the other children—the boy failed to appear in school and was lost sight of until his arrest as a beggar.

The worker was unsuccessful in her appeal to the father to allow the boy to return to school and to submit to medical treatments. The father's beliefs were in conflict with both. The boy had experienced considerable freedom while wandering with his father and he too refused to return to school or to his mother. The boy had accepted the father's belief that the mother was possessed of the devil and developed fears of her.

Psychiatrists tell us that men like Mr. Paulton exhibit psychopathic traits. A social worker is incompetent to make a diagnosis of Mr. Paulton's behavior and personality but suspicion is aroused as to his sanity. The social worker can only examine the grounds for such suspicion in order to decide whether to refer the matter to a psychiatrist. Needless to mention that Mr. Paulton refused to listen to proposals for an examination. From his point of view the worker and the psychiatrists were sinners and could be saved only by accepting his faith.

What is a worker to do in such a case? The man and the boy are completely isolated from friends, relatives, home, and fellow believers. There is no one who could appeal, reason, explain, or exert any pressure on the father, and the boy is under

[1] Reported to writer by Mrs. Ruth E. White, Imperial Valley.

his complete domination and control. The worker believed that there was nothing left for her to do but to file on the father on charges of contributing to the delinquency of his minor child, detain the child to assure his appearance in juvenile court for a hearing, and recommend placement in a foster home under the strict supervision and custody of the probation officer.

The Case of Robert.[1]—Robert, thirteen, has average intelligence, and is in the eighth grade. He was referred by his teacher because of his quiet manner and his tendency to daydream. In the interview with the social worker, the mother spoke of her concern over his poor work and her regret that he had no friends, but otherwise she was aware of no difficulty.

The boy's father is a skilled worker, making a comfortable income. He is sociable, enjoying his lodge meetings and an occasional evening of pool. He prefers a younger son who is like him in personality and whose part he invariably takes against Robert.

Because of the father's attitude, the mother defends Robert, but is unaware of her partiality for him. As a girl, she wanted to join an Episcopalian sisterhood, but her mother would not allow it. She found marriage disappointing and discovered her only solace in innumerable church activities. Throughout the interview, she was inclined to resist the visiting teacher's assumption that Robert was unadjusted. When finally pressed as to the boy's reaction, she arose and, after exacting a promise that the social worker would not tell Robert, opened the door into a small adjoining room. In it the boy had constructed a chapel, with two small pews and an altar decorated by a crucifix and candles and an altar cloth he had himself embroidered. Here he spent most of his time alone, conducting church services. He intends to become a minister. His mother believes that she is not responsible for his religious fervor, but at the same time recounts an experience that occurred a few months before his birth, when she vowed to dedicate the child to the church if God would induce her husband to cease scoffing at religion. She considers that her prayer was answered and that the child has naturally turned to the church.

When the social worker pointed out the possibility that her ambition for the boy would not be realized unless he learned to make social contacts, she agreed to urge him to spend more time playing outdoors with the boys, and gave her consent to his joining the harmonica club at school. However, when the visiting teacher suggested that the chapel be dismantled on the pretext of her need for a sewing room, she objected that nothing would be accomplished, for Robert would only reconstruct the chapel in his own room. The harmonica club proved ineffective, for although Robert attended regularly, he took no interest in the other boys, and used the harmonica at home to play hymns.

Since numerous attempts at relieving the mother's identification with the boy and the father's rejection of him were unsuccessful, and the child himself

[1] See ELIZABETH DEXTER, "Treatment of the Child Through the School Environment," *Mental Hygiene*, XII (April, 1928), 358–365.

remained inaccessible to any discussion of his problem, the social worker turned to the minister and the family physician in the hope of getting some control of the situation.   The physician, who had known Robert since birth, was amazed at what was going on in the home.   He readily offered his cooperation and agreed to urge outdoor activity for the sake of the boy's health.   The minister had wondered at Robert's intense enthusiasm, but was unaware of the lengths to which it had carried him.   He exerted his influence to discourage the boy's absorbing interest and undertook to discuss his problem with the mother.   He also tried to foster a friendship between his son and Robert.

Five months of treatment, for the most part carried on indirectly through the teacher, minister, and physician, appear to have accomplished little more than a superficial change in the original situation.   The parents' attitudes are too firmly fixed, and the boy's behavior is too deeply entrenched, to give way to the healthier family relationships that are necessary to free the boy from his emotional entanglement.   This case, as is often true of cases of serious maladjustment, did not come under treatment until the situation was largely unmanageable.   What can then be achieved is sufficiently disproportionate to the effect involved to make it seem more and more important that cases be detected in an earlier, more helpful stage.

Case of Ernest J.—Mr. John J., forty-five, appealed for help in dealing with his nine-year-old boy, whom he had discovered masturbating.   He explained that prayer had had no effect, the boy was "a perverse sinner, given over to the pleasures of the flesh, and in grave danger of eternal damnation" if he could not somehow achieve some saving grace.   To save the boy from himself he had compelled him to sleep in handcuffs and was prepared to use drastic measures in order to save him.   When the worker undertook to explain the relative unimportance of such sex practices, and the danger of focusing too much attention on it, the father immediately undertook to enlighten and eventually to save the worker from such heretical beliefs.   The father's misinformation, his literal-mindedness, and narrow, inflexible philosophy of life had developed a fanaticism with powerful religious sanctions which did not bode good for the boy's future.   At the time the boy was too young to appreciate the situation to the full and was inclined to avoid parental pressures by any avenue of escape which offered.   In fact, he was already staying away from home as much as possible and building up delinquency attitudes.

Success in dealing with such parents depends to a considerable extent upon familiarity with the religious ideology and thought forms.   If the worker can use these with facility, it may be entirely possible to interpret sound social practice in language which carries conviction to the parents.   Since sects are conflict groups it is very easy to set up a violent conflict between the parents and the worker—who in extreme cases seems to them little better than an emissary of the Evil One.

Less extreme cases and those people who do not live in such complete social isolation as Mr. Paulton and his boy may be appealed to, and, if that fails, some degree of social pressure used through the family or fellow believers. A "practitioner" of a sect of some repute told the writer not long ago that one of the best things to do is to rest the case with the leader of the church, whose policy it is to see that the members—when under the care of a public agency—comply with the rules and regulations of that agency. In most cases, however, the worker may have to resort to placement in a foster home of the children involved. (See the case of Noble Morrell, pp. 381–385.)

Organized Religion and Community Organization.—The Rt. Rev. Mgr. Thomas J. O'Dwyer,[1] Executive Director, Catholic Welfare Bureau of Los Angeles, writes as follows regarding organized religion of any denomination or creed in relation to community organization.

Long ago someone once said—"As the twig is bent, so the tree will grow." The saying has become dull through too much usage. It has lost its fresh ring. But it is as true as ever. When we realize how so many human tendencies, for better or worse, originate in the habits of childhood, we know how important it is for a child to have false outlooks corrected early. . . . It is most fortunate, in my opinion, when organized religion enters the scene in the sponsoring of a family case work service. A family case worker can affect a young life—many young lives, for that matter—long before a youngster has shown the slightest evidence of becoming a behavior problem. That is because, in their comprehensive family rehabilitation program, family case workers deal with all the delicate human relationships within the four walls of a home. . . . They can instill mutual respect and the sense of moral responsibility. They can arrange for religious instruction. They can show how the home can represent an example in good government, through the wise rule and guidance of parents, the obedience of children, and each member's regard for the rights of all the others. Thus, the beginnings of good citizenship start in the home. The formulation of intelligent family programs consonant with the religious, racial and national backgrounds of such families is the function of the family case worker. . . . Often a starting point may be the religious or moral re-education of the parents, that the home be made safe for the rearing of little ones. At any rate, the family case worker has the first opportunity to affect young lives for the better, to lessen the possibility of these young people reaching that state we broadly describe, in sociological language, as pre-delinquent.

[1] Paper especially prepared for this volume, July 20, 1936.

A family case worker with a religious agency has a wider opportunity to do so than a family case worker with a public welfare agency. The latter arrives upon the scene only when a family has either reached destitution or has already become a menace to public health and safety through parents, children, or both having come to the attention of the school or police authorities. . . . Thus the family case worker with a private agency invariably is upon the scene at an earlier stage in the family's history; and may do much to prevent its members from falling into destitution, crime, or delinquency, those unhappy developments which first bring the public agencies upon the scene.

The religious welfare agency may enter upon the scene, moreover, at three different periods. First, the entry of the family case worker just discussed. Second, the entry of the family or children's case worker or both, when a child's behavior problem first becomes apparent. Third, the entry of either such case worker or both, in treating the problem of delinquency in cooperation with the public authorities. . . .

In the case of either the pre-delinquent or the delinquent, much good can be done by private agencies developing Big Brother and Big Sister movements. . . . The man who undertakes to guide and counsel, and be an example, to some one problem boy, should do so in cooperation with the program mapped out by a professional children's case worker. The same applies to a woman extending her personal friendship to a girl.

For a good many pre-delinquents and delinquents come from homes broken by divorce, separation or the death or desertion of one or both parents. Such unfortunate boys and girls certainly need a friend, someone to look up to, to confide in and trust. An evening a week spent by a good man or good woman with such a youngster can mean much. The Big Brothers and Big Sisters have done much for thousands of such young people. Private agencies should do all in their power to develop such a movement. It would do much to prevent many problem youths from reaching the state where they must be placed in reformatories. It would do much to remould the lives of those released from institutions. . . .

Too much cannot be said about the right of young people to a participation in the normal gaiety of youth. It is not right that young people should be deprived of normal enjoyment because they are short of money or perhaps without any money. That is just the time when they need to meet, to laugh, to dance, to hear music. It must be remembered that monotony and loneliness also are contributing factors to delinquency. The normally gay youth is less susceptible to evil influence than those made morbid and resentful by a sense of enforced isolation from normal social activities.

If I seem to have digressed from the actual programs of religious agencies in the direct prevention and treatment of delinquency, it is because I know we agree that such programs cannot meet with very much success unless they are coordinated with intelligent community social planning.

In this connection it seems to me that the clergy of all denominations, as well as judges, and probation officers, educators, clubwomen, legislators, the press, merchants, farmers, industrialists and labor leaders should be interested in community social planning, in the activities of Councils of Social Agencies and Coordinating Councils. Leading citizens of all faiths, as members of these councils meet and act in behalf of the best interests of the whole community. With their sociological approach, they survey the business, industrial and agricultural factors of this community. They study the influence of destitution, unemployment, and inadequate income upon crime and delinquency. Wide social vistas can open up for them. They can pool their findings with groups interested in social justice; in wages, hours and working and living conditions, and in the mutual responsibilities of employers and employees. They can do all this, not in the interest of any class, but in the interest of the entire community. The members of the Councils can, I believe, profitably scrutinize, and perhaps revalue, some of the most cherished institutions of secular life, and take steps to remedy them, for the sake of youth.

In fact, all persons must become interested in a thorough reconstruction of our present social order if we are to get at the roots of juvenile delinquency. We all have to accept a wider province for the mission of social welfare. We have to realize that not only the poor and the needy require social welfare measures. We have to realize that some book, magazine and newspaper publishers, and some stage and motion picture producers, play a part in contributing to juvenile delinquency. We cannot blind ourselves to these influences. We cannot fail to deal with those responsible, if we are to cope with juvenile delinquency. No matter how splendid a civic atmosphere is created in any community, it must be realized, it is not isolated from the rest of the world. It is subject, to a great degree, to outside influences. There are books, magazines, newspapers and motion pictures originating in other parts of the nation, near and far. Sometimes, while not grossly indecent, they do not stand for very high ideals. They proffer interpretations of facts and events in which the ideals or goals of the characters involved are certainly far from edifying. Life, in many books, magazines, stage and screen plays, and newspapers, appears to be a parade of scandal, gossip, murder, robbery and assault, with no moral drawn. All human society seems to move through a nightmare. The finer aspects of life and human nature are not touched upon to any appreciable extent. As adults and children alike are exposed to this constant intellectual pestilence, is there any wonder that there is juvenile delinquency, and that it is hard to combat?

In our scrutiny and revaluations of the institutions of society, we must not overlook some of our heretofore most cherished notions of public education. The intellectual incertitudes of youth today, the failure of many young men and women of college years to find in life any meaning beyond the biological, has sown confusion, crime and suicide. These are the youths who have been taught by so-called liberal professors to flout the existence of God, to deny the validity of the Ten Commandments, and to regard sex morality as old-fashioned. Their minds have been formed by conceptions of life, history and the individual that are one-sided and futile, and that often not only deny God and immortality, but represent religion as an out-moded superstition. How can we ask these little ones to respect authority when they have been taught that there is no authority for anything? How can we ask them to respect the dignity of fellow human beings when they have been educated to believe that a human being is 98 cents worth of chemicals, and is an animal who happens to be a little more highly organized than other animals?

Facts and figures, available to all of us, show us how few of all the children who get into trouble are active communicants of any church at the time. Facts and figures, stark and irrefutable, show us how much divorce, and the broken home, have been responsible for the degradation of these little ones. Yet the child grows up in a society where men and women who have plighted their troth "for better or worse, for richer or poorer, till death do them part," have regarded that sacred pact as a trivial utterance. What can we say to the child, how can we ask him to hold any agreement, pact or covenant sacred, to believe at all in honor, in courage and in tenderness, in a society that permits his home to be broken by divorce on the most shallow grounds?

And that is not all. This same society is one in which many bankers, industrialists and merchants have not, in their attitudes towards human beings, regarded them as beings created to the image and likeness of God. In the name of inordinate profits, they have been willing to underpay millions of men, women and children, thwarting their lives, breaking them on the wheels of industry, making it sorely difficult for them to live in health and decency by depriving them of adequate housing, food and clothing. In the face of attempts to regulate their operations, many of these same bankers, merchants and industrialists cry out that they are being deprived of their rights as individuals. They attempt to make it appear as if sound objectives of distributive justice are no different than the harsh materialism of Marxist Communism.

They control a great many powerful newspapers, and fill them with misleading statements. How is a younger generation to be asked to go straight, to love integrity and honesty, when some of the so-called big men of our country, the men who should be good examples to them, are the sponsors of so much deceit? How ask them to treat those close to them fairly when highly extolled bankers, industrialists and merchants are not dealing fairly? How ask them not to steal when outstanding men object to governmental regulations minimizing the possibility of promoters stealing the savings of widows and orphans by selling them worthless securities?

It seems to me that the problem of juvenile delinquency is so bound up with all these considerations, that social welfare measures must be applied to all society if the problems of youth are to be coped with. We must reclassify our conception of what constitutes a criminal. We must, I think, regard all those who flout the Ten Commandments and the teachings of Christ as criminals, whether they do so openly, covertly, or by implication through their social attitudes. We must regard every activity as criminal that lessens or destroys faith, hope and love; that demeans human dignity; that denies that economic law should be in line with moral law; or that stirs class hate. We must change our national consciousness. We must realize that rich and poor alike have been accepting immoral, materialistic conceptions of life that have poisoned the entire intellectual atmosphere.

I have mentioned these things because it seems to me that the broadest, deepest coping with juvenile delinquency involves the combatting of false values held equally by all classes. We must, I believe, try to convince people in all social strata that their chief concern should not be with making money, or with selfish pleasure, but with loving God and neighbor, if they are to be examples to youth. We must try to convince them they have a higher goal than any attainable in this world; that "the survival of the fittest" is an absurd theory; and that unrestrained competition is heart-breaking and health-breaking, if we are to give them perspective and a sense of proportion, and if we are to expect their children to possess perspective and a sense of proportion. We must ask more people to live critically instead of blindly; that their influence will be felt by the young, the citizens of the years to come.

We, who are members of organized religious denominations, in addition to our immediate professional duties, can do these things and many more, towards decreasing juvenile delinquency. We can encourage the purchase of newspapers, magazines and books that uphold decent values. We can support sound values in the drama. We can stand for social justice, but against class hate. We can lift our voices against whatever seems conducive of confusion, unwholesomeness or despair, in art or letters or legislation. And above all, we can encourage the religious education of youth, turning the hearts of the young towards God, who is their only abiding light and hope. Then we shall be helping in the creating of a social atmosphere in which the Ten Commandments will be more widely regarded as the criteria of right and wrong. Then we shall be giving youth standards to live by. Then we shall be striking at the roots of crime and suicide and delinquency.

Suggestions to the Religious Leader.—Burt offers the following suggestions to religious leaders in dealing with delinquent youth.[1]

With almost all delinquents, boys or girls, rich or poor, it is the positive rather than the negative aspects of religious teaching that should chiefly be enforced. If a direct reference to such things is necessary, virtues and not vices should most of all be dwelt upon. For the rest, bad habits like intemperance and unchastity are better depicted, not as horrible iniquities, or as sins against some high theological code, but simply as hygienic follies—faults which, persisted in, will stop the child from keeping himself physically and mentally fit: indeed to set a boy training with others for some athletic event will often be a far better preventive against over-indulgence than any amount of lecturing on the Christian duties of abstinence. Always the quiet example will be much more effective than the eloquent sermon, and the indirect method will yield the richest fruit. In too earnest a religious zeal there are risks as well as benefits, and the majority of older delinquents are least likely to be antagonized when moral effort is placed before them, not as essentially a form of self-repression or as a sign of saintly piety, but rather as the harmonious culture of all sides of human nature, each in just proportion to the rest.

The White House Conference on Child Health and Protection[2] makes the following statements regarding development of religious ideals.

Fundamental Needs of the Child

1. The need for right or correct notions of conduct, for a code of life growing out of a knowledge of personal rights and personal obligations that accompany these rights and are inherent in the individual; these are derived from one's personality and dignity and are to be differentiated from legal rights or privileges. These moral rights are built on the concept of the ideal. The ideal is the law of life, and morality in

---

[1] BURT, *op. cit.*, pp. 236–237.
[2] *The Delinquent Child*, pp. 139–142.

its widest sense is the relation between responsible behavior and the ideal.

2. The need for motives sufficiently strong to assure loyalty to these norms of conduct, even at the sacrifice of selfish personal gratification; these spring from one's direct relation with God.

3. The need for help and assistance to make the practice of these ideals of conduct an actuality in daily life.

There is a vast difference between resolution and accomplishment. For example, while the following of religious precepts and counsels is altogether inviting and comforting in the abstract, in practical everyday life it is often difficult and uninviting. The discipline of will to have courage, irrespective of personal inclination or public opinion, to follow that which has been taught, is achieved only through forces within or, in the belief of many, is bestowed by grace.

Correct notions of conduct and motives sufficiently strong to make them operative must be developed in the child's mind not alone by teaching, but through actual demonstration of patterns of sincere and honest living. These must parallel his physical, intellectual, and emotional development, in order that they shall become an integral part of the character of the growing man, and be sufficient to guide him effectively in all their ramifications of his daily conduct.

In other words, conduct is the outgrowth of conviction that certain courses of conduct are *right* and others *wrong*, plus motives strong enough to influence the individual to act according to that conviction. If we conceive it to be the province of religion to deal with the threefold relationship of the individual to himself, to others and to God, then it is the duty of religion to instruct the child as to his obligation to himself, to others and to God. Further and no less important, religion is to furnish him motives for conforming to the obligation implied in each of these relationships, motives sufficiently strong to enable him, in the concrete events of daily life which are continually presenting themselves, to live up to his convictions. Official representatives of religion in some special and substantial manner assist the child to reduce to actual practice these correct notions or ideals of conduct. In other words, religion includes a way of life, as well as a doctrine or a belief. Just how this duty is or will be accomplished, depends upon the means used by the individual church. In general, they may be divided into subjective and objective means; subjective, as to the individual, in that religion is a force from within rather than from without, objective as to the church in that religion is there expressed in various forms. Among those means are worship, prayer, sacrament, meditation and reflection, reading the Bible and other religious writings, observation of special pious customs, intelligent performance of charitable service to one's fellowmen. The aim of the church is to give the child a satisfactory philosophy of life; a sense of belonging to something bigger and nobler than himself; a sense of security which comes, not from the outside, but from peace within.

To assist the individual in obtaining these goals, churches have instituted or inaugurated various aids. The most usual are the regular periods of worship; special seasons of prayer; pious customs; the giving of instruction through day schools and Sunday schools; everyday worship and mid-week worship; revivals, missions, and retreats; keeping the church open at all times, thus inviting meditation and reflection in a favorable atmosphere; pastoral visiting of members; life adjustment institutes, and special social activities under church auspices, such as settlements, young people's societies, church clubs, study clubs, open forums, boy and girl scout activities, and organized and unorganized social activities of various types.

Not only does the child have needs in relation to the church, but the church also has certain needs in relation to the child. These may be listed as: (1) tradition and stability, which must not be confused with inflexibility; (2) keeping the teaching of religion as its dominant purpose; (3) relating religion to everyday life; (4) closer cooperation between the church and the home in the development of social values; (5) studying impartially the experience of the other friends of childhood for the purpose of correcting social conditions which defeat a realization of the religious ideals.

In stating these needs it must be kept in mind that religion, in its basic principles and in most of its application to concrete situations, is both conservative and radical. It has tradition and stability and at the same time, in setting forth ideals in the application of these basic principles, it is centuries ahead of time. Churches sometimes lag behind in application of some of their principles to various newly arisen domestic, economic, social or international conditions. Many churches, however, of all denominations are molding and enlarging their activities and inaugurating programs to meet these complexities of modern life. On the other hand, there are great unevenness and wide gaps, within even the same denomination. Programs in many places are as yet mainly paper ones.

The social worker with insight can gain several major clues from the foregoing discussion: Parents and youth do not often divorce themselves from the church if the church has been in a position to recognize and meet their needs. There is little use advocating or ordering church attendance without creating a desire for it in one who has been weaned away from it. It is essential to know the interests, religious hankerings, previous training, devotion to particular beliefs in order to adapt the available influences to individual needs.

In the matter of attendance at church or Sunday school the child is very much swayed by local custom. If his fellows attend, he will regard it as natural and attend as a matter of course. There must needs be group sanctions in such matters. Workers will find it a very difficult matter to induce the child to swim against the current of his gang, his neighborhood, or his family. In fact, insistence upon such nonconformity may contribute to his further disorganization. One needs to make certain also that disinterest in religious matters is not an expression of negativism to parents or others with whom the child is in conflict. Religion is but one aspect of life, and the role it can play in the life of the individual or the group necessarily depends upon other aspects of life.

The worker should enlist the cooperation of the local clergy not only regarding the religious needs of the family and the children but regarding community problems. The worker needs to stress the necessity of bringing together the church and the delinquent who have seemingly parted ways.

Selected Bibliography

1. BLACK, ARCHIBALD: *Opening Roads: Addresses for Young People*, The Macmillan Company, 1936.
2. BOWER, W. C.: *Religious Education in the Modern Church*, The Bethany Press, 1929.
3. CABOT, RICHARD: *What Men Live By*, Houghton Mifflin Company, 1914.
4. GILKEY, JAMES GORDON: *Getting Help from Religion*, The Macmillan Company, 1936.
5. GIBRAN, KAHLIL: *The Prophet*, Alfred A. Knopf, Inc., 1936.
6. KUPKE, O.: *The Religious Development of Adolescents*, The Macmillan Company, 1928.
7. MACLEAN, A. H.: "Idea of God in Protestant Religious Education," *Teachers College Contributions to Education*, No. 410, Columbia University, 1930.
8. MATHEWS, SHAILER: *New Faith for Old*, The Macmillan Company, 1936.
9. PIAGET, JEAN: *The Child's Conception of the World*, Harcourt, Brace and Company, 1929.
10. SCHMIEDELER, EDGAR, and M. ROSE MCDONOUGH: *Parent and Child*, Chap. XIII, "Religious Education in the Home," D. Appleton-Century Company, Inc., 1934.
11. THOMPSON, C. J. S.: *The Hand of Destiny*, Rider and Company, 1933.
12. VORWAHL, H.: "Die Religion der Jugend," *Viertel-jahrschrift für Jugendkunde*, III (1933), 143–152.

13. White House Conference on Child Health and Protection: *The Delinquent Child,* pp. 137–165.

Suggestions for Further Study

1. How can the probation officer aid in instilling respect for religious institutions in the offender?

2. What can be done to interest all churches in probation work?

3. What does Mr. Cooley mean by "the Opportunity of the Church"?

4. What are the fundamental needs of the child in relation to the church? How can these needs be met?

5. What special provisions are there for religious instruction of youth?

6. What use can the probation officer make of day schools (denominational)? of religious vacation schools? camps under church auspices? scouting? Big Brother organizations?

CHAPTER XXIV

THE ROLE OF THE SCHOOL[1] AND VOCATIONAL GUIDANCE[2] IN THE ADJUSTMENT OF DELINQUENT AND PROBLEM YOUTH

Individualized versus Mass Education.—Many short stories, novels,[3] biographies, and autobiographies,[4] as well as scientific treatises[5] depict the life of the child who by inclination or ability is not a fit subject for close confinement over lessons and tasks which bring little or no immediate satisfaction.

Uncongenial school and distasteful educational occupations have been shown by research students to do considerable mental and moral harm. "The particular form which maladjustment takes differs from one case to another and it is the greatest weakness of most schools that they so seldom trouble to analyze the reason for their failure."[6] The individual teachers are rarely in a position to analyze the trouble, first because they are overburdened with large classes and long teaching hours and secondly, because—even though they are child pedagogues—they seldom possess the necessary sociological and psychological acquaintance with the social worlds of the children to enable them to recognize and deal effectively with serious problems. Frequently the child confesses his hatred for school to the teacher. This situa-

---

[1] See Mary B. Sayles, *The Problem Child in School.*

[2] For a discussion of vocational guidance and employment for youth see Luella Cole, *Psychology of Adolescence*, pp. 357–384; A. J. Jones, *Principles of Guidance;* E. L. Thorndike and Others, *Prediction in Vocational Success;* E. B. Watson, *A Source Book for Vocational Guidance.*

[3] Booth Tarkington, *Seventeen, Penrod;* Mark Twain, *Tom Sawyer, Huckleberry Finn.*

[4] G. Stanley Hall, *The Confessions of a Psychologist;* Henry Adams, *The Education of Henry Adams;* see also in Luella Cole, *Psychology of Adolescence*, bibliography, pp. 493–497.

[5] Clifford Shaw, William Healy, Cyril Burt, John Slawson, Miriam Van Waters, and Others, *op. cit.* (in the preceding chapters; see index) see also M. V. O'Shea, *The Child, His Nature and His Needs.*

[6] Cyril Burt, *The Young Delinquent*, p. 74.

tion is in most instances held to be "the fault" of the parents, who are regarded as not instilling sufficient respect for school or as "uncooperative," or the blame is shifted to lack of mental ability, lack of emotional stability, lack of physical stamina, or the gang, or the court, or anything except such factors as the rigid and standardized school curriculum, old-fashioned and frequently incompetent schoolteachers, and inflexible rules and regulations. There is no doubt that the home, the court, the child, and others present serious problems to the school as well as to each other, but to fail to recognize the school's shortcomings is to shut one's eyes and ears to one of the most serious tensions which perplex the adolescent world, particularly, the "lost generation," to borrow Miss Davis' term.[1]

Consider the case of the sixteen-year-old girl[2] to whom school work became such a perplexing problem that she became a habitual truant, and, when the school authorities threatened to arrest her and her mother, she ran away from home and, after several weeks' acquaintance with a sailor, married him without her mother's knowledge and consent, resorting to lying about her age, residence, and occupation, all while the attendance officer, probation officer, juvenile police, and mother were looking for her.

The girl is intelligent, reliable, and devoted to the mother, but the particular school work baffled her seriously. She failed in Spanish, mathematics, and chemistry. No doubt there were subjects in the high-school curriculum which would have resulted in the girl's taking less serious steps which may possibly lead to lifetime regrets. There were also undoubtedly other contributing causes to the girl's hasty marriage to a strange sailor, but the school situation precipitated the crisis. From the girl's and the mother's story, it is doubtful whether any other situation would have driven her away from home. In this case the school was not even aware as to why this intelligent girl failed and what courses might have interested her and kept her in school.

Whatever form school unadjustment assumes and whatever its symptoms, a full study should be made before any action is taken. It is evident from the foregoing chapters that no systematic plan of treatment can be undertaken without study of the individual case. But the study must be made of the child in his vital rela-

---

[1] See Maxine Davis, *The Lost Generation.*

[2] Reported to writer by a juvenile court referee.

tion to his social world, in these instances focusing attention upon the school world. The school does now realize, as does the rest of the world, that it has a definite responsibility in the failure of many of those whom it regards as "normal children."

If school unadjustment were the only disastrous result, there would perhaps be comparatively less ground for worry. School unadjustment leads to truancy, ganging, predatory activities, child marriages, sex delinquency, and a host of other difficulties which bring boys and girls to the juvenile courts and reform schools and which give rise to some specific pathological behavior pattern.

The school may rightly say that the problem children were problems long before they arrived at school, that they have only carried over their maladjustments from the home to the school-room, and that they respond to teachers in ways conditioned by parents. That is undoubtedly frequently true, but unless

. . . the teacher has developed genuine insight into problems of personality, including her own, she is more than likely to fix in the child some undesirable, destructive emotional attitude, and this far more through what she is, what she does, than what she teaches.

The school is not responsible for the emotional attitudes with which pupils enter, but the school should frankly realize that success, or failure, will be determined, not by intelligence of students, nor by richness of course of study but in the degree of skill with which it develops the emotional life of children [and meets their problems]. In each student crises arise, seemingly without adequate basis, the every day matters of the first school success, or failure, first punishment, humiliation, reward, criticism, ridicule, undetected cheating, or unmerited approval will serve as the core around which a cluster of emotional habits will cling.[1]

Transfer to Another School.—If the school is unable to adjust a child's problems within its own particular setup, he may profit by a transfer. A child may be transferred from one school to another for two major reasons. First, he may have formed obnoxious associations and staunch alliances with other pupils baser than himself, and it is necessary to sever these intimacies. Secondly, the school may be ill adapted to the needs of the particular child and his teachers may have grown weary of him and uncongenial. The choice of a new school is often a hard problem.

[1] MIRIAM VAN WATERS, *Youth in Conflict*, pp. 89–90, 97.

The worker does not desire to start an epidemic of delinquency in a new school by transferring a contagious element. The interests of the group are paramount and should be considered before the interests of the individual child. The worker should be guided in making the choice by tolerant attitudes of the faculty toward troublesome cases, the general congenial atmosphere of the school and school grounds, the opportunities for freer activity and for training of character as well as of intellect. Perhaps these are only praiseworthy expressions pointing toward an ideal to be sought rather than a condition actually achieved in many schools. Painstaking workers—acquainted with opportunity rooms, special teachers, and courses of study—maintain that in every district one can find some excellent facilities for a small number of cases to which school authorities are willing to devote extra time and energy when they become acquainted with the need.

Children who show marked physical anomalies, who are exceptionally large or exceptionally small for their age, often show marked improvement when they are removed from their grade—either in their own school or transferred—and are placed with children more nearly their own size. An ungraded room may meet the requirements of the school and child at the same time. Children can be cruel to each other, and a sensitive child, nagged and scoffed at, will develop many complexes and compensating delinquencies while in a more congenial atmosphere these youths can make an adjustment rather easily and overlook remarks derogatory of them.

Unfortunately, the child designated as a problem by the school is generally transferred to a school of lower educational requirements, which, because of prevalency of problems among its students, is called a "special school." The sensitive child may be humiliated by such a transfer and the more intelligent child is deprived of the challenge to work harder and measure up to his ability, while the suggestible child will find it a prolific source of contamination. Many special schools have achieved a high grade of professional standards, but many still remain of questionable repute academically and socially. Dr. Van Waters' experience with this type of case is of importance:

He [the boy] may be roughly handled by the attendance officer, turned out of his school by the principal to be sent to a "Special School" or Parental Class, where, without further investigation, some hardy young teacher, intellectually and socially not far advanced beyond the delinquent, herds him with "bad boys" and young "rough necks" and ignorantly administers "swats" with a paddle to make him manly, and baseball to make him "a regular guy" without slightest reference to the needs of childhood.[1] The boy may be placed in such a school at eight years of age, and there spend the remainder of his school life. Educational reform may sweep the general school system, the curriculum may become rich and plastic, but these "parental" schools will be administered on theory of punishment, not education. At best the boy forms permanent associations with gangs of "young toughs," almost illiterate, at worst he is maimed physically and mentally.[2]

There is not the careful and judicious sorting of children assigned to special schools which the situation warrants. As Burt maintains: "the one thing essential is not to change, but to choose, the school," and it might be added "to choose it with care and discretion in the interests of the child."

At times schools refuse to transfer a child to another school, believing that such procedures cast a reflection upon their methods and their authority. If the school undertook to adjust itself to the needs of the child, no transfer would be necessary in many instances, but to leave the conditions unchanged or to place the burden of adjustment upon the child is to assume a highly unprofessional attitude. At times, perhaps this situation is more true of girls than boys. They are unadjusted not to the curriculum and to the teacher, but to the social atmosphere of the school.

Janet, fifteen, was the oldest of four daughters of a widowed janitress living in the basement of an apartment house in a high-grade residential district. Many of the girls in her class came to school in linen, voile, and silk frocks, or carefully laundered ginghams with fine trimmings. Janet developed a serious inferiority complex over her meager wardrobe, accompanied by tensions, restlessness, and that sickening feeling which arises when one is unfavorably compared with his fellows. The family welfare worker—a regular visitor in the home—recognized the

---

[1] Reference here is to widespread practice of maintaining discipline classes, or "parental schools," under the Board of Education, for the correction of truancy and other delinquencies.

[2] *Op. cit.*, p. 91.

signs of emotional maladjustment.   Friendly and warm relationships were of little or no avail.   When Janet began to show signs
of neurotic behavior, the child guidance clinic was consulted.
Its only suggestion was a transfer to a school within the same
distance but on the other side of the dividing boulevard.   Janet
was not deprived of any scholarship opportunities but in the new
school social differences were less pronounced.   To justify the
transfer to Janet, the change was proposed to her in the light of a
working scholarship in the office which was offered her in the new
school.   This worker associated change with new resources and
offered it as a promotion.   With continued friendly contacts with
the worker, Janet's inferiority was greatly decreased.[1]

The Teacher as Pedagogue and Child Welfare Worker.—As
indicated there are in every school and frequently in every class
unadjusted children.   The teacher must, therefore, be more than
a pedagogue.   She must also be a child welfare worker, equipped
to recognize problems, to trace them to their source, to know
about child nature and personality traits and to fit the educational
system to his needs.   That means individualization to a far
greater degree than has heretofore been understood by many
school authorities and curriculum makers in the educational field.
If the school considers mass methods more economical, it is
shutting its eyes to the backbreaking burdens of financial cost
of juvenile courts, reform schools, penitentiaries, and G-men
and of the social costs of demoralized and wasted lives.   It is of
interest to note that the modern educators themselves have
sounded individuality as the keynote of modern education, yet
few of them have put it into actual operation.

With regard to social work in the schools, the United States
Children's Bureau[2] maintains:

The fact that practically all juvenile delinquents are children of school
age does not mean that the school itself is responsible for their delinquency.   The child's personality may have been warped in his very
early years.   His revolt against school authority and discipline may be
an indication of some deep-seated difficulty which has its roots in his
past or in his home environment.   It may be the danger signal presag-
ing more serious conflict with all authority in the future.   Whatever
the cause may be, it is usually during his school days that the child's

---

[1] Case reported by Joan Moore of Chicago Public Schools.
[2] *Facts about Juvenile Delinquency*, Publication No. 215 (1935), pp. 16–19.

most serious delinquencies develop, and the school is therefore most intimately involved in the whole problem of delinquency. . . .

The delinquency committee of the White House Conference . . . pointed out that "before the school lies the promise of a real program for the prevention of delinquency." Part of this promise lies in the fact that the school must realize increasingly that the child it teaches has a life outside of that which is passed in the classroom and that he must be taught and treated and guided in the light of this fact, that the school must sincerely and vitally interest itself in the environment of the child it tries to teach. In many instances, as the committee points out, "this will involve . . . educating the family, industry, and so forth to their responsibilities rather than seeking to relieve them."

However well trained and understanding the teacher may be, the task which this responsibility on the part of the school implies is not one which she can carry single-handed. The school organization must provide for various services to assist in preventing or solving the various problems of school maladjustment and dissatisfaction which are fertile sources of delinquency. These services include the following:

1. *Health Services.*—Expert help in the physical well-being of the child should be available through physicians, dentists, hygienists, and nurses.

2. *Attendance Departments.*—Every school system should include on its staff attendance officers especially trained in social case work. They should receive compensation corresponding to the pay of the teaching staff; and, as is the case with the teaching staff, the number appointed should be based on the number of children to be served if effective results are expected. The duties of the attendance officer should include systematic visiting of schools; conferences at the schools with children, teachers, and parents; visits to homes; and the maintenance of cooperative relationships with social agencies and legal authorities, school physicians and nurses, special classes, visiting teachers, and other special services for the school child.

3. *Visiting Teachers and School Counselors.*—The "visiting teacher," as defined by the National Committee of Visiting Teachers, is a social worker, trained in mental hygiene, who studies and treats the maladjusted school child in his home setting, advising with the parents and relatives, with the teacher and the school authorities, and with social agencies, if these are necessary in handling the case. While training for social work is necessary, teaching experience is often recommended because of the understanding it gives of the school problems and their practical adjustment. In communities in which visiting teachers are an essential part of the school system, they are making an extremely valuable demonstration of the service that should be available for all children having personal or family problems that handicap their school

adjustment. This service should be closely coordinated with child-study departments, administration of school attendance laws, special classes, and vocational guidance.

In some schools the person who makes adjustments between home and school in the case of children who are not satisfactory in scholarship or behavior or both is called a counselor. The title is unimportant. What is important is that the work be done by a person with training in social case work.

4. *Special Schools and Classes.*—Many schools are finding that certain truant and delinquent children can be handled effectively in special classes. These are not the "truant rooms," "disciplinary classes," "ungraded classes," and the like that segregate problem children to the relief of the school but often to the detriment of the child, whose hatred and distrust of school may be aggravated by thus being labeled a bad character. As the schools develop more effective social case work, special classes will be organized on the basis of the treatment indicated rather than the offense committed. Schools are recognizing more and more that when a thorough mental, physical and pedagogical examination of the child reveals that his needs cannot be met in a regular class, he should be placed in a special class equipped to deal scientifically with his particular difficulty. Such classes include classes for children who have physical handicaps (as of vision or hearing); classes for children with mental handicaps; classes for retarded children who are not mentally deficient; and classes for gifted children for whom the challenge of a different school curriculum may be the solution of behavior problems caused by lack of interest and satisfaction in their school work.

Especially interesting programs in schools for children with behavior problems have been developed in Chicago and Cleveland. Two such schools in the Chicago public-school system are the Montefiore, established in 1929, and the Moseley, established in 1930, for the study and treatment of boys who are maladjusted in regular day schools, being truant and incorrigible and therefore well started on the way to delinquency. Complete physical, psychological, and social study is given, also psychiatric study if needed. An individual record folder and a full case history are kept for every boy. These schools serve children from elementary, junior-high, and parochial schools—or about two-thirds of the city's area. The Thomas A. Edison School (operated since 1921, renamed in 1925) in Cleveland has also developed a comprehensive program for boys presenting problems of misconduct and truancy.

5. *Educational and Vocational Guidance.*—Provision should be made in the school course for an adequate program of educational and vocational guidance. Such a program would include a sufficient number of well-trained and experienced counselors in the schools to make adjust-

ments for every child that will prevent discouragement and prolong his school life. In some cities bureaus of vocational guidance and placement are organized under the same department as that of school attendance. Teachers and others dealing with children presenting behavior problems should make the fullest use of the vocational service.

6. *Child-study Departments and Clinics.*—Many schools refer problem children to child-guidance clinics where these exist. A few have behavior clinics of their own. Child-study divisions and psychological or psychiatric clinics are provided in some pedagogical difficulties. Figures reported to the White House Conference indicate a universal school need for help in understanding and providing for the needs of the child who finds difficulty in adjusting himself to the demands of the school or who fails to develop normal avenues of self-expression, achievement, and social cooperation.

The more progressive schools have already seriously considered their own and the children's problems and have shown a quickened sense of responsibility toward young persons in conflict.

Self-government programs, use of the project method, enriched courses of study, more attention paid to diagnosis of individual differences, greater flexibility in discipline, vastly more heed given to beauty, to arts, literature, music and natural science, an increasing respect for personality, more cautious approach in matters of truancy, backwardness, dullness and anti-social behavior, more reading and more genuine living on the part of teachers, above all, more life, more adventure and color are transforming the schools into true social groups instead of barracks of military discipline, and factories for the mechanical molding of "raw" flesh and blood. Within the true social group any conflict that takes place between child and adult will be stimulating to each.[1]

Dr. Van Waters in discussing the personality traits of teachers and their behavior patterns writes:

The teacher should have ability to detect early signs of emotional maladjustment in children, should feel respect for complexities of personality, above all should understand why force in dealing with emotional disorders is blind, stupid, useless and often cruel and dangerous. The teacher herself should have made adequate adjustment to life, should not look to children to supply her with opportunities for outlet to anger, fear, wish to dominate, or to be dominated. She should not use affections of children to gratify her need of love and approval;

[1] VAN WATERS, *op. cit.*, p. 110.

her own adult human relationships should be established satisfactorily. The most important personality attribute of the successful teacher is ability to create and foster a sense of vitality and enthusiasm for life. In this sense her attitude should be parental, that is to say, in the interests of health and virility.[1]

Again, as Dr. Van Waters maintains, if the school sometimes mishandles cases, there are compensating heartening exceptions. "It all depends on the attitude of mind toward delinquency training, skill and good-will of the teacher." She cites a number of cases which were effectively handled, one of which we quote.[2]

The Case of May.—A sickly orphan who had been brought up in the home of a conscientious woman, mother of a girl about May's age. May suffered jealousy. One day the clothing of the daughter of the home was found slashed and snipped into pieces. May denied doing it. She was locked in a room and fed bread and milk (which she refused) until the woman finally, to avoid scandal, took May to court. May was resolute in denial. The court explained that at present it was not necessary to discover the mystery of slashed clothes; the important thing was the shocking mental and physical state into which the child had worked herself. After examination and physical restoration, May was placed in a home where she attended a small high school; the principal was asked to cooperate in reconstruction of May. Years of effort by this socially minded woman are now being rewarded. May took a purse from school within a few weeks of admission. No attempt by the principal was made to "prove" this, or to compel a painful "confession." May was told the probabilities pointed to her; if she wished she could make restitution. It was explained to her that stealing is a grave symptom of inner trouble; all her friends were now trying to help her, and pending the "cure" it would be best for her to work out of school hours to repay incidental losses. She need not "confess" in words; no force would be used to make her pay if she felt innocent. Three times in two years May yielded to impulse to steal small articles; each time she made restitution. For over a year there has been no stealing; delinquency with boys broke out recently. The court offered to remove the troublesome girl from high school.

"No," said the principal. "This girl is making steady progress in school. Her attitude is not rebellious; it is that of one appealing for help. This is our job; unless we fail, or the girl begins to injure others, we are going to keep May in school."

May is about to graduate after four years' intelligent supervision in this high school.

[1] *Ibid.*, p. 99.
[2] *Ibid.*, pp. 102–103. Reprinted by permission of New Republic, Inc. For the relation of the high school to the problem of delinquency see also Luella Cole, *Psychology to Adolescence*, chaps. VIII and XIII; also Walter A. Lundeen, *Juvenile Delinquency*, chap. V.

FURTHER NEEDS OF THE SCHOOL IN RELATION TO DELINQUENCY

Those who have studied the problems of school in relation to youth[1] agree that schools are in need of a reorganization. Of course, the schools themselves have arrived at that conclusion, but as many of them see the problem it is largely one of lack of finances. That is important but there are many needs which can be met with little or no additional expenditure of money.

In general and briefly, the schools need to pay more attention to projects of the children's own choice and interests and less attention "to a preparation for life." John Dewey[2] has for many years stressed that schools need to concentrate *on life*, as it surrounds the child here and now, and his future will be enriched and more abundant. It might be inferred that often routine school work interferes with education.

Schoolteachers should pay more attention to the children who do not display a lively interest, who are subdued and suppressed. They are perhaps of least trouble to a busy teacher, but such manifestations indicate abnormalities which need the attention of a sympathetic counselor. The active, curious, extrovert child may often become a nuisance to an overburdened teacher and thus come in conflict with her, but socially he is not a serious problem, while the suppressed child is.

Many schools are meeting and other schools should meet the need for sex instruction in junior and senior high schools. "It is a serious matter to mingle youth of both sexes during adolescence with no adequate sex instruction available either in home or at school."[3] The average age of the expectant unmarried mother in two Florence Crittenton Homes in two large metropolitan centers was fifteen years.

Guidance must come from a source expert in adolescent difficulties; girls should be under supervision of a wise woman counselor; boys under a man physician, teacher or other male of absolute clarity and integrity. It must be remembered that hypocrisy is resented bitterly, and can never be concealed from young people. Equally resented is

[1] VAN WATERS, *op. cit.;* THOMAS D. ELIOT, *The Juvenile Court and the Community;* WILLIAM I. THOMAS and DOROTHY S. THOMAS, *The Child in America;* EDWIN J. COOLEY, *Probation and Delinquency.*

[2] See *Democracy and Education.*

[3] VAN WATERS, *op. cit.,* p. 109.

the cold "unfeeling" type of supervision and criticism that youth with insight fears or holds in contempt, for it is based either on shallowness or something more abnormal.[1]

Someone has suggested that the school authorities should not flee from some of the problems presented by youth. The school, instead of barring and forbidding the obscene literature which boys and girls handle under cover, should show it alongside the reproductions of classical paintings and sculpture of nude men and women and explain the motives of the producer of each and thus set standards of beauty and morality. The school should discuss the "thrillers," the crime-inflated press, the demoralizing influences in city life, not in the spirit of moralizing, but as the current topics of the day. It would thus set standards and provide bases for judgment of the life and the pace in the modern city.

As Dr. Van Waters has repeatedly pointed out, competition is a poor instrument in the schoolroom. Pressure of competition causes detectable and undetectable suffering among sensitive children, which does not produce values as it is assumed to do in business. The injured loser only too frequently seeks compensation and defenses along socially destructive channels.[2]

Andrew B. Steele, Chief Probation Officer, Jackson County Juvenile Court, Kansas City, Missouri, in an article on "The New Educational Philosophy as it affects Delinquents,"[3] shows keen insight into the problems of the relationship between the juvenile courts and the schools, from which we quote only in part:

CONTRIBUTIONS OF THE JUVENILE COURT TO THE SCHOOL

The juvenile courts have contributions to make to the schools in the problem of dealing with delinquent children. Professor Harry Overstreet has suggested that we are controlled by central ideas. The central idea in the juvenile court procedure has been consideration of the delinquent child—a friendly attitude toward the child and his problems. It has refused to blame the child for his delinquency. It has refused to consider the delinquent child as different and apart from other children. It has freed itself from the impedimenta of the doctrines of total deprav-

[1] Ibid., p. 109.
[2] See op. cit., passim.
[3] Year Book, National Probation Association (1932–1933), pp. 150–153.

ity, individual responsibility, freedom of choice, the magic of authority, and the divine rights of parents, teachers, and others in positions of authority. It has accepted with their implications the newer sociological and psychological ideas, that where there is delinquency, there is a delinquent situation; that individual responsibility is completely overshadowed by parental and social responsibility in cases of delinquency; and that the authority must be respectable, intelligent and sympathetic. It is quite significant that the juvenile courts have not had to change this central idea during these times of new orientations. Rather, they have been reinforced by the larger social movements of family case work, public health, mental health, and the newer psychology and sociology. It must be recognized to the everlasting credit of the pioneers in the juvenile court movement that they looked in the direction of giving the delinquent the feeling of being respected, of having a share in and of still belonging to the group, in the positive building up of regard for authority, loyalty to his fellows, and a feeling of security in his being.

It would be misleading to infer that the schools have overlooked these principles. The child-centered school has certainly taken them into account, and it has succeeded remarkably well in bringing its educational practices into line with the needs of the children. The foolish notion that regard for the pupil's needs means that the child himself is aware of his needs, and the equally foolish notion that adults must know what a child ought to need, do not concern us here. The one is mistaken sentimentality, while the other is probably a hang-over from the days when adults considered children little grown-ups. It goes without saying that the needs of children can be found out only through thoroughgoing research.

THE NEW EDUCATIONAL PHILOSOPHY AS IT AFFECTS DELINQUENTS

The case in point here is that the vested interests of the academically minded still present stubborn resistance to the education of all the children of all the people according to their interest and needs. These ladies and gentlemen need to ponder the suggestions in a philosophy of education given to the world by Emerson ninety-one years ago: "You are trying to make that man another you. One's enough. . . . The secret of education lies in respecting the pupil." Knowledge for the sake of knowledge, and art for art's sake still wage a rather successful struggle against the more realistic ideas of "knowledge in use," and art for the purpose of creative expression in modern living. There is still a clearly recognized gap between what many children get in school and what they need. This has particular bearing on the case of the delinquent child. If the truth about it were known, it is quite likely that the athletic and extra-curricular programs of many schools more nearly meet the needs of many pupils than their regular classroom programs; that is, if the test is to be the behavior of these pupils as useful, healthy and happy members of the social group.

Nearly every juvenile court is confronted with the rapid increase in delinquency in the fourteen-year-old group. The ever present elements in the situation are conflict with authority and vocational maladjustments, accompanied all too frequently by school failure. Is it not time to question the nature and function of school authority just as we have questioned the nature and function of parental authority when it has resulted in serious conflict? Is it not about time to ask the schools to give more attention to the vocational interests and needs of the unsuccessful in school, especially since compulsory attendance laws compel older and older boys and girls to continue in school? Is it not about time to think about a reinterpretation of success in life? How much longer are we going to worship the shoddy idea of "success in a big way"?

The nature and function of authority in a democracy was one of the first problems that confronted our sires in this republic. Since the days of the Declaration of Independence our fundamental idea of authority is that "governments derive their just powers from the consent of the governed." To begin with, men admitted that this was their natural right. The idea grew and it was later realized that it must also apply to the just as natural right of women. Then, through the unifying processes that go on while we are not aware, the last generation has begun to give serious attention to the question of the application of the principle in the governing of children. Children, too, are coming into their rights when it is realized that they must participate if they are to grow up in the ways of democracy. The fear that this does away with authority is just the same fear as of old—the fear of loss of prerogatives. It is much simpler to take it as a change from the idea of authority as force and position, to the idea of authority as intelligent leadership valued for its inherent worth. This simply decrees that authority must be respectable if it is to be respected. Government must respect the governed. Or, to put it another way, government must serve the governed. Men naturally respect authority that offers them security and leadership.

A man has no more important activity than his vocational pursuits. Work is a biological necessity. Has it not been pointed out that since their social beginnings men have played, they have worked, they have loved, and they have worshipped? There must be something fundamental in the nature of things that makes this so. The mess we are in just now would indicate that it is about time to put a few first things first. Wise men have always held work to be of the first importance in human affairs. Is there any good reason to think there will be any change in this respect as long as men are biologically men, and the world in which they live is constituted as it is? One might facetiously add that Old Man Biology has been on the job a long time and is not to be denied. Man's work is not only a means of supplying him with the necessities of life, but beloved work has a deeply satisfying and unifying effect on his personality. In view of the social and personal importance of vocational activity, one who deals with delinquents must wonder why in so many instances we have an educational set-up that makes a child's vocational needs and interests lead him directly into conflict rather than into cooperative endeavor with school authority.

As long as we continue to measure success wholly in terms of ability to juggle symbols or to accumulate wealth and power, great masses of the population are doomed to failure. This applies especially to the boys and girls who fail in school and come into conflict with authority. If more attention could be given these individuals, there would be less reason for conflict between these individuals and the social order. One who has witnessed the gratifying results growing out of placing dull normal and borderline children in special school groups where they are allowed to succeed in their own rights, is encouraged to hope that the practice can be extended with respect to the vocational needs and interests of many children. Successful achievement in the tasks assigned goes hand in hand with more wholesome social attitudes and gains in self-respect and usefulness. It is a revelation to see school failures drop the anti-social attitudes which characterize them when they are compelled day after day to face the fact that they must fail by standards set for their more fortunate fellows, and take on new life when success is placed within their reach. There are many indications here that respect for these individual differences would materially diminish the numbers that are being fed into the army of the delinquent and maladjusted, and make for a more wholesome and happier national life.

Credit must be given progressive school authorities for working in the direction of a more inclusive school program. They are extending the provisions for the children of differing capacities and interests. They recognize the fact that children cannot be separated in school from the experiences they have outside the school walls. More and more attention is being given to health and the experiences of children in their homes and neighborhoods. This requires a new relationship between the home and the school, and the vital factor in bridging this gap is the visiting teacher. It surely can be no mere coincidence that the attitude of the visiting teacher toward the maladjusted and the delinquent child is quite in line with that of the enlightened probation officer. One is increasingly struck with the overlapping functions of these workers.

These factors in the situation should cause all of us to be more active and determined in lending assistance to forward looking schoolmen and schoolwomen who are advancing with a clear vision to a nobler social order through educational programs better suited to the needs of the children.[1]

The Montefiore School[2] Social Laboratory.—The Montefiore School on the West Side of Chicago has a psychological clinic and a social service department operating within the school building. As the psychologist told the writer upon a visit to this school: "It makes all the difference in the world in understanding the personality of the child and his needs when you are right on the spot to see the various difficulties into which these children get with each other or with teachers and do not have to depend on a rationalized or half-forgotten account by a tense child or an irate teacher." Such a clinic is in a unique position to serve as an observation post of the needs and problems of children as they arise in over one-third of their waking time and in group associations.

The Montefiore School, which was organized in 1919 as a special school for the truant and problem boys in the district, maintains a laboratory station. It has fully equipped offices for doctors, nurse, dentist, psychologist (who had considerable training in sociology), and psychiatrist.

Doctors, nurse, dentist, psychologist, psychiatrist, and truant officer, a teacher who does personnel work, a special speech teacher, a teacher of remedial teaching, as well as carefully selected classroom teachers try to find out all they can about the needs of the boys enrolled. The school aims to prevent juvenile delinquency by caring for problem boys many of whom often become delinquent boys.

It is the purpose of the school to enrich its program to fit education to the needs of the problem type of boy and to understand their problems so well that the boys will cease to be truants or behavior cases and will learn to conform socially to their school environment and in part overcome the difficulties of their home and civic environments.

In short the school aims to teach: (1) Cleanliness of body, mind and speech; (2) ideals of courtesy to each other, to parents, to teachers and

[1] See also ETHEL REYNOLDS, "The Visiting Teacher in the Cincinnati Public Schools," in Sheldon Glueck and Eleanor T. Glueck (Editors), *Preventing Crime*, pp. 133–153.

[2] See EDWARD H. STULKEN, "The Montefiore Special School for Problem Boys," in Sheldon and Eleanor Glueck, *Preventing Crime*, Chap. XI.

to the public; (3) the fundamentals of education, Reading, English, Writing, Mathematics, Civics, etc.; (4) the rules of good health and the necessity for the correction of all physical defects. . . .

One of the best of the special features in connection with the work of the Montefiore School is the work of two recreation men furnished by the Board of Education, who spend all of their time in teaching the various groups of boys how to play, and to get along together in groups. The work of one recreation man proved so valuable during the first year that the school was in operation that a second playroom, equipped with games invented and made by the teachers and pupils, was opened in February, 1931. This room has quite the air of a boys' clubroom and proves of value in giving the problem boy experience in playing with other boys.[1]

This school, as careful observation and the testimony by some court officials points out, accomplishes its aims through the maintenance of small classes, supervised project work, organized recreation activities, supervised library reading, creation of reading habits, shopwork; correct eating habits and dining-room decorum are a part of the instructional work of the school. The school was organized to prevent juvenile delinquency and to adjust problem boys in a special day school without recourse to court action or custodial care. Since 1930, delinquency has been steadily declining in the districts in which these boys live.[2] The writer was told that approximately $75,000 was saved to the taxpayers in 1935 through the activities of this school in behalf of the delinquent boys. The school works in very close cooperation with the court and the Probation Department as well as with a host of other social agencies. "Society has too patently been neglecting the early danger signals of personality maladjustment and of criminality in not providing school clinic facilities for the study and treatment of problem children. . . . This enterprise cannot be nibbled at; it must be undertaken on an extensive scale and as an integrated program before tangible results can be expected," conclude the Gluecks[3] after their finding that "in a substantial proportion of criminal careers the danger-signals of anti-sociality are evidenced very early in life."[4]

[1] Montefiore School, *Sixth Annual Report* (1934–1935).
[2] Verified by the Juvenile Court of Cook County.
[3] *One Thousand Juvenile Delinquents*, pp. 277–278.
[4] *Ibid.*, pp. 276–277.

Reciprocal Responsibilities of Court and School.—Excerpts from the following two articles, which are supplementary to each other and are written by an educator, Jane Cartwright,[1] Director of the Luella Cummings Home in Toledo, Ohio, and by a juvenile court judge, the Honorable Carl B. Hyatt, of Ashville, North Carolina (at present with the Department of Justice), indicate what the reciprocal responsibilities of court and school are:

The established policies of agencies define their scope of work, but this is not true of the public schools. Their work has no boundaries. Aside from their major problem of education, they are in a position to know the child rather intimately; they are in a position to see indications of all kinds of neglect or other difficulties; they are at hand when the child first shows signs of deviation from normal development; they have the first opportunity to detect the problems that later feed the stream of delinquency. What they can do about these problems of course depends largely upon their facilities, the personnel of the schools and their cooperation with other agencies, particularly the juvenile court. This is well illustrated by a policy that was put into action some time ago in Toledo by Ralph Dugdale, Assistant Superintendent of Schools and Director of the Attendance Department. He was given power by the juvenile judge to subpoena parents and their children in cases of truancy or similar difficulty. Two half days each week are set aside for conferences with these parents. The result is that about 90 per cent of the cases are satisfactorily adjusted in the school department, leaving few for court disposition. In this way greater chances for understanding are possible, and both child and parents are usually saved the experience of court contact. Julia Lathrop once said "A child's welfare is best served by keeping everything normal about him, keeping him a school child even if he diverges from the straight and narrow paths. In recent years there has been increasing emphasis upon the assumption by educational authorities of responsibility for the treatment of problem children as essentially an education, and not a judicial function."

Though our school systems do much to contribute to the adjustment of children's lives they are producing certain types of problems, in that they are not as yet able to furnish educational opportunities meeting all children's abilities and interests. Mr. Dugdale, three years ago, conducted a most interesting experiment. For this experiment twenty of the hardest, most difficult school boys were selected, all of whom had had continuous bad court records. Each of these boys was interviewed and each gave as a reason for his conduct a dislike for school; each

[1] "Community Cooperation versus Delinquency," *Year Book, National Probation Association* (1932–1933), pp. 34–35.

expressed a desire to do a particular type of trade work. For the sake of the experiment nothing was allowed to stand in the way of giving these boys what they wanted. They were given the opportunity for the desired trade training and but one of these boys has had a recurrence of a court charge.

In the last analysis it is the juvenile court that very largely serves as a hub, around which the majority of agencies and institutions dealing with the welfare of children must rotate. It is the instrument of law and legal power, which so necessarily dovetails into the operation of agencies. The court stands in a position to set standards, and to lead in public opinion but the success of its so doing depends upon how well they are making use of community forces.

CAN THE JUVENILE COURT BE A SUCCESS IN ITSELF?[1]

It is a question in my mind whether we are not tending in the direction of the ultimate abolition of the juvenile courts in their present setting and the establishment of social readjustment elsewhere. Perhaps we shall discover that socialized education can locate, diagnose and solve most problems now appearing before the juvenile courts; that probational staffs or clinical guidance, at present recognized as part of the court, can operate without a definite connection with it. One authority has stated that 90 per cent of the case work now under the supervision and direction of the courts can be as successfully disposed of by other agencies.

At present, probably the establishment of a substitute for a juvenile court is idealistic; but it is an accepted principle that the juvenile court can be strong only in the same proportion as it constructively coordinates all the numerous activities brought into being by human needs. It cannot meet the problem of the individual passion, urge, weakness, or strength except through the agency adapted to deal with his maladjustment.

Our zeal for courts and court activities frequently blinds us to the subtle forces behind and beyond the courts. It so frequently makes it impossible for us to see and understand that the influences which make and mar human happiness and adjustment are really beyond the reach of the law. The law is necessary and fundamental, but stripped of outside agencies, it is effective only as a policeman's club and is completely unable to adjust itself to the individual's needs and the finer shadings of life. Unless there is a mutual helpfulness between the court and outside agencies, there is little left for the law except physical force. But physical force on the part of the law can be reduced in proportion

[1] Carl B. Hyatt, "The School, the Juvenile Court and the Social Attitude," *Year Book, National Probation Association*, (1931), pp. 46–47.

that the responsibility is shifted to social agencies outside. Real advance in social problems is made, not through the courts, but through those activities that readjust, create and train the individual.

May we assume that as soon as schools are ready to deal with child problems—involving change of attitude and habit—from an individual rather than a mass approach, many types of delinquencies can be turned over to them? Will not educators with certain judicial powers be more successful than judges trying to play the role of educators? But who should deal with delinquencies which are the result of social, economic, and communal disorganization? What do even the most progressive schools and courts offer? Which agencies, resources, workers should coordinate their efforts in social readjustment and personality reconditioning?

THE ROLE OF EMPLOYMENT AND VOCATIONAL GUIDANCE IN THE ADJUSTMENT OF DELINQUENT AND PROBLEM YOUTH

At one time we believed that employment was the salvation of man and child, since it kept them out of mischief and did not give the devil an opportunity to play havoc with idle hands. Later we began, particularly in the case of minors, to scrutinize the nature of their employment, the conditions under which they work, the associates they have during work hours, and so on. It was realized that children's health may be seriously undermined, their development retarded, and their morals gravely endangered under certain working conditions. More recently we have begun to compare the advantages of remuneration and of being occupied with the disadvantages of too early social emancipation from the controls of parents and home which frequently accompanies economic independence of juveniles. Again we are reminded of the saying of one father: "There is just as much control in the home as there ever was, only it has changed hands." There is another consideration: when millions of bread-winners are out of employment we must decide carefully whether or not to advise a minor to enter employment and possibly displace an adult wage earner.

In advising a particular juvenile to seek employment the social worker must therefore consider the following questions: (1) Will the child's health, morals, mental development suffer by engaging in this particular job? (2) Will the child be exploited in any way? (3) Is there a danger that the authority in the home will be reversed and that social control by the home will be undermined if he gains some degree of economic independence? (4) Will he displace a wage earner? Even in this age of great individualization the child should realize the insecurity of the industrial worker. (5) Are there opportunities for advancement or is it a blind-alley job? In certain jobs a few tricks are quickly learned but the person works futilely to extricate himself from the mire.

Often one's future is ruined or his ambitions frustrated by lack of opportunities for education and vocational training while young. The social worker should take a long view of the situation even though solution to the immediate pressing problems seems to be employment. Minors should remain at school as long as is possible and expedient. It is often discouraging to the social worker to watch a young boy or girl waste time at school while the family could profit by the earnings. What needs to be done in these cases—all other things being equal—is to provide aid to the family and stimulation to the student to make better use of his time. The need is not for more workers but for better trained workers. Only adequate education and training can supply to the individual that sense of satisfaction which comes from a job well done. Young people in our modern industrial order meet many disheartening situations as it is, without becoming demoralized because of lack of efficiency and training. The lack of efficiency is human wastage which cannot be easily retrieved in later years. Of course, it often happens that the most efficient persons, and persons not suffering from serious personality difficulties, must join the ranks of idle unemployed during a depression, but the large employment agencies testify to the fact that the number of these persons was at a minimum on their lists while the "borderline cases" were their most serious problem.

At times one hears a social worker say that "selling papers can do no harm to the boy," that he knows "prosperous businessmen whose paper-selling in boyhood was their making." It must be remembered that urban conditions have greatly changed since these businessmen were boys, that in many cities the population has doubled and trebled, that the traffic hazards were practically unknown in those days, that the whole moral tone of our country has changed since the war, and that two, three, or four scores of years ago there were many more opportunities for energetic people with a minimum of training and education than there are at present.

When there are no dangers which might result from injudicious or hasty engagement in employment of minors, the worker may advocate seeking a job for an older boy or girl on part- or full-time basis, depending upon the nature of the case. When the child is employed, the worker should concern himself with the effect upon the child, particularly when the transition from school work to industry is too great or too rapid. Clearly he needs more supervision rather than less since he has entered another social world with numerous other possibilities both for advancement and for retardation or disorganization. Particularly is that true of girls who work as salesladies, counter girls, waitresses,[1] usherettes, mother's helpers,[2] or boys who work as messengers or bellhops.[3] It should not be assumed at any time that when a "girl is planted in a nice home as a mother's helper" she will not need as much supervision or even more than when she was at her own home. The question frequently arises whether or not to tell the employer of the child's offense and the agency's interest in the case. Obviously, it depends upon the intelligence of the employer, the nature of the case, and other circumstances, but under any conditions it is unwise to give the child the feeling that his employer is being deceived. There are employers who do not understand, but frequently the difficulty lies in the wrong approach to him rather than in his lack of ability to appreciate the situation. If the employer is to be taken fully into confidence, a study must be made of him and the approach should be carefully planned and slowly executed.[4]

Vocational Guidance.[5]—In cases of older boys and girls the worker should interest himself in the type of occupations which are best suited to their peculiar bent. It is not only discouraging and destructive for restive youths to be placed in blind-alley

---

[1] See FRANCES DONOVAN, *The Woman Who Waits.*

[2] See WILLIAM I. THOMAS, *The Unadjusted Girl.*

[3] See THEODORE DREISER, *An American Tragedy.*

[4] See PAULINE V. YOUNG, "The Employer," in *Interviewing in Social Work*, pp. 154–159.

[5] See White House Conference on Child Health and Protection, *Vocational Guidance;* see also the case of James R., pp. 343–344, 346.

jobs,[1] with no prospects to relieve the monotony and dull
drudgery, but it is embittering and tends to develop cynicism
in them as they grow older and must remain unskilled for the
rest of their working lives.

The offenders who are studied at the clinic might receive some
suggestions from the psychologist. Attempts should be made to
correlate the youth's interests and aptitudes with vocational
placement. Material gain is of prime importance in a family
dependent on children's earnings. Even when no other considerations are taken into account than financial gain, the social
worker will realize that an ill-chosen job is often more harmful
than no job at all. Experience and statistics testify that
attempts to reduce placement in blind-alley jobs have reduced
the sum total of adolescent offenses.[2]

The movement for vocational guidance for youths, and
particularly for offenders, is still uncharted. Here and there
attempts have been made at scientific placement of youths in
suitable callings, but the industrial order has offered too few
opportunities.

Frequently the problem does not center around a choice of a
vocation but around a conflict of plans. Parents have high
ambitions for their children. Often they wish to accomplish
vicariously the success which they have never attained in their
own youth. The children, however, have other interests but
they do not wish to disappoint their parents, or the parents are so
insistent that they will not allow an independent choice and will
not face reality nor resign themselves to a compromise. The
child's own thwarted ambitions form a foundation for emotional
maladjustment and ultimately for misconduct.

Under these circumstances the worker will need to explain to
the parents the desirability of their children following an occupation suitable to their intellectual equipment and temperamental
traits. The parents must also become aware of the significance
of open conflict or hidden disappointment when their growing
son or daughter does not or cannot follow his or her choice.
Many sixteen-year-old girls may suddenly decide to get married
to a chance acquaintance only to escape conflict at home or a

[1] See E. S. BOGARDUS, *The City Boy and His Problems*, pp. 101–109;
FREDERICK J. ALLEN, *Principles and Problems in Vocational Guidance.*

[2] BURT, *op. cit.*, p. 194.

feeling of failure which besets them when they are unable to follow the vocational pursuits not of their own choice. Boys and young men may leave home and take to the road for the same reason.

The Case of Charlotte.—Such cases repeat themselves in girl's courts. Charlotte, at the age of sixteen, married a young man of twenty-seven, without her mother's consent or knowledge. "It broke my heart to be married without the family, but I knew that it was either a secretarial course at school or elopement. I had struggled with school for two years. The course did not interest me. The truant officer was after me. My mother would not believe that I was not interested in the course. I had no one to turn to. I was not what you might call boy-crazy. I met Bob at my cousin's house. He looked a kind and clean-cut boy and had a steady income. He is a sailor. . . . I knew him almost a month when I married him. . . . I realize now that our marriage is a mistake, but the secretarial course was also a mistake."

Dr. Leta S. Hollingworth states that in this situation "parents seem almost never to be able to follow the advice given them. Having cherished for about fifteen years the belief that their son would be what they wish, they cannot reconcile themselves to the disappointment of giving up their cherished dreams."[1] It may be maintained, however, that when parents face a crisis they are more likely to accept compromises.

If a child suffers too severely when he must disappoint a parent, it may be possible to induce him to redirect either his own interests or those of his parents into some nonvocational hobby to be pursued in his leisure hours.

At present the danger lies not so much in conflict of vocational plans, in lack of vocational orientation, or in inadequate equipment, as it does in lack of opportunities open to the young, once they become qualified. In an industrial world where a man in the prime of life becomes an industrial discard and the youth become the lost generation, the fundamental difficulty lies far deeper than an individual worker or agency can control. The only thing that the worker can do is to understand the source of the offender's unadjustment and to hold out the hope to him that in the rapid reorganization the country is undergoing and the tremendous shifts in population which are taking place from city to country, plans will also be made for youth's new day.

[1] *Psychology of the Adolescent*, p. 86.

Another source of industrial frustration of which the worker should take cognizance arises from the relative decline in the demand for skill in industry. No longer are the large numbers of highly skilled workers needed in our present machine age. The worker cannot raise high hopes in youths which must later be blasted as these people must adjust themselves to the role of machine tenders. They should be aided in finding life satisfactions not only in their work but in their hobbies, in their play, in reading. The unimaginative, the mentally dull, the emotionally highly stabilized may suffer little from such a situation as awaits many of them in a machine civilization, but for others, unless outlets are found and the situation interpreted, it may give rise to serious tensions. For the former blind-alley jobs may perhaps be suitable, despite the fact that American tradition expects every boy to rise.

The social worker must also recognize the fact that when a job-seeking person is rebuffed by employers time after time he may become work-shy. To put the full responsibility on him to find and hold a job is often too much. He needs help and encouragement in finding it and supervision after obtaining it. Considerable interpretation of the employment situation is needed to dispel any notions that the individual alone is at fault or that there is no use in looking for employment or in obtaining an education. There are many opportunities for qualified young people and the situation in some respects is growing better.

Selected Bibliography

1. BALDWIN, SARA E., and ERNEST G. OSBORNE: *Home-school Relations*, Progressive Education Association, 1935.
2. DEXTER, ELIZABETH H.: "Treatment of the Child through the School Environment," *Mental Hygiene*, XII (April, 1928), 358–365.
3. ———: "The Child's Adjustment to School Life," *Year Book, National Probation Association* (1932–1933), pp. 160–162.
4. ELIOT, THOMAS D.: *The Juvenile Court and the Community*, The Macmillan Company, 1914.
5. ———: "Case Work for Quasi-delinquent Children by Educational and Other Non-court Methods," *Journal of Delinquency*, IX (January–March, 1925), 1–50.
6. ———: "The Juvenile Court and the Educational System," *Journal of Criminal Law and Criminology*, XIV (May, 1923), 25–45.
7. DOLTON, ISABELLA: "The School and the Juvenile Court," *Year Book, National Probation Association* (1931), pp. 48–60.

8. HARPER, WILLIAM J.: "The School and Court Relationships Concerning Behavior Problems," *Year Book, National Probation Association* (1932–1933), pp. 163–167.

9. JACKSON, LEROY F.: "The School and the Court; An Interpretation of Function," *Year Book, National Probation Association* (1932–1933), pp. 154–159.

10. KENNEDY, WILLIAM: "Responsibilities and Opportunities of the Public School as a Social Service Instrument," *Proceedings of the National Conference of Social Work* (1927), pp. 447–454.

11. KEPPEL, E. P.: "Education for Adults," *Yale Review*, XV (April, 1926), 417–432.

12. MARTENS, ELISE H.: "Berkeley's Coordinated Program of Child Adjustment," *School Life*, XVI (October, 1930), 23–24; (November, 1930), 56–58.

13. OPPENHEIMER, J. J.: *The Visiting Teacher Movement*, 1924. Reprinted for the Public Education Association of New York.

14. PERRY, CHARLES M.: "Limitations of the Public School as a Social Service Instrument," *Proceedings of the National Conference of Social Work* (1927), pp. 441–447.

15. PLANT, JAMES S.: "As the Twig Is Bent," *National Conference of Social Work* (1929), pp. 182–190.

16. SAYLES, MARY B.: *The Problem Child in School*, The Commonwealth Fund, 1925.

17. STEELE, ANDREW B.: "The New Educational Philosophy as It Affects Delinquents," *Year Book, National Probation Association* (1932–1933), pp. 149–153.

*18. WHITE HOUSE CONFERENCE ON CHILD HEALTH AND PROTECTION, *The Delinquent Child* (IV C2), pp. 38–43, 79–96, 101–133 (school); 246–256 (police); 137–165 (church); 193–224 (recreation); 262–264; 266–267.

Vocational Guidance and the Child in Industry

19. BINFORD, JESSIE: "Understanding the Delinquent," *Year Book, National Probation Association* (1931), pp. 24–25.

20. COLE, LUELLA: *Psychology of Adolescence*, Farrar & Rinehart, Inc., 1936, Chap. XI, "The Vocational Misfit."

21. FITCH, JOHN: *Vocational Guidance in Action*, Columbia University Press, 1935.

22. HANNA, JOSEPH V.: "Vocational Factors in Delinquency," *Year Book, National Probation Association* (1932–1933), pp. 189–197.

23. HATHWAY, MARION: *The Young Cripple and His Job*, University of Chicago Press, 1928.

24. HUGHES, GWENDOLYN S.: *Mothers in Industry*, New Republic, Inc., 1925.

25. JONES, A. J.: *Principles of Guidance*, McGraw-Hill Book Company, Inc., 1930.

26. JONES, ABRAM NICHOLLS: "Employment Problems of Probationers," *Year Book, National Probation Association* (1932–1933), pp. 198–202.

27. LeMesurier, Mrs. L. (Editor): *A Handbook of Probation and Social Work of the Courts*, "Probation and Work Finding."

28. McGill, Nettie: *Children in Street Work*, U. S. Children's Bureau, Publication No. 183 (1928).

29. ———: *Child Workers on City Streets*, U. S. Children's Bureau, Publication No. 188 (1929).

30. New York State Crime Commission, *A Study of Environmental Factors*, 1929, pp. 53–63.

31. ———: *From Truancy to Crime: A Study of 251 Adolescents* (1928).

32. ———: *Crime and The Community: A Study of Trends in Crime Prevention.* Subcommission on Causes and Effects of Crime, pp. 143–151; 272–289 (1930).

33. Thorndike, E. L., and Others: *Prediction in Vocational Success*, The Commonwealth Fund, 1934.

*34. Van Waters, Miriam: *Youth in Conflict*, pp. 111–123.

35. Watson, E. B.: *A Source Book for Vocational Guidance*, H. W. Wilson Company, 1930.

*36. White House Conference on Child Health and Protection, *The Delinquent Child*, pp. 169–189.

Suggestions for Further Study

1. What is the new educational philosophy as it affects delinquents?

2. What is meant by "knowledge in use"? Do the schools in your community impart this kind of knowledge?

3. What is the role of the visiting teacher? What functions does she perform in your community?

4. What does Cooley mean by "dynamic and socialized schools"?

5. Define character education. How do William I. Thomas and Dorothy S. Thomas define it? (See *The Child in America*, pp. 272–294.) What are the methods of character education?

6. What is the relation of the school to community organization? parental education? coordinating councils?

7. What role should the school play in vocational placement of children? vocational education? interpretation of the present economic system? in leisure-time activities?

8. What role should the school play in the adjustment of minor offenses? of emotional maladjustments?

9. What should be the function of the school guidance clinic? the staff?

CHAPTER XXV

THE ROLE OF RECREATION IN THE ADJUSTMENT OF DELINQUENT AND PROBLEM YOUTH

The recreation leader of the old school of thought viewed delinquency largely as misdirected energy and as the result of thwarted desire for adventure and new experience during the hours of spare time and inactivity so characteristic of modern city life. It is true, as H. H. Lou observes, that much of the delinquent behavior of children is not readily distinguishable from the recreational activities of their nondelinquent friends, "for the wish for new experience may take different forms of activities, good and bad."[1]

The recreation leader of the newer school of thought recognizes the fact that any conditions in family life or in the social group which promote repression and handicap the child directly or indirectly promote conflicts in the child which cannot be removed merely by supplying "proper recreational activities."

Recreation and leisure-time activities are regarded by many as important factors in the program for crime prevention and not from the narrower point of view as benefits to individual persons or families. Frederick Thrasher, as can be judged from his discussion of the Lower West Side New York Leisure Time Conference,[2] looks upon these leisure-time activities largely as programs in crime prevention:

The principle of district recreational planning with a view to crime prevention was applied in the spring of 1934 with the organization of the Lower West Side Leisure Time Conference as a permanent department of the Council of Lower West Side Social Agencies. This Conference, which is composed of representatives of all the recreational groups and interests of the community, has as its general purpose to develop an integrated program of leisure time activities for all children

[1] *Juvenile Courts in the United States*, p. 157.
[2] "Crime Prevention through Community Planning," reprinted by the Lower West Side Social Agencies (New York City) from *The University of Chicago Magazine*, March, 1935.

and adolescents of the Lower West Side irrespective of race, creed, or economic level. It has stated its immediate objectives as follows:

Fact Finding.—To provide a scientific basis for a community leisure time program through furnishing all agencies with useful facts and information.

Conference and Co-operation.—Increased co-operation and better understanding among all agencies dealing with leisure time problems.

Outdoor Play Facilities.—(a) Utilization of vacant land, play streets, and roofs to provide additional facilities and reduce traffic hazards; (b) co-operation with Park Department and playgrounds.

Summer Activities and Camps.—To study vacation activities and to promote wider opportunities for camping.

Co-operation with Public Housing Authority.—For the development of recreational facilities as an integral part of slum clearance projects.

Prevention of Delinquency.—Co-operation with Juvenile Aid Bureau of the Police Department for a better organization of leisure time facilities for preventing delinquency.

Leisure Time Adjustment of Problem Children.—Co-operation with Public Schools of area, Bureau of Attendance, and Children's Court to make available more adequate leisure time activities for problem children.

Circulation of Toys.—To co-operate with the Toyery in promotion of more adequate facilities for this work.

Wider Use of School Plant.—Promotion of wider use of school buildings and grounds for leisure time activities after school hours and in vacations.

Wider Use of Church Plant.—Promotion of wider use of church facilities for wholesome leisure time activities.

Better Films Council.—Development of a Lower West Side Motion Picture Council to improve public taste in pictures and provide more opportunities for children to see suitable films.

Radio Committee.—To study the role and possibilities of the radio in relation to the use of leisure time.

Reading and Exhibits.—Promotion of more extensive use of libraries and museums.

Volunteer Workers.—Fuller utilization of local leadership for recreation: (a) Fuller co-operation with parents and parents' organizations; (b) fuller utilization of Big Brothers as recreational advisors.

Parent Education.—Promotion of parent education and organization to facilitate more adequate leisure time activities for children.

Experimental Block Program.—To develop experimentally and evaluate programs of leisure time activities for all children of given blocks where recreational problems are acute.

Recreational Advisement.—Development of specialized personnel to organize leisure time programs for individual children referred by agencies.

Leisure Time Information Bureau.—Development of a clearing house for all information as to local leisure time activities and resources.

Recreation for Handicapped Children.—Development of special facilities for children who are hard-of-hearing, cardiac, etc.

Education of the Public.—As to importance of wholesome leisure time activities for children and adolescents and stimulation of increased support of existing leisure time activities.

New Facilities.—Study of leisure time resources of community and development of more adequate or needed new facilities.

While the above objectives were formulated for purposes of educating the community, rather than to achieve academic precision, they are based upon local researches and they embody an application of sociological principles essential to effective community planning. Definite, though uneven, progress has been made in the realization of each of these objectives. A few examples may be cited. . . . About 50 per cent of the children of this area are unreached by an organized recreational agency. The growing recognition of the failure of supervised recreation to reach the boys on the local block led the Leisure Time Conference to develop its play street program, which was designed to occupy the leisure time of children not reached by other agencies. Seven play streets were set aside by action of the Board of Aldermen, and a director and staff of emergency workers were provided by the city. During the summer of 1934 a daily average of about 1,000 children enjoyed a variety of games and leisure time activities on these play streets. Seven hundred boys participated in stick-ball tournaments and 900 boys were taken to big league baseball games at the Yankee Stadium. At the end of the summer the program was continued after school hours and on week-ends and some indoor facilities were made available for use of the children in inclement weather. This program is being guided by a Steering Committee (of the Leisure Time Conference), which is composed of representatives of the recreational agencies of the community. This committee has frequent meetings to discuss policies and plans for the development of the program. . . .

It should be noted that the Leisure Time Conference makes contacts with numerous agencies such as the church, the school, the library, the radio, committee, and others engaged in the interests of the parents, educational agencies, housing authorities, the police department, and others. But the efforts of the conference in relation to these agencies are directed *only* toward the promotion of wholesome leisure-time activities. Of course, it is a Leisure Time Conference and should undoubtedly not concern itself with the other numerous needs of the underprivileged child. But the question may be raised as to how a community planning program can be organized effectively and economically when the other needs—social-economic, mental hygiene, educational, medical, religious, and others not met by leisure-time activities—are not taken into account by a conference carrying on a program on such a wide scale as indicated above?

Is it wise to isolate "leisure-time needs" by one conference and allow other conferences and agencies to make contacts again with the schools, churches, police, housing authorities, the parents, and others in order to deal with the wider and often more pressing needs, mentioned above? Surely, the schools, the homes, the churches, and others can offer more than just recreational facilities. Is not the conference undertaking too much unilateral specialization along activities which have not been conclusively proved to be the "lifesaver" in delinquency? There must be a large number of children on the Lower West Side of New York who do not avail themselves of these activities but who are not delinquent. At least a study—with a control group—by the writer in Russian Town yielded such results.[1] Every intelligent person will agree that wholesome play and recreation are indispensable in the lives of all persons, but other things must be taken into account in the intricate life pattern of families, persons, and communities, living in a changing social-economic and moral order.

The Relation of Group Work to Case Work.—Robert C. Taber, Boys' Club and Settlement Representative, Council of Social Agencies, Philadelphia, raises the pertinent question in a paper read before the Pennsylvania Conference on Social Welfare, Group Work Division—"Will Increased Wholesome Leisure Time Activities Alone Prevent Juvenile Delinquency? If not, What Will?"[2] We quote him in part:

Leisure time activities alone, no matter how wholesome or how extended, cannot prevent juvenile delinquency. Leisure time activities have an important role to play in a prevention program but there are definite limitations as to what can be accomplished through this medium. A full recognition of this fact is necessary at the very beginning if we

[1] See *Pilgrims of Russian-Town*, Chap. IX.
[2] Manuscript, Feb. 28, 1936, pp. 1–8. Quoted by permission of Mr. Taber.

are to give recreation an importance which is not out of all proportion to its actual effectiveness. . . .

What is there in the very nature of delinquency which makes it a problem that recreation alone cannot meet? It would seem to me that there are certain generalizations concerning delinquency which can be made without treading upon dangerous ground.

In the first place, there is no one cause of delinquency and, consequently, there can be no one solution. Every delinquent child presents his own unique problem. As human beings, we are not only born with different physical, mental and emotional equipment but the forces which have gone into our life experiences are dissimilar. . . . How could a recreational agency be expected to give the time necessary to know any great number of its members on such an intensive basis?

Secondly, a goodly portion of delinquent behavior is symptomatic, just as certain physical maladies are symptoms of an underlying disorder. In other words, there is seldom a direct cause and effect which can be simply traced. Causal factors frequently lie far beneath the surface and require deep insight on the part of the worker if they are to be reached. . . . The fact that delinquent behavior is so frequently symptomatic makes it an unwise practice to refer juvenile delinquents to recreation centers in a wholesale fashion. It is not that leisure time activities have nothing constructive to offer, but that such a practice would mean that we would be blind to other phases of the problem which cannot be met by the recreation center.

A third consideration has to do with the difference in our ways of solving difficulties. . . . How could leisure time activities alone prevent delinquency when we choose different methods of achieving a satisfactory adjustment? They could not possibly meet the needs of all individuals. It would seem to me that this point warrants further consideration inasmuch as it represents a stumbling block for many of us as group workers when we set about to plan a preventive program.

The child who is unusually fearful is overwhelmed by a group. The strange faces and the new experience of sharing with others makes him feel that he is in a foreign land. He finds it so difficult to make a place for himself within the group that he drops out after one or two visits. Unless he receives personal help or unless some fortuitous circumstance brings about a change in him, he may never become affiliated with an organized group. He will keep to himself as much as possible. Oftentimes this same person feels comfortable in an individual relationship with a case worker and can work through some of his fear.

On the other hand, there are children who find more freedom within a group than in a relationship with a case worker. For them, the meeting with a worker alone is a terrifying experience because they feel caught, whereas their meeting with a group gives them the comforting support of the other members. The attention of the leader is not concentrated on one person but on the group as a whole, and therefore, the relationship is not so intensive. . . .

Again, the recreation center is limited in what it can offer the child whose problem has reached the acute state. . . . I recall the case of a boy who found out for the first time at the age of sixteen that he had been adopted. He became infuriated with his foster mother and his usual quiet behavior suddenly changed to deliberate and intentional revengeful acts against her. She had been an unusually good mother to him but that did not make the shock any easier for him to bear. He ended up by running away for nearly a year during which time all efforts to locate him were unsuccessful. I think that you will agree that if anyone had been able to reach him during his depressing period and had invited him to attend a recreation center, he would have been completely indifferent toward the invitation. His indifference would not be due to any failure on the part of the recreation center but to the fact that recreation was not the thing that was most concerning him at the moment. The very idea of mingling with other boys who were enjoying themselves might be repulsive to him. He needed to go away from people where he could think his problem through for himself. . . .

In Philadelphia we have been engaged for nearly three years in an experiment with boys who have been discharged by the Juvenile Court. Each boy is referred to a center in his own neighborhood and visits are made to his home for a period of several months. A survey was made of 1,600 cases and some interesting figures resulted. Out of the total, we found that 18 per cent were active members of some organized group when the initial visit was made; that 58 per cent had never been affiliated with a recreation center despite the fact that facilities were available within ten blocks of their homes; and that the remaining 24 per cent had been members at one time but were inactive at the time of our first interview. . . . A goodly portion represented boys who were definitely opposed to participation in supervised play. They preferred the adventure and freedom of the street where they were practically a law unto themselves. They could not adjust to authority of any kind with perhaps one exception. They could tolerate the authority necessary to hold their group together but they could not accept the simplest of rules which must, of necessity, be set up by any recreation center if its work is to be anything but chaos. In other words, an individual must have already achieved a certain sense of adjustment if he is to find organized group experience attractive. If those figures and illustrations have any validity, we cannot infer that the provision of recreation facilities will assure good use of leisure time. On the contrary, we must recognize that the poor use of leisure time on the part of many delinquents, is just another indication of their lack of capacity to make a satisfactory adjustment.

To be sure we have not done all that we can as group workers in meeting this wide range of problems, and yet I feel certain there are limits as to what we can do. Perhaps this process of defining limits will be helpful to us in that we need to know what we cannot accomplish before we are free to concentrate our efforts upon that area in which we can be effective. If we continue to feel responsible for the whole program of juvenile delinquency, we shall be overwhelmed by it and become lost in the struggle. On the other hand, if we can see recreation in its proper relationship to other services, we can be more helpful. . . .

The boy who is busily occupied is less apt to be exposed to undesirable influences and, therefore, runs less risk of getting into trouble. More important, however, than the amount of time he spends at the center is what the time he does spend there means to him. It can be satisfying experience in that it provides for the expression of the fundamental urges within him. He can achieve power in a constructive way by becoming a leader and by taking certain responsibility for phases of the program. He may find satisfaction in becoming a respected member of a group. The wide range of activities lend themselves to the constructive use of the participants.

The group experience gives him an opportunity to learn the all important lesson of sharing and cooperating with others. The importance of human relationships in living cannot be over-emphasized. So much of importance hinges on our capacity to get along with other people—our economic, social, and personal security. Inasmuch as supervised play does provide another group experience in addition to the group experience in family and school relationships, it becomes an exceedingly important contribution to the development of a child.

The recreation centers also meet a day by day need. It goes along with the child over a period of time in contrast to a case work service, which usually involves a temporary relationship in which help is found for a specific problem. It represents an element of stability, something which acts as a hitching post in the important process of finding one's self. . . .

The Case of Frank Ryder.—A concrete illustration will clarify the point: Frank Ryder's case shows that a recreation center could not be of direct help with his specific problem because of the pressing nature of his difficulty. He is fifteen years old, born of an Irish family who have always lived in a small house in bad repair within a block from the waterfront. He is one of six children with only one child younger than himself. He has a twin brother by the name of Thomas. Mr. Ryder has a very soft quality as a person but has become embittered toward his neighbors. He feels that they are all against him because of his effort to keep Frank on the right track. He has finally washed his hands of any responsibility toward Frank, in fact he has not spoken to Frank for one whole year. Mrs. Ryder is an exceedingly emotional and dramatic person who gets highly wrought up on the slightest provocation. Her own mother died of epilepsy. She is very dictatorial and domineering over the father. She herself is given to having frequent spells and it is obvious that she lives in mortal terror of having her own condition diagnosed as epilepsy. She shields all of the children against the father. Her husband has become resigned to his position of providing for the family and no longer attempts to play a part as head of the family. He seems to have set himself apart from his family as he has from his neighbors. He keeps to himself entirely with one exception. He is exceedingly fond of his one-year-old granddaughter. All of his affection seems to center about her.

Frank, himself, is an ungainly boy whose one outstanding characteristic is antagonism toward everything and anything. He speaks of himself as the black sheep in the family. He is physically handicapped as the result of a trolley accident in which he lost part of his foot.

A goodly portion of the tension which existed in this family could be traced back to this accident. It had taken place when he was eight years old, and during the seven years that followed Frank had become very demanding and antagonistic until he arrived at the point where his own parents turned to the court in desperation because he had gotten beyond their control. They had him arrested with the hope that it would scare him. He was placed on probation by the court and at the same time referred to our agency. Upon inquiring from the settlement house in his neighborhood, we found that he had been a member of their center since he had been a youngster. He was known as a general trouble maker, as a decided misfit. He deliberately went out of his way to antagonize the different members of the staff. He intentionally disrupted the activities program in any way that he could. Occasionally the workers had been obliged to suspend him from attending but each time he would return and very rapidly slip back into his old ways.

It was obvious that the recreation center alone could not help him in making an adjustment. It required *individual attention of a case worker as well*.

As we came to know Frank and his family, we found that his mother made a pet of him after the accident. She would be seen sitting on the doorstep with Frank's head in her lap. She would stroke his head and meanwhile complain to the neighbors of his injury, saying that he had been the "sheik" of the family and now his good looks had been marred forever. In her sympathy for Frank she spoiled him by doing anything he wanted. She shielded him from his father so that Frank missed the ordinary firmness which any father must exercise in bringing up his children. He quite naturally expected everyone to bow to his demands and to have his battles fought for him. As he began to enter into the period of adolescence he missed the protection of his mother. She could not extend her control into his school and neighborhood life. He found that his new associates ignored his demands. He got no special consideration from them and became very antagonistic toward them. It was the only weapon he could fall back upon. He did not know how to win a place among his associates through a constructive kind of behavior, and he, therefore, turned to this destructive channel which he found effective.

Added to this was an incident which occurred between him and his father. A year before Mr. Ryder had caught Frank entering the house by climbing over the roof. He had punished Frank and a group of older boys learned of it. On New Year's eve, when they had been celebrating with liquor, they encountered Mr. Ryder and told him he was discriminating against Frank. He became infuriated and the boys finally attacked him. He escaped and ran into his home. As he did so, a shot was fired which barely missed him. He was certain that Frank had gotten these boys to "gang up on him" and from that point on he positively refused to speak to his son. Needless to say, a tremendous amount of ill-feeling existed in that home. They didn't trust each other and were continually taking out their feelings on each other in some subtle way. . . .

The case worker enabled the father to express a tremendous amount of his resentment and he finally arrived at the point where he would speak to Frank and take some responsibility for him. However, Mr. Ryder can never fully forgive Frank even though he now knows that his son did not get the boys "to gang up" on him. He cannot give Frank what he might otherwise have given him in his relationship as a father. Mrs. Ryder now enjoys a freer relationship with her husband and has taken over the responsibility for Frank with Mr. Ryder in lieu of sharing nothing with him. Frank has made a better adjustment in that his antagonistic attitude has diminished as the tension of the family has lessened. Through his regular interviews with the case worker he learned to take some responsibility for his own actions. He is no longer entirely irresponsible. However, he has a long way to go.

Frank had attended a settlement house regularly for many years, but as previously stated, he had been very antagonistic and disruptive. As the result of his relationship with the case worker, he had expressed and was relieved of a tremendous amount of resentment and came to feel more comfortable in his home relationship. This partial adjustment carried over into his settlement activities. He helped the staff by doing little things for them. The workers gradually gave him more responsibility as he was ready, and he took great pride in giving assistance. He worked in harmony with them for the most part. The settlement activities provided a medium for self-expression which brought him a sense of "power with," instead of "power over" people. The recreation center carried along with Frank long after the case worker ceased his visiting. In fact, it will continue to serve Frank in his need for the expression of his positive self. In this instance case work and group work have worked together in his behalf.

Harry M. Shulman,[1] formerly of the New York State Crime Commission, brings out similar points in connection with his studies of delinquency in Brooklyn and Manhattan.

National and local recreational agencies operate on several diverse theories. The more conservative seem to feel that recreation is a substitute program for delinquent activities, and that the extension of recreational facilities to fill in the entire free time for the child will combat delinquency by affording him no opportunity for delinquent behavior. Other recreational agencies have faith in the transfer of attitudes acquired in supervised recreation, and feel that children trained in ideals of sportsmanship will communicate these ideals to other children who have not had direct contact with recreational programs. Certain agencies are primarily concerned with the overcoming of physical and mental disabilities or the utilization of special aptitudes, on the theory that the problem child has developed conflict around an inferiority which must be compensated for by giving him opportunity for success. Many of the older child guidance agencies, dominated by the psychological point of view, have worked on this principle. . . . Problem children do not adapt themselves well to normal groups. They are not merely normal children who steal, or stay out late, or play truant. These behavior manifestations are symptomatic of deeper underlying conflicts with their families and society. These children often have distorted personalities. They have deep feelings of inferiority, are oversensitive, and crave response and security. They are frightened by the size of the average community center or club. They are awed by the complexity of its system and irked by the inflexibility of its rules.

[1] "Social Agency Coordination for Crime Prevention," *Year Book*, *National Probation Association* (1935), pp. 218–222.

These excerpts clearly indicate that perhaps too much reliance is placed on group recreation and play groups in the adjustment process of problem youth. It has been frequently assumed that "group play can do no harm but will do some good," like sunshine and fresh air for any physically ill patient. While that is undoubtedly true in many instances, it may be distinctly harmful in others, as was shown by Shulman and Taber. Therefore, the worker needs to use care and discretion as to when to rely on mass recreational opportunities as a major factor in the adjustment process and when to use them in conjunction with other resources.

Frederick M. Thrasher made an exhaustive study "of a Boys' Club, newly opened in a crime-breeding area of New York City. The Club was established [for boys of seven to eighteen years and older] because delinquency was prevalent in this area. . . . The Study measured the influence of this Club during its initial four years from 1927–1931, utilizing the descriptive, ecological, statistical, and case study methods."[1] The conclusions drawn from these case studies are of importance:[2]

The case-studies made by the Study revealed that the Club had a negligible influence upon its problem members during the Study period. The acute behavior problems in these cases precipitated by various combinations of family disorganization, dire poverty, school maladjustments, gang activities, association with older hoodlums and underworld characters, demoralizing experiences on the streets and in institutions of commercialized amusement and neighborhood hangouts—these influences for the most part were beyond the power of the Boys' Club to neutralize, particularly in the limited time each week which the average Boys' Club member spent in club activities involving as they did, little real guidance from the Club personnel.

Five years have elapsed since Thrasher made certain recommendations, one of which might be quoted in full.[3]

Surely an institution organized so definitely with the avowed purpose of preventing delinquency should have at least one full-time specialist on the staff with psychological, psychiatric, and sociological training who could apply the recognized methods of scientific study and treatment to

[1] "The Boys' Club and Juvenile Delinquency," *The American Journal of Sociology*, XLII (July, 1936), 66–80.

[2] *Ibid.*, p. 78.

[3] *Ibid.*, p. 78.

the very numerous problem boys, both potential and actual, who become a direct responsibility of the Boys' Club.

The extent to which Thrasher's recommendations have been adopted by the club in question can be judged from the following statement:[1]

Record-keeping has been made more efficient. Attendance has been improved and turnover reduced. A staff-member with psychiatric training has been added to the Club's personnel to handle difficult cases. The attitudes of the boys of the neighborhood have become more cordial. The program has been enriched by the addition of handicrafts and shop-work. The boys have given more time in the gymnasium by the later scheduling of tournament events. A representative of the Bureau of Attendance of the Public Schools has been added to the staff to route all known truants in the area into the Club. This man, whose function is not known to the boys, provides the means of reaching an important class of known potential delinquents, namely, truants.

A social stocktaking, so to speak, is of importance in keeping up to date with modern and scientific methods in the adjustment of individual cases or in the whole program of crime prevention. The progressive recreation departments frequently review their activities and change their program and approach to meet the changing conditions of the times and of the particular community. These departments are also using the case work approach more and more to problems which cannot be adjusted by mass recreation.

It should be noted that in the cases of James R. (pp. 333 *ff.*) and Peter Smith (pp. 407 *ff.*) recreational activities were planned and directed from the standpoint of the family and social situation of the boys, and from the standpoint of their particular interests. Furthermore, the probation officer knew that Peter Smith had several boy friends, alliance with whom did not seem perilous. However, he sought to combat the influence of an unorganized group and to supplant it with the silent supervision of an organized club whose specialty it is to provide legitimate pastimes. He recognized that since clubs differ greatly as to their nature, activities, fees, government, and general atmosphere, it was essential to choose the organization keeping in mind the

[1] *Ibid.*, p. 79.

requirements and the circumstances of Peter's case.   Cooley's[1] experience in his former connection with his work at the Court of General Sessions is of significance.

DIRECTING THE SPARE TIME ACTIVITIES OF DELINQUENT AND PROBLEM YOUTH

Directing and superintending the delinquent's spare-time activities was a far harder task than that of placing him in a fitting occupation. Once more the best approach was that of discovering the probationer's own tastes and inclinations through consultation and repeated contact. Changes of recreation involved, first of all, a new outlook on life, changes of associates and friends, the making of new contacts, and the breaking up of cherished habits of conduct. . . .

The probationer, bent upon indulging himself in various amusements, could be induced to relinquish them only after he had been convinced of their disadvantages and of the existence of more absorbing and constructive types of recreation.   In most cases, discussion or argument produced but little result.   It was generally possible, however, through the use of repeated suggestion and through arousing the curiosity and interest of the probationer, to induce him to experiment with new types of recreation.   Experience with these new forms often engaged his permanent interest and assured his continued participation therein.

In each case the probation officer sought to discover some particular hobby that would fire the enthusiasm of the young delinquent.   Usually this device was found successful, and the new found interest often proved a safe and sufficient substitute for previous disorderly habits.

Probationers preferring sports and outdoor recreation were encouraged to join athletic clubs and gymnasia, while others, who were interested in less strenuous activities, were induced to become members of settlements, clubs, and civic organizations located in their neighborhood. More serious individuals, often of the introvert type, who shunned contact with their neighbors, were interested in hobbies and attractions which provided them with wholesome diversions during their spare moments.

Recreation ideation and habits, however, were extremely difficult to change.   It was soon found that the delinquent's concept of recreation was in many instances very limited and in some cases scarcely extended beyond the crude interests of alcohol, sex, and gambling.   To materially change this situation, to broaden and elevate concepts of recreation, to eliminate the misdirected leisure time so frequently attendant upon delinquency, and to direct basal instincts and energies into channels of

[1] EDWIN J. COOLEY, *Probation and Delinquency*, pp. 134–136.

sublimation represented one of the most difficult problems of work with delinquents. In many cases, it was only after slow, painstaking effort that an improvement in leisure time pursuits, could be effected.

Cyril Burt is of the opinion that the adolescent girl is in far greater need of supervised and special recreation than the adolescent boy. Hard work, physical exercise, even strenuous bodily activity "have always been counseled as a means of chastening the instincts of the flesh."[1] Club activities, supervised dances and parties, avoiding isolated pairs, should be encouraged.[2] (See case of Marilyn Smith, pp. 296–315.)

Recreational Facilities.[3]—Every large city and many towns in America have developed suitable recreational activities and amusements to appeal to varied tastes and moods. Indoor and outdoor sports, swimming, organized games, hikes, dancing, art galleries, concerts, museums, motion pictures—intelligently chosen—are among the facilities which at least the large cities contribute to wholesome entertainment which "fire the enthusiasm of the young defaulter." Elizabeth Pendry and Hugh Hartshorne devote a large book, *Organizations for Youth*, to a comprehensive discussion of the resources in a community program of recreation and education through recreation for adults and youth. These authors list every conceivable type of formal organization, discuss its history, growth, philosophy, method, program, administration, methods of motivation, and evidences of success. It should prove of value to every worker in the recreational field. The problems are: Which of these varied organizations are the most suitable for the particular offender, and how shall he be put in contact with them to his best advantage?

In most large cities the Council of Social Agencies has an up-to-date inventory of agencies for leisure-time activities. The Los Angeles County Probation Department has compiled a useful handbook for its workers and all leaders of youth, *Youth's New Day*,[4] which provides a classified list of social agencies. This

[1] *The Young Delinquent*, p. 233.

[2] See WILLIAM HEALY, *The Individual Delinquent*, Chaps. IV, XI.

[3] See reports of the Cleveland Recreational Survey; L. L. THURSTONE, *Delinquency and Spare Time;* see also MARTIN H. and ESTHER NEUMEYER, *Leisure and Recreation.*

[4] Published by Los Angeles Lions Club, 1935.

handbook lists not only playgrounds, schools with playgrounds open after school hours, settlements and social centers, and preventive "character-building" agencies, but divisions of welfare relief, health agencies, hospitals, clinics, churches, family welfare agencies, employment agencies, etc. These various agencies are listed by district with a brief characterization of the general conditions in the district, the juvenile population, and the juvenile delinquent population.

Handbooks of this type are useful to a worker for purposes of reference; they are useful to the community leaders in knowing the presence or absence of facilities for youth; and they are useful for general research purposes and studies correlating the number and kind of agencies for youth and the rate of delinquency in a given district.

The White House Conference on Child Health and Protection[1] makes some very pertinent remarks with regard to recreational agencies and their activities:

During the last thirty or forty years settlement and neighborhood agencies, boys' and girls' clubs, community centers, Boy Scouts, Girl Scouts, Campfire groups, and the recreation movement have developed to meet the needs of thousands of young people and have made notable contributions to our civic life. We are now, however, at a period when an intensive study of the general influence of all these agencies should be made, not only from the point of view of what they accomplish in terms of their own membership, but also from the point of view of their general effectiveness in clearing away from childhood those handicapping influences within the individual which spread from child to child like a contagion. The individual must be studied more in relation to his group association, or in relation to his friend or friends, than has been done in the past. Daily, the full force of group influences is being borne in upon us. The challenge before community agencies is to reach out into the districts they are serving by providing leadership of a quality which can win the children on the wing. Intensive knowledge of the neighborhood is required, knowledge of local personalities and of local thought.[2] Cooperation of the adults of the districts must be won in meeting the needs of the child on the basis of the child's free choice of associations. The agency should pay as much attention to those who do not come to it as to those who do.

[1] *The Delinquent Child*, pp. 201–208.
[2] For a study of conflicts between recreational activities and group norms, see Pauline V. Young, *Pilgrims of Russian-Town*, pp. 139–142.

Moreover, back of the effort with individuals must be the constant effort to strengthen home life and conditions of living. . . .

Organized Municipal Recreation Groups.—Privately organized groups have reached comparatively few children and as the need and appreciation for community recreation have grown, our municipalities have extended their functions to support and supervise recreational centers, playgrounds, beaches, forest preserves, camps. As these become larger, and take children in cities far from their homes and neighborhoods, they have many of the dangers of commercial centers, since children and young people meet in them without the safeguards of any other association and cannot know whether they are finding good or bad companionship. The time has come when these municipal groups need evaluation. Without this evaluation we must not be content to extend what would seem in themselves to be good institutions. Are these great, highly organized recreational groups making patterns for our children and deadening individual tastes, abilities, creative powers, just as modern industry and business methods do?

Do these planned, regulated, supervised activities surpass the simpler, but more creative outlets for which all children should be given an opportunity?

Are we depending too much on large group activities to the exclusion of the development of neighborhood workers who could foster and develop small groups?

Are these municipal groups adapting their work to the delinquent?

Must we not consider their dangers, political domination, lack of leadership and educational programs, failures to meet individual needs?

Playgrounds.—In considering juvenile delinquency the query constantly arises, to what degree will a well organized recreation program lessen delinquency? In 1929 Andrew G. Truxal, reviewing figures which claimed to show the reduction of delinquency after the establishment of playgrounds, came to the conclusion that there seemed to exist a significant correlation between the absence of juvenile delinquency and the presence of play areas. He maintains, however, that too much emphasis has been placed upon recreation as a single factor and too much claimed for the effect of playgrounds. Mr. Truxal is undoubtedly right in being conservative. Nevertheless, the evidence that comes from many sections of the country indicates that playgrounds are a leverage in prevention. This appears logical, since playgrounds provide for boys and girls outlets for action meeting their natural impulses for physical and mental activity. Certainly, there is nothing more dangerous than pent-up vitality and mental energy not focused on constructive interests.

Leadership.—The playground not only provides open space for activities, but leadership, the influence of one, or more men and women to stimulate children's participation in a program. The personalities of leaders should be such that they will know, and be known by, the individual child. The day for squad work on the playground is over. The present demand is for a high degree of individualization. No longer is the activity the keynote, but the person in relation to the activity. Further, the playground official of the future will be rather a community agent than a playground director, because full responsibility will be placed upon him for reaching children where they are, which seems, in most cities, to be the city streets. The background of child life must be known as it is seen, not only on the playground but on the streets and in the alleys.

Most important, too, is the fact that children cannot be dissociated from adults. This means a wide and inclusive program participated in by the older folks as well as by the younger. . . .

Individual children must be reached in the home setting, and known in relation to their playmates, and a fine analysis must be made of the tastes, abilities and interests of the given boy or girl. The playground leader, then, is responsible for the individual and to a high degree for the social setting of which that individual is a part. . . .

The importance of the recreation leader is brought out by this quotation from Clifford R. Shaw's *Delinquency Areas:* "The play group is a spontaneous form of primary relationship which reflects community life and is very significant in determining attitudes, habits, and standards of conduct in the juvenile . . . the behavior of the members. Some gangs become so powerful in their hold on members that the patterns persist and actually dominate the community."

Clearly, if this be true, every effort should be made to fill our city streets with influences that establish elements of right conduct rather than wrong. This cannot be done, however, if leaders are tied to given playgrounds their entire time. Every playground should have certain workers-at-large in a neighborhood. It is surprising and startling to walk through the congested sections of almost any city and to see the streets swarming with children and a nearby playground comparatively empty. And—the city street! Listen to the language. No control of conduct there. Watch the aimless and enervating action. Notice the pathetic acceptance of leadership from an older boy or girl and listen to the often ribald suggestions of a corner gangster. The challenge to the playground is the city street. Playgrounds can no longer wait for children to come to them, but their personnel must find children where they are, mingle with them, and win them to those elements of the playground program which meet their inclinations, and which give free rein to their desires for spontaneity. We are just at the beginning of the development of method in this respect. Cincinnati, through so-called *Play*

Street has made a national demonstration. The results of the efforts of the Playgrounds Association of Philadelphia and of Community Service, Inc., of Boston in increasing the patronage of the public recreation facilities in those two cities, by discovering the naturally organized groups and giving them something to do which leads them to the playgrounds and athletic fields, point the way to major developments in the next few years.

Many years ago Jane Addams wrote in her book, *The Spirit of Youth and the City Streets*, that the object of settlement work was not to take children off the streets but to make the streets safe for children. It is advocated that every playground should have certain workers-at-large[1] in neighborhoods where children tend to congregate and play on the streets.

An Experiment in the Use of Recreation in Treating Delinquents.—M. L. Pettit, formerly Probation Officer, Juvenile Court, South Bend, Indiana, now Professor of Sociology, University of Notre Dame, reports on "An Experiment in the Use of Recreation in Treating Delinquents."[2] The excerpts are self-explanatory.

Some four years ago, in tabulating data concerning the social causes of maladjustment among boys, it appeared to the investigators that in about 75 per cent of the cases, inadequate recreation or antisocial companionship depending upon recreation were among the contributing causes. In some instances, it was the boy and his gang, in other instances it was the individual boy and chance associates. In some cases, the whole social background of the boy was excellent; in other cases, the reverse of this situation was true. The question naturally arose as to what means were available, and as to what methods were used in dealing with these problems. Were these isolated problems of the boy, or the boy and his gang; or were they problems of certain geographical or delinquency areas?

It was ascertained that the "repressive method of rehabilitation" was generally used in the attempted solution of these cases. If the antisocial activity or offense, as many of our courts still call it, was a gang activity, it seemed as though the main direction of the rehabilitative processes centered around the break-up of the gang. Gangs were presumed to be vicious breeders of crime—and detriments to the com-

[1] See GERALD J. LINARES, "The Director-at-large Plan of San Francisco Recreation Commission," in Sheldon and Eleanor Glueck (Editors), *Preventing Crime*, Chap. V.

[2] *Year Book, National Probation Association* (1931), pp. 61–65.

munity. One of the probation rules most frequently used was: "The probationer shall not associate with boys who have violated any law or who have not a good reputation in the community."

It was comparatively easy for the probation worker to "order" his charge to discontinue association with his gang or to discontinue some type of antisocial recreation. But it was extremely difficult for the boy to sever these bonds of loyalty, good fellowship, and perhaps his only opportunity for recreation, which "quitting the gang" implied. The strange and phenomenal part of the situation, so far as the probation officer was concerned, was that if the boy's relation with the gang was other than merely nominal, he rarely severed this relationship. Penalties might follow, but the gang remained intact. Probation reports showed that the cultural level of the boy or the degree of his social experience, particularly so far as home training was concerned, made little or no difference. The leader of the gang was the master of the boy's destiny.

Another feature of the problem presenting itself was the question of the delinquent boy whose maladjustment seemed to be primarily coupled with his inability to find the proper type of recreation or the proper associates,—the introvert who suddenly tried to shift himself out of his social rut and to join the normal activities of his psychosocial age level. Numerous cases were found where this situation had resulted in a social misstep and the adventure had ended in the juvenile court.

These investigators reasoned that a new philosophy and a new plan were needed in dealing with boys before the court. Repressive rehabilitation is not rehabilitation. It was felt that the pertinent question in regard to the boy's activities is not what has he done, but, why has he done it in this particular manner rather than in a socially normal manner? We decided that these boys whose chief deficiency seemed to be a lack of means of expressing the normal social activities of adolescence, or else a socially abnormal method of expressing them, should be given an opportunity of doing something instead of "don't doing" something.

The philosophy of our experiment became, "Any boy who is within the range of normalcy, that is, not noticeably deficient mentally or physically, and who is delinquent because of lack of proper leisure time guidance in his program or because of improper associates, will be given the proper program to meet these determined needs." It was felt that if diagnostic accuracy could be reasonably expected, normal programs could be substituted for socially abnormal programs and boys would be rehabilitated through their own volition.

Furthermore, it was felt that all cases before the court regardless of causation should be determined as to a definite leisure time program and if it were found that such programs were insufficient to meet the needs of the boy, they should be strengthened as a matter of juvenile court responsibility. The gang, for instance, is not fundamentally antisocial in nature. It is a natural phenomenon of the gregarious tendencies of adolescence. The difficulty lies not in the gang but in the gang's lack of a supervised program. It is the community organizations who fail to reach the boy and not the boy who should shoulder the responsibility. . . .

The general conclusions suggested by our experiment are:

1. The problem of the delinquent gang may be independent of, but generally is a problem of delinquency area. Delinquent gangs may be rehabilitated under their own leadership through the use of recreational programs fitted to their needs. Both the Boy Scouts and the Y.M.C.A., if they can be induced to see this phase of their work, are effective. Scouting is probably more effective than the Y.M.C.A., however, as its program may be brought into the district where it is needed. It is a part of the work of the probation staff to convince these organizations that they should undertake this type of work.

2. Delinquency areas may be controlled and often eliminated through the proper recreational set-up.

3. In dealing with the individual boy, success depends upon accurate psychological and sociological groupings; a wise choice of program, and placement with boys who will accept the newcomer as a member of the group. Both the Y.M.C.A. and the Scouts were successful in this type of work, although the Y.M.C.A. had the larger percentage of success due to the number of types of work possible in a centralized building program.

4. Approximately 60 per cent of all individual cases supplied with proper recreation were rehabilitated. Where it was found impossible to supply recreational adequacy, the reverse was true. All gangs supplied with recreational programs were rehabilitated while our one attempt to break up a gang resulted in failure.

5. The Boy Scouts and the Y.M.C.A. without changing their programs are equipped to deal with the delinquent boy. Such changes as are necessary to meet the need of the individual boy and gang are not deviations from the regular program but merely a shifting of emphasis.

What Constitutes Wholesome Recreation in Particular Cases? When the worker suggests employment in leisure-time activities he should ask himself: What do these activities have to offer to the youth which would appeal to youth as worth while and stimulating? Would he receive adequate and intelligent supervision? Would he have a chance to develop potential leadership qualities? Would these activities tend to overbalance the excitement and thrill of commercialized recreation or the values to him of the gang?   Would these activities tend to keep the child away from a home where he is needed or whose norms are in conflict with the particular recreational program?   "The family that plays together stays together," is a slogan adopted from National Recreation Association by many cities for their campaigns to promote home play.[1]   Do the activities advocated promote such play?   These and other questions need to be carefully considered before "ordering" an offender "to choose only wholesome recreation."

The worker needs also to remember the powerful and alluring appeals made by the motion pictures, by gambling houses, road-houses, obscene literature and a crime-gorged press, gangsters, and others.   Youth lacks discretion in choosing the proper play groups and forms of recreation.   The facilities must be sought out, explained, and checked upon with regard to providing the adventure, security, and response which a child seeks from play activities and groups.

A group of public-spirited women, alumnae of the University of Chicago and members of the Mortar Board, have launched upon a plan under the intelligent leadership of their president, Mrs. Marion Farley, and in cooperation with and guidance of the Juvenile Court of Cook County, Chicago, which promises fruitful results.   These women, working in very small groups, three to every eight or ten children, have undertaken to familiarize young wards of the Juvenile Court with what may be termed the better types of recreational facilities available in their own neighbor- hoods and in the city at large.

Irene Kawin, Chief Deputy Probation Officer of the Juvenile Court of Cook County, found that their wards knew only the cheapest forms of recreation, which frequently added to their delinquency patterns.   The probation officers dealing with these cases cannot devote the time and the court cannot afford the money necessary for conducting outings and visits to public recreational and educational institutions.   The members of the Mortar Board volunteered their services in February, 1934, and have continued since that date.[2]

[1] JAMES E. ROGERS, *The Child and Play*, quoted by M. H. and E. S. Neu- meyer, *Leisure and Recreation*, p. 357.

[2] Personal communication from Miss Kawin, Jan. 9, 1936.

A brief summary of one letter from Mrs. Marion Farley, their president, indicates that a trip has been taken practically every month since the above date for a group, or groups, of children. The number of children varies from five to thirty, depending on the nature of the trip. Only in two or three instances has a child shown lack of interest, and very few of the original group of women have discontinued their services. The volunteers do not attempt to do any professional work or to learn the facts surrounding the cases. Their primary concern is to provide fun and educative recreation to a group of children designated by the probation department as having ability to profit by the opportunities and able to get along in a group.

The trips included visits—with guide service—to the Merchandise Mart, Field Museum, Lincoln Park Zoo, Industrial Museum, the World's Fair, Cook County Forest Preserves, the coal mine and cotton exhibit at the Field Museum, motion pictures of various habitat groups at museums, picnics during the summer months at the public parks, Valentine, Easter, and Christmas parties at some park field house, at which time the children made the decorations, cards, and arranged for the program.[1]

Mrs. Farley further reports:

The most outstanding change which we have noted in the children since our first contacts with them is the apparent desire of each of them to participate whole heartedly in the activities of the group. This has seemed significant to us because we have both boys and girls and their ages vary considerably. We were at first in doubt as to whether the more sophisticated girl would retain a rather sullen and bored attitude. This attitude disappeared in the course of time because of the delegation of authority to them in recognition of their seniority and because they became friendly with the Mortar Boards who are older and who played all the games and enjoyed them. Probably at first these girls thought the group's fun beneath their dignity, but in time they found enjoyment in joining in with the rest. Also the boys, who are very lively, found they had a good time making Valentines with the group as well as playing baseball. The way in which these youngsters have adjusted themselves in such a mixed group has been a very interesting process.

We have noted an attitude on the part of the older children that they must watch out for the little ones, that is, to see that they don't get

[1] Adapted from a report sent by Mrs. Farley to writer on Feb. 23, 1936.

lost and that they always have their full share of refreshments. There has been a similar lack of the selfishness which is so often apparent when children play together. This responsibility that the older ones assumed of their own accord was not at all apparent at first. . . .

We have endeavored to give this group a series of trips which they could repeat, if they wished, with their families or other friends. For the most part, we have made use of community resources of various types and we have made a point of explaining that no tickets were needed and the arrangements could be made by following certain procedures. Although the children have learned a lot in their various trips, we have not tried to impress that fact. We have rather sought to give these children good and genuine fun. We have spent as much time as possible out of doors and in places where there was room to run and chase without being told to "get off the grass." In other words, our philosophy has been that just plain fun, in a group, is of itself highly beneficial to children. . . . We are all trying to show these youngsters how they can find good times for themselves and their families.[1]

The experiment of the Mortar Board is interesting and promising, particularly in view of the fact that throughout Mrs. Farley's report are evidences of sympathetic insight and genuine ability on the part of these members to deal with a group of children as well as with individual situations which with other people might prove compromising. Here are a few instances in point.

Jane Jones appeared for the afternoon outing in a long black dress, a chiffon velvet wrap, and high heeled slippers. There was only one thing to do to prevent her from feeling completely out of place and so we delegated the important functions of the afternoon to her. She purchased the pop corn balls and peanuts and decided on the place and time to eat them, and when the time came, she distributed the food.

Two of the girls told the Mortar Board members of the experiences they had had in "homes" and discussed quite seriously and in an interested manner, how many babies one could carry about at one time, and how many times a day a baby had to be changed. . . . We have been pleased to note that the older girls who at first seemed indifferent to the activities of the group have accepted the friendship of the Mortar Boards and have concerned themselves with helping the younger ones to have a good time and not get lost.

Only those children who expressed a desire to join the outings participated. There was no persuasion, no pressure, no reward,

[1] Personal communication from Mrs. Farley, Mar. 6, 1936.

no punishment. There was no reference to their faults, to misbehavior, to court records. There was genuine interest both on the part of the children and their leaders, and both groups seemed to enjoy themselves equally.

The experiment provides stimulation through group activities, new experience, response, information as to the facilities and methods of securing wholesome recreation at a minimum cost and capable of being enjoyed by both old and young members of the family.

It must be pointed out, however, that in the management of such delinquent groups lie grave dangers. It is a general principle in social work that groups should not be selected on the basis of delinquency, dependency, or any pathological traits because it is almost impossible to control the moral atmosphere which tends to pervade such groups. Furthermore, there is great danger that the pleasurable activities of such groups may be interpreted by other children who are nondelinquent as rewards for delinquency and the latter may seek to alter their behavior patterns. The sounder method perhaps would be to include these children in unselected groups of so-called normal children, since all children tend to follow the group patterns. Apparently, due to very careful management, these dangers seem to have been avoided in the Chicago groups, through vigorous activity, careful selection of cases from communities whose nondelinquent children would not envy them these minimal activities, and through careful supervision.

"The Way Out."—The comment expressed by the White House Conference on Child Health and Protection regarding "the way out" is apropos here:

When the child can find near at home, with companions of his own choice, opportunity for all that his ever widening sphere of craving and interests demands, when his community, including all groups, private, municipal, commercial, holds as its greatest asset the security and development of all of its children; when the spirit of the neighborhood reflects our most ideal teaching, then will the community help to minimize those behavior problems that handicap the lives of so many children.

Our responsibility was expressed years ago by Jane Addams in *The Spirit of Youth and the City Streets:* "We may either smother the divine fire of youth or we may feed it. We may either stand stupidly staring as it sinks into a murky fire of crime and flares into the intermittent blaze of folly, or we may tend it into a lambent flame with power to make clean and bright our dingy city streets."[1]

Selected Bibliography

*1. ADDAMS, JANE: *The Spirit of Youth on the City Streets.*
2. BUSCH, H. M.: *Leadership in Group Work,* Association Press, 1934.
3. CURTIS, HENRY S.: *Education through Play,* The Macmillan Company, 1915.
4. FORMAN, HENRY J.: *Our Movie Made Children,* The Macmillan Company, 1933.
5. HANMER, LEE F., "Recreation," *Encyclopedia of the Social Sciences,* Vol. XIII, pp. 176–181. See also play, amusements, sports, playgrounds, clubs, motion pictures, etc.
6. JACKS, L. P.: *Education through Recreation,* Harper & Brothers, 1932.
7. KINGMAN, JOHN M. (Editor), and EDWARD SIDMAN: *A Manual of Settlement Boys' Work,* National Federation of Settlements, 1935.
8. MASON, B. S., and E. D. MITCHELL: *Social Games for Recreation,* A. S. Barnes & Company, 1935.
9. MITCHELL, ALICE: *Children and Movies,* University of Chicago Press, 1929.
10. NEUMEYER, MARTIN H., and ESTHER S.: *Leisure and Recreation,* A. S. Barnes & Company, 1936, Chap. XVIII, "Community Recreation: Semipublic and Private Agencies," pp. 324–363.
11. NEWSTETTER, W. I.: "Boys' and Girls' Clubs," *Encyclopedia of the Social Sciences,* Vol. II, pp. 667–670.
12. PANGBURN, W. W.: "Recreation," *Social Work Year Book,* Russell Sage Foundation, 1935.
13. PENDRY, ELIZABETH R., and HUGH HARTSHORNE: *Organizations for Youth,* McGraw-Hill Book Company, Inc., 1935.
14. PETTIT, M. L.: "An Experiment in the Use of Recreation in Treating Delinquents," *Year Book, National Probation Association* (1931), pp. 61–68, 1934.
15. ROGERS, JAMES E.: *The Child and Play,* D. Appleton-Century Company, Inc., 1932.
16. SMITH, C. F.: *Games and Game Leadership,* Dodd, Mead & Company, Inc., 1932.
17. STEINER, JESSE F.: "Recreation and Leisure Time Activities," in *Recent Social Trends in the United States,* McGraw-Hill Book Company, Inc., Chap. XVIII, pp. 912–957, 1934.
18. THOMPSON, CHARLES S.: "All Nations Boys' Club, Los Angeles," in Sheldon and Eleanor Glueck (Editors), *Preventing Crime,* McGraw-Hill Book Company, Inc., 1936.
19. WILLIAMSON, MARGARETTA: *The Social Worker and Group Work,* Harper & Brothers, 1929.
20. STONE, WALTER L.: *What Is Boys' Work?* Association Press, 1931.

[1] *The Delinquent Child,* p. 224.

Suggestions for Further Study

1. What is meant by "the repressive method of rehabilitation"? How does this method compare with what W. I. Thomas calls "the ordering-and-forbidding technique"?

2. How is it possible to tell when certain methods are "repressive" to a given individual?

3. What is meant by "rehabilitation through own volition"? How is this accomplished?

4. What is meant by "proper recreation" in a given case? What are the criteria of proper recreation?

5. Why is recreation an essential part of a child's life?

6. How does recreation in the modern city compare with that of the rural districts?

7. In what light should the general conclusions suggested by the South Bend experiment be viewed? What are the shortcomings of such an experiment? the advantages?

8. In what way does a change in recreation involve a new outlook on life?

9. What are the advantages of E. J. Cooley's suggestions regarding provision of constructive recreation?

10. What recreational activities are available in your community? religious? secular? public? private? organized? spontaneous? How are these coordinated? Which activities are enjoyed the most by the children? Why?

11. How can recreational agencies induce the expression of creative powers?

12. The White House Conference Report raises the following questions:

a. Do these planned, regulated, supervised, activities surpass the simpler, but more creative outlets for which all children should be given an opportunity?

b. Are we depending too much on large group activities to the exclusion of the development of neighborhood workers, who could foster and develop small groups?

c. Are the municipal groups adapting their work to the delinquent? (*The Delinquent Child*, p. 205.) How would you answer these questions in regard to your community?

13. To what extent should the playground leader reach the child through the home setting? through his associates? through the community? his community?

14. How can the probation officer influence public opinion and bring public opinion and pressure to bear on the community to control commercialized recreation?

CHAPTER XXVI

THE COORDINATING COUNCIL MOVEMENT AND THE LOCAL COMMUNITY

It is estimated that there are more organizations for youth—municipal, county, state, national, international in scope—than for any other social group in this country. Problems of youth attract a great deal of attention and arouse a great deal of sympathy. A large number of public and semipublic, private and semiprivate agencies have launched various programs and have developed independent organizations, societies, clubs, republics, leagues, councils, orders, plans, codes, committees, brotherhoods, federations, associations, ideas, agencies, settlements, and so on.[1] To this motley array the schools, the churches, and some national and language groups add their welter of organizations. The lack of coordination of efforts, of policies, of procedures, of services of these various organizations is appalling and disconcerting. Erle F. Young writes:[2]

It is little wonder that conflicts of interest have developed, and that unhealthy competition between organizations is rife in the struggle for available funds, public attention, and exclusive responsibility for certain desirable classes . . . or special programs of action. Only too frequently in the resulting chaos the interests of the juvenile have been well-nigh lost sight of by the very agencies whose special guardians they were presumed to be. In-coordination of effort is not merely a matter of wastage of effort and funds but a certain proportion of juvenile disorganization can probably be directly charged to the resulting inefficiency of the institutions concerned. Many students now insist that one of the first necessary steps in social advance is the integration of the efforts of all responsible agencies.

The Origin of the Movement for Coordination.—The first pioneer plan for coordinating the work of local departments

[1] See ELIZABETH PENDRY and HUGH HARTSHORNE, *Organization for Youth.*

[2] "The Coordination Council Plan in Los Angeles County," *The Journal of Criminal Law and Criminology*, XXVI (May, 1935), 34.

interested in the welfare of youth and their communities was started when the Chief of Police, August Vollmer, in Berkeley and the Assistant Superintendent of Schools, Dr. Virgil Dickson, realized that their departments were dealing with some of the same problems of children. At first they met once a week for luncheon to discuss these problems and as time went on they gradually included other officials and social workers who could help in working out a plan of adjustment for individual children. This group adopted the name "coordinating council," writes Kenneth Beam.[1] This council was formed in 1919 in Berkeley, California. The Berkeley experiment was recommended by the State Commission for the Study of Problem Children in 1929 for adoption elsewhere.

Robert H. Scott, Judge of the Juvenile Court, Los Angeles County, defines the Coordinating Council as "a clearing house where sincere, devoted, intelligent individuals and organizations discuss mutual problems of child, family, and community welfare; while the [coordinating council] can be inspiring success we naturally should not rely upon that or any similar movement to be a power-house to supply energy to all its related organizations."[2]

Los Angeles County, under the leadership of Kenyon J. Scudder and Kenneth S. Beam, of the Probation Department, and Judge Samuel Blake of the Juvenile Court, followed the lead and organized in 1932 the Los Angeles Coordinating Council,[3] adapting the plan of the Berkeley Council to local needs. This council is a voluntary organization including within its membership such persons as court officials, probation officers, school attendance officers, police juvenile officers, representatives of service clubs, civic organizations, group workers and case workers from private and public agencies, and lay persons.

As early as 1928 Judge Robert H. Scott organized an extensive Juvenile Court Committee with some 800 citizens from the general community as members participating in learning and disseminating the facts, functions, and the work of the Juvenile Court. This large body of citizens soon became aware that the

[1] "The Coordinating Council Movement," *Year Book, National Probation Association* (1935), p. 201.

[2] *Los Angeles Bar Association Bulletin,* XI (May 21, 1936), p. 222.

[3] The reader is urged to see two pamphlets by Kenyon J. Scudder and Kenneth S. Beam, *Why Have Delinquency?* and *Who Is Delinquent?*

sources of delinquency were embedded in the disorganizing forces of the community. Many of the leaders of this community became community-conscious, and when the coordinating council movement germinated in Los Angeles the social soil was ready for it. Undoubtedly much of the success which this movement has achieved in Southern California is due to a large extent to the early work of the Juvenile Court Committee.

Its underlying philosophy is based on the fact that mobilization of resources and coordination of effort are essential for effective work and that the causes of delinquency are too diverse and too complex to be dealt with by any one group working alone. The philosophy is embodied in the definition of a coordinating council formulated by Francis H. Hiller, in a "Report of a Brief Study of the Coordinating Councils." He says:

> A coordinating council may be described as an association of public and private welfare agencies and civic bodies to coordinate their work, to discover and estimate more accurately than heretofore the demoralizing influences in their community and neighborhood, and to plan and act jointly for the betterment of conditions, most frequently with special reference to the prevention of juvenile delinquency.[1]

In July, 1936, there were 110 councils in California, 60 of which were organized in Los Angeles County. An additional 104 councils are scattered in eighteen other states in the Union, ranging from one council each in New Jersey, New Hampshire, North Carolina, Oklahoma, to 24 councils in Pennsylvania, 21 in Michigan, 10 in Illinois, while the rest of the states have 2, 4, 6, 8, or 9 councils each.[2] In Los Angeles County there is a central executive board with representatives from the local committees and from the various county and city departments and other special groups interested in children's behavior problems. It is evident that the movement is spreading comparatively rapidly in some localities, particularly in Southern California. At the Attorney General's Conference on Crime, held in 1934, a resolution was adopted recognizing the work of the coordinating councils and urging state and national sponsorship of them.

The Program of the Coordinating Councils.—The first councils, according to Beam, were interested solely in the adjustment of

---

[1] Mimeographed, Dec. 14, 1935, p. 1.

[2] KENNETH S. BEAM, "Roster of Councils," mimeographed, 1936.

individual behavior problems of particular children, and representatives of various schools, health and welfare agencies of the police and probation departments formed an *adjustment committee*. To this committee behavior problems of children were presented in sufficient detail to enable it to make a referral to the appropriate agency for treatment. The committee itself did no case work. It operated on the belief that through the consideration of cases and plans and of the programs of the suitable agencies the various members of the committee will become familiar with the programs, equipment, administrative setup, and points of view of the representing agencies and will, therefore, be in a position for more effective cooperative effort. Mr. Hiller observes:[1]

The question arises why these cases should not be referred directly by the police or schools to the appropriate agency. The answer is that participation in the council has created a situation with a spirit of mutual understanding and confidence, which has resulted in the referral of more cases than previously and what is more important, earlier than they otherwise would have been. When police officers, for example, find boys on the streets late at night or in undesirable places or engaged in some minor misconduct, the procedure in the past was usually to warn them or at most to take them to the station house and send for their parents. Probably from a quarter to a third of all cases of boys coming to the attention of the police are of this character. Previously nothing more was done about them. Such indifference gave rise to the question, "Does a kid have to break into jail before the community will give him a lift?" These cases, through the adjustment committees, now come to the attention of some social agency which may render a helpful service in time to prevent the development of more serious delinquency.

Later the interests of the councils embraced the development of constructive play and leisure-time facilities for youth and elimination of unwholesome community conditions which have a direct bearing on delinquency problems. With the development of these wider interests representatives of many of the so-called character-building agencies were invited to join the councils, and a *character-building committee* was formed; and with the inclusion of representatives of civic organizations, such as men's and women's clubs, parent-teacher associations, the American Legion, an *environment committee* was formed and was assigned the specific

[1] *Op. cit.*, p. 15.

task of improving both home and community environments.[1] However, there is a great diversity in the matter of committees, observes Kenneth Beam. Some councils have no committees at all but do all their work in one general meeting.[2]

The programs, nature of meeting, efficiency, and procedures vary widely from council to council and committee to committee, depending largely upon the quality of the local leadership, professional standards and attitudes of the members, personal interests in publicity of certain members who have been termed "publicity hounds," as well as on the amount and quality of provision for leisure time of youth and the degree of local community organization and support. Equally varied are the objectives and purposes of the various councils. The following fundamental principles concerning coordinating councils grew out of the discussion at the San Diego meeting, 1934, of the California Conference of Social Work.

a. The Council should provide a careful study of the various areas in the community in order to determine the problems and needs of the community in dealing with juvenile delinquency.

b. The Council should coordinate into one plan the various services offered by all the social agencies in the area, to combat juvenile delinquency. This is the task of the Adjustment Committee of the Council.

c. The Council should provide all the agencies in its area with the facts by which they can evaluate their program and by which they can be directed in their efforts and plans for expansion.[3]

These fundamental principles indicate the uniqueness of the coordinating councils and distinguish them from the Council of Social Agencies, which is furthermore organized on a city-wide rather than on a neighborhood basis, and which gives immediate consideration to problems of agency organization and relationships rather than to community conditions.

Erle F. Young states:[4]

The widest possible latitude has been given each local council. The simplicity of the council organization has made possible whatever

[1] BEAM, "The Coordinating Council Movement," pp. 202–203.
[2] "Delinquency Prevention through Coordination," mimeographed (1936), p. 4.
[3] *The California Conference Bulletin,* XVIII (November, 1934), 12.
[4] *Op. cit.,* pp. 36–37.

activity special conditions and local interests have suggested. Certain problems, for example, the sale of liquor to minors, are county-wide, if not state-wide. A plan has therefore developed to devote at least a portion of the work of all councils to these wider interests, following a schedule of topics agreed upon at a meeting of officers of all councils. Topics listed for discussion in the immediate future include such matters as social legislation, liquor and youth, the summer camp program, church and youth, and home life of modern youth.

Annual conferences give further opportunity for securing united effort and developing a common point of view. By these means the weaker councils, which have had difficulty in developing concrete activities, are provided with a minimum program and are stimulated to action.

The activities of the central committee have led to a number of city-wide and county-wide projects. The State Employment Relief Administration has provided a high-grade personnel including many unemployed professionals. A group of such persons was organized and assigned to the playgrounds to supplement the work of the professional personnel. Some were assigned to help the individual councils and the probation department. Various survey projects were set on foot. A careful study of delinquency by elementary school districts has provided for the first time useable local statistical pictures of the delinquency situation in the city. A directory of all recreational and character-building facilities was also prepared.

The leadership of the movement in Los Angeles County is in the Juvenile Probation Department and the Juvenile Court. However, probation officers do not act as officers in the local councils. A high degree of local autonomy and local control is thus assured while at the same time providing the necessary intimate contact of the local community with the juvenile court; this easy access to the court frequently results at first in "dumping" the local difficult children on the court. Through the adjustment committee this tendency is soon sharply counteracted and local community resources are called into play. The net result has been a sharp reduction in the number of cases referred by many communities to the court.

The above comments, though relating to the Los Angeles Council, are equally applicable to the plan of many other councils.

What Do the Councils Accomplish?—Mr. Beam reports that many groups and individuals ask the above question. The present writer had made a preliminary study of the activities and opinions—in connection with the article by Erle F. Young— of various councils members who are in executive positions both in their own agencies and in the councils with which they are intimately connected. Some saw specific advantages, which may be quoted in part.

The council makes the juvenile delinquency problem a community problem rather than that of some one agency. Social workers moreover are discovering that it is not simply a matter of "cases"; it is a matter also of the "community." . . .

It provides a sympathetic approach to the child and a better understanding of his problems. Successful treatment depends largely on that type of approach. In particular we are humanizing the approach of the police, the sheriff, and the probation officer. . . .

The council arouses an interest in prevention and induces officials to think in such terms. . . .

We have now a suitable technique for referring cases to the right agency. It is showing community leaders the value of case studies. . . .

The surveys sponsored by the council have given us real information on community situations with which we have been struggling. Furthermore, it is now good form to pool our information rather than utilize it simply for self-promotion. . . .

The council puts every agency "on the spot." We are all coming to know each other's affairs and a failure on the part of one is soon common knowledge. We are all challenged therefore to put forth our best effort in order to maintain our status. We no longer operate in the dark or go our own way unheeding of the opinion and plans of other workers. . . .

Most of us have not changed our procedures very much as yet but the Police Department is a notable exception. They have instructed their officers to give full cooperation and have begun referring certain cases to the adjustment committee which heretofore received no special attention. That includes about 25 per cent of the cases coming to the attention of the Police Department. It is a great step forward in organization. . . . [1]

To these statements may be added one by Mr. Hiller:

The carrying out of the council's programs has been greatly facilitated by work relief projects in many areas under the state emergency relief administration. Hundreds of workers have been so employed in Los Angeles County, chiefly on the making of surveys of social conditions under the direction of the central executive and research committee but these workers have also been assigned to aid many of the neighborhood councils in carrying out some of their projects.

[1] Erle F. Young, manuscript, pp. 4–5.

Scudder and Beam have stated that they "do not expect the full effect of the councils to be felt for another generation."[1] It is clear that a satisfactory evaluation of the council plan cannot be made when it has been operating only four years and a half. Erle F. Young believes that such an evaluation can be accomplished only after the institution has been tried under more varying conditions and over a longer period of time. "That it has been successful in certain communities and in dealing with certain problems is a well established fact. Whether these successes can be repeated in other communities and with other types of problems"[2] is just now being learned. Excerpts from interviews with some of the members referred to before will illustrate not only certain problems which these members in Los Angeles have found to be at times very disconcerting, but also the fact that the agencies need far greater integration than has been achieved to date.

It is very true that to a large degree the social and civic workers have learned to get along better together and to discuss their problems with each other, but each then goes back to his own organization and continues his work in his accustomed routine way. As yet there has been no real reorganization of any agency. This is a very difficult matter. . . .

One of the greatest difficulties has been that, from the point of view of the local agency, the program has been developed and sponsored outside of the community and independently of the agencies concerned. It is, in fact, a child of the probation department, turned over to us for foster care. We have had very little to do with the planning and those who have imagination and organizational ability have had little chance to make any original contributions, while those who are unimaginative and lack organizational ability consider it an abstraction, or as something of a routine procedure which they work out faithfully but frequently ineffectually. However, there is considerable leeway in the local councils. . . . [3]

---

[1] *Who Is Delinquent?* p. 51.

[2] "The Coordinating Council Plan in Los Angeles County," p. 38.

[3] Mr. Hiller observes that in Oakland the councils "to a considerable degree have had their programs and policies handed down to them. In Los Angeles . . . it has been the policy of the central executive committee . . . to avoid all appearance of dictation to or control of neighborhood units. Leadership, nevertheless, is furnished by the members of the central councils, particularly through the county probation department." *Op. cit.*, p. 8.

Another serious difficulty of a similar nature is the relation of the agencies to delinquent children. In some communities the children are now being over-importuned to join organizations and participate in activities. Many things are offered them. They are invited to pageants, programs, picnics, and so on in large numbers where everything is arranged for them. Children and parents are impressed by such affairs and come to the conclusion that it is not necessary to earn the privilege of belonging to clubs or to earn the pleasures provided them. . . .

At present these communities are frequently over-run with schools, playgrounds, character-building agencies and community affairs. A very unhealthy competition has developed between social agencies for the available juvenile clientele. That seems paradoxical in view of the principles of the council and of the large number of unchurched and unorganized boys and girls, but it is the actual situation in some few communities. . . .

We social workers are a very busy people at our own tasks. An additional committee to attend is a real burden for most of us. . . .

Most of us have had little experience at organization work and little ability for it while most of the work of the council calls for just that. . . .

We have few of the leading people on our councils. We do have the responsible social workers but they cannot accomplish the tasks they have set for themselves without the active help of the real leaders in the community. Hence we have failed to clear the neighborhoods of disorganizing forces, low grade movies, dance halls, saloons, and the like. . . .

It is true that we social workers, through council activities, have come to know our problems better, to work together more harmoniously and have drawn into our groups many lay persons but our difficulty is that as yet no real technique for adjusting juvenile problems is known. All of the good-will in the world and all possible cooperation will not remedy many situations. We simply do not know what to do or how to do it. Conferences, committee meetings, paper plans are no solution for these situations. Much further real research is needed. . . .

We are quite innocent of any formulated social philosophy. Since organization is itself presumed to be a good thing we have apparently assumed that that is what is needed in this case. There is a good reason to think so, of course, but we do not have any carefully formulated point of view such as the juvenile court movement had. That makes us almost wholly empirical in our approach but gives us a very confused picture of what it is all about.[1]

[1] See YOUNG, "The Coordinating Council Plan in Los Angeles County," pp. 38–39.

The number of people making the above observations are comparatively few.

Mr. Beam, while making an extensive study of the coordinating councils in several states for the National Probation Association in 1936, reports various activities which are a direct result of the council's discovery of need, backing, planning, and selecting the agency to carry the plan into effect. The council serves as a medium but some agency actually does the work.[1] Among the major activities may be listed some ten: (1) sociological studies of neighborhoods made by graduate students in certain universities; (2) education of the public regarding the work of the councils, through published booklets, articles in local papers, radio programs, forums, and lectures; (3) closer coordination of the work of member agencies; (4) development of recreational and library facilities; (5) service for individual children through the adjustment committees; (6) development of a public-school behavior clinic (in Berkeley); (7) special attention to young people from sixteen to twenty-five years of age; (8) promotion of better films; (9) agitation against child labor and sale of liquor and salacious literature to minors; (10) referral of problem cases to the schools or child welfare agencies without recourse to the juvenile court.

The councils have been able to keep out of court many children whose problems were, at least momentarily, adjusted by more informal and noncourt procedure. Also, social workers have become more "community-minded" and less "agency-minded"; communities have awakened to the needs of children; and unification of forces and concerted action is a very helpful procedure to all concerned. Then there are what Mr. Hiller[2] calls "intangible values."

Most participants in the work of the councils feel that their most valuable contribution is in the fostering of inter-agency cooperation, acquaintance and understanding, in the stimulus to better and more extensive work, and in community education in problems of child welfare and delinquency. Some testify to their astonishment at discovering how little known to each other were some of the most active agencies. Organizations have been stimulated and challenged by facing together serious community problems. The presence of representatives of

[1] *Op. cit.*, p. 7.
[2] *Op. cit.*, pp. 16–17.

religious and civic organizations creates a psychological situation in which each agency is more eager to do its best. The head of a police department, for example, admitted that his department probably acted much more promptly and thoroughly in getting evidence upon which they abolished gambling places near a high school, by reason of the fact that the problem was presented by school officials and two or three citizens at a meeting of the coordinating council of which a police officer was also a member. Of course the schools could have referred the problem to the police without the intervention of a council but the reference was facilitated by the acquaintance of the school and police representatives and action was encouraged by the knowledge of the police department that representative citizens and organizations in the neighborhood wanted this thing done and would applaud them for doing it.

The educational value of the council movement is undoubtedly considerable. The activities of civic groups in child welfare work have been directed through participation in the councils into channels mapped out with reference to a study of community needs, whereas formerly each group was left to choose more or less at random whatever activity had the strongest emotional appeal. The results of surveys and news of activities of the member organizations are taken back to the various organizations by delegates. In many neighborhoods the councils have organized educational courses for the public, particularly for parents, combining with the educational addresses some entertainment feature to increase the attendance. As a result, instead of the usual rather select group who attend a parent-teacher meeting, as many as 2,000 parents have been brought out for the "community nights" in some districts.

Electrical transcriptions . . . for use in informing organizations of the work being done in delinquency prevention, are an exceedingly effective educational device. . . . The transcriptions give the audience a vivid sense of being actually on the scene of action.

Suggestions Concerning the Coordinating Council Movement. The intelligent and farseeing leaders in the movement realize that the young councils, because of the immensity of the problem, have made but a modest beginning in the planning for child welfare and in community reorganization. It is suggested that the councils concentrate more on the real fundamental issues in our complex American life, and that they engage the interests not only of social workers, public officials, and laymen but also of a larger number of the more experienced of the social scientists and the social engineers.

It is suggested that the councils learn the modern trends in social group work and promote and stimulate organizations which are youth's own choice, born of creative ability under intelligent guidance rather than organizations *for* youth created and handed down to them by adults and maintained under varying adult policies and motives. The prewar German Youth Movement will well repay study on this point,[1] as well as the boys' brotherhood republics in this country.[2]

It is suggested that the councils learn the more modern trends in community organization and stimulate and develop indigenous leadership and promote self-direction of groups and support whatever values there may be in native institutions.

Another point of view could be taken on this subject and the question raised as to whether or not the local communities can supply the indigenous leadership now supplied from the outside, and in general whether such a procedure is workable and expedient? We see some disheartening examples of the misuse and ineffectiveness of democratic government. The principles underlying democratic government, on the other hand, are unimpeachable and they should be utilized to their fullest extent in every energetic enterprise involving the lives and destinies of other individuals and groups. There are representatives of successful merchants, of the professions, of the lay group of the communities in which these councils function, but as yet, not a single member is a representative of the very folks whose lives are being "planned," "guided," or "adjusted." May we assume that the "common people," the "clientele," cannot supply intelligent representatives who can be educated, if necessary, in social ethics and in discreet relations with their neighbors? Many experiments by social workers in "client participation"[3] have proved too valuable to be disregarded in this field without trial.

Alida Bowler writes that many people expressed great satisfaction

---

[1] See bibliography p. 596, Nos. 20–25.

[2] See WEBB WALDRON, "No Adults Allowed," *Reader's Digest*, XXVIII (April, 1936), 79–82.

[3] ELIZABETH DUTCHER, "When Clients Participate," *The Survey*, LXX (February, 1934), 41–43; see also MARY VIRGINIA BOOK, "As the Andrews Family Sees It," *The Family*, XIV (January, 1934), 308–310.

in seeing community after community face their responsibility to youth and childhood and settle down to an organized effort to meet that responsibility.   They report that when these communities now have to file petitions in juvenile court, it is no longer with a "good riddance of bad rubbish" attitude.   It is much more likely to be with expressions of regret that the community has been unable to solve the problems of this child without the aid of outside agencies.   There is a real recognition of the fact that he is definitely a product of things his community has done, or permitted to be done, to him and of things it has failed to do for him.[1]

Miss Bowler is undoubtedly using the term "community" to mean a constellation of secondary organizations, such as the schools, the police, the welfare agency.   As such, the community is performing a valuable service through concerted action and unified forces, but the primary group organizations, the family, the church, the mutual aid groups, the labor union, and others are not considered as possible assets in working out a plan of action, and therefore such procedure neglects fundamental principles of sound community planning.

Certain social workers and public officials may object to extensive participation and representation of the people whose destinies are under consideration in council plans and meetings. Undoubtedly tact and discretion are needed in this work just as much as in any other line.   But it cannot be said that the council committee members know the wishes, goals, policies, and culture of many of the very groups they attempt to serve.   This is particularly true of the large number of immigrant groups and communities with which the councils are concerned.   They are not truly in contact with the life of these groups and can, therefore, have no true power over them.   In these situations there is little insight and little social imagination, to use Cooley's terms.[2] Individual teachers and social workers may at times seek the views and consult the leaders of immigrant groups regarding the problems encountered with their children, but intimate views are difficult to grasp by one who does not "think and feel immigrant"; the minds of these leaders seem impenetrable and remain largely untouched.   One young Russian leader asks:

[1] "Experiments in Preventing Juvenile Delinquency," *Year Book, National Probation Association* (1934), pp. 165–166.

[2] See CHARLES H. COOLEY, *Human Nature and the Social Order*, pp. 140–142.

Why do the Americans always want to make us over and to run things their way? If our way works with Russians, why change and borrow trouble? It takes a Russian to run things for Russians. But we are not given a chance. . . . We can Americanize ourselves in our own way. We can be good Russians and good American citizens at the same time.[1]

Again it may be argued that American social agencies—which are secondary group organizations—have attempted to fulfill the functions which should be left to the local native and indigenous institutions to fulfill only because the latter had failed to do so. We can only point out that modern social case work as well as modern social group work and community organization have vindicated the policy that under no circumstances should anything be done for individuals or for groups which they can be stimulated to do for themselves. Numerous groups have demonstrated remarkable ability for leadership and community organization, according to Allen T. Burns, a profound student of community problems. As to the other groups we do not know. They have never been sufficiently stimulated nor given the opportunity and intelligent backing. Under such circumstances the functions assumed by outsiders are rarely more than an imposition and an artificial and ineffectual substitute for those institutions which are "freely developed by initiative and cooperation of the people themselves."[2] Under such circumstances outside leadership can never be anything but a foreign power dedicated to proselyting or "uplift" work among people who would attain greater efficiency if stimulated to work out their own plans.

There are many communities which can supply indigenous leadership, which should be exploited to its fullest extent. Native leaders know how far and how rapidly they can go in the adjustment process. They know the emotions which this process calls into play, they can feel the pulse of the community, so to speak, and can recognize the danger signs by the frank and constant personal reactions of their fellow members. As one intelligent Mexican leader[3] said, "Our children are not losing faith in us.

[1] PAULINE V. YOUNG, *Pilgrims of Russian-Town*, p. 234.

[2] WILLIAM I. THOMAS and FLORIAN ZNANIECKI, *The Polish Peasant in Europe and America*, p. 1526.

[3] PAULINE V. YOUNG, "Social Problems in the Education of the Immigrant Child," *American Sociological Review*, I (June, 1936), 427.

They feel that our means for social control are sanctioned by the Americans."

We shall repeat what has already been stated in connection with case work with individuals: "There are leaders and there are runners." The group and social institutions which have become the concern of the councils need leaders drafted from their own midst as well as supplied from the outside, but they do not need "runners" of any kind to run their lives. Everyone wishes to have a decent chance to guide his own life, under intelligent native leadership. To adopt the words of Donald Young, author of *American Minority Peoples*,[1] these groups will become adjusted automatically, if given a chance without oppression and exploitation.

It is suggested that the councils concern themselves with the far-reaching effects of social and economic disorganization and what the Gluecks call "the mountain of deleterious urban social conditions" and become more active in the promotion of appropriate social security acts and needed social legislation in general.

Undoubtedly the coordinating council movement will in the near future direct its efforts toward social legislation in favor of the establishment of minimum wages, of abolition of child labor, development of socialized medicine, of slum clearance, of health and food protective measures, of broader and more effective principles of public education and vocational guidance, and a host of other needed developments which retard the advancement of child welfare.

It is suggested that the councils learn more of the pressing need for parental education and concern themselves with the establishment in every community of permanent parent-guidance clinics conducted by experts.

It is possible to give full assent to various points of view and policies in dealing with the problems of child and community welfare yet to face an impasse in dealing effectively with these problems. The great barrier to early success lies in almost total lack of tested ways and means. Of course, we must recognize our problems first in order to plan effectively a positive course of action. Experimental programs are urgently needed. This field awaits the appearance of social technicians thoroughly conversant with the culture and the intimate life of the various

[1] See pp. 457–466.

neighborhood groups, endowed with creative imagination, and backed by thoroughgoing research before attempting any solution of problems. So far the situation has been complicated by the fact that agencies have attempted to "solve" problems without adequate knowledge of "what works" and "what does not work" in the adjustment of the serious life problems of individuals, communities, and groups.

On the basis of the expressed problems which the social agencies are facing, the following suggestions might be offered:

It is suggested that the agencies work in closer cooperation with the central executive committee among whose various functions is to plan with individual agencies as to how to adapt their work to the unique needs of the whole community. The central executive council having a broad view of the entire community is in a position to supply the perspective of the total situation which might be difficult to attain by any one agency.

It is suggested that—since the council itself does no social or community work, which is properly left to be carried on by the social agency—the social agency take more initiative in effective cooperative planning and in reorganizing their communities. When the social agencies complain of ineffective work it reminds one of the constant cry that democracy is failing, yet the very people who complain are the last ones to participate in public affairs or even to vote.

It is suggested that the social agencies interpret to the children in the community the advantages of the various activities organized for their benefit. There is no reason why the children should not be offered the same "opportunities to earn the privilege of belonging" to a new club—if that has proved to be a desirable procedure—as were offered in the old clubs.

It is suggested that the social agencies disregard the possibilities for immediate gains for a particular agency but view the coordinating council movement in its broader ramifications and realize that by becoming "community-minded" rather than "agency-minded" the individual agency will make its biggest strides.

The coordinating council movement, however, has already assumed far-reaching significance because of its aims of coordination of effort of members and agencies, of programs of wide variety of organization in the field of child welfare. If the councils have accomplished nothing else than coordination of work of public and private agencies—legal, educational, recreational, and welfare—it has accomplished its goal.   For this reason we may agree with Hiller, that "the councils will undoubtedly change as to methods and policies but not as to fundamental purpose." "It is now a lusty movement well worth the attention of students of social organization and worthy of development and experimentation in other communities under good leadership."[1]

Mr. Kenyon J. Scudder, who has been closely associated with the work and organization of the Coordinating Council movement in California, writes as follows with regard to the coordinating councils and crime prevention and community organization.[2]

Community Action and Crime Prevention.—Crime and delinquency will never be reduced until the community decides to do something about it.   More than half the youngsters coming into the Juvenile Courts of America are ordinary children who quickly adjust themselves when given an opportunity.   The other half are less fortunately endowed with a mental capacity somewhat below normal, and these unfortunate youngsters are entitled to better care and attention than the community has seen fit to give.   If we would keep these youngsters out of trouble we must make available to all children the fine facilities in the community which are now restricted to a select few.   Too often these select few are the ones who need it the least.   If this program is good for these certainly it should be expanded for those who are underprivileged and who now cannot afford to join.

A recent study of some 14,000 Juvenile Court cases in Los Angeles County during the years 1929, '30, and '31, indicated that less than 14 per cent of these children belonged to any kind of a character-building organization.   Eighty-six per cent found their comrades in the street.   Is it any wonder that they found themselves in trouble?   It is natural for youth to organize in gangs.   The Boy Scout troop is a gang; the Hi-Y group is a gang; but these are gangs under trained leadership with a constructive purpose.   A gang of delinquents is organized but it lacks decent leadership and purpose.   Yet, these destructive gangs can be turned into fields of usefulness and good citizenship.   And this is what the Coordinating Council program is trying to do.

When a child is in trouble in a neighborhood, the easiest thing to do is to take him out.   Too often the community clamors for this kind of service from public agencies.   They are afraid that one child will

[1] Erle F. Young, manuscript, p. 8.

[2] Paper especially prepared for this volume, Aug. 1, 1936.

contaminate the others and yet they assume no responsibility for conditions over which this child has no control, and which have contributed definitely to his delinquency. . . . It has been said that the Juvenile Court was never designed to prevent delinquency; it was planned as a better method of combating delinquency after its occurrence, and as such it has amply fulfilled the expectations of those who sponsored its beginning. Its function was, and still is, diagnostic and not prophylactic. With the last statement we agree. However, that was yesterday. Now the Juvenile Court has a new function. We now stand upon the threshold of a new era. New forces are at work. The community is beginning to organize. It is looking around. It is shaking itself out of its lethargy. It is anxious to clean up unsatisfactory conditions which affect youth.

Juvenile Courts and Probation Departments have in their possessions vital information about local conditions. Too often this is withheld. Public and private agencies, officials and lay people must be drawn closer together. Sheldon Glueck tells us: "In many communities most of the facilities for effective coping with pre-delinquency, delinquency and crime already exist; they require effective integration."

The Juvenile Court and Probation Department of Los Angeles County became very much incensed over the old policy of dropping cases into the Court. The community shed these cases like an old skin. It didn't want them; neither did it want them returned. And yet, when these cases were returned to the community often the agencies and organizations got together and rendered very valuable service and made many splendid adjustments.

But these agencies and organizations were in the community before the child got into trouble. The facilities did exist but they required effective integration. For this reason the Juvenile Court and Probation Department sponsored the Coordinating Councils.

When this movement started many agencies and organizations became very much concerned. Was this a new child which was to be dumped on the community, this organization known as the Coordinating Councils? Was somebody going to have to feed it and nurse it? Or was it going to be able eventually to stand on its own feet?

It is always easy to find people who will criticize a new movement. People do not like change. They have been so long embedded in their individual ruts that they glance with suspicion upon anything new. "We didn't do things that way in the past." . . . "We question the advisability of this program." . . . "Isn't this a fifth wheel?" . . . "Don't we attend enough meetings now?" . . . "We are very busy people and we have our own programs to consider." . . . "Then, after all, how do we know that the bringing in of lay people is going to help our program. In fact, they'll muddy up the water."

Mr. Justin Miller refers to these people as the "Prima Donnas" of social work. They do not want to do any community planning, neither do they wish to be disturbed in the regular routine of their work.

Fortunately these are but a few of the fine people who are interested in the Coordinating Council work. These complaining drones have very little interest outside of their own social agency. They fear lay people. On the other hand, Professor Lindeman, of the New York School of Social Work, in speaking to the Coordinating Councils in Los Angeles, recently said, "We must learn how to work out means and methods of collaboration between laymen and professionals. These Councils ought to be the places where the best trained professional people will find themselves strengthened and their efforts enlivened by the presence and experience of lay citizens."

As we review the chronological histories of each of the sixty-four Councils, we find that in some instances action has been slow, in others rapid, but in practically every Council a fundamental change has come about—the awakening of a new social consciousness.

Throughout the organization process we have all frowned upon undue publicity. Council meetings rarely reach the papers until the group have become well established. We cannot afford to have these Councils looked upon as "purity squads" or "cure all" groups, where the community can dump all of its problems. When we do that, the councils are through. The Coordinating Council is not another social agency. Rather, it is an opportunity for all groups interested in community and child welfare to get together and to coordinate their efforts.

These Councils have actually reduced delinquency in certain areas. In others they have started many worth while projects and have enlisted community support for the fine programs offered by its members. In January, 1935, the Los Angeles Crime prevention Bureau reports:

"There were 3,013 boy arrests in 1934 as compared with 3,552 in 1933. This means a reduction of 509. This large decrease of approximately 13 per cent cannot be attributed to any change in the policy of the Police Department affecting juvenile arrests. There are now many more Police Officers assigned to juvenile work than ever before, and for this reason fewer cases should escape their attention. We must, therefore, attribute this marked decrease in delinquency to other influences of which the Coordinating Councils would seem to deserve the lion's share. Their work with 'First Offenders' and pre-delinquents has been undeniably effective, as shown by this unbiased Annual Report."

Community Projects Encouraged by the Councils.—Only a few community projects encouraged by the Councils can be listed here. They include:

a. Summer Camping.—Forty-two Councils are actively participating and more than 3,200 children will be given camping experience this summer. This represents an increase of 35 per cent over any previous year.

b. Vacation Church Schools.—Last year there were 110 such schools. This summer 214, over 100 per cent increase. The churches are working together for the first time. Most of these new schools were in neglected areas. The results have been very satisfactory.

c. Toy Loan Libraries.—Eleven toy libraries located in neglected areas receive their supply from a central shop. These libraries circulate more than 5,000 toys each month.

d. Prevention of Sale of Liquor to Minors.—Fifty-four Councils are definitely active in curbing the sale of alcohol to minors. They have cleaned up many acute situations.

e. Community Dances.—Eleven Councils are most active in sponsoring or backing community dances in their council areas.

f. Special Trips.—Many special trips are planned for children in certain areas through a "Youth Activity Committee." Thousands of children have visited new scenes, attended ball games, races, parks and museums. These children could not afford to go themselves. Many lay groups have been called upon to make these trips possible.

g. Censorship of Salacious Literature.—A case study was made of thirty questionable magazines under the direction of Dr. Martin H. Neumeyer, Sociology Department, University of Southern California. Ten were finally selected and were removed from the news stands by means of Court action.[1]

h. Leadership Training Courses have been sponsored by character building organizations in districts participating. This has resulted in several new groups being formed in neglected areas.

i. Motion Picture Estimate Service has been established in the Los Angeles Public Library. Anyone can call the library and ask about any motion picture, particularly as to its desirability for children.

These are but a few of the accomplishments of the Councils in Los Angeles County.

In December, 1935, Miss Katharine Lenroot, Chief of the United States Children's Bureau, addressed representatives of the Coordinating Councils of Los Angeles. She had been preceded by Miss Hester B. Crutcher, Director of the Delinquency Unit of the Children's Bureau, who was in Los Angeles making a study of Coordinating Councils. Miss Lenroot prefaced her remarks by referring to Miss Crutcher's study, and also that she had followed the Coordinating Council program very carefully through the Coordinating Council Bulletin and other publications. She then proceeded to point out five outstanding accomplishments which could be credited to the Coordinating Council program.

[1] See *Coordinating Council Bulletin*, Los Angeles County (July, 1935), "Perverted Children."

1. *Changed Public Attitude toward Delinquency.*—The first thing of importance is a change in the public's attitude toward delinquency. This question of attitude has been, perhaps, the most difficult problem with which those interested in providing for adequate methods of dealing with juvenile delinquency have been confronted.

2. *A Positive Approach to Community Problems.*—The Councils I visited this morning were considering such things as the liquor problem, salacious literature, health problems, and all those things which are involved in community housekeeping and which can definitely help to set your neighborhood in order, so as to eliminate some of the things which are most detrimental to the development of youth.

3. *Better Understanding of Agencies for Community Service.*—It is quite apparent that in coming together in Adjustment Committees, Character Building Committees and Environment Committees you are dealing at first hand with the resources of the community for service to the family and for group activities of various kinds, obtaining a knowledge of their functions, methods and programs.

4. *Preparation of the Community to Attack New and Difficult Problems.*—Community organization on a neighborhood basis brings all the agencies together and should help to make the community able to attack new and difficult problems. I was interested at the Downtown Council this morning in certain studies that are being made there which ought to lay a basis for a constructive program of this kind.

5. *Broader Understanding of Economic, Political and Social Problems.*—This type of organization is of significance because it affords an opportunity for many people to work together for community service in ways that cannot help but broaden our understanding and appreciation of great underlying economic political and social problems. I think that you have special opportunity here in Los Angeles to forward this ideal for American society and I want you to feel that in doing this you will be making a contribution of significance to the State and to the Nation, and perhaps to mankind as a whole.

It is of great significance that while Miss Lenroot was in Los Angeles only two days she found time to attend two Coordinating Councils and to address the Officers of the Councils at an evening meeting.

Sanford Bates, Director of Federal Prisons, in addressing the California Coordinating Councils at the California Conference of Social Work which met in Los Angeles in April, 1936, said:

"We know what's right; we know what's wrong with our community; we have enough knowledge and so on; we have schools enough, usually playgrounds enough; we have doctors who are skillful enough to treat the individual child; we have child clinics if we know where to find them; we have the tools and the materials. The thing we lack is the organized, dynamic conscience of the community that brings these forces to bear upon the conditions that need remedying. I think that's what makes the Coordinating Council Movement so significant, so prophetic."

At the National Conference of Social Work which met in Atlantic City in May, 1936, the first Annual Conference of Coordinating Councils was held. This was attended by more than four hundred delegates from all over the United States.[1]

Evaluation of the Coordinating Councils.—The Council of Social Agencies of Los Angeles, through its Character Building Division, prepared the following evaluation of the local Coordinating Council movement. This was done to clarify for the Council of Social Agencies many questions concerning the place of the Coordinating Council movement in the community. In preparing this evaluation for the approval of the Executive Committee and the Council of Social Agencies due consideration was given to the fact that the local Coordinating Councils were still in a formative period. The statement follows:

Constructive Achievements

1. The Coordinating Councils have developed closer cooperative effort among professional and lay workers, as related to the field of social work, in local committees.

2. The work of the Coordinating Councils has offered each agency an opportunity for self-evaluation and criticism, and makes possible comparison of its work with the work of other agencies in similar fields.

3. A consciousness of community responsibility and community planning has been engendered by the Coordinating Councils within the local areas involved among professional and lay people, as related to the field of social work, especially in relation to the problems of delinquency prevention.

4. Much valuable information concerning neighborhood resources and local problems has been secured through surveys conducted by the local Coordinating Councils under the supervision of a central research committee.

5. The Coordinating Councils have assisted in the enrichment of community recreational and character-building activities by the assignment of workers of the S.E.R.A. and other governmental projects.

6. Commendable freedom from arbitrary central control has tended to develop in each community local leadership and responsibility. In the course of such developments, constructive direction from a central advisory board should be continued in matters of organization, policy and program in order that mistakes may be avoided.

7. In particular, the Coordinating Councils have fostered community movements beneficial to youth, among which are: Suppression of salacious literature; referral of cases of predelinquent children to specific agencies best equipped to meet their needs; dissemination of accurate information regarding liquor control laws, etc., in relation to minors.

[1] See various addresses on "The Community Approach to Delinquency Prevention," *Yearbook of the National Probation Association* (1936), pp. 1–155.

Dangers to Be Guarded Against

1. There is danger of local Coordinating Councils proceeding too hastily in dealing with problems of individuals and in planning new activities to meet community needs.   This is observed most frequently in groups where adequate skilled leadership with experience in community planning is not available.

2. There is an ever-present danger that local Coordinating Councils will set themselves up as new agencies.

3. In metropolitan areas where a Council of Social Agencies exists the discovery and reporting of needs, problems and resources are considered to be responsibilities of the Coordinating Council, but in the development of a community program, clearance, guidance and direction should be given by the Council of Social Agencies.

4. In organizing such a movement on a state or national basis, serious consideration should be given to adequate representation of the collective organizations—private and public—and of civic and service organizations.

At the first Conference of Coordinating Councils of California in San Francisco in May, 1935, eighty-six Councils were represented.   In reporting on the accomplishments of the Coordinating Councils at this meeting, Dr. Norman Fenton, Director of the California Bureau of Juvenile Research, made several important statements based upon the returns to a questionnaire sent out to all Coordinating Councils in California.

"Let us pause to examine how the Coordinating Council may be of help in community betterment.   In the field of juvenile delinquency, for example, there has seemed to be no fundamental organized Community consciousness.   Each agency of government has laid the problem of delinquency on the doorstep of some other agency.   All public officials have, with unanimous voice, blamed the situation upon the home and the parent.   The community itself has decried the inefficiency of the public service, thinking perhaps by this criticism of its public officials, to absolve itself of responsibility for error.   Instead of voicing recriminations and rationalization, the Coordinating Council accepts the challenge of delinquency, faces the problem and studies it thoughtfully. Practical recommendations are made.   The community consciousness is strongly behind their accomplishment.   No wonder that where Councils exist the everyday life of children has already been improved, and incidentally the community life of adults."

The Coordinating Councils of Los Angeles County are hardly under way.   It will be many years before the real accomplishments of this movement can be measured with any degree of accuracy.   Committees, organizations and lay people, however, are being drawn together as never before.   There now is evidence of a community consciousness which is taking hold with firm hand upon unsatisfactory community conditions affecting youth. Coordinating Councils are merely one method of approaching the problem of delinquency and crime. Social facilities must be coordinated and made available to all children rather than to a select few. The Coordinating Council plan brings all of these groups together. Its primary object, however, is not limited to a reduction of delinquency and crime, but a sincere determination to make the community a better place in which to live.

The Child and the Community.—The philosophy upon which the work of the delinquent child in relation to the community should be based is well expressed by Jessie Binford in her article "Understanding the Delinquent,"[1] from which we quote in part:

The child's needs for security and development can never be fully met by his home, his school, his church or industry. He needs group life, widening interests; he craves the adventure and the opportunities to act as an independent human being which are to be found in what we call "the community." All children, privileged and underprivileged, take what the community has to offer. Adults make it what it is and when it does not satisfy the needs of the children or thwarts and exploits them, then the responsibility is theirs, and no clinics or juvenile courts or reformatory institutions can very fully adjust them.

If a child's earlier and most intimate group fail him, he will, while still very young go forth into his community to satisfy his longing for affection, appreciation, companionship, adventure and will respond to what he finds there with an immature evaluation. What attracts and satisfies him the most may be the very thing that will make him socially unadjusted, delinquent or criminal.

However, under any circumstances, the child will eventually seek the community because of his need for it. His family may try to delay having him meet complete experience and adventure, but it is more and more difficult to do so, because families live so much more outside their homes. Apartments, hotels, clubs, with all their ready-made, mechanical devices, and without yards for play, are chosen to live in partly for economic reasons, and are preferred by many. Crowded city areas for both the rich and the poor mean that all the children are in the community for their leisure time. To meet this situation, community groups and agencies are consciously attempting to attract children and to draw them into what they have to offer, although they may have little conception of their part in completing the life of the child, or that he must be especially safeguarded because he is too immature for all experiences. The community has not yet realized that it is responsible for building to satisfy the fundamental needs of the child, and that it

[1] *Year Book, National Probation Association* (1931), pp. 26–29.

must not only offer opportunity for creative play, companionship and adventure, but must also protect children and young people from negative, demoralizing recreation.

This new, most modern situation is being met to a certain extent by conscious planning on the part of certain private, municipal and commercial groups. They make it easy for parents who wish to evade responsibility, and it is only those that are least constructive that are taking in all children.

There are also those less concrete and obvious community agencies and influences—the press, the spirit of the neighborhood, the lawlessness of the present day. Through these, patterns are formed in the early years, of childhood and youth, which symbolize our morality, our integrity, our philosophy of life.

Apartment life and its consequences, the restriction of the physical area of family life, the easy access of outside influences through the news, the automobile and the radio; perhaps never before have community influences had a larger part in the life of the individual. The great commercialization of recreation, the national organization of character building agencies, the syndication of news and opinion, the wholesale standardized recreation of municipalities—perhaps never before have community influences been so utterly beyond the control of the individual.

We can better understand and help the delinquent child only when we evaluate and analyze community groups and influences in relation to individual behavior, and make a basic attack on them in communities where "traditions teach delinquency, and where crime is the most interesting play of children."

Recommendations were made by the various sub-committees considering the child in relation to these social institutions. Sometimes present steps are in the wrong direction—we considered it even more disturbing that we often so thrill over them as to forget that they have validity only as they lead on to other steps. There are three implications in the entire delinquency report that transcend all others—representing those goals which we are always to keep before us.

Generations that have gone before have primarily stressed the clear duty that environment has for the child, and this we reaffirmed, and in doing so, emphasized that in all social relationships adults who have the guardianship of a child have:

1. A duty to develop in him regular and correct habits of living.

2. A duty to provide such richness of wholesome ideas and interests as will answer his ideational needs. It is not sufficient to use casual amounts of constructive and healthy material as coloring matter for the great masses of sensationalism and artificial stimulation to which the child is subjected.

3. That the guardians of the child have the duty to present in their own living such patterns of honesty, sincerity and courage as shall challenge the child's emulation. In an age when mechanical devices bring distant wonders and the spread of wealth provides ease and comfort beyond our wildest dreams, it is of the greatest importance that all adults realize that by no such trickery is wholesome life produced. It is only in the examples of sincere living that the child finds the dynamic impulse for his own wholesome development.

We affirmed the recognition of delinquent conduct as one of the natural outcomes of those clashes of interest, prerogative and need that are inherent in the matter of living as a social group. Finding fault, laying blame—that most paralyzing and childish of all our human interests—in the past has largely invaded our philosophy as to delinquency. The point in hand is not so much that delinquency is inevitable as that we appreciate the naturalness and ubiquity of those processes which lead up to it. This is fundamentally a matter of recognizing that the stresses which bend the delinquent are of precisely the same character as those which bend our own lives. The needs which have been pictured are those which are of the lives of all of us. All of us, too, have to meet the most unyielding moulds of the various institutions which surround us. As we see the delinquent as a part of this natural and inevitable clash we naturally bring into our concepts a dispassionate attitude which (perhaps for the first time) will allow us to consider the problem of delinquency in a way that leads to some real solution. Thus can we place ourselves in a position to test out our work with the child, whether we focus on the treatment of the child's problem in relation to himself, his family, the state, the school, industry, the church or community forces.

Selected Bibliography

1. ADDAMS, JANE: *The Spirit of Youth and the City Streets*, The Macmillan Company, 1909.
2. ADDITON, HENRIETTA: *City Planning for Girls*, Social Service Monograph No. 5, University of Chicago Press, 1928.
3. BEAM, KENNETH S.: "The Coordinating Council Movement," *Year Book, National Probation Association* (1935), pp. 200–213.
4. ———: "Delinquency Prevention through Coordination," mimeographed, 1936.
5. BOWLER, ALIDA C.: "Experiments in Preventing Juvenile Delinquency," *Year Book, National Probation Association* (1934), pp. 162–166.
6. CARTWRIGHT, JANE: "Community Cooperation versus Delinquency," *Year Book, National Probation Association* (1932–1933), pp. 31–35.
7. CHUTE, CHARLES L.: "Probation in a Community Social Welfare Program," *Year Book, National Probation Association* (1932–1933), pp. 20–30.

8. DEARDORFF, NEVA R.: "Child Welfare," *Encyclopedia of Social Sciences,* Vol. III, pp. 373–380.

8a. DICKSON, VIRGIL E.: "The Berkeley Coordinating Council," *Mental Hygiene,* XIII (July, 1929), 514–519.

9. HART, HASTINGS: *Preventive Treatment of Neglected Children,* Russell Sage Foundation, 1910.

10. HEFFNER, DORA SHAW: "The Los Angeles Coordinating Council Plan," *Year Book, National Probation Association* (1934), pp. 114–125.

11. HILLER, FRANCIS H.: "Coordinating Councils, Report of a Brief Study," mimeographed, 1935.

12. NEUMEYER, MARTIN H.: "The Los Angeles County Plan of Coordinating Councils," *Sociology and Social Research,* XXX (May–June, 1935), 460–461.

13. REEDER, RUDOLPH: *Training Youth for the New Social Order,* Antioch Press, 1933.

14. SCUDDER, KENYON J.: "The Los Angeles County Coordinating Council," in Sheldon and Eleanor Glueck (Editors), *Preventing Crime,* McGraw-Hill Book Company, Inc., 1936.

15. SCUDDER, KENYON J., and KENNETH S. BEAM: *Why Have Delinquents?* Pamphlet, Rotary Club of Los Angeles, 1933.

16. ———: *Who Is Delinquent?* Pamphlet, Rotary Club of Los Angeles, 1934.

16a. VOLLMER, AUGUST: "Coordinated Effort to Prevent Crime," *Journal of Criminal Law and Criminology,* XIX (August, 1928), 196–210.

17. WALTZ, HENRY W.: "The Probation Officers and Community Organization," *Year Book, National Probation Association* (1934), pp. 104–113.

18. YOUNG, ERLE F.: "The Coordinating Council Plan in Los Angeles County," *The Journal of Criminal Law and Criminology,* XXVI (May, 1935), 34–40.

19. YOUNG, PAULINE V.: "The Social Settlement and the Changing City," *Sociology and Social Research,* XIX (September–October, 1935), 63–70.

The German Youth Movement:

20. BLÜHER, HANS: *Wandervogel, Geschichte einer Jugendbewegung,* Verlag Hans Blüher, Charlottenburg, 1919.

21. CHEVALIER, EMILE: "The German Youth Movement," *Living Age,* CCCXXIX (April 10, 1926), 99 ff.

22. LASKER, BRUNO: "The Youth Movement in Germany," *Survey,* XLVII (December 31, 1921), 489–493.

23. RAYMOND, MARCEL: "The German Youth Movement," *Living Age,* CCCXXXIII (September 1, 1927), 417 ff.

24. STÄHLEN, OTTO: *Die Deutsche Jugendbewegung,* Deichertsche Verlagsbuchhandlung, Leipzig, 1930.

25. YOUNG, ERLE F.: "The German Youth Movement," *Sociology and Social Research,* XVI (March-April, 1932), 367–379.

Suggestions for Further Study

1. Read Charles L. Chute, "Probation in a Community Social Welfare Program," *Year Book, National Probation Association* (1932–1933), pp. 20–

30, and discuss: (*a*) What should be the functions of a probation department in any community? (*b*) How can these functions be attained in your community? (*c*) What are the obstacles which prevent proper functioning? (*d*) How may these be overcome in your community? (*e*) What are the criteria of good probation work? What are the bases of evaluation? (*f*) What conclusions does the author arrive at from his research? (*g*) What is the value of social research in probation work?

2. How does Miss Cartwright define "community cooperation"?

3. What is the community's responsibility in delinquency?

4. What role does the probation officer play in bringing about "community cooperation"?

5. Attempt to answer some of the questions raised by Miss Cartwright regarding your own community.

6. Of what value is this article to you in your daily work?

7. What are the community forces which influence the life of children and young people? What are the needs of the child which the community can supply?

8. What problems are created by motion pictures?

9. According to Jessie Binford, what are "the duties of adults who have guardianship of children"? How can these duties be fulfilled?

10. In what respects is the coordinating council movement a force in the adjustment of the offender?

11. How do Professors Neumeyer and Young (Erle F.) differ in their analysis of the coordinating council plan?

12. How do you account for the divergent views expressed by various social workers regarding the value of the coordinating councils in Los Angeles?

13. What are the possibilities of such a movement?

14. Read carefully the various articles on "The Community Approach to Delinquency Prevention," in *Yearbook of the National Probation Association* (1936), pp. 1–151 and indicate the philosophy upon which this approach is based.

15. What considerations do you need to take into account when you set out to organize a coordinating council in your community?

16. Why is the coordinating council movement promising of results in a crime prevention program? in a program of community reorganization?

CHAPTER XXVII

THE ROLE OF THE JUVENILE COURT CLINIC[1]

One of the most striking facts with regard to the conscious life of any human being is that it is interwoven with the lives of others. It is in each man's social relations that his mental history is mainly written, and it is in his social relations likewise that the causes of the disorders that threaten his happiness and his effectiveness and the means for securing his recovery are to be mainly sought.— JAMES J. PUTNAM, *quoted by Mary Richmond, Social Diagnosis, p. 4.*

Many writers point out that one of the most outstanding contributions of the juvenile court movement is the development of children's clinics associated with the courts for the scientific study and understanding of personality problems.[2]

What Is a Clinic?—Louis Wirth[3] says that the notion of a "clinic" is

derived from the Greek "reclining" and has come in medicine to be applied to bedside treatment. To some the term "clinical" may appear to be synonymous with "abnormal," since the need for treatment, in the older conception of medicine, seems to imply the existence of a disease or a pathology. Modern clinical medicine, however, seems to be characterized chiefly by the "case method" of study of the individual, rather than by its emphasis of the pathological.

Dr. William Healy furnished much of the stimulus to the present-day clinical movement in America. He and his associates established in Chicago in 1909 the first American clinic (a gift from Mrs. Ethel Dummer)—in connection with the Juvenile Court of Cook County—under the name of the Juvenile Psycho-

[1] For a comprehensive discussion of child guidance clinics see Lawson G. Lowrey, *A Child Guidance Clinic, Its Purposes and Methods of Service,* and George S. Stevenson and Geddes Smith, *A Child Guidance Clinic: A Quarter Century Development,* also *The Child Guidance Clinic and the Community* (a symposium); for a discussion of the court clinic, see H. H. Lou, *Juvenile Courts in the United States,* pp. 199–203.

[2] *Ibid.,* p. 199.

[3] "Clinical Sociology," *American Journal of Sociology,* XXVII (July, 1931), 50.

pathic Institute,[1] which name was in later years changed to Institute for Juvenile Research. The first court clinic is recognized as having originated under the leadership of Harvey Humphrey Baker of Boston, who realized that there was a great deal more to know about the child than the judge and the probation officer could learn unassisted by social scientific experts.

The clinic is a coordinated attempt in the study and treatment of personality and conduct disorders of children and youth, using the arts of the psychiatrist, psychologist, or psychometrist, and the social worker. The form of organization and the functions which the clinic assumes differ in various localities, but those described by Dr. Lawson Lowrey[2] are typical of most clinics:

The director of such a clinic is a physician with special training in psychiatry, particularly that phase which deals with childhood problems. The psychiatrist is a physician trained in nervous and mental diseases, who views the problems presented from the standpoint of physical health. The psychologist, who is trained in determining mental abilities and disabilities, views them from the standpoint of the individual's abilities and disabilities and educational requirements. The social worker, who is trained in the application of social methods of investigation and treatment, considers them from the standpoint of the social factors involved.

The aim of the clinic is to concentrate on children "who through their activities and behavior in the home, school, or community exhibit difficulty in achieving a satisfactory adjustment to the demands of every day life."[3]   Dr. Bernard Glueck also observes that while the clinic deals with various serious personality problems of children as well as with feeble-minded and defective children, its work should properly be only with children capable of more or less normal adjustment.[4]

The Procedure of the Clinic.—The procedure which the clinic has developed differs from clinic to clinic but in general it seems to conform to the following type, according to Louis Wirth.[5]

---

[1] See RALPH P. TRUITT, "Community Child Guidance Clinics," in *The Child Guidance Clinic and the Community*, pp. 1–16.

[2] *Op. cit.*, p. 4.

[3] BERNARD GLUECK, "Child Guidance," *Encyclopedia of the Social Sciences*, Vol. III, p. 394.

[4] *Ibid.*

[5] *Op. cit.*, p. 51.

(*a*) The case comes to the clinic with a statement of the problems presented as seen by the referring agency or person; (*b*) which is followed by the collection of data by the various investigators of the clinic; (*c*) there follows discussion among the specialists for the purpose of arriving at the facts; (*d*) which are then analyzed with a view of agreeing on a diagnosis; (*e*) to be followed by the formulation of a program of treatment; (*f*) whereupon attempts are made to carry out the program; (*g*) accompanied by periodic reexaminations and evaluations of the program adopted, and the diagnosis upon which it was based; (*k*) with the further effort of arriving at valid generalizations of principles and an improvement of techniques.

Thus the clinic in actual practice is a matter of teamwork, requiring the combined and almost simultaneous efforts of the physician, psychiatrist, psychologist, and social case worker. As Dr. Bernard Glueck maintains:[1]

As every problem in child guidance is a problem of the "setting" or "situation" of the individual child it can be dealt with adequately only by taking into account all the relevant elements. It is of little remedial value to label a child thief, truant, or coward if he steals, runs away from school or is easily intimidated, for behind these simple categories lurks a complexity of phenomena which can be understood only after a thorough study of the individual child and of the social and psychological setting of which he is part.

Since the establishment of the first clinics the following significant tendencies have been observed:

First, there has been a change of emphasis from study of misconduct and delinquency to a study of conduct and the whole field of behavior. The contributions of psychology and psychiatry are no longer conceived to be limited to the task of defining whether a given delinquent is feeble-minded or insane but are rather applied to the understanding and treatment of human behavior as a whole, normal as well as abnormal. Accordingly, while the early institutions were generally called "Psychopathic Institutes," the more recent institutions are mostly entitled "Child Guidance Clinics." Secondly, the emphasis of most of these clinics is laid on community service rather than on service to juvenile courts only, as in the past. It soon became evident that work with children who present behavior problems would be more effective if the problems were recognized and dealt with before the behavior had

[1] *Op. cit.*, p. 394.

become so serious as to necessitate some form of court action. This means that it became increasingly necessary for the psychiatric clinics for children to establish direct contacts with public schools, with social agencies, and with homes.[1]

In recent years the clinic has come more and more to recognize the role of the social factors, and now we find in the literature on child guidance and mental hygiene a more extensive discussion of the problems of social relations and social conflicts which undoubtedly in many instances give rise or contribute to oversensitiveness, obstinacy, constant quarreling, timidity, and other undesirable personality traits which Dr. Glueck lists as problems for the clinic to overcome. Personality traits are fostered and developed in and by the social group. Without the social group, no matter what the individual's potentialities are, his personality traits remain just as undeveloped as those of Casper Hauser, who for sixteen years or more was kept in strict social isolation in a cellar.[2] Before emerging from his confinement his reactions and traits were those of an animal.

The more progressive psychiatrists realize that while they are better oriented to regard the unadjusted person as the central object of study, they should not overlook the social world as the most potent sources from which disorganization and personality unadjustment spring. Some clinicians, they say, are chiefly concerned with the child's reactions—mental, emotional, and physical—to the surrounding world. But as clinicians do not study this world, then it must be argued that the child is apt to be considered by them in abstraction as an entity in itself, artificially divorced from reality, a procedure which is neither practical, logical, nor possible. Dr. Glueck, as many others, however, maintains that in "the process of adjustment [of the child], which often involves the remaking of the environment, the social worker is of key importance."[3] Thus, "the environment," one of the major sources of unadjustment, is left to the art of social workers to deal with. Hence social workers actually assume a far greater importance in clinic work than is generally realized. It is through their influence that the social factors in

[1] Lou, *op. cit.*, p. 203.
[2] See PAUL J. A. VON FEUERBACH, *Casper Hauser;* PHILIP HENRY STANHOPE, *Tracts Relating to Casper Hauser.*
[3] *Op. cit.*, p. 394.

behavior problems have been called to the attention of the psychiatrist.   Also, as Wirth[1] writes:

The social workers in many instances have assimilated the psychiatric viewpoint, with the apparent result that a new type of psychiatry seems to be emerging, distinguished from the older by its emphasis on the situational factors in personality development and behavior problems. In one modern child guidance clinic the interest in physical treatment has been almost completely displaced by "social-psychiatric" treatment.

Dr. Lowrey,[2] Director of the Institute for Child Guidance, New York City, says:

In general, treatment proceeds (as is common in child guidance clinics) through the joint efforts of psychiatrist and social worker and frequently the psychologist.   The Institute does practically nothing in the way of physical treatment, referring cases needing such to the family physician (or family specialist) or to the clinics to which the patients would ordinarily go.   So far as the major efforts are concerned, the most important phases of the treatment are contributed by the psychiatric social worker in her attempt to remold attitudes in the home, the school and elsewhere, and by the psychiatrist in his work with the individual patient, or, in many instances, with parents, where the psychotherapeutic problem is at a level beyond that to which the social worker is prepared to go.

A further hampering factor in clinic operation is the "laboratory point of view" which many specialists bring to this work. One rarely hears of psychiatrists and psychologists leaving the close domains of their offices and studying the child in the "environment," the school, the home, the street, gangland, and delinquency areas, "which need remaking," as Clifford Shaw, Frederick Thrasher, E. W. Burgess, John Landesco, and a host of other of the younger sociologists have done.   The older sociologists took the challenge rather seriously that "they are a bunch of armchair philosophers" and the younger group have gone out to face the environment, social reality which surrounds us at every point, in our inner, outer, conscious, subconscious, and unconscious mind.   The clinicians need the sociologist to

[1] *Op. cit.*, p. 55.
[2] Lawrence G. Lowrey, *Report* [of the Institute] *for the Year Ending June* 30, 1928, p. 23.

study the environmental factors if they are to avoid the indictment that they are a group of "office-chair philosophers." We must recognize, of course, that some of the leading psychiatrists of the country, notably Adolf Meyer, have insisted that the essential function of the clinician was to see all the elements in the total picture which the patient shows.[1] But the puzzling thing is that the clinician, with his insistence on thoroughgoing study, should so generally rest satisfied with seeing that "total picture" and the actual social world of the patient through the eyes of a social worker, and furthermore, that he should entrust the social worker to work out, not only the technique, but the principles involved in remolding the environment. His own contacts with that world in the individual case are limited to such indirect and secondhand contacts as he can make with the patient across the interviewing desk or can gather from the reports of case workers.

The emphasis upon psychogenic theories in many cases has caused the psychiatrists to view the role of the family, the gang, the neighborhood, the general community through a veil darkly. Yet he proposes to proceed in remolding this individual, not so much through the manipulation of psychic forces, as through control of the social environment.

We hear of the rather common complaint of social agencies and individual social workers that, after preparing elaborate social histories of patients who are examined by psychiatrists, the report of the psychiatrist—in addition to a few diagnostic labels—frequently consists of a brief review of the case history with the conclusion which competent case workers could draw for themselves. This reaction undoubtedly is an exaggeration, yet the experience is too common to disregard it wholly. The objections furthermore relate to the practice that after prolonged and costly study, the recommendations of the clinic are frequently of little practical value or merely recommend the removing of the child from his home. Certainly "remaking of the environment" means more in the long run than a change of residence or placement in a foster home in which the environment is more congenial. Ultimately the child must return to his previous residence and his own home.

The Court Clinic and the Child Guidance Clinic.—So far what has been said about the clinic applies to a considerable degree to

[1] *Ibid.*, p. 25.

both court and noncourt clinics. The privately endowed clinics supported by community chest funds are generally called child guidance clinics, and these often serve the community as a whole and are interested in delinquent as well as nondelinquent children. The larger court clinics, though their form of organization as described by Dr. Lowrey is practically the same as those of the child guidance clinics—with the exception that the social worker in the court clinic is the probation officer—differ in the following important respects.

The privately endowed child guidance clinics are community agencies and study, diagnose, and attempt treatment of the whole child. The purpose of the clinic attached to a juvenile court, which is supported by the taxpayer, is[1] "to supply the judge, who is to be the administrator of the treatment, with knowledge as to the kind of individual before him, as well as the kind of treatment which will best meet the needs [of the individual] . . . and the needs of society with reference to him." Says Dr. Alfred LaBine: "The clinic . . . furnishes the court information on the conditions of mental health or disease of [the offender] . . . and an opinion as to what may be expected in the future."[2] This opinion practically takes the form of recommendations as to treatment.

The court clinic is not a research agency to the extent that the child guidance clinic is. The court clinic concentrates exclusively on children who are dealt with by the juvenile court and most frequently, though not always, on those children who are detained in a juvenile detention home. The court clinical staff rarely sees the parents or guardians of the offender for purposes either of diagnosis or of treatment of the case. Neither does it refer or recommend problems of parents to social agencies and to an Institute of Family Relations. Not all children are given or are in need of a psychiatric examination. Frequently only the "most serious cases" are seen by the psychiatrist, and not a few of these are subjected to a most cursory examination owing to the large numbers of children passing through the court clinic.

[1] "Community Child Guidance Clinic," in *The Child Guidance Clinic and the Community*, p. 1.

[2] "The Psychiatrist in a Criminal Court," *Year Book, National Probation Association* (1932–1933), p. 138.

Authorities agree[1] that practically all the work done to date in the field of delinquency and problematic behavior of children has been diagnostic in character. Diagnosis is the first step toward intelligent treatment. Treatment is much more complex than diagnosis, yet generally treatment is left to the social worker and the probation officer. While "across-the-table conferences" and diagnostic procedures of the clinic are invaluable and indispensable they need to be followed up by intimate contacts, study, and adjustment by the clinician of the social setting, which produces maladjustment. Only such procedure would take fully into account both major factors—constitutional and situational—which comprise the total situation of the child.

There are certain serious difficulties which hinder wider development of the court clinics: clinical study, observation, and treatment are exceedingly expensive. Since they are supported by tax funds, they are frequently limited as to staff, equipment, and competency of the staff they attract. Furthermore, the points of view of the clinicians have not been widely accepted by court officials, judges, and probation officers. On this point, Walter C. Bell of the Division for Juvenile Training, Department of Public Welfare of Massachusetts, writes:[2]

Intelligence Classifications.—Far too much emphasis has been placed upon the classification of a child as feebleminded or not. Most court psychiatric service was inaugurated to determine just this, or to diagnose definite mental disorder for the court's information, and in many instances this service has never been allowed to grow much beyond this stage. Except for the definitely committable cases the question of feeblemindedness is of relative unimportance. Such a concept of the function of a clinic on the part of the court has been a real handicap to the psychiatrist.

"The early belief that feeblemindedness was in general and by itself a very important cause of crime," says Sutherland, "has never been definitely substantiated." A recent interesting study of first offenders of average intelligence and defective intelligence, and of repeaters of average intelligence and defective intelligence from the standpoint of success and failure, showed that 35 per cent of the first offenders of

---

[1] Milton E. Kirkpatrick, "The Contribution of Child Guidance Theory to the Treatment of Behavior," *Year Book, National Probation Association* (1935), p. 149, also F. H. Allen, *ibid.*, pp. 131–148.

[2] "Some Emphases in Psychiatric Service," *Year Book, National Probation Association* (1932–1933), pp. 111–116.

average intelligence were failures while 39 per cent of those of defective intelligence were failures.   In the study of the repeaters, 66 per cent of average intelligence were failures as against 70 per cent of those of defective intelligence.   In other words the results were practically the same; and we are led to the conclusion that there is little or no difference in adjustment or in the likelihood of success between those of average intelligence and those of defective intelligence either in first offenders or repeaters.

In an age of mechanization and standardized routine living, intelligence is a much overrated commodity. . . . But what contributes most to [one's] ultimate success and proper adjustment is "P.Q." or personality quotient, plus whatever special abilities he may have.   All of us know the feebleminded who get ahead by sheer force of personality and who, after a few preliminary adjustments in which we may play some small part, go along steadfastly and persistently without deviation and often adapt themselves successfully to specialization in modern industry against which the more aggressive, the more assertive and intelligent minds often rebel. . . .

The probation officer [as a result] having pigeon-holed his delinquent has dismissed his problem with the feeling that after all this is a feeble-minded child and that as far as he is concerned he plans to waste mighty little effort on him. . . . Let us guard against a "sheep and goats" attitude of mind.   Let us consider every child from the standpoint of his needs and of the particular problems which he presents and ask our psychiatrist not only to name and classify these needs, but to instruct us in their relative importance and to help us build up a constructive program of treatment and adjustment.

Psychiatric Service for the First Offender.—By contrast, far too little emphasis has been placed upon using psychiatric service for the first offender.   There is no reason for assuming that he represents some special caste.   All offenders are first offenders at some time in their careers; and many nominal first offenders are second and third offenders who haven't previously been caught.   Our tendency has been to go lightly with first offenders.   We are all familiar with the plea so dear to lawyers to be lenient on the ground that "this is his first offense"— and we ourselves lean toward this attitude and in many instances, rightly too.

When a second offense appears, we begin to sit up and take notice and increase our efforts all along the line and unfortunately it is not until the third or fourth offense that we begin to suspect our own conclusions and call in help from the psychiatric clinic.   This is clearly a procedure following the law of diminishing returns, and for a probation officer who has to "spread himself thin" over a large number of cases and conserve his time and energy, it is often a clear waste of effort. The clinic which sees such a boy for the first time after repeated appearances in a number of courts is not only getting marked down goods, but being short changed at the same time. Let us make an increased use of the clinic for the first offender. Where there is trouble due to emotional or other conflicts, physical needs or definite mental problems requiring therapy or prolonged study and readjustment, the court must continue its supervision and work along with the clinic. Where these are not present, leniency for the first offender may not only be well in order, but very wise and proper. It is a great art to know when to stop, not only in reading a paper but in dealing with the delinquent before the court. Too often we do not stop soon enough.

[Relation of] the Clinic and the Probation Officer.— . . . At present, it is like all poor relations; you are apt to be suspicious of them; you like to feel a little remote and superior to them and yet you are always expecting that, at any moment they will descend upon you to spend the summer.

First of all there are the difficulties associated with terminology, technique and approach. There is no reason why a probation officer should be a trained psychiatrist. The obligation to get his stuff across to the courts and the probation officer so that they can not only understand it, but make use of it, rests entirely with the psychiatrist—just as it does with the chemist or physicist when he deals with the lay person. Such an effort may prove invaluable to him because, after all, it may assist him in clarifying and vitalizing his own ideas. Vagueness and uncertainty like many a poor dish are often completely disguised with a rich sauce, the formula of which is not known to anyone but the man who serves it.

Moreover, where the problem presented shows clearly the need for mental hygiene or therapy, the clinic should be prepared to give it. . . . No probation officer should attempt it. . . .

The Clinic and the Community.—If the clinics are to be of real assistance to the court in a plan of treatment, they must know something of the community in which they function and the resources which it offers for care or treatment, but they must know a great deal more about the community in which the child lives and the social forces which surround its life. The sociological aspects of their problem seem temporarily to be eclipsed by the psychiatric aspects, but they are none the less important. When the psychiatrist proceeds from the field of diagnosis to the field of treatment he steps immediately from one world to another. It is of little use to prescribe a plan of treatment for a person based on the assumption that he is living in the Ideal State when he really lives in Back Street Alley. As the psychiatrist cannot have all knowledge for his province any more than the probation officer can, he must get this community picture elsewhere. This he can get from the probation officer who either lives or works in that community, and who should know, not what resources one would hope for, but actually those that are available and open to him.

This implies a close correlation between the clinic and the court, sitting together in conference, joining in discussion and study, and striving for some method of evaluation of results. The probation officer must be prepared to protest the intangible and substitute the feasible but he must constantly be aware that sometimes those who see a thing from a distance get a better picture than those who stand too close.

The Needs of the Court.—To bring about this kind of relationship and make this extended use of the clinic possible where resources are limited, the court in its turn must develop some sifting out process and some ability to state clearly to the clinic just what service it wishes. Otherwise referrals become routine and new contacts become just more grist to the mill. The court may roughly divide its requirements as to kinds of service into these three groups:

a. A purely diagnostic service with recommendations.

b. Cases which the clinic will carry cooperatively with the probation officer for repeated study and advice.

c. Those that the clinic will carry for specialized treatment with its own psychiatric social worker, where the contact of the probation officer will be only nominal.

After all, this psychiatric service is an expensive thing and as such, when it is provided by public monies, it becomes a matter viewed with considerable skepticism and conjecture by the layman. At this present stage, the courts must be in a position to say that it is of real practical assistance if they are to justify it. Otherwise, when the demand for economy sets in, it may be the first item to be lopped from the budget.

The following case summary is one in a large number of cases which could be cited to illustrate that while clinics submit to the court very carefully diagnosed cases and sound recommendations, the court does not always heed their advice.

CASE SUMMARY OF EDWARD EDWARDSON[1]

Fourteen years of age—born Dec. 2, 1921; eighth grade. Edward was picked up on Dec. 20, 1935, by a police officer in the suburbs of S. while asleep at the front door of a residence. He was placed under voluntary probation to the Police Juvenile Bureau in S. and returned to his parents. On Jan. 26, 1936, the boy ran away from home, was gone several days, slept in an abandoned garage or in the night shows on Main Street. He was

[1] Case transcribed with permission of K. County Juvenile Court.

picked up by police officer and taken to Juvenile Detention Home. There he was defiant, threatened to run away, was unwilling to submit to discipline and to carry out orders.

The Social History.—The parents are dependent on unemployment relief and are allowed $86 a month for themselves and their eight children, between the ages of sixteen years and two years of age. They expect a ninth child in two months. They plan to move to R., a town 150 miles distant, where the father was promised work as a truck driver. The father is fifty-one years of age, born in Canada, in good health, has grammar-school education; he is a carpenter by trade but has been out of work for three years. The mother is thirty-two years of age, born in Missouri, has grammar-school education, is "high strung, nervous, and extremely abusive in her language." The house ($15 a month rent) is ill-kept, crowded, and poorly furnished.

The mother refused to call for Edward at Juvenile Detention Home, accusing the authorities of being too lenient. She regards the boy as "worthless, out of his right mind, incorrigible." She entered "on a very serious tirade" against the boy, maintained that he had always made trouble and is unable to get along because he wants his own way, and when he can't have it, he runs away. The parents want the boy away from home as he does damage to the other children.

Development History of Edward.—Second among eight children; normal birth; walked at eighteen months; used to beat his head on floor unless he had his own way; had temper tantrums at early age; was cruel to animals and children; was punished by severe beatings. Parents do not agree on discipline.

Clinical Examination of Edward. *Physical Examination.*—Shows him well developed though undernourished. Is in need of herniotomy after general physical condition is improved. Wassermann negative, puberty early. Possibly diabetic.

Psychological Examination.—Physical age 14:9, mental age 14:8, I.Q. 99. Average normal; normal adult insight into social situations. Reasons well; shows reflective and serious effort; friendly, sociable boy. Has good imagination; has a sense of humor.

Psychiatric Examination.—First psychiatric examination, on Dec. 20, 1935, was very superficial and revealed hyperactivity, tensions, and suffering due to rejection by mother. No abnormalities.

Behavior Report.—At Detention Home on four days' observation: loud, uncouth, aggressive, willing and responsive, fair sport; housework fairly done.

Later Psychiatric Examination.—2–9–36. Emotionally unstable; feels his rejection strongly; he believes life cruel to him; deals similar treatment back to those who constitute his environment. His rejection is symptomized in enuresis, nightmares, early tantrums. He desires to look nice, to have some money, to be a Mussolini. He believes that "a hard fist is the best answer." He says that he never picks a fight but waits until others start it. At home he "fights and talks back because he loses his temper quickly; is sassy to his mother, although he gets many beatings for it. Wants to go on the road and go on and on." He is sure that his parents don't want him, and that nobody likes him.

The boy states that he is nagged at home, is deprived of any affection and privileges which the other children receive, is not allowed to go fishing with his brother. He admits his own irritability but knows that he is not welcome, and, therefore, runs away. He wants to live in the country. He says: "I really don't enjoy life; I want to go on hikes, go fishing, but I never get to go anywhere."

Clinical Recommendations.—The boy needs a feeling of security and sense of belonging and of being wanted, loved, appreciated, trusted. He is an outgoing sociable, affectionate person, responds to kindness and understanding. He needs an outlet for physical energy. He wants to live on a ranch.

Disposition of the Case of Edward E.—The boy was placed in R. Home for Boys under the supervision of the probation officer, Feb. 17, 1936. The boy ran away from R. Home as he was unhappy there and unable to make an adjustment to the many varieties of boys in the home. The Superintendent refused to take him back, finding him "an impossible person to deal with."

Subsequent History.—Edward was picked up almost immediately by a police officer, and as the boy was being returned to Juvenile Detention Home he escaped at the door. He was picked up later in the day and kept in detention.

Placement in the State School for Boys was recommended but due to its overcrowded condition he would have had to wait for several weeks before he could be admitted. Commitment to the State School was deemed necessary in spite of the fact that the boy had not committed delinquencies and had not violated any law of the state nor any local ordinances, but was regarded "sufficiently incorrigible at home and in an institution for boys to warrant commitment." While awaiting admittance the boy was sent back to his home. He ran away after a few days' stay.

On Mar. 13 the boy was apprehended by police officer and was sent to Juvenile Detention Home. He admits having stolen a bicycle valued at $40 from A. B., at S. A., but abandoned it. Later held up a man with a toy revolver and took a dollar from him. Then he went to Bridge F. to hide; there he was approached by a sex pervert but escaped from him. He went to C., stole another bicycle valued at $40, and went to L. and left the bicycle in an auto park. (The boy's account coincides closely to the facts obtained in a police investigation.)

4-20-36. Edward was committed to the State School.

4-23-36. The boy ran away from State School. While out he stole four automobiles and burglarized a grocery store, taking crackers, sweets, canned goods, and 150 pennies.

4-30-36. Edward was apprehended and a petition was filed by a police officer charging him with, *Count One:* grand auto theft; *Count Two:* making use of personal property without consent of owner and in his absence. The boy was detained in Juvenile Detention Home awaiting the hearing. Neither of the parents appeared in court for the hearing. The father was out of town on a trucking job and the mother had been recently confined after the birth of the ninth child.

Behavior Reported by Psychiatrist.—Edward threatened and attempted to jump out of the tenth-story window. He feels his rejection by his parents keenly. He had a fight at the Detention Home because a boy insulted his mother. He seeks recognition and response from the nurse; craves sympathy from attendants. He does not get along well in a group; he feels rejected and asks if he is mentally deranged as his mother believes. Continues asking the nurse if she thinks he is crazy. He is very unhappy and is overwhelmed with and fearful of his outcome.

He is responsive to sympathetic understanding and praise with pathetic eagerness. His good behavior depends on affectional bonds and understanding between self and person in charge. With encouragement he does remarkably well.

His greatest fear is commitment to a State Industrial School, which would be very unfortunate and would provide the basis for grave behavior in the institution as well as upon release. Careful placement in a home in the country with people who can give him affection, guidance, and understanding is still recommended.

Disposition of Case.—5–1–36. Case was heard in Juvenile Court. Neither parent appeared for the hearing. The father had not returned from his trucking job and the mother had recently given birth to the ninth baby. Edward was ordered to be committed to the State Industrial School at the recommendation of the probation officer while the recommendations of the psychiatrist were disregarded. (Note that Edward is only fourteen years and six months old.)

The following case summary of Neil Neilson is another case in point.

CASE OF NEIL NEILSON[1]

Sixteen years old. No. 00516. 11–22–35. The boy is in court for unlawfully taking a bicycle from high school of the value of $50, the property of S. P. The boy acknowledges and admits that he stole the bicycle herein indicated; that he hid it in a cave and tore it to pieces. The boy's attitude is not cooperative. He is rather morose and stubborn. There are ten children in the family, ranging in ages from one year up to this boy and an older girl. The family is in dire financial straits, and it would appear to be to the benefit of this boy, from the standpoint of discipline as well as that of financial aid, that he should have an opportunity at County Forestry Camp and receive the training, education, and remunerative help to be offered there. He wants to live on a farm and among "people who would like him."

It is recommended that Neil Neilson be declared a ward of the Juvenile Court, under Sub. 13, Sec. 1, of the Juvenile Court Act, in that the allegations in the complaint are found to be true; that he be placed in Juvenile Hall Detention Home for a thorough physical and mental examination; that he be released to the Probation Officer to be placed at County Forestry

[1] Case transcribed with permission of the Court of S. County.

Camp 10; the funds accumulating to his credit to be held in trust pending further order of the court; continue the matter thirteen weeks for further report. Secure medical report, however, before the order is put in full force and effect.

Referee of the Juvenile Court.

Clinical Report. Neil Neilson.—Date: Nov. 27, 1935.

Social History.—The patient's marked feeling of insecurity in relation to both parents from a very early age has contributed greatly to his persecutory trend—the conviction that he is an outcast in every social situation. Father was in "delicate" health until adolescence—wandered early from the family fold. He was about twice mother's age at the time of marriage. Parental disharmony because of father's chronic alcoholism has had important repercussions for the patient, particularly since father has been more constantly in the home since depression. Patient resents extremely correction by father when the latter has been drinking and "holds a grudge" against him. Maternal grandfather a Civil War veteran, died when mother was nine. Mother felt deprived—left school upon completion of the grades to work in a laundry. She has given birth to ten children in close succession. Patient is the second. He was preceded by a girl and followed by three others. Mother is nervous and irritable—whipped patient severely and to excess until he was three because of his negativism. Symptoms of emotional insecurity and environmental pressure can be discerned in retention of infantile modes of satisfaction—such as early thumb sucking, enuresis until the age of nine, nail biting, etc. There was speech difficulty until patient started to school. History of excruciating earache from infancy until 1930 when T. & A. were done. Hearing impairment was reported at one time. Until comparatively recently, patient is said to have been "whipped constantly" by the school group who were "determined to conquer" him. He is academically retarded. As in the home situation patient has thus had security further threatened at school. Response to this kind of treatment has been in terms of rejecting all symbols of authority on the grounds that they "have it in for him," which in turn leads to "threats to get even." Patient is "not a mixer"—feels he has no friends. Is frequently depressed. Home is cheerless and wretched. Patient evinces interest in athletics and is reported to have some mechanical aptitude.

Physical Examination.—11–13–35. General physical condition good. Tonsils out. Puberty Post. Wassermann (6–12–34) negative.

Psychological Examination.—12–6–35. Stanford Binet, physical age 16:1; mental age 13:4; I.Q. 83. Classification not determined. Superior in analysis or where creativeness is necessary. Barely passes twelve-year vocabulary but passes sixteen-year abstract words. Weak in work where a visual memory is an important factor toward success. Very slow and halting reader. (Visual disability plus inferior attention control.) Sullen appearing. Wide and inconsistent scatter (eight through superior adult). Responds quickly at times and at other times remains silent, refusing to answer when examiner tries to question him further. Shows a good persistency of effort, but is weak in tests where retention is the necessary factor toward success.

Behavior Report.—11–16–35. Three days observation. Behavior in general excellent. He was quite stubborn, glum, and uncommunicative at first because he resented coming to Juvenile Hall. He ignored the group and listened to the radio. He has become more friendly lately but continues to be reserved and inarticulate. He doesn't seem to be a "good mixer."

Psychiatric Examination.—11–26–35. The patient as he appears first before the examiner presents a picture of smouldering wrath ready to burst out on slight provocation. He sits with head hanging, eyes averted, and with conscious careful determination not to be, as it were, caught with his defenses down. He does not engage in spontaneous conversation and as this is being elicited through initial questioning he replies abruptly, as concisely as possible, with no offer of elaboration or further explanation. He tells of "never liking school" and of therefore "being bad." He derives satisfaction from this negative behavior in that he has caused trouble to the other person. His attitude is verbalized in "I get back on them—plenty!" This attitude was expressed again as regards his experience in camp. Rapport is established only after much time has been consumed and much positive effort on the part of the "analyst." The patient has undoubtedly from early infancy had a predominance of influences and experiences of destructive and unsatisfying value to him. "Spankings" and other evidences of rejection as well as hostility have laid the basis for his feeling of unwantedness and even positive persecution as the same experiences of the home were repeated in the school and in each social group entered by him. Through inhibition and repression he learned early to find some compensation in manifesting behavior unacceptable and therefore provocative of a sort of interest and attention. History indicates that at an early period patient symptomatized his then already pent-up painful experiences in cruelty to animals. He had need—it was also noted—of clinging to infantile satisfactions rather than to move on to mature adult personality integration. He is an extremely sensitive person whose rejection has been so acute that he has built up various poses and attitudes which make him appear "hard" and impregnable. He is, however, unconsciously seeking acceptance, security, and affection on some level. To the emotional factors in home and school which have so frustrated patient has been added that of dire poverty and economic strain and stress to such a point that patient feels himself only a burden in the home.

Recommendations.—Nothing of constructive value can be contributed to the patient or by him until he is given some experience from which he derives a sense of "wantedness," of acceptance or security and of being appreciated for his individual self. His life's experiences have contained a preponderance of unsatisfying ones and the patient needs definitely this positive feeling of security and appreciation in the group. What comes as compulsion and without consideration for his real wishes only follows in line with all the other many frustrations of his life. He has expressed a wish to live on a ranch and to be self-supporting. It would undoubtedly contribute a great deal to his ego-satisfaction to do this. The patient has further expressed interest in mechanical training—yet it seems that this outlet has not been so far available to him. The patient should be with calm, unemotional people who know patience in relationships with other humans and some sympathetic understanding that deep-seated painful conflicts and emotional experiences are symptomatized in this gruff "bad" behavior. This patient can be expected to respond well if led through kindness and simple consideration and understanding.

Medical Director.

Disposition of the Case.—Boy placed at County Forestry Camp 10.

The question arises why were the recommendations by the psychiatrist, who to all appearances made a careful study of the boy, and whose recommendations were sound, disregarded? The probation officer maintained that in the case of Edward "It was no use even trying to put such a boy on a farm, as he would run away after the first day." The judge maintained that the "psychiatrist does not know what the court is up against, since the community was getting tired of Edward's escapades and his case had gotten into the newspapers. How long should the public be imposed upon with the vagrancies of such a boy? The psychiatrist doesn't know the world nor the difficulties of farm homes in our Community." Obviously all are correct. The judge based his thinking on his general knowledge of boy behavior and reactions of the community. The clinic based its thinking on the concrete knowledge of these boys under careful study. In view of general case work principles and philosophy the clinical recommendations are sound.

Suggestions for Improvements in the Practices of the Court Clinics.—We can perhaps do no better at present than to rely on the Gluecks'[1] study and their recommendations regarding possible improvements in the court clinic with regard to contacts with the offender, his social study, value of "own story," and importance of clinic's role in treatment.

Contacts with Clinic— . . . The nature of the personality problems presented by delinquents is such that one or two examinations and psychiatric interviews do not, as a rule, enable the clinical worker to grasp the motivating forces involved, or to establish that rapport with the delinquent which is indispensable to even a superficial determination of the mental mechanisms underlying his misconduct. We are convinced that every original examination by the clinic should be deemed tentative, and should be made largely for the purpose of giving the court a rough sketch of the case as a basis for an experimental *original* disposal of it. There should then be at least one reexamination, within a few

[1] *One Thousand Juvenile Delinquents*, pp. 252–259.

weeks after the original one, when more reliable data as to the delinquent's background have been obtained and when information as to his
response to the experimental treatment can be taken into account. In
cases which require it, several more clinical contacts should be provided
for—a procedure that would be feasible if the clinic were an integral
part of the court.

Materials before Clinic and Court—. . . If clinical work deserves to be
done at all, it deserves to be done with great thoroughness; for only in
this way can the full potentialities of the clinical approach be determined.
It would be far better for a clinic to devote its efforts to a relatively small
number of cases, in order to find out what can be done by intensive
investigation and treatment, than to skim the surface in many hundreds
of cases and thus make relatively little progress, or arrive at questionable conclusions.

Some of the clinic's social data are obtained from the probation
officers; moreover the situation not infrequently changes between the
time of the clinical investigation and the disposition of the case by the
court. For those reasons, in addition to the one already mentioned
and others to be indicated, a much more intimate relationship between
clinic and court is called for. . . .

The clinic must supply the court not only with a summary but with a
duplicate of pertinent detailed reports in support of it. Particularly
helpful would be a copy of "the boy's own story"[1]—a clinical document
that sometimes throws light on the motivations of his misconduct and
ought therefore by all means to be considered by the judge and the
probation officers.

Turning now to the content of the summary, it is exceptional for the
clinic to indicate why and how certain factors (e.g. poverty, drunkenness of father, the mother's going out to work) have been *causative* in
any particular case. The mere presence of such factors in a situation
should not be taken as necessarily indicating their etiologic significance.
There are many boys who come of poor families and/or whose parents
are drunkards and/or who suffer from other handicaps who, nevertheless, do somehow not become delinquent. The clinician should therefore do his utmost to determine the mechanisms of causation as they
operate in the particular case, and should give the evidence in support
of his conclusion that a certain factor or complex of factors is causal.

Clinic . . . a Treatment Agency— . . . If . . . a Clinic . . . is to
play a truly effective role, it seems indispensable that it should guide
the technical features of *the treatment program* adopted by the court. . . .

The Clinic's Relationship to the Court.—Society entrusts the treatment
of juvenile delinquents to courts rather than to clinics. Yet judges

---

[1] [For samples, see Clifford Shaw, *The Jack-Roller*.]

need the aid not only of clinics but of all other available resources that might have something to contribute to the treatment process. Logically and functionally, a clinic should be an integral part of a court, even though the other necessary services cannot be, by reason of their multiplicity and because their major concern is not with juvenile delinquency.

The psychiatrist would undoubtedly stress at least two additional points: (1) the necessity for much better training and equipment for probation and other court officers who might more thoroughly understand and be instrumental in carrying out clinical recommendations as well as court instructions, and (2) an ever alert attitude toward discovering means of establishing the practical resources (school, home, recreation, etc.) helpful in a constructive program in dealing with offenders. The lack of these resources in some communities makes the clinical recommendations "impracticable."[1]

Further Recommendation: The Inclusion of a Sociologist.—To the Gluecks' recommendations we should like to add the inclusion of a sociologist on the clinical staff. This procedure would fortify the clinic at its weakest point. From the cases cited in this volume it becomes apparent that we can support Burt's contention that delinquency and problematic behavior are at bottom social rather than psychological concepts.[2] This contention is particularly significant since it is the result of a study of 600 cases of juvenile delinquents and especially since Burt is himself a psychologist. Furthermore, Dr. Healy, a widely recognized psychiatrist, found in a study of 4,000 repeated juvenile offenders that "72.5 per cent were definitely mentally normal . . . the feebleminded appear among serious delinquents from five to ten times more frequently than in the general population, but, even so, they form not more than one-fifth as many as the mentally normal. Our total is 13.5 per cent clearly feebleminded,"[3] state Healy and his associate Augusta F. Bronner. The figures of John Slawson, a psychologist, correspond almost exactly with those of Healy and Bronner. Slawson writes: "We find among the total population of delinquents tested, which is 1,543, that

---

[1] Comment by Dr. George J. Mohr (Chicago psychiatrist) in letter to writer, Sept. 14, 1936.

[2] CYRIL BURT, *The Young Delinquent*, p. 15.

[3] *Delinquents and Criminals; Their Making and Unmaking*, pp. 150–151.

13.4 per cent are tested intelligence deficients."[1] Burt says: "I find that, of the juvenile delinquents whom I have tested with the Binet-Simon tests, 8 per cent, and no more, are mentally defective."[2] Of course, it is exceedingly important to identify the feeble-minded in order to provide institutional or other proper care for them.

So far too few studies of juvenile delinquents have been made by psychiatrists relative to mental disease to give us the extent of psychoses and neuroses among the juvenile population, but the very fact that only a relatively small number of offenders ever see the psychiatrist is indicative of the assumption that the extent of mental disease is considered insignificant.

The 3,000 cases of juvenile delinquency studied at various times by the writer[3] could definitely have profited by a sociological approach to behavior, which would have aided in the understanding of those phases of behavior which could not be adequately understood through biological, psychological, and psychiatric approaches. These cases, of which only a few representative samples have been included in this volume, indicate that the child's behavior is in reality what Burgess[4] would call "a constellation of a number of roles, each oriented with reference to a social group in which the child has a definite place." Wirth observes that "a boy, whose parents have had the bad judgment to name him Percival or Oswald, may, in a given cultural milieu of his associates, be suffering from as significant a stigma as if he had one leg or a harelip. It is not desirable that the sociologist should displace the physician, the psychologist, the psychiatrist, nor the social worker, but he should bring to them the insight which his approach furnishes not merely in order to modify their viewpoint but to understand the child's behavior more completely as a social phenomenon."[5]

The sociologist through his cultural approach points out that a given problem or delinquency is such only by virtue of the fact that the community on the basis of its existing mores at the time

[1] *The Delinquent Boy*, p. 160.

[2] *Op. cit.*, p. 286.

[3] See note, p. 320.

[4] See E. W. BURGESS, "The Study of the Delinquent as a Person," *The American Journal of Sociology*, XXVIII (May, 1923), 657–680.

[5] *Op. cit.*, p. 59.

considers it a problem or delinquency. The Russian Molokan newly wedded couples by the elders of the church were considered bound by holy and spiritual bonds of matrimony, but these couples, married by the elders alone, were considered in America as illegal unions and not a few of the young brides and grooms were arrested and sent to juvenile detention or jail.[1] Marilyn Smith (see pp. 34 *ff.* and 296 *ff.*), who absented herself from school, was considered a truant, and the school was ready to take legal action in the matter, but had she attended a higher school in Germany, where attendance is disregarded, her behavior would not have been viewed as problematic. Further, had she lived in a Samoan family, where intermingling of the sexes is free at a comparatively early age, the parents would have had no fears regarding actual or potential problems.[2]

Thus, as Wirth[3] expresses the accepted point of view of the sociologists, they proceed on

the hypothesis that human beings everywhere live in social groups and that the conduct of the individuals, however it may differ from others, is always expressive of the culture of the group. But a child, for instance, in our type of civilization is seldom just a member of one group, except during the earliest period of life, but of many intersecting and conflicting groups and may at times show behavior traits which are at variance with the standards of the group of which we are accustomed to regard him as a member. These differences in group standards may be gross or they may be very subtle. A child's loyalty to the dictates of his gang may account for his disobedience of the rules of family life. Or the subtle influences of the personality of a teacher may change the honesty curve of children passing from one school room to another.[4]

[1] See PAULINE V. YOUNG, *The Pilgrims of Russian-Town*, pp. 144–146.

[2] Moreover, the psychologist and psychiatrist, because of their lack of this cultural point of view, are continually making errors of judgment in their therapy, by advising courses of conduct that seem to meet the individual desires or inclinations of the patient, without regard to the fact that the patient is not merely an individual but also a social animal and that the courses of conduct suggested will bring him into social conflicts which may be worse than the original disease. This is, I think, particularly true of the psychoanalysts. It seems to me this is one of the strongest arguments in favor of a social approach to problems of behavior, in actual and clinical practice. [Comment by Paul Popenoe of the Institute of Family Relations.]

[3] *Op. cit.*, pp. 60–61.

[4] See M. A. MAY and H. HARTSHORNE, *Character Education Inquiry, Studies in Deceit*. For a discussion of this question in which psychiatrists

Furthermore, the studies (by Burt, Glueck, Zorbaugh, Wirth, Thomas, Bogardus, Burgess, Park, and others, frequently referred to in this volume) on the relationship between the social milieu and behavior patterns point clearly to the urgent necessity of studying unadjusted youth in the vital relation to their culture, their family, their social institutions, mores, social controls, and community life in general. Eleanor Glueck's[1] study on "Culture Conflicts and Delinquency" shows that "culture conflicts in one way or another play a considerable role in the delinquency of children." The writer's studies of delinquent and nondelinquent Russian Molokan boys[2] indicate that such factors as (1) race, (2) nationality, (3) economic status, (4) broken homes, (5) dependency, (6) health, (7) mentality, (8) temperamental traits, (9) psychoses, (10) genetic factors fail to explain the differences in the behavior of the adjusted and unadjusted groups. They can, however, be clearly differentiated in terms of their contacts with urban life and social institutions, and standards which often produce culture conflicts. Without an understanding of these basic conflicts delinquency becomes meaningless and the adjustment of personality problems well-nigh impossible. Shaw's studies at the Institute for Juvenile Research supply ample evidence that sociologists can and do contribute to the understanding and treatment of behavior problems. In a way, whatever success the writer has had in the adjustment—even though some may regard it as temporary—of Marilyn Smith was due almost wholly to the fact that the problem was considered as arising in an uncongenial social environment and inadequate social relations between the parents and daughter. As soon as these relations were altered the personality and conduct of the girl changed.

Psychiatrists are interested in what is occurring in the mental and emotional life of a patient as a result of inner experiences or in the processes in which psychic mechanisms work. They con-

---

and social scientists participated see *Proceedings of the First Colloquium on Personality Investigation*, American Psychiatric Association, New York, December 1–2, 1928, especially pp. 49–54.

[1] *Journal of Mental Hygiene* (in press).

[2] "Urbanization as a Factor in Juvenile Delinquency," *Proceedings of the American Sociological Society*, July, 1930, 162–166; see also "Differentiation of Delinquent and Non-delinquent Boys," *Zeitschrift für Sozialforschung*, III (April, 1934), 79–81.

centrate on the individual and the unique ways in which mental processes operate in individual cases. Sociologists concentrate on the person as a member of social groups and see his behavior as a result of social experiences and group relations as well as of unique individual equipment and urge a study of both.

In summary we may say that the sociologist's field training and viewpoint contribute to a better understanding of the child's behavior, which is a response to the cultural setting and conflicts and to the interplay of social attitudes between himself and the social group of which he is an inseparable part. The sociologist contributes to a better understanding of a child's emotional life, his fears, loyalties, attachments, or aversions which arise in response to other persons or things, or ideas, or ideals of the given group in which the child lives. The sociologist contributes to a better understanding of the cultural factors which loom large in a society in transition from a rural to an urban organization of life; from primary group to secondary group controls; from immigrant to native. The sociologist contributes to a better understanding into the motives and attitudes of the child, which are in response to the social wishes for new experience, security, recognition, and response. The sociologist contributes to a better understanding of the child's conscious, subconscious, and unconscious mind, which inevitably is conditioned by his contacts with, responses to, or memories of social life. The sociologist contributes to a better understanding of the factors of personal and social disorganization and reorganization in terms of community disorganization and reorganization. The sociologist's point of view can enrich the resources of the clinic through an introduction of the cultural approach to delinquency.

PREDICTION OF SUCCESS OR FAILURE ON PROBATION BY THE COURT CLINIC

The most difficult problem in the administration of probation has been that of selecting suitable subjects for this method of treatment. Clearly not all delinquents can be put on probation, and the likelihood of success varies greatly from one person to the next. In the past it has been necessary to rely upon common sense and good judgment unaided by any scientific methods of predicting success or failure in the given case. What has been needed is a method of stating in terms of probability the expected reaction of the probationer to this form of treatment. As we have seen this reaction is the resultant of the interaction of a multitude of factors, such as his age, sex, gang experiences, home life, neighborhood connections, mental status, and so on. A prediction method must take account of as many of these factors as possible. Under the leadership of E. W. Burgess, George Vold, Elio D. Monachasi, Sheldon Glueck, and others (see bibliography) such expectancy rates have been prepared for several institutions and communities. The logic of this method is simple. The parole or probation experiences of the given institution are tabulated in a way which classifies each individual in terms of each of the factors determined upon and these results are then tabulated in terms of (a yardstick of the future behavior) success or failure. Using these experience tables as a yardstick the future behavior of any new prospective probationer can then be stated in such terms as: the chances for successful probation in this case are, say, 76 in 100. Such a ratio is exceedingly valuable, when used in connection with all other available data, for making the practical decision. The clinic might very well compute the probability for success in each case and include it in the report to the judge for his use in disposing of the case. As Sanford Bates points out

No expert in any other profession attempts to speak with authority unless and until he has at his command the record of past experiments in his field. Too long have we worked in the darkness of absolute ignorance or depended upon empirical methods. The use of modern statistical analysis will shed light in many dark places in the field of probation, parole, and prison administration.[1]

Undoubtedly the addition of a statistician to the clinic staff should be recommended. He should observe these cautions: (1) the figure is only a probability and the unlikely may occur; (2) as Bates says: "The prognostic tables should never be a substitute for executive or judicial judgment but will be a logical means of applying the accumulated experience of the past . . . to the important problems of the future";[2] (3) each institution, department, and community needs to develop its own experience tables and not rely upon those of other groups,

[1] SANFORD BATES, *Prisons and Beyond*, p. 120.
[2] *Ibid.*, p. 120.

which may strongly reflect unique elements in their peculiar situations.

THE VALUE OF THE COURT CLINIC

Undoubtedly the court clinic will undergo change and modification as time goes on but it has already demonstrated its worth, in spite of certain shortcomings.   Its substitution of the medical for the moral or for the legalistic point of view in matters of conduct constitutes a real advance over previous approaches. Its substitution of psychotherapy over judicial pronouncements is another important advance in the control of juvenile behavior. The clinic's insistence on proper habit formation in early childhood has done much to prevent certain forms of misconduct.

The shift in emphasis from a legalistic, a priori procedure to a scientific inquiry and consideration from various points of view by several specialists has done much to place the work of the court on a sound basis.   While the clinic cannot be expected to offer any miraculous way of modifying human behavior without a change in the social-economic structure of society, its work has already demonstrated how helpful a study of the total situation can be in the adjustment of the delinquent youth.   And as Lou says: "These specialists have carried the principles and practices of child psychology and psychiatry side by side from the laboratory into the courts of law, and have carried the individualized study and treatment as far as the contributions made by medicine, biology, sociology, education and other social sciences, together with their constructive imagination, permit."[1] Heretofore many isolated attempts have occurred to deal with the child, to educate him, to punish him, to pray over him, to scold him. These isolated attempts only tended to segment him into bits, or as Dr. Van Waters points out, the school has considered him "as a pupil, the physician a patient, the church a soul, the court a ward, the community a pest, the social agency a client; more than anything else the child guidance clinic has succeeded in reassembling the child."[2]

Selected Bibliography

1. ALLEN, FREDERICK H.: "The Influence of Psychiatry on Social Work," *Year Book, National Probation Association* (1935), pp. 131–148.

[1] *Op. cit.*, p. 202.
[2] *Youth in Conflict*, p. 232.

2. ANDERSON, HAROLD H.: "Discipline," University of Iowa Child Welfare Pamphlets No. 11 (Nov. 12, 1932).

3. BELL, WALTER C.: "Some Emphases in Psychiatric Service," *Year Book, National Probation Association* (1932–1933), pp. 111–116.

4. BINGHAM, ANNE T.: "What Can Be Done for the Maladjusted?" *Mental Hygiene*, IV (April, 1920), 422–433.

5. BOWLER, ALIDA C.: "Experiments in Preventing Juvenile Delinquency," *Year Book, National Probation Association* (1934), pp. 153–166.

6. *The Child Guidance Clinic and the Community* (a symposium), The Commonwealth Fund, 1928.

7. GLUECK, BERNARD: "Child Guidance," *Encyclopaedta of the Social Sciences*, Vol. III, The Macmillan Company, 1930.

8. ———: "Psychiatric Treatment and Probation," *Mental Hygiene*. VIII (October, 1924), 873–892.

*9. GLUECK, SHELDON, and ELEANOR T. GLUECK: *One Thousand Juvenile Delinquents*. See Chap. IV, "The Clinic of the Judge Baker Foundation," pp. 46–62.

10. GROVES, ERNEST R., and PHYLLIS BLANCHARD: *Readings in Menta. Hygiene*, Henry Holt & Company, 1936.

11. JARRETT, MARY C.: *Mental Clinics: An Account of their Development in the United States*, National Committee for Mental Hygiene, 1927.

12. KENWORTHY, MARION E.: "Psychoanalytic Concepts in Mental Hygiene," *The Family*, VII (November, 1929), 213–223.

13. KIRKPATRICK, MILTON M.: "The Contribution of Child Guidance Theory to the Treatment of Behavior," *Year Book, National Probation Association* (1935), pp. 149–167.

13a. LA BINE, DR. ALFRED C.: "The Psychiatrist in a Criminal Court," *Year Book, National Probation Association* (1932–1933), pp. 138–141.

14. LEE, PORTER R., and MARION E. KENWORTHY: *Mental Hygiene and Social Work*, The Commonwealth Fund, 1930.

15. LEMESURIER, MRS. L.: *A Handbook of Probation and Social Work of the Courts*, National Association of Probation Officers, London, 1935, Chap. XVI, "Probation and Child Guidance."

16. LEVY, DAVID: "On the Problem of Delinquency," *Year Book, National Probation Association* (1932–1933), pp. 95–110.

17. LOWREY, LAWSON: *A Child Guidance Clinic, Its Purposes and Methods of Service*, National Committee for Mental Hygiene, 1924.

18. McCORD, ELIZABETH: "The Value of the Psychiatric Approach for All Children's Caseworkers," *Proceedings, National Conference of Social Work*, 1928.

19. PALMER, LEO J.: *Psychiatry and the Social Adjustment of Probationers* (pamphlet), New York State Department of Correction, Division of Probation, 1932.

20. PLANT, JAMES E.: "The Relationship of the Psychiatric Clinic to the Juvenile Court," *Journal of Mental Hygiene*, XIII (October, 1929), 708–718.

20a. STEVENSON, GEORGE S., and GEDDES SMITH: *Child Guidance Clinics, A Quarter Century Development*, The Commonwealth Fund, 1934.

21. RICHARDS, ESTHER LORING, *Behavior Aspects of Child Conduct*, The Macmillan Company, 1933.

22. ————: "Behavior Problems," *Social Work Year Book* (1935), pp. 42–47.

23. ROLLER, ANNE: "Berkeley Experiments with Controls," *Survey*, LXV (Oct. 15, 1930), 79–80.

24. TAFT, JESSIE: "Mental Hygiene Problems of Normal Adolescence," *Mental Hygiene*, V (October, 1921), 741–751.

24a. THOM, DOUGLAS A.: "The Normal Adolescent," *Yearbook of the National Probation Association* (1936), pp. 253–265.

*25. THOMAS, WILLIAM I. and DOROTHY S. THOMAS: *The Child in America*. See particularly Chap. X, "The Psychiatric Approach."

26. THRASHER, F. M.: "The Problem of Crime Prevention," *Year Book, National Probation Association* (1934), pp. 6–22.

27. WAXTER, THOMAS J. S.: "Psychiatry in the Juvenile Court," *Year Book, National Probation Association* (1932–1933), pp. 117–125.

28. WIRTH, LOUIS: "Clinical Sociology," *American Journal of Sociology*, XXVII (July, 1931), 49–66.

29. WOODS, ELIZABETH L.: "The School and Delinquency: Every School a Clinic," *National Conference of Social Work* (1929), pp. 213–221.

Prediction of Success or Failure on Probation

1. BRUCE, ANDREW, E. W. BURGESS, ALBERT J. HARNO, and JOHN LANDESCO: *The Workings of the Indeterminate-Sentence Law and the Parole System in Illinois*, Chap. XXX, 1928.

*2. GLUECK, SHELDON, and ELEANOR T. GLUECK: *One Thousand Juvenile Delinquents*, "Predicting Behavior of Delinquents," pp. 185–190.

3. HOUSTON, JOHN W.: "The Right Selection of Probation Cases," *Journal of Criminal Law and Criminology*, XII (Feb., 1922), 577–581.

4. MONACHESI, ELIO D.: *Prediction Factors in Probation*, The Hanover Press, 1932.

5. SOCIAL FORCES, VII (June, 1929), see articles by Burgess, Cooley, Eliot, Lawes, Rice, Sutherland, and others.

6. VOLD, GEORGE B.: "Do Parole Prediction Tables Work in Practice?" *Publications of the American Sociological Society* (May, 1931), pp. 136–138.

Suggestions for Further Study

1. What is the history of psychiatric service for delinquent children?

2. What is the significance of the clinic (a) in the investigation of juvenile delinquency, (b) in the treatment of juvenile delinquency?

3. Who are some of the outstanding clinical psychiatrists?

4. What are the significant tendencies in the psychiatric clinic movement?

5. How can the probation officer profit by the recommendations made by the Gluecks regarding changes in clinical procedure?

6. What psychiatric service is available to the adult delinquent?

7. How does the philosophy of the clinic for juvenile offenders differ from that of the adult offender?

8. How does Mr. Bell's analysis of the psychiatric service in court cases differ from that presented by Bernard Glueck, "Analytic Psychiatry and Criminology?" in Sheldon Glueck, *Probation and Criminal Justice*, pp. 197–222?

9. What is meant by "causal factors derived primarily from social forces," "causal factors derived primarily from personality drives"? Illustrate.

10. What is meant by "inner psychic difficulties"? How do these arise? Illustrate. Are they independent of the social relationships and the outer environment of the person? If so, to what extent? If not, indicate the degree of social relationships entering into the situation.

11. What is the value of prognostic tables? the limitations?

BIBLIOGRAPHY OF BIBLIOGRAPHIES

The selected bibliographies at the end of chapters and in footnotes contain over 500 separate titles. These can be traced through the authors or subject index. Space forbids their repetition at this point. We can only list recent books containing bibliographies of the more recent publications.

1. BURT, CYRIL, *The Young Delinquent*, D. Appleton-Century Company, Inc., 1925.
2. *The Child, the Family and the Court*, References on, United States Department of Labor, Children's Bureau, No. 193 (1933).
3. COLE, LUELLA: *Psychology of Adolescence*, Farrar & Rinehart, Inc., 1936.
4. Commonwealth Fund, *Publications*, 1936.
4a. CULVER, DOROTHY C.: *Bibliography of Crime and Criminal Justice*— 1927–1931, H. W. Wilson Company, 1934.
5. *Encyclopedia of the Social Sciences*, The Macmillan Company, 1930– 1935. See particularly articles on "Child Welfare," "Case Work," "Social Work," "Clinic," "Juvenile Court," "Criminal Court," "Crime," "Police," "Education," "Motion Pictures," "Child Labor," "The Community," "Probation," and others.
6. KUHLMAN, A. F.: *A Guide to Materials on Crime and Criminal Justice*, H. W. Wilson Company, 1929.
7. LEVY, DAVID, and MARY COBURN: *Books Suggested for Library Pertaining to Behavior Problem Children*, Mental Hygiene, XIV (April, 1930), 445–462.
8. LOU, H. H.: *Juvenile Courts in the United States*, University of North Carolina Press, 1927.
9. MANGOLD, GEORGE B.: *Problems of Child Welfare*, The Macmillan Company, 1936.
10. *Mental Hygiene*, Literature for Beginners; for Advanced Readers (pamphlets).
11. *National Probation Association Selected Readings* (pamphlet).
12. NIMKOFF, MEYER: *The Child*, J. B. Lippincott Company, 1934. Bibliography on the child and his family—school—work—aesthetic—and religious experience.
13. ———: *The Family*, Houghton Mifflin Company, 1934. Bibliography on structure, functions, background of the modern American family in the psychosocial and economic setting.
14. Russell Sage Foundation, *Bulletin*, published bimonthly in various useful fields.
14a. SHURTLEFF, CAROLINE: "An Annotated Bibliography in Juvenile Delinquency" (mimeographed), prepared for the Attorney General's Advisory Committee on Crime, Justin Miller, Chairman, 1936.
15. *Social Work Year Book*, 1929–1935: see for similar subjects listed under No. 5.

15a. SULLINGER, EARL, *Social Determinants in Juvenile Delinquency*, John Wiley & Sons, Inc., 1936.

16. U. S. Children's Bureau, *List of References on Juvenile Courts and Probation in the United States*, No. 194 (1923).

17. University of Iowa, *Child Welfare Pamphlets*, University of Iowa (various dates).

17a. WALLIN, J. E. WALLACE: *Personality Maladjustments and Mental Hygiene*, McGraw-Hill Book Company, Inc., 1935.

18. White House Conference on Child Health and Protection, *The Delinquent Child; Education for Home and Family Life; Parent Education; The Adolescent in the Family; Home and School Cooperation; Child Labor; The Handicapped Child*. The Century Company, 1932.

19. YOUNG, PAULINE V.: *Interviewing in Social Work*, McGraw-Hill Book Company, Inc., 1935.

20. ZNANIECKI, FLORIAN: *Social Actions*, Farrar & Rinehart, Inc., 1936.

APPENDIX

Books for Parents and Youth

The following list of books contains fiction, biography, and scientific treatises which may be recommended, with discretion, to parents, and boys and girls of high-school age. It is recommended that the social worker become familiar with the books before recommending them to others. Most of these books are available at public libraries.

1. ABBOTT, M. A.: *The Boy Today.*
2. ARLITT, ADA HART: *Adolescent Psychology.*
3. AUBREY, E. E.: *Religion and the Next Generation.*
4. AYLING, JEAN: *The Retreat from Parenthood.*
5. BARNES, C.: *School Girl.*
6. BENEDICT, AGNES E.: *Children at the Crossroads.*
7. BENNETT, ARNOLD: *Clayhanger.*
8. BLANCHARD, PHYLLIS: *The Adolescent Girl.*
9. BLATZ, WILLIAM E., and HELEN BOTT: *The Management of Young Children.*
10. BOORMAN, W. R.: *Personality in Its Teens.*
11. BROMFIELD, L.: *The Good Woman; The Green Bay Tree.*
12. CAIN, J. M.: *The Postman Always Rings Twice.*
13. CANFIELD, DOROTHY: *The Bent Twig.*
14. CARR, R. S.: *The Rampant Age.*
15. CASTLE, E. B.: *Fathers and Sons.*
16. COBB, STANWOOD: *Discovering the Genius within Us.*
17. COLE, LUELLA: *Psychology of Adolescence.*
18. CONDE, BERTHA: *What's Life All About?*
19. COWAN, MRS. EDWINA EUNICE (ABBOTT), and AVIS D. CARLSON: *Bringing Up Your Child.*
20. DANE, C.: *Regiment of Women.*
21. DELL, FLOYD: *Love in the Machine Age; Mooncalf; Janet Marsh.*
22. DENNETT, MARY WARE: *Sex Education of Children.*
23. DICKERSON, ROY E.: *So Youth May Know.*
24. DREISER, THEODORE: *An American Tragedy.*
25. DUTTON, LOUISE: *Going Together.*
26. ELLIOTT, GRACE L.: *Understanding the Adolescent Girl.*
27. EMERSON, HAVEN: *Alcohol: Its Effects on Men.*
28. FALLADA, H.: *Little Man, What Now!*
29. FISHER, V.: *Passions Spin the Plot.*
30. FOREST, ILSE: *Child Life and Religion.*
31. FRANCE, A.: *Revolt of the Angels.*
32. GALE, ZONA: *Preface to a Life.*

33. GRAHAME, KENNETH: *The Golden Age.*
34. HANLEY, J.: *Boy.*
35. HILLYER, JANE: *Reluctantly Told.*
36. KENWICK, EVELYN: *The Child from Five to Ten.*
37. KIRSCH, J. M.: *Sex Education and Training in Chastity.*
38. KNOPF, OLGA: *The Art of Being a Woman.*
39. LACY, J. S.: *Tuning In with Our Children.*
40. LAWRENCE, D. H.: *The Rainbow; Women in Love; Sons and Lovers.*
41. LEACOCK, STEPHEN: *Humor! Its Theory and Technique.*
42. LEONARD, EUGENIE A.: *Concerning Our Girls and What They Tell Us.*
43. LEWIS, EILUNED: *Dew on the Grass.*
44. LINCOLN, VICTORIA: *February Hill.*
45. MILLAY, KATHLEEN: *Against the Wall.*
46. MILLIN, S. G.: *God's Step Children.*
47. MYERS, G. C.: *The Modern Parent; Building Personality in Children.*
48. MYERSON, ABRAHAM: *When Life Loses Its Zest.*
49. O'SULLIVAN, M.: *Twenty Years A-growing.*
50. PARSONS, PHILLIP A.: *Crime and the Criminal.*
51. PIAGET, JEAN: *The Child's Conception of Physical Causality.*
52. PITKIN, WALTER B.: *The Psychology of Happiness.*
53. PLATT, Dr. CHARLES: *The Riddle to Society.*
54. ROBERTSON, E. A.: *Ordinary Families.*
55. SHELLOW, S. M.: *How to Develop Your Personality.*
56. STEKEL, Dr. WILLIAM: *A Primer for Mothers.*
57. STONE, IRVING: *Lust for Life.*
58. STRECKER, EDWARD A., and KENNETH E. APPEL: *Discovering Ourselves: A View of the Human Mind and How It Works.*
59. TARKINGTON, BOOTH: *Seventeen; Alice Adams; Gentle Julia.*
60. THURSTON, E. T.: *The Turmoil; Milennium.*
61. VAN AMMERS, KULLER: *The Rebel Generation.*
62. VAN WATERS, MIRIAM: *Youth in Conflict; Parents on Probation.*
63. WEMBRIDGE, ELEANOR ROWLAND: *Other People's Daughters; Life among the Low-brows.*
64. WEST, REBECCA: *The Judge.*
65. WESCOTT, G.: *The Grandmothers.*
66. WHARTON, EDITH: *The Old Maid; The Children.*
67. WILLIAMS, FRANKWOOD E.: *Adolescence.*
68. WOLFE, W. B.: *How to Be Happy, Though Human.*
69. WRIGHT, MELVIN: *How to Get Along with People.*
70. YOUNG, PAULINE V.: *Pilgrims of Russian-Town.*
71. ZWEIG, STEFAN: *Amok.*

NAME INDEX

A

Abbott, Grace, 25, 27, 176n, 250, 251, 390, 492
Abbott, M. A., 629
Acheson, Eunice M., 378
Ackerly, Spafford, 99–102
Addams, Jane, 30, 250, 561, 568
Addis, R. S., 377n
Additon, Henrietta, 24, 268, 285, 595
Adler, Herman M., 254, 454
Aichhorn, August, 30, 128, 293, 294, 325, 355, 362, 390
Alexander, Franz, 293n, 391
Allen, Frederick H., 89, 95, 390, 539, 605n, 622
Anderson, Forrest N., 94, 377n
Anderson, Harold H., 623
Anderson, J. E., 377n
Arlitt, Ada Hart, 629
Aubrey, E. E., 629
Augustus, John, 176
Ayling, Jean, 629

B

Baker, Harry J., 135
Baker, Harvey Humphrey, 174, 250, 599
Baldwin, Roger N., 172, 252
Baldwin, Sara E., 541
Barnes, Harry Elmer, 176n, 250, 539n
Bates, Sanford, 251, 590–591, 621
Baylor, Edith M. H., 377n, 379n, 390, 392
Beach, Everett C., 116n
Beam, Kenneth S., 571, 572, 574, 575, 577, 579, 595
Beaman, Florence, 379n
Beard, Belle Boone, 251

Belden, Evelina, 169, 172, 193, 194, 251
Bell, Marjorie, 18, 499
Bell, Walter C., 605–608, 623
Bender, John, 66
Benedict, Agnes, 31, 32, 453, 623
Bennett, Arnold, 629
Berman, Louis, 293n
Bernard, Jessie, 401n
Bernreuter, Robert G., 401n
Bernstein, Salome S. C., 397n
Binford, Jessie, 542, 593–594
Bingham, Anne T., 623
Bissel, Elizabeth, 254
Black, Archibald, 453, 501, 515
Black, Jack, 254
Blades, Leslie B., 254
Blake, Samuel, 571
Blanchard, Phyllis, 64n, 79n, 298n, 379, 391, 453, 623, 629
Blatz, W. E., 377n, 629
Bloodgood, Ruth, 226n, 254
Blüher, Hans, 596
Blumer, Herbert, 282n
Bogardus, E. S., 97, 103
Book, Mary V., 581
Boorman, W. R., 298n, 629
Bott, H., 377n
Bowen, Joseph T. (Mrs.), 251
Bowen, Ruth, 397n
Bower, W. C., 515
Bowler, Alida, 226n, 254, 581–582, 595, 629
Bowman, Le Roy, 399
Bradley, Alice, 76
Branham, V. C., 378, 390
Breckenridge, Sophonisba P., 203, 251, 454
Bridgman, R. R., 454
Brinker, Dorothy, 103
Bristol, Margaret C., 104, 112

631

Fitch, John, 542
Flexner, Bernard, 27, 166, 170, 171*n*, 172, 173, 252
Ford, J., 120*n*
Forman, Henry J., 568
Forrell, A. A., 305
Fosdick, Raymond, 258*n*, 285
Fowler, H. W., 110, 112
Francis, E. A., 481–482
Frank, Lawrence K., 64*n*, 67*n*, 391, 455
Franke, Herbert, 254
Fuller, Helen, 258

G

Gariepy, Marguerite R., 397*n*
Gates, Charles A., 156*n*, 170
Gay, Eleanor, 336
Gee, Wilson, 54
Gibran, Kahil, 515
Gilkey, James H., 453, 515
Glueck, Bernard, 599, 600, 623
Glueck, Eleanor T., 19, 24, 103, 252, 285, 391, 614–616, 623, 624
Glueck, Sheldon, 13, 19, 24, 103, 135, 246, 252, 291, 293*n*, 391, 472, 614–616, 623, 624
Goddard, H. H., 378
Goldstein, Jonah J., 23, 58, 126, 236, 239, 252, 269, 396*n*
Gross, Hans, 361*n*, 391
Groves, Ernest R., 64*n*, 79*n*, 89, 391, 396*n*, 397*n*, 379, 453, 455
Gullett, R., 292*n*

H

Hagerty, Frank W., 289*n*
Hagerty, James E., 467*n*, 491
Haines, Alice, 378
Hall, Jerome, 252
Hall, William Clark, 252
Halperin, Irving, 252
Hamilton, Gordon, 21, 104, 111, 112, 330, 391, 462, 465–466
Hamilton, Mary E., 258*n*, 285
Hancock, Bess, case by, 139–146

Hanmer, Lee, 568
Hanna, J. V., 542
Harno, Albert J., 624
Harper, William J., 477, 542
Hart, Ella B., 455
Hart, Hastings, 595
Hart, Hornell, 455
Hartshorne, Hugh, 397*n*, 453, 557, 618
Hathway, Marion, 475, 542
Hauser, Casper, 601
Hauser, Phillip, 282
Hayner, Norman, 282*n*
Haynes, Fred E., 470
Healy, William, 8, 12, 31, 54, 58, 62, 93, 121, 135, 367, 391, 598, 616
Heffner, Dora, 596
Henley, William Ballentine, 175*n*, 176–177, 251
Henting, Hans, 254
Hexter, Maurice B., 32
Hill, Octavia, 54
Hiller, Francis, 238*n*, 391, 479, 572, 573, 576, 596
Hindus, Maurice, 20
Hoffman, Charles W., 28, 239–240, 251
Hollingworth, Leta S., 310*n*, 540
Holton, Karl, xii, 228
Hopkins, Cornelia, 378
Houston, John W., 391, 624
Hughes, Elizabeth A., 58, 89
Hughes, Gwendolyn S., 24
Hulbert, Henry S., 252
Humm, Doncaster G., 401*n*
Hurbert, H. S., 255
Hurd, Harvey W., 173
Hurley, T. D., 171
Hurry, J. P., 120*n*
Hutzel, Eleanor, 59, 277, 282, 285
Hyatt, Carl B., 216–217, 534, 535–536

J

Jackson, L. P., 568
Jackson, Le Roy, 542
Jacobsen, C., 292*n*

SUBJECT INDEX

A

Accommodation, social, 98–99
Administrative law, 171–257
Adults, education, 395–406
  probation, 13, 218, 270
  recreation, 560
    (*See also* Contributing to delinquency; Home; Parents; Probation)
Age, chronological, 9, 180
  legal, 193–194
  mental, 91, 102, 336, 410, 427, 605–606, 612–613
  social, 9
Agencies, dealing with delinquents, 24–30, 467, 534–536, 570–597
    (*See also* Cooperation with agencies)
  family welfare, 449, 583
  private, and coordinating councils, 574–580, 585–588
Approach, to child, 40–43, 277–279, 294–315, 323–327, 333–348, 355–356
  to community, 570–597
  to parents, 296–315, 436–440
    (*See also* Interaction; Interviewing)
Arrest by police, 82, 270
    (*See also* Police, field cases)
Assets in case, study of, 130–131, 134, 411
Assistance League of Southern California, case by, 371
Attitudes, behavior sequence in origin of delinquency, 93, 123
  of case worker, rating of, 486–487
  changing of, 296–315, 341, 353–372, 390
  importance of study of, 33–43, 54–57, 63–64, 67n

B

Berkeley Coordinating Council, 571
Bibliography, of bibliographies, 627–628
  on clinic, 622–623
  on coordinating councils, 595–596
  on delinquency, 30–31
  on diagnosis, 135
  on guides in study, 103
  on hearing, juvenile court, 69–70
  on investigation, 89–90
  on law, administrative, 250–251
  on police, juvenile, 285–286
  on reading matter, 629–630
  on recording, 112
  on recreation, 569
  on religion, 515–516
  on report to court, 148
  on school, 541–542
  on treatment, social, 390–393, 455–456
  on worker, 491
Big Brothers Association, 33, 43–50, 259, 261, 380–381, 414–418, 425
Big Sisters Association, 412
Boston, Juvenile Court of, 206, 210, 246, 614–616
Boys' club (*see* Club, boys')
Boys' court, Chicago, 194, 211–212
Budgetary guidance, 76, 343, 396
Burglary, cases of, 356–361, 407–421, 608–611

C

California, provisions for juveniles in, 144–145, 192, 193, 201, 218–220, 238n, 243, 259, 262–268, 443, 527
    (*See also* Los Angeles County)